CONCEPTS · STRATEGIES · PRACTICE

Global Marketing

TEXT AND READINGS

CONCEPTS • STRATEGIES • PRACTICE

Global Marketing

TEXT AND READINGS

Syed H. Akhter

Associate Professor of Marketing and
International Business
Marquette University

SOUTH-WESTERN College Publishing

An International Thomson Publishing Company

Acquisitions Editor: Robert B. Jared
Production Editors: Sue Ellen Brown and Sharon L. Smith
Production House: Books by Design
Cover Design: Larry Hanes
Internal Design: Russel Schneck
Marketing Manager: Stephen E. Momper

SI68AA

Library of Congress Cataloging-in-Publication Data

Akhter, Syed H.
  Global marketing: concepts, strategies, and practice /
by Syed H. Akhter:
    p.   cm.
    Includes index.
    ISBN 0-538-83176-6
    1. Export marketing.   I.   Title.
HF1416.A43   1994
658.8′48—dc20   94-17710
                                                              CIP
                                                              AC

2 3 4 5 6 7 MT 0 9 8 7 6 5

Printed in the United States of America

I⟨T⟩P
International Thomson Publishing

South-Western College Publishing is an ITP Company. The ITP trademark is used under license.

To Marita

PREFACE

In the last two decades we have witnessed a gradual shift in focus from domestic to international, to multinational, to global marketing. This shift in focus reflects the socioeconomic, political, and technological developments that have changed the way business is conducted. The breakup of the Soviet Union, the creation of the European Union, the formation of the NAFTA, the rapid growth and integration of the Asian Pacific economies, the ascendence of market economies, and the alliance of computer and communication technologies have all increased the significance of global marketing.

Products, services, and capital are increasingly exchanged in the borderless global economy. Firms that once relied on a single-country market are now vigorously competing for market shares in a dynamic, complex, interdependent, and competitive global market. The global expansion of business has blurred the distinction between domestic and foreign markets and has made it difficult to determine the origin of products and the nationality of firms.

These developments pose many challenges to marketers. For example, they have to adapt to the complex and fast-changing business environment and make decisions that enhance the competitive position of their firms in the global marketplace. They have to forge alliances between themselves and constituents such as governments, financial institutions, advertising agencies, and middlemen to market their products effectively and efficiently across countries. Furthermore, to achieve success, they need to understand the concepts, strategies, and practice of global marketing.

THE STRUCTURE OF THE TEXT

This book is divided into two parts. The first part consists of 12 chapters. The first chapter is an introduction to global marketing followed by four chapters focusing on the economic, financial, political, and cultural environments of global marketing, respectively. Chapters 6 through 9 cover the marketing mix variables (product, price, place, and promotion) as they relate to global marketing. Chapter 10 explains global business involvement in terms of market entry strategies, Chapter 11 covers topics related to global marketing strategies, and Chapter 12 deals with the ethics of global marketing.

The second part of the book includes 44 readings, four for each of the chapters, 2 through 12. In selecting these readings, the objective was to offer comprehensive coverage of key topics. Rigorous, interesting, and provocative, the articles expand and elaborate on specific conceptual and practical issues in global marketing.

Several features of this text are noteworthy. First, complex global marketing concepts are explained in a clear and straightforward way. Second, examples from different regions of the world illustrate the use of concepts and strategies, making the subject matter both interesting and meaningful. Third, the chapters are kept at a reasonable length to facilitate understanding and teaching. Fourth, the combination of text with readings provides access to foundation materials and key topical areas in global marketing, and gives instructors the freedom to select and customize the coverage of materials on different topics. And fifth, the most recent data available are used to explain global marketing developments and practices.

SUPPLEMENTARY MATERIAL

An Instructor's Manual with a test bank is available. The test bank includes true/false, multiple choice, and fill-in-the-blank questions. Other supplementary materials include lecture outlines and discussion questions for each chapter. For each reading, a synopsis and discussion questions are also provided. Instructors interested in adopting a simulation exercise can use Export to Win, South-Western College Publishing.

ACKNOWLEDGMENTS

This book would not have been possible without the contributions and support of many people. I thank the authors whose articles are included in this book. Their contributions help us to understand the exciting and challenging field of global marketing. I sincerely appreciate the thoughtful comments of Tailan Chi, University of Wisconsin-Milwaukee, A. Ben Oumlil, The University of Dayton, and Lisa Spiller, Christopher Newport University. My special thanks to the following reviewers who evaluated the first draft of the book and provided many helpful suggestions in the selection of readings:

Sanjeev Agarwal
Iowa State University

David M. Andrus
Kansas State University

S. Tamer Cavusgil
Michigan State University

Esra F. Gencturk
University of Texas-Austin

Paris Gunther
University of Cincinnati

Richard T. Hise
Texas A&M University

Michael Minor
University of Texas-Pan American

Gordon P. Stiegler
University of Southern California

John Weber
Notre Dame

Van R. Wood
Texas Tech University

My thanks to an excellent team at South-Western College Publishing: Jeanne Busemeyer, Randy Haubner, and Rob Jared, Acquisition Editors; Sue Ellen Brown and Sharon Smith, Production Editors; Scott Person, Senior Marketing Manager; and Steve Momper, Marketing Manager; and Pamela Person, Project Sponsor, deserve special thanks for turning an idea into a finished product. It has been a pleasure working with them. I also thank Herb Nolan of Books By Design for coordinating the final phase of the book's production. And finally, I thank my family for their support and love.

Syed H. Akhter
Marquette University

BRIEF CONTENTS

READINGS

CONTENTS

11 Strategic Global Market Management 146

12 Ethics and Global Marketing 159

CHAPTER **ONE**

I think there is a world market for about five computers.
Thomas J. Watson, Chairman of the Board, IBM, 1943

Global Marketing

The term *global marketing* is frequently used to refer to the marketing of products and services in different countries. Rather than using the term *international marketing* or even *multinational marketing,* many firms with operations in more than one country are increasingly using the term *global marketing* to define their marketing activities. Global marketing, global corporations, and global economy are today's watchwords. We live in a global economy and we are served by global corporations who engage in global marketing. But what are the distinguishing characteristics of global marketing?

Consider the following. Rather than conducting marketing activities on a country-by-country basis, global marketing focuses on a firm's marketing activities in all of the countries where the firm is currently operating and expects to operate in the future. Rather than developing marketing strategies for a country as an independent market, global marketing develops strategies for a country as an integral part of the firm's global marketing plan. Rather than ignoring the effects of implementing marketing plans in one country on operations in other countries, global marketing makes this consideration an important component of its planning process. And rather than treating a country as domestic or foreign, global marketing considers each country as a part of the global market. Overall, global marketing takes into consideration the total marketing activities of a firm and strives for synergism in analysis, planning, implementation, and control. More important, when a firm engages in global marketing, it considers the world as its market and its marketing activities as coordinated efforts to enhance its global competitive position.

In contrast to the political reality of a world divided into countries with defined borders, the economic reality today is that of a borderless world connected by communications satellites, linked by supersonic jets, and united by economic interdependence. In this borderless economy, global sourcing, global production, and global competition have blurred the distinction between domestic and foreign markets. To achieve an advantage in today's highly competitive global economy, many marketers have begun to think and act globally. Take the case of Jim Easton, the chairman of Easton Aluminum, Inc., a firm based in Van Nuys, California. When designing a new hybrid arrow for archers, Jim Easton had to choose whether to develop the technology for the world market or for the American team competing in the Olympics in Barcelona. As chairman of the company, he decided that if he were going to develop an arrow shaft with his own money, he would sell the product all over the world.[1] For Jim Easton and many others, the world is the market. The idea of the world-as-market is increasingly shaping how global marketers think about and conduct marketing activities.

DEFINING GLOBAL MARKETING

The definition of global marketing can be built upon the definition of marketing adopted by the American Marketing Association (AMA) in 1985. This new definition states the following: "Marketing is the process of planning and executing the conception, pricing, promotion, and distribution of ideas, goods, and services to create exchanges that satisfy individual and organizational objectives."[2] Although this definition does not capture the full essence of marketing, it has many distinguishing features.

First, this definition does not restrict marketing to exchange activities that are motivated by profit alone; it includes nonprofit marketing activities. Thus, the activities not only of IBM but also of the Red Cross or the World Health Organization, or even Billy Graham (the TV evangelist), are included within marketing. Second, by including not only products but ideas and services, the definition broadens the domain of marketing. Third, it includes two important sets of marketing activities—those that precede the production of goods or services and others that follow it. And fourth, it includes all four elements of the marketing mix (product, price, place, and promotion) and considers them equally important.

Building on the definition of marketing adopted by the AMA, global marketing is being defined herein as the coordinated performance of marketing activities to create exchanges across countries that satisfy individual, organizational, and societal objectives. This definition makes three important additions to the one adopted by the AMA. First, it indicates that global marketing activities are conducted across countries without labeling these countries as domestic or foreign. Second, it emphasizes coordination of global marketing conducted across different country markets. And third, it suggests that global marketing

---

[1] Timothy K. Smith, "U.S. High-Tech Sports Gap Is All Henry Ford's Fault," *The Wall Street Journal,* August 5, 1992, A15.

[2] "AMA Board Approves New Marketing Definition," *Marketing Educator,* spring, 1985, 1.

should be motivated not only by the achievement of individual and organizational goals but societal goals as well. The inclusion of societal goals in the definition of global marketing is instructive because both profit and nonprofit corporations operate within a social system. Thus, the success or failure of these corporations is influenced by how the society responds to their activities. By being socially responsible, environmentally accountable, and ethically conscientious, global marketers enhance the survival and growth potential of their firms.

THE GLOBAL MARKETING ENVIRONMENT

In Figure 1.1, we illustrate the global marketing environment of a firm. Certain key points about this environment should be noted. First, consumers are the focal point of the global marketing environment. The task of a global marketer is to enhance his firm's competitiveness by making product, price, place, and promotion decisions that satisfy consumers' needs and wants better than the competition. However, it is important to note that these marketing decisions are influenced by the economic, financial, political, and cultural environment of each country as well as by the broader regional and global environment. This realization is the hallmark of a global marketer.

WHY SHOULD FIRMS ENGAGE IN GLOBAL MARKETING?

If a firm has captive consumers in one country market and can sell at a profit whatever it produces, it may not feel the need to seek marketing opportunities elsewhere. For many firms in the United States this has been the case. The United States, which for a long time has been the largest economy in the world, was able to support the production and marketing activities of many U.S.-based businesses. As these firms achieved their objectives by operating only in the United States, they were neither motivated nor forced to seek overseas marketing opportunities.

However, as the integration of the global economy is proceeding at a rapid pace, firms with marketing operations limited to the United States are finding themselves unable to compete with firms operating in multiple country markets. Thus, what once was a fairly captive market for these firms is slowly being chipped away by more aggressive and efficient domestic and global competitors. Furthermore, having relied solely on the U.S. market, these firms are finding that they are not only losing their market shares in the United States, but that they have nowhere else to go. In short, staying in one market has made them vulnerable to competitive attacks.

Recent developments in the telecommunications and transportation industries have created a highly integrated and competitive global economy. In this economy, the push for global marketing is coming from many directions. Concern with survival and growth, intensive competitive pressures, promising marketing opportunities in numerous countries, and globalization of markets are some of the factors encouraging firms to engage in global marketing. These are explained below.

Survival and Growth

Two long-term objectives of a firm are to survive and grow. To achieve this, firms must be competitive. As trade among countries increases, firms that rely only on one country market will find it increasingly difficult to achieve their long-term goals of survival and growth. However, firms that successfully expand their marketing activities in multiple countries learn to satisfy consumers in diverse operating conditions. Having established their marketing presence in different countries, these firms learn to manage their marketing activities more efficiently and effectively. Their accumulated experience makes them formidable competitors. If they are attacked in one market, they in turn have the option of attacking their competitors in other markets. For example, Fuji—the leading

FIGURE **1.1**   The Global Marketing Environment

color film manufacturer in Japan—outbid Kodak for the sponsorship of the 1984 Los Angeles Summer Olympics. Fuji's share of the U.S. film market jumped from 6 percent to 8 percent by the end of 1984. Kodak had to decide what to do about Fuji's competitive move. It launched an aggressive campaign in Fuji's home market. In Japan, Kodak increased its advertising, more than tripled its staff, started a Japanese research facility, and created a new subsidiary to deal strictly with Japan. Not only did Kodak increase its marketing presence in Japan but it also served notice to Fuji about what to expect if it attacks Kodak again in the United States.[3] Firms operating in only one market do not have this option. In short, by engaging in global marketing, a firm makes itself less vulnerable to competitive attacks and more prepared for success.

Increasingly, firms are expanding their business and marketing operations worldwide to capitalize on the growing opportunities in developed and developing countries. By expanding their operations beyond the frontiers of one country, firms have been able to achieve economies of scale in their operations, preempt competitive attacks, solidify their competitive position, and, above all, enhance their survival and growth potential. There is a growing realization among firms that if they rely exclusively on one country for their business, they not only forgo attractive marketing opportunities in other countries but also make themselves vulnerable to competitive attacks in their own domestic markets.

Table 1.1 provides data for selected U.S.–based firms that have expanded their worldwide marketing activities. The table indicates the percentage of sales revenue these firms earn from markets outside the United States. The 1990 sales figures and the growth rate of the firms for nine years ending in 1990 are also presented. Two things are clearly evident from the table. First, many of the firms listed in the table earn close to or more than 50 percent of their revenue from outside the United States. In 1990, for example, Boeing, Coca-Cola, Colgate-Palmolive, Digital Equipment, Dow Chemical, Exxon, Gillette, and Hewlett-Packard all earned more than 50 percent of their sales revenue from markets outside the United States. Second, many of these firms have been able to achieve high growth rates in sales. Hewlett-Packard grew at the rate of 15.6 percent, and Digital at 16.8 percent for nine years ending in 1990. Overall, the data in Table 1.1 indicate the increasing involvement of many U.S.–based firms in global marketing.

Diversification and Competitiveness

By going global, a firm diversifies its product and market portfolios and improves its competitiveness. All businesses are affected by cyclical and seasonal

---

[3] W. Chan Kim and R. A. Mauborgne, "Becoming an Effective Global Competitor," *The Journal of Business Strategy,* January/February 1988, 33–37.

fluctuations. However, those operating in multiple country markets are more able to offset the adverse consequences of these fluctuations. Furthermore, by diversifying, a firm is able to increase the size of its market. This allows the firm to achieve economies of scale in its marketing activities and enhance its overall competitiveness.

TABLE **1.1**   Sales of U.S.–Based Companies Outside the United States

Company	1990 (%)	Sales Growth Rate, % (1982–1990)	1990 Sales (Mil. U.S. $)
Black & Decker	42%	14.5%	4,832
Boeing	58	12.2	27,595
Bristol-Myers Squibb	39	12.8	10,300
Coca-Cola	61	6.3	10,236
Colgate-Palmolive	67	0.9	5,691
Cray	41	25.8	804
Digital Equipment Corporation	55	16.8	12,943
Dow Chemical	52	5.8	19,773
Exxon	77	(0.3)	105,519
Gillette	67	7.1	4,345
H.J. Heinz	42	6.8	6,647
Hewlett-Packard	54	15.6	13,233
Kellogg	41	9.3	5,181
Polaroid	46	3.7	1,972
Procter & Gamble	39	8.6	24,081
Upjohn	40	5.3	3,033
Wrigley	39	6.9	1,111
Xerox	38	7.7	16,951

Source: Adapted from Gary Hoover, Alta Campbell, and Patrick J. Spain (eds.), *Hoover's Handbook 1992*, The Reference Press, Austin, TX.

Attractiveness of Country Markets

The United States is an extremely attractive market because of its size. It is the largest economy in the world. In 1992, its population was approximately 255.5 million and its gross domestic product (GDP) approximately $6 trillion. However, even in this attractive market a firm cannot sell more than a certain number of products. The quantity is determined by the number of potential buyers with the purchasing power and willingness to buy the product. Firms operating only in one country market limit their growth to the size of the market. However, firms can expand the size of their market by establishing their marketing presence in other countries. Take the case of Japan and Germany, two highly attractive markets in terms of market size. In 1992, the population in Japan was approximately 124.3 million and its GDP was close to $3.7 trillion. In Germany the population in 1992 was about 80.7 million and its GDP approximately $1.9 trillion.[4] Thus, by going to different countries, a firm is able to increase its market size and capitalize on marketing opportunities that exist in these markets.

Maurice G. Hardy, president and chief operating officer of Pall Corporation, the world's largest manufacturer of specialty filters, advises small and midsize firms to go to different countries for two crucial reasons: first, to keep the competitors in their own countries; and second, to take advantage of opportunities in the growing economies in Europe and the Pacific. By following his own advice, Hardy was able to achieve an overall growth of 20 percent annually for his company. In 1961, sales volume was about $7 million; by 1988 it increased to $429 million. The company was able to achieve this growth by expanding its operations in European, Middle Eastern, and Asian countries.[5]

Globalization of Markets

The markets for goods, services, capital, technology, and even labor are becoming global. Companies can sell products, raise capital, set up research and development centers, hire executives, and provide consulting services in different countries. It is in this sense that the markets are becoming global. As more and more products and services are traded among countries, the more global the market becomes; the more global the market becomes, the more products and services are exchanged.

Globalization of markets does not mean that all products are traded worldwide. Governments impose restrictions on what can be produced in their countries, exported from their countries, and imported into their countries.

---

[4] "The World Economy in Charts," *Fortune,* July 26, 1993, 96.

[5] Maurice G. Hardy, "Going Global: One Company's Road to International Markets," *The Journal of Business Strategy,* November/December 1989, 24–27.

These restrictions have kept the markets from becoming truly global. Trade restrictions among countries, however, are gradually being curtailed through bilateral and multilateral negotiations. This easing of restrictions is making markets more global for different products and services. Coca-Cola and Singer, for example, are proving that global markets can be accessed. Each company sells its products in more than 150 countries.

WHAT IS UNIQUE ABOUT GLOBAL MARKETING?

Although global marketers consider the world as one market and different country markets as components of this world market, they recognize that the business environment in each country is different. The differences result from many factors including the economic, financial, political, and cultural makeup of each country. Together, these differences set the parameters within which marketing activities can be conducted. As global marketing involves operating in more than one country market, global marketers must contend with a more complex global environment than do marketers confined to one country market. The factors that make global marketing unique are explained below.

Economic Environment

The economic environment of each country is different. These differences result from variations in the purchasing power of consumers, competitive intensity within different industries, and the general economic health of an economy. Countries rely on two major policy tools—fiscal and monetary—to manage their internal economic conditions. Fiscal policies affect the tax rates and spending programs of the government. Monetary policies, however, regulate the quantity of money within an economy. Collectively, these policies influence employment, inflation, investment, and economic growth within a country. These in turn affect the activities of global marketers. As each country has its own fiscal and monetary policies, global marketers have to deal with a different set of policies in each country market. This is not the case with marketers who operate in only one country market.

Financial Environment

With a few exceptions such as Liechtenstein, which uses the Swiss franc, each country has its own currency. The price of one currency in relation to another is defined as the *exchange rate*. For instance, if we are interested in finding how many yen can be exchanged for one dollar, we are interested in finding the exchange rate or the price of yen in terms of dollars. If one dollar can be exchanged for 100 yen, the exchange rate or the price of 100 yen is one dollar.

Conversely, we can also determine how many cents can be exchanged for one yen. If one dollar can be exchanged for 100 yen, one yen can be exchanged for a cent. For global marketers, an understanding of exchange rates is important because price ratios among currencies fluctuate. And this fluctuation can adversely or favorably affect the performance of a firm. For example, in the 1980s, the value of the dollar rose by approximately 50 percent against other major currencies. As a result, American goods became prohibitively expensive to foreign buyers, and foreign goods became attractively cheap to American buyers. In 1987, merchandise exports from the United States were equal to $250.28 billion, while merchandise imports were equal to $409.77 billion. This gave rise to a trade deficit of $159.49 billion, the highest in U.S. international trade history.[6] Thus, what determines the change in price ratios of different currencies and how these changing ratios can affect a firm's marketing of products and services in different countries are important considerations for global marketers.

Political Environment

Governments play an important role in regulating both domestic and international trade. To manage its trading activities, each country develops its own set of tariff and nontariff barriers that affect global marketing. A *tariff* is defined as a tax paid to customs officials on imported products or services. When a firm in the United States imports mineral water from France and pays tax to customs officials on this imported product, the tax is called a tariff. There are two main types of tariffs: *specific tariff* and *ad valorem*. When U.S. customs officials collect a fixed amount per physical unit of import, such as dollars per kilogram of sugar or dollars per car, it is called a specific tariff. When customs officials collect tax as a percentage on the estimated value of imported merchandise, the tariff is referred to as ad valorem (on the value). In addition to taxing imports, governments impose other restrictions that can adversely affect global marketing activities. These restrictions include import quotas, complicated exchange controls, buy-domestic policies, and administrative red tape to harass foreign sellers. Together, these restrictions are called *nontariff barriers*. For global marketers, an understanding of how tariff and nontariff barriers can affect global marketing activities such as entry strategies, market share, product content and quality, and profitability is critically important.

Cultural Environment

Global marketing is conducted across countries. To understand how consumers will respond to marketing activities, global marketers should know about the

---

[6] International Monetary Fund, *Balance of Payments Statistics Yearbook*, Washington, DC, 1992.

culture of each country where they operate. As consumers in each country operate within their cultural environment, they evaluate and respond to marketing offerings in different ways. Nonetheless, due to the increasing flow of information from one country to another, cultural characteristics are becoming similar in many ways. For global marketers, this raises the question of how global marketing strategies should be developed and implemented across different country markets. While cultural differences influence adaptations in marketing offerings, cultural similarities encourage standardization. Reconciling the pulls toward standardization and adaptation of global marketing strategies makes global marketing unique. Balancing cultural differences and similarities plays a significant role in planning global marketing activities.

MARKETING MIX POLICIES

Although the four elements of marketing mix (product, price, place, and promotion) are generally classified as controllable variables, global marketers realize that they do not exercise total control over them. That is, they cannot produce and market whatever they like wherever they like. Marketing decisions are made within the regulatory constraints of a country. These constraints cannot be ignored because each country, by instituting its own set of regulations, affects the activities of global marketers.

Each government develops a set of policies that affect the marketing mix activities of global marketers. For example, product strategies can be affected by a local content law that requires firms to manufacture a certain portion of the product in the country where the product is being marketed. A government may require firms to receive approval from the government before raising or lowering the price of their products. Restrictions can be imposed on the amount of money global marketers can spend on promotional activities. Governments can also make global marketers distribute products through a particular distribution channel or to areas specified by the government. As each government develops a unique set of regulations that affects marketing activities, the development of a global marketing plan and its implementation become a highly complex task. Without a good understanding of the myriad regulations affecting their marketing activities, global marketers cannot operate effectively.

WHY SHOULD WE STUDY GLOBAL MARKETING?

Global marketing affects not only businesses and nations but also individuals. As consumers, we are affected through global marketing by the product choices offered in the marketplace. Just take an inventory of the products you have in your home and see how many countries are involved in satisfying your needs and wants. The delectable chocolate we buy is the end result of transactions among multiple country markets. For example, the cocoa comes from Ghana, peanuts from Sudan, corn syrup from Iowa, coconuts from the Philippines, and sugar from Ecuador. The paper to wrap the chocolate comes from trees in Canada and the tinfoil from Thailand. The truck that brings the chocolate to the store is made in Japan.[7] Thus, global marketing combines the diverse resources available in different countries to produce a product we can enjoy. Overall, as global marketing activities among nations increase, the choices available to us also increase.

We are also affected by global marketing through the job opportunities available to us. As the significance of global marketing increases, the available jobs and the skills required for these jobs will also change. Firms will look for employees who can understand and manage the complexity of dealing with different environments and different people. Thus, marketers, in addition to understanding the developments taking place in the global economy, need certain skills to conduct global marketing activities effectively and efficiently.

ABB, a global electrical equipment giant, is a world leader in high-speed trains, robotics, and environmental control. Created by a merger between ASEA (a Swedish engineering group) and Brown Boveri (a Swiss competitor), ABB is bigger than Westinghouse and capable of going head-to-head with General Electric. ABB's chief, Percy Barnevik, stresses that today's managers need "patience, good language ability, stamina, work experience in at least two or three countries, and, most important humility." He further notes that people in his company who are on the fast track spend up to thirty hours a week either traveling or attending conferences and evening seminars, in addition to their regular work.[8]

SUMMARY

Global marketing is defined as the coordinated performance of marketing activities to create exchanges across countries that satisfy individual, organizational, and societal objectives. Four important reasons motivating firms to engage in global marketing are survival and growth, diversification and competitiveness, attractiveness of country markets, and globalization of markets. The practice of global marketing is becoming increasingly critical for firms because it is in the global marketplace that the battle for market shares is being fought. Thus it makes sense for marketers to think and act globally.

---

[7] "As the World Learns," *The New York Times*, April 9, 1989, sec. 4A, 22–23.

[8] Carla Rapoport, "A Tough Swede Invades the U.S.," *Fortune*, June 29, 1992, 76–79.

The global environment (economic, financial, political, and cultural) within which marketing activities are conducted is constantly changing. The changing environment creates both opportunities and threats for firms. To develop effective global marketing strategies, firms need to understand economic, financial, political, and cultural developments taking place in the world. These considerations make global marketing a challenging and exciting field of study.

As consumers we are affected by global marketing in what, where, and how we can buy. We are also affected by global marketing in terms of where, how, and for whom we work. The impact of global marketing on our lives is pervasive. Thus, to better understand the forces shaping our world and to stay ahead of the competition, we need to study global marketing.

CHAPTER **TWO**

Of all human powers operating on the affairs of mankind, none is greater than that of competition.

Henry Clay

The Economic Environment

 Global marketing activities are influenced by local, regional, and global economic conditions. Understanding how these three layers of the economic environment affect marketing activities is critical for deciding what type of products to market, where to market them, how to position them, how much to charge for them, and how to promote and distribute them. The three layers of the economic environment are illustrated in Figure 2.1. The local economy, shown in the center, is surrounded by the regional and global economies. The regional economy itself is encompassed by the larger global economy. The relationship between the three layers is interactive. Thus, what happens at the local level affects the regional and global economies, and vice versa.

The purpose of analyzing the overall economic environment is to facilitate effective decision making. In general, the better the analysis, the better the decision. Analysis of the economic environment requires valuable resources such as time and money. As these resources have opportunity costs, they should be used judiciously: marketers should know what to analyze, how to analyze, and, above all, how to interpret the findings. In the following sections we discuss each of the three levels of the economic environment and end this chapter with an analysis of the globalization of the U.S. economy.

THE LOCAL ECONOMY

By *local economy* we mean the economy of the country where marketing activities are being conducted or will be conducted. The local economy should be carefully analyzed, because the behavior of firms and consumers within a country is directly affected by the local economic environment. In analyzing the local economic environment, a global marketer generally focuses on three

FIGURE **2.1**   The Economic Environment

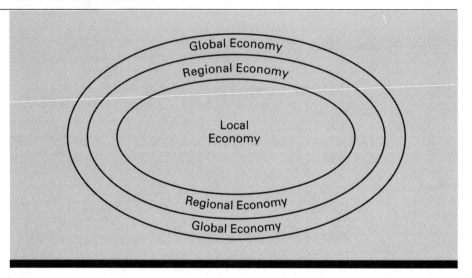

things: the economic conditions of consumers, the overall economic situation in the country, and the nature of competition within the country. By focusing on these elements, a global marketer can determine marketing opportunities and threats within a country. Thus, for example, the decision to establish a marketing presence or to expand operations in a country where a firm is already present is influenced by the outcome of the analysis of the local economic environment.

The Consumers

Global marketers realize that consumers' decisions to purchase products are greatly influenced by their *disposable income,* which is income after tax. Disposable income determines, for example, whether consumers can buy durables such as cars, houses, and stereos, or acquire services such as lawn care, plastic surgery, or dental insurance. Disposable income also determines whether consumers can buy such simple convenience items as soap and shampoo. In particular, disposable income determines not only what consumers buy, but also when, where, and how much they buy. Knowing about the disposable income of different groups of consumers (target markets) helps a global marketer determine the marketing mix that will be most appropriate for each target market within a country.

The Country

The economic condition of consumers is inextricably tied to the economic health of their country. If the economy is growing and real wages are increasing, consumers in general will experience an increase in their purchasing power. However, if the economy is in a recession and real wages are declining, consumers will experience a decline in their purchasing power. Thus, it is important for global marketers to determine the general economic health of a country. Some of the important variables in determining the economic health of a country are gross domestic product (GDP); GDP per capita (GDP divided by population); GDP growth rates; savings and investments rates; inflation and unemployment rates; imports and exports; inflow and outflow of foreign direct investments; number of global corporations operating within the country; structure of industries; and commercial, fiscal, and monetary policies of the central government. By determining the economic condition of a country, a firm is able to develop and adjust both short- and long-term plans to achieve its global marketing goals.

When analyzing the economic conditions of a country, firms should be aware that the data available at the country level, either aggregate or per capita, reveal only the general economic health of the country and not the specific economic conditions of different groups of consumers. To determine the economic conditions of groups of consumers within a country, an analysis of these groups should be conducted separately. Most often marketers forget this simple statistical fact and try to infer the economic state of separate target markets from data pertaining to the country as a whole.

For example, GDP per capita, although a useful indicator for classifying countries into different income groups, does not give an accurate picture of the potential of target markets within a country. In general, GDP per capita will either underestimate or overestimate the income of specific target markets. This is because a country's economy is made up of several segments of people, and each segment is different from the others in terms of its purchasing power. For example, in 1986 the GDP per capita in the United States was $17,735.[1] However, the income of the bottom 20 percent of U.S. households was less than $15,000, while that of the top 20 percent was more than $50,000.[2] Thus, to determine the market potential of a target market, that market should be clearly identified, located, and measured.

Consider the following. With a GDP per capita of approximately $263 in 1990, China can be considered one of the poorest countries in the world.[3] If GDP per capita is assumed to indicate the purchasing power of every consumer

---

[1] *Economic Report of the President,* U.S. Government Printing Office, February 1992.

[2] Paul Wonnacott and Ronald Wonnacott, *Economics,* New York: John Wiley & Sons, 1990.

[3] Euromonitor, *International Marketing Data and Statistics 1993,* London.

within China, firms will erroneously conclude there is no market potential for high-value-added products. However, there is an emerging group of consumers called *dakuan* and *kuanye* (which roughly translate into "fat cats"). These consumers are buying Italian suits, French cosmetics, and European fountain pens. Some retailers are planning to sell Rolex watches with a price tag as high as $20,000 to this highly attractive market.[4] Global marketers can leave potentially profitable markets untapped by drawing erroneous conclusions from aggregated data. When examining data, global marketers should know what type of data they are dealing with and what type of conclusions are justifiable.

The Competition

To understand the competition's current strategies and envision their likely future strategies, global marketers should study the nature of the competition. The success of any marketing strategy depends on the strength of competitive analysis. Without this, a firm will not become aware of its current position and future performance vis-à-vis its competitors. Porter[5] has identified five basic forces that determine the state of competition in an industry: rivalry among existing firms, potential impact of new entrants, power of suppliers, power of buyers, and substitute goods. These forces collectively shape the competitive intensity of an industry, and its profitability. They also indicate that competition in an industry goes well beyond the established players. However, the prominence of each force varies from industry to industry. As Porter notes, in the oceangoing-tanker industry the key force is probably the buyers, while in the steel industry the key forces are foreign competitors and substitute materials. Thus, it is important to know how the different competitive forces will affect a firm's current and future performance.

THE REGIONAL ECONOMY

The performance of a country's economy is influenced by its economic relations with other countries. Countries make different arrangements with each other to manage their economic relations. These arrangements can lead to the formation of a free-trade area, a customs union, a common market, and an economic union. Their common characteristics are shown in Figure 2.2. In a *free-trade area*, member countries remove trade barriers among themselves, but

---

[4] Nicholas D. Kristof, "China: Rolex Watches, Italian Suits Are Symbols of Emerging Class of Super-Rich," *The Milwaukee Journal*, September 27, 1992, J3.

[5] Michael E. Porter, *Competitive Strategy: Techniques for Analyzing Industries and Competitors*, New York: Free Press, 1980.

FIGURE **2.2**   Forms of Economic Integration

	Removal of Internal Tariffs	Common External Tariffs	Free Flow of Capital and Labor	Harmonization of Economic Policy
Free-Trade Area	≡≡≡			
Customs Union	◆◆◆◆◆	◆◆◆◆◆		
Common Market	••••••	••••••	••••••	
Economic Union	○○○○○	○○○○○	○○○○○	○○○○○

keep their own national barriers against the rest of the world. In a *customs union,* member countries not only remove all trade barriers among themselves but also adopt a common set of external barriers against the rest of the world. In a *common market,* member countries form a customs union and further allow free movement of labor and capital. In an *economic union,* member countries unify their full economic policies and create a single economy with one currency and unified fiscal and monetary policies.

Of late, cooperative activities among countries within three major regions—Western Europe, Asian Pacific, and North America—have been drawing the world's attention. These arrangements are having a significant impact on the composition and pattern of regional and global trade. To survive and grow in today's highly complex and competitive economy, firms need to understand these regional developments and their strategic implications. This understanding will help executives assess potential opportunities and threats in different product and geographic markets. Assessing competitive opportunities and threats, and evaluating the strengths and weaknesses of their firms, are important activities that help executives achieve competitive advantage in the global marketplace. In the following section, we focus on economic developments in three important regions of the world: Western Europe, Asian Pacific, and North America—commonly referred to as the Triad.

FIGURE **2.3**   The European Union's Origin

1951	On April 18, 1951, six European countries, Belgium, France, the Federal Republic of Germany, Italy, Luxembourg, and the Netherlands signed the European Coal and Steel Community (ECSC) Treaty in Paris, France.
1955	The Foreign Ministers of the six countries agreed to begin negotiations to establish the European Economic Community (EEC) and the European Atomic Energy Community (EAEC).
1957	The six signed the Treaty of Rome, establishing the EEC and the EAEC.
1973	On January 1, 1973, Denmark, Ireland, and the United Kingdom became member states, creating a community of nine.
1978	The European Community (EC) was formed by the merger of the ECSC, EEC, and EAEC.
1981	Greece joined the EC.
1986	Spain and Portugal joined the EC, creating a community of twelve.
1987	Member countries approved and enacted the Single European Act (SEA), which called for a fully unified market by 1992.
1990	EC Heads of State agreed in Dublin on April 28, 1990, to take decisive steps towards European unity as conceived in the SEA.
1992	The Treaty of European Union, known as the Maastricht Treaty, was signed in Maastricht, the Netherlands, in 1992, which among other things called for a central banking system, a common currency, and a framework for expanding the Union's political role.

The European Economic Integration

One of the most significant economic developments in Western Europe is the creation of an integrated market in the European Union (EU). (See Figure 2.3 for key dates in the EU). After lifting the many tariff and nontariff barriers that hinder the flow of products, capital, and labor, Belgium, Luxembourg, Denmark, France, Germany, Ireland, Italy, the United Kingdom, the Netherlands, Greece, Spain, and Portugal will form a large, integrated market. The gradual elimination of internal tariff and nontariff barriers within the EU will create a highly competitive but attractive market. The combined GDP of the EU in 1991 was $6.1 trillion, with a population of 345.8 million. (For comparative data on the Triad, see Table 2.1.)

Many have suggested that the EU will become a tariff fortress, but this is not likely. Trade relations are influenced by the reciprocity rule. Thus, if the EU erects new trade barriers against other countries, those countries may erect trade barriers against the EU. If the EU closes its doors to firms from other

TABLE 2.1   Population and Gross Domestic Product

	Population (Mil.) 1991	G.D.P (Mil. U.S. $) 1991
European Union		
Belgium	10.00	$ 196,873
Denmark	5.20	112,084
France	57.00	1,199,286
Germany	80.10	1,574,316
Greece	10.30	57,900
Ireland	3.50	39,028
Italy	57.80	1,150,516
Luxembourg ('90)[a]	0.38	8,700
Netherlands	15.10	290,725
Portugal	9.90	65,103
Spain	39.00	527,131
United Kingdom	57.60	876,758
TOTAL	345.88	$6,098,420
North America		
United States	252.70	$5,610,800
Canada	27.30	510,835
Mexico	83.30	282,526
TOTAL	363.30	$6,404,161
Asia Pacific		
Hong Kong	5.80	$ 67,555
Singapore	2.80	39,984
South Korea	43.30	282,970
Taiwan ('90)[b]	20.20	155,736
Malaysia	18.20	46,980
Indonesia	181.30	116,476
Thailand	57.20	93,310
Philippines	62.90	44,908
Japan	123.90	3,362,282
TOTAL	515.60	$4,210,201

Source: World Bank, *World Development Report 1993*.
[a]Euromonitor, *European Marketing Data and Statistics 1993*, 28th ed., Euromonitor Publications, London.
[b]Euromonitor, *International Marketing Data and Statistics 1993*, 17th ed., Euromonitor Publications, London.

countries, those countries may close their doors to EU firms. Reciprocity in trade relations is a powerful inducement for countries to keep their markets open. The question before the EU is how well it can protect the interests of its firms without launching a trade war.

The EU is motivated by a desire to provide an enhanced competitive edge to EU firms in relation to non-EU firms. To achieve this goal, existing rules and regulations affecting different aspects of business activities are being gradually and carefully modified. Measures that have already been approved cover capital movements, banking, technological standards, automobile exhausts, and profes-sional recognition. Furthermore, agreement among EU members is likely on public contracts, mergers and takeovers, and television broadcasting.[6] Overall, the EU has the potential of becoming more competitive as its firms consolidate their resources through mergers, acquisitions, and, above all, rationalizations—the application of modern methods to achieve efficiency.

The Asian Pacific Economies

In the Asian Pacific region, during the last decade South Korea, Taiwan, Hong Kong, and Singapore have emerged as major economic players in the global market. Currently, these newly industrialized countries (NICs) are in the process of consolidating their resources to target specific industries for product devel-opment and market expansion. By focusing on high-value-added products and diversifying their markets, these countries have become strong competitors in markets traditionally considered strongholds of American, German, and Japa-nese firms. These NICs already compete in autos, telecommunications, electron-ics, and other state-of-the-art technologies such as fiber optics and computer chips. In addition to the four NICs, four other Asian Pacific countries—Malaysia, Indonesia, Thailand, and the Philippines—are poised to become formidable competitors in high-value-added products.

Japan, having established itself as a global economic power, is playing a significant role in shaping the industrial development of the Asian Pacific region. For example, Japan's Ministry of International Trade and Industry (MITI) has prepared blueprints to develop new industries in neighboring Asian countries, particularly Thailand, Malaysia, Indonesia, and the Philippines. The plan proposes making Malaysia one of the foremost producers of word proces-sors, answering machines, and facsimile devices. Indonesia is targeted for tex-tiles, forest products, and plastics.[7]

As Japan's role increases, and as other developing economies in the region improve their economic competitiveness, intraregional trade in the Asian Pacific region will increase. Economic growth in Asian Pacific will be fueled by three

---

[6] Mark Nelson, "Measure for Measure," *The Wall Street Journal,* September 22, 1989, R8.

[7] Bernard Wysocki, "Guiding Hand: In Asia the Japanese Hope to 'Coordinate' What Nations Produce," *The Wall Street Journal,* August 20, 1990, 1, A4.

important developments: increasing domestic demand, expanding business involvement overseas, and growing competitiveness of firms based in this region. The growth of manufacturing, marketing, and financial activities in Asian Pacific will transform the region into a highly attractive market for products and services. It is in this market that Japan's influence is increasing, while America's is clearly waning.[8]

The North American Free Trade Agreement

The North American Free Trade Agreement (NAFTA) among the United States, Canada, and Mexico is an important step towards integrating the economies of the three countries. The NAFTA will reduce tariffs and quotas; liberalize trade in several areas including agriculture, autos, textiles and apparel, trucking, and government procurement; grant favorable treatment to investors; and establish agencies to investigate environmental and labor abuses.[9]

The assumption guiding the formation of NAFTA is that increasing the size of the North American market by reducing trade barriers will enhance the competitive edge of North American firms. The combined GDP of the United States and Canada was $6.1 trillion in 1991, with a population of 280 million. By including Mexico in the pact, the combined GDP of the three countries increases to $6.4 trillion, and the population to 363.3 million. Overall, NAFTA will result in a higher GDP and population than the EU. (For comparative data on the Triad, see Table 2.1.)

THE GLOBAL ECONOMY

Four major developments characterize the global economic environment: increasing trade and investment, increasing interdependence, increasing competition, and increasing complexity. These developments are affecting the structure, conduct, and performance of firms throughout the world.

Increasing Trade and Investment

In 1960, world exports totaled $118.8 billion, and by 1991 had increased to over $3.4 trillion.[10] This phenomenal growth was fueled by two forces: the expansion of marketing activities beyond the confines of national borders, and the growing

---

[8] James Sterngold, "Japan Builds East Asia Links, Gaining Labor and Markets," *The New York Times*, May 8, 1990, A1.

[9] United States Department of State, *U.S.–Canada Free Trade Agreement*, Washington, DC, June 1988.

[10] International Monetary Fund, *International Financial Statistics Yearbook* 1989 and 1992, Washington, DC.

efforts of governments to increase exports from their own countries. Firms realized that to achieve economies of scale and to improve their competitiveness, they would have to expand their operations to multiple countries. Governments also realized that earnings from exports could be used to stimulate domestic economic growth and development. Thus, marketing considerations, coupled with export-enhancing governmental policies, increased world trade phenomenally. (See Table 2.2 and Figure 2.4 for data on world exports and the share of the five largest exporters—the United States, Germany, Japan, France, and the United Kingdom—for selected years.)

Compared to exports, foreign direct investment has been expanding at an

TABLE 2.2   Exports (Billions U.S. $)

Country	1960	1970	1980	1991
U.S.A.	20.601	42.659	225.57	422.16
Germany	11.417	34.228	192.86	402.84
Japan	4.055	19.317	130.44	314.79
France	6.867	17.879	116.03	217.02
U.K.	10.606	19.428	110.13	184.96
World	118.8	290.5	1910.9	3441.7

Source: International Monetary Fund, *International Financial Statistics Yearbook* 1989 & 1992, Washington, DC.

FIGURE 2.4   Percentage of World Exports 1960–1991

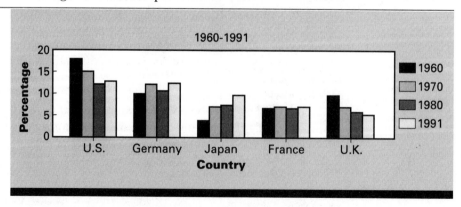

Source: International Monetary Fund, *International Financial Statistics Yearbook* 1989 & 1992, Washington, DC.

even faster rate. By 1989, the total worldwide stock of foreign direct investment stood at approximately $1.5 trillion. Between 1983 and 1989, foreign direct investment outflows increased at the rate of 29 percent a year. During this same period, world exports grew at 9.4 percent, and world gross domestic product grew at 7.8 percent.[11] Foreign direct investment is playing a significant role in the transfer of technology, managerial know-how, and financial resources from one country to another. The United States, the United Kingdom, Germany, France, and Japan are the five major countries from which foreign direct investments originate. Both increasing foreign direct investments and increasing trade have made the global economy more interdependent.

Increasing Interdependence

Increasing trade in goods, services, and capital among countries and the growing involvement of global corporations in multiple countries have created an interdependent global economy. The economic fate of one country is inextricably tied to economic events in other countries. For example, a country's growing economy encourages imports from other countries. As more products are imported from a country, it in turn experiences economic growth. Likewise, when a country is experiencing a downturn in its economy, the effects are not confined to its domestic economy alone but to those of its leading trading partners as well.

Increasing Competition

As firms expand their business and marketing operations globally, they increase the intensity of competition in each country. Recently, the number of firms with global operations has increased in many industries. In the auto industry, for example, the United States, Germany, and Japan were once the major global players. Recently, South Korea has joined the competitive arena, and Malaysia is poised to establish its marketing presence in the auto market. In many other industries including medical equipment, optics, computers, and farm equipment, the number of firms with a global presence has increased considerably. Increasing global competition is forcing firms to develop better ways of satisfying consumers. As such, firms are focusing on all four elements of the marketing mix (product, price, promotion, and place) to achieve a competitive advantage.

Increasing Complexity

The global economy has also become more complex because of increasing trade and investment, increasing interdependence, and increasing competition. Fiscal and monetary policies designed for a country's domestic economy affect the

---

[11] United Nations, *World Investment Report,* New York, 1991.

economic performance of other countries. For example, inflationary monetary policies in the United States will affect not only the United States, but also its major trading partners in Europe and Asian Pacific. The close link among the economies of different countries has created an extremely complex global economy. Economic events in a country are not isolated. They have repercussions in other economies.

THE GLOBALIZATION OF THE U.S. ECONOMY

In terms of market size, the United States is the largest economy in the world. Ironically, it was the size of the U.S. economy that discouraged many businesses in the past from establishing marketing presence in other countries. In 1960, U.S. merchandise exports as a percentage of GDP was close to 4 percent. Recently, however, this situation has changed. In 1990, U.S. merchandise exports as a percentage of GDP increased to over 7 percent.[12] The increasing involvement of American firms is motivated by the realization that they can no longer rely exclusively on domestic purchasing power for future growth. In today's business environment, competitive pressures from local and foreign firms are eroding domestic market shares of many U.S. firms and forcing them to explore marketing opportunities in different countries. It is important to note that while U.S. exports as a percentage of GDP has increased, the share of U.S. exports as a percentage of world exports has declined from 17.3 percent in 1960 to 12.3 percent in 1991 (see Figure 2.4).

To enhance their competitive position, American marketers are exploring different options such as exporting, licensing, and investing. There is a growing realization among American firms that reluctance to engage in committed global marketing will hurt not only them but also the U.S. economy.[13] Operating in the global market provides a firm greater discretion in developing new products, establishing new markets, and cross-subsidizing products and markets. Cross subsidization is the use of financial resources accumulated in one market to fight a competitive battle in another.[14] As the global involvement of U.S. firms increases, their competitiveness increases as well.

---

[12] *Economic Report of the President*, U.S. Government Printing Office, February 1992.

[13] Somkid Jatusripitak, Liam Fahey, and Philip Kotler, "Strategic Global Marketing: Lessons from the Japanese," *The Columbia Journal of World Business* 20, spring 1985, 47–53.

[14] Gary Hamel and C. K. Prahalad, "Do You Really Have a Global Strategy," *Harvard Business Review* 85, July/August 1985, 139–148.

SUMMARY

The three layers of the economic environment that influence the conduct of global marketing activities are the local economy, the regional economy, and the global economy. In examining the local economic environment, a firm focuses on three variables: the economic conditions of consumers, the economic condition of the host country, and the competitive environment of the industry. In analyzing regional economies, a global marketer focuses on economic relations among countries within a region. The emphasis is on understanding how the removal or imposition of trade barriers within a region would affect the flow of products and services from one country to another.

Countries cooperate to manage their economic relations. The level of cooperation is reflected in economic arrangements made to facilitate trade. These arrangements can result in the formation of a free-trade area, a customs union, a common market, or an economic union.

Global marketers realize that to successfully establish their marketing presence in a host country they have to understand economic developments taking place at the global level. In recent years, global trade and foreign direct investments have been increasing rapidly, making the global economy more interdependent, competitive, and complex.

The United States, with the largest economy in the world, plays an important role in the global economy. Both exports from and imports into the United States have been increasing. Growing U.S. involvement in global trade and investment means that economic, political, and social developments in other countries have a bearing on the performance of the U.S. economy. For firms, this is an important consideration in developing global marketing strategies.

CHAPTER THREE

When it is a question of money, everybody is of the same religion.

Voltaire

The Financial Environment

A firm's marketing involvement varies from country to country. In some countries, a firm may be involved in sourcing, producing, and marketing. In others, the operations may be limited to exporting. Regardless of the level of marketing involvement in a country, a firm must be able to operate successfully within the complex global financial environment. In this chapter we will focus on the following topics: the financial system within which global marketing activities are conducted, management of exchange risk, financial institutions that help global marketing activities, and global currency markets.

Global marketing activities require moving funds from one country to another, converting one currency to another, conducting transactions in different currencies, and managing the future value of different currencies. Understanding and managing the key elements of the financial environment can mean the difference between success or failure in global marketing. For many businesses, managing different currencies acts as a deterrent to engaging in global marketing; but for a few, it makes global marketing both challenging and rewarding.

The impact of financial considerations is significant to marketing decisions. Critical decisions such as where a firm can sell its products, and how, when, how much, and by whom it gets paid are determined in part by financial considerations. For example, a firm interested in selling products to distributors in different countries has to deal with a host of issues: how to set the price of the product in the currency of each country; how the distributors' financial ability will affect the terms and methods of payment; what effects each country's banking regulations will have on the conversion of one currency to another. It is important for a firm to understand how these issues will affect its global marketing activities. Crossnational differences in the financial environment create the uncontrollable constraints within which a global marketer operates. Knowing how global marketing activities can be managed advantageously within these constraints is critical for deciding how, when, and where global marketing activities should be conducted.

THE FINANCIAL SYSTEM

The global financial system in place today is a well-organized, fine-tuned system. It allows a firm to hedge and speculate, convert one currency into another, and transfer large amounts of money from one country to another in the foreign exchange markets. Foreign exchange markets are markets for the purchase and sale of foreign currencies (foreign exchange). These markets are not located at any single physical location where buyers and sellers of foreign exchange meet. The markets are a network of computer systems, telephones, cables, and other communications media that banks and foreign exchange dealers use to complete transactions. The major foreign exchange markets are found in leading financial centers such as London, New York, and Tokyo. Understanding how the global financial system works can be enhanced by examining some of its key elements and features, which we discuss in the next section.

Acceptability and Convertibility

Each country has its own currency, which serves as the common measure of value and medium of exchange. A country's currency is commonly accepted within its territory for conducting economic activities and business transactions. In the United States, consumers use dollars to buy products and services. In Bangladesh, they use takas. Although an American marketer may not accept takas in exchange for his products, a Bangladeshi trader will happily accept dollars for his products.

Some currencies are readily accepted in exchange for products and services. These currencies, among others, are the German mark, American dollar, British pound, French franc, and Japanese yen. And there are other currencies that global marketers do not readily accept in exchange for their products and services. Among many others, these currencies include the taka of Bangladesh, rupee of Sri Lanka, pound of Sudan, and franc of Mali. The acceptability of a currency, in general, is determined by the economic position of its country in the global economy. A taka, for example, is not readily acceptable because Bangladesh is not a major player in global trade. There is not much that Bangladesh can sell in the world market at a competitive price. The acceptability of a currency is also influenced by how easily it can be exchanged for another currency. A currency that can be freely converted, such as the American dollar, is more readily accepted than a currency that cannot be freely converted, such as the pound of Sudan.

Hard Currencies

Hard currencies are readily accepted, easily converted, and freely traded in foreign exchange markets. These are primarily the currencies of developed countries such as the United States, Japan, Germany, France, the United Kingdom, Switzerland, and other western European countries. These currencies are preferred by businesses both in developed and developing countries because they can easily be traded in foreign exchange markets. Thus, a Nigerian marketer may sell her products to an Egyptian on the condition that the buyer in Egypt pays for the merchandise in American dollars or German marks rather than in the Egyptian pound. In general, hard currencies are appealing to global marketers precisely because they are readily accepted, easily converted, and freely traded.

Soft Currencies

Soft currencies are not freely traded in the foreign exchange markets. These currencies are neither readily accepted nor easily converted. The currencies of countries such as Somalia, Albania, Romania, Pakistan, and Afghanistan are considered soft currencies. In general, currencies of less developed as well as developing countries are grouped under the soft currency category. Although global marketers do not generally prefer to deal in soft currencies, the risks associated with soft currencies are far fewer today than they were a decade ago. Increasing global trade has increased both the demand for and supply of soft currencies. With improved communications networks among different financial centers and institutions, the soft currency markets are gradually developing. As the risk associated with soft currencies diminishes, global marketers are exploring the different possibilities that can make dealing in soft currencies competitively advantageous.

Exchange Rates

The price of one currency in terms of another is called the *exchange rate*. If one dollar can buy two marks, the price or exchange rate of marks in terms of dollars is $.50 per mark. When the exchange rates of a currency are determined by demand and supply conditions alone—without the influence of governmental interventions—this is referred to as *floating exchange rates*. Both the demand and supply of a country's currency are influenced by developments in its domestic economy and the global economy. Among the factors that influence a currency's demand and supply, the following are considered important: inflation, interest rates, productivity changes, speculators' expectations, economic growth, trade deficit, and political stability.

One important variation of floating exchange rates is managed float. When the exchange rates of a currency are determined by government-managed demand and supply, it is referred to as *managed float*. In a managed float system, the rates are allowed to respond to market conditions, but only within limits considered acceptable by governments. For example, in a managed float system, a central bank may intervene when appreciation of a country's currency undermines the trading competitiveness of its firms or when depreciation of its currency increases the risk of inflation within the country.[1] As interventions by a central bank may require buying or selling foreign exchange, the maintenance of foreign reserves becomes necessary.

The floating exchange rate system, which began in 1973, lasted until 1985. The system worked fairly well until 1982, when the U.S. current account deficit began to grow at a disturbing rate. The Group of Five (the United States, Japan, Germany, the United Kingdom, and France), concerned about the global financial situation, met at the Plaza Hotel in New York and agreed to begin managing exchange rates.[2] The Plaza agreement was the beginning of a change in the global financial system.

Depreciation and Appreciation

When the exchange value of a currency increases, it is said to have appreciated; when the exchange value of a currency declines, it is said to have depreciated. When one currency appreciates in relation to another, the other has depreciated. Consider this example. Suppose that on January 1, 1 dollar could be exchanged for 2 marks. But on January 7, 1 dollar was selling for 2.2 marks. The dollar has appreciated because its exchange value has increased, and the mark has depreciated because its exchange value has declined. It takes 2.2 marks to buy a dollar that once cost 2 marks. Thus, in a relative sense, the appreciation of one currency is the depreciation of the other. In today's global financial markets, the exchange rates of major currencies fluctuate from second to second.

Most of us become familiar with the depreciation or appreciation of a currency when we travel abroad and convert one currency into another—say, dollars into yen. On August 26, 1992, American tourists in Japan could get 124.82 yen per dollar. However, on September 30, 1992—five weeks later—a dollar could be exchanged for only 120 yen. This represents a depreciation of the dollar. As a result, American tourists probably bought fewer Japanese goods, because their price in terms of dollars had increased.

Depreciation or appreciation of a currency can have a significant impact on how firms conduct marketing activities. Take the case of Valmont Industries, a Nebraska manufacturer of irrigation systems, street light systems, and power supplies. In the early 1980s, when a strong U.S. dollar made American goods too expensive for exporting, Valmont responded by building a factory in Madrid, Spain. The company supplied irrigation systems to its European customers from this plant. However, when the dollar became weak in the late 1980s,

---

[1] Daniel R. Kane, *Principles of International Finance,* London: Croom Helm Ltd., 1988.

[2] John C. Pool, Stephen C. Stamos, and Patrice F. Jones, *The ABCs of International Finance,* Lexington, MA: Lexington Books, 1991.

Valmont increased exports from its Nebraska plant. It had become cheaper for the company to sell products manufactured in Nebraska than those manufactured in Spain. For Valmont, fluctuating exchange rates posed a dilemma: while exports from its U.S. plant increased, sales revenue from products manufactured abroad went down.[3]

MANAGING EXCHANGE RISKS

Financial considerations play an important role in marketing decisions. When a new product is introduced in a country, funds may be required in the currency of that country. Profits from one country may need to be converted to the currency of another country where the firm wants to establish production facilities. Firms may need to put aside for future use currencies obtained from the sale of products.

A firm must manage its worldwide financial resources to meet overall corporate objectives. Getting the greatest value from the company's currency pool is only one of the challenges. To successfully manage the financial aspects of global marketing, a firm should know how the foreign exchange market works. In a foreign exchange market, there are two main types of currency transactions: spot and forward transactions. *Spot transactions* are generally completed within one or two business days. *Forward transactions* are completed on an agreed-upon future date, usually no more than six months. Both spot and forward transactions can be used to manage the four types of exchange risks to which a firm is exposed in global marketing.

Types of Exchange Risks

The four types of exchange risks are transaction exposure, translation exposure, tax exposure, and economic exposure. These risks evolve because of fluctuations in exchange rates. *Transaction exposure* is the risk associated with converting a currency to another currency at a later date. Let us assume that you had 100,000 yen on September 1, and the exchange rate on that day was 200 yen per dollar. Thus, on September 1 you could have bought $500 for 100,000 yen. However, if you waited to convert your 100,000 yen into dollars at a later date, the exchange rate might not be the same as it was on September 1. These fluctuations in exchange rates create the transaction exposure. Companies usually consolidate their transactions in one currency at the end of a year. *Translation exposure* occurs when the exchange rate at the time of consolidating all transactions into one currency is different from the time when the transactions were

---

[3] Louis Uchitelle, "Manufacturers Group Urges Big U.S. Push for Exports," *The New York Times*, February 9, 1991, 17, 21.

completed. *Tax exposure* occurs when the tax liability of a company changes because of changes in the exchange rates. *Economic exposure* is a comprehensive term that refers to the total long-term exposure of a firm to changes in exchange rates, and how these changes can affect the present value of future cash flow.

To understand how a firm can protect itself from a potential loss due to exchange rate fluctuations, consider the following simplified example. On January 1, 1993, a U.S. firm sells 100 laser printers to a German company for 100,000 German marks, with payment due on March 1, 1993. The January 1 exchange rate is 2 marks per dollar. Thus, in dollars, the price of 100 laser printers is $50,000. Let us assume that on March 1, 1993, the exchange rate changes to 2.25 marks per dollar and that on January 1 the U.S. firm could not have predicted this change. What happens on March 1? The U.S. firm gets 100,000 marks and converts them to dollars. As the March 1 exchange rate is $1.00 = 2.25 marks, the U.S. firm gets only $44,444.44, a loss of $5,555.56 How can this U.S. firm protect itself from potential losses due to exchange rate fluctuations? Explained below are three methods.

Natural Hedging. *Natural hedging* involves buying and selling in the same currency. Thus, on March 1, 1993, rather than converting marks into dollars, the U.S. firm can use its 100,000 marks to buy products and services in Germany. Although the dollar has rallied, it does not have adverse effects because the firm is not converting marks into dollars. Natural hedging is quite common among firms with subsidiaries in different countries.

Currency Forwards. The U.S. firm can also protect itself by entering into a *forward contract* in a foreign exchange market. For example, the firm can sign a contract to buy $50,000 for 100,000 marks on March 1, 1993. These transactions are usually arranged through a bank. By signing the deal, the firm is assured of receiving $50,000 in exchange for its 100,000 marks on March 1, 1993. Even though the dollar rallies on March 1, 1993, the firm is protected from a loss of $5,555.56.

Options. A *foreign-exchange option* is another alternative the U.S. firm could consider to protect itself from potential losses due to exchange rate fluctuations. Under this option, the U.S. firm enters into a contract to buy or sell foreign exchange on a particular date. However, unlike the forward contract—in which the firm is obligated to fulfil the contract—foreign-exchange options grant the firm the right, but not the obligation, to honor the contract. This means that on the day the contract matures, the firm can choose not to complete the transaction. Whether the firm completes the transaction depends on the difference between the exchange rates agreed upon in the contract and the spot rate on the maturity date.

Suppose that the U.S. firm, on January 1, 1993, enters into a contract with a foreign exchange dealer to buy $50,000 for 100,000 marks on March 1, 1993.

The firm also buys an option from the dealer for $500 that gives it the right to buy $50,000 for 100,000 marks on March 1 but does not obligate it to do so. What would the firm choose to do on March 1? Would it buy $50,000 for 100,000 marks? The answer depends on what the exchange rate of marks is in terms of dollars on March 1, 1993.

Three things can happen in a foreign exchange market on March 1, 1993. The dollar can appreciate, depreciate, or stay at the same level as it was on January 1. Let us assume that on March 1 the dollar appreciates to 2.25 marks per dollar, as we have indicated earlier. Should the U.S. firm exercise the option and receive its $50,000 for 100,000 marks from the bank? Yes—because, if the firm were to exchange 100,000 marks in foreign exchange markets, it would only get $44,444.44 on March 1. However, if the dollar depreciates to, say, 1.80 marks per dollar, should the firm exercise the option? No. Why not? Because it can get $55,555.56 in foreign exchange markets for its 100,000 marks. What would the firm do if the exchange rate remains the same? The firm would be indifferent to exercising its option.

We have discussed above how a firm can use natural hedging, currency forwards, and options to protect itself from potential losses from exchange rate fluctuations. We will next examine how different financial institutions help U.S.–based firms increase their global marketing involvements.

FINANCIAL INSTITUTIONS

Financial institutions play an important role in facilitating business transactions conducted across countries. A global marketer should be familiar with financial institutions that can help in marketing. We will deal with two financial institutions that play an important role in enhancing the global activities of American firms.

Commercial Banks

Most commercial banks in the United States have international banking departments. These departments are generally staffed by people who are specialists on specific countries. These specialists can provide useful information to a firm that is considering marketing in a foreign country, as well as to firms that have extensive operations in multiple countries. Many large banks, to assist their clients, either have their own branches in foreign countries or maintain correspondent relationships with banks in these countries. Commercial banks can facilitate global marketing by

◆ providing free consulting services to firms interested in establishing marketing presence in different countries

◆ preparing documents, facilitating collections, and arranging for payments

♦ exchanging currencies and providing financing and hedging facilities
♦ collecting foreign invoices, drafts, letters of credit, and other financial documents
♦ transferring funds to other countries and providing credit information on foreign buyers
♦ giving letters of introduction and letters of credit to marketers

Export-Import Bank

The Export-Import Bank (Eximbank), an independent U.S. government agency, facilitates the financing of U.S. exports. Its objective is to provide loans, guarantees, and insurance to finance the purchase of U.S. goods and services in foreign countries. To achieve these goals, the Eximbank provides a number of services to U.S. businesses. Its six main financial programs are direct loans, guarantees, engineering multiplier program, operation and maintenance service program, working capital guarantees, and export credit insurance.

Direct loans provide capital to foreign buyers of U.S. goods and services. Guarantees provide repayment protection to U.S. and foreign commercial lenders for their loans to foreign buyers of U.S. goods and services. The engineering multiplier program stimulates exports of U.S. architectural design and engineering services. It provides financing in support of project-related design services or feasibility studies that may generate further exports of U.S. goods and services. The operation and maintenance services program provides loans or loan guarantees to train local personnel in the operation or maintenance of plant systems and procedures. The working capital guarantee program, a loan guarantee program, provides eligible exporters with access to working capital loans from commercial lenders who would not make these loans without a guarantee from Eximbank. The export credit insurance program protects U.S. exporters from the failure of foreign buyers to make payments for their purchases. In providing these services, the Eximbank does not compete with private financing, but supplements it to help U.S. businesses achieve their exporting goals.

THE GLOBAL CURRENCY MARKET

According to a 1990 survey by the Bank for International Settlements, $650 billion a day of foreign exchange is traded worldwide. The major players are large banks, multinational corporations, global money managers, individual speculators, and tourists.[4] The integration of the global economy, the expansion

---

[4] George Anders, "Answers to Commonly Asked Questions About Currency Trading in a Wild Week," *The Wall Street Journal*, September 17, 1992, A7.

of the capital market, the revolution in communications, and the acceleration of foreign-exchange transactions have considerably reduced the ability of a government to control the global financial market.

Eurocurrency

Innovations in private financial markets, coupled with technological developments that make instantaneous communications possible around the world, are driving forces behind the creation of a worldwide wholesale market for currencies. Governments and businesses can borrow funds in this large and complex market, also referred to as the *Eurocurrency market.* A Eurocurrency is a claim against a bank in a currency different from that of the bank's home country. The prefix *Euro* is now commonly used to refer to currencies traded outside their origin. Thus, Eurodollars are U.S. dollars deposited in banks outside the United States. Likewise, Euroyen are Japanese yen deposited in banks outside Japan. There is a large market for this Eurocurrency. The phenomenal growth of the Eurocurrency market has been motivated by many factors, including depositors' desire to keep currency holdings a secret, avoid regulations and taxes, and maintain control over deposits.

The size of the Eurocurrency market has grown at a phenomenal rate. In the ten-year period ending in 1987, total net deposits of Eurocurrency increased from \$478 billion to \$2,377 billion. The largest share of the market, around 66 percent, was held by dollar-denominated deposits (\$1,569 billion). Comparatively, the total figure of dollars held in the United States by commercial banks and thrift institutions in savings, time, and demand deposits was \$2,376 billion in 1987.[5]

Asian Dollar Market

The Asian dollar market is playing an important role in encouraging trade between the Asian Pacific countries and the rest of the world. The Asian Pacific countries—especially Japan, South Korea, Taiwan, Singapore, and Hong Kong—are playing a significant role in today's global economy. The increasing trade between Asian Pacific and the rest of the world has created both a demand for and supply of major currencies, but especially U.S. dollars. The Asian dollar market consists of a group of banks in Singapore and Hong Kong that accept deposits and make loans in U.S. dollars.

European Monetary System

In March 1979, the EU agreed to set up a European Monetary System (EMS) as part of Europe's increasing unification. Within this monetary system, ex-

---

[5] Bruce G. Resnick, "The Globalization of World Financial Markets," *Business Horizons,* November/December 1989, 34–41.

change rates were to remain nearly fixed. The agreement also called for a new European central bank and the creation of a new currency, the European Currency Unit (ECU). Since 1979, the performance of EMS has been mixed. Although the commitment allowed deviations of 2.5 percent from the initial declared par value, exchange rate fluctuations have been much wider.

SUMMARY

Global marketing activities are conducted within the global financial environment. This environment is active, dynamic, and beyond the control of global marketers. The motivating forces for change in this environment are diverse, ranging from technological developments to political visions. Global marketers need to understand the mechanics of this financial environment. This understanding will help them achieve a competitive advantage in the global marketplace.

Global marketers should recognize that buyers have many sources for their purchases, and a variety of possible financial arrangements. Thus, it is up to marketers to make their products and financial arrangements more attractive than those of their competitors. Marketers can obtain a competitive advantage by better understanding the needs of buyers and by making flexible financial arrangements. Rigidity in conducting marketing activities comes from not knowing how best to use the financial environment to one's own advantage.

Consider this simple but instructive example to understand how different financial arrangements can give a firm a competitive advantage. You wish to buy a computer for your home office but currently do not have cash on hand. There are two retailers selling the same brand of computer. One retailer allows you to buy on credit with full payment due after 60 days. The other retailer refuses to sell on credit and wants cash for his computer. Who will get your business? The point is that creative financial arrangements can enhance a global marketer's competitive position just as they enhance those of a local retailer. To operate effectively in today's global economy, a global marketer should have a working knowledge of how the national and global financial environments work and how they can be effectively used for conducting marketing activities. In particular, a global marketer should know about the global monetary system, the financial institutions, and the currency markets.

CHAPTER FOUR

Free trade, one of the greatest blessings which a country can confer on a people, is in almost every country unpopular.

Thomas Babington

The Political and Legal Environment

Governments play an important role in regulating business and marketing activities. The role of a government as regulator is coming under greater scrutiny as global marketing involvements of firms continue to increase at a rapid pace. The constraints imposed by governmental regulations determine to a great extent what a firm can and cannot do within a country. For global marketers, it is important to understand why and how governments regulate business activities. And to manage governmental regulations, global marketers should also be aware of how they can analyze and respond to the regulatory environment of a country. We examine these critical issues in this chapter.

Global firms operate in a country with the consent of the government. Generally, a government imposes certain restrictions on a firm's operations before it allows the firm to operate. The firm, in turn, may set certain conditions and requirements of its own. Negotiations between the government and the firm are influenced by the objectives each wants to achieve, and thus the role that each expects the other to play. When negotiations between the two lead to an agreement, the agreement spells out the rules of the game and provides broad guidelines for the firm's activities within the country.

The agreement between the government and the firm that sets the stage for the firm's operations in the country seldom remains in effect for long. Over time, the government may intervene and impose additional conditions on the firm's operations. Governmental interventions that "interfere with or prevent business transactions, or change the terms of agreements, or cause the confiscation of wholly or partially foreign owned business property," are referred to as *political risk*.[1] The question is why governments intervene in the business and marketing operations of a global firm. This is the subject of the next section.

---

[1] V. Fred Weston and Bart W. Sorge, *International Managerial Finance*, Homewood, IL: Richard D. Irwin, 1972, 60.

WHY DO GOVERNMENTS INTERVENE?

Governmental interventions in the activities of a global firm are motivated by different factors, including the self-interest of the government. To stay in power or get reelected, a government needs the support of many constituencies, including labor unions, religious organizations, farmers, small and large businesses, and environmental groups, among others. When one of these groups—say, a labor union—claims that the activities of a global firm are adversely affecting local firms and local employment conditions, the government may feel compelled to take actions against the firm to placate the labor union. Hitachi, a Japanese electronic manufacturer, was authorized by the British government to operate a TV assembly plant in northern England. A British labor union launched a bitter campaign, claiming that Hitachi would destroy the domestic industry and eliminate in the long run two thousand jobs. Due to the seriousness of the protest, the government backed out of the agreement and Hitachi had to leave.[2]

Governmental interventions in the activities of a global firm are also influenced by macrosystemic concerns, which Boddewyn and Cracco[3] have grouped under three categories: national interest, national sovereignty, and national identity. One of the major functions of a government is to protect the national interest of the country. Thus, after claiming that the national interest of the country is at stake, a government may intervene in the activities of a global firm. The Peruvian government, for example, nationalized the Banco Continental, a Chase Manhattan Bank subsidiary, after declaring banking a strategic sector of the economy. Governments also set a limit on foreign ownership of strategic industries such as telecommunications, defense, transportation, and news media for reasons of national sovereignty. To safeguard national identity, promotional activities of businesses may be regulated. For example, in Saudi Arabia human nudity and images of pigs are forbidden in ads to protect the national identity.

TYPES OF INTERVENTIONS

Governmental interventions affect different aspects of a firm's activities. In an extreme case, a government may ask a firm to close its operations and leave the

---

[2] R. F. Janssen, "Hitachi Bid to Build Television Plant in Britain, Creating Jobs, Provokes a Storm of Opposition," *The Wall Street Journal*, November 1, 1977, 46.

[3] Boddewyn, J. J. and E. F. Cracco, "The Political Game in World Business," *Columbia Journal of World Business,* January/February 1972, 7, 45–56.

country. And in a less drastic case, a government can institute a policy that requires a firm to seek governmental approval before raising or lowering prices. As the business and marketing activities of a global firm are linked across countries, governmental interventions in one country can affect the firm's operations in other countries. The increasingly active role of governments in regulating a firm's activities necessitates the understanding of what a government can do to materially affect the performance of a firm in a particular country as well as elsewhere.

Ownership and Control

Confiscation, expropriation, and domestication are three types of intervention that are considered extremely severe because they affect the ownership and control of a firm within a given country. Confiscation occurs when a government takes over a firm's local operations and does not compensate the firm for its loss. When a government takes over a firm's local operations and provides compensation, it is called expropriation. Domestication is the process whereby a government forces a firm to relinquish ownership and control of its local operations to nationals. These three types of intervention have received much press because of their severe effect on global firms.

Although cases of confiscation and expropriation have been numerous, especially in economically less developed countries, these extreme forms of governmental intervention are expected to decline. The reasons for their decline are that governments realize that they send the wrong signal to potential investors when they confiscate or expropriate global firms' assets; governments have discovered that they have been unable to achieve their socioeconomic and political goals through confiscation or expropriation; and governments now realize that they can achieve their societal goals by other types of intervention that are less extreme as well as less pernicious.

Foreign Exchange, Export, Import, and Taxation

Governments have numerous other options with which to regulate and control the activities of a global firm. Exchange controls, export requirements, import restrictions, and tax regulations are a few of these regulatory options. For example, when faced with a scarcity of foreign exchange, a government can establish exchange controls. This would mean that a firm may not be able to convert its earnings into another currency, or that to obtain foreign exchange from the government for importing raw materials, it may have to pay a higher rate than the market-determined exchange rate. To earn foreign exchange, a government can also demand that a certain amount of the firm's output be exported. Import restrictions, however, can effectively force a firm to buy raw materials locally. Tax laws can also be changed. Often, after letting a firm establish operations in the country, the government changes its tax rate for the global firms to increase tax revenue. In addition to these regulatory options, a government can also regulate the four elements of the marketing mix: product, price, place, and promotion.

The Marketing Mix

Governmental interventions in the marketing mix take different forms. The local content law, one of the most popular interventions in the product category, requires that a certain portion of a product marketed within a country be locally manufactured. In regulating price, the government can set a price ceiling—that is, an upper limit on the price a firm can charge in the market. Requirements can be imposed on a firm to distribute its products in places where it may not be profitable to do so. The government can also demand that the firm use a local advertising agency to develop its promotional campaigns. In controlling the activities of a global marketer, a government is limited only by its imagination. The options are myriad and the effects are varied. It is important, however, not to conclude that governments indiscriminately use their power to interfere in the activities of global firms. As explained earlier, governmental interventions are motivated by different reasons, and a global marketer should attempt to ascertain what they are.

ASSESSING POLITICAL RISK

One important task for a global marketer is to assess political risk in a country. Assessing political risk means that a marketer has to estimate the likelihood of governmental interventions in his firm's business and marketing activities. For instance, when will a government impose import restrictions or ask the company to change its product content? Or, when will the political environment in a country change so dramatically that extreme forms of intervention such as confiscation and expropriation become inevitable? A global marketer realizes that it is difficult to predict precisely when and how a government will intervene in his firm's marketing activities. However, rather than operating in the dark, a global marketer must use different methods to assess the impact of future developments in the political environment on his firm's performance.

Assessing political risk is critical because changes in the political environment can affect what can be sold in a country, how it can be sold, and even for how much it can be sold. As the risk of extreme forms of intervention such as confiscation and expropriation has declined, political risk analysis now focuses on subtle shifts in governmental policies that can turn a profitable enterprise into an unprofitable one. The assessment of political risk is becoming increasingly important because of the growing global business involvement of firms. In the following section, we discuss the different methods commonly used for assessing the potential for political risk within a country.

Experts' Opinions

Firms frequently seek opinions from current and retired government officials who have been involved in foreign affairs, and from academics who have analyzed international relationships. The firm's interest is to find out what type of political developments can occur in a country and how these developments will affect the firm's activities. Government officials, due to their experience and contacts, have gained familiarity with the political figures and conditions in various countries. They often have firsthand knowledge of the political situation in a country and can provide an educated opinion on what can happen there. For instance, they may predict which political party will come to power and what its economic agenda will be. Or, they may estimate how long the present government will stay in power and how it will affect the activities of the global firm. Henry Kissinger, secretary of state in the Nixon administration, has built a reputable consulting firm based on his personal contacts with foreign leaders and his insights on political developments. Besides government officials, academicians also provide valuable information. Having extensively studied economic and political developments, academicians often serve as consultants to major global firms.

In-House Research

Many large corporations have an in-house research department that monitors and studies political developments. Borg Warner, whose major businesses are industrial products, air conditioning, chemicals, transportation equipment, and financial services, uses its own managers and executives to monitor political risk in countries where it operates and in many where it does not. The company rates a country on five factors: political stability, economic conditions, labor situation, government controls, and external (e.g., diplomatic) relations. The most desirable countries are those with political stability, low inflation, mild tax policy, and generous investment incentives. Controls of various sorts and poor labor conditions are considered worrisome.[4]

Secondary Sources

Due to the significance of political risk and its implications for global firms, many private companies are in the business of estimating political risk in different countries and making their findings available at a price to businesses and the general public. As the study of political risk is extremely involved, requiring large data bases and sophisticated statistical analysis, it is not economi-

---

[4] Charles M. Newman and I. James Czechowitz, *International Risk Management: Management and Practices,* Morristown, New Jersey: Research Foundation of Financial Executives Institute, 1983.

cal for many firms to engage in their own analysis. For these firms, it is far more economical to obtain the services of private firms that provide risk indexes for different countries. Some of the leading sources of information on political risk are the following: BERI (Business Environment Risk Index), Business International (BI), Frost & Sullivan, and PSSI (Political System Stability Index).

The BERI index provides estimates of political risk in forty-eight countries on a regular basis. BERI also publishes reports detailing a country's credit worthiness over five years.[5] BI estimates the likelihood of risks such as nationalization, regime change, and foreign exchange repatriation restrictions; Frost & Sullivan publishes economic data about different countries and analyzes political situations.[6] PSSI estimates the probability of political events that can change the profitability of an investment.[7]

MANAGING POLITICAL RISK

As marketing activities are influenced by political developments, marketers need to influence and shape these developments as best they can. In so doing, a firm has to be careful not to overstep the bounds of acceptable ethical behavior. Bribing public officials to influence decisions is neither appropriate nor acceptable. However, in many countries, as in the United States, firms can lobby, persuade, and convince public officials to make decisions that are favorable for both the country and the firm. Before regulatory decisions are made, public officials need information. Firms should therefore share their information with officials so that subsequent decisions are acceptable to both the government and the firm.

The views presented above suggest that global marketers should be effective political actors as well as astute marketers. What this means is that global marketers should not only be able to sell toothpaste but also be able to create political conditions that will help them achieve their marketing goals. In addition to lobbying, firms can take proactive measures to reduce political risk in a country: they should try to identify with the country, help the host country achieve its societal goals, promote vertical integration, stay ahead of intervention, and insure against political risk.

---

[5] Jose De La Torre and David H. Neckar, "Forecasting Political Risks for International Operations," in Spyros Makridakis and Steven C. Wheelwright, eds., *The Handbook of Forecasting: A Managerial Guide,* 2nd ed. John Wiley & Sons, 1987, pp. 373–416.

[6] James C. Baker and Anaam Hashmi, "Political Risk Management: Steering Clear of Risky Business," *Risk Management,* October 1988, 40–47.

[7] Jeffrey D. Simon, "Political Risk Assessment: Past Trends and Future Prospects," *Columbia Journal of World Business,* fall 1982, 62–71.

Identify with the Country

It is in the interest of a global firm to identify with its host country and not maintain an image of foreignness. Political conditions seldom stay the same. With changing political conditions, some firms come under attack. A firm may be boycotted; or worse, its employees may be threatened. To avoid such adverse effects of political risk, firms should make sure they are considered part of the community. Honda spent generously on advertising to show that the products it sells in the United States are American, not Japanese.

Help the Host Country Achieve Its Societal Goals

In addition to achieving their business and marketing goals, global firms should help the host country achieve its societal goals. Goals such as acquiring better management skills, improving productivity, and increasing employment are extremely important to a host country. Global firms can participate in implementing policies that go beyond the achievement of business and marketing goals to include societal goals. For example, a global firm can encourage local participation in all aspects of its activities, from increasing the number of local employees in the management cadre to increasing the use of local raw materials.

Promote Vertical Integration

Identifying with the host country and helping it achieve its societal goals involve taking actions within the host country. By vertically integrating its corporate activities across countries, a firm can reduce the probability of governmental intervention. *Vertical integration* takes place when a firm links its activities across countries so that each unit is dependent on the other. A vertically integrated business discourages extreme forms of intervention such as confiscation because the government is unable to operate the confiscated unit without the help of the firm's other units located in other countries.

Stay Ahead of Intervention

Poynter[8] suggests that the probability of governmental intervention increases when the bargaining power of a host country increases. In general, a host country's bargaining power increases when it can replace resources normally supplied by the global firm and when it can control the firm's access to the local market, raw materials, labor, and capital. Thus, to discourage intervention,

---

[8] Thomas A. Poynter, "Managing Government Intervention: A Strategy for Defending the Subsidiary," *The Columbia Journal of World Business,* winter 1986, 55–65.

firms should upgrade their bargaining power. This can be done in many ways. They can stay ahead of the technical and managerial capabilities of the host country by introducing new products and technology and by increasing exports. However, firms should keep two things in mind when endeavoring to upgrade their bargaining power. First, they need to know when to do it; and second, how to do it locally as well as worldwide.

Insure Against Political Risk

In addition to taking proactive measures to reduce the adverse consequences of political risk, global firms can purchase insurance to cover such risks. Two important agencies from whom a global firm can purchase insurance are the Overseas Private Investment Corporation (OPIC) and the Foreign Credit Insurance Association (FCIA). The OPIC, formed by the U.S. government in 1969, offers three kinds of political risk insurance. It covers losses from currency inconvertibility, expropriation, and events such as war and revolution. The FCIA, an association of leading U.S. companies in the marine and casualty insurance field, was formed in 1961. FCIA provides insurance to U.S. exporters of goods and services against commercial and political risks that may arise from buyers' failure to pay for commercial and political reasons.

SUMMARY

Governmental interventions in business and marketing activities are of great concern to global marketers because they introduce new parameters in a firm's operations. These interventions affect different aspects of a firm's activities, such as ownership, control, exports, imports, taxation, and the marketing mix. It is important, however, to realize that governmental interventions are motivated by a desire to achieve certain goals. These may include reducing unemployment, increasing the use of domestic resources, protecting the environment, conserving foreign exchange, and improving the standard of living.

An extreme form of intervention is the confiscation of a business. The government, in this case, takes away property without compensating the owners for their loss. Such extreme forms of intervention have declined in recent years; governments have begun to realize that they can achieve their socioeconomic and political goals by imposing price controls or requiring the use of local resources.

Global marketers should recognize that political risk cannot be totally avoided. Thus, to safeguard their interest, they should try to estimate the likelihood of political changes that may adversely affect their business and take measures to discourage such interventions. Firms assess political risk in a country by seeking experts' opinions, conducting in-house research, and using secondary sources. And to manage political risk, global marketers employ strategies such as identifying with the host country, helping the host country achieve its socioeconomic and political goals, promoting vertical integration, and staying ahead of intervention.

CHAPTER **FIVE**

Understanding is the beginning of approving.

Andre Gide

The Cultural Environment

This chapter examines the cultural environment within which firms conduct global marketing activities. Beginning with a discussion of the characteristics of culture, the chapter focuses on high-context versus low-context culture, and monochronic versus polychronic culture. The chapter also covers issues related to verbal and nonverbal communications, self-reference criterion, and cultural universals.

Being primarily a social activity, marketing involves interactions among people, products, and institutions. These complex and subtle interactions are shaped by the cultural environment. Buyers' interactions with sellers, consumers' with products, and institutions' with consumers are all influenced by culture. In addition, culture determines the prepurchase, purchase, and postpurchase activities of consumers: How consumers react to marketing communications, how they reach a decision to purchase a product, which product they purchase, and how they consume the product are all shaped by culture. Therefore, global marketers need to examine culture to understand these and many other social activities.

For example, greetings are expressed differently in different societies. The Russians kiss each other on the cheek; the Japanese bow; the Indians put their palms together in a prayer position and bow slightly; and the Americans shake hands. Each country develops its unique system of customs and relationships. And if we are not familiar, for example, with the customs in Russia, we may not know how to react to a sudden kiss on the cheek. The study of culture helps us understand what and why people do what they do.

For global marketers, the knowledge of culture is essential for developing marketing strategies. Whether consumers reject or accept a particular marketing offering is to a great extent determined by the cultural forces operating on their cognitive, affective, and conative behavior. To understand consumers' behavior and to become an effective decision maker, a global marketer must understand the subtleties and dynamics of culture.

CHARACTERISTICS OF CULTURE

Culture is one of those elusive phenomena that we all seem to recognize but find difficult to define. Scholars, however, agree that culture is all encompassing. It includes the entire heritage of a society and reflects a total way of life. Broadly defined, culture is that complex whole that includes knowledge, belief, art, law, morals, customs, and any other capabilities and habits acquired by human beings as members of society.[1] Although the culture of each country is distinctive in many ways, all cultures share some common characteristics. In the next section, we discuss some of the common characteristics of culture.

Culture Is Prescriptive

Culture prescribes acceptable forms of behavior to people living within a community. Our cultural bank of knowledge guides us along the acceptable course of action. For example, culture prescribes how we should get married and raise children, how we should buy and use products, and how we should interact with our elders. We do not have to develop a unique solution to every problem we face in our daily lives. The acceptable course of action, however, may be different from culture to culture. For example, when people buy their groceries at a supermarket in the United States, they do not stand at the checkout counter and haggle over prices with the cashier. They pay the listed price, get the merchandise, and check out. But in many countries, such as India and Nigeria, haggling is common and is considered both a skill and an essential component of the social fabric.

Culture Is Learned

It is commonly said that people are not born with culture but that they acquire it. A child is born with genetic information but not with a cultural heritage. We acquire the culture of the community in which we grow up. A young boy growing up in a village in Nicaragua and a young boy growing up in New York City will learn very different things. Each will learn to adapt to his culture and assimilate its values. This process is called *enculturation*. As people move through different stages of life, they learn to distinguish right from wrong, and what is acceptable from what is not. This knowledge becomes a part of the cognitive component of an individual. Having learned how to respond to different problems, we know how to act in different situations.

---

[1] J. F. Sherry, Jr., "The Cultural Perspective in Consumer Research," in *Advances in Consumer Research*, ed. R. J. Lutz, vol. 13, Chicago: Association for Consumer Research, 1986, 573–575.

Culture Is Dynamic

As culture influences our behavior, we in turn influence its content by our behavior. The relationship between behavior and culture is interactive. We change because of cultural changes. Likewise, our culture changes over time because we change our ways of doing things. For example, a retailer, who buys in bulk for the first time to lower the price of merchandise has found a new way of doing things. Eventually, this new way of buying in bulk and selling in volume will change the merchandising culture. As new ways of doing things become acceptable, old cultural traditions are replaced by new. But this always takes time. People do not accept change easily. In fact, they resist it. New ways of doing things are more acceptable if they closely conform with accepted ways.[2]

Culture Is Subjective

People interpret their environment in their own subjective ways. Different cultures, for example, subjectively interpret numbers, shapes and sizes, and symbols. These subjective meanings develop within the context of a culture. In the United States, the number 4 has no significance other than numeric; but in Japan it has unfavorable connotations because the words *four* and *death* are pronounced the same. In Kenya, the number 7 or any number ending with 7 is considered bad luck; in the United States, there is the "lucky 7." Colors also have subjective meanings. In Greece, black is a negative color, while in Italy the color purple is negative. So it is with nature: The owl is a symbol of wisdom in the United States, but in Madagascar it has negative connotations.[3] *(sagesse)*

LOW-CONTEXT AND HIGH-CONTEXT CULTURES

Both verbal messages and nonverbal cues determine the full meaning of communication. However, people in different cultures process and interpret verbal messages and nonverbal cues differently. These disparities have been classified along a continuum of low-context to high-context cultures.[4]

---

[2] Everett M. Rogers, *Diffusion of Innovations,* 3rd ed., New York: Free Press, 1983.

[3] Business America, "Adapting Export Packaging to Cultural Differences," December 3, 1979.

[4] Edward T. Hall and Mildred Reed Hall, *Understanding Cultural Differences,* Yarmouth, ME: Intercultural Press, 1990.

Low-Context Cultures

In low-context cultures such as North America, Germany, and Switzerland, communication is explicit and precise. The message is conveyed in words. The context of communication is not as important as conveying a message. Therefore, what is said is more important than how it is said or where it is said. Although Germans and Americans share some common characteristics as members of low-context cultures, they also exhibit significant differences. Compared to Americans, Germans are more formal when they speak to each other. They address even close colleagues as "Herr Schwartz" or "Frau Frank." There it is also customary to address professional people as, for example, Herr Doctor or Frau Directorine.[5]

High-Context Cultures

In high-context cultures such as those of Asia, Latin America, and the Middle East, the setting in which communication takes place is very important. Thus, not only what is being said—but how and where it is being said—is of great significance. In these cultures, words are not the only carriers of the message. Meanings are derived from context as well.

MONOCHRONIC AND POLYCHRONIC CULTURES

Hall and Hall examined how individuals from different cultures process information and manage their work.[6] They classified people under two groups: monochronic and polychronic. People who process information in a direct, linear fashion and focus on one thing or action at a time are *monochronic*. They operate on rigid schedules and are strictly punctual. For them, time is linear, having a beginning and an end. In contrast, people who work at several tasks at one time are referred to as *polychronic*. The emphasis in polychronic cultures is on completing human transactions rather than holding to schedules.

Recognizing how others view the concept of time and manage their work can be extremely helpful in developing effective global communication strategies. Japanese businesspeople, for instance, claim that Americans are "pushy" because they want to get down to business as quickly as possible. In return, Americans claim that Japanese are closed off because they take a long time to get down to business. Until we understand how members of different cultures

---

[5] Roy Terry, "Manners Mean a Good Deal," *Financial Times,* November 17, 1992, 5.

[6] Hall and Hall, *Understanding Cultural Differences,* 13–15.

view time and personal relationships, it will be difficult to satisfactorily conduct negotiations, arrange meetings, and actualize transactions. Global marketers from a monochronic culture must pay close attention to the mores of a polychronic culture. Likewise, global marketers from a polychronic culture must be sensitive to the behavioral patterns of a monochronic culture. Misinterpretation of cues may result in cultural faux pas—and in lost business.

CULTURE AND VERBAL COMMUNICATION

Language plays an important role in giving a culture its unique characteristics and flavor. Differences in verbal communication across countries are immediately obvious to global marketers. For example, Egyptians speak Arabic and Americans speak English. Britons speak English, and so do people living in Australia, Ireland, and New Zealand. However, the English spoken in Australia and in the United States is not the same. Global marketers should be cognizant of variations in verbal communication not only in countries where different languages are spoken, such as Japan and Germany, but also in countries where the same language is spoken, such as the United States and the United Kingdom.

To make communication effective, global marketers should understand the linguistic uniqueness of each culture. People express their appreciation and understanding of the world through languages. They interpret their world and what is important to them through language. The Arabic language has more than six thousand different words for *camel*, its parts, and its apparatus. The Inuit use many different words to define the subtle differences in snow. And the Americans can talk about a car in a way that may elude the Saudis. Our language reflects the things that are important to us and how we interact with them.

Many firms erroneously assume that what works in one country will work in another. This has led to the use of the same advertisement in different countries. Although in some cases the message was translated in the local language, the ads were basically the same. The following will make you wonder how big corporations could commit such big blunders: An American airline proudly advertised its plush on-board "rendezvous lounges" to travelers to Brazil, not knowing that *rendezvous* in Portuguese means a room rented for lovemaking. Mistakes also occur when foreign businesses translate other languages into English. For example, a sign in an airline ticket office in Copenhagen, Denmark, read, "We take your bags and send them in all directions." These advertisements are potent reminders of what can go wrong when a firm fails to incorporate language differences in its promotional campaigns. Other such examples are shown in Figure 5.1.

FIGURE **5.1**   Translation Errors from Foreign Languages to English

Country	Location	Translation
Romania	Hotel	The lift is being fixed for the next day. During that time we regret that you will be unbearable.
Japan	Hotel	You are invited to take advantage of the chambermaid.
Austria	Hotel	In case of fire, do your best to alarm the hotel porter.
Switzerland	Hotel	Because of the impropriety of entertaining guests of the opposite sex in the bedroom, it is suggested that the lobby be used for this purpose.
Russia	Hotel	If this is your first visit to the USSR, you are welcome to it.
Norway	Cocktail lounge	Ladies are requested not to have children in the bar.
Mexico	Hotel	The manager has personally passed all the water served here.
Switzerland	Restaurant	Our wines leave you nothing to hope for.
Poland	Restaurant	Salad a firm's own make; limpid red beet soup with cheesy dumplings in the form of a finger; roasted duck let loose; beef rashers beaten up in the country people's fashion.
Thailand	Dry cleaners	Drop your trousers here for best results.
Hong Kong	Dress shop	Ladies have fits upstairs.
Italy	Doctor's office	Specialist in women and other diseases.
Sweden	Furrier	Fur coats made for ladies from their own skin.
Denmark	Airline ticket office	We take your bags and send them in all directions.
Hungary	Zoo	Please do not feed the animals. If you have any suitable food, give it to the guard on duty.

Adapted from Mike Kelly, "Side-Splitting Translations: These Phrases Will Tickle Your Funny Bone," *The Milwaukee Journal,* November 25, 1990, p. H5.

CULTURE AND NONVERBAL COMMUNICATION

People communicate both verbally and nonverbally. When they are angry, they express anger not only in words but also with facial expressions, body language, posture, gait, intonation, volume, and breathing rate; and often, words are not even used. In these cases, actions do speak louder than words. Nonverbal communication is both forceful and significant. It adds to the total meaning of communication. Global marketers should understand the nonverbal aspects of communication within a particular culture to avoid marketing blunders. In the following section, we examine some of the important variables that constitute different aspects of nonverbal communication.

Time

In the United States, the following questions are commonly heard: "Do you have time?" "Where has the time gone?" "Can you give me a little time?" In general, these questions reflect how Americans view time. Time is given a physical shape. People can have it, save it, and give it. Time is viewed as linear and fixed in nature. It is divided into seconds, minutes, hours, days, weeks, months, years, decades, and centuries. The phrase "time is money" is also a reflection of how time is viewed. Losing time means losing money. Progress is measured in terms of time; that is, how fast we can travel, cook, and compute. Our perception of time determines how we communicate with each other. Some cultures have a different perception of time: Time is on a continuum, not so neatly divided into seconds and minutes. Global marketers should understand these subtle differences to make communication effective.

Space

To a great extent, the perception of space is determined by how much space is available to us. Compare the attitudes toward physical space in Japan and the United States as a reflection of the size of each. Japan is a small country, approximately 372,313 square kilometers (143,750 square miles). Comparatively, the United States is large, approximately 9,363,166 square kilometers (3,615,122 square miles). Consequently, the perception of space in Japan and the United States is very different. What appears small to Americans may be perceived as large by Japanese standards. Japanese have learned to economize space. Their kitchens are smaller and so are their home appliances. When Sears entered the Japanese market, it sold its appliances in a corner of Tokyo's Seibu Department Store. But the company's products did not sell. Japanese consumers had no use for the American appliances, which were simply too big.[7] For Americans, the bigger the better. For Japanese, the more compact the better.

Cross-cultural differences in the perception of space and objects have implications for such marketing concerns as product size, retail store layout, and office design. To many Chinese in Hong Kong, *feng shui* (the art of placement, of balancing and enhancing the environment) is essential in management. Western and Oriental banks, restaurants, and other businesses regularly employ feng shui experts to enhance their working environments and gain a competitive edge in the Asian market. Among other firms, Citibank, Chase Asia, PaineWebber, McKinsey & Company, the Morgan Bank, and the offices of the *Asian Wall Street Journal* all use feng shui. McKinsey & Company is a New York–based management consulting group that opened an office in Hong Kong in 1986. The building, the floor, and the office were chosen for lucky numbers—most had auspicious 8 in them. A feng shui expert was hired by the firm on the advice of the architect. The expert chose the location of the reception area, selected the color red for the lobby, and recommended the addition of a rock to the manager's office.[8]

Symbols

Symbols are communication shorthand that render the meaning of a phenomenon in abbreviated forms. Color, for example, is commonly used in different cultures to signify different attributes. In the United States, brides marry in white, while in India they marry in red. Numbers also have meanings beyond their numerical value. As indicated earlier, some numbers are considered lucky and others unlucky. Products also have symbolic meanings. A refrigerator, for example, is considered a luxury product in India and thus a status symbol, and in many houses is placed in the living room rather than the kitchen. In Germany, where refrigerators are common necessities, it would be highly unlikely to see one sitting in the living room.

Negotiations

Negotiation styles vary across cultures. In some cultures, people simply shake hands and the agreement is sealed. There are no lawyers and there are no written contracts. A word and a handshake are sufficient for each party to complete an agreement. In the United States, however, documents and lawyers are indispensable in closing a deal. Agreements spell out minute details. What is to be done and when and by whom are clearly explicated in the contract. As cultures vary in terms of how they form agreements, global marketers should

---

[7] Yumiko Ono, "Surging Market, A Japanese Retailer Finds Southeast Asia Is The Place To Grow," *The Wall Street Journal,* September 4, 1992, A1.

[8] Sarah Rossbach, *Interior Design with Feng Shui,* New York: Penguin Books, 1987.

recognize these nuances to avoid serious problems in negotiating contracts, arranging sales, and organizing meetings. The art of negotiation is to make each party feel it has gained something.

Gifts

Exchange of gifts is an important social activity. Gifts serve to strengthen bonds between people. Although receiving and giving gifts are common to all cultures, variations occur in what one can give, when gifts can be given, how much can be given, where gifts should be given, and to whom gifts should be given. These questions should be considered by a global marketer before receiving or giving gifts.

SELF-REFERENCE CRITERION

People interpret unfamiliar events based on their own cultural values. The unconscious reference to our cultural values is referred to as the *self-reference criterion* (SRC). Lee[9] recommends a four-step process to avoid committing mistakes that may arise from the unconscious reference to our cultural values.

1. Define the business problem or goal in terms of your cultural traits, habits, or norms.
2. Define the business problem or goal in terms of the foreign cultural traits, habits, or norms. Make no value judgments.
3. Isolate the SRC influence in the problem and examine it carefully to see how it complicates the problem.
4. Redefine the problem without the SRC influence and solve for the optimum business goal.

The four-step process listed above serves as a reminder that our own cultural knowledge may not always be relevant or adequate for interpreting new cultural stimuli. To improve their managers' effectiveness in coping with new situations and dealing with people from different countries, many firms have instituted multicultural training programs. British Petroleum and Motorola, for example, put their managers through short courses to make them culturally competent.[10]

---

[9] James A. Lee, "Cultural Analysis in Overseas Operations," *Harvard Business Review*, March/April, 1966, 106–114.

[10] Bob Hagerty, "Trainers Help Expatriate Employees Build Bridges To Different Cultures," *The Wall Street Journal*, June 14, 1993, B1, B6.

CULTURAL UNIVERSALS

The issue of *cultural universals* has received considerable attention both from academicians and practitioners. Cultural universals are tendencies found in every culture. Murdock[11] has developed a list of cultural universals. These include age-grading, athletic sports, bodily adornment, calendars, cleanliness training, community organization, cooking, cooperative labor, dream interpretation, courtship, dancing, etiquette, family feasting, gift giving, joking, mourning, property rights, religious ritual, sexual restrictions, status differentiation, visiting, weaning, and weather control.

The desire to love, to look beautiful, and to be appreciated is shared by all cultures. However, what it means to look beautiful and how to achieve beauty often vary from culture to culture. Although a person living in a village in Mali may not have the same concept of beauty as someone living in Manhattan, the two are united by their common desire to look beautiful.

Cultural universals play an important role in marketing products and services. Global marketers know that certain traits are present in all cultures. For example, Ponds is able to market its seven-day beauty plan worldwide. The marketing plan and the product are successful because beauty is a cultural universal, and Ponds is promoting the idea that its product can help anyone become beautiful.

SUMMARY

Understanding the culture of the target market before developing and implementing the marketing mix is an important step toward successful global marketing. Cultural variations as well as similarities demand attention from marketers. The challenge for a marketer is to understand the two and make decisions accordingly. There is no single prescription for success. Both standardization and adaptation of the marketing mix have worked successfully. Marketers need to make decisions based on their understanding of each target market. That is, they should know how the market will respond to their strategies.

Culture influences every facet of our lives, including the consumption of products and services. For example, what we consume, how, when, where, and even why we consume are all influenced by culture. Thus, it is important for a global marketer to understand how culture influences our behavior. To better

---

[11] George P. Murdock, "The Common Denominator of Cultures," in *The Science of Man in the World*, ed. Ralph Linton, New York: Columbia University Press, 1945.

understand people from different cultures, global marketers can use the concept of high-context and low-context cultures. People from a high-context culture derive meanings not only from what is said but also where and how it is said. In contrast, people from low-context cultures focus on what is said rather than where and how it is said.

Individuals also process information and manage time differently. People who process information in a direct, linear fashion and work on one thing at a time are considered monochronic. Those who do not think of time as linear and work on several things at one time are considered polychronic. In communicating with target markets, negotiating contracts, or arranging meetings, global marketers need to focus on both verbal and nonverbal communications. Perceptions of time, space, symbols, and appropriate negotiating behavior differ according to culture. Recognizing these differences and taking culturally conducive actions enhance a global marketer's ability to achieve a competitive edge.

CHAPTER **SIX**

We are what we repeatedly do. Excellence, then, is not an act, but a habit.
Aristotle

Global Product Strategies

T he marketing mix consists of four separate but interrelated elements. Commonly known as the four Ps of marketing (product, price, place, and promotion), these elements are the basic ingredients global marketers work with. Developing products to satisfy consumers, pricing products to achieve a competitive edge, distributing products to make them available at the right place and time, and promoting products to encourage consumer patronage are a marketer's essential tasks.

A product's appeal is enhanced when all four elements of the marketing mix are combined synergistically. Although each component is important for delivering satisfaction to consumers, product is the most significant. After a consumer buys a product, its performance will determine whether he or she will buy the product again. If the product fails to perform as expected, the other three elements of the marketing mix—price, place, and promotion—will not easily persuade the consumer to purchase the product again. Consumers may be swayed to buy a product once or even twice, but not repeatedly, if it invariably fails to perform the desired functions or if, for that matter, a better substitute is available.

Procter & Gamble, one of the leading manufacturers of consumer products, virtually created the throw-away diaper market in Japan in 1977 when it began marketing its Pampers diapers. By 1981, P&G controlled 90 percent of the diaper market in Japan. In 1982 a Japanese sanitary napkin maker, Uni-Charm, introduced a highly absorbent granulated polymer diaper. Kao Corp. and a cosmetic giant, Shiseido Co., also entered the diaper market. When Uni-Charm entered the market, its diapers were better designed and better suited for Japanese consumers. It researched the buying habits of European and American consumers for two years and polled 300 Japanese mothers on their opinions of foreign diapers before introducing its products. By 1985, Pampers' share declined to about 7 percent. P&G lost its market prominence not only because it gave up its technological lead but also because it failed to focus on consumer needs. Japanese consumers complained that Pampers did not meet their expectations for high-quality products.[1]

The economic and social justification for a firm's existence is that it can produce and deliver products more efficiently than an individual can. Factors of production such as capital, technology, labor, management, and information are assembled and organized by a firm to produce products of value. These products are then taken to markets, where they compete for market share and consumer patronage. The attempt by each firm to establish its presence in a market intensifies competition. As a rule, a firm's success in this competitive environment is largely determined by how well it conceptualizes, develops, introduces, and manages products.

This chapter focuses on the following issues: product concept, product development, product introduction, product adoption, and product management. The last two sections of the chapter deal with the composition of products exported from the United States and research and product development in selected countries.

WHAT IS PRODUCT?

To most people, products are things that are palpable, useable, and disposable: for example, cars, towels, and radios. Marketers, however, hold a much broader view. To them, a product is something that has exchange value. As such, products are not limited to physical objects, but include ideas, organizations, and people.

Ideas, organizations, and people must be marketed just like tangible products. Ideas that encourage greater understanding of cultural diversity as well as those that promote the development of a regional trade zone require effective marketing. In the case of the North American Free Trade Agreement (NAFTA), the governments of the United States, Canada, and Mexico used marketing communication strategies to convince their citizens that NAFTA is a viable economic agreement beneficial to all three countries. Organizations such as the Sierra Club and Red Cross rely on the same pool of marketing principles and strategies that PepsiCo and Nestlè use to market their products. And the effective marketing of a politician, whether of the United States or France, is as critical for his or her success as it is for the success of a bar of soap. In the United States, as well as elsewhere, when politicians prepare for a debate or speech, they not only consider how their message will appeal to voters but also

---

[1] Barbara Buell and Zachary Schiller, "How P&G Was Brought to a Crawl in Japan's Diaper Market," *Business Week,* October 13, 1986, 71–74.

FIGURE **6.1**   The Total Product

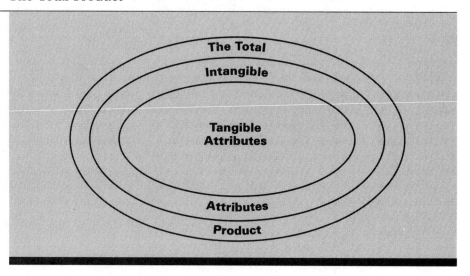

how the design of their suits, the color of their ties, the expressions on their faces, and the delivery of their speeches will affect voters' perceptions.

The Total Product

Products consist of tangible and intangible attributes, which are illustrated in Figure 6.1. The tangible attributes include such elements as raw materials, size, weight, features, design, and packaging. The intangibles include brand image, styling, and the additional benefits and services that marketers include with a product: installation, free delivery, interest-free credit, lifetime warranty, after-sale service, and no-questions-asked return policy.

Conceptualizing a product in terms of tangible and intangible attributes provides a global marketer with numerous options to differentiate a product and appeal to specific segments of the market. Theodore Levitt notes that in the future, competition will not take place between what firms produce in factories but "between what they add to their factory output in the form of packaging, services, advertising, customer advice, financing, delivery arrangements, warehousing, and other things that people value."[2]

Consider the watch, for example. The basic function of a watch is to keep time. If it performs reliably and accurately, it is considered a good watch. Based

---

[2] Theodore Levitt, *The Marketing Mode,* New York: McGraw-Hill, 1969, 2.

only on the criterion of keeping time, a Timex digital is as good as a Rolex; both keep time accurately and reliably. Although in terms of keeping time there may not be a difference between a Timex and a Rolex, the two are not the same. A Rolex watch has specific tangible and intangible attributes that collectively create its distinctive image of status, prestige, style, and quality. These attributes are different from those associated with a Timex. As such, the target markets are not the same for Rolex and Timex. People who wear Rolex are making a statement about their status, lifestyle, and values; people who wear Timex are doing the same. But the two statements are different.

PRODUCT DEVELOPMENT PROCESS

A firm strengthens its competitive position by regularly developing and adding new products to its product lines. Firms that lag behind in this endeavor weaken their market position and increase their vulnerability to competitive attacks. The success of global firms such as Sony and 3M is built on developing products that give them an edge in today's highly competitive marketplace. By developing successful products for new or existing markets, a firm strategically positions itself to take advantage of growing business opportunities. Ralph Larsen is the chairman and chief executive officer of Johnson & Johnson, a major producer of health-care products, biotechnology, advanced surgical technology, and disposable contact lenses. He attributed his company's impressive record of success to ". . . scrambling relentlessly for new products, equipment and technology— and accepting occasional failures." The firm's record seems to support Larsen's point; in 1991, a third of Johnson & Johnson's sales came from products introduced within the past five years.[3]

The development of new products is an involved and costly process requiring the use of scarce and valuable resources. When a firm develops and introduces an unsuccessful product, it drains its resources. However, when it develops, introduces, and manages a successful product, it strengthens its competitive position and boosts management's confidence. To achieve competitiveness, many firms are forming joint ventures in production and product development. Mercedes-Benz, the German luxury car manufacturer, and Ste. Suisse Microelectronique et d' Horologerie (SMH), the Swiss company that makes Swatch watches, formed a joint venture to build microcompact cars, nicknamed Swatchmobile. A little more than 8 feet long and $4^{1}/_{2}$ to 5 feet wide,

---

[3] Elyse Tanouye, "Balancing Act: Johnson & Johnson Stays Fit by Shuffling Its Mix of Businesses," *The Wall Street Journal*, December 22, 1992, A1, A4.

FIGURE 6.2   Product Development Process

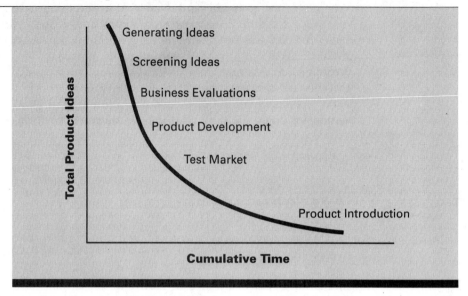

the cars will be rolled out in 1997 and targeted to city dwellers who want small, inexpensive, and easy-to-park cars.[4]

The process for developing a new product (summarized in Figure 6.2.) is the same whether a firm is developing a single standardized product for every country it operates in or an adapted product for each country. In either case, the process begins with the generation of ideas followed by screening of ideas; business evaluation of ideas; development of the product (a prototype); test marketing of the product; and, finally, introduction of the product in the marketplace. How effectively these six crucial steps are executed determines a firm's success in developing new products and gaining a competitive edge.

Generating Ideas

The first step in product development is an exercise in creatively identifying consumer needs and wants and showing how they can be satisfied. At this stage, product ideas are generated for tapping new or existing markets, complementing existing product lines, or improving existing products. Product ideas can come from many sources, including consumers, competitors, employees, inventors, private research organizations, and universities.

As competitive pressures build and product development costs increase,

---

[4] Ferdinand Protzman, "Off The Wrist, Onto The Road: A Swatch On Wheels," *The New York Times*, March 5, 1994, 19.

firms are being forced to look worldwide for promising ideas. Products faring well in one country are considered for introduction in others. Kellogg, for example, studied the European muesli cereals—a mixture of fruit, grains, and nuts—and developed its highly successful Mueslix cereal for the American market.[5] At Unilever, the world's third-largest food company, the top food executive and his three-man team scour the world for food ideas that can be transferred from one country to another.[6] Global firms, in contrast to firms whose operations are localized, enjoy an advantage in generating product ideas because of their exposure to marketing environments in various countries.

Screening Ideas

The second step in product development is screening ideas. Global marketers know from experience that all ideas generated in the first step may not be appropriate for and relevant to the firm's needs. Thus, ideas are divided into two categories: acceptable and unacceptable. The division is based on criteria such as the compatibility of an idea with the firm's marketing operations, the ability of the firm to convert an idea into a product, the fit between an idea and the philosophy of the firm, the sales potential of an idea, the contribution of an idea to the firm's competitive position, and the profit-making potential of the idea.

Misclassifying or ignoring a promising idea can result in lost revenues or costly failures. When Ron Zarowitz became a manager at Chrysler in 1985, he proposed the idea of built-in child seats. His idea was rejected; he persisted. In 1987, the company finally agreed to discuss the idea, which then remained in discussion for two years. By 1992, after long deliberations, the first built-in child seats were included in Chrysler's minivan as an option, with great success. After missing out on the opportunity for years, Chrysler was selling the vans as fast as it could produce them.[7]

Business Evaluation

The aim at this stage is to subject ideas that passed screening to cost-benefit analysis, and determine whether they have business potential. Many questions are addressed. For example, what will the demand be for the product, and how will it change in the future? How will the competitors respond, and what effect will their response have on the product's performance in the marketplace? How

---

[5] Michael J. McCarthy, "U.S. Companies Shop Abroad for Product Ideas," *The Wall Street Journal,* March 14, 1990, B1, B6.

[6] Bob Hagerty, "Unilever Scours the Globe for Better Ideas," *The Wall Street Journal,* April 25, 1990, A13.

[7] Brian Dumaine, "Closing the Innovation Gap," *Fortune,* December 2, 1991, 56–62.

will the product be marketed in different countries—that is, will it be adapted or standardized? Which countries are suitable for marketing the product, and which are potential targets for later introduction?

When evaluating ideas for their business potential, the analysis should focus on their commercial viability not only in the firm's existing markets but also in markets where the firm intends to operate in the future. The inclusion of both existing and prospective markets in the analysis forces a firm to think strategically and take a long-term perspective. Ideas that pass through business evaluation are taken to the next stage of the process, product development.

Product Development

In the product development stage, details of a product are worked out and the tangible and intangible attributes are specified. Considerations influencing the development of a product include the product's core benefits, positioning, degree of standardization, and the role of price, place, and promotion in enhancing the product's appeal. To develop a competitive product, cooperation among marketers, engineers, customers, and the research and development (R&D) team is becoming increasingly important. For example, Boeing, the largest exporter in the United States, has radically changed the way it develops its planes. In the past, Boeing's planes were designed by its prominent design engineers. In contrast, the present design process involves the added participation of airlines that will fly the plane, mechanics who will service it, and the many others who will help build it, price it, and market it.[8]

Test Market

The success or failure of a product is ultimately determined by how consumers respond to it in the marketplace. If consumers buy a product repeatedly, the product is successful; if they do not, it is a failure. An important way to obtain information about initial consumer response is to select a few representative markets for test marketing. Results can then be used in deciding whether the product should be introduced.

Test marketing decisions for a global firm depend in part on whether the firm's product will be adapted or standardized. The test marketing of an adapted product is conducted in the country where the product is to be marketed. However, for a standardized product, a firm may select a few representative countries, test market the product, and, based on the results, launch the product in all of its country markets. The cost of test marketing a standardized product in every market would be prohibitive and the benefits not cost-justified. By carefully planning and executing test marketing in a few

---

[8] Jeremy Main, "Betting on the 21st Century Jet," *Fortune*, April 20, 1992, 102–117.

representative countries, a firm is able to generalize the results to other countries.

Colgate-Palmolive Company, a multinational which markets its products in more than 160 countries, follows a "lead country" strategy in which it launches or tests a product in several countries and then follows through globally. For example, after some pretesting, Colgate launched Palmolive Optims shampoo and conditioner in the Philippines, Australia, Mexico, and Hong Kong in 1991. The company is now rolling out the product in Europe, Asia, Latin America, and Africa.[9]

Product Introduction

Global firms have to resolve whether their products should be standardized or adapted. There is some confusion as to what a standardized or an adapted product actually is. We define a standardized product as one that is marketed in more than one country without any modifications. An adapted product is one that has been modified to meet the specific characteristics of a target market in a country.

The decision to standardize or adapt depends on the economic, financial, political, and cultural environments of countries where the firm intends to market a product. Generally, when the marketing and consumption conditions are similar across countries, a standardized product can be developed. And when these conditions are different, product adaptation becomes necessary. When establishing its marketing presence in Japan, Kentucky Fried Chicken Japan (KFCJ), adapted its packaging and menu for its Japanese patrons, who are connoisseurs of fried food. Rather than dumped into take-out boxes, as in the United States, in Japan the chicken pieces are neatly arranged in prescribed patterns. The menu in Japan is also adapted to local tastes, and includes such items as smoked chicken, a three-piece fried fish plate, and an assortment of ice cream and sherbet cups, among other things.[10] Another example: After selling its dark, doe-eyed, and flat-chested Barbie in Japan for more than a decade, Mattel Inc. decided to sell the same doll in Japan that it sells in the rest of the world, the blue-eyed voluptuous Barbie. The firm also decided to sell directly to retail outlets, bypassing the wholesalers; and to appeal directly to children, bypassing the parents. By using the standardized strategy, Mattel expects to increase its sales in Japan to $200 million by the end of the year 2000.[11]

---

[9] Christopher Power, "Will It Sell in Podunk? Hard to Say," *Business Week,* August 10, 1992, 46–47.

[10] "KFCJ 'Does Chicken Right'—for Japan's Tastes," *Nation's Restaurant News,* November 14, 1988, F100, F102.

[11] Pauline Yoshihashi, "Now a Glamorous Barbie Heads to Japan," *The Wall Street Journal,* June 5, 1991, B1.

The standardization strategy is based on the premise that consumers everywhere share some common values, beliefs, and consumption patterns, and thus a standardized product can be developed to satisfy their needs and wants. In contrast, the premise underlying the adaptation strategy is that consumers in different countries are not the same, and therefore require adapted products to satisfy their needs and wants. Each school of thought has its advocates. So far, however, empirical evidence supporting either position unequivocally is lacking. In deciding whether to adapt or to standardize products, a firm should heed a central consideration—that is, how best to satisfy consumers. Adamantly following either the standardization or the adaptation strategy will surely yield suboptimal results. Let us examine the strengths of each option.

Advantages of Standardization. The advantages of standardization are numerous. First, by making a product in large quantities, a firm is able to achieve economies of scale; that is, it is able to reduce the per-unit cost of production by manufacturing more of the same item. Second, by reducing the cost of production, it is able to reduce the price of the product and thereby achieve price competitiveness in the marketplace. Third, by standardizing, a firm is able to present a uniform image of its products in all countries. Although the advantages of standardization are compelling, the implementation of this strategy should be based on its effect on demand.

Advantages of Adaptation. Product adaptation offers many advantages to a firm. A firm is able to achieve a good fit between product attributes and consumer expectations. By adapting its products, a firm can expect to appeal to a wider segment of the population and thus expand its market penetration in each country. These advantages, however, should be weighed against the effect of adaptation on the cost of producing a product. Adaptation may force a firm to produce in small quantities, thus raising the per-unit cost. If this results in a higher price than consumers are willing to pay, the adaptation strategy has not been successful.

Must standardization and adaptation be framed as an either-or proposition? Although standardization and adaptation are generally treated as two distinct approaches, a practical representation would depict them on a continuum, with standardization at one end and adaptation at the other. Firms could then move along this continuum to achieve an optimum of each.

Mandatory Product Adaptations. In some cases, a firm may have no choice but to adapt its product to meet the regulatory and operating conditions within a country. Without making the required changes the firm may not be able to sell its product. These adaptations are called mandatory adaptations. Governmental regulations, technological requirements, cultural imperatives, and measurement standards force firms to change the design, packaging, content, and labeling of products.

Governmental regulations are the most persuasive reasons for adapting products. A firm cannot sell its products in a country without meeting the product specifications developed, imposed, and monitored by the government. When Quaker Oats launched Gatorade in France in 1991, the product did not meet the standard for a health beverage, so the company had to add extra vitamin B_1.[12]

Technological considerations often determine whether a product can be used in a country. Many products, especially electronic goods, must be adapted to local conditions for storage, use, and disposal. For example, products designed to run on 110–120 voltage must be adapted to run properly in countries where the voltage is 220. Furthermore, technological infrastructure in less developed economies can also make product adaptations necessary. In the early 1970s, Boeing encountered a technological roadblock when it tried to expand its market to less developed countries. It found that its 737 jet bounced a great deal and the brakes failed on landing because the runways in these countries were short and soft. Boeing fixed the problem by adding thrust to the engine, redesigning the wings and landing gear, and installing tires with lower pressure. These adaptations were highly successful and made the 737 one of the best-selling planes.[13]

Cultural imperatives may necessitate product adaptations. Consumers, in general, like to use products that are culturally acceptable to them. When Johnson & Johnson introduced its baby powder in Japan, it did not sell well. Japanese mothers feared that the powder, when sprinkled from a bottle, would fly all over the house and contaminate their kitchens. Johnson & Johnson changed the package to a flat box and added a powder puff. The product soon caught on with Japanese mothers.[14]

Measurement standards are often different across countries. Products are usually measured in volume, length, weight, or quantity. The system of measurement adopted by almost every country in the world, except for the United States and a few others, is the metric system. Thus, products shipped from the United States have to be adapted to meet the measurement standards in other countries. Likewise, products coming into the United States from other countries must be adapted to meet American measurement standards.

PRODUCT ADOPTION

When introducing a new product in a country, global marketers like to estimate the adoption rate of the product. The adoption rate refers to the number of

---

[12] Joann S. Lublin, "Slim Pickings: U.S. Food Firms Find Europe's Huge Market Hardly a Piece of Cake," *The Wall Street Journal*, May 15, 1990, A1, A20.

[13] Andrew Kupfer, "How to Be a Global Manager," *Fortune*, March 14, 1988, 52–58.

[14] "Learning How to Please the Baffling Japanese," *Fortune*, October 5, 1981, 122–126.

people in a target market who adopt a product over time. The faster a new product is adopted by consumers, the faster the company can establish its marketing presence, recoup its product development costs, and earn profits. The following five factors are critical in influencing the rate of adoption: relative advantage, compatibility, trialability, complexity, and observability.[15]

Relative Advantage

Relative advantage refers to a product's ability to satisfy consumer needs and wants better than competing products. The greater the relative advantage of a product, the higher will be its adoption rate. When Federal Express promised to deliver mail within twenty-four hours, it was quickly adopted in the U.S. because it offered a service whose relative advantage was speed and reliability. When Whirlpool's consumer research revealed European preferences for a microwave oven that worked like a conventional one, Whirlpool introduced the VIP Crisp microwave in 1991. The Crisp has a broiler coil for top browning and a unique dish that sizzles the underside of the food. The Britons could fry their bacon and eggs, and the Italians could make their pizza crust crispy. Crisp soon became the best-selling microwave in Europe.[16]

Compatibility

The compatibility criterion refers to how closely a new product fits the existing cultural norms, values, and tastes of the target market. Compatible products are likely to be adopted faster than incompatible ones. H. J. Heinz, a major food company, discovered that its marketing efforts were most successful when it adapted its products to local cultural preferences. The company regularly uses focus groups to determine what kind of taste and image consumers in different countries prefer. In Sweden and Central Europe, for example, the company successfully sells hot ketchup, Mexican ketchup, and curry ketchup, in addition to the classic sweet ketchup.[17]

In every society, people develop distinctive ways of doing things that become an intrinsic part of their culture. When a new product challenges these cultural norms, it meets with resistance. The more entrenched the accepted ways of doing things, the more resistance there will be. In general, products that are compatible with the existing cultural norms are more readily adopted by consumers.

---

[15] Everett M. Rogers, *Diffusion of Innovations*, 3rd. ed. New York: Free Press, 1983.

[16] Sally Solo, "How to Listen to Consumers," *Fortune,* January 11, 1993, 77–79.

[17] Gabriella Stern, "Heinz Aims to Export Taste for Ketchup," *The Wall Street Journal,* November 20, 1992, B1, B9.

Trialability

Trialability refers to the ease with which consumers can sample a new product. A product that does not involve high risk, economic or otherwise, will be adopted faster than a high-cost, high-risk product. Disposable razors rank high on the trialability criterion because they are low on both price and risk.

Complexity

Products that are difficult to understand or complex to use take a long time to gain acceptance among consumers. The easier it is to use a product, the more likely that consumers will adopt it. Calculators were rapidly adopted in every country because they were easy to use and convenient. To add, subtract, multiply, divide, and perform other mathematical functions, consumers only needed to push the right keys and read the result in the display window.

Observability

Observability refers to how easily the benefits of a product can be observed and understood. Products whose benefits are visible will be adopted faster than those whose benefits are not as visible. Examples of products that are highly observable and successful include the Walkman, automated bank tellers, cellular phones, and Post-it notes.

PRODUCT MANAGEMENT

The product-market portfolio matrix is a useful tool for managing the performance of products in different countries. The matrix reflects a firm's market position in a country based on its competitive strength and the attractiveness of the country. The competitive strength of a firm is determined by the market share of the product, the overall fit between the attributes of the product and consumer expectations, the ability of the firm to effectively market the product, the positioning of the product, the level of cooperation in the distribution channel, and the profit potential of the product. The attractiveness of a country is determined by its market size, growth rate, competitive environment, governmental regulations, and political stability.

A product-market portfolio matrix for two companies, A and B, marketing the same product is represented in Figure 6.3. Company A has a strong market presence in Germany and Italy and a weak position in the United States and Japan. In contrast, company B has a strong presence in the United States and Mexico and a weak position in Germany and France. If each company chooses

FIGURE **6.3**   Product-Market Portfolio Matrix

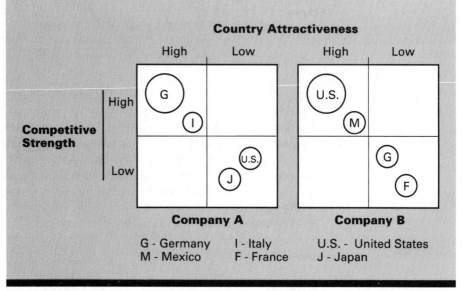

Source: Adapted from J. C. Larreche, "The International Product-Market Portfolio," AMA Educators' Proceedings, American Marketing Association, Chicago, 1978, p. 277.

to do so, it can attempt to change its market position in each country and improve the performance of the product by taking strategic actions.

Company A is strong in Germany and Italy but weak in the United States and Japan. What are its options? If company A wants to strengthen its position in the United States, for example, it will have to deploy more resources to this market. This can be achieved by diverting the resources from Germany or Italy, where the company is strong, to the United States, where it is weak. In implementing this strategy, however, the management should realize that company B may not sit idly but retaliate. What can company B do? It can lower its price or increase its promotion in the United States. Or it can put pressure on company A in Germany by increasing its marketing involvement there.

What a competitor may do in response to a firm's strategy is difficult to predict. The options are many and so are their effects. Before developing and implementing marketing strategies, it is important for a firm to understand its own strengths and weaknesses and those of its competitors. Strategies are goal specific. A firm should explicitly delineate what it wants to achieve in every country and how. Furthermore, it should anticipate competitors' responses and develop a plan to better prepare for contingencies. The product-market portfolio matrix encourages a firm to work out the probable effects of strategies and counterstrategies within a country as well as globally.

THE U.S. ECONOMY AND THE PRODUCT COMPOSITION OF ITS EXPORTS

The types of products exported from a country indicate its economic strength. Based on this measure, the United States is one of the strongest economies in the world. Contrary to popular opinion, exports from the United States do not consist primarily of agricultural products or raw materials but of high-value-added products. In 1965, 23.7 percent of U.S. exports comprised agricultural products. By 1990, the share of agriculture products in total exports declined to 10.3 percent (see Figure 6.4).

The fifty largest exporters in the United States are shown in Table 6.1. Among other high-value-added products, major exports of these U.S. firms consist of commercial and military aircraft, motor vehicles and related parts, computers and related equipment, aerospace products and jet engines, military hardware and missile systems, electronics and consumer products, chemicals and pharmaceuticals, health and imaging products, and farm and industrial equipment.

Global competition is increasing in every industry. Currently, the United States enjoys a dominant position in pharmaceuticals and forest products; shares its leadership with Europe and Japan in aerospace, chemicals, food, scientific and photographic equipment, petroleum refining, and telecommunications equipment; fears a continued decline in computers, industrial and farm equipment, motor vehicles, and metals; and struggles to keep up in electronics.[18]

---

[18] Andrew Kupfer, "How American Industry Stacks Up," *Fortune*, March 9, 1992, 30–46.

FIGURE **6.4**   U.S. Agriculture Exports as a Percentage of Total

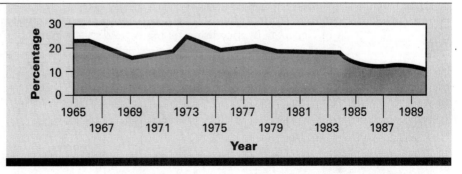

Source: The Economic Report of the President, U.S. Government Printing Office, Washington, DC, 1992.

TABLE **6.1**   Top 50 U.S. Exporters

Rank 1991	Rank 1990	Company	Major Exports	U.S. Exports 1991 mil U.S. $	% change from 1990	As % of total sales %	As % of total sales Rank	Total Sales 1991 mil U.S. $	Total Sales Fortune 500 Sales Rank
1	1	BOEING Seattle, WA	Commercial and military aircraft	17,856.0	11.0	60.9	1	29,314.0	12
2	2	GENERAL MOTORS Detroit, MI	Motor vehicles, parts	11,284.7	9.4	9.1	39	123,780.1	1
3	3	GENERAL ELECTRIC Fairfield, CT	Jet engines, turbines, plastics, medical sys.	8,614.0	20.8	14.3	25	60,236.0	5
4	5	IBM Armonk, NY	Computers, related equipment	7,668.0	23.8	11.8	31	64,792.0	4
5	4	FORD MOTOR Dearborn, MI	Motor vehicles, parts	7,340.0	3.4	8.3	41	88,962.8	3
6	6	CHRYSLER Highland Park, MI	Motor vehicles, parts	6,168.0	23.3	21.0	12	29,370.0	11
7	9	McDONNELL DOUGLAS St. Louis, MO	Aerospace prod., missiles, electronic systems	6,160.0	74.1	32.9	5	18,718.0	21
8	7	E.I. DU PONT DE NEMOURS Wilmington, DE	Specialty chemicals	3,812.0	(12.4)	10.0	34	38,031.0	8
9	10	CATERPILLAR Peoria, IL	Heavy machinery, engines, turbines	3,710.0	8.0	36.4	4	10,182.0	45
10	8	UNITED TECHNOLOGIES Hartford, CT	Jet engines, helicopters, cooling equip.	3,587.0	(0.5)	16.9	15	21,262.0	16
11	13	HEWLETT-PACKARD Palo Alto, CA	Measurement and computation prod. and sys.	3,223.0	14.5	22.2	11	14,541.0	26

		Company, location	Products						
12	12	PHILIP MORRIS New York, NY	Tobacco, beverages, food products	3,061.0	4.5	6.4	46	48,109.0	7
13	11	EASTMAN KODAK Rochester, NY	Imaging, chemicals, health products	3,020.0	2.1	15.4	21	19,649.0	18
14	14	MOTOROLA Schaumburg, IL	Commun. equip, cellular phones, semicond.	2,928.0	4.5	25.8	8	11,341.0	39
15	27	ARCHER-DANIELS-MIDLAND Decatur, IL	Protein meals, vegetable oils, flour, grain	2,600.0	123.6	30.3	6	8,567.7	60
16	17	DIGITAL EQUIPMENT Maynard, MA	Computers, related equipment	2,200.0	14.6	15.7	19	14,024.2	28
17	24	INTEL Santa Clara, CA	Microcompter components, modules, systems	1,929.0	60.4	40.4	3	4,778.6	106
18	18	ALLIED-SIGNAL Morristown, NJ	Aircraft and automotive parts, chemicals	1,729.0	(5.9)	14.6	23	11,882.0	36
19	30	SUN MICROSYSTEMS Mountain View, CA	Computers, related equipment	1,606.0	43.7	49.3	2	3,259.8	146
20	15	UNISYS Blue Bell, PA	Computers, related equipment	1,598.0	(27.5)	18.4	13	8,696.1	58
21	21	RAYTHEON Lexington, MA	Electronics, environmental sys., aircraft prods.	1,556.0	8.4	16.6	17	9,355.5	51
22	20	WEYERHAEUSER Tacoma, WA	Pulp, paper, logs, lumber	1,550.0	(0.6)	17.8	14	8,701.6	57
23	22	DOW CHEMICAL Midland, MI	Chemicals, plastics, consumer specialties	1,376.0	2.4	7.1	44	19,305.0	20
24	19	GENERAL DYNAMICS St. Louis, MO	Tanks, aircraft, missiles, gun systems	1,370.0	(15.6)	14.3	24	9,548.0	50
25	28	MERCK Rahway, NJ	Health products, specialty chemicals	1,342.0	16.1	15.6	20	8,602.7	59

(continued)

TABLE 6.1   Continued

Rank 1991	Rank 1990		Major Exports	U.S. Exports 1991 mil U.S. $	% change from 1990	As % of total sales %	Rank	Total Sales 1991 mil U.S. $	Fortune 500 Sales Rank
26	25	3M St. Paul, MN	Industrial, electronic, and health products	1,275.0	6.3	9.6	36	13,340.0	29
27	33	INTERNATIONAL PAPER Purchase, NY	Pulp, paperboard, wood products	1,200.0	9.1	9.4	37	12,703.0	31
28	23	UNION CARBIDE Danbury, CT	Chemicals, plastics	1,200.0	(6.3)	16.3	18	7,346.0	66
29	31	TEXTRON Providence, RI	Aerospace and consumer products	1,171.0	6.2	14.9	22	7,840.1	63
30	34	HOECHST CELANESE Bridgewater, NY	Chemicals, plastics, fibers, pharmaceuticals	1,158.0	6.7	16.9	16	6,856.0	75
31	26	WESTINGHOUSE ELECTRIC Pittsburgh, PA	Electrical product, electronic systems	1,141.0	(4.5)	8.9	40	12,794.0	30
32	35	MONSANTO St. Louis, MO	Herbicides, chemicals, pharmaceuticals	1,128.0	4.5	12.6	30	8,929.0	53
33	37	XEROX Stamford, CT	Copiers, printers, document processing sys.	1,040.0	15.6	5.8	47	17,830.0	22
34	36	ALUMINUM CO. OF AMERICA Pittsburgh, PA	Aluminum products	967.0	4.4	9.7	35	9,981.2	46
35	41	ABBOTT LABORATORIES Abbott Park, IL	Drugs, diagnostic equipment	957.0	17.5	13.8	27	6,921.7	74
36	16	OCCIDENTAL PETROLEUM Los Angeles, CA	Agricultural products, coal	951.0	(54.2)	9.2	38	10,304.8	43

		Company	Location	Product						
37	29	COMPAQ COMPUTER	Houston, TX	Computers, related equipment	950.0	(15.3)	29.0	7	3,271.4	145
38	39	FMC	Chicago, IL	Armored military vehicles, chemicals	913.0	7.7	23.3	10	3,931.5	119
39	38	MILES	Pittsburgh, PA	Chemicals, health and imaging products	877.0	1.4	14.2	26	6,197.4	85
40	47	COOPER INDUSTRIES	Houston, TX	Petroleum and industrial equip., elec. products	835.0	26.0	13.5	28	6,162.6	86
41	40	ROCKWELL INTL.	El Segundo, CA	Electronics, automotive parts	828.0	(0.8)	6.9	45	12,027.9	35
42	43	HONEYWELL	Minneapolis, MN	Building, industry, and aviation control sys.	808.0	7.7	13.0	29	6,220.9	83
43	45	BRISTOL-MYERS SQUIBB	New York, NY	Drugs, medical devices, consumer products	807.0	8.9	7.1	43	11,298.0	40
44	50	LOCKHEED	Calabasas, CA	Aerospace products, electronics, missile sys.	794.0	35.0	8.1	42	9,809.0	47
45	32	EXXON	Irving, TX	Petroleum, chemicals	744.0	(32.4)	0.7	50	103,242.0	2
46	42	DEERE	Moline, IL	Farm and industrial equipment	713.0	(5.9)	10.1	33	7,055.2	72
47	44	AMOCO	Chicago, IL	Chemicals	712.0	(4.2)	2.8	49	25,604.0	14
48	46	TENNECO	Houston, TX	Farm, construction, and auto equipment	692.0	(2.7)	4.9	48	14,035.0	27
49	49	ETHYL	Richmond, VA	Specialty and petroleum chemicals	655.0	10.5	25.4	9	2,574.8	173
50	48	REYNOLDS METALS	Richmond, VA	Aluminum, aluminum and plastic products	603.0	(5.6)	10.4	32	5,784.5	93
		TOTALS			130,406.7				987,755.1	

Source: *Fortune*, June 29, 1992.

COMPETITIVE PRODUCT DEVELOPMENTS

Although the United States is a major player in some critical industries, the global competitive picture has changed enormously during the last twenty years. Japan has assiduously developed itself into a major competitor for such high-value-added products as electronics, telecommunications, biotechnology, auto-mobiles, and heavy machinery. South Korea, Taiwan, Singapore, and Hong Kong have also shifted their production emphasis to products such as automobiles, computers, electronics, and heavy equipment. Similar developments are taking place in Europe.

Competition in all industries will be intense. As countries attempt to maintain and gain a competitive advantage, the worldwide competitive picture will change. One way to estimate the future competitive environment for new products is to examine the R&D expenditures in different countries. Table 6.2 compares R&D expenditures in the United States, the United Kingdom, Germany, and Japan. Germany's commitment to the aerospace industry is clearly visible. It spends 23.78 percent of sales on R&D in this industry. Japan leads in consumer products and is second in telecommunications, leisure, motor, and electronics. The United States leads in manufacturing, telecommunications, and leisure products. The United Kingdom does not lead in any sector. Based on the data presented in the table, we can hypothesize that in the future Germany will be competitively stronger in the aerospace industry and Japan in consumer products.

SUMMARY

The success of a global firm is determined by how well it develops, introduces, and manages products. In today's economy, a firm achieves success by developing products faster than the competition, introducing products earlier than the competition, and satisfying consumer needs and wants better than the competition. A global firm operating in multiple countries must consider differences in operating environments in each country before making product-related decisions. The guidelines for making these decisions are provided by the marketing concept that suggests that product-related decisions should be consumer oriented.

The development of a new product consists of six major steps: generation of ideas, screening of ideas, business evaluation of ideas, development of the product, test marketing of the product, and finally, introduction of the product. Global marketers are in a uniquely advantageous position—exposed to the marketing environments of other countries, they are able to obtain successful ideas from one country and transfer them to others.

TABLE **6.2** International Comparison of R&D Spending by Top 100 Spenders

	R&D % of Sales				
	All Industries	Motor	Chemical	Consumer Products Excluding Food	Electrical & Electronics
U.K.	1.69	2.77	3.56	0.53	4.25
U.S.	3.80	3.60	4.50	1.60	5.60
Germany	5.09	4.73	5.79	4.37	9.09
Japan	3.71	4.12	3.88	8.59	5.78

	R&D % of Sales				
	Aerospace	Leisure	Manufacturing Including Mechanical Engineering	Metals & Mining	Tele-communications
U.K.	3.34	0.36	0.79	0.57	1.85
U.S.	4.20	6.80	4.10	1.70	5.50
Germany	23.78	—	3.67	1.81	—
Japan	—	3.62	3.23	0.73	4.34

Source: *Financial Times*, October 9, 1992, p. 10.

When introducing products in different countries, marketers must resolve the issue of product standardization and adaptation. Should the firm market the same product in all countries, or should it develop an adapted product for each country market? Both have their advantages and disadvantages. Before making the decision, global marketers should assess the needs and wants of the target markets and then decide whether a standardized or an adapted product is most suitable.

Managing products in multiple countries is a complex task. The product-market portfolio matrix provides a framework that can aid a firm in making decisions to improve its competitive position. The matrix is based on two factors: the attractiveness of a country and the competitive strength of the firm in the country. A firm examines these two factors for each country where it operates and determines what strategies it can adopt to enhance its competitive position. However, while developing strategies, the firm must remember that competitors will not sit idly but will respond to the its actions. Therefore, an important element of the strategy development process is to anticipate where, when, and how the competitors will respond.

The economic strength of a country is determined by the type of products it exports. By this measure, the United States is one of the strongest economies in the world. Exports from the United States consist mostly of high value-added products such as aircraft, motor vehicles, computers, aerospace products, jet engines, military hardware, missile systems, electronics, consumer products, chemicals, pharmaceuticals, imaging products, and farm and industrial equipment. Although the United States has been the market leader in many of these high-value-added products, competition in many product categories is on the rise. Germany and Japan have increased their expenditures on R&D activities and are poised to introduce new and innovative products.

CHAPTER SEVEN

Everything is worth what its purchaser will pay for it.

Publilius Syrus

Global Pricing Decisions

O f the four elements of marketing mix—product, price, place, and promotion—only price generates revenue for a firm; the other three produce cost. Besides generating revenue for a firm, price is an important strategic weapon for gaining a competitive advantage in the marketplace. When Japanese color TV manufacturers entered the U.S. market in 1967, they priced their products between $50 and $100 less than comparable units of U.S. manufacturers.[1] This pricing strategy helped the Japanese firms achieve a competitive edge and establish marketing presence in the United States. Thus, how much revenue a firm earns and how effectively it enhances its market position are greatly determined by how competitively it prices its products.

Pricing decisions are not easy to make. In setting a product's price, a marketer has to consider two sets of conditions: internal and external. Internal conditions are specific to the firm and encompass its objectives, business philosophy, and cost structure. External conditions refer to market conditions both within a country and globally. They include, among others, governmental regulations, market conditions, and consumer characteristics.

Internal and external conditions influence pricing decisions differently. For example, rising costs of raw materials may force a firm to increase its price, but governmental regulations such as price controls may determine whether the firm can do so, and by how much. In Venezuela, despite surging raw material costs, Procter & Gamble and other manufacturers were granted few price increases because of government-instituted price controls.[2] Likewise, internal cost structures and external competitive conditions may encourage a firm to set

---

[1] "Electronics Companies Feel More Competitive," *Business Week,* April 21, 1973, 25–26.

[2] Alecia Swasy, "Foreign Formula, Procter & Gamble Fixes Aim on Tough Market: The Latin Americans," *The Wall Street Journal,* June 15, 1990, A1, A7.

its price lower in one country than in others; but concern about dumping accusations may discourage such action.

Although a firm has to consider numerous factors in setting a price, two considerations are paramount: first, will the firm maximize profit by setting the price at a particular level; and second, will consumers think they are getting "value" for their money if they purchase the product at this price. Firms cannot survive without making a profit; and consumers will not buy a product in a competitive market if they do not get "value" for their money. These two critical considerations, profit maximization and consumer satisfaction, provide the context within which the influence of other factors (e.g., governmental price controls or competitive responses) is evaluated and incorporated into a pricing decision.

In this chapter, we examine the following global pricing issues: the different pricing methods that can help global marketers make pricing decisions, the strategic issues involved in making global pricing decisions, the terms of payment, and the modes of payment used in global transactions.

PRICING METHODS

The five commonly used methods for setting a price are markup pricing, standard pricing, target return pricing, market based pricing, and strategic pricing. Markup, standard, and target return pricing are cost oriented—they consider a product's cost in determining its price, while ignoring market conditions. In contrast, market-based and strategic pricing are market oriented—they determine price based on market conditions as well as cost considerations. Although any one of these methods may not result in the price the firm settles on, these methods provide useful reference points for making pricing decisions.

Markup Pricing

A simple method for determining the price of a product is through markup pricing. The price is determined by adding a markup to the unit cost of the product. The necessary information for using this method is the fixed cost, variable cost, expected sales, and specified markup. Assume that the variable cost of producing a leather briefcase is $50 and the fixed cost $400,000. The firm expects to sell 10,000 units and earn a 10 percent markup on sales. The price based on this markup is $100 (see Table 7.1). Had the firm wanted to earn a 15 percent markup on sales, the price would have been $105.88.

The appeal of markup pricing is in its simplicity. However, it has its drawbacks. Markup pricing fails to take competitive conditions into account and ignores consumer responses to varying prices. By ignoring these factors, a firm runs the risk of either overpricing the product—in which case it is unable to maximize profits—or underpricing, in which case it loses money on every unit

TABLE 7.1   Pricing Methods

Markup pricing: The following information for a leather briefcase manufacturer is given:

Variable cost	$50
Fixed cost	$400,000
Expected sales (units)	10,000

The unit cost is calculated as follows:

$$\text{Unit Cost} = \frac{\text{Fixed Cost}}{\text{Expected Sales}} + \text{Variable Cost}$$

$$\$90 = \frac{\$400,000}{10,000} + \$50$$

Assume that the firm wants to earn a 10 percent markup on sales. The markup price is given by:

$$\text{Markup Price} = \frac{\text{Unit Cost}}{1 - \text{Desired Return on Sales}}$$

$$\$100 = \frac{\$90}{1 - 0.10}$$

Target return pricing: The following information for a table lamp manufacturer is given:

Total investment	$500,000
Desired return	20%
Unit cost	$60
Expected sales (units)	10,000

$$\text{Target return price} = \frac{\text{Desired Return} \times \text{Total Investment}}{\text{Unit Sales}} + \text{Unit Cost}$$

$$\$70 = \frac{0.20 \times \$500,000}{10,000} + \$60$$

sold. Considering the inherent weaknesses, why should we even bother to discuss markup pricing? Although this method is not an optimal way to approach the problem of pricing, it does provide some valuable information. It estimates price based on different markups and different levels of expected sales, which can be helpful in negotiating with a government threatening to impose price restrictions or a buyer willing to purchase only a fixed amount of the product.

Standard Pricing

When a firm uses the standard pricing method it charges the same price for its products in every country. Generally based on the projected unit cost, the price of a product is set in one currency, which is then converted to its equivalent value in other currencies. Consider the case of a U.S.-based firm. To implement standard pricing, it converts the dollar price of a product to its equivalent value in other currencies using current exchange rates. For example, if the dollar price of one of its products is $50 and the yen-to-dollar rate is 130 yen to 1 dollar, the firm will charge 6,500 yen in Japan. Likewise, if it sells this product in France and the exchange rate between the French franc and dollar is 5 francs to 1 dollar, it will charge 250 francs in France.

From a marketing perspective, charging the same price in all countries is not the most logical choice, because competitive conditions and consumer responses vary across countries. Besides lacking in marketing orientation, standard pricing is also difficult to implement in today's floating-exchange-rate environment. A dollar-based standard price will require frequent changes in the price of the product in other countries to reflect the fluctuating values of their currencies. Notwithstanding these drawbacks, one redeeming virtue of this method is that it protects a firm from the accusation of price discrimination, as the price charged is the same in all countries.

Target Return Pricing

With target return pricing, the firm establishes a target rate of return on its investments and sets the price accordingly. An example of a price determined by target return is presented in Table 7.1. The necessary information for using this method is total investment, desired target return, unit cost, and expected sales. Assume that a lamp manufacturer invests $500,000 and expects to earn 20 percent on its investment. The unit cost of its table lamp is $60 and expected sales are 10,000 units. Given this information, the price based on the target return pricing method is $70 (see Table 7.1).

Certain features of target return pricing are notable. First, a firm will achieve the desired rate of return on its investment if its sales and cost estimates are accurate. Second, if either the expected rate of return or sales figures or both are changed, the price arrived at will be different. In general, this pricing method shares the same drawbacks as the other two methods discussed above. However, the major drawback of target return pricing is its lack of marketing orientation: it does not take competitive conditions and consumer characteristics into account in setting a price. The focus of this pricing method is on the firm rather than on the consumers and the market.

Market-Based Pricing

In contrast to the three pricing methods discussed above, market-based pricing, as the name implies, takes into consideration market and regulatory forces when determining price. Thus, if market conditions vary by country, prices also vary. From a marketing perspective, this is a reasonable approach to setting a price.

However, its implementation can raise serious problems for a firm. If the firm is charging a comparatively higher price in one country, neither the government nor the consumers there will like the price discrepancy. The government may demand an explanation or even fine the firm for overpricing. Hoffman-La Roche, producers of Valium and Librium, followed a pricing strategy that led to substantial price differences among countries, which prompted a series of overpricing cases in Germany, Holland, and the United Kingdom against the firm. The litigation led to a £3.75 million fine in the United Kingdom for overpricing.[3] Another potential problem of market-based pricing arises when the price differences among countries encourage traders to buy products in low-price markets and sell them in high-price markets. This practice, called gray marketing, is discussed later.

Strategic Pricing

With strategic pricing, a minimum standard price is set for all countries, but local managers within each country are free to increase the price if domestic conditions warrant. When establishing the minimum standard price, head office executives evaluate the local and global competitive environments, the cost structure of a product, and the objectives of the firm, among other criteria. The managers within each country, however, can choose to sell at the suggested price or increase it, depending on local competitive conditions, consumer characteristics, channel margin requirements, and governmental regulations. Close coordination between the head office and local management is essential for successfully implementing this pricing method. Strategic pricing offers some built-in advantages. A firm is able to achieve uniformity in its pricing strategies by setting a minimum standard price for all countries. It also achieves diversity by incorporating the influence of local conditions in its pricing decisions. In particular, the strategic pricing method joins the global view of the executives at the head office with the domestic perspective of the managers within each country.

STRATEGIC ISSUES IN GLOBAL PRICING

Global firms link business and marketing activities across countries to achieve competitiveness and enhance profit. Raw materials or components are often produced in one country and transferred to another for conversion into final products. Products are then assembled or manufactured in one country and

---

[3] "Body Blow to the Trustbusters," *The Economist*, February 16, 1980, 88.

sold in others. These movements of raw materials, component parts, and finished products among countries raise various pricing and regulatory issues.

Consider this scenario. Assume that market conditions in Germany are more favorable for charging a higher price than in South Korea. A firm, therefore, charges a higher price in Germany than in South Korea. What are the implications? First, if the price difference is large enough, it will encourage *gray marketing*—that is, traders would buy products in South Korea at a low price and sell them in Germany at a high price. Second, the government of South Korea may accuse the firm of dumping its products in South Korea. Third, the German government may accuse the firm of overcharging and demand compensation. Fourth, competitors may seek a price advantage by lowering their price in Germany. These probable responses show the complexity of global pricing decisions. In this section, we focus on five strategic pricing issues: price escalation, transfer pricing, fluctuating exchange rates, parallel imports, and dumping.

Price Escalation

When products are shipped from one country to another, costs are incurred. Some of the costs, which include tariffs and export documentation fees, are unique to the movement of products among countries. These costs generally escalate the price of a product. Table 7.2 illustrates how these costs and channel margins can increase the price of a product from $16.38 in the exporting country to $21.53 in the importing country.

Managing Price Escalation. A firm's competitive position suffers when the price of a product escalates to a level greater than what a majority of consumers in the target market are willing to pay. To bring the price down, global marketers can consider several alternatives. First, if tariffs in a country are lower for components than for the finished product, a firm may come out ahead by shipping the parts to that country and assembling them there. For this option to work, the savings in tariffs must be greater than the cost of assembling the product in that country. A second option in bringing the cost of a product under control is downsizing—that is, removing some of the costly features of the product. This strategy may be appropriate for countries where state-of-the-art features in a product do not give a firm any perceivable advantage and thus can be innocuously removed. A third option requires shortening the distribution channel, thus eliminating the profits of some intermediaries from the price. In using this strategy, however, a firm should heed the warning that one can eliminate a distribution channel but not its functions. Shortening the channel may mean that the firm has to perform some functions that the eliminated channel member was performing. If the costs of performing these functions are greater than what was paid to the channel member, this strategy may not be feasible. The fourth and most important alternative is for the firm to focus on

TABLE 7.2 Sample Cost Plus Calculation of Price Escalation

	Price in the Exporting Country	Price in the Importing Country
Factory price	$10.00	$10.00
Domestic freight	.50	.50
	10.50	10.50
Export documentation		.50
Transport (CIF)		1.00
Landed cost		12.00
Tariff (15% of landed cost)		1.80
		13.80
Wholesaler markup (20% on cost)	2.10	2.76
Retailer markup (30%)	3.78	4.97
Final price	16.38	21.53

increasing its productivity so that it can reduce costs and subsequently lower prices.

Transfer Pricing

Another strategic issue of great importance is that of transfer pricing. This refers to the price charged for goods and services transferred intraorganizationally—that is, from operating units in one country to operating units in other countries. Transfer pricing strategies can be classified under two groups: market based and nonmarket based. Market-based transfer pricing relies on the prevailing market price for transfering products between operational units. Nonmarket-based transfer pricing uses a wide array of transfer pricing methods such as negotiated prices, cost-based prices, mathematically programmed prices, and dual prices.[4]

---

[4] Mohammad F. Al-Eryani, Pervaiz Alam, and Syed H. Akhter, "Transfer Pricing Determinants of U.S. Multinationals," *Journal of International Business Studies*, 3, 1990, 409–425.

As global firms have increased their worldwide activities, the significance of transfer pricing has grown. Transfer pricing is important to global firms because it affects the profits and rewards of their affiliates. Transfer pricing is also important to governments because it affects the amount of taxes they can collect from corporate affiliates. We discuss these issues in the following sections.

Transfer Pricing and Taxation. The use of transfer pricing to skirt taxes is a widely discussed topic. As taxes are paid on profits, a firm supposedly can reduce its tax burden by showing lower profits in countries where tax rates are higher, and higher profits in countries where rates are lower. Consider this simple example. The affiliates of a global firm are located in two countries, X and Y, and they transfer goods to each other. The tax rates in country X are lower than in country Y. How could these two affiliates price their goods to manipulate taxes? The country X affiliate would charge a high price (overinvoice) when it transfers goods to the country Y affiliate, and the country Y affiliate would charge a lower price (underinvoice) when it transfers goods to the country X affiliate. By charging a higher transfer price, the affiliate in country X would show a higher profit in the country where the tax rate is lower. And by charging a lower price, the affiliate in country Y would show a lower profit in the country where the tax rate is comparatively higher. Thus, by over- and underinvoicing, a firm is able to reduce its tax burden (see Table 7.3 for a simplified example of how a firm increased its total tax burden when one of the affiliates lowered the price it charged to another affiliate from $20 to $15.

The foregoing explanation on the use of over- and underinvoicing for manipulating taxes makes a number of simple assumptions that cannot be ignored. First, it ignores the influence of factors other than tax reduction on the pricing decision of a firm. Second, it supposes that the government is unaware of what the firm is doing to manipulate its tax burden. Third, it assumes that the government is unable to establish the market price of a transferred product.

To discourage firms from using transfer pricing for manipulating taxes, many governments have established guidelines for determining the transfer price of a product. The U.S. government policy on transfer pricing is stated in Section 482 of the United States Revenue Act of 1962. The main points are:[5]

1. Market prices are generally preferred by the Internal Revenue Service (IRS) based either on a comparable uncontrolled price method or a resale price method.

2. The IRS will accept cost-plus markup if market prices are not available and economic circumstances warrant such use.

---

[5] Scott S. Cowen, Lawrence C. Phillips, and Linda Stillabower, "Multinational Transfer Pricing," *Management Accounting*, January 1979, 17–22.

TABLE 7.3   Effect of Transfer Pricing on Tax Burden

	Scenario A			Scenario B	
	Affiliate Seller in country (x)	**Affiliate Buyer in country (y)**		**Affiliate Seller in country (x)**	**Affiliate Buyer in country (y)**
Price	$20.00	$22.00	Price	$15.00	$22.00
Cost of product	–$10.00	–$20.00	Cost of product	–$10.00	–$15.00
Profit	$10.00	$ 2.00	Profit	$ 5.00	$ 7.00
Country tax rate	10%	20%	Country tax rate	10%	20%
Affiliate tax	$ 1.00	$ 0.40	Affiliate tax	$ 0.50	$ 1.40
Combined tax burden	$1.40		Combined tax burden	$1.90	

3. The actual cost methods are not acceptable.

4. Negotiated prices are acceptable as long as the transfer price is comparable to the price charged to an unrelated party.

Federal tax officials in the United States maintain that American distributors of foreign-made goods have been reducing their tax liability by paying higher prices to their parent companies and showing lower profits. Of the 36,800 foreign-owned firms filing tax returns in 1986, more than half reported no taxable income. To aid the IRS in collecting taxes, Congress has given the agency broad authority to assess taxes on foreign-owned companies. In particular, the IRS can fine firms up to $10,000 a month, with no limits on the cumulative penalty, for failing to cooperate and provide records.[6]

Exchange Rate Fluctuations and Pricing Decisions

The relation between price and exchange rate is complex. After considering the influence of internal and external factors, a firm sets the price of its product for a country. This price is specific to that country, and although the firm may not change the price, it will continuously vary in relation to other currencies

---

[6] Robert Pear, "I.R.S. Investigating Foreign Companies Over Units in U.S.," *The New York Times,* February 18, 1990, 1, 17.

because of fluctuating exchange rates. Consider this example. The price of an electric razor in the United States is $60 and the exchange rate of the dollar and Swedish krona is $1 = 7 krona. If we converted $60 to krona, it would come to 420 krona. Thus, in Sweden the price of the electric razor is 420 krona. Now assume that the krona appreciates and the new exchange rate is $1 = 6.5 krona. What is the price of the electric razor in krona? Although the dollar price is still the same, $60, the price of the razor in Sweden has decreased to 390 krona.

Exchange rate fluctuations have far-reaching consequences for global marketers. If the price differential due to exchange rate fluctuations is large enough to cover shipping costs from one country to another and also give a profit to traders, it will promote gray marketing. Furthermore, such price differentials can also lead to the accusation of dumping. A firm cannot control exchange rate fluctuations, but it can learn to manage the effects to its own advantage. To do this, a firm should understand the influence of varying exchange rates on its marketing activities and learn to manage them profitably.

The declining value of a currency can have contradictory effects on a firm's performance. Take the case of Hurco Company, a manufacturer of machine tools and electronic controls, which sold 40 percent to 45 percent of its products in Europe. When the dollar weakened against other currencies in 1990, Hurco was able to increase its market share in Europe as well as raise its price in dollars. While a weak dollar enabled Hurco to charge Europeans higher prices, it also made the firm pay higher prices for products it bought from Spain and Japan.[7]

Gray Marketing or Parallel Imports

Market conditions in different countries are seldom alike—inflation rates, market potential, competitive intensity, governmental regulations, and consumer characteristics generally vary. If a firm uses market-based pricing, the price for the same product may be different across countries. These price variations encourage traders to buy products in a low-price country and sell them in a high-price country, a phenomenon referred to as *parallel imports* or *gray marketing*. Gray marketing takes place outside the firm's authorized distribution channel. And the greater the price variation among countries, the higher the occurrence of gray marketing. In the United States the growth of gray markets was fueled by the strong dollar in the early 1980s. The gray market for luxury cars grew 2,000 percent between 1981 and 1986. Of the 101,000 cars Mercedes-Benz sold in the U.S. in 1984, 22,000 were sold by gray marketers.[8]

Pricing policies alone do not encourage gray marketing. Fluctuating exchange rates can also be the cause. If the value of, say, the Australian dollar

---

[7] "Few Quick Bucks: How Dollar's Plunge Aids Some Companies, Does Little for Others," *The Wall Street Journal,* October 22, 1990, A1, A4.

[8] Larry S. Lowe and Kevin F. McCrohan, "Minimize the Impact of the Gray Market," *The Journal of Business Strategy,* November/December 1989, 47–50.

appreciates in relation to the yen, traders will be tempted to buy products in Japan and ship them back to Australia. Likewise, if the yen appreciates, traders will be encouraged to buy products in Australia and ship them back to Japan. Essentially, traders engage in gray marketing when the difference in price is large enough for them to meet the cost of moving products from one country to another and earn a profit.

Managing Gray Marketing. Gray marketing results in two or more prices for a product in the same country. One price is that of the authorized distributors, the other of gray marketers. Manufacturers and distributors are concerned about gray marketing because of its adverse effects on manufacturers' credibility and distributors' market shares. What can global marketers do? Not much. Several companies, including Johnson & Johnson, Merck & Co., Yves Saint Laurent, Christian Dior, and Shelton Inc. have fought back against gray marketers by taking legal action and pushing for more governmental restrictions on gray marketers.[9] Such attempts, however, have not been very effective. If marketers do not narrow the price differential among countries, gray marketers will continue to buy in one country and sell in another.

To discourage gray marketing, a firm can try to differentiate its products in different countries by adding or deleting features from a product. However, such an action should be based on competitive conditions and consumer characteristics, and not on the desire to stop gray marketing. An important drawback of introducing a different version of the same product in different countries is that it may increase the cost of the product as well as the costs of packaging, promoting, and transporting the product. In turn, these may reduce the competitiveness of the firm. Other options—tracking the gray marketers, educating consumers, or even taking legal action—have not proven effective in curtailing the gray market.

Dumping

In Article VI of the General Agreement on Tariffs and Trade (GATT), *dumping* is defined as offering a product in export markets at a price below normal value. Normal or fair value is defined as the price charged by a firm in its home market. When a firm does not sell the product in its home market, the highest comparable price charged in third markets, or its cost of production, may be used to determine normal value.[10]

There are three common types of dumping: sporadic, predatory, and per-

---

[9] "There's Nothing Black and White About the Gray Market," *Business Week*, November 7, 1988, 172–180.

[10] Michael P. Leidy and Bernard M. Hoekman, "Production Effects of Price- and Cost-Based Anti-Dumping Laws Under Flexible Exchange Rates," *Canadian Journal of Economics*, November 1990, 873–876.

sistent. *Sporadic dumping* occurs when a firm sells its products at a low price to reduce its surplus inventory. *Predatory dumping* occurs when a firm sells its products at a low price to drive out competitors and gain control over the market. *Persistent dumping* occurs when a firm charges a high price in a country where it enjoys protection and a low price in a country where it has to compete. Although these three types of dumping are conceptually distinguishable, in practice it is difficult to tell them apart.

Antidumping laws similar to those of the United States exist in the European Union, Australia, Canada, and in some developing countries. In March 1993, the European Commission took action to protect the EU bicycle makers from "unfair" Chinese competition. Bicycle manufacturers from France, Germany, the Netherlands, Spain, and the United Kingdom complained in 1991 that Chinese imports were undercutting EU products by an average of 44 percent. While EU bicycle sales increased by 32 percent between 1989 and 1991, the share of EU manufacturers declined from 33 percent to 27 percent. At the same time, Chinese manufacturers increased their share from 4.6 percent to 10.5 percent. The commission noted that "The pressure from Chinese exporters on the price of bicycles sold in the Community has eroded EC industry's profitability and undermined its investments." It imposed provisional antidumping duties of 34.4 percent of the net price before customs clearance on Chinese bicycles imported into the Union.[11]

U.S. manufacturers frequently accuse their foreign competitors of dumping products in the United States. For example, the National Knitwear and Sportswear Association accused Hong Kong, South Korea, and Taiwan of dumping sweaters made with synthetic fibers, especially acrylics, on the U.S. market.[12] The Big Three auto makers—GM, Ford, and Chrysler—charged Japanese companies (mainly Toyota and Mazda) with dumping minivans in the United States.[13]

In the United States an antidumping case involves a two-step investigative procedure. First, the U.S. Commerce Department determines whether an imported product is being sold at prices below those prevailing in the exporting countries. If so, the investigation moves to the second stage. At this stage, the International Trade Commission (ITC) investigates whether an American industry "is being or is likely to be materially injured or is prevented from being established" because of such imports. If the conclusion is affirmative, the accused firm must pay an antidumping duty in addition to the normal tariff.

---

[11] Andrew Hill, "EC Penalises Bicycle Imports," *Financial Times,* March 12, 1993, 6.

[12] Eduardo Lachica, Steven Jones, and James McGregor, "Trial Balloon?: New Wave of U.S. Protectionism Feared as Asia Is Accused of Dumping Sweaters," *The Asian Wall Street Journal,* February 10, 1989.

[13] Paul Ingrassia and Eduardo Lachica, "U.S. Car Makers Charge Japanese with Dumping," *The Wall Street Journal,* June 3, 1991, A3, A4.

This may force the accused firm to increase the price of the product—which is, in fact, why the antidumping case was initiated in the first place—to make the firm less price competitive.

Charging a low price for a product is a strategic decision firms frequently make to gain a competitive advantage. This does not necessarily mean that the price is lower than the actual cost of the product. From a consumer's perspective, a lower price is desirable. However, from the perspective of a firm, especially one that desires protection from competition, this is not at all desirable; it intensifies competition. Competing on price means that the firm has to evaluate its strategic orientation, performance standard, reward structure, and consumer orientation and make decisions that will enhance its competitiveness.

TERMS OF PAYMENT

Over time, a number of terms of payment have evolved for conducting international transactions. Each with a specific meaning, these terms are the lingua franca of international traders. Anyone interested in global marketing must know what these terms are, what they mean, and how they can be profitably used with buyers with different levels of experience in the international movement of goods. In moving goods from one country to another, many expenses are incurred, such as those for loading, shipping, and insuring goods. The price quoted to an overseas buyer must indicate which expenses are included in the seller's price. Some buyers, for example, may not want to deal with the loading, shipping, and insuring of goods they buy from a foreign country. They are interested primarily in knowing how much they will have to pay for the goods delivered to them at their home port. The term used for quoting this price is different from the term used for quoting a price to a buyer who wants the goods delivered at a port in the seller's country. Some of the common terms of payment useful for preparing a quotation are discussed next.

EXW (ex works). The price includes the charge for the goods at a named point of origin such as a factory or a warehouse. The seller agrees to place the goods at the disposal of the buyer at the specified place on the specified date.

FAS (free alongside ship). The price includes the charge for the goods and their delivery alongside a vessel at a named port of export. The seller handles the cost of unloading and wharfage; all other charges, such as loading, insuring, and transporting the goods, are left to the buyer.

FOB (free on board). The price includes the charge for the goods and all costs up to and including delivery of goods aboard a vessel at a named port of export. Other charges are the responsibility of the buyer.

C&F (cost and freight). The price includes the charge for the goods and their transportation cost to an overseas port of import. Insurance cost is paid by the buyer.

CIF (cost, insurance, and freight). The price includes the charge for the goods, insurance, transportation, and miscellaneous charges to the point of debarkation from the vessel at a named overseas port of import.

CPT (carriage paid to) and CIP (carriage and insurance paid to). These two terms are used in place of C&F and CIF, respectively, for shipment by modes other than water.

Each option mentioned above can be selectively used to gain a strategic advantage. A firm's buyers often have different levels of exposure to the international movement of products. Some feel comfortable in dealing on an EXW basis, working out the shipping details themselves. Others, however, may prefer CIF, not wanting to handle the arrangements of loading, shipping, and insuring the goods. Global marketers can benefit by being flexible in setting the terms of payment that accommodate the needs and experiences of their buyers in different countries.

MODES OF PAYMENT

The payment arrangements that a firm makes with an overseas buyer determine the risk the firm is willing to assume. In the early stages of a business relationship with an overseas buyer, a firm must take all necessary precautions to ensure payment for goods sold. Later, however, mutually beneficial arrangements can be made for delivering goods and receiving payments. The different payment methods involving varying levels of risk and security are discussed next.

Cash in Advance

From a firm's perspective, receiving cash in advance for goods is a highly desirable option. Its advantages include security of payment and availability of funds for meeting sales commitments. However, from the buyer's perspective, this is not a desirable arrangement. Having made the payment, the buyer can only hope that the goods will be delivered on time and as promised. In global transactions, this method of payment is generally used when buyers and sellers know each other or when products traded are high-priced.

Open Account

Through this method, a firm sends the goods to the buyer, who is expected to pay at a future date by terms already agreed to. Open account is a convenient mode of payment because it eliminates excessive paperwork. After receiving the goods, the buyer pays as stipulated in the agreement. The feasibility of this method, however, depends on the credit worthiness of the buyer. Thus, before selling goods on open account, the exporter should secure a credit report on the buyer and check the political, economic, and commercial risks in the importing country. Open account is commonly used for intrafirm transactions, that is, when affiliates of a firm sell to each other.

Letter of Credit

A letter of credit is a conditional payment mechanism. It is a document issued by a bank to a seller on the instructions of a buyer. It authorizes the seller to receive from the bank a specified sum of money under the terms stipulated in the letter of credit. The terms usually require the seller to present documents such as the commercial invoice, a clean bill of lading, and insurance policy to the bank within a specified time.

Before making a payment, the bank verifies that the documents submitted by the seller meet the requirements of the letter of credit. If there is a discrepancy between the documents required and those submitted, the discrepancy must be *cured* before payment is made. Full compliance with the letter of credit is mandatory. A letter of credit may authorize immediate payment upon presentation of documents (called an *at sight* letter of credit) or future payment at some agreed-upon date (called a *time* or *date* letter of credit). The various types of letters of credit are discussed next.

Revocable. A revocable letter of credit can be altered or canceled by the buyer after it has been issued by the buyer's bank.

Irrevocable. An irrevocable letter of credit cannot be altered or canceled without an agreement between the buyer and the seller.

Confirmed. A confirmed letter of credit is a letter of credit whose validity has been confirmed by the seller's bank. With a confirmed letter of credit, the seller is assured of payment by her bank even if the buyer or the buyer's bank defaults.

Confirmed Irrevocable Letter of Credit. A letter of credit that is both confirmed and irrevocable cannot be altered or canceled without the consent of the seller. The seller is assured that she will receive payment, if not from the buyer's bank then from her own. This option gives the seller maximum protection. We examine the typical steps involved in making payment by a confirmed irrevocable letter of credit.[14] To simplify the exposition, we assume that the buyer (importer) is in Germany and the seller (exporter) in Malaysia.

---

[14] U.S. Department of Commerce, *A Basic Guide To Exporting,* January 1992.

1. In accordance with the terms of the sales contract, the buyer in Germany applies to a bank to issue a letter of credit to be confirmed by a Malaysian bank.

2. The buyer's bank prepares an irrevocable letter of credit, including instructions to the exporter concerning shipment, and sends the letter of credit to a Malaysian bank, requesting confirmation.

3. The confirming bank in Malaysia adds its obligations and forwards the confirmed credit to the exporter.

4. The exporter reviews all conditions in the letter of credit, prepares the shipment, and arranges with a freight forwarder to deliver the goods to the specified destination.

5. When the goods are loaded, the forwarder completes the necessary documents and gives them to the exporter. The exporter presents these documents along with the letter of credit to the confirming bank.

6. The confirming bank reviews the documents. If they are in order, the bank pays the exporter and mails the documents to the buyer's bank for review.

7. The buyer's bank reviews the documents. If they conform, it debits the buyer's account, and gives the documents to the buyer to claim the goods.

Draft or Bill of Exchange

A draft, also called a bill of exchange, is a negotiable instrument, drawn up by the seller, stipulating payment by the buyer of a fixed amount at a specific time. Upon shipping the goods to the buyer, the seller delivers the draft and shipping documentation to his bank, which then forwards the draft and documents to the buyer's bank. The buyer's bank presents the draft to the buyer, who is required to sign, date, and write *accepted* on the face of the draft. After the acceptance is complete, the buyer's bank hands over the shipping documentation needed for the buyer to claim the goods.

When the buyer pays for the goods depends on the terms of the draft. There are three commonly used drafts: sight, time, and date. If the draft is payable on presentation, it is a *sight draft*. If payment can be made within a specified period of time, anywhere from 30 days to 180 days, it is a *time draft*. And if the contract stipulates payment on a specific date in the future, it is a *date draft*. As a negotiable instrument, an accepted draft can be sold at a discount to a bank. If, however, the buyer defaults on the draft, the seller is ultimately responsible for payment.

Forfaiting

A form of financing, *forfaiting* allows a seller to receive payment for goods from a bank rather than from the buyer. The bank buys the buyer's IOU from the seller at a discount and assumes responsibility for collecting payments. The seller can sell the IOU on a nonrecourse basis; that is, once she sells the promissory note, the bank assumes full risk for collecting payments. The bank, in turn, can sell the IOU in the secondary market that exists for forfait transactions.

Consider the case of Integrated Ceramic Technology, Inc. (Incetek), a small American manufacturer of machinery used for producing electronic components. Incetek found a Czechoslovakian company, Tesla, willing to place an order of $4 million but on the condition that payment be spread over several years. Incetek found a German bank willing to buy Tesla's IOU. And Tesla was able to find a Czech bank willing to provide a guarantee that the company would meet its four-year repayment schedule. Through this forfaiting arrangement, Incetek was able to successfully close the deal.[15]

Countertrade

Buyers do not always have money to pay for goods; however, they may be willing to engage in countertrade to secure the goods they need. The sale of goods or services that are paid for in whole or in part by goods or services is called *countertrade*. Mirus and Yeung state that countertrade arrangements are a "rational response" to environmental constraints and market imperfections, and that they do not necessarily represent inefficient economic transactions.[16] Four of the most common countertrade arrangements are barter, counterpurchase, compensation deals, and buyback arrangements.

Barter. In a simple barter no money changes hands. Goods or services are exchanged for goods or services. Brazil exchanged food products, aluminum, steel and iron products, paper, tires, and vehicles for petroleum from Iran and Iraq; typewriters and refrigerators for Algerian petroleum; and petrochemicals, tractors, and manufactured goods for rice from Thailand.[17]

Counterpurchase. In a counterpurchase agreement, the seller sells his products for cash and agrees to purchase products from the buyer for a specified amount, often the same amount paid by the buyer. Products that are commonly offered for counterpurchase consist of traditional exports (agricultural commodities, fertilizers, bulk chemicals, minerals), goods in surplus or subject to

[15] Bill Black, "Forfaiting Keeps You from Forfeiting Foreign Orders," *European Trade Report,* March 15, 1991, 1, 15.

[16] Rolf Mirus and Bernard Yeung, "Economic Incentives for Countertrade," *Journal of International Business Studies,* fall 1986, 27–39.

[17] Pompiliu Verzariu and Paula Mitchell, *International Countertrade: Individual Country Practices,* U.S. Department of Commerce, August 1992.

quotas (industrial and consumer goods, coffee, and textiles), and low-technology components.[18]

Compensation Deals. In a compensation deal, both goods and cash are involved in the transaction. The seller agrees to receive part of the payment in cash and the rest in goods. For example, the agreement may specify a 40 percent cash payment and the remaining 60 percent to be paid with goods.

Buyback Arrangements. In a buyback arrangement, the seller agrees to buy a certain amount of goods produced by the buyer or accept as payment a certain portion of the output produced with the use of the equipment sold by the seller. For example, Occidental Petroleum negotiated a $20 million deal with the former Soviet Union. Under the contract, Occidental agreed to build several plants and receive ammonia as partial payment over a twenty-year period.[19]

SUMMARY

The pricing decisions of a firm can be based on methods that are cost oriented, such as markup pricing, standard pricing, and target return pricing. Or they may be based on methods that rely on market conditions but do not ignore cost considerations. These methods are market-based pricing and strategic pricing. In setting the price of a product, global marketers face a challenging dilemma. If price is based on market conditions, it varies across countries because market conditions in different countries usually vary. This situation may encourage gray marketing as well as governmental interventions. However, if a firm sets a standard price for each country, it may underprice the product in some countries and overprice it in others. And this may result in lost revenue or reduced market shares or both.

The notion of a single, worldwide price is not feasible in today's global economy and floating-exchange-rate regime. Not only are market conditions different across countries, but exchange rates between different currencies also fluctuate continuously. This makes it difficult for a firm to maintain a standard price in all countries. A firm benefits from using a pricing method that incorporates market conditions, local as well as global, and consumer characteristics. Although market- and consumer-oriented pricing methods are not without

---

[18] Pompiliu Verzariu, *International Countertrade: A Guide for Managers and Executives,* U.S. Department of Commerce, August 1992.

[19] Joseph R. Carter and James Gagne, "The Dos and Don'ts of International Countertrade," *Sloan Management Review,* spring 1988, 31–37.

problems, they are the only methods that force a firm to take market dynamics into account before making pricing decisions.

Pricing decisions should be made to maximize profits and enhance the firm's competitive edge. To achieve these two goals, a firm should first analyze its internal conditions, market conditions within the target country, and the global business environment. The results of this analysis will be useful in managing various strategic pricing issues such as price escalation, transfer pricing, gray marketing, dumping, and fluctuating exchange rates.

Over time, a number of terms have developed to indicate the price of a product. The most common are EXW (ex works), FAS (free alongside ship), FOB (free on board), C&F (cost and freight), CIF (cost, insurance, and freight), CPT (carriage paid to), and CIP (carriage and insurance paid to). These pricing arrangements allow a firm to adapt to the varying needs and experiences of its transnational buyers.

An important concern of global marketers is to receive payments for goods sold. In some cases, a firm can receive payments in advance and in others after the goods are delivered to the buyer. The modes of payment, such as cash in advance, open account, letter of credit, bill of exchange, forfaiting, and countertrade involve different levels of risk and security. In selecting a mode of payment, global marketers need not take undue risk. With familiar buyers, they can conduct transactions on an open-account basis, but with unknown buyers, a confirmed irrevocable letter of credit is recommended.

CHAPTER EIGHT

Work all day. Work all night. Deliver. On time. On budget. On schedule.
George Shaheen

Global Logistics Channels

In this chapter we cover the following topics: the importance of global channels, direct and indirect channels of global distribution, designing a distribution channel within a host country, managing channel alliances, evaluating channel performance, and just-in-time distribution.

The globalization of markets, increasing competitive pressure, emerging business opportunities, and the desire to survive and grow are encouraging firms from both developed and developing economies to expand their operations globally. Firms that operate globally seldom conduct totally independent business operations within a single country. Sourcing, producing, and marketing activities are usually linked between countries. Raw materials are purchased in one country and transported to another for conversion into component parts. Component parts are produced in one country and transferred to another for assembly into final products. Products assembled or manufactured in one country are sold in others. As firms expand their operations globally, the issue of moving raw materials and finished products economically and efficiently from one country to another has assumed renewed importance.

Nike, a major designer, producer, and distributor of high-quality athletic and leisure footwear, sells its products in more than sixty countries.[1] Nike sources the critical components of the footwear in the United States and ships them overseas for manufacture and distribution. It contracts with manufacturing facilities in Hong Kong, South Korea, Singapore, Taiwan, Thailand, and the People's Republic of China. Depending on the country, Nike sells its products through independent distributors, its own distribution subsidiaries, or exclusive distributors who are responsible for selling to retailers.[2]

---

[1] Gary Hoover, Alta Campbell, and Patrick J. Spain, eds., *Hoover's Handbook*, Austin, TX: The Reference Press, 1991.

[2] "Nike Outdoes Competition in Delivery to Customers," *Global Trade*, March 1988, 8.

All major corporations, whether they are based in the United States or in South Korea, have expanded their operations beyond the frontiers of a single country. Colgate-Palmolive (U.S.), Nestlè (Switzerland), Sony (Japan), Siemens (Germany), Hyundai (South Korea), and many others operate worldwide. Such expansion has made the distinction between domestic and global distribution unimportant. Successful corporations realize that survival and growth will depend on adopting a worldwide, global view of business.[3]

Moving goods internationally is generally more complicated and expensive than moving them domestically. To achieve a competitive advantage, it is important for firms to organize the flow of inputs and outputs in a way that not only makes them available at the right place and at the right time but also at the right price.

The movements of raw materials, components, and products can be grouped into two categories. The first is the movement of raw materials or components from one country to another for conversion or assembly into products; this is referred to as the *global flow of materials*. The second is the movement of finished products from the country where they are assembled or produced to countries where they will be marketed; this is referred to as the *global distribution of products*. The effective management of the movement of products from one country to another, and the delivery of these products to consumers within a country, requires an understanding of global distribution channels and the functions they perform.

A *global distribution channel* consists of a group of individuals and organizations that direct the flow of products from a manufacturer to consumers across countries. The channel members perform various functions. Among others, they collect, analyze, and transmit market information to a firm; initiate and maintain contacts with buyers in different countries; receive, process, and execute orders; arrange for shipping, insuring, and delivering the products; take title to the products; and make the sale.

Channel intermediaries are of two types: *merchant middlemen* and *agent middlemen*. Merchant middlemen are independent business organizations whose business decisions are guided by profit motives. They take title to the goods and assume risks for the products they purchase. Agent middlemen do not take title to the products, but may represent the manufacturer, negotiate contracts, or bring buyers and manufacturers together to negotiate a sale. When authorized by a firm, agent middlemen can make binding contracts on its behalf. In general, an agent middleman is a representative of the firm.

For a global marketer, there are two important goals to achieve in managing the global distribution of products: first, to effectively and efficiently move products from the *home country*, where they are produced, to *host countries*, where

---

[3] Paul S. Bender, "The Challenge of International Distribution," *International Journal of Physical Distribution and Materials Management* 15, 1985, 20.

FIGURE **8.1**   The Indirect and Direct Channel of Distribution

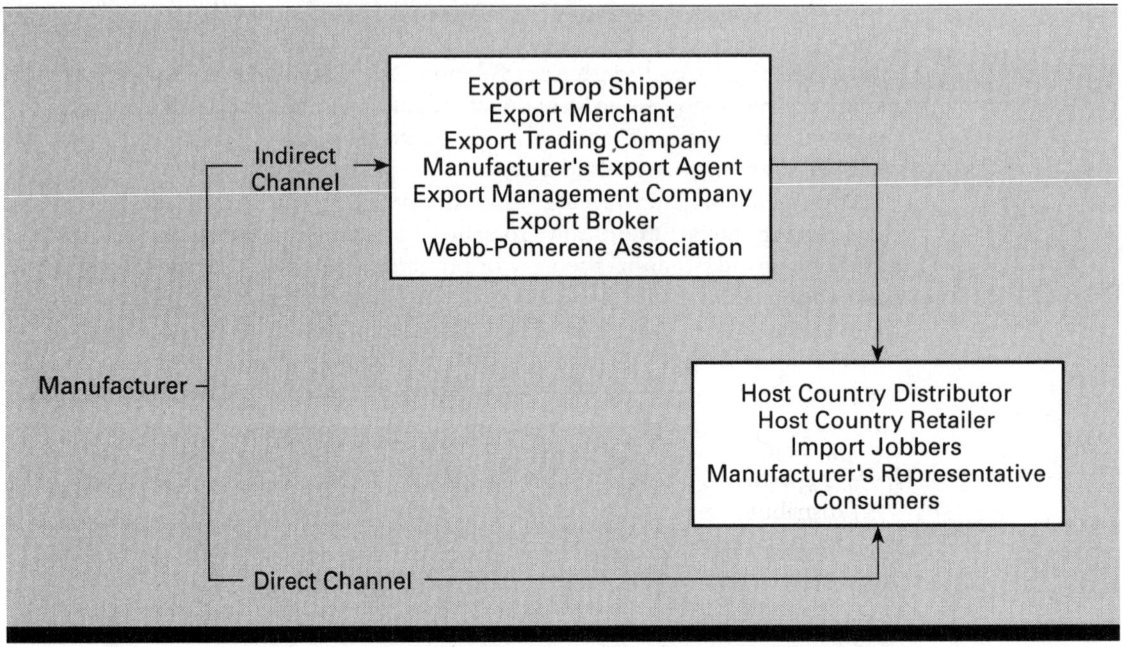

they will be marketed; and second, to deliver these products to consumers within a country market satisfactorily and competitively.

There are two main options a firm can use to move products from a home country to host countries: the direct channel and the indirect channel (see Figure 8.1). Through a direct channel, the firm deals directly with intermediaries (middlemen) within a host country to market its products there. With the *direct channel*, a firm can also choose to sell its products directly to consumers in host countries without using the services of intermediaries. An *indirect channel* requires the use of home country intermediaries to market products in host countries. In this case, the firm does not deal with any intermediaries or consumers in host countries; this function is the responsibility of the home country intermediaries.

THE DIRECT CHANNEL OF GLOBAL DISTRIBUTION

When electing to develop a direct channel, a firm has to be convinced that it can perform distribution functions more effectively than the intermediaries in the home country. By dealing directly with intermediaries or consumers in host countries, it can gather market-related information to establish its marketing presence in these countries. Furthermore, setting up a direct channel allows a company to achieve greater control over its distribution activities and earn higher profits. However, the direct channel is not without its drawbacks. If the firm is unfamiliar with the business environment in host countries, or if it lacks resources or managerial commitment, it may encounter difficulties in managing the intermediaries and developing an appropriate marketing package.

In the following sections, we explain the types of intermediaries involved in a direct channel. It is important to bear in mind that these descriptions are based on the common functions these intermediaries perform. There may be some exceptions that depart from these descriptions.

Host Country Distributors

A host country distributor is a merchant middleman who purchases products from the firm and then resells them at a profit to retailers or to final consumers. This distributor often enjoys exclusive rights to sell products in the country or in a specific region within the country. Because the distributor buys from the firm, the firm has access to funds for its cash-flow needs. The company can also exercise some control over the final price of the product and aftersale service to consumers.

When a firm uses a distributor to establish marketing presence in a host country, the company is interested in making a long-term commitment to stay in that market. As such, distributors should be carefully selected. Selecting the right host country distributor requires patience and long-term thinking. Before signing the contract, a firm should familiarize itself with prospective distributors, evaluate them on their organizational and technical ability to support the company's business, investigate cultural differences, and examine local laws in the distributor's native country.[4]

A distributor contract can include a number of provisions. According to Robinson,[5] the following are important:

1. Duration and termination.
2. Territory.
3. Special reservations by seller to sell directly or at reduced commission to certain categories of buyers.

---

[4] Richard M. Lucash, James Geisman, and William Contente, "Choosing an Overseas Distributor," *Small Business Reports* 16, August 1991, 68–71.

[5] Richard D. Robinson, *International Business Management: A Guide to Decision Making*, Hinsdale, IL: The Dryden Press, 1978, 75.

4. Products and/or services covered.

5. Tax liabilities.

6. Payment and discount terms.

7. Right to fix and/or change prices and other terms.

8. Sales support to be given by both parties.

9. Responsibility for custom clearances.

10. Limitation on right of assignment of rights.

11. Information to be supplied by an agent or distributor to the seller.

12. Inventory maintenance.

13. Services and information to be supplied by seller and on what terms.

14. Clarification of warranties.

15. Right to audit.

16. The arbitration system to be used.

Host Country Retailers

Rather than dealing with a distributor, a firm may decide to deal directly with a host country retailer. This is a merchant middleman who buys products from the firm and resells them to consumers. Although the term *retailer* is commonly used across countries, the structure, performance, and orientation of retailers vary from country to country.

Compared to the retailing structure in the developed economies of the United States, the United Kingdom, Germany, and France, the Japanese retailing system has often been characterized as traditional, antiquated, and obsolete. This generalization is based on the large number of small retail stores that operate in Japan. In 1985, for example, Japan had 1.6 million retail stores, each serving on average 74 people. By contrast, in the United States there were more than 1 million retail stores, each serving 228 people (see Table 8.1 for data on other countries).

The view that the Japanese retail structure is traditional or antiquated is challenged by Goldman. Based on an analysis of the institutional structure of retailing in Japan and the United States, he concludes that although the food retailers in Japan and the United States are vastly different, the nonfood retail sector in the two countries is quite similar. For example, there were 7.9 (1985) nonfood retail stores per thousand persons in Japan, while in the United States there were 6.8 (1982) stores, a comparable number. However, the difference was quite large for food stores—5.5 stores per thousand people in Japan versus 0.7 stores in the United States.[6]

---

[6] Arieh Goldman, "Japan's Distribution System: Institutional Structure, Internal Political Economy, and Modernization," *Journal of Retailing*, summer 1991, 154–183.

TABLE **8.1**   Structure of Retail Trade

Country	Year	Retail outlets (000s)	Pop. per outlet	Retail staff (000s)
Algeria	1971	3.6	5,146	18
Argentina	1974	445.8	40	1,868
Australia	1986	160.2	100	929
Brazil	1980	885.6	143	2,817
Egypt	1981	2.1	20,000	48
Ghana	1983	1.5	8,693	16
Guatemala	1982	.88.2	84	n/a
India	1978	450	1,450	n/a
Iran	1971	214	175	328
Israel	1982	30	144	83
Japan	1985	1,628.6	74	633
Kenya	1987	4.3	4,930	250
Malaysia	1980	96	142	247
Mexico	1975	463.6	122	985
Morocco	1972	4	3,900	20
New Zealand	1983	30	107	129
Nigeria	1982	22.2	4,045	266
Pakistan	1976	276	325	502
Saudi Arabia	1981	80.3	130	174
Singapore	1986	15.5	166	63
South Africa	1983	58.1	408	373
South Korea	1986	637.7	63	1,221
Tanzania	1983	1.6	12,963	17
Thailand	1988	6.7	7,910	42
United States	1984	1,035	228	9,834
Zimbabwe	1982	1.2	5,843	13

Source: Adapted from *International Marketing Data and Statistics,* London: Euromonitor Publications Limited, 1990

A new development, the internationalization of retailing, is proceeding at a rapid pace with a significant impact on global distribution. Aldi, a German food discounter that operated only in Germany a decade ago, has now expanded its operations to seven European countries with some 3,300 stores. Sweden-based Ikea (furniture), Italy-based Benetton (fashion clothing), and Britain-based Body Shop (toiletries) are expanding their retailing operations in Europe as well as in the United States.[7] In a survey of twenty-six British retailers with international operations, the three most important reasons given for international expansion were niche opportunities within the market, the size of the market, and the level of economic prosperity within the market.[8]

U.S.-based retailers have also expanded their operations into other countries. Toys "R" Us, for example, has opened stores from Singapore to Germany. It is estimated that by 1997, it will have 406 international units generating sales of $4.2 billion annually.[9] Other U.S.-based retailers that have expanded their operations internationally include J.C. Penney (Canada, U.K., Mexico); Tiffany (Italy, U.K., Germany, Switzerland, Hong Kong, Japan); The Gap (U.K., Germany, Canada); and Estee Lauder (Hungary, Russia).[10]

Import Jobbers

Import jobbers are merchant middlemen in a host country. They buy products from a firm and sell them to other intermediaries such as wholesalers or retailers within the country, or directly to consumers. Because import jobbers are not granted exclusive territorial rights for selling products, a firm can deal with several of them in a host country.

Manufacturer's Representatives

A manufacturer's representative in a host country is an agent middleman who does not buy or take title to the products, but works primarily to represent the firm to existing and potential customers. The territorial jurisdiction of this intermediary may extend from a region in a country to a group of countries. A company should exercise extreme caution in selecting its representatives in host countries. In many countries the laws are skewed in favor of the repre-

---

[7] Peter F. Drucker, "The Retail Revolution," *The Wall Street Journal,* July 15, 1993, A14.

[8] Nicholas Alexander, "Retailers and International Markets: Motives for Expansion," *International Marketing Review* 7, 1990, 75–85.

[9] Annetta Miller, Lourdes Rosado, Peter McKillop, and Don Kirk, "The World 'S' Ours," *Newsweek,* March 23, 1992, 46–47.

[10] Alison Fahey, Christy Fisher, and Kate Fitzgerald, "International Intriguing: As Domestic Sales Lag, U.S. Retailers Probe Foreign Markets," *Advertising Age,* January 29, 1990, S1, S2.

sentatives, making it difficult to terminate relations with them even if they are performing unsatisfactorily.

Consumers

A firm may choose to sell products directly to consumers in host countries. This option is often riddled with regulatory and administrative inconveniences. Import regulations, duty payments and clearance procedures, and mishandling of products can deter a company from using this alternative. However, as many countries are reducing regulatory hurdles and streamlining the delivery of products, this alternative is beginning to show potential for establishing marketing presence in host countries. The example of Harrod's illustrates how firms can directly and successfully reach consumers in different country markets. Harrod's, a London department store, ran a full-page advertisement in *The New York Times* on December 29, 1985. The advertisement featured an international 800 number that consumers could call to charge their purchases. The ad generated sales amounting to more than $300,000. Products were shipped from London to consumers in the United States.[11]

THE INDIRECT CHANNEL OF GLOBAL DISTRIBUTION

Through an indirect channel, a firm uses intermediaries in its home country to establish marketing presence in host countries. In selecting a channel partner, the company needs assurance that the intermediaries can perform the distribution functions better than it can. To a great extent, these intermediaries become an international organ of the firm, performing most of the functions that an export department would normally handle.

In choosing an indirect channel, a firm may be motivated by its own lack of experience in host countries or even a dearth of resources to develop a direct channel. Many companies rely on intermediaries to establish their marketing presence in a host country. However, after the sales volume reaches a particular level, some of these firms may choose to develop their own in-house department to handle the operations in host countries. The following represent indirect channel options.

Export Drop Shippers

The export drop shipper provides a link between a firm and a buyer in a host country. Upon receiving an order from a buyer, the export drop shipper

---

[11] *International Direct Marketing Guide,* Alexandria, VA: Braddock Communications, 1990.

requests the company to ship the product directly to the buyer. The buyer pays the drop shipper, who then pays the firm. Because drop shippers provide only minimal promotional help and do not hold inventory, they can pass the savings on to both buyers and sellers.

Export Merchants

The export merchant purchases products directly from a firm and sells them in host countries. All risks associated with the account in the host country are assumed by the export merchant. The advantage of dealing with an export merchant is that a company is able to establish its marketing presence in host countries without much effort. However, in dealing with an export merchant, a firm also relinquishes control over the marketing and promotion of its products in host countries. Thus, if the export merchant has not priced the product competitively or created a favorable image of the product, it may adversely affect product acceptance.

Export Trading Company (ETC)

The Export Trading Company Act was passed in 1982. Its goals are to promote and encourage the formation of export management and export trading companies, reduce uncertainty about applying U.S. antitrust law to export operations, expand the options available for export financing by permitting bank holding companies to invest in ETCs, and reduce restrictions on trade finance provided by financial institutions. An ETC can either act as the export department of firms or take title to the products and export on its own account.

Manufacturer's Export Agent (MEA)

A manufacturer's export agent is an agent middleman in the home country who represents a firm to potential buyers in host countries and provides selling services to the concern. The MEA is an individual or company that does business in its own name rather than the firm's. The contract between the company and the MEA specifies such details as the countries to be covered, products to be handled, methods of compensation, terms of sale, and duration of the contract. Although the services offered by these agents are limited, their broad knowledge makes them valuable for establishing marketing presence in certain host countries.

Export Management Company (EMC)

An EMC is an agent middleman that virtually functions as the export department of a firm, providing it with extensive marketing services. Serving as an export department, an EMC may take full or partial responsibility for locating customers, promoting products, conducting marketing research, and shipping and delivering products in host countries. It may also collect payments from overseas customers and guarantee payments to the firm. In return, the EMC may earn a commission or salary, or receive a retainer along with a commission or other fees.

To a firm new to exporting, an EMC provides expertise in the early stages of its involvement in overseas markets. The EMC can be used to test product acceptability or to introduce products in country markets where a firm does not have a marketing presence. By handling products of several clients, an EMC can provide various export-related services at a competitive price. The option of selecting an EMC appeals to companies that do not want to make extensive financial or personnel investments but desire a marketing presence overseas.[12]

There are also disadvantages in using an EMC. The EMC may not be willing to make the type of investments necessary to capitalize on marketing opportunities in host countries. It may demand startup costs before representing the firm in host countries. It may underrepresent the company by not aggressively pursuing marketing opportunities. Furthermore, the use of an EMC reduces the gross margin, impedes direct communication with customers, and lessens the ability of a firm to correctly measure market potential.

Export Brokers

Export broker is an all-inclusive term for an agent middleman who, for a fee or commission, brings buyers and sellers together. An export broker can make offers to buyers and negotiate the most attractive terms for the firm it represents. Usually, the relationship between a company and an export broker is sporadic. Contacts between the two are made if the broker has located a buyer for the firm's products in host countries.

Webb-Pomerene Association

Based on the Webb-Pomerene Act of 1918, American firms can combine their resources to expand exports from the United States without being subjected to the Sherman Antitrust Act. Members of the association, however, are not permitted to form agreements that discourage or reduce competition within the United States. The association performs several useful functions for its members. It promotes products in host countries, locates buyers, provides market information to member companies, receives orders from buyers and transmits them to members, arranges for the transportation of the products,

---

[12] Walter H. Nagel and Gaston Z. Ndyajunwoha, *Export Marketing Handbook*, New York: Praeger, 1988, 35–36.

negotiates insurance costs, and organizes efforts to reduce trade barriers. Collectively, its activities help member firms reduce the cost of locating markets and maintaining and expanding marketing presence in host countries.

DESIGNING A DISTRIBUTION CHANNEL WITHIN A HOST COUNTRY

When designing a distribution channel within a country, a firm has to consider such important factors as consumer characteristics, product characteristics, market characteristics, cost structures, and coverage. We discuss these next.

Consumer Characteristics

In developing a channel, the primary concern of the company is to maximize the delivery of benefits to consumers. As such, understanding the behavior of the target market is essential for developing a channel. For example, marketers should know where, when, what, how, and why consumers buy products. Kentucky Fried Chicken (KFC) entered the Japanese market in 1970. Based on its American formulas and strategies, it selected suburban locations for its stores. The units suffered anemic sales and tepid consumer response. KFC was considering withdrawing from the Japanese market when Shin Ohkawara, who became the president and CEO of KFC Japan in 1984, opened the stores in central urban locations. Ohkawara's site selection worked: KFC Japan has more than 725 outlets.[13]

Product Characteristics

The characteristics of a product play an important role in developing a channel. For products that require aftersale service, the criteria for selecting channel members may include the ability to deliver the required service to consumers. However, personal care products can be sold either through stores or directly to consumers. Avon, a marketer of personal care products, has successfully sold directly to consumers in many countries. When Avon entered the Chinese market, the firm and its marketing approach were both novel to the Chinese. Avon met its six-month sales projections during the first two months, and expects sales to reach $50 million to $60 million within five years. Its sales force consists of doctors, lawyers, teachers, and computer scientists.[14]

---

[13] "Pioneer Manager Catapults KFC to Success," *Nation's Restaurant News,* November 14, 1988, F100, F102.

[14] Andrew Tanzer, "Ding-dong, Capitalism Calling," *Forbes,* October 14, 1991, 184–186.

Market Characteristics

To gain a competitive edge, a firm should examine market characteristics and assess the strengths and weaknesses of the existing distribution structure. Marketers frequently adapt the distribution of the products to local conditions or create their own distribution system. Nestlè is a good example: In Bangkok, Thailand, shopkeepers cruise the waterways in boats filled with Nestlè's products. And in some African communities, young women, carrying Nestlè's products on trays balanced on their heads, are part of the company's distribution channel.[15] Electrolux, a manufacturer of home appliances, initially sold its products in Japan through stores. It soon discovered that working with these powerful stores was becoming difficult. Electrolux took a strategic decision that worked to its advantage. It pulled out of the stores and began selling its products directly to consumers, door-to-door.[16] Levi's, however, penetrated the Brazilian market by opening a chain of 400 Levi's Only stores. These account for 65 percent of Levi's $100 million in sales in Brazil.[17]

Cost

There are two types of channel-related costs: the cost of developing the channel and the cost of maintaining it. Development costs are the initial expenditures a company incurs in organizing the channel. These may include the cost of researching the market, negotiating with prospective channel members, and setting up the physical facilities. Maintenance costs include the salary of the sales force and employees, promotional expenses, margins and markups of channel members, and other operating costs. In determining the cost of a distribution channel, firms should be aware that providing and expanding customer services are not without costs. As the level of customer service is increased, so does the cost of providing it. Global marketers have to balance the increasing cost of providing services with the satisfaction that consumers derive from these additional services and the amount of money they are willing to pay in return.

Consumers expect many services from channel members: on-time delivery, a large assortment of products, no-questions-asked return policy, credit facilities, and home delivery. The relative importance of these services to consumers influences the service mix offered by the channel. When the Japanese economy slowed down, consumers were willing to trade-off service for lower prices. As the relative importance of price increased, discount stores became popular.

---

[15] Norris Willatt, "How Nestlè Adapts Products to Its Markets," *Business Abroad,* June 1970, 31–33.

[16] Michael Berger, "Breaking All the Rules," *International Management,* February 1990, 58–59.

[17] Maria Shao, Robert Neff, and Jeffrey Ryser, "For Levi's, a Flattering Fit Overseas," *Business Week,* November 5, 1990, 76–77.

Tsuneo Okubo, president of Retail Science, a Tokyo research organization, notes that the recent emergence and rapid growth of large, specialized discount stores for all kinds of goods is the biggest change in Japan's distribution structure in the past twenty years.[18] The emergence of large discount stores in Japan has coincided with slowed economic growth.

Coverage

In some countries, wholesalers and retailers operate only within the major metropolitan areas. Within a metro city, these retailers may cover only a few blocks. Thus, if a firm wants to reach consumers beyond the city's jurisdiction, the services of numerous middlemen may be required. In other countries, wholesalers and retailers may cover the entire country. Because of these variations, a company may need to adapt its channel design in each country.

MANAGING CHANNEL ALLIANCES

The alliance between a firm and a channel has to be managed so that each can help the other. Relationships between a firm and its channel members evolve over time. A company's marketing objectives in a country may change, or the channel members themselves may want to change the roles they play in product distribution. The government may also impose certain constraints on the relationship between channel and firm. These and other changes are normal, requiring a company to pay special attention to its dealings with channel members. A relationship based on trust and mutual advantage ensures that the objectives of the firm and the channel members are achieved. Furthermore, a firm's goals can be realized by establishing clear lines of communication to channel members, to motivate and control them.

Communicating

The strategic alliance between a company and its channel can work only if the two establish an effective communication link. In countries where the firm has an office, personal communication between firm and channel is possible. However, in countries where independent channels represent the firm and the firm does not have a physical presence, it should develop a link to communicate its goals to the channel and receive performance feedback. Recent developments in telecommunications, such as videoconferencing and conference calls that allow cross-country communication, can be effectively used by marketers to reach their channels.

---

[18] Yumiko Ono, "Bargain Hunting Catches On in Japan, Boosting the Fortunes of Discount Stores," *The Wall Street Journal*, May 19, 1992, B1, B9.

Motivating

In many ways, channel members have the same goals as manufacturers. They want to establish marketing presence in a country and maximize the return on investment. Establishing an alliance ensures that both the manufacturer and the channel are able to achieve their marketing goals. What a channel member does for a manufacturer greatly depends on how the channel evaluates the importance of the manufacturer to its survival and growth. Motivation to carry and promote a manufacturer's products depends on whether a channel can make a profit by doing so. A manufacturer, however, can enhance its attractiveness by training channel members, providing promotional displays, and participating in cooperative advertising.

Controlling

Controlling a channel involves developing criteria for measuring performance of channel members, evaluating the channel's performance against these criteria, and taking corrective actions to reduce the difference between the desired and the actual performance. To control effectively, a firm should communicate to the channel the criteria to be used for measuring performance. Furthermore, the concern should institute a system for receiving timely information on the channel's performance and for taking corrective measures. Controlling the activities of channel members across countries is difficult. First, companies may not get reliable data from channel members. Second, the cost of obtaining useful data may not justify their value. And third, changes in the competitive environment may make the measurement criteria irrelevant.

EVALUATING CHANNEL PERFORMANCE

After a distribution channel has been established, its performance needs to be measured periodically. Some common measurement criteria are sales, service, and inventory. The first criterion, sales analysis, involves the comparison of a channel's actual sales against expected sales. This useful measure provides information on how effective the channel has been in achieving its sales goals. The data also provide information to the firm about its own marketing program, which can be useful for taking remedial actions. Sales analysis can further be broken down by products, customers, and territories.

The second criterion for evaluating channel performance is the level of service. Aftersale service for many products, such as automobiles and home appliances, is important to consumers. They want to know what to do if a product fails to perform. Meeting this need has become an important vehicle for gaining a competitive advantage. Firms promise aftersale service as an incentive to consumers to purchase their products. Thus, if channel members cannot adequately provide these services, the firm's future sales are adversely affected. Firms set service standards for their channel members and expect their standards to be met. One effective way of ascertaining the level of service is to query consumers. A company can send out a questionnaire and inquire about service quality. Information received from this survey measures the actual performance of the channel, which is then compared to the standard set by the firm.

The third measure of performance is the level of inventory maintained by a channel member. Firms usually set as a standard a level of inventory that channel members are expected to maintain. However, the standard varies for wholesalers and retailers. The idea behind this measure is that by keeping goods in stock, a wholesaler or retailer will be able to meet demand. (This measure is declining in importance as businesses are discovering the virtues of just-in-time delivery, which we discuss next.)

JUST-IN-TIME DISTRIBUTION

The just-in-time (JIT) approach is perhaps the most innovative way to manage inventory, production, and delivery. Its aim is to eliminate waste and maximize efficiency. JIT is the Americanized version of *Kanban*, a system developed by Toyota during the 1950s and 1960s in Japan for delivering components and materials to locations within plants. Kanban "is basically the system of supplying parts and materials just the very moment they are needed in the factory production process so those parts and materials are instantly put to use."[19] Ideally, in a just-in-time system, the products should arrive when they are needed, neither earlier nor later. The four principles underlying a JIT system are zero inventories, short lead times, small and frequent replenishment, and zero defects.[20]

SUMMARY

Increasing competitive pressure, globalization of markets, emerging business opportunities, and the desire to survive and grow are encouraging firms to expand their operations globally. As this expansion unfolds, companies must be able to move raw materials and finished products economically and efficiently

---

[19] Bruce D. Henderson, "The Logic of Kanban," *The Journal of Business Strategy*, winter, 1986, 6.

[20] John J. Coyle, Edward J. Bardi, and C. John Langley, *The Management of Business Logistics*, St. Paul, MN: West Publishing, 1992.

from one country to another. Products should reach their destination not only at the right time and place but also at the right price. Firms can achieve a competitive advantage by streamlining their global logistics channels.

There are two primary options a firm can use to move products from a home country to host countries: direct channel and indirect channel. In the direct channel, the company develops its own distribution system in host countries to market products to consumers. The numerous options in the direct channel include host country distributors, host country retailers, import jobbers, manufacturer's representatives, and consumers. An indirect channel requires the use of home country intermediaries to market products in host countries. In this case, the firm does not deal with intermediaries or consumers in host countries; that is the responsibility of the home country intermediaries. The options in the indirect channel include export drop shipper, export merchant, export trading company, manufacturer's export agent, export management company, export broker, and Webb-Pomerene Association.

The organizing principle underlying the development of a channel is total consumer satisfaction. Factors that influence the development of a channel are consumer, product, and market characteristics; cost; and coverage. The performance of a distribution channel should be periodically reviewed by developing performance criteria and evaluating the channel's performance against these criteria.

CHAPTER NINE

The key to success for Sony, and to everything in business, science, and tech-nology for that matter, is never to follow the others.

Masaru Ibuka

Global Promotion Strategies

In today's intensely competitive environment, promotion plays a decisive role in establishing a firm's marketing presence. Whether a company sells its products in one country or many, the goals of promotion are the same: to increase the perceived value of a product and convince consumers to adopt it. It is important to remember, however, that promotion alone cannot make a product successful. For example, couturier Christian Lacroix's signature fragrance received heavy promotional fanfare, but it failed to elicit an enthusiastic response because consumers just did not like the product.[1] Although promotion can enhance a product's appeal, it cannot ensure its success. All four elements of the marketing mix should work together synergistically to enhance a firm's competitive edge in the marketplace.

One of the first lessons of global promotion is that people across the world are unique in some ways and similar in many others. They dress, talk, and eat differently. Their life-styles, values, mores, and beliefs are also different. The French enjoy wine with their meals, while the Saudis prohibit the consumption of liquor; the Germans prefer to be greeted formally, while the Americans are generally informal. A 1990 Procter & Gamble advertising campaign for Camay soap was highly successful in Europe but was considered rude in Japan. The advertisement showed a husband barging in on his wife sitting in a bathtub. While the French and the British thought the advertisement was sexy, the Japanese saw bad manners.[2] But regardless of their culture, people are also similar in many respects. They want to look beautiful, share joyous moments,

---

[1] Patricia McLaughlin, "Ethereal Perfume Ads Go to Great Lengths to Disguise Whatever It Is They're Selling," *The Milwaukee Journal*, February 21, 1993, G2.

[2] Ken Wells, "Selling to the World: Global Ad Campaign, After Many Missteps, Finally Pays Dividends," *The Wall Street Journal*, August 27, 1992, A1, A8.

and express feelings through art, music, and dance. The musical instruments in India may not be the same as those in France, but the songs they accompany often have the same themes of love, hope, and joy.

Cultural similarities and differences are important considerations for a firm because they influence how consumers interpret and respond to promotional stimuli. Brand names such as Kodak, Xerox, and Rolex have traveled well across countries, but Nova, which means "no go" in Spanish, did not fare well as a brand name for a car in Latin America. Consider the following examples of unintentional mistakes that have caused their sponsors embarrassment. Braniff airlines ran an advertising campaign intended to emphasize the comfort of leather seats. The Spanish version read "sentado en cuero," which idiomatically is a request to be seated in the nude. Other examples include Kentucky Fried Chicken's "finger lickin' good," which came out in Chinese as "eat your finger off"; and Pepsi's "come alive," which came out in its Asian version as a call to bring ancestors back from the grave.[3]

It is important for a firm to understand how people interpret words, symbols, colors, and numbers, among other things, before developing its promotional campaigns. Other factors influencing the development of a promotional campaign include the objectives of the firm, media availability, agency availability, competitive situation, and governmental regulations. As promotion involves communicating with target markets, we begin by analyzing how the communication process works.

THE COMMUNICATION PROCESS

The communication process, illustrated in Figure 9.1, consists of a series of steps involved in the flow of information from a sender to a receiver and back to the sender. It is initiated by a sender, who encodes a message and sends it through a medium to a receiver, who decodes the message and responds. The response of the receiver provides feedback to the sender. The communication process is enveloped by noise, which causes distortion in the encoding, delivering, and receiving of a message. The elements of the communication process are defined as follows:

- ◆ **Sender.** An individual, group, or organization that sends a message to a target audience.
- ◆ **Encoding.** The process of organizing thoughts and ideas into a symbolic form by the sender.

---

[3] Richard N. Weltz, "How Do You Say 'Oops!'" *Business Marketing*, October 1990, 52–53.

FIGURE **9.1**   The Communication Process

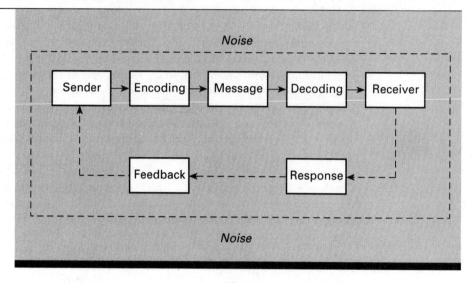

- **Message.** The symbols that a sender transmits to a receiver through a medium or media.
- **Medium of Transmission.** That which carries the encoded message from a sender to a receiver. The medium can be aural (e.g., radio); visual (e.g., magazine); or audiovisual (e.g., TV).
- **Receiver.** Also known as an audience or a destination; an individual, group, or organization that receives the message.
- **Decoding.** The process of inferring meanings from a message by a receiver.
- **Response.** The receiver's actions after being exposed to a message.
- **Feedback.** The response that the sender receives from a receiver.
- **Noise.** Elements in the communication process that cause a discrepancy between the encoded and the decoded messages. Among other causes, the inability of the sender to encode a message properly or the inability of a medium to faithfully transmit a message can cause discrepancies between the intended and the received message.

Each element plays a role in generating effective communication. The sender should encode the message clearly, the medium should transmit the message reliably, and the receiver should receive the message accurately. In general, discrepancy between the intended and the received message is reduced when sender and receiver share a common field of experience. In other words, when they share language, life experiences, social class, moral values, orientations, and stage in life-cycle, discrepancy in communication is reduced. When we communicate with our friends and family, it is not always necessary to analyze their social and psychological characteristics. Our common field of experience allows us to communicate spontaneously and freely. Even a small gesture may carry the weight of many words.

Marketing communication, however, is different from social communication. When the sender is a firm and the receiver is a target market, the onus for reducing ambiguity rests with the firm. Consumers usually do not like to spend much time decoding messages. The clearer the message, the easier it is for them to understand. In communicating with a target market, the objectives of a firm are to formulate a clear message, deliver it effectively, and measure the results reliably.

To communicate with its target markets, a company can select from four alternatives: advertising, sales promotion, personal selling, and public relations. Collectively these four options are referred to as the promotional mix. To gain a better appreciation of each of the four elements of the promotional mix, we will discuss each individually.

GLOBAL ADVERTISING

Advertising is any paid form of nonpersonal communication in which the sponsor can be identified. Advertising is often controversial. Some people enjoy the artistic beauty of an advertisement and value its informational content; some see it as a tool for selling products that consumers could do without; and some say it is an agent for perpetrating cultural hegemony. For example, when Eurodisney aired its advertisements in France, some of the French equated the ads with American cultural imperialism.

Reactions to advertisements are not easy to predict. The Benetton advertisement that showed AIDS victims dying in hospitals surrounded by relatives and friends evoked mixed emotions. Some thought it a tasteless attempt to achieve popularity, others saw it as a sincere effort to increase public awareness of AIDS.

The controversies surrounding advertising are not likely to disappear. However, a few points can help put the matter in perspective. To begin with, advertising is beneficial both economically and socially. The economic benefits stem from what advertising does in the marketplace. Consider the following. Advertising generates sales. As sales increase, production increases to meet the growing demand. As production increases, the per-unit cost of the product goes down because of economies of scale. As cost goes down, a firm is able to reduce the price, which in turn increases sales. Furthermore, advertising encourages competition, which forces companies to improve productivity and product quality. The social advantages ensue from the increased level of economic activities that generate employment and a higher standard of living; overall, consumers benefit by paying a competitive price for a high-quality product.

PLANNING AN ADVERTISING CAMPAIGN

Planning a global advertising campaign requires a clear specification of advertising objectives. De Beers, the huge South African cartel that controls 90 percent of the world's diamond supply, began advertising in Japan to persuade its reluctant citizens to buy diamond engagement rings. In the 1940s, fewer than 5 percent of affianced Japanese bought diamond engagement rings. After a relentless advertising campaign by De Beers, eight out of ten brides now wear diamond rings.[4]

To achieve its objectives, a firm has to make strategic decisions related to the advertising message (product attributes to be emphasized); advertising budget and allocation (the amount of money to be spent on advertisements, and where); media plan (the composition of the media for delivering the message); agency (whether local agencies, a global agency, or some combination will handle the account); regulations (constraints on advertising); and measurement procedure (the evaluation of advertising effectiveness).

Advertising Message

A crucial decision for a global firm is determining the advertising message for each target market. In developing this message, a company has to decide between a *standardized* message for all country markets or an *adapted* message for each country. The arguments for selecting each approach flow from the assumptions made about the target market. Basically, if target markets across countries are similar, a standardized approach is recommended; and if they are different, an adapted approach is preferable.

As with products, the decision to adapt or standardize a message should be guided by consumer characteristics. If consumption systems and buying motives are different across countries, a standardized message will not be effective. Maxwell House, much to its disappointment, found that Germans had little respect for "American coffee"; and Procter & Gamble discovered that Crest's fluoride appeal meant little or nothing to the British public.[5]

---

[4] Stefan Kanfer, "A Cartel More Durable than Diamonds," *The New York Times,* September 26, 1993, F11.

[5] S. Watson Dunn, "Effect of National Identity on Multinational Promotional Strategy," *Journal of Marketing,* October 1976, 50–57.

An advertising message increases its appeal by being congruent with the religious, political, and cultural sentiments of the target market. Words, pictures, or symbols considered offensive by the audience should be assiduously avoided in an advertisement. Every culture has its own list of taboos. In Poland, for example, references to the Church or to sex should not be made in an advertisement; and in Mexico, criticism against the government is not tolerated (see Figure 9.2 for advertising taboos in selected countries).

Budget and Allocation

An advertising budget is determined by internal and external conditions. Internal conditions include management orientation, advertising objectives, and resources available to a firm. External conditions that influence the determination of an advertising budget include governmental regulations, competitors' advertising strategies, market attractiveness, and media restrictions, among others.

FIGURE **9.2**   Taboo on TV

Egypt	Sex; anything more than a little kiss
Poland	References to the Church or sex
Hong Kong	Indecent matter; obscene or vulgar language
Iran	Women whose heads, arms and legs are not covered; drinking
Most Arab countries	Nudity, sex, enthusiastic necking; criticism of the head of state; criticism of any religion
Brazil	Explicit sex and violence during prime time; references to government repression
Mexico	Criticism of the government
Thailand	Anything remotely critical of the royal family
Japan	Criticism of the imperial family or religious sects
Israel	Any shot of a political candidate; terrorists' opinions
Turkey	Ethnic problems
Indonesia	Anything offending religion
South Africa	Any reference to Jesus Christ; all expletives containing the word *God*, including "Oh, God"

Source: John Lippman, "Television Is Fast Changing the Way the World Works, the Way It Plays, the Way It Goes to War and Makes Peace," *The Milwaukee Journal*, December 20, 1992, J1, J3.

Advertising expenditures by medium vary greatly by country. In 1987, 35.9 percent of Argentina's advertising expenditures went to the print media, whereas in India, the percentage was 71. In Israel, outdoor/transit advertising attracted 17.5 percent of total advertising expenditures; in the United States only 1.2 percent was spent on this medium (see Table 9.1).

Media Options and Country Characteristics

In selecting a medium, global marketers are guided by two major considerations: effectiveness and economy. Media plans that satisfy these criteria generally vary by country because of differences in media characteristics. The availability, cost, quality, frequency, and reach of media vary across countries. Although countries are different in terms of media characteristics, economically developed countries show less variation among themselves than they do between themselves and less developed countries (see Table 9.2).

Recent technological developments are changing the way advertising works. Expanding communication networks have created a challenging problem for global firms. Not very long ago, a company could develop an advertising campaign for one country without worrying about how it may affect its consumers in another. Consumers watched, listened to, and read what was available through the domestic media. Their exposure to foreign material was limited. Satellite transmission of TV and radio programs, increasing travel, and mass distribution of videocassettes have all changed this. Now people not only watch, read, and listen to news, sports, and entertainment programs from other countries, but are also exposed to foreign advertisements. This phenomenon of cross-country transmission is more prevalent in developed economies, especially European, than in developing ones. But this too is changing. Cross-country transmission of information in developing countries is becoming more common.

To communicate with target markets, a global marketer can select from an array of media options such as television, radio, magazine, newspaper, direct mail, catalog, facsimile, video, and cinema. Media selection should be guided by the strengths and weaknesses of each medium and the goals of the firm. In the following section, we discuss the aforementioned media options.

Television. Television is a highly sophisticated technological medium. Almost every country in the world today has TV broadcasting capabilities. In developed economies, TV reaches every part of the country; advertisers can select from an array of channels that cater to specific and general audiences. In the United States, for example, viewers have access to more than one hundred channels when they subscribe to cable TV. In Europe, satellite television allows Europeans to watch programs from other European countries. By contrast, less developed economies, because of limited resources and inadequate technological infrastructure, have TV broadcasting systems that operate only within the major

TABLE **9.1**   Percent of Advertising Expenditure by Media in Selected Countries (1987)

Country	Print	TV	Radio	Cinema	Outdoor/ Transit	Other
Argentina	35.9	36.7	12.7	3.5	11.2	0
Australia	47.8	34.3	9.2	1.5	7.2	0
Brazil	40.4	51	8.5	0	0	0
Egypt	n/a	n/a	n/a	n/a	n/a	n/a
Guatemala	n/a	n/a	n/a	n/a	n/a	n/a
India	71	17.9	3.7	1.6	5.9	0
Iran	n/a	n/a	n/a	n/a	n/a	n/a
Israel	55.6	8.2	15.4	3.3	17.5	0
Japan	35.7	35.3	5.2	9.2	14.6	0
Malaysia	51.9	43	1.5	0.2	3.5	0
Mexico	17.6	48.4	19.8	1.1	13.2	0
New Zealand	51	28	13	0	7.9	0
Pakistan	n/a	n/a	n/a	n/a	n/a	n/a
Singapore	59.8	32.9	3	0.6	3.7	0
South Africa	63.5	31.8	0	1.4	3.4	0
South Korea	49	44.8	6	0.3	0	0
Thailand	31.4	48.3	19.5	0.8	0	0
United States	34	21.9	6.7	0	1.2	36.2
Zimbabwe	61.1	21.8	12.4	2.6	2.1	0

Source: Adapted from *International Marketing Data and Statistics*, London: Euromonitor Publications Limited, 1990.

cities; but the number of viewers per TV may be very high. In 1987, when the population in the United States was 243 million, there were 195 million TVs in use. In contrast, with a population of over 100 million, Nigeria had only 550,000 TVs (see Table 9.2 for data on media in selected countries).

As a medium for communicating with target markets, TV has inherent limitations. In some countries, such as Pakistan, advertisements are bunched

TABLE 9.2   Media Access in Selected Countries (1987)

Country	Daily Newspapers	TVs in Use 1986 (000s)	Radios in Use 1986 (000s)	Fixed Cinemas
Algeria	5	1,610	5,000	216
Argentina	188	6,650	20,000	919
Australia	62	7,500	20,000	703
Brazil	314	26,000	50,540	1,397
Egypt	12	4,000	15,000	185
Ghana	4	146	2,650	7
Guatemala	5	300	500	115
India	1,334	5,000	60,000	12,696
Iran	23	2,600	3,250	294
Israel	26	1,125	2,000	214
Japan	125	71,000	100,000	2,116
Kenya	4	115	1,800	40
Malaysia	40	1,800	6,850	425
Mexico	312	9,490	16,000	2,172
Morocco	10	1,208	4,800	240
New Zealand	32	1,200	3,000	172
Nigeria	14	550	16,000	240
Pakistan	105	1,500	10,000	650
Saudi Arabia	12	3,210	3,850	n/a
Singapore	10	550	775	57
South Africa	23	3,100	13,000	n/a
South Korea	14	7,900	40,000	482
Tanzania	2	13	2,000	34
Thailand	25	5,200	9,300	682
United States	1,687	195,000	510,000	16,032
Zimbabwe	3	130	480	32

Source: Adapted from *International Marketing Data and Statistics,* London: Euromonitor Publications Limited, 1990.

together and shown in blocks before the feature program. In many countries, viewing hours vary; twenty-four-hour programming is not common the world over. In some countries, certain products cannot be advertised on TV and commercials have to be locally produced. MTV Europe, for example, has to black out commercials for low alcohol beer in Norway because of regulations against beer advertisements. In Poland commercial lyrics must be sung in Polish; and in Australia commercials have to be filmed using an Australian film crew and actors; imported commercials are prohibited.[6]

Radio. Radio is emerging as an effective vehicle for advertising products globally. Its popularity in developed economies, especially the United States, has increased recently. In large U.S. cities, radio stations cater to segmented markets by delivering specialized programs such as news; weather; country, rock, pop, hard rock, oldies, classical, and instrumental music; talk radio; religious broadcasting; and ethnic programming. By contrast, less developed economies do not offer such varieties. In many of these countries, radio broadcasting is controlled by the government, and the program format is determined by public authorities.

As the data in Table 9.2 indicate, per-capita availability of radios in less developed economies is much lower than in developed economies. In Zimbabwe, for example, the population in 1987 was more than 9 million, but there were only 480,000 radios in use. In contrast, Singapore, with a population of over 2.5 million, had 775,000 radios. As literacy rates are generally low in less developed economies, radio advertising is an excellent medium for reaching the uneducated in urban and rural areas. As the importance of radio is increasing, it is receiving greater regulatory attention. Advertising regulations that control content, duration, frequency, and timing will influence the use of radio for advertising in many countries.

Magazines. Magazines have become a highly specialized medium for delivering information to target markets. There are not only magazines that focus exclusively on sports, but magazines that specialize in winter or summer sports. And within summer sports, there are magazines that focus only on golf, tennis, or soccer. Magazines such as *Reader's Digest, Time, Newsweek,* and *Playboy* are famous throughout the world. Regional or local versions of these magazines enjoy high readership and are popular among the educated. In many countries that once were colonies—India and Algeria, for example—magazines are available in the national language of the country as well as in the language of the former colonial rulers. In countries that were under French rule, French is still widely used; and in those where the British ruled, English is commonly used.

---

[6] Wells, A1, A8.

Newspapers. As an advertising medium, newspapers offer many advantages. They can deliver messages to target markets economically and quickly. Newspapers in many less developed economies do not have data on the demographics of their target markets, which makes it difficult to develop an advertising plan. In some less developed economies the poor quality of newspapers once posed a serious problem for advertisers. Unsatisfactory reproduction of advertisements, substandard paper quality, and unreliable delivery plagued the medium. Recently, however, these problems have been rectified in many countries. But other problems associated with space limitation and content specifications still exist. In Saudi Arabia, newspapers such as *Al Madina, Arab News,* and *Saudi Gazette* are important vehicles for advertising. However, all newspapers are subject to religious and governmental restrictions. For example, not only are references to alcohol and pork forbidden, but even images of toy stuffed pigs and piggy banks cannot be shown.[7]

Direct Mail. Direct mail allows a firm to effectively target a potential market and reliably measure the effectiveness of the campaign. Direct mail is more common in developed economies. Its increasing use there has been expedited by technological innovations in the collection, storage, analysis, and dissemination of information. Events such as the increasing participation of women in the work force have also encouraged the use of direct mail. In less developed economies, however, direct mail opportunities are currently limited because of lack of reliable lists, undependable mail delivery, and low literacy rates. Notwithstanding these drawbacks, in less developed economies direct mail can prove useful in the urban areas, where the middle class usually live.

Catalogs. Firms are increasing the use of catalogs to advertise their products. However, the use of catalogs is currently restricted to the developed economies such as the United States, Canada, Japan, and Europe. Customers can place their orders by mail or telephone and receive shipments by mail. As with direct mail, the use of catalogs is not common in less developed and developing economies due to lack of reliable lists, costly and unreliable mail, and low literacy rates.

Facsimile. Technological developments are creating new and challenging opportunities for advertising products. Firms can send copies of their advertisements over telephone lines to target markets. The advertisements are reproduced by the fax machine in homes or offices. However, faxing advertisements is surrounded by controversy. While the ads are printing, they tie up a company's fax machine and can delay the transmission of important business

---

[7] Marian Katz, "No Women, No Alcohol; Learn Saudi Taboos Before Placing Ads," *International Advertiser,* February 1986, 11–12.

messages. Furthermore, the person receiving the fax has to pay for the paper on which the ad is printed. When these and other controversies are resolved, there will be an increase in the use of fax for advertising.

Videos. Unlike radio or TV, video does not limit firms to 30- or 60-second commercials. While companies send videos to consumers in developed economies to promote their products, the use of videos in developing and less developed economies has taken a different form. Businesses advertise their products in movie videos. Advertisements are interspersed throughout, similar to commercials for network TV movies in the United States. When consumers rent movies, they rent commercials as well.

Cinema. Movies are popular entertainment worldwide. The use of cinemas for advertising is more prevalent in less developed economies, where movies—being inexpensive—are the prime source of entertainment. Movies are generally shown in cinemas, but in some countries mobile theaters go from village to village.

Billboards. As an advertising medium, billboards are popular in all countries. Advertisements are displayed for a contractually determined time at a particular location. Thus, the choice of location is critical. The advertisement should be located on a route that the target market takes for traveling. Determining who uses the route, when, and how frequently is easier in developed economies. In further contrast, billboards in developed economies line the highways, whereas billboards in less developed economies are primarily concentrated in urban centers.

Advertising Regulations

Regulations affect every aspect of advertising. The production, message, timing, delivery, frequency, duration, and placement of advertisements all can become targets for government regulations. The advertising regulatory climate varies by country. Recently, for example, Taiwan's Department of Health banned baby formula advertisements from newspapers, magazines, and the electronic media.[8] And in Singapore, revealing lingerie is now banned from TV advertising by the government-controlled Singapore Broadcasting Corporation.[9] Governments offer many reasons for regulating advertising, such as a desire to promote local businesses, protect local culture, and safeguard consumers' interests. To successfully develop and implement advertising campaigns worldwide, a global firm has

---

[8] "World Newswatch," *Advertising Age International,* November 23, 1992, 1–2.

[9] Ian Stewart, "Sensitive Censors: Singapore Orders TV Ads to Show Less Skin," *Advertising Age International,* November 23, 1992, 1–13.

to familiarize itself with the existing regulations and learn to adapt its promotional package accordingly.

Agency Selection

A global concern can make three basic choices in selecting an advertising agency: it can select an agency to handle its advertising globally, select a local agency in each country, or combine both options—local agencies handling advertising in some countries and a major agency in the rest. The selection of an advertising agency is influenced by how a firm organizes its global marketing activities; that is, whether it is centralized, regionalized, or localized. Other key factors influencing agency selection include the nature of the company's products, the size of the internal advertising and public relations staff, and the size of the communications budget.[10] Another consideration guiding the selection is what the firm wants to do itself and what it wants to delegate to an agency.

The advantages that local agencies once had over global agencies are slowly diminishing. Local agencies, with operations confined to one country and managed by indigenous people, were able to develop advertising campaigns consistent with the local culture. They knew the idioms, the customs, the mores, and the idiosyncracies of the target market and developed commercials that did not diverge from social norms. Although they lacked the resources, experience, and expertise of a larger, global agency, their familiarity with the target market enhanced their appeal. The advertising environment, however, is changing. Recently, many agencies have expanded their operations to multiple countries and hired local people to run the affiliates. This allows them to manage their clients' accounts in countries where the clients previously used local agencies. The presence of global agencies in countries such as India, South Korea, and Thailand has increased the number of acceptable agency options and improved the performance of local agencies.

GLOBAL SALES PROMOTIONS

Sales promotions are short-term promotional activities to increase sales. The focus is on using incentives to gain attention, create interest, stimulate desire, and generate a favorable response from the target market—usually the purchase of a product or service. For sales promotions to succeed, marketers must work within the legal, political, economic, and cultural constraints of a country.

The growth of global sales promotions has been impressive. In almost every country, firms engage in some type of short-term promotional activities to

---

[10] Robert F. Roth, *International Marketing Communications,* Chicago: Crain, 1982.

generate sales. However, the promotions are used more frequently and extensively in developed economies. Kashani and Quelch note that in developing countries, free samples and demonstrations are the most widely used consumer promotion tools. However, coupons—whose use is widespread in the developed countries—are rarely used in developing countries.[11] Sales promotions appeal to target markets because of the immediate benefits they offer to consumers.

Sales promotions can be grouped under two broad categories: consumer directed and trade (channel) directed. Consumer sales promotions are designed to encourage people to purchase products or patronize particular stores. Trade sales promotions are geared toward channel members, and are designed to encourage them to carry a firm's products or to push the products to the next channel member.

Consumer Sales Promotion Techniques

Although designed to encourage short-term sales, consumer sales promotions help firms achieve their long-term objectives. When businesses engage in sales promotions, they communicate with their customers. This communication should be carefully planned to elicit the desired response from customers. The sales promotions directed toward consumers are as follows: coupons, rebates, free samples, premiums (mail-in and in-pack), bonus packs, trading stamps, and contests and sweepstakes. We discuss these next.

Coupons are certificates that entitle the holder to a price reduction on the purchase of a specific product. As an incentive, coupons serve two functions. For consumers who already use the product, coupons make a purchase economically attractive; and for those who do not use the product, coupons reduce the economic risk of trying it. Consumers can redeem coupons in a store to receive the product at a lower price. Although couponing is highly popular in the United States, it is still resisted in Europe. In 1990, for example, roughly 3,000 U.S. manufacturers distributed 279.4 billion coupons, compared with 5.1 billion distributed by 750 manufacturers in the United Kingdom. In France, retailers still oppose couponing; major retailers in Holland and Switzerland refuse to accept coupons; and in Germany the discount given on a coupon cannot exceed 1 percent of the product's value.[12]

Rebates serve the same two functions as coupons. Consumers buy a product, then submit the following to the manufacturer: proof of purchase, usually a dated cash-register receipt with the purchase price circled; the universal product code (UPC) from the product's package; and a completed rebate form. Upon receipt of these items, the manufacturer sends a refund to the consumer.

---

[11] Kamran Kashani and John A. Quelch, "Can Sales Promotion Go Global?" *Business Horizons,* May/June 1990, 37–43.

[12] Laurie Petersen, "Get Ready for Global Coupon Wars," *Promote,* July 8, 1991, 20, 22.

While coupons and rebates require consumers to pursue the benefits, **free samples,** as the name suggests, are samples of the product distributed free of charge to consumers. Generally, along with a free sample, consumers receive a coupon that they can redeem when they purchase the product. The idea behind free samples is to encourage consumers to try the product at no cost. If consumers like the product, they will purchase it. Clairol, a manufacturer of personal care products, successfully increased sales in the United Kingdom, Sweden, and Germany by distributing free samples.[13]

Mail-in premiums are product offers that consumers can redeem when they send in proof of purchase, such as the cash-register receipt or UPC. **In-pack premiums** are, as the name implies, packaged along with the product being promoted. To receive the promotional benefit, consumers need only purchase the product. **Bonus packs** normally contain an extra quantity of a product in a package without an increase in price. The extra product is a bonus to consumers.

Trading stamps are stamps consumers receive when they buy products from a store. This program is generally designed to motivate consumers to patronize the store rather than purchase a product. After acquiring a number of stamps, consumers are entitled to receive the promised merchandise, either free or at a discount.

Contests and sweepstakes are another form of promotional activity. They enhance name recognition and stimulate sales by attracting consumers' attention to a product or firm with the promise of cash prizes or other goods.

Trade Sales Promotion Techniques

Trade sales promotions are often used to persuade channel members to carry products or increase sales. They are also used to motivate salespersons to improve their performance. Trade promotions consist of sales contests, price-off offers, advertising allowances, display allowances, free goods, or push money.

Sales contests are used to motivate increased sales. Under this plan, channel members and salespeople are rewarded for achieving a certain sales volume. **Price-off** offers are economic incentives for purchasing products. Channel members are given a discount from the price of a product. This technique is used to motivate dealers to carry a new product or buy products in large quantities. A firm can increase its product visibility by offering two types of trade allowances (advertising and display) to its channel members. **Advertising allowances** are given to retailers for advertising the company's products. **Display allowances** compensate retailers for exhibiting a special display of the firm's product. A company can also offer channel members **free goods** or **push money**

---

[13] "Worldwide Beauty Hints: How Clairol Markets Glamour in Any Language," *Business Abroad,* March 6, 1967, 23–25.

(compensation to channel members), to encourage them to carry and push products.

GLOBAL PERSONAL SELLING

Unlike advertising, which relies on one-way communication from sellers to buyers, personal selling involves interactions between salespersons and buyers for establishing long-term exchange relationships. The survival and growth of a firm depend not on making a single sale but on convincing buyers to purchase repeatedly. It is repeat purchases that make a firm successful. Although personal selling is expensive, it effectively convinces customers to purchase products. The face-to-face interaction allows a buyer to ask questions and a salesperson to answer them. Thus, it is an effective way of selling products that require special handling and servicing.

The job of a salesperson is to keep buyers happy by solving their product-related problems. The relationship between buyer and salesperson is based on trust. Thus, salespeople should promise what they can deliver and not make false claims about their products. The promises made and the services rendered by a salesperson are critical in generating sales and maintaining the loyalty of buyers.

Salespeople are the link between buyers and sellers. Their two primary functions are keeping buyers satisfied and keeping the firm informed. Being closer to the market, salespeople are aware of competitive developments that create opportunities and threats in the marketplace. For example, changes in consumer preference and taste may create opportunities; and the introduction of one product may threaten the prospect of another. These and other developments should be transmitted to the head office.

Personal Selling

The activities of a salesperson are diverse and numerous. The responsibilities may include not only finding a buyer but also keeping the buyer happy. The tasks of a salesperson can be grouped under the following five categories: planning, prospecting, preparing, selling, and following up.

Planning. Selling begins with planning. At this stage, a salesperson decides what needs to be done, how, and when. Approaching the job of selling in an ad-hoc manner does not yield the desired results. Planning is essential for all sales-related activities.

Prospecting. Prospecting refers to finding and cultivating new customers. Depending on the business, a salesperson relies on various sources for information on new prospects. Existing customers can be a reliable source for locating new ones. Trade shows, directories, firm's records, and advertisements are other avenues. After preparing an initial list of customers, a salesperson prunes the list for prospects who will be contacted later.

Preparing. Preparation is essential before meeting or calling on a buyer. Knowledge about his own and competitors' products helps a salesperson make an effective presentation to customers. Furthermore, relevant data about the buyer's business and his needs indicate how the products the salesperson is offering will help the buyer achieve his long-term objectives. The better prepared a salesperson is, the better his performance will be in convincing buyers to purchase his products.

Selling. Selling can be divided into four stages: approaching the customer, making the presentation, answering questions, and closing the sale. Whether a buyer is approached by telephone, mail, or in person, the approach may to a great extent determine what follows. The objective may be simply to make contacts or gather information on the buyer's needs. If the approach is successful, the salesperson may get an opportunity to make a presentation on the product. During and after the presentation, it is important for the salesperson to be able to answer buyer's questions. Finally, the presentation should lead to the closing of the sale by persuading the buyer to purchase the product.

Following up. The sale is not the final step. A quick follow-up is important for restoring confidence and inquiring about the delivery of the product and its performance. The follow-up is necessary in establishing a solid link with the customer, who may wish to purchase again or advise friends and colleagues to do so.

Managing the Global Sales Force

As marketing activities of firms involved in high-technology and high-value-added products are expanding globally, the importance of global personal selling is also increasing. To successfully conduct global marketing, companies may have to organize their own sales force. This would call for recruiting, selecting, training, motivating, and evaluating the sales force in different countries. Furthermore, the firm will also have to decide whether a centralized or decentralized organization is suitable for managing the sales force.

Sales Force Compensation

Compensation of the sales force is based on straight salary or straight commission, or a combination of both. A *straight salary* involves paying a fixed amount to a salesperson. This gives the salesperson a sense of security and is easier for the firm to administer. However, if the sales force is not motivated, this method may result in reduced sales. The *straight commission* is based on the amount of sales generated. There are two types of straight commission: fixed and varying percentage rates. With a fixed percentage, the rate of commission does not vary with sales; with the varying method, the rates vary with the amount of sales. The main advantage of the straight commission is that it encourages salespeople to perform. However, the disadvantage is that after a salesperson has achieved the specified quota, he may not push for more sales. To avoid this, the sales force may be given a combination of fixed salary and commission.

GLOBAL PUBLIC RELATIONS

Global public relations is evolving from its traditional role of issuing press releases to promoting strategic alliances between a company and various entities such as trade unions, customers, governments, media, special interest groups, stockholders, and employees. As business activities of global firms continue to expand, the significance of public relations increases. People around the world receive more information now than ever before. They are generally aware of a company's activities within their own country as well as in others. A misunderstanding between a firm and any one of the groups can disrupt the flow of products from one country to another, which can be catastrophic for the firm. Thus, maintaining and promoting harmonious relationships between a company and the public is the primary goal of global public relations.

Public Relations Tools

Public relations officers rely on speeches, special events, public service programs, news releases, and information services. Speeches by company officials are instrumental in creating and establishing a favorable image. Firms can also organize special events within a company as well as outside to create a favorable image. Public service programs include encouraging employee participation in building a school or raising money for a charitable purpose. News releases to the media about the development of a new product, a new appointment, or any other significant activity can heighten the awareness of the people about the positive contributions of the firm. Information services provide a forum for answering questions that the public may have regarding the company's products or activities. It is a valuable vehicle for promoting a favorable image. Four important areas that deserve special attention are employee relations, customer relations, press relations, and government relations.

Employee Relations. Employees constitute the backbone of a firm. Keeping them informed and motivated about the company's activities increases their loyalty. Productivity and product quality will be enhanced. As their firm's ambassadors, employees interact with their community. Thus, an important aspect of a company's image is created by its employees and how they represent their firm to the community.

Customer Relations. Customers' responses to a firm's offerings determine whether it succeeds or fails. Public relations managers should convey a message that the firm cares for its customers, that they are important to the company. In particular, customer safety should be emphasized.

Press Relations. In every country, the press plays an important role in shaping consumer and governmental attitudes toward business firms. It is important to realize that the press not only reports news but also shapes public opinion. Public relations officers can establish positive relations with the press by holding press conferences, releasing image-enhancing information, and inviting the press to public meetings.

Government Relations. A business operates in a country with the consent of the government. Developing relationships with government officials can expedite the work of a firm. When there is a problem that involves the government, the public relations officers will know whom to contact to resolve the problem. Positive relationships with government officials also help a company establish itself as a good citizen.

SUMMARY

The two major goals of promotion are to increase the perceived value of a product and to convince consumers to adopt the product. This is achieved by communicating effectively with consumers. Communication between a firm and its target market is facilitated when the sender and the receiver of a message share a common field of experience. To communicate with their target markets, marketers rely on four elements of the promotional mix: advertising, sales promotion, personal selling, and public relations.

Advertising is any paid form of nonpersonal communication in which the sponsor is identifiable. To make advertising effective, global marketers should carefully plan the objectives, message, target market, advertising appropriation, media plan, and measurement procedure. In selecting media for advertising, global marketers have many options. These include television, radio, magazine, newspaper, direct mail, catalog, facsimile, video, and cinema. Governmental regulations affect every aspect of advertising, such as production, timing, delivery, frequency, duration, and placement.

Sales promotions are short-term programs that encourage sales. Although their objectives are short-term, promotion should be planned to achieve a long-term competitive edge in the marketplace. Sales promotions are directed toward consumers and channel members. Consumer sales promotions encourage consumers to buy products, whereas trade sales promotions encourage channel members to push a firm's products.

Personal selling is two-way communication between a buyer and seller. This involves planning, prospecting, preparing, selling, and following up. Three common methods of compensating a sales force are straight salary, straight commission, or a combination of both.

Public relations forge a strategic alliance between a firm and the public. Public relations officers need to pay special attention to employees, customers, government officials, and the press. Speeches, special events, public service programs, news releases, and information services are some of the tools that global marketers use to achieve their goals.

CHAPTER TEN

Make opportunities happen.

Mary Kay Ash

Global Business Involvement: Market Entry Strategies

Global firms conduct business within a country with varying levels of involvement. Between the two options of exporting and manufacturing, a company has considerable leeway in choosing its level of involvement. For example, it can export its products to a country without getting involved in activities associated with exporting. Or it can license its technology to another firm, which can produce and market the products.

The type of marketing a company can undertake within a country is greatly determined by its mode of entry. An indirect exporter, for example, can sell products within a country but may not be able to manage and control marketing activities as effectively as a firm involved in both manufacturing and marketing. Likewise, a company that licenses its technology can establish its marketing presence in a host country but may lose some control over the production and marketing of products. In general, the ability to control marketing activities increases with the level of business involvement within a country.

ENTRY STRATEGIES

Firms use a variety of entry strategies to establish marketing presence in host countries. Among others, these strategies include exporting, licensing, franchising, management contracting, contract manufacturing, turnkey operations, foreign direct investments (joint ventures and wholly-owned subsidiaries), and strategic alliances. The decision to select a particular entry strategy reflects what a firm wants to achieve, how it wants to achieve it, and, above all, what role it expects to play within a country market. Thus, for a global marketer, it is important to know the level of involvement associated with each entry strategy, and its advantages and disadvantages. This knowledge will be helpful in selecting an appropriate entry strategy for each product and achieving a competitive edge in the global marketplace. We discuss the different entry strategies next.

Exporting

Historically, exporting has been the most popular entry mode for establishing marketing presence within a host country. Countries encourage their firms to export because, in general, employment is increased, competitiveness improved, and foreign exchange earned. Encouraged by home governments, motivated by competition, and influenced by a desire to expand, businesses all over the world have made a concerted effort to increase their exports. As a result, world exports increased twenty-nine-fold, from $118.3 billion in 1960 to $3441.7 billion in 1991. The three largest exporters in the world are the United States, Germany, and Japan. The U.S. share of world exports in 1960 was 16.5 percent, declining to 12.3 percent in 1991. Germany and Japan, however, increased their share of world exports from 9.6 percent and 3.4 percent in 1960 to 11.7 percent and 9.1 percent in 1991, respectively.[1]

Firms can select from two major exporting options: direct and indirect. When a company engages in *direct exporting*, it performs all the necessary activities to sell its products within a host country. These activities include determining market potential, finding a buyer, locating channel members, and dealing with the administrative functions of exporting such as preparing documents, arranging transportation, and insuring the merchandise. When a firm engages in *indirect exporting*, it delegates these tasks to an intermediary, such as an export management corporation (EMC) that is willing to work for a fee or commission or both.

Advantages and Disadvantages.
Exporting offers many advantages. First, it is usually the preferred mode of entry for a firm new to global marketing because it minimizes political risk. Second, it is an effective entry strategy when market potential in a host country cannot be accurately determined. Third, it allows a concern to sell its products in host countries either through independent intermediaries or through its own distribution channel when it wants to exercise greater control over marketing activities. Fourth, it prepares a company to increase business involvement by manufacturing in a country if market conditions become attractive. And fifth, it lets a firm terminate its business relationship without incurring significant costs when political or economic conditions within the host country deteriorate.

Notwithstanding the numerous advantages, exporting also has certain drawbacks. For example, fluctuating exchange rates and governmental interventions can adversely affect the earnings of an exporter. If an exporter gets paid in the

---

[1] International Monetary Fund, *International Financial Statistics Yearbook*, Washington, DC, 1989, 1992.

buyer's currency, and if this currency depreciates when payment is received, it will result in a financial loss to the exporter. Consider the following. On January 1, 1996, a German exporter sells 1,000 portable telephones to a British firm for 1 million pounds. On this day, the exchange rate is 2 deutsche marks per pound. If the German exporter gets paid on this day, she can exchange £1 million for DM 2,000,000. But if she gets paid on, say, March 1, 1996, and the exchange rate on that day is 1.75 marks per pound, she will get only DM 1,750,000.

A company can also get hurt by governmental interventions. The imposition of additional tariffs can reduce the price competitiveness of an exported product, and the application of new standards can effectively bar a product from entering the country unless the required modifications are made. In addition to these drawbacks, exporters may find it difficult to respond quickly to market changes and maintain control over marketing activities unless they have a physical presence in the country. This loss of control can prevent a firm from establishing the desired image of its products in a host country.

Licensing

The rapid expansion of global marketing makes licensing a popular entry strategy. Licensing involves payment of a fee or royalty by a licensee in exchange for the use of a patent, trademark, product formula, company name, or anything of value. The core of a licensing agreement is the transfer of intangible property rights from a licensor to a licensee.

The majority of licensing takes place among developed economies. In a comparative analysis of licensing behavior of firms based in five countries (United States, United Kingdom, Sweden, Germany, and Japan) in 1975, it was found that the United Kingdom, Germany, and the United States were net licensors, with the United States showing the least propensity to license from abroad. Japan was the keenest importer of foreign technology and a net licensee, and Sweden was a marginal net licensee.[2]

Advantages and Disadvantages. Licensing is a cost-effective way for a firm to expand and establish marketing presence in host countries. When, for example, exporting is no longer feasible because additional tariffs result in loss of price competitiveness, a company can license its proprietary technology and maintain marketing presence in the country. Licensing also gives a firm the opportunity to enter countries where it cannot engage in production because of resource and organizational constraints or because of economic or political risk. In short, licensing provides a cost-effective way to earn revenue and establish marketing presence in a host country.

---

[2] Jeremy Clegg, "The Determinants of Aggregate International Licensing Behaviour: Evidence from the Five Countries," *Management International Review*, 30, 1990, 231–251.

From a country's perspective, licensing agreements are beneficial because they can increase the inflow of sophisticated technology and managerial expertise. Both developed and developing countries encourage certain types of licensing to improve their economic performance and competitiveness. For example, South Korea—a highly prosperous developing country—has identified six areas in which it will encourage licensing agreements during the period 1987–2001 to improve its economic performance and competitiveness. The six areas are as follows:[3]

1. Computers, software, semiconductors, and information networks.
2. Fine chemicals and biotechnology.
3. Technology for designing, engineering, developing, automating, molding, and testing product quality.
4. Energy conservation and alternative energy development.
5. Health, environmental protection, and other social services.
6. Marine and aeronautical industries.

Licensing agreements also have many disadvantages. They can restrict the ability of a firm to take full advantage of market potential within a host country; they can create a competitor in third markets; they can make a firm lose control over the use of its technology and the quality of its products; and they can result in conflict if the licensee is responsible not only for the manufacturing of the product but also for its marketing.

The drawbacks of licensing should encourage a firm to safeguard its interests by including provisions in the contract that stipulate its recourse in the event of noncompliance or unauthorized use of the contract. Not having such provisions can create a marketing dilemma for a licensor, best illustrated by the following example. A New York apparel maker licensed its name in Europe and has been facing decreasing international profits because of quality problems. Although the clothing produced by the licensees in Europe fell below American standards, the licensor could not regain the rights to its own brands because of the licensing agreement.[4]

Franchising

As a mode of entry, franchising is similar to licensing. In a franchise agreement, the franchisor grants the franchisee permission to use a patent, trademark, product formula, company name, or anything of value. In addition, the fran-

---

[3] Thomas J. Ehrbar, *Business International's Guide to International Licensing,* New York: McGraw-Hill, 1993.

[4] Julie Amparano Lopez, "Going Global," *The Wall Street Journal,* October 16, 1992, R20.

TABLE **10.1**   Global Growth of U.S. Franchisors (1985)

Host Country	Number of Franchisors	Number of Outlets
Canada	239	9,054
Asia (less Japan & Middle East)	74	1,452
Caribbean	88	803
Australia	75	2,511
Continental Europe	73	4,398
United Kingdom	68	2,291
Japan	66	7,124
Mexico	36	542
New Zealand	22	402

Source: International Trade Administration, *Franchising in the Economy 1985–87,* U.S. Department of Commerce, 1987.

chisor provides operational and managerial help (e.g., raw materials, equipment, training, and financing) to the franchisee. In return, the franchisor receives an initial franchising fee and regular payments of a percentage of sales. Since the 1940s, a new form of franchising has developed called *business format franchising.* Primarily developed in the United States, business format franchising involves an "ongoing business relationship between franchisor and franchisee that includes not only the product, service and trademark but the entire business format itself . . . a marketing strategy and plan, operating manuals and standards, quality control and continuing two way communications."[5]

After growing rapidly in the 1950s and 1960s, U.S. franchisors expanded their overseas operations vigorously in Canada, Japan, Continental Europe, and Asia (see Table 10.1). U.S. franchisors were encouraged to expand their business because of the perceived foreign market potential and the interest of foreign franchisees, rather than any immediate concern about domestic market saturation.[6] For example, McDonald's, Pizza Hut, and Kentucky Fried Chicken—all

---

[5] International Trade Administration, *Franchising in the Economy 1985–87,* Washington, DC: U.S. Department of Commerce, 1987, 3.

[6] Bruce J. Walker and Michael J. Etzel, "The Internationalization of U.S. Franchise Systems: Progress and Procedures," *Journal of Marketing,* April 1973, 38–46.

thriving U.S. businesses—have successfully expanded their businesses in the major markets of the world.

Advantages and Disadvantages. The advantages of franchising are similar to those of licensing. A franchisor is able to enter host countries and establish marketing presence without large outlays of resources. Such expansions increase a franchisor's revenue, making franchising an attractive mode of entry. Marks & Spencer, a major British retailer, has successfully used franchising to expand its global presence and establish the St. Michael name in the European and Pacific markets with minimal capital investment. The franchisees in turn benefit from a proven system and the support of a major British retailer.[7]

The drawbacks of franchising are the same as those of licensing. For example, a franchisee may not maintain the product quality or level of service specified in the contract. This makes it difficult for a franchisor to maintain a uniform product or service image across country markets. Thus, to protect itself from such contingencies, a franchisor must specify in the contract its recourse in the event of noncompliance by a franchisee.

Contract Manufacturing

Under a contract manufacturing arrangement, two major options are available: a firm can either supply a manufacturer with parts and have the manufacturer assemble them, or it can have the manufacturer fabricate the whole product according to specifications. The business, however, retains marketing responsibilities.

Advantages and Disadvantages. By engaging in contract manufacturing, a firm capitalizes on its expertise in marketing products, while delegating manufacturing tasks and responsibilities to a contractual partner. Contract manufacturing is an economical way to expand business activities. The three main disadvantages of contract manufacturing are that it can make the contractual partner a potential competitor; result in loss of control over the manufacturing of the product; and create scheduling problems whereby the company may not be able to get the products on time.

Management Contracting

In management contracting, a firm provides management expertise and technical know-how to another concern or to a government. Although the manage-

---

[7] Maureen Whitehead, "International Franchising—Marks & Spencer: A Case Study," *International Journal of Retail & Distribution Management,* March/April 1991, 10–12.

ment team basically acts as consultants, it may also get involved in operational activities.

Advantages and Disadvantages. Management contracting provides numerous advantages, which include the following:[8] a firm can use excess managerial talent, which for political and/or economic reasons it does not wish to dismiss; it can establish contacts with businesses and government officials in host countries and explore opportunities for future business involvements; it can easily remit fees for managerial services; and it can use its involvement with a plant or company to provide resources to one of its nearby operations. An important disadvantage of management contracting is its limited duration. After the contract is over, the firm may have to leave the country unless it has negotiated a new contract with another company.

Turnkey Operations

Under this arrangement, a firm agrees to complete a project before handing it over to the owner. The responsibilities of the company generally include the design, construction, and operation of the project. In some cases, the agreement may also require the firm to train executives and workers to enable them to run the facility. Turnkey agreements are usually made with governments who have large public service and construction projects, such as building hospitals, highways, and ports.

Advantages and Disadvantages. The most attractive features of turnkey operations are that they are large, long-term, and profitable. However, these characteristics also make turnkey operations precarious. In particular, the element of uncertainty increases because of the long life of the project. For firms, it may be difficult to predict how a change in the government may affect the outcome of a project.

Foreign Direct Investment

Increasingly, firms are using foreign direct investment to establish marketing presence in host countries. It has been estimated that while world exports grew at a compounded rate of 9.4 percent between 1983 and 1989, world foreign direct investment outflow grew at the compounded rate of 28.9 percent. The reasons for the high growth rate and the increasing importance of foreign direct investment include the following:[9]

---

[8] M. Z. Brooke, *International Management: A Review of Strategies and Operations,* London: Hutchinson, 1986, 82.

[9] United Nations, *World Investment Report 1991: The Triad in Foreign Direct Investment,* New York: United Nations Centre on Transnational Corporations, 1991.

1. Strong recovery of the world economy.
2. Emergence of Japan as a major investor.
3. Rise of newly industrializing economies such as Singapore, Taiwan, and Hong Kong as investors.
4. Growth in the number of cross-border mergers and acquisitions.
5. Economic integration of the EC.
6. Rise in the service sector in the global economy.
7. Liberalization of regulations on the movement of capital flows.

Foreign direct investment involves a major commitment of resources. Such investments can take two forms: *joint ventures* and *wholly-owned subsidiaries*. In a joint venture (JV), two or more firms form a partnership and share in ownership, risk, profit, and control of the business. More specifically, a joint venture has the following characteristics:[10]

1. Contribution by partners of money, property, effort, knowledge, skill, or other asset to a common undertaking.
2. Joint property interest in the subject matter of the venture.
3. Right of mutual control or management of the enterprise.
4. Expectation of profit, or presence of "adventure."
5. Right to share in the profit.
6. Usual limitation of the objective to a single undertaking or ad-hoc enterprise.

Under the broad term *joint venture,* three major types can be identified: a JV between a foreign-owned concern and a privately owned local firm, a JV between a foreign-owned firm and a local state enterprise or the local government, and a JV between a number of foreign-owned companies without any local participation. Firms that once were bitter competitors are now forming joint ventures to improve their competitive position, achieve a global presence, cut costs, and raise capital. For example, rivals such as General Electric (the American industrial giant) and Fanuc Ltd. (Japan's leader in factory automation) have formed a JV—GE Fanuc Automation Corp.—to improve their competitive positions.[11] Compared to a JV, a wholly-owned subsidiary is totally owned by a foreign-owned concern. The firm assumes full responsibility for strategic

---

[10] J. Fred Weston, Kwang S. Chung, and Susan E. Hoag, *Mergers, Restructuring, and Corporate Control,* Englewood Cliffs, NJ: Prentice-Hall, 1990, 331.

[11] Terry Atlas, "Global Markets Make Partners out of Rivals," *Chicago Tribune,* April 25, 1989, 1, 18.

and operational functions, exclusively assumes the risks, and enjoys the financial rewards.

Advantages and Disadvantages. Both joint ventures and wholly-owned subsidiaries give a firm more control over business activities in a host country than do the entry strategies discussed earlier. In addition to greater control, JVs and wholly-owned subsidiaries provide entry into closed markets, opportunities for achieving vertical integration, access to raw materials and supplies, and freedom in responding to competitive challenges and changes within a country market. The disadvantage of a JV is that disagreements between partners may unfold, resulting in unresolvable conflicts. In the case of a wholly-owned subsidiary, the disadvantage is greater risk associated with economic changes and governmental interventions.

Strategic Alliances

Strategic alliances allow firms to share their resources to gain a competitive edge in the marketplace. Unlike joint ventures that require companies to contribute specified amounts of resources to create an independent business organization, strategic alliances promote cooperation between firms without creating a new business organization.[12] The alliances are motivated by a desire to share technology, production, and marketing resources. Microsoft and Digital formed an alliance to integrate efforts in object-oriented software, in which software is written in separate modules and later connected.[13] Strategic alliances are taking place mostly among companies in the three main economic regions: North America, Asia Pacific, and Europe.

Advantages and Disadvantages. Increasing competitive pressure is forcing firms to join together for a sustainable competitive advantage. By creating these alliances, firms gain access to markets, distribute large R&D expenses, share complementary resources, and spread risks. However, in a strategic alliance there is also the possibility that a company may lose its competitive strength by sharing its technology or marketing expertise with a competitor. Furthermore, if the alliance is taking place among firms that are culturally different, misunderstandings and ineffective communication can occur, which can adversely affect the alliance.[14]

---

[12] Robert Porter Lynch, "Building Alliances to Penetrate European Markets," *The Journal of Business Strategy*, March/April 1990, 4–8.

[13] "Microsoft, Digital to Work on Object Software Jointly," *The Wall Street Journal*, November 30, 1993, B6.

[14] Philippe Gugler, "Building Transnational Alliances to Create Competitive Advantage," *Long Range Planning*, February 1992, 90–99.

why not strategic alliance?

FACTORS INFLUENCING ENTRY STRATEGIES

Entry strategies have to be developed for each product and for each country. Both internal and external conditions influence the selection of these strategies. The internal conditions include the objectives of a company, management orientation, resources, and type of product. The external conditions include market potential, competitive environment, home country regulations, host country regulations, and political risk. In the next section, we focus on internal and external conditions and their influence on the selection of entry strategies.

Internal Conditions

The four internal factors that influence the selection of an entry strategy are the firm's objectives, management orientation, available resources, and type of product.

Objectives. Objectives indicate what a business wants to achieve in a country in relation to a particular product. As such, objectives guide the selection of entry strategies. For example, the objective of getting rid of excess inventory does not call for a highly involved entry strategy. The company may decide that the most suitable approach in this case is to use the services of an export broker and engage in indirect exporting. However, a firm that desires a strategic presence in a country will consider options such as direct exporting or even higher levels of involvement such as joint ventures.

Management Orientation. Influenced by experiences and biases, management orientation plays an important role in the selection of entry strategies. Often, countries with high market potential are ignored because managers do not want to deal with them. And, in some cases, expensive investments are made in countries based on personal preferences rather than market potential. Biases and preferences are invariably present in decision making, and they may prevent managers from making the right decision. Before selecting an entry strategy, marketers should determine whether their decisions are based on a good fit between market potential and the firm's capability to exploit it, or on a preconceived notion about the country.

Resources. Entry strategies require varying amounts of resources. For example, building a factory in a country requires more resources than exporting products to the country. As businesses do not have unlimited resources, they make entry decisions within the constraints imposed by available resources. Thus, although market potential in a country may justify the building of a factory to meet local demand, limited resources may compel a firm to engage in licensing.

Type of Product. The type of product plays an important role in selecting an entry strategy. High-value, technologically sophisticated products such as cameras or mainframe computers cannot be optimally produced in every country where they are marketed. Besides insufficient demand, inadequate technological infrastructure may not justify their production. Thus, a firm may choose to export these items. In contrast, many convenience products such as soap and beverages can be produced in many countries. Pepsi Cola, for example, can be bottled almost everywhere it is marketed.

External Conditions

Selecting an entry strategy is also influenced by external conditions, which include market potential, competitive environment, home country regulations, host country regulations, and political risk within a country.

Market Potential. Before deciding whether exporting, direct investing, or any other entry strategy will be the most suitable, a company has to determine how much can be sold and how much can be earned within a country market. A small and unattractive market does not warrant a huge deployment of resources. However, if market potential is encouraging, a firm may decide to establish either a joint venture or a wholly-owned subsidiary, both of which demand high levels of involvement and deployment of resources. In considering the influence of market potential on entry strategies, it is important to remember that market potential is not static. It can be increased by employing effective marketing strategies or decreased by implementing ineffective strategies. The potential of a market is measured in relation to the effectiveness of the marketing effort.

Competitive Environment. The competitive environment refers to two important facets of a market: the existing competitive situation and expected competitive developments. The existing competitive situation reveals the strengths and weaknesses of competitors by focusing on their entry strategies, marketing programs, R&D efforts, and market shares. Expected competitive developments are those anticipated due to political, technological, and socioeconomic restructuring. Collectively, the competitive environment determines what a firm can profitably do within a country, and thus which entry strategy it should adopt to attain a sustainable competitive advantage.

Home Country Regulations. Companies do not have complete autonomy in selecting their entry strategies. Regulations within a home country may determine the type of entry strategies they can adopt. In the United States, for example, exports of certain high-technology products are regulated by the government. These restrictions prohibit U.S.-based concerns from selling their products to certain countries even when market potential is high. Other developed countries have similar restrictions that limit the entry alternatives available to their firms.

Host Country Regulations. The selection of an entry strategy is also influenced by host country regulations. In many countries, the government may require local participation in ownership, preventing a foreign company from establishing a wholly-owned subsidiary.

Political Risk. Entry decisions are influenced by assumptions about future developments in a country. Even if market potential is high, a firm will hesitate to establish a production facility in a country if it expects developments to adversely affect its business. In this case, it may choose to export rather than make the products within the country. However, if expected developments look promising, the company may choose to manufacture the products within the country rather than exporting or licensing them.

STAGES OF BUSINESS INVOLVEMENT

Firms develop their business involvement in a country in stages. The internal and external conditions change over time, requiring changes in the level of business involvement. Companies may enter a market first by exporting products and later by producing them in the same country. Various hypotheses have been offered to trace the stages of a firm's business involvement. One that has received considerable attention is the international product life-cycle hypothesis, which we discuss next.

The International Product Life-Cycle Hypothesis

Developed by Vernon,[15] the product life-cycle hypothesis distinguishes three stages in the life of a product: the new-product stage, the maturing-product stage, and the standardized-product stage. These stages show how firms change their involvement in different countries based on the stage of a product.

The New-Product Stage. The first stage in the cycle, the new-product stage, is characterized by certain distinguishing features. A company based in an economically developed country manufactures and markets a new product in its home country. It stays in its home market to be close to consumers and make product adaptations based on their responses. Although the firm exports the

---

[15] Raymond Vernon, "International Investment and International Trade in the Product Cycle," *Quarterly Journal of Economics,* May 1966, 190–207.

new product to other developed countries, domestic sales are the main source of revenue at this stage. As the demand for the product is relatively price-inelastic, and as there is no competition, a company can charge a high price and recover its R&D costs. At this stage, the firm also enjoys some form of patent protection in the innovating country.

The Maturing-Product Stage. This is the second stage in the cycle. Demand for the product begins to increase in other developed economies; this is initially met by increasing exports. However, higher demand and increasing tariff and nontariff barriers in the developed countries influence the innovating firm to set up production facilities in those countries. As production begins abroad, exports from the innovating country decline. Competitive pressure intensifies at this stage because other businesses begin to enter the market. The price of the product is reduced to meet competitive challenges. The developed countries make the product not only for their domestic markets but also for export.

The Standardized-Product Stage. At this stage, the product becomes standardized, leading to fierce price competition. To meet the competitive challenges, firms look for low-cost production sites. Production begins to move to developing countries, where labor cost is lower. Over time, production increases in the low-wage countries, who begin to export the standardized product to developed countries. At this last stage, the high-wage developed countries become net importers of the product, while the low-wage developing countries become the major exporters.

The international product life-cycle model is intuitively appealing. It can be applied to products such as radios, calculators, and televisions. These products were first introduced in the United States, but now they are imported into the United States from developing economies. The model also shows how the comparative advantage of nations changes over time in relation to new and standardized products. At first, new products are developed and introduced in the large, lucrative markets of the United States, Japan, and Germany. However, later on, as the product becomes standardized, the low-wage developing countries become the major producers. The implication of the model is clear: continuous product innovation is the key to success for developed economies.

SUMMARY

The type of marketing a firm can conduct within a country is greatly determined by how it chooses to enter the market. A company has many entry options to select from: exporting, licensing, franchising, management contracting, contract manufacturing, turnkey operations, foreign direct investments (joint ventures and wholly-owned subsidiaries), and strategic alliances. The selection of an entry strategy is influenced by internal and external factors. Internal factors include a firm's objectives, management orientation, available resources, and type of product. External factors include market potential, competitive environment, home country regulations, host country regulations, and political risk.

The international product life-cycle hypothesis traces the three major stages in the life of a product: new product, maturing product, and standardized product. In the first stage, a new product is introduced and marketed in a developed economy. In the second stage, production begins in other developed economies. In the final stage, the product is produced in low-wage developing countries and imported into developed countries.

CHAPTER ELEVEN

Success depends on previous preparation, and without such preparation there is sure to be failure.

K'ung Fu-tse (Confucius)

Strategic Global Market Management

In strategic global market management, two critical questions demand continuous attention: where should a firm be, and how should it get there. The first question deals with a company's future position in terms of market share, product performance, and customer satisfaction, among others. The second involves the development of a strategy—a game plan—for achieving the goals of a firm. Without answering the first question, a company cannot tackle the second. Specifically, global marketers need to know where they want to be before they can determine how to get there.

Business strategies are based on assumptions about expected behavior of various actors in the marketplace, including governments, consumers, special-interest groups, and competitors. A strategist develops business scenarios based on these assumptions and formulates a plan of action. From the list of business scenarios, the most probable is selected and the corresponding strategies are implemented. Strategies specify the course of action a firm intends to take to achieve its organizational goals. The details of a strategy specify when, where, how, why, and by whom these actions will be performed.

As competitive pressures on businesses increase, so does the importance of formulating and implementing cost-effective and result-producing strategies. Firms cannot expect to survive and grow by leaving their activities to chance. Success is not a random event, it is a planned outcome.

Competition is the essence of our global economy. In this competitive environment new businesses will come into being, and some of the old ones will disappear. Firms can no longer expect success without acting swiftly and without adapting to the changing competitive environment. Effective strategies are indispensable to a company's survival and growth. Achieving, maintaining, and enhancing a competitive position requires an understanding of how economic, political, and social restructuring will affect the future marketing environment and the conduct of business.

In the following sections, we discuss concepts and issues related to global marketing strategies. In particular, we focus on strategic analysis, strategic options, strategic predispositions, and global competitive situations affecting the development of strategies.

STRATEGIC ANALYSIS

Strategic analysis is demanding. It involves identifying a firm's internal strengths and weaknesses and determining opportunities and threats in the marketplace. The benefits from this process are enhanced by the participation of managers from all levels of an organization. How well managers understand their strengths and weaknesses, and how effectively they capitalize on opportunities and threats, determine how successful they will be in the marketplace.

Strengths and Weaknesses

Determining strengths and weaknesses is a two-step process. First, a firm identifies the key strategic factors that contribute to success in a given business; and second, it rates itself on these elements relative to its competitors. The key factors that provide a company its competitive edge can be grouped under four broad but related categories: technology, marketing, information management, and management skill. Technology includes factors that indicate a firm's expertise in turning concepts into desired products. Marketing includes factors that reveal the ability of a company to develop, introduce, promote, price, and distribute products and services. Information management includes factors that specify how a firm acquires, analyzes, interprets, disseminates, and uses information. And management skill includes factors that indicate the decision-making ability and behavior of managers.

A firm has to identify key success factors specific to its given business. (For example, in the fast-food industry, location and price advantage may be critical.) After identifying the key success factors, a company needs to rate itself on each and determine how much better or worse off it is compared to its competitors. A comparative analysis of strengths and weaknesses reveals how a firm can use its resources to effectively establish marketing presence.

Firms succeed by consistently delivering better value than the competition. As in other spheres of life, success in business is not a random outcome. In general, the likelihood of a company's success in a competitive environment is increased when it acquires characteristics that enhance its competitive edge.

Opportunities and Threats

At this stage of strategic analysis, firms identify opportunities and threats that already exist and that are likely to evolve due to socioeconomic, technological, and political developments. After the opportunities and threats have been identified, they should be ranked according to magnitude—that is, whether the identified opportunities and threats are significant or trivial. Six important areas that businesses need to examine for determining opportunities and threats are customers, special-interest groups, competitors, governments, technologies, and markets.

STRATEGIES

Strategic analysis is followed by the formulation of strategies. Strategies, as mentioned earlier, are goal-directed plans of action. They can be developed for a product, a business unit, or a whole corporation. A product strategy, for example, can focus on modifying an existing product to improve its acceptability in the marketplace. A business-unit strategy can focus on moving resources from a comparatively strong business unit to a comparatively weak one. And corporate strategies can focus on the selection of the scope of marketing presence—national, regional, or global. Although we discuss the three types of strategies separately for pedagogical reasons, it is important to note that they work synergistically to help a firm achieve its short-term and long-term goals. The three types of strategies are discussed next.

Product-Market Growth Matrix

The product-market growth matrix delineates four basic growth strategies. These strategies result from interactions between products and markets. Two types of products (existing and new) and two types of markets (existing and new) are considered in this four-cell matrix (see Figure 11.1).[1]

Market Penetration. This is a growth strategy that uses existing products to expand into existing country markets. The goal is to increase market shares by penetrating country markets already served by a firm. To increase its market share, a company can convince existing customers to increase their purchases, attract customers from competing products, and motivate new customers to purchase the product. When a firm follows a growth strategy of market

---

[1] H. Igor Ansoff, "Strategies for Diversification," *Harvard Business Review*, September/October 1957, 113–124.

FIGURE **11.1**   Product Market Growth Matrix

	Existing Markets	**New Markets**
Existing Products	Market Penetration	Market Development
New Products	Product Development	Diversification

Source: H. I. Ansoff, "Strategies for Diversification," *Harvard Business Review,* September/October 1957, 113–124.

penetration, it can expect increased demand. To meet this demand, production is boosted, resulting in greater economies of scale. This in turn allows a company to lower its price and increase the product appeal to a wider market segment.

Product Development. This is a growth strategy founded on creating new products or adapting existing products for existing country markets. This strategy is based on identifying existing customers' unmet needs that can be satisfied with new products. In some cases, rather than developing a new product, a firm modifies existing products to satisfy customers. A product development strategy can be considered feasible under different market conditions: when a company thinks that consumers' loyalty to existing products will extend to new ones it introduces; when a firm must counter the introduction of a new product by a competitor; or when a company wants to solidify its market position and discourage future competitors.

Market Development. This involves selling existing products in new markets. These markets can be either in countries where the firm currently operates or in other countries. Within existing country markets, new markets can be developed by identifying new users of the product or by expanding the distribution channel. To establish marketing presence in other countries, a company can select from a list of options including exporting and licensing. The choice is influenced by market potential, political constraints, and the firm's objectives. By following the market development strategy, a business can expect the same advantages that accrue from market penetration—that is, greater demand, greater production, lower cost, lower price, and even greater demand.

Diversification. This involves the introduction of new or adapted products into new country markets. A firm that is well established in developed economies may choose to expand its operations into developing or less developed economies. In many instances, a company may find that the product it sells in developed economies can be modified to make it acceptable in other types of economies. Or, a firm may develop new products to meet the infrastructural and socioeconomic constraints of these countries. In either case, developing and less developed economies are providing significant opportunities for marketing not only low-value but also high-value products.

Strategic Business Unit (SBU) Portfolio Strategy

Global firms usually conduct diversified business activities. They operate in multiple countries and market myriad products and services. To achieve efficiency in management, a global firm often divides its total operation into cohesive units, commonly referred to as strategic business units (SBUs). The division is generally based on geography or product or both. For example, a concern operating in five countries may consider each as its SBU; it may divide its products into multiple product groups and create an SBU for each group; or it may combine geography and product groups to create an SBU. In the last two cases, a company can have only one SBU in a country if only one product group is being marketed, or multiple SBUs if multiple product groups are being marketed.

The popular Boston Consulting Group (BCG) growth-share matrix is a useful tool for developing strategies for SBUs (see Figure 11.2). The two dimensions of this four-cell matrix are the growth rate of a market and the

FIGURE **11.2**   Strategic Business Unit Portfolio Strategy
The BCG Growth Share Matrix

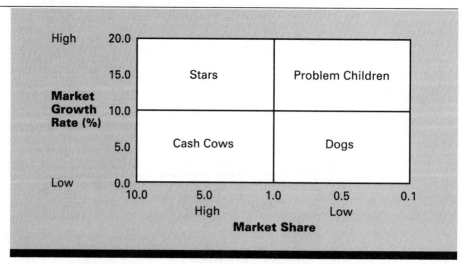

Source: Barry Hedley, "Strategy and the Business Portfolio," *Long Range Planning,* February 1977, 10.

relative market share of SBUs. The vertical axis measures the market growth rate; the horizontal measures the market share of SBUs relative to the market share of major competitors. The midpoint on the horizontal axis is 1.0, indicating market share equal to that of the major competitor. An SBU's position to the left of the midpoint indicates that the firm has a leading market-share position, whereas a position to the right of the midpoint indicates that the company is behind its major competitor.

The growth-share matrix is divided into four quadrants. The SBUs assigned to each quadrant are labeled stars, problem children, cash cows, and dogs. The stars are in the northwest cell of the matrix, problem children in the northeast cell, cash cows in the southwest, and dogs in the southeast. The strategies based on the growth-share matrix focus on the allocation of resources among the different SBUs.

Stars. These are in the high-growth market enjoying high market shares. As the market is growing at a high rate, they need cash to support their growth. However, as their market shares are also high, they generate a great deal of cash.

Problem Children. These are in the high-growth market but have low market shares. Their need for cash will be high, as they have the potential of becoming stars.

Cash Cows. These are in a low-growth market but have high market shares. This position allows them to generate a great deal of cash, which can be used to improve the position of other SBUs.

Dogs. These are in a low-growth market, and their market share is also low. For an SBU, this is not an enviable position. The dogs may end up requiring cash indefinitely, without improving their position.

As indicated earlier, the strategies based on the growth-share matrix focus on allocating resources among the SBUs. These strategies may take one of the following forms: redistributing resources from less promising to more promising SBUs, establishing new SBUs through acquisition or expansion, or divesting less promising SBUs to free resources for promising SBUs.[2]

Corporate Competitive Strategy

The competitive environment of a global firm varies by product and country. In some countries, a company faces strong, entrenched competitors with well-established brands; in others, the competitors not only have weak brands but

---

[2] James C. Leontiades, *Multinational Corporate Strategy: Planning for World Markets,* Lexington, MA: Lexington Books, 1985.

FIGURE **11.3**   Corporate Competitive Strategy

		Market Share Objective	
		High	Low
Scope of Operations	Global	Global High Share Strategy	Global Niche Strategy
	Regional	Regional High Share Strategy	Regional Niche Strategy
	National	National High Share Strategy	National Niche Strategy

Adapted from James C. Leontiades, *Multinational Corporate Strategy*, Lexington, MA: Lexington Books, 1985.

lack resources to strengthen their market position. These differences in competitive situations encourage global firms to vary the scope of their operations from national to regional to global. With each option, a global concern can choose from two levels of market penetration: low market share versus high market share. The two strategic dimensions, scope of operations and market share objectives, give a company six strategic options, as shown in Figure 11.3.

Global High-Share Strategy. This strategy is usually followed by large global firms. They have to coordinate activities to achieve a high share of the global market.[3] This strategy is usually implemented for standardized products. Slight variations in products may be made to meet the environmental constraints of different countries. Through mass production, firms achieve economies of scale, which give them the cost advantage they need to gain a competitive edge.

Global Niche Strategies. Here, companies select a market niche where they can avoid confrontation with major competitors. The purpose is to establish a global presence but with specialized products. The firm relies on patents or its goodwill to ward off competitors, and strengthens its global position by relying on its distinctive competitive advantage.[4]

Regional High-Share Strategies. Companies that follow regional high-share strategies attempt to achieve high market share within a particular region. They

---

[3] Thomas Hout, Michael E. Porter, and Eileen Rudden, "How Global Companies Win Out," *Harvard Business Review*, September/October 1982, 98–108.

[4] Frederick E. Webster, Jr., "Marketing Strategy in a Slow Growth Economy," *California Management Review*, spring 1986, 93–105.

may, for example, divide the world into six major regions (North America, South America, Western Europe, Eastern Europe, Asia Pacific, and Africa) and then focus on one or two regions. Regional high-share strategies provide the advantage of mass production, enabling a firm to compete on price. A company may pursue this strategy when markets are homogeneous within a region but heterogeneous across regions.

Regional Niche Strategies. In following regional niche strategies, firms select specialized markets within a region to establish their marketing presence. The argument in favor of this strategy is that market conditions in countries within a region may be similar; thus, by following this strategy, a company can capitalize on market opportunities. Collectively, the different countries within a region can represent a large market that makes mass-scale production possible.

National High-Share Strategies. Just because they are large, global firms do not necessarily have to follow a global or regional strategy for all products. Variations in market conditions and internal strengths and weaknesses can motivate a business to follow a national high-share strategy. That is, a company may sell the product in only one country and attempt to achieve a high share of the single-country market.

National Niche Strategies. With this strategy, a firm specializes in a small segment of the market within a country. The market is small, and thus unattractive to other global firms. However, if the potential of this market looks promising, other companies may enter to exploit the opportunities. National niche strategies are motivated by a desire to serve the specialized needs of a market segment within a country.

The six competitive strategies presented above allow a firm to adapt its strategic posture based on market conditions. Markets are not homogeneous because economic, political, social, and technological conditions vary across countries. A company can capitalize on these differences by matching its strategies with opportunities and threats in the marketplace.

STRATEGIC PREDISPOSITIONS

Strategic decisions of global marketers are partly influenced by four major types of strategic predispositions: ethnocentrism, polycentrism, regiocentrism, and geocentrism.[5] Among the different factors that shape these strategic predispositions are administrative experiences and leadership styles of the CEOs, their

---

[5] David A. Heenan and Howard V. Perlmutter, *Multinational Organization Development: A Social Architecture Perspective,* Reading, MA: Addison-Wesley, 1979.

values and beliefs, the history of the firm, and myths and folktales permeating the company.

Ethnocentrism

Ethnocentrism refers to a predisposition to base all strategic decisions on home country values and interests. The domestic market is considered the most important, and a preference is exhibited for putting home country personnel in key positions around the world. Marketing mix decisions are made at headquarters, and products are developed based on the needs of home country consumers.

Polycentrism

Polycentrism refers to a predisposition to base strategic decisions on the culture and values of each country where a firm operates. The country markets are considered a series of domestic or national markets. A preference is shown for hiring local people to manage the business. Marketing mix decisions are made in each country, and products are developed based on local needs.

Regiocentrism

Regiocentrism refers to a predisposition to base all strategic actions on the culture and values of a specific region. The world is divided into separate regions such as North America, Asia Pacific, and Western Europe, among others. Each region is considered different from the others politically, socially, and economically. Managers are recruited, developed, appraised, and assigned on a regional basis, and the firm tries to establish its viability and legitimacy at a regional level. Marketing mix decisions involving products, advertising, pricing, and distribution are also made regionally.

Geocentrism

Geocentrism refers to a predisposition to take all strategic actions based on worldwide opportunities. Using a global-systems approach to decision making, a geocentric company integrates its subsidiaries around the world into a network of businesses. People are hired based on competency, not nationality; headquarters and subsidiaries consider themselves a part of a global entity, and not national or regional units. Marketing mix decisions are made by consultation, and global products adaptable to local conditions are developed and introduced.

SOME GLOBAL STRATEGIC CONSIDERATIONS

The recent economic and political developments in Europe, North America, and Asia Pacific have generated a heated debate about the future of global trade. There seems to be a growing consensus among academicians and public officials that the nature of competition has changed. The end of the cold war augurs the beginning of a new type of competition among nations. Countries, especially the developed ones, will compete not on the basis of military power but economic strength. As such, in the future, countries will rearrange their priorities and redirect resources from military hardware to consumer and industrial wares.

The global economic and political restructuring has changed the economic and geopolitical reality not only for countries but also for firms. Developments in the European Union, the North American Free Trade Area, and the Asia Pacific Economic Cooperation region are significantly affecting the conduct of business. Global marketers need to understand the ensuing ramifications to competitively position their firms in tomorrow's competitive arena. They also need to know how developments will affect their future competitive advantages and, thus, their future performance. The influence of these developments on some of the strategic business decisions is discussed next.

Production Location and Sourcing

As global firms expand global business, production location and sourcing decisions increase in importance. In the past, these decisions were largely influenced by cost considerations. That is, either the least expensive supplier or manufacturing site was selected. The appeal of this approach was ease of implementation. Basically, different alternatives were measured and arranged in terms of cost, and the one with the lowest cost was selected.

In today's economy, production and sourcing decisions are influenced not only by cost but also by noncost parameters. A company that focuses on cost alone will lose sight of broader strategic goals such as establishing, maintaining, and expanding market shares in different countries. Had Japanese companies based their decision to assemble or build products solely on the criterion of cost minimization, the United States would not have been their most logical choice. The decision to start production there was influenced by an understanding of the strategic importance of the American market as well as the objective of achieving cost efficiencies. Furthermore, by establishing assembling and manufacturing plants in the United States, Japanese firms exhibited their commitment to the American economy. And, by creating jobs and exporting products from the United States, they became good citizens.

The Double Squeeze

In the past, competition for high-value-added products, such as electronics, autos, medical equipment, and computers, has been the exclusive domain of American, European, and Japanese firms. The newly industrialized countries—South Korea, Hong Kong, Taiwan, and Singapore (commonly known as the NICs)—competed only in low-value-added products such as raw materials, intermediary products, and textiles. Recently, however, the competitive thrust of these countries has changed significantly. Not only are their businesses competing in low-value-added products, but they have also effectively entered markets for high-value-added products such as optics, telecommunications, medical equipment, and computers. As a result, the NICs are squeezing companies from the developed economies at both ends of the product mix—low- and high-value-added products. In the future, the NICs will provide competition not only in their own backyards but also in the American, European, South American, and African markets. Overall, the entry of NICs in high-value-added products, both consumer and industrial, has intensified the battle for market shares.

Business and Politics

The U.S. government, as well as others, is playing an active role in obtaining, maintaining, and enhancing the competitive advantages of its domestic firms. For example, Motorola accused Japan of hoarding radio spectrum and violating trade agreements to provide spectrum to foreign companies. The U.S. trade representative at the time, Carla Hills, threatened retaliation with duties and penalties on Japan's exports to the United States. Japan relented and Motorola began its Japanese operations in October 1991.[6] The alliance between government and business is motivated by the realization that the resources available to each can be managed synergistically to the benefit of both.

Post-Marketing Concerns

The marketing grid (see Figure 1.1) shows the consumer at the center of concentric circles, surrounded first by the four elements of marketing mix (product, price, place, and promotion) and then by domestic environmental constraints (economic, social, technological, and political). Recently, another outer circle has been added, showing the global environmental constraints. The marketing grid, focusing on consumers, has served marketers well by forcing them to think of consumers when formulating and implementing marketing strategies.

Following the precepts of the marketing grid, firms have successfully devel-

---

[6] Andrew Kupfer, "Ma Bell and Seven Babies Go Global," *Fortune*, November 4, 1991, 118–128.

oped and introduced new products and have profitably managed existing ones. The implications of the marketing grid are clear. Operating within environmental constraints, marketers should make product, price, place, and promotion decisions to satisfy consumers. Companies that provide higher value for the dollar (or the rupee) are better able to strengthen their market presence and achieve profit goals.

In tomorrow's marketing era—the era of ecological, social, egalitarian, and ethical concerns—the focus will not only be on satisfying needs and wants of target markets but also on allaying concerns of various special-interest groups. Organized around specific issues such as protecting the environment or encouraging economic participation of disenfranchised people, special-interest groups represent the concerns of different segments of the population. By focusing on a particular issue, they achieve clarity of purpose as well as immense economic and political power.

Firms will increasingly find their business activities being judged not only by the bottom line, but also by the impact they have on society. For example, the marketing of natural furs brought animal-rights activists out in force. Many outlets in the United States subsequently stated that they would not carry fur products in the future. In certain cities the confrontation among retailers, wearers of fur coats, and animal-rights activists became quite ugly. Environmentalists and other special-interest groups will force companies to be sensitive about how products are developed, manufactured, and marketed. As these groups exert political and economic pressure, companies will not only have to become socially and ethically conscious but also develop political skills for better managing their presence in different country markets.

SUMMARY

To survive in a competitive environment, marketers must be able to exploit business opportunities. Only forward thinking and global vision will enhance their competitiveness. Political, economic, technological, and social developments are making the global economy more interdependent and interrelated. In this highly competitive and fast-paced economy, success or failure will depend on how marketers perceive, understand, and interpret world events and then act upon them.

Global marketers formulate strategies to achieve a sustainable competitive advantage. When a firm possesses the key success factors for its industry that competitors cannot easily copy, it strengthens its position. Dealing with competitive situations as they arise leaves a business strategically unprepared to capitalize on business opportunities and avert competitive threats. The better an executive's understanding of these developments, the better prepared he or she is to manage a company's long-term performance.

As competitive pressures in the European, American, and Asian Pacific markets increase, firms must reconsider their strategies. This should be influenced by the new economic and political realities, and not by past failures or successes. Business opportunities and competitive threats are created by changes in the environment in which businesses operate. To survive and grow, companies need to adapt to the changing global economic and political climate. Otherwise, they will be unable to manage competitive threats and exploit business opportunities.

CHAPTER **TWELVE**

Whoever does not know how to find the way to his ideal lives more frivolously and impudently than the man without an ideal.

Friedrich Nietzsche

Ethics and Global Marketing

The influence of global corporations spans all economies. With the growing importance of global corporations, public concern about the effects of corporate activities on individual lives and the environment is mounting. This is reflected in the debate currently raging among academicians and practitioners on what constitutes an ethical business practice.

As ethics is nudging its way onto center stage, firms from both developed and developing economies are formulating codes of conduct to guide their employees in making ethical decisions. Promotional campaigns are being launched that not only tout the advantages of products but also project companies' ethical positions. For example, the Body Shop advertises its nonexploitative trade with indigenous people in less developed countries; Timberland boot company condemns racism in Germany; and Benetton promotes ethnic tolerance.[1]

Ethics focuses on what is morally right or wrong. In determining whether a business decision is ethical or unethical, global marketers normally rely on precepts stating that firms should not hurt and deceive people; hold back significant product-related information; engage in unlawful activities; or make false promises. Although these precepts are useful in judging the ethical content of a decision, they cannot be easily applied to all situations.

Consider the following: The use of insecticides such as DDT is banned for household consumption in the developed economies because it harms the environment, wildlife, and people. However, a company from a developed country sells the product for household use in a less developed country. Is this ethical? If not, who is acting unethically—the firm marketing the product, the host government allowing the firm to market the product, the consumers using

---

[1] Jane Sasseen, "Companies Clean Up," *International Management*, October 1993, 30–31.

the product, or all three? Consider another case. A company is bidding for a billion-dollar construction project. The executives have been told that their chance for getting the contract is small if they do not bribe government officials. They bribe the officials but do not win the contract. Is this business practice ethical? If not, who is acting unethically—the firm, the government official, or both?

If you decided that it is unethical to market DDT for household consumption because it adversely affects the health of people, can you apply the same standard to the marketing of tobacco and alcohol? Furthermore, can it be categorically stated that marketing any product that adversely affects human beings or the ecological system is unethical?

WHY ETHICS?

The primary goal of a firm is to make a profit. Profit is indispensable because it provides investors the return they expect from their investments, businesses the resources they need to survive and grow, governments the taxes they need to build roads and bridges, and people the jobs they need to raise their standard of living. However, in the pursuit to maximize profit, it is not unusual for companies to make decisions that hurt consumers, employees, and the environment. For example, Ford did not correct a known defect in one of its cars—the Pinto—that made it susceptible to gas tank explosions;[2] Metropolitan Edison concealed information from the press about the Three Mile Island nuclear accident;[3] and B. F. Goodrich, to win certification, rewarded employees who falsified data on aircraft brakes.[4] Sears, a large retailer, recently acknowledged that it was overcharging consumers for car repairs. And BMW, in one of its ads in the United States, made some astounding claims about its new 740i V-8 engine. The ads indicated that the engine suffered "no sign of wear" during a continuous 100,000 mile top-speed test. When pressed to show the test results, BMW retracted the claim and acknowledged that the test had run only 78,125 miles and had not been continuous.[5] These are but a sample of corporations that engage in unethical practices. Gellerman[6] reports that managers rationalize their misconduct by thinking that their actions are

---

[2] Rogene A. Bucholz, *Fundamental Concepts and Problems in Business Ethics*, Englewood Cliffs, NJ: Prentice-Hall, 1989.

[3] Mike Gray and Ira Rosen, *The Warning*, New York: W. W. Norton, 1982.

[4] Kermit Vandivier, "The Aircraft Brake Scandal: A Cautionary Tale in Which the Moral is Unpleasant," in A. G. Athos and J. J. Gabarro, eds., *Interpersonal Behavior: Communication and Understanding Relationships*, Englewood Cliffs, NJ: Prentice-Hall, 1978, 529–540.

[5] "Experts Slam Door on BMW," *The Milwaukee Journal*, August 1, 1993, A18.

[6] Saul W. Gellerman, "Why 'Good' Managers Make Bad Ethical Choices," *Harvard Business Review*, July/August 1986, 85–90.

- within ethical and legal limits;
- in the individual's or the corporation's best interests;
- safe because they would never be discovered or publicized; and
- helpful to the company—therefore, the company would condone them and even protect those engaging in them.

The tension between the financial imperatives of survival in the marketplace and the ethics of marketing has been noted by Camenisch.[7] Although unethical activities may temporarily improve a firm's performance, the long-term consequences are generally unfavorable. The managers of a fast-food chain in England were able to temporarily increase their sales by telephoning a bomb scare to a competitor. But the chain's reputation suffered nationally when it was found out.[8]

For a business, the discovery of unethical practices can be embarrassing, if not devastating. When a firm engages in unethical activities, it has to defend its behavior in public and place its long-term survival at stake. Therefore, it needs to detect the danger signs that can indicate its propensity for engaging in unethical behavior. Cooke has identified fourteen such signs of ethical risk.[9] A firm puts itself at ethical risk when it

1. Emphasizes short-term revenues above long-term considerations.
2. Ignores or violates internal or professional codes of ethics.
3. Looks for simple solutions to ethical problems and is satisfied with quick fixes.
4. Does not want to take an ethical stand when there is a financial cost to the decision.
5. Creates an internal environment that either discourages ethical behavior or encourages unethical behavior.
6. Sends ethical problems to the legal department.
7. Looks at ethics solely as a public relations tool.
8. Treats its employees differently than its customers.
9. Institutes unfair or arbitrary performance-appraisal standards.
10. Lacks procedures or policies for handling ethical problems.
11. Provides no mechanism for internal whistleblowing.
12. Lacks clear lines of communications within the organization.

---

[7] Paul F. Camenisch, "Marketing Ethics: Some Dimensions of the Challenge," *Journal of Business Ethics* 10, 1991, 245–248.

[8] Sasseen, 30–31.

[9] Robert Allan Cooke, "Danger Signs of Unethical Behavior: How to Determine If Your Firm Is at Ethical Risk," *Journal of Business Ethics* 10, 1991, 249–253.

13. Shows concern only for the needs and demands of the shareholders.

14. Encourages people to leave their personal ethical values at the office door.

When consumers, suppliers, and other stakeholders lose faith in a company, it is the company that suffers. It takes a long time to build consumers' trust; it does not take long to lose it. In a competitive environment, a firm cannot expect to survive for long if it ignores ethical considerations. The inclusion of ethics in business decisions does not imply a disregard for profit motives. On the contrary, by incorporating ethical considerations, a company not only becomes a good corporate citizen but also enhances its survival and growth potential. The expeditious recall of adulterated Tylenol illustrates that ethics is good business. When Tylenol was relaunched with better safety features, it immediately regained its market share and established itself once again as the leading analgesic on the market.

Sims recommends three strategies to promote ethical behavior in organizations.[10] First, ethical consciousness in an organization should be encouraged by its chief executive. Second, a formal process should be developed and used to support and reinforce ethical behavior. Third, philosophies of top managers and immediate supervisors should focus on institutionalizing ethical norms and practices at all levels of the organization.

ETHICAL PHILOSOPHIES

Global marketers make numerous decisions about product, price, distribution, and promotion. For example, they decide where and how a product should be tested, how much it should cost, how it should be advertised, and where the product should be distributed. On the surface these decisions may seem innocuous and devoid of ethical implications; but they can be ethically challenging under certain circumstances. Consider the case of marketing cigarettes in less developed economies. In developed economies, increasing health concerns and a growing awareness of the hazards of smoking have persuaded nonsmokers not to take up smoking and encouraged smokers to quit. Recognizing the adverse effect of this trend on sales, many tobacco companies have begun an aggressive marketing campaign in less developed countries, where people are not as well informed about the consequences of smoking. Should the tobacco industry pursue these markets? Argue your case from the perspective of the firm; the

---

[10] Ronald R. Sims, "The Challenge of Ethical Behavior in Organizations," *Journal of Business Ethics* 11, 1992, 505–513.

people in the targeted countries; and the governments of these countries, which allow firms to sell cigarettes.

Marketing decisions have to be made. For some, the temptation is strong to ignore ethical considerations because of economic, political, and cultural differences. For example, to save money, firms send nuclear and chemical waste to less developed economies that are inadequately equipped to handle such by-products. Contaminated food and untested medicine are also sold in less developed economies—often with the consent and approval of the host government. In all these cases, not only the businesses but the governments disregard ethical considerations—at the expense of the people.

Companies deal with ethical issues on a daily basis. In a recent survey, marketing managers in the United States indicated some of the issues that pose the most difficult ethical or moral predicaments. These issues include bribery, fairness, honesty, price, product, personnel, confidentiality, advertising, manipulation of data, and purchasing.[11] Marketers develop heuristics, rules of thumb, and guidelines to deal with these ethical issues and dilemmas. These approaches can be categorized under four philosophies, whose major points are discussed next.

Utilitarianism

Utilitarianism focuses on the consequences of actions. An action is judged to be right if it results in the greatest good for the greatest number of people. This principle encourages people to judge actions by their consequences and to select the one that best maximizes net benefits for society. However, it is important to note that in applying the principle of utilitarianism, a decision maker has to define what constitutes a society. Does the term *society* include the people living within a particular country or a group of countries or even the world? Without this classification, it would be difficult to measure the effects of an action: what may be good for the French may not be good for the British. Furthermore, critics contend that by focusing on the distribution of utility, utilitarianism can cause severe harm to a small group of people while benefiting a large group.[12] This outcome is considered by many as unethical.

Egoism

Like utilitarianism, *egoism* focuses on the consequences of an action. However, unlike utilitarianism, egoism places the long-term interests of an individual—not

[11] Lawrence B. Chonko and Shelby D. Hunt, "Ethics and Marketing Management: An Empirical Examination," *Journal of Business Research* 13, 1985, 339–359.

[12] Donald Robin, Michael Giallourakis, Fred R. David, and Thomas E. Moritz, "A Different Look at Codes of Ethics," *Business Horizons,* January/February 1989, 66–73.

society—in the forefront.[13] This principle encourages a person to take actions that advance his or her self-interest. The two important weaknesses of ethical egoism are that it would not take a stand against even the most blatant infractions (e.g., discrimination, pollution, marketing of unsafe products); and it cannot resolve conflicts involving the egoistic interests of two or more people.[14]

Deontology

Deontology focuses on universal principles of right and wrong. Actions are judged independent of their consequences. What is important is not the consequence of an action but the motives and the character of the person performing the action.[15] An important criticism of deontology is that there may be situations when lying, for example, may not be unethical. If lying can save an individual or a society from injury, it may not be considered unethical.[16]

Relativism

Relativism suggests that the determination of right and wrong is culture specific, and that there are no universal rules applicable to all situations. Thus, what is considered ethical in one society may not be in another. A drawback of relativism is that it can provide executives with the justification they need to take unethical actions. By contending that consumers everywhere do not value safety equally, they may disregard the harmful effects of their products in certain countries. Such decisions may not be in the best interest of either the consumers or the company.

The four philosophies discussed above focus on either actions or outcomes. As such, they can lead to more than one "right" decision. Their major drawback is that they do not provide specific guidance to decision makers. Two managers within a firm may end up with different decisions by following different philosophies, or even the same philosophy. So, what can managers do when making marketing decisions in different countries? It is important for them to realize that societies across the world do not differ widely on some of the fundamental moral issues. For instance, no society encourages its citizens to lie, cheat, and steal. Thus, if executives respect consumer safety and truth in advertising in one country, they should respect these criteria in others.

---

[13] R. E. Reidenbach and D. P. Robin, "Toward the Development of a Multidimensional Scale for Improving Evaluations of Business Ethics," *Journal of Business Ethics* 9, 1990, 639–653.

[14] John Tsalikis and David J. Fritzsche, "Business Ethics: A Literature Review with a Focus on Marketing Ethics," *Journal of Business Ethics* 8, 1989, 695–743.

[15] Tom L. Beauchamp and Norman E. Bowie, *Ethical Theory and Business,* 2nd ed., Englewood Cliffs, NJ: Prentice-Hall, 1983.

[16] Robin et al., 68.

ETHICAL CODES FOR MARKETING

To guard against unethical and inconsistent behavior, firms have formulated codes of conduct that help managers ask the right questions before making decisions. Ranging from general to specific, these codes focus on business-related activities, and thus guide managers to choose an action that is congruent with the firm's philosophy. For example, J.C. Penney requires that its advertising not be deceptive in any manner, and Coca-Cola expects its employees and agents to comply with all applicable legal requirements.

A comparison among U.S. companies and European firms from three countries (United Kingdom, France, and the former West Germany) revealed that Europeans and Americans emphasize different aspects of business when developing codes of conduct. For example, all European codes addressed the question of employee conduct, in contrast to only 55 percent of American firms. However, more than 80 percent of American companies developed their codes in relation to customers, compared to only 67 percent of European firms. And, while 86 percent of American companies refer to their relations with the government and suppliers, fewer than 20 percent of European firms cover these two topics.[17]

Although ethical codes provide guidance in decision making, they may not cover every contingency. Thus, a firm might have a general checklist for determining the ethical structure of a decision. A seven-step checklist is presented below.[18]

1. Recognize and clarify the dilemma.
2. Get all the facts.
3. List all your options.
4. Test each option by asking, Is it legal? Is it right? Is it beneficial?
5. Make the decision.
6. Double check the decision by asking, How would I feel if my family found out about this? How would I feel if my decision were printed in the local newspaper?
7. Take action.

The checklist is designed to make managers aware of the assumptions involved in their decision making. Managers do not have to go through this checklist every time they make a decision; that would be cumbersome and

---

[17] Catherine C. Langlois and Bodo B. Schlegelmilch, "Do Corporate Codes of Ethics Reflect National Character? Evidence from Europe and the United States," *Journal of International Business Studies*, 1990, 519–539.

[18] John R. Schermerhorn, *Management for Productivity*, New York: Wiley, 1989.

counterproductive. Instead, when they are uncertain about a situation, they can rely on the checklist to lead them toward the right decision.

FACTORS ENCOURAGING ETHICAL CONSIDERATION

Internal factors such as moral values, and external factors such as technological, socioeconomic, and political environments encourage executives to consider the ethical ramifications of their decisions. Some of these important external factors are discussed next.

Information Technology

Developments in information technology have significantly changed the world during the past two decades. Satellites link the global economy, and information flows from one country to another almost instantaneously. In a sense, the political division of the world, which focuses on territorial demarcation, has been blurred by the massive flow of information. People must pass through border checkpoints, but information can flow almost unhindered across countries. These developments in information technology have brought about an important realization among executives: They can no longer expect to treat a country as a separate, isolated entity. What happens in one country can be heard and seen readily in others. For example, the news of a fatal gas leak at a Union Carbide plant in India was transmitted all over the world soon after it happened. The instantaneous transmission of news is making firms rethink and reshape their ethical postures.

Visible Destruction

Business activities are coming under greater scrutiny because of visible environmental destruction the world over. Deforestation, water pollution, overflowing garbage dumps, depletion of the ozone layer, and chemical and nuclear waste are issues of great concern. Deforestation is likely to have severe ecological consequences on many species, including our own. Some lakes are so polluted from industrial discharge that they cannot be used for swimming and fishing. Some garbage dumps are so full that city officials are having to shop for alternative locations in other cities and countries. The ozone layer, which protects us from the ultraviolet rays of the sun, has depleted, increasing the probability of skin cancer. And nuclear and chemical waste have been dumped in oceans and rivers, causing extreme danger to aquatic creatures and people living in surrounding areas.

These visible signs of destruction illustrate how some businesses have been disregarding ethics and acting irresponsibly. In the United States, approximately one-fourth of the waste produced by pharmaceutical firms is classified as hazardous.[19] In Ireland—where many U.S. pharmaceuticals operate—the Department of Environment estimates that of the 58,000 tons of hazardous waste produced each year from 1986 to 1988, between 4,000 and 5,000 tons "disappeared." Poor record-keeping may account for some of the disappearance, but the bulk of it was probably dumped illegally or found its way into drains.[20]

Special-Interest Groups

Organized around such issues as environmental protection or greater economic participation of disenfranchised people, special-interest groups are exerting pressure on firms to act responsibly and ethically. These groups have effectively highlighted the fact that business activities are to be judged not only by the bottom line, but also by the impact they have on a society. The economic and political pressure these groups wield will encourage businesses to raise their ethical standards. Heightened ethical sensitivity will have an impact on how, where, when, and by whom products are manufactured, marketed, and disposed of.

Market Forces

In a competitive environment, market forces determine who will succeed and who will fail. To succeed, firms have to encourage repeat purchases of their products. This is achieved by acting ethically—that is, by delivering what has been promised; by respecting customers; by providing reliable information; and by ensuring consumer satisfaction. Companies that behave ethically give their customers a sense of security and encourage loyalty. Conversely, unethical behavior disillusions consumers, making them switch from one firm to another. Market forces in the long run favor those companies that act ethically.

In the United States, there is a growing realization of the need to make ethics effective. Firms are trying to achieve two interrelated purposes: First, there is a desire to ensure compliance with company standards of conduct; second, there is a growing conviction that strong corporate culture and ethics are vital to survival and profitability.[21] As a result, many companies have created an in-house ethics department. Some have instituted R&D programs to develop environmentally safe products; others have formulated nondiscriminatory em-

---

[19] John Dobson, "Ethics in the Transnational Corporation: The 'Moral Buck' Stops Where?," *Journal of Business Ethics* 11, 1992, 21–27.

[20] K. Keohane, "Toxic Trade-Off: The Price Ireland Pays for Industrial Development," *The Ecologist* 19, 1989, 144–146.

[21] *Corporate Ethics: A Prime Business Asset,* New York: The Business Roundtable, 1988, 6.

ployment policies. In conjunction, technological developments, visible environmental destruction, special-interest groups, and market forces are persuading
firms to act ethically.

SUMMARY

As global trade in products and services continues to expand vigorously, firms'
activities are coming under greater scrutiny. The question of what constitutes
an ethical business practice has moved to the forefront. Some companies have
developed a code of conduct to guide their employees in making ethical
decisions, though these codes can serve their purpose only if they are used.
Many concerns overlook ethical considerations to improve their short-term
profitability. This strategy is not only short-sighted but replete with dangerous
consequences. Unethical decisions can result in loss of life, destruction of the
environment, and denial of equal opportunities.

Managers use heuristics and rules of thumb to make ethical decisions. These
heuristics can be grouped under four major philosophies: utilitarianism, egoism,
deontology, and relativism. Utilitarianism focuses on the greatest good for the
greatest number of people; egoism places the long-term interests of an individual in the forefront; deontology emphasizes universal principles of right and
wrong; and relativism suggests that the determination of right and wrong is
culture specific.

Ethical issues have become important for various reasons. The information
revolution, visible destruction of the environment, special-interest groups, and
market forces are motivating businesses to consider the ethical content of their
decisions. Global firms should be aware of the consequences of their activities;
the onus to act ethically is on them. However, when a firm engages in an
unethical activity, it is not the only culpable party. The blame is shared by the
government officials whose job it is to monitor marketing activities.

THE WORLD ECONOMY AFTER THE COLD WAR

C. Fred Bergsten

Three global transformations are well under way as we enter the 1990s. First, the reforms in the Soviet Union and Eastern Europe, if successful, will end the Cold War and most East-West confrontation, and will allow substantial reductions in military arsenals. Second, the salience of security issues will decline sharply; economics will move much closer to the top of the global agenda. The international position of individual countries will derive increasingly from their economic prowess rather than their military capability. The relative power of the United States—and, even more, of the Soviet Union—will fall; Europe's— and, even more, Japan's—will rise. Third, the world economy will complete its evolution from the American-dominated regime of the first postwar generation to a state of U.S.-European-Japanese "tripolarity." An economically united Europe will be the world's largest market and largest trader. Japan is already the world's largest creditor and the leader in many key technologies. Its GNP will exceed three-quarters of America's by the year 2000 at the growth and exchange rates that now seem likely.

International relations will look very different by 2000 as a result of these transformations. The hierarchy of nations will shift considerably. The Big Three of economics will supplant the Big Two of nuclear competition as the powers that will shape much of the 21st century.

The United States is the only superpower in both military and economic terms. It alone will remain in the top rank as the nature of world affairs changes. Indeed America may soon be the only military superpower. Such status, however, will be of decreased utility as global military tensions are substantially reduced and international competition becomes largely economic.

Moreover the United States is in relative economic decline, caught in a scissors movement between increasing dependence on external economic forces and a shrinking capacity to influence those forces. The share of international trade in the American economy has tripled over the last four decades, and is about as great as in the economies of Japan or of the European Community [EC] as a group. The United States has become the world's largest debtor country and will continue to rely on capital inflows of over $100 billion per year to finance its external deficits for the foreseeable future.

By contrast the American share of world output has been halved during the postwar period. America's share of world trade is less than the EC's, and its exports are not much greater than West Germany's alone. The global role of the dollar has fallen steadily as the Deutsche mark and the yen become more widely used in international finance.

In the short to medium term, America's international economic position is likely to decline further. Economic growth is now much more rapid in Asia and Europe, and seems likely to continue there at four percent a year or so through most of the next decade, compared to an annual growth rate of between two and two-and-a-half percent in the United States. Productivity increases in Japan and many other Asian countries are considerably higher than in America. Europe is buoyed both by the onset of economic unification in the West (almost certain to go beyond "completion of the internal market" to an Economic and Monetary Union, or EMU) and by economic revival in Eastern Europe. By 2000, the Big Three economies will be more alike than different on most key counts: levels of GNP and external trade, and degree of dependence on international trade and financial flows.

A central question for the world of the 1990s and beyond is whether the new international framework will produce conflict over economic issues or a healthy combination of competition and cooperation. History suggests that there is considerable risk of conflict, which may even spill over from the economic sphere to create or intensify political rivalries. Such a pattern contributed to the breakdown of global order prior to 1914 and again in the interwar period. Now is the time to create a global framework to avoid such tensions in the future.

The world must adjust to this fundamental shift in economic relationships among its major countries as security arrangements change. Ironically, the end of the Cold War could sharply heighten the prospect of a trade war. Throughout the postwar period, the overriding security imperative blunted trans-Atlantic and trans-Pacific economic disputes. The United States and its allies, particularly West Germany, frequently made economic concessions to avoid jeopardizing their global security structures. Cold War politics in fact sheltered the economic recoveries of Europe and Japan, and America's support for them. The United States seldom employed its security leverage directly in pursuit of its economic goals; indeed, security and economic issues remained largely compartmentalized in all of the industrial democracies.

Removal of the "security blanket" could erode this separation. Indeed the United States and others could be tempted to use security issues to seek economic advantage. Such a policy would make it considerably harder to maintain cooperation in both the economic and security dimensions. At the same time, since East-West confrontation has provided the rationale for much of America's international engagement throughout the postwar period, ending the Cold War may suggest to some Americans that the country should largely withdraw from such engagement, including in the economic domain.

In short there is an intimate interaction between the basic international political and economic transformations: removal of the security blanket increases the risk of economic conflict, which could erode security ties. The ultimate paradox of the twentieth century would be a realization of the Marxist prophecy of an inevitable clash among the capitalist nations just as the political conflict spurred by Marxist ideology is waning. The "end of history" might not be so dull after all.

This risk of economic conflict is already acute. Japanese politician Shintaro Ishihara has predicted that "the 21st century will be a century of economic warfare." Such conflict is most likely to surface between the United States and Japan.

Japan's position is clearly changing. Its global current-account surplus fell from $87 billion in 1987 to $57 billion in 1989, a figure representing less than two percent of its GNP. The growth of Japan's imports from the United States during the same period was six times greater than the growth of its exports to the United States. Manufactured goods now comprise more than half of total Japanese imports. Japan has displayed a willingness to continue financing a large portion of America's deficits, even when the dollar was falling steadily during 1985–1987, and to contribute substantially to global funding needs elsewhere (Third World debtors, foreign aid recipients, even Eastern Europe). The image of an omnipotent "Japan, Inc." was eroded considerably in early 1990 by the sharp decline of Tokyo's stock market and the yen, and the apparent inability of the Japanese authorities to stop it.

Yet American frustration with Japan remains high. Japan's bilateral trade surplus with the United States remains large, and may soon start rising again because of the weakening of the yen over the past two years and slower Japanese growth. There remains much exasperation over the Japanese market's seeming impenetrability to many imports and most foreign direct investment. A major concern is Japan's concentrated pursuit of superiority in a wide range of strategic high-technology industries, including many in which the United States retains a substantial competitive advantage.

The debate has taken an ominous new direction in both countries. In America, many who consider themselves internationalists—including many mainstream economists—have come to agree that Japan is "different" and should be treated differently. The latest negotiating effort between the two countries, the Structural Impediments Initiative, addressed some of these differences, but it is unlikely to produce rapid results. If it does not, this will strengthen the view that a new strategy is required.

Attitudes are changing in Japan as well. Dismay bordering on disdain is coming to dominate Japanese reactions to America's continued failure to correct its budget and trade deficits, raise the national savings level, improve the education system and boost competitiveness at the company level. At the same time, the fragility of Japan's political system and a redirection of its policies to improve domestic living standards provide powerful pressures for turning inward. Hence Japan may not accept another round of "bashing" from America.

With respect to Europe, fears are widespread that a truly united continent will see itself as so self-sufficient, and be so preoccupied by regional developments, that it will have little interest in promoting global economic cooperation.

Indeed the European Commission's own study of the unification of the European market predicts that imports from outside the community will decline in almost every sector as a result of the removal of remaining trade barriers.[1] Blueprints for EMU suggested by the European Commission and by Bundesbank President Karl Otto Pöhl refer to the outside world in only the most cursory fashion.[2] These concerns are heightened by the prospect of a broadening of Europe's economic union to embrace Eastern Europe, which will undoubtedly seek extensive preferential access to the West European market and thus further inhibit liberalization of the EC's global policy.

One motive for European unity is restoration of global leadership for the continent, to reclaim the limelight enjoyed by virtually all of its member countries during earlier periods of history. In a world dominated by economic issues, the quest for economic leadership could be a major driving force.

This drive could be healthy if, supported (or led) by convergent policies in the United States and Japan, it could propel Europe toward a cooperative leadership position in the global economic structure. But Europe could also swing in a confrontational direction, as it has with its current policies on agriculture and aircraft. The West German model of close ties between banks and industries, sometimes with government support, is an approach that could arouse foreign ire. France's historical mercantilism is clearly still alive, as demonstrated by its repeated efforts to hold Japanese competition at bay. The involvement of East European countries could add to *dirigiste* thinking in the EC. If market-oriented Great Britain were to opt out of the EC during this critical transition period, the risk of confrontation would be enhanced.

Finally, America's confidence in its international economic position has been shaken. Trade "hawks" have argued, with some success, that the reduction in the security imperative now opens the way for unilateral actions to promote U.S. trade interests. And it is true that the United States can now afford to be less solicitous of its allies—American leverage is enhanced, to an extent, by the declining need to place overriding priority on political cohesion and thus to mute its economic demands.

U.S.-Japanese economic tension has already intensified, and U.S.-European economic confrontation could erupt as well. Any significant downturn of the U.S. economy could trigger an outbreak of protectionism. Renewed growth in the external deficit could discredit the strategy, crafted in 1985–1987 by then Secretary of the Treasury James Baker and the other finance ministers of the

---

[1] See Commission of the European Communities, "The Economics of 1992," *European Economy*, March 1988, Table A-5, pp. 180–81.

[2] See *Report on Economic and Monetary Union in the European Community*, prepared by the Committee for the Study of Economic and Monetary Union, Commission of the European Communities, April 12, 1989; also see "Basic Features of a European Monetary Order," a lecture presented by Karl Otto Pöhl, Paris, Jan. 16, 1990.

Group of Seven leading industrial nations, to respond to trade pressures primarily through currency changes and macroeconomic policy cooperation—particularly since such cooperation has already virtually disappeared. A new financial crisis or failure of the several ongoing trade negotiations, bilateral and multilateral, would intensify the tendency to "blame the foreigners."

How might such economic conflict evolve in the 1990s and beyond in a world dominated by nonmilitary concerns and three great economic powers? One possibility is the emergence of blocs, each centered on one of the Big Three. There are widespread perceptions that the world is already headed in this direction. An economic bloc already exists in Europe and will clearly broaden (to include more countries) and deepen (to encompass more functions) over the coming decade.

At the moment, however, the development of blocs in Asia or the Americas seems unlikely. Asian trade is split in three directions: within the region, with the western hemisphere, and with Europe and the Middle East. Most Asian countries thus focus primarily on expanding multilateralism and their global relationships. Annual income disparities within the region are huge, ranging from over $20,000 per capita in Japan, through South Korea and Taiwan at about one-fourth that level, to Southeast Asia at much less and China at a few hundred dollars; hence meaningful economic integration is virtually impossible. Politically, no country in the region wants to enter a bloc led by Japan unless all other avenues are effectively closed.

Similar considerations pervade the Americas—except perhaps for Canada and Mexico, because they depend so heavily on trade with the United States. The rest of Latin America has diversified trade, a far different standard of living and a historical antipathy to entangling ties with the "Colossus of the North." Moreover, nearly every country in the hemisphere is a debtor and needs financial help from the rest of the world. Closer consultative arrangements among the Americas might be desirable, but an economically significant bloc is no more likely than in Asia, barring a substantial breakdown at the global level.

However, to head off eventual self-fulfillment of the prophecies that trading blocs will develop, it will be essential to reinvigorate global economic cooperation and its institutions. This is one key reason, encompassing both economics and politics, to place a high priority on achieving such cooperation. Another reason is to provide time for Europe to achieve its ultimate aspiration of political union, which would render concerns over that "bloc" as obsolete as concerns about preferential treatment within the United States of America.

The second question affecting potential economic conflict is how each of the Big Three would relate to the others. At present the economic powers frequently find themselves aligned with different partners on different issues: America and Europe seek to open Japan's markets for manufactured goods; America and Japan push Europe to avoid any new discrimination against outsiders; Europe and Japan criticize the United States on its budget deficit and trade unilateralism. Shifting coalitions generally provide a healthy basis for systemic stability, if they occur within a framework of agreed international rules and institutional arrangements.

Historian Robert Gilpin notes, however, that "almost all [students of international relations] agree that a tripolar system is the most unstable configuration."[3] History and game theory both suggest a strong tendency for each of the parties in such an arrangement to fear that the other two will line up against it permanently, leading each to adopt excessive policies. Given the inevitable self-perception of vulnerability on the part of each of the three parties, two will, in fact, tend to ally against the third under conditions of rough tripolar equality—possibly to create their own "bi-gemonic" dominance.

In the United States, there is a widespread view that conflict among the Big Three would evolve into an alliance between America and Europe against Japan. Japan would be viewed as an outlier on both trade and investment issues, and thus a target for the other industrial, and perhaps many developing, countries. Racial overtones would be widely perceived even if unintended.

A second possibility is that the United States and Japan would band together against a united Europe. If Europe is the only true bloc, and thereby becomes the world's largest and most powerful economic entity, the other global actors may need to coalesce against it for traditional balance-of-power reasons. Such an outcome would be much more likely if Europe were to turn inward and to discriminate overtly against outsiders.

Americans need to be aware, however, of a very plausible third possibility: a European-Japanese nexus. These regions are likely to enjoy higher growth rates than America during the coming critical transitional period—perhaps by a substantial margin. Their economic policies, especially toward international issues, have tended to be more stable and predictable. They will thus offer attractive markets and business partners for interpenetration, via both trade and investment, as reflected in the recent linkup between Mitsubishi and Daimler-Benz to conduct joint aerospace research and possibly cooperate in automobile production.

Perhaps most important, doubt about America's future dynamism is widespread in Europe and Japan (and other parts of Asia). Europeans and Japanese may come to feel that the United States will reform its domestic policies only if they join together to provide external pressure to do so. Any major protectionist steps by the United States would feed these doubts and drive the two together. Helmut Schmidt and Valéry Giscard d'Estaing created the European Monetary System in the late 1970s partly as a buffer against economic instability emanating from America. Similar linkups between Asia and Europe are clearly possible in the 1990s and beyond.

The emergence of any of these possibilities as permanent configurations

---

[3] *War and Change in World Politics* (Cambridge: Cambridge University Press, 1981), p. 235.

would be extremely destabilizing for global politics as well as economic affairs. The region targeted by such an "alliance" would almost certainly turn inward as the external pressures strengthened domestic forces already seeking such a course: protectionists in America, regionalists in Europe, traditionalists in Japan. The target area would probably seek to form (or expand) its bloc of nearby supporters, and the other areas would retaliate in kind. All economies would suffer, and there would be a genuine risk of trade warfare.

There is good news, however. The Big Three enter the new era as political allies with strong security ties and democratic governments. Their cooperation over the past four decades, while uneven, has largely avoided major crises and has proven superior to all historical antecedents. The extensive interpenetration of companies and financial markets throughout the three regions militates against a breakdown of cooperation. Thus there is hope that a new era of interaction between economics and security could be very different from the pre-1914 and interwar periods, when the struggle for world economic leadership coincided with political hostility.

The bad news is that the world economy has enjoyed prolonged periods of stable prosperity only when under the hegemonic leadership of a single country—the United Kingdom in the latter part of the nineteenth century and the United States in the first postwar generation.[4] It has never experienced successful "management by committee."

But there will be no new hegemon to supplant the United States. Neither Japan nor even a fully united Europe could achieve anything like the global dominance, even in the economic sphere alone, that is needed to support such a role. Hence effective international economic cooperation will depend on the achievement of joint leadership by the Big Three economic superpowers, just as nuclear deterrence was maintained by the Big Two military superpowers. There is simply no alternative.

The postwar economic powers have proved exceedingly adept at responding to crises with sufficient skill to avoid lasting economic effects. But there have been a number of close calls: American leadership nearly faltered in responding to the Mexican debt crisis in 1982, enormous protectionist momentum was permitted to build in the United States before dollar adjustment and credible trade policies were launched in 1985, and extensive financial disruption resulted from the plunge of the dollar in 1987. Moreover the movements of globalized financial markets could now overwhelm the efforts of individual governments, or even several countries acting in concert. New sources of conflict among nations could well result from contemporary changes in global politics and economic capabilities.

The system no longer provides strong defenses against such threats. As a

---

[4] See Charles P. Kindleberger, *The World in Depression. 1929–1939* (Berkeley: University of California Press, 1973).

result, currency misalignments and instability have become endemic; large trade imbalances persist; protectionism and neomercantilism have intensified; Third World debt remains unresolved; policy cooperation is ad hoc and fragile.

To restore effective systemic defenses, America, Japan and a uniting Europe must join to provide collective leadership. The Big Three need to start acting as an informal steering committee for the world economy—reinvigorating the existing institutional structures, creating new ones and initiating concrete steps to utilize them consistently.

Such leadership must rest on firm internal foundations in each area. The United States has to make the difficult adjustment from hegemon to partner. It can do so only by restoring its international competitive economic position and, at a minimum, halting a further buildup of foreign debt. These changes would be even more essential for the United States if cooperative global management should turn out to be unattainable. In that case it would become necessary to defend the country's interests aggressively in a world economy characterized by widespread confrontation and even hostility.

The United States will have to increase its government spending in some areas directly related to the country's international competitiveness. Examples include expenditures on education, research and development, export finance and direct help for key industries. It is eminently logical to use part of the "peace dividend" that may result from lessened defense outlays to finance these expenditures, since they will be aimed at achieving many of the same national goals—preserving America's world role and national security—as the military programs that will be cut.

Elimination of the overall budget deficit, however, remains crucial for foreign policy as well as economic reasons. The budget deficit is the chief cause of the trade deficit, which in turn requires the United States to borrow huge sums abroad and thus adds greatly to its external dependence and its insecurity. In addition, as long as the United States drains resources from the rest of the world, it cannot be a net financial contributor to other countries. Indeed the United States competes with others for scarce world savings. Hence America's greatest contribution to recovery in Eastern Europe or the Third World would be correction of its own fiscal position.

President Bush got it backward in his inaugural address when he asserted that "the United States has the will but not the wallet." The reality is that this country has plenty of wallet but a deficiency of will. The United States is both the richest nation in the world and the least taxed. If the peace dividend and other expenditure cuts do not finance the needs of the coming years, revenue increases will be essential.

Changes of this nature call for fundamental alterations in American attitudes. The traditional mind-set in this country, derived from nearly a century of global dominance and a virtually self-sufficient continental economy, has been to adopt whatever public policies and corporate strategies fit the domestic environment. The rest of the world was largely ignored in the formation of policy.

There are a number of stunning recent examples of this abiding phenomenon. The Tax Reform Act of 1986 ignored the international position of the United States and probably made it harder for American firms to compete abroad. Budget policy, as just noted, remains the underlying cause of the huge buildup of foreign debt. Foreign exchange intervention policy ignored the decimation of much of American industry and agriculture caused by the soaring dollar in the first half of the 1980s. The Export-Import Bank, America's only effective governmental tool for promoting overseas sales, ran out of money in 1988 when such sales were finally booming.

Americans will have to start viewing themselves as part of an integrated global economy, and pushing their government and firms to behave accordingly, if they are to prosper and remain world leaders into the 21st century.[5]

Japan faces the opposite problem. As in the United States, a small minority recognizes the basic change in the country's international position and seeks new policies. (Such arguments inspired the Maekawa Commission reports, for example.) For Japan, this requires adopting the mind-set of a huge creditor country that is confident of its ability to compete throughout the world. It means dropping Japan's perception of itself as a vulnerable island nation that must "export or die" and protect its own market and firms against "powerful outsiders." Indeed, participation as an equal partner in effective tripolar management of the world economy could provide a new rationale for Japanese foreign policy and might have considerable appeal to Japan, as it would play to the country's obvious comparative advantage.

Japan has already begun to change impressively. But much more is needed quickly: further increases in imports of both manufactured (including high-technology) products and agricultural goods, a conspicuous expansion in the presence of foreign investors, eschewal of infant industry protection and industrial policies, additional reductions in its trade surpluses with the rest of the world and especially with the United States. Japan has repeatedly demonstrated an enormous aptitude for reform, as in its responses to the two oil shocks and the doubling of the yen in 1985–1987. It can clearly do so again if convinced that such change is a national imperative, although the historical record suggests that continued outside pressure will be needed to galvanize such a strategy.

Europe faces a distinctly different problem: maintaining an outward, global orientation and beginning to operate as a unit in the world arena while completing the enormously complicated task of forging a truly unified regional economy. The key is probably the extent and speed of unification itself. Smooth completion of the process by the mid-1990s, for example, should generate enormous self-confidence in Europe and an appetite for moving simultaneously

---

[5] A detailed strategy of "competitive interdependence" for the United States is presented in C. Fred Bergsten, *America in the World Economy: A Strategy for the 1990s*. Washington, D.C.: Institute for International Economics, November 1988.

on global reforms. By contrast, internal divisions and failures could sap both the capacity and will to look outward.

Fortunately German unification seems likely to speed the process. It will intensify the desire of France, most of the other countries, and Germany itself to achieve Thomas Mann's call for "Europeanization of Germany instead of Germanization of Europe" through full economic integration of the continent. The inevitable engagement of the East Europeans may create a two-speed Europe for a while, but the previous EC membership of several less industrialized countries was already pushing in that direction.

The substantive key is EMU, which now seems likely by mid-decade. The continental countries outside Germany have made a fundamental decision to link their currencies to the Deutsche mark, and need EMU to provide political legitimacy for a European zone of monetary stability. Germany has lost the ability to modify its exchange rate vis-à-vis the rest of Europe, since the other countries follow virtually all of its currency and monetary moves, and so sees a compelling need to complete the transition to a full monetary union that will produce a "Germanization of European money rather than a Europeanization of German money." The unification of Europe for trade policy purposes made possible the liberalizing leaps of the Kennedy and Tokyo rounds of the General Agreement on Tariffs and Trade (GATT); EMU should make possible similar leaps in global monetary affairs.

Some observers, including Europeans who want an outward-oriented continent, argue that new global economic initiatives are premature until Europe has completed its regional structure. But the EC seems able to negotiate the Uruguay Round in the GATT while continuing to complete its internal market. It is imperative that EMU be made compatible with stable global monetary arrangements—and thus there is a strong case for devising them in parallel. It would in fact be dangerous to wait until Europe is fully organized to work out the needed international reforms, both because the delay itself could produce serious conflict and become some of the most desirable avenues for global progress could be foreclosed.

If the Europeans were unwilling to negotiate on this timetable or if a unified Europe resisted joining the global initiatives suggested here, perhaps to seek economic hegemony on its own, the United States and Japan might have to proceed bilaterally for a time. America and Japan already took such a step in creating the initial currency "reference ranges" with the Baker-Miyazawa agreement of October 1986, which was subsequently generalized at the Louvre Accord in February 1987. The U.S.-Japanese Structural Impediments Initiative probably heralds similar talks at the global level, as already suggested in several communiqués of the Group of Seven.

But an American-Japanese Group of Two would be decidedly inferior to a Group of Three that included Europe. It could create negative reactions in Europe and feed perceptions that a U.S.-Japanese bloc was being formed. On the other hand, as with monetary arrangements in 1986–1987, U.S.-Japanese bilateralism could be a useful tool to increase the proclivity of the Europeans to cooperate, by indicating that the other economic superpowers would be willing and able to proceed without them.

The overall result of these internal changes would be a considerably different Big Three: a newly competitive America, a newly internationalized Japan, and an economically integrated Europe.

Absent such internal developments, each area will lack the internal self-confidence or the international respect needed to play its part in global leadership. But achievement of these crucial changes in each of the Big Three can be promoted, perhaps decisively, by the adoption of new international policy commitments and specific steps to implement them.

First, political leaders of the Big Three need to recognize publicly the dramatic changes in the global environment and declare their intention to construct and maintain a stable international economic order based on shared leadership and mutual responsibility. Such a commitment should be enunciated at the Houston summit this July, the first of the 1990s, to set the essential political framework and begin to define the needed initiatives.

Such a commitment would obviously be credible only if it encompassed effective follow-through steps to translate principle into practice. Money and trade would be the most essential components of such a package. The Big Three should start the process by launching the construction of a new international monetary regime to replace the Bretton Woods system that collapsed in 1971–1973. No system worthy of the name has existed since that time, with enormous costs for the world economy. But stable and effective monetary arrangements are as crucial to the world economy as national monetary stability is key to each individual country.

The preferred course is to build in evolutionary fashion on the "reference ranges," the "economic indicators" to guide policy cooperation that were agreed upon at the Tokyo summit in 1986, and the European Monetary System itself. The key countries would set zones for their currencies that, given reasonable consistency of domestic policies, would avoid large current account imbalances (and thus limit both financial risks and protectionist pressures). The zones would be shifted in response to differences in national inflation rates and to major changes in the world economic environment, such as large jumps in oil prices, but the countries would otherwise pledge to adopt new policies as needed to preserve them. Over time, the zones could be narrowed if experience with the system suggested the feasibility of doing so, perhaps leading ultimately to a regime similar to Bretton Woods or the EMS.

The details would of course take time to develop. In any event, global negotiation should proceed in parallel with the European regional effort. Moreover the new regime should be implemented only when actions have been taken that promise correction of today's continuing trade imbalances.

On trade, the immediate key is a successful completion of the Uruguay

Round that would convincingly resume market liberalization and refurbish the credibility of the GATT. Realization of the Uruguay Round's full agenda would move significantly in these directions by expanding international disciplines on agriculture and safeguard measures, broadening the rules to encompass services and intellectual property rights, reintegrating textile trade into the GATT, and improving the process for settling disputes. A strong push from the Houston summit will be essential to achieve these results, just as the summits of the late 1970s were decisive in galvanizing a successful conclusion to the Tokyo Round.

Much more is needed, however, to make the needed leap in the effectiveness of global trade arrangements. The Big Three should thus push for the implementation of four sweeping new reforms by 2000: (1) elimination of all tariffs on all industrial trade; (2) a complete ban on all quantitative trade barriers including "voluntary export restraint agreements"; (3) a sharp expansion in the independence and mandate given the GATT to police the system; and (4) creation of an instrument similar to the GATT for investment issues to provide a stable framework for international corporate activities (and help resist protectionist pressures in this area, notably in the United States).[6] An even bolder approach would be agreement to finally establish the "International Trade Organization," to cover all these issues and many more, that was originally intended to be the comprehensive "third leg" of the postwar economic system (along with the International Monetary Fund and World Bank).

These proposals should be taken up promptly after the conclusion of the Uruguay Round. The so-called bicycle theory posits that trade policy either moves steadily toward liberalization or topples in the face of protectionist pressures. Launching a new negotiation toward such major steps would keep the "bicycle" moving forward without delay, avoiding the post-negotiation malaise that permitted substantial protectionist pressures to flourish after the conclusion of both the Kennedy and Tokyo rounds. It would also help ensure the outward orientation of the EC by maintaining its engagement in multilateral trade bargaining through to the culmination of its new regional compact.

Initiatives by the Big Three to reform and dramatically improve the international monetary and trade regimes along these lines, as well as to make substantial changes in their internal economic structures, would clearly mark the beginning of a new era of collective leadership of the world economy. It would indicate that each area was fully aware of the new global environment, in both political and economic terms. It would show that each could adopt a new mind-set: for America, a willingness to share power with others; for Japan, an

---

[6] A Free Trade and Investment Area among OECD countries has been proposed by Gary Clyde Hufbauer in "Beyond GATT." *Foreign Policy*, Winter 1989–1990. A similar GATT-wide structure would be far superior, however, because it would include at least the more advanced developing countries and strengthen (rather than cripple) the GATT as an institution.

acceptance of international responsibility; for Europe, a willingness to act jointly on global economic and monetary, as well as trade, policy.

Thus the Big Three could assert control of issues that will inexorably emerge as central to world events if the Cold War does in fact dissipate. They would preempt the risk that removal of the security blanket and economic rivalry itself would generate severe international conflict. They would create an orderly framework for managing some of the elements that will dominate relations among them in the years ahead.

The continuing erosion of the present economic regime, and the failures of recent cooperative efforts, do not bode particularly well for the ambitious reforms proposed here. However, the history of international economic management is replete with cycles of backsliding that eventually grew so serious that the political leadership of key countries was forced to undertake large-scale initiatives to get back on track.

For America, there are important strategic reasons to launch new initiatives. The United States still retains enormous economic power. It is enjoying an extended period of growth, job creation and deregulation that is widely admired—and financed—by the rest of the world. America's security preeminence will remain vital through the East-West transition period, especially in Asia (including Japan), where the security situation has not changed nearly as much as in Europe. The United States has much closer relations with both Europe and Japan than either has with the other, enhancing its ability to shape the evolution to a new world economic order.

The value of America's bargaining assets, however, is likely to fall further in the years ahead. It thus behooves the United States to move sooner rather than later to further construction of a new system that will promote global economic and political stability, as well as its own national interests. Initiatives to do so would indicate that the United States had both the intellectual capacity and the political will to try to shape the historical transformations now under way and is ready to assert continuing international leadership in the post–Cold War era.

THE STRATEGIC CHALLENGE OF THE EVOLVING GLOBAL ECONOMY

Raj Aggarwal

Driven by significant advances in technology, telecommunications, and transportation, the global economy is currently in a period of rapid change characterized by:

- ◆ Shifting strategic and commercial advantages;
- ◆ Increasing international integration; and
- ◆ The emergence of new economic power centers.

In recent years, many government and corporate managers have often been "blindsided" by these developments that begin and develop outside their normal sphere of attention.

The global economy is beginning to feel the economic and social impact of the commercialization of at least three major categories of new technologies: biotechnology, microprocessor-based information processing, and telecommunications. These new technologies, designed to supplement human intellectual and genetic abilities, are based on the creation, manipulation, and transmission of electronic and genetic information. And these technologies are likely to transform the global economy even more fundamentally than the industrial revolution, when human and animal power was supplemented by mechanical power.

The economies of most nations and regions have become more open to international influences, and their relative economic importance is shifting. Newly industrialized countries (NICs), especially those located in the Orient, are making their presence felt in global markets. International financial markets are playing a more important role than any domestic financial market.

This globalization of product and financial markets has been accompanied in most countries by a sale of nationalized enterprises to private investors. There has also been a shift to greater dependence on free-market mechanisms, even in such champions of social control as the Soviet Union and the People's Republic of China (PRC).

How significant are these trends, and how can a business continue to compete successfully in this changed environment?

Globalization of Product and Financial Markets

Recent decades have witnessed significant technological advances in international communications and transportation. The availability and cost-effectiveness of these innovations have facilitated the international transmission of technology and cultural values. Thus, production and marketing are becoming increasingly global—not only for mature industrial products such as textiles, steel, farm equipment, and autos, but also for such items as consumer electronics, computers, and semiconductors.

Driven by technology and the logic of comparative advantage, world trade has grown much faster over the last few decades than has world Gross National Product (GNP). Global exports and imports were about one-fifth of global GNP in 1962. This figure had increased to about one-fourth by 1972 and to more than one-third by 1982.[1] This remarkable increase in international trade is reflected in the increased openness of almost all national economies to international influences.

As an example, the proportion of U.S. GNP accounted for by exports and imports is now more than one-fifth, double what it was two decades ago. This production is even higher for manufactured goods (see Figure 1). The U.S. Department of Commerce estimates that the U.S. exports about one-fifth of its industrial production and that about 70 percent of all U.S. goods compete directly with foreign goods.[2]

Some states within the U.S. are even more dependent on the international economy. For example, Ohio ranks fourth in terms of manufactured exports. At least one-seventh of its manufacturing employment depends directly on exports, and more than half of all Ohio workers are employed by firms that depend to some extent on exports.[3] Thus, for most companies there is no such thing as a *domestic* market.

This increase in world trade and investment is also reflected in the recent globalization of financial markets. The external currency market, commonly known as the Eurodollar market, was at $3.6 trillion at the end of June 1986.[4] It is now larger than any domestic financial market. Thus, companies are increasingly turning to this market for funds. For example, U.S. companies raised almost $40 billion in these external financial markets in 1985, representing about 30 percent of the funds raised.[5] Even companies and public entities that have no overseas presence are beginning to rely on this market for financing.

---

[1] See C. P. Beshouri, "The Global Economy," *Federal Reserve Bank of Atlanta Economic Review,* August 1985, p. 51.

[2] See the President's Commission on Industrial Competitiveness, *Global Competition: The New Reality* (Washington, D.C.: The Commission, 1985), p. 9.

[3] Raj Aggarwal, "The Global Economy: Challenges of Newly Industrialized Countries," *The Ohio Economy* 2 (No. 3, Second Quarter 1986), p. 2.

[4] Morgan Guaranty Trust Company, "Global Financial Change," *World Financial Markets,* December 1986, p. 15.

[5] Morgan Guaranty Trust Company, p. 18.

FIGURE 1   U.S. Trade as a Share of U.S. Manufacturing Output

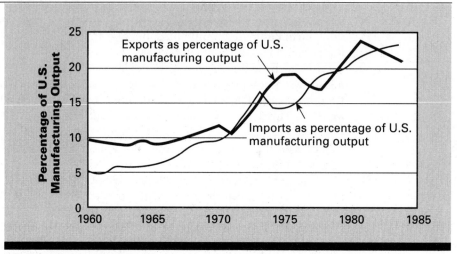

Source: U.S. Department of Labor, Bureau of Labor Statistics, 1984; Organization for Economic Cooperation and Development, 1984.

Note: For 1985, the percentages are 19 for exports and 24 for imports. Estimates for 1986 put exports at 17 percent of U.S. manufacturing output and imports at 25 percent.

In addition to the rise of these external markets for funds, most national financial markets are becoming better integrated with global markets because of the rapid increase in the volume of interest rate and currency swaps ($20 billion in 1985). The foreign exchange markets have also grown rapidly. The weekly trading volume in these globally integrated markets, at about $1 trillion, now exceeds the annual trading volume on the world's securities markets.[6] Because of these changes, any financing decision now must consider conditions in global, not just domestic, financial markets.

Decline of U.S. Dominance in Global Markets

In addition to the globalization of product and financial markets, the relative importance and role of regional and national economies are also undergoing rapid change. As an example, the importance of the U.S. economy is declining.

While the U.S. economy created almost 19 million new jobs (a labor force increase of 23 percent) in the 1970s, it did not keep pace with the productivity increases of its competitors. In the previous quarter-century, while per capita productivity increased at a 1.2 percent annual rate in the United States, it

---

[6] See Raj Aggarwal, "Managing for Economic Growth and Global Competition: Strategic Implications of the Life Cycle of Economies," in *Advances in International Comparative Management*, Richard N. Farmer, ed. (Greenwich, CT: JAI Press, 1986), p. 21.

FIGURE **2**   International Comparison of Productivity Growth and Capital Formation, 1960–1983

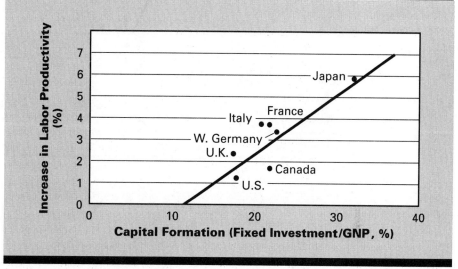

Source: U.S. Department of Commerce.

increased at a 2.3 percent annual rate in the U.K., 3.4 percent in West Germany, 3.7 percent in France, 5.3 percent in South Korea, and 5.9 percent in Japan.[7]

This low rate of increase in U.S. productivity seems to be related to its low savings rate—about one-third of the Japanese rate—and a low rate of capital formation (see Figure 2). In recent years, the United States has also suffered from low expenditures on non-military research and development as a percentage of GNP when compared to the percentage spent by such competitors as West Germany and Japan.

While the United States remains the largest economy, its share of global high-technology exports and its share of global GNP are declining (see Table 1). Concurrent with these changes in international trade patterns, similar changes are occurring in the global patterns of international portfolio and direct investment. As an example, both direct and portfolio investment in the United States have been increasing faster than U.S. investments overseas.

The declining dominance of the U.S. economy is reflected in the declining proportion of U.S. firms among the world's largest 100 industrial firms (see Table 2). The increased global importance of non-U.S. firms is also reflected in the fact that European and Japanese direct investment in the United States now exceeds U.S. direct investment in Europe and in Japan.

---

[7] The President's Commission on Industrial Competitiveness, p. 28.

TABLE **1**   Global Shares of GNP

Region	1960	1980	Change	Annual Growth to 2000 (est.)
North America	29%	25%	–4%	3–4%
Western Europe	30%	26%	–4%	2–3%
Soviet Bloc	19%	17%	–2%	4–5%
East Asia	10%	17%	+7%	7–8%
Other Countries	12%	15%	+3%	5–6%

Sources: *Euro-Asia Business Review* 4 (No. 1), and *Euromoney* (October 1982).

TABLE **2**   World's Largest 100 Industrials

Area	1960	1970	1980	1985
U.S.	70	64	45	47
Western Europe	28	27	42	26
Japan	2	8	8	14
Developing Countries	0	1	5	13

Source: Annual lists as compiled by *Fortune*.

Just as the United States replaced Britain in the early part of this century, Japan is now well on its way to replacing the United States as the largest creditor in the world. According to the Bank for International Settlements, the Japanese now have the largest share of global banking assets.[8] For the first time since 1914, the United States has become a net international debtor. At the end of 1985, the United States had the largest foreign debt of any country in the world.[9]

Rise of the Newly Industrialized Countries

One of the most significant characteristics of this changing global economy is the rise of the developing countries, especially those located in the Orient. For

---

[8] See 1986 Annual Report of the Bank for International Settlements, Basel, Switzerland, p. 37.
[9] Bank for International Settlements, p. 15.

the past forty years, the less developed countries (LDCs) have experienced much faster rates of economic growth and industrialization than have the developed countries. Since the 1950s, LDC GNP has grown more than fivefold.

In the 1970s the LDCs supplied only 5 percent of the manufactured goods imported by developed countries. Now they supply more than 20 percent of their own demand for manufactured goods and more than 8 percent of the overall demand in the developed countries.[10] The ranks of the top twenty exporting nations now include such LDCs as South Korea, Taiwan, Hong Kong, Singapore, China, Mexico, and Brazil.

As Table 2 shows, over the last quarter century, companies from the LDCs have increased their presence among the world's largest 100 industrial companies from zero to thirteen. Over the same period, foreign direct investment (FDI) by these and other LDC companies grew to more than $20 billion, an annual growth rate of about 17 percent versus a growth rate of 10 percent for FDI from the developed countries.[11] In the United States, FDI from the LDCs now accounts for more than 14 percent of the total. For firms located in the United States and other developed countries, the LDCs represent not only growing markets but also, in many cases, a source of new competition.

As Table 1 indicates, economic growth in the Asian Pacific region has far outpaced any other region of the world. The consensus among economists is that in the next fifteen to twenty years, the economies of the Far East are expected to grow at the highest rate (8–10 percent per annum), followed by South Asia (6–8 percent), Latin America (5–6 percent), East Bloc (4–5 percent), North America (3–4 percent), and Western Europe (2–3 percent). These economic growth rates are reflected in trade and investment data.[12] The Pacific Rim countries now account for a higher share of world exports (38.4 percent in 1984) than do the countries of Western Europe.[13]

The volume of U.S. trade with the Asian Pacific group of countries has exceeded its trade with Europe since 1981. By 1995 U.S. trade with the Asian Pacific countries is estimated to be double that of its trade with Europe.

According to a 1985 study by the California Department of Commerce, "The Pacific Rim countries represent a $3 trillion-a-year market growing at a rate of $3 billion a week."[14] With the recent rise of the Asian Pacific economies, the global economic center of gravity is continuing its historical westward movement.

Technology and the NICs The growth of the newly industrializing countries (NICs) is reflected in the global activities of firms from these countries. At the

---

[10] Lionel H. Olmer, *U.S. Manufacturing at a Crossroads: Surviving and Prospering in a More Competitive Global Economy* (Washington, D.C.: U.S. Department of Commerce, 1985), p. 23.

[11] Beshouri, p. 51.

[12] "Across the Globe Economic Growth Picks Up," *Euromoney,* May 1984, p. 293.

[13] "Trade Winds Blowing Across the Pacific," *The Economist,* May 3, 1986, p. 79.

[14] *Facts on the Pacific Rim* (Sacramento: California Department of Commerce, 1985), p. 4.

top end of the technology scale, U.S. dominance in semiconductors and computers is being challenged by Japanese, Korean, and Taiwanese firms. In semiconductors, the Japanese and Koreans are now significant global competitors in memory chips, and the Japanese compete in some semicustom chips. In computers, the Japanese are major global competitors in mainframes and in personal computers (PCs), while Korean and Taiwanese firms are producing inexpensive versions for the PC market. For example, the Leading Edge (IBM PC-compatible) computer, which is enjoying great success in the U.S. market, is made by Daewoo Corporation of Korea.

Japanese dominance in mature industries (for example, steel, shipbuilding, chemicals, consumer electronics, and automobiles) is being threatened by firms from Korea, Taiwan, Brazil, Mexico, and other NICs. For example, the world's largest plastics firm is now Taiwanese (Formosa Plastics), the largest petrochemical complex is in Jubail, Saudi Arabia, and the largest selling import car in Canada is Korea's Pony, made by the Hyundia Corporation. Brazil is being used by Volkswagen and others as an export base for autos, Mexico is being used by Ford as an engine manufacturing base for its North American auto operations, and all three U.S. automakers plan to supply the U.S. market with significant numbers of autos imported from Korea and Taiwan. Samsung and Tatung are now moving from being private-label suppliers to developing brand-name recognition for electronic products in the U.S. market.

There are numerous other examples of NIC manufacturers displacing advanced-country manufacturers not only in maturing global markets but also in some high-technology industries. It is, however, less well known that manufacturers in a second group of NICs at a lower level of economic development—for example, India, Thailand, Indonesia, and Mexico—are displacing manufacturers from the first group of NICs in the more mature industries, such as textiles and metal castings and fabrication. New economies seem to continually develop expertise in a technology as it matures and then to displace firms in more advanced economies.

In recent times this process of economic evolution seems to have been hastened by the decreasing costs of international transportation and communication and by the commercialization of new technologies in the highly developed countries. There is also evidence of technological leap-frogging, where some NICs acquire highly sophisticated technological capabilities. For example, China and India have developed fairly sophisticated aerospace and nuclear industries, while Brazil and Israel are exporting significant quantities of aircraft and other military hardware.

Hope for U.S. Manufacturing Technology may reduce the role of labor costs. With the advent of robotics and other computer-based intelligent machines, the efficiency of U.S. manufacturing seems to be improving. At least for some sectors sensitive to quality and style and in manufacturing where labor costs are a small percentage, U.S. manufacturing may once again be able to compete effectively with production bases in low-cost overseas locations.

While U.S. manufacturing has been about one-fourth of GNP since the 1950s, it may now be at the stage agriculture reached half a century ago—experiencing a steady decline in the number of workers, but poised for a large increase in output.

NIC Firms in Global Markets

What is the nature of the competitive challenge posed by these changes in the global economy and by the emerging firms from the NICs?

Foreign operations by firms from the NICs tend to follow certain patterns. NIC companies invest overseas to protect the markets they have developed through exports and to seek new markets for growth. They generally go overseas for risk reduction and to overcome government restrictions in their home countries. They seek reliable and lower cost sources of raw materials and technology. Their FDI is generally concentrated in countries similar in cultural characteristics, generally lower on the ladder of economic growth, and geographically nearby. However, there are important exceptions, as indicated by Korean and other NIC firm activity in U.S. markets.

NIC firms usually go overseas by means of joint ventures with local partners. Unlike U.S. companies, they hardly ever undertake wholly-owned foreign operations. Their foreign operations, again unlike U.S. companies, are not highly integrated or centrally controlled. They start by focusing on simple, standardized products, and their foreign operations may be labor intensive compared to similar local operations of firms from the developed countries. They usually start with a low-cost operation serving small markets, markets which may be considered too small and uneconomical for firms of developed economies. They generally do not engage in much product differentiation or nonprice competition. They tend to use a high proportion of local inputs and to work closely with local ethnic groups. Their relationship with the host government is usually good.

NIC firms usually operate with low levels of overhead expense. Although direct compensation and managerial benefits are low, top management often is given a significant ownership stake in the operation.

Thus, the NIC firms seem to have a well-defined niche when they engage in FDI. Although these firms share some characteristics with other multinational corporations (MNCs), they are very different in some key aspects which give them some distinct competitive advantages. FDI by these NIC firms is likely to grow rapidly in coming years and to become relatively more important as a competitive force in global markets.

Possible Responses to NIC Competition

What is the best response to this competitive threat from the NICs? In order to develop some answers to this question, it is useful to keep in mind, *first*, that the changes in the relative standing of the various economies and the globalization of product and financial markets are driven by fundamental forces such as technology and telecommunications. Thus, it may not be easy or wise to attempt to reverse or oppose these changes. Opposition is likely to be expensive, and it probably will only buy time.

Second, it seems that the world economy is undergoing extensive technology-driven structural changes. The relative importance of various industries and countries is changing more rapidly than in earlier times.

Companies in the United States and Western Europe must face up to the fact that Japanese low-cost production is being replaced by even lower cost producers from the "new Japans": Hong Kong, Korea, Singapore, and Taiwan.[15] Industries at successively higher levels of technology are facing this threat. Consequently, companies in these industries must engage in a never-ending process of moving to higher value-added operations, using ever higher levels of technology. How can this be accomplished successfully when it usually is impossible to know the exact nature of industries with emerging technologies?

Bureaucratic systems were developed in an age when change was much slower. These systems are not very good at responding to rapidly changing markets and technologies. In addition, a large, modern economy may be too complex a system to manage or even to understand. Therefore, government control or management of an economy may be an exercise in frustration.

Almost every country in the world seems to be discovering these limitations of bureaucratic systems, as evidenced by the global movement toward the privatization of government-owned and -run companies. Government companies are being sold in countries ranging from the United Kingdom and France to Turkey and Thailand. Even the PRC and other centrally planned economies are beginning to transform their economic systems to take greater advantage of systems that reward individual initiative, which is the essence of free enterprise.

To stay competitive in rapidly evolving global markets, the United States must depend on a system that can respond quickly and efficiently to change. A number of fields, from quantum mechanics to sociobiology, are coming to similar conclusions regarding the nature of optimal growth strategies in an uncertain environment. It seems that the most effective long-run strategy for large, complex systems to adjust to rapid environmental changes is a process of trial and error undertaken in the form of numerous random changes among the individual units.

It seems that the economic system best able to keep an economy growing and competitive in an increasingly dynamic global economy is a market-force-driven free enterprise system with appropriate, but minimal, government regulation. This is especially true for the United States, whose role in the global economy seems to be that of developing and exploiting ever newer technologies.

---

[15] For details, see, for example, Aggarwal, "Managing for Economic Growth and Global Competition" and *Global Competition: The New Reality.*

Consequently, if we are to stay competitive in the global economy, the United States must continue to encourage innovation in our companies and economy. We should continue to emphasize corporate and social systems that encourage and reward entrepreneurship. Our tax and investment banking systems should ensure a continuing supply of venture capital and the ability to retain the rewards of taking the risks inherent in new ventures.

Similarly, companies should also develop systems to encourage and reward entrepreneurship.[16] Worker input should be valued, and employees should feel they have a stake in the success of the company. Traditional approaches to merit pay systems should be supplemented by a heavy emphasis on profit sharing and decentralized decision making to encourage individual initiative and risk taking, even in large corporations.

To avoid the problems that prevented other cultures and economies from adjusting to change, the United States needs to shift the focus of public policy more toward the generation of a bigger economic pie and somewhat away from the recent obsession with its distribution. It is also important that the United States cut government spending and reduce the growing budget deficit. Funding the deficit leaves less capital with a higher cost for business and industry. In addition, the United States must continue to encourage and reward a higher savings rate to fund higher levels of R&D and new capital spending.

The global economy is facing a new period of rapid change, driven at one end by the newly emerging information-processing and biological technologies and at the other by the successive emergence of countries at ever lower levels of economic development as global competitors. With the rapid rise of the Asian Pacific region, the global economic center of gravity continues its westward move toward the Orient. In response, developed countries must continue to encourage higher levels of savings and investment in new capital equipment and the development of new technology.

In view of the rapid pace of economic change, all countries must continue to develop corporate and public policies that focus on encouraging and rewarding individual initiative in responding to market signals. Government and corporate managers increasingly operate in product and financial markets that are global in nature and that are characterized by shifting competitive and technological advantages. To ignore these significant changes in the global economy is to invite disaster.

---

[16] See Joel A. Ross, "Corporations and Entrepreneurs: Paradox and Opportunity," *Business Horizons* July–August 1987.

READING 3 **TAILORED TRADE: DEALING WITH THE WORLD AS IT IS**

Pat Choate ◆ Juyne Linger

The United States is floundering in the global marketplace, incurring devastating losses in market position, profits, equity, and jobs. The real problem is less with America's products than it is with America's trade policy. We face the prospect of continuing economic loss until American business and political leaders recognize the fundamental differences between U.S. and foreign economic systems. Today the key trade issue is not free trade versus protectionism but diminishing trade versus expanding trade.

We are operating with an obsolete American trade policy, an artifact of the mid-1940s when the United States and Britain dominated the global economy, tariffs were the principal obstacle to trade, and U.S. supremacy was uncontested in virtually all industries. In the intervening decades, economic circumstances have shifted radically. U.S. trade policy has not.

Today America's trade policy seems frozen by intellectual and political inflexibility, paralyzed by the relentless conflict between proponents of "free" and "fair" trade. The free traders argue that American markets should be open, and the movement of goods and services across national borders unrestrained. The fair traders assert that access to American markets should be restricted until U.S. businesses are granted equal access to foreign markets. They contend that free trade is impossible as long as other nations erect barriers to U.S. exports.

Of course, both are correct: fair trade requires equal access and equal access leads to free trade. The problem is that both sides base their positions on the same two long-held and now outdated premises:

1. Global commerce is conducted under the terms of the General Agreement on Tariffs and Trade (GATT) and dominated by the United States and similar economic systems abroad.

2. Multilateral negotiations are the most effective way to resolve pressing trade issues.

Both assumptions are wrong. The 40-year-old GATT now covers less than 7% of global commerce and financial flows. More important, world trade is no longer dominated by the free-trade economies. Today, nearly 75% of all world commerce is conducted by economic systems operating with principles at odds with those of the United States.

The loss of dominance by the free-trade economies must bring a dramatic shift in the overall goal of U.S. trade policy. The United States has long operated on the premise that a multilateral world requires multilateral negotiations. But reliance on multilateral negotiations has become a risky proposition at best. The bulk of U.S. trade negotiating efforts over the past four decades has taken place in multilateral talks under the auspices of the GATT (see sidebar, "A Look at the GATT" on page R26). Indeed, U.S. policymakers have mistaken the GATT negotiation process for an end in itself. Making the GATT work has become an American trade objective. But as the number of GATT signatories has more than quadrupled from 23 countries in 1948 to 94 today, the task of forging a multilateral trade policy consensus has become virtually impossible.

The new players—all with their own trade objectives and most with economic systems unlike Uncle Sam's—are often reluctant to engage in substantive multilateral trade negotiations. When nations finally do confer, moreover, new rules come slowly: the Tokyo Round of trade talks began in 1973 and did not end until 1979.

While multilateral talks drag on, the United States misses opportunities for international economic cooperation and trade expansion. The new reality is that a multilateral world requires more options, both inside and outside the GATT, than multilateral negotiations provide.

Of course, a new trade strategy alone will not ensure U.S. success in the fast-paced, competitive global marketplace of this century and the next. The economic future of the United States depends on two linked economic agendas: one internal, the other external.

The internal agenda would focus on the competitiveness of American industry—on creating an economic environment in which business, workers, and unions can combine to turn out products that are competitive in price, quality, service, innovation, and marketing. This agenda would require changes in macroeconomic and microeconomic policies: reducing the federal budget deficit, lowering the cost of capital, reducing pressures for quick results and short-term earnings, rebuilding the public infrastructure, commercializing new technologies, and upgrading the competence of American workers.

The external agenda would focus on expanding trade. That agenda demands a more practical, less ideological national trade strategy. Its first requisite is a pragmatic approach for dealing with foreign economic systems and competitive practices that are often vastly different from those of the United States. Its second is a negotiating strategy that will give America the means and flexibility to expand commerce with other nations by dealing with them as they are, rather than as we wish they were.

Five Competing Economic Systems

America's involvement in the global economy has passed through two distinct periods: a development era during which the United States sought industrial self-sufficiency in the eighteenth and nineteenth centuries, and a free-trade era in the early- and middle-twentieth century during which open trade was linked

A Look at the GATT

The General Agreement on Tariffs and Trade (GATT) is the principal multilateral agreement covering world trade. Its purpose is to foster unrestricted multilateral trade by binding participating nations to negotiate trade rules and by mandating penalties for any deviation from these obligations. In June 1987, 94 nations were contracting parties to the GATT, which is administered by a secretariat of 350 headquartered in Geneva. Its budget for 1987 is SFr 61,122,300—approximately $40 million. The GATT has many fundamental flaws, most of which can be traced to its origins.

Immediately following World War II, the United States championed the creation of a global economic system which rested on the World Bank, the International Monetary Fund (IMF), and the International Trade Organization (ITO). The ITO was to be a supranational organization that would deal with global trade in its entirety—imports, exports, adjustment, employment, and differing economic practices. The United States envisioned an ITO with substantial powers, much like the IMF, to confront nations that refused to eliminate trade-distorting barriers and practices.

Beginning in 1946, 23 nations began negotiating a charter for the ITO. As part of a larger effort, these nations also began multilateral negotiations in the summer of 1947 to reduce tariffs. It was anticipated that this agreement would be folded into the ITO. The tariff treaty was completed in January of 1948 and the participating nations became signatories to the GATT. By the end of 1948, the negotiators for the 23 participating nations completed the ITO charter, later called the Havana Charter, and referred it for the approval of their governments.

The ratification of the ITO, however, became embroiled in American politics and was rejected by the Congress. The residual was the GATT "interim" agreement. By default, therefore, the GATT became the principal multilateral agreement on global trade.

As a tariff accord, the GATT was fine. As the

with prosperity. Now America has entered a third, more dangerous era—an age of global economic interdependence.

Today, as most business leaders will readily attest, everything is globalized. Finance. Technology. Research and product development. Customer service. Capital and investment flows. Production facilities. Distribution networks. Marketing.

With surprising swiftness, the United States has shifted from relative economic self-sufficiency to global interdependence. In 1960, trade accounted for only 10 percent of the country's GNP. By the mid-1980s, that figure had more than doubled. American farmers now sell 30 percent of their grain production overseas; 40 percent of U.S. farmland is devoted to crops for export. In fact, more U.S. farmland is used to feed the Japanese than Japanese farmland. American industry exports more than 20 percent of its manufacturing output, and one out of every six manufacturing jobs depends on foreign sales. Within the U.S. market, more than 70 percent of American industry now faces stiff foreign competition.

foundation for global trade, it is fundamentally flawed. Specifically, GATT coverage was limited to merchandise trade and tariffs. Because it was a contractual agreement, enforcement depended on the voluntary arbitration of disagreements between signatories.

To remedy these deficiencies, the United States has led other nations in six additional GATT negotiations—in 1949, 1951, 1956, 1960–62, 1962–67, and 1973–79. The eighth and most recent series of negotiations, the Uruguay Round, was begun in 1986. Most striking about these negotiations is that the time lag between each has grown, while succeeding negotiations take longer to conclude. If the past is a guide to the future, the Uruguay Round will not be completed until the mid-1990s.

Now as in the past, the GATT has four principal limitations. First, it neither recognizes nor bridges the vast differences between the world's five economic systems. Rather, the basic goal of the GATT is to advance free trade and open markets through the reduction of market-retarding obstacles.

Second, GATT coverage is limited. The GATT covers roughly 80% of world trade in merchandise. However, trade in services, agriculture, textiles, and investment and capital flows are presently excluded. Consequently, the GATT only covers 5% to 7% of global economic activity.

Third, the GATT dispute-settlement mechanisms are ambiguous, slow, and unenforceable. For example, the United States pleaded unsuccessfully for 12 years for the European Community (EC) to reduce its import barriers to American citrus. In 1982, the United States took the issue to the GATT; in 1985, a GATT panel found in favor of the United States; the EC ignored these findings, precipitating a minor trade war. This example is so common that most nations are unwilling to involve the GATT in trade disputes.

Finally, and as a direct result of its other weaknesses, the GATT's low credibility limits its capacity to correct the global trade system's weaknesses. Furthermore, its existence hampers the creation of alternatives. Indeed, GATT's inability to change has made the agreement not merely an obstacle, but a threat to expanded world trade.

But while the economy has been changing its course and business leaders adjusting their practices, American trade policies remain locked in the past. U.S. trade policy still rests on three pillars:

1. Open markets and free trade are the most efficient means to expand global trade and, therefore, should form the economic model that guides world commerce.
2. Multilateral negotiations are the best means to open markets and promote free trade.
3. The United States has a primary responsibility among nations to advance free trade.

There is, however, a fundamental flaw in this thinking: other nations' economies are not like the United States' economy, nor will they be, nor should they be. Other countries compete in the world marketplace using vastly different assumptions, serving vastly different ends than America's. Economic systems differ in ways both manifest and subtle, reflecting basic differences in history, culture, national aspirations, and politics.

Five types of economic systems confront the United States. Four of them are not founded on our free-trade economic model: centrally planned (like the Soviet Union); mixed (France); developing (Mexico); and plan-driven (Japan). Only the Anglo-American system is rooted in a free- and fair-trade approach.

Within this framework, there are, of course, variations. The mixed economy of France differs in many ways from the mixed economy of Sweden; Japan's version of a plan-driven system differs from South Korea's plan-driven economy; and even between America and Canada there are clear distinctions. Yet each model possesses characteristics that are important to the design of future U.S. trade policies. It is possible, for example, to sketch the differences among the five systems by comparing them along four dimensions: the role of government in the economy; the ownership of industry; the relationship between process and results in the system; and how trade is conducted.

In the rule-driven, market-oriented Anglo-American economic model, for instance, government sets the economic backdrop but takes few direct positions on which industries should exist, grow, or decline. In contrast, plan-driven economies, like Japan's, and mixed economies, like Sweden's, skillfully blend the strength of government with the flexibility of the marketplace. Once decisions are made, government backs them with resources and, at strategic moments, with trade protection.

In free-market and plan-driven economies, private ownership of business and industry is the rule. The mixed economies, like France's, are based on a combination of state and private ownership, market and nonmarket decisions. Major industries are either owned by the state or tightly regulated. The major enterprises in the centrally planned economies, of course, are state owned.

The Anglo-American economies are process oriented; once rules are established, market processes dominate. The plan-driven economies are results oriented; business and government shape a national "vision" that often includes targeting certain industries like semiconductors or computers. To guide the economy toward desired results, governments of plan-driven economies will provide special financing, encourage joint research, and offer adjustment assistance like worker retraining. The mixed economies rely on a combination of market processes and government planning. The command economies are dominated by state planning.

The process-oriented Anglo-American economies are heavily influenced by economists and lawyers who make, interpret, and enforce the rules under which market processes operate. Because the plan-driven economies are results oriented, they have far less need for lawyers and economists to make and enforce rules. As recently as the mid-1970s, Japan's huge Ministry of International Trade and Industry had only two Ph.D. economists. Instead, politicians and business leaders direct the results-oriented economies. In trade talks, therefore, U.S. and Japanese trade negotiators often have different orientations: the Americans focus on rules that will facilitate market processes while the Japanese focus on measures that can advance their national economic vision.

Negotiations are handled differently in the different systems as well. In the Anglo-American economies, trade is conducted mainly by business. In the mixed and planned economies, trade often involves negotiations with both business and government. In the centrally managed economies, the government alone conducts trade.

Even the vocabulary of trade is dramatically different; in centrally managed economies, the concept of trade liberalization means increasing the number of government agencies that can negotiate their own trade arrangements. Under Mikhail Gorbachev's program of *glasnost,* for example, the Soviet Union's Ministry of Foreign Trade must share its monopoly over trade negotiations with 21 other ministries and 72 state enterprises, each of which can now make its own trade deals. But even under trade liberalization, in all cases trade is still with the state.

In fashioning their economic systems, the developing nations have borrowed from each of the other four systems, patching together combinations of public and private sector initiatives. In virtually all these countries, however, government predominates in designing and implementing a national trade strategy.

American policymakers, devoted to free trade and open markets, have ignored the often vast differences between U.S. and foreign economic systems. Rather, they still operate on the free-trade premise that policies that are neutral to the fate of American industries will produce the same market-oriented benefits globally as they do domestically. Consequently, American trade policies are doing enormous harm to U.S. industry.

Even where there is ample evidence of harm—as in the case of consumer electronics—industries have been unable to get relief from predatory foreign practices like dumping, theft of American intellectual property, foreign regulation that forces U.S. companies to move plants and jobs offshore as a condition of market entry, and nontariff barriers that restrict exports of America's most competitive goods and services. Free-trade advocates have exacerbated the problem of gaining legitimate relief by discrediting reciprocal market access as a negotiating strategy. And they mistakenly brand tough negotiating tactics as protectionism.

Multilateral negotiations via the GATT have been unable to bridge the differences among the world's five economic systems. If we continue to depend on these agreements, the United States must resign itself to failure: we will effect no major changes in the global trade system by the end of the 1980s. And by then the cumulative U.S. trade deficit for the decade is likely to exceed $1 trillion.

Despite America's spirited urging of other nations to adopt the U.S. economic model—reliance on market forces, free trade, and deregulation—this system has enjoyed little appeal abroad. It suits us, but it would never fit many other nations—and they know it. Consequently, U.S. trade policy is at a crossroads: we can either continue to urge other nations to adopt our free-trade economic model or we can change U.S. trade policy to deal with other nations as they are, rather than as we wish they would be.

Clearly, only the second course makes sense. It is pure folly for us to presume that we can somehow convince other nations to abandon economic systems that serve their interests and adopt a system that serves ours. Nor can we blindly continue to look the other way. America can no longer afford its missionary work on behalf of global free trade. When the United States had huge trade surpluses and was the world's largest creditor, we could afford to give other nations special trade concessions as a means of inducing them to become free traders. But now that the United States has chalked up an unprecedented $400 billion in indebtedness and faces unprecedented trade deficits far into the future, a "beggar thyself" policy to help our neighbors is impractical. We need a new U.S. trade strategy.

Shifting to Tailored Trade

To meet the challenges of global competition, the United States must have trade-sensitive fiscal, monetary, and exchange-rate policies. And the government must vigorously enforce domestic trade laws. But while these actions are necessary, by themselves they are not sufficient to reverse America's trade losses. Beyond sound macroeconomic policies and the production of fully competitive goods and services, America also requires results-oriented trade policies to:

- Deal effectively with foreign economic systems and competitive practices that are quite different from its own.
- Resolve trade disputes in a timely manner.
- Address trade comprehensively—imports, exports, investment, and competitive practices.

There is a recent benchmark for such a strategy: the newly negotiated U.S.–Canadian bilateral trade pact. This agreement—a strong sign that the otherwise arthritic U.S. trade strategy may have some flexibility—has produced a sweeping change in the trade arrangements between the world's two largest trading partners. It created a framework and time schedule for eliminating tariff and nontariff trade barriers between them. Moreover, the U.S.–Canada talks were completed in less than 16 months, breakneck speed for trade negotiations. And they were comprehensive, covering imports, exports, and investment.

At the same time that the two nations established a larger framework for their bilateral trade, they addressed and partially resolved several thorny micro issues, such as the 1965 Automotive Products Trade Agreement and Canadian restrictions on U.S. investment. Finally, and perhaps most important, the agreement established a powerful and quick dispute-settlement mechanism, based on arbitration panels composed of experts.

The U.S.–Canadian trade negotiations illustrate what bilateral arrangements can produce. Because U.S. trade policymakers have been fixated on a multilateral strategy, other trade expansion possibilities have been regulated to a secondary status, constrained in scope, or used as a placebo for powerful U.S. interests. The recent Market-Oriented Sectoral Specific (MOSS) negotiations with Japan, for example, concentrated on a narrow range of goods and services, like easing restrictions on U.S. lawyers practicing in Japan.

Bilateral arrangements have their limitations, of course. They would expand trade, for example, but only between the participating countries. Moreover, a system of global trade based exclusively on bilateral or "plurilateral" (involving several nations with mutual interests) relations could easily create so much fragmentation and discrimination that net global trade would be reduced.

When carefully drawn, however, bilateral or plurilateral arrangements can also facilitate the expansion of trade. Such arrangements are quite common; most other nations conclude them as a matter of course. As the U.S.–Canadian agreement illustrates, these agreements have great potential for expanding U.S. trade.

A tailored-trade approach would elevate bilateral and plurilateral negotiations from a secondary to a primary role. This would enable American representatives to match the negotiations to the economic system with which we were negotiating. For example, talks would draw free-trade arrangements with free-trade economies, managed-trade agreements with managed-trade economies, and appropriately tailored, mixed agreements with those economic systems in between. At the same time, there are some crosscutting issues, such as improved protection of intellectual property rights, that need to be negotiated across the five economic systems in either a plurilateral or multilateral forum (see Table 1).

A tailored-trade approach would be pursued through a parallel negotiation strategy using governmental structures and holding concurrent discussions with any nation willing to join in. The United States would, in effect, announce that its door is open to all countries ready to bargain. A parallel approach in which talks can proceed bilaterally, plurilaterally, or multilaterally gives the United States the flexibility to negotiate with cooperative trading partners, even if some nations refuse to participate. The momentum created by parallel negotiations represents a formidable incentive for uncooperative nations to end their delaying tactics and participate in trade talks. Very simply, those nations that participate earn the benefits (see Table 2).

The major benefit, of course, is access to the U.S. market. Ironically, the massive trade deficit that compels the United States to reform its trade policies also generates enormous negotiating leverage; America is the largest market for dozens of nations. The threat to close U.S. markets to nations unwilling to open

TABLE 1   Non-Anglo-American systems account for 73% of world trade . . .
(in millions of current U.S. dollars)

Economic System	Total Value	Percent of World Trade
Anglo-American	1,062,759	27
Centrally Planned	464,439	12
Developing	575,957	15
Mixed	1,297,263	33
Plan-Driven	527,957	13
Total	3,927,987	100

Source: Calculated from merchandise trade data in the World Bank's *World Development Report 1986* (New York City: Oxford University Press, 1987) and the CIA's *Handbook of Economic Statistics 1986* (Washington, D.C.: Central Intelligence Agency, 1986).

their markets to American goods, services, and investment is the best—perhaps the only—negotiating chip the United States possesses. Any meaningful, self-interested U.S. trade policy must use this tool to expand market access for nations that do negotiate trade expansion agreements and limit market access for nations that do not.

TABLE 2   . . . and 67% of world GNP
(in billions of current U.S. dollars)

Economic System	Total Value	Percent of World GNP
Anglo-American	4,384.1	33
Centrally Planned	1,857.4	24
Developing	2,524.5	14
Mixed	1,310.5	19
Plan-Driven	4,384.1	10
Total	113,179.9	100

Source: Calculated from data in the U.S. Arms Control and Disarmament Agency's *World Military Expenditures and Arms Transfers 1985* (Washington, D.C.: ACDA Publication 123, 1985) and the CIA's *Handbook of Economic Statistics 1986.*

To be sure, America must not succumb to the lure of old-fashioned protectionism: there will always be those who would rather erect barriers to foreign goods and services than improve their own ability to compete. At the same time, U.S. policymakers must be sophisticated enough to discern the difference between closing U.S. markets to avoid foreign competition and threatening to close them as a device to open foreign markets. The former shrinks trade, the latter expands it. Our national interests lie with expanded trade. But in a more complex world of competing economic systems, a sophisticated negotiating strategy must recognize that the path to our ultimate goal is rarely straight. In fact, sometimes it may even appear to point in the opposite direction, away from expanded trade, as a way of finally reaching the desired destination.

Top priority should go to the most pressing trade issues. Almost two-thirds of the U.S. trade deficit in recent years has been with Canada, Japan, South Korea, Taiwan, and Germany. It is only common sense that we seek bilateral negotiations with these countries. Rather than wait for cumbersome multilateral talks to grind forward, the United States should quickly seek direct negotiations aimed at reducing current imbalances. The Canadian pact shows that this approach will work. And it should show the other countries that agreement has benefits.

While the goal of a tailored-trade strategy will always remain the same—to expand trade—the focus and negotiating tactics will vary from one economic system to the next. The primary focus of tailored-trade negotiations with free-trade economies, for instance, is to open markets. These negotiations seek to eliminate obstacles that impede market transactions: tariffs, subsidies, nontariff barriers, and performance requirements, for example. By improving the market processes in the free-trade economies, trade can be expanded between these nations.

Tailored-trade negotiations with the plan-directed economies, such as Japan's, would be results oriented, concentrating on outcomes, timetables, and responsibilities. These talks would focus on a wide array of issues including levels of permissible trade imbalances, the composition of trade, allowable market shares, investment in both countries, and practices like dumping in third markets.

Negotiation with the plan-driven market economies, particularly Japan, South Korea, and Taiwan, is essential because those nations are both the most secure U.S. allies in the Pacific and among the principal sources of U.S. trade deficits. They are also America's main economic competitors and popular models for the economic policies of other nations. Together they represent the second-largest market in the world. American companies cannot hope to compete successfully in the global marketplace if they cannot penetrate these plan-driven markets while rival companies based within those countries continue to enjoy unrestricted access to the American market.

Tailored-trade agreements with the mixed economies will focus on a combination of market-opening processes and results-oriented outcomes. These negotiations are timely since many of the European countries have become increasingly nationalistic, retarding foreign investment and imports to shield their domestic markets and champion companies. Indeed, the largest of these economies, the Federal Republic of Germany, has shrunk from either engaging in GATT negotiations or helping the United States give macroeconomic stimulus to the global economy. Using the carrot and the stick of the U.S. market, we can remind the Germans that they share responsibility for world economic growth.

Tailored-trade talks with the command economies will attempt to establish managed-trade arrangements. While trade with the command economies offers many theoretical possibilities, there are formidable obstacles. For more than a decade, American companies have looked at the People's Republic of China as a tremendous market. But U.S. companies that invest in China have no protection except their contracts. U.S. sales to the Soviet Union are limited by Soviet insistence that foreign companies take all or partial payment through countertrade, such as exchanging capital goods for oil and gas. To gain foreign currency, the command economies often dump their products on world markets, thereby undercutting competitive U.S. companies. Before trade with the managed economies can expand much, these and dozens of other critical issues must be resolved.

Tailored-trade agreements with developing nations would involve a combination of market-opening processes, results-oriented arrangements, and managed trade. This reflects the mix of economic systems, often within one nation, used by the developing countries. Of these negotiations, the most important are with Mexico, a nation deeply mired in debt, economic stagnation, and fast population growth.

Tailored-trade agreements need to be supplemented by negotiations on crosscutting issues, problems that are part of the current global economy regardless of economic system. Counterfeiting, for instance, concerns several advanced industrial nations, including Britain, Japan, and Sweden, each of which operates with a different system. Another worry is the burgeoning number of offset requirements—arrangements that vary in complexity from barter requirements to complicated coproduction and technology transfer requirements. Plurilateral negotiations are best for addressing such issues.

If there is a future for the GATT, it is as a second-tier forum in which to resolve issues like these. There will always be problems of definition—what constitutes a government subsidy, for example—which can be tossed to the GATT to handle. But the United States ought not to deceive itself about the future role of the GATT or the best way to represent America's interests in the global economy. A tailored-trade strategy can give America the means and flexibility to expand commerce with other nations by bridging economic differences and making U.S. trade policy far less ideological and far more practical.

READING 4   THE LOGIC OF GLOBAL BUSINESS: AN INTERVIEW WITH ABB'S PERCY BARNEVIK

William Taylor

ABSTRACT.   Percy Barnevik, president and CEO of ABB Asea Brown Boveri, is a corporate pioneer. He is moving more aggressively than any CEO in Europe, perhaps in the world, to build the new model of competitive enterprise—an organization that combines global scale and world-class technology with deep roots in local markets. He is working to give substance to the endlessly invoked corporate mantra, "Think global, act local."

Headquartered in Zurich, ABB is a young company forged through the merger of two venerable European companies. Asea, created in 1890, has been a flagship of Swedish industry for a century. Brown Boveri, which took shape in 1891, holds a comparable industrial status in Switzerland. In August 1987, Barnevik altered the course of both companies when he announced that Asea, where he was managing director, would merge with Brown Boveri to create a potent new force in the European market for electrical systems and equipment.

The creation of ABB became a metaphor for the changing economic map of Europe. Barnevik initiated a wrenching process of consolidation and rationalization—layoffs, plant closings, product exchanges between countries—that observers agreed will one day come to European industries from steel to telecommunications to automobiles. And soon more than a metaphor, Barnevik's bold moves triggered a wholesale restructuring of the Continent's electrical power industry.

The creation of ABB also turned out to be the first step in a trans-Atlantic journey of acquisition, restructuring, and growth. ABB has acquired or taken minority positions in 60 companies representing investments worth $3.6 billion—including two major acquisitions in North America. In 1989, ABB acquired Westinghouse's transmission and distribution operation in a transaction involving 25 factories and businesses with revenues of $1 billion. That same year, it spent $1.6 billion to acquire Combustion Engineering, the manufacturer of power-generation and process-automation equipment.

Today ABB generates annual revenues of more than $25 billion and employs 240,000 people around the world. It is well balanced on both sides of the Atlantic. Europe accounts for more than 60% of its total revenues, and its business is split roughly equally between the European Community countries and the non-EC Scandinavian trading bloc. Germany, ABB's largest national market, accounts for 15% of total revenues. The company also generates annual revenues of $7 billion in North America, with 40,000 employees. Although ABB remains underrepresented in Asia, which accounts for only 15% of total revenues, it is an important target for expansion and investment. And ABB's business activities are not limited to the industrialized world. The company has 10,000 employees in India, 10,000 in South America, and is one of the most active Western investors in Eastern Europe.

In this interview, Percy Barnevik, 49, offers a detailed guide to the theory and practice of building a "multidomestic" enterprise. He explains ABB's matrix system, a structure designed to leverage core technologies and global economies of scale without eroding local market presence and responsiveness (see the sidebar "The Organizing Logic of ABB" on page R38.) He describes a new breed of "global managers" and explains how their skills differ from those of traditional managers. He reckons candidly with the political implications of companies such as ABB.

The interview was conducted at ABB's Zurich headquarters by Harvard Business Review associate editor William Taylor.

HBR: Companies everywhere are trying to become global, and everyone agrees that ABB is more global than most companies. What does that mean?
Percy Barnevik: *ABB is a company with no geographic center,* no national ax to grind. We are a federation of national companies with a global coordination center. Are we a Swiss company? Our headquarters is in Zurich, but only 100 professionals work at headquarters and we will not increase that number. Are we a Swedish company? I'm the CEO, and I was born and educated in Sweden. But our headquarters is not in Sweden, and only two of the eight members of our board of directors are Swedes. Perhaps we are an American company. We report our financial results in U.S. dollars, and English is ABB's official language. We conduct all high-level meetings in English.

My point is that ABB is none of those things—and all of those things. We are not homeless. We are a company with many homes.

Are all businesses becoming global?
No, and this is a big source of misunderstanding. We are in the process of building this federation of national companies, a multidomestic organization, as I prefer to call it. That does not mean all of our businesses are global. We do a very good business in electrical installation and service in many countries. That business is superlocal. The geographic scope of our installation business in, say, Stuttgart does not extend beyond a ten-mile radius of downtown Stuttgart.

We also have businesses that are superglobal. There are not more than 15 combined-cycle power plants or more than 3 or 4 high-voltage DC stations sold in any one year around the world. Our competitors fight for nearly every contract—they battle us on technology, price, financing—and national borders are virtually meaningless. Every project requires our best people and best technology from around the world.

The vast majority of our businesses—and of most businesses—fall somewhere between the superlocal and the superglobal. These are the businesses in which building a multidomestic organization offers powerful advantages. You want to be able to optimize a business globally—to specialize in the production of components, to drive economies of scale as far as you can, to rotate managers and technologists around the world to share expertise and solve problems. But you also want to have deep local roots everywhere you operate—building products in the countries where you sell them, recruiting the best local talent from the universities, working with the local government to increase exports. If you build such an organization, you create a business advantage that's damn difficult to copy.

What is a business that demonstrates that advantage?

Transportation is a good one. This is a vibrant business for us, and we consider ourselves number one in the world. We generate $2 billion a year in revenues when you include all of our activities: locomotives, subway cars, suburban trains, trolleys, and the electrical and signaling systems that support them. We are strong because we are the only multidomestic player in the world.

First, we know what core technologies we have to master, and we draw on research from labs across Europe and the world. Being a technology leader in locomotives means being a leader in power electronics, mechanical design, even communications software. Ten years ago, Asea beat General Electric on a big Amtrak order for locomotives on the Metroliner between New York and Washington. That win caused quite a stir; it was the first time in one hundred years that an American railroad bought locomotives from outside the United States. We won because we could run that track from Washington to New York, crooked and bad as it was, at 125 miles an hour. Asea had been pushing high-speed design concepts for more than a decade, and Brown Boveri pioneered the AC technology. That's why our X2 tilting trains are running in Sweden and why ABB will play a big role in the high-speed rail network scheduled to run throughout Europe.

Second, we structure our operations to push cross-border economies of scale. This is an especially big advantage in Europe, where the locomotive industry is hopelessly fragmented. There are two companies headquartered in the United States building locomotives for the U.S. market. There are three companies in Japan. There are 24 companies in Western Europe, and the industry runs at less than 75 percent of capacity. There are European companies still making only 10 or 20 locomotives a year! How can they compete with us, when we have factories doing ten times their volume and specializing in components for locomotives across the Continent? For example, one of our new plants makes power electronics for many of the locomotives we sell in Europe. That specialization creates huge cost and quality advantages. We work to rationalize and specialize as much as we can across borders.

Third, we recognize the limits to specialization. We can't ignore borders altogether. We recently won a $420-million order from the Swiss Federal Railways—we call it the "order of the century"—to build locomotives that will move freight through the Alps. If we expect to win those orders, we had *better* be a Swiss company. We had better understand the depth of the Swiss concern for the environment, which explains the willingness to invest so heavily to get freight moving on trains through the mountains to Italy or Germany and off polluting trucks. We had better understand the Alpine terrain and what it takes to build engines powerful enough to haul heavy loads. We had better understand the effects of drastic temperature changes on sensitive electronics and build locomotives robust enough to keep working when they go from the frigid, dry outdoors to extreme heat and humidity inside the tunnels.

There are other advantages to a multidomestic presence. India needs loco-

The Organizing Logic of ABB

ABB Asea Brown Boveri is a global organization of staggering business diversity. Yet its organizing principles are stark in their simplicity. Along one dimension, the company is a distributed global network. Executives around the world make decisions on product strategy and performance without regard for national borders. Along a second dimension, it is a collection of traditionally organized national companies, each serving its home market as effectively as possible. ABB's global matrix holds the two dimensions together.

At the top of the company sit CEO Percy Barnevik and 12 colleagues on the executive committee. The group, which meets every three weeks, is responsible for ABB's global strategy and performance. The executive committee consists of Swedes, Swiss, Germans, and Americans. Several members of the executive committee are based outside Zurich, and their meetings are held around the world.

Reporting to the executive committee are leaders of the 50 or so business areas (BAs), located worldwide, into which the company's products and services are divided. The BAs are grouped into eight business segments, for which different members of the executive committee are responsible. For example, the "industry" segment, which sells components, systems, and software to automate industrial processes, has five BAs, including metallurgy, drives, and process engineering. The BA leaders report to Gerhard Schulmeyer, a German member of the executive committee who works out of Stamford, Connecticut.

Each BA has a leader responsible for optimizing the business on a global basis. The BA leader devises and champions a global strategy, holds factories around the world to cost and quality standards, allocates export markets to each factory, and shares expertise by rotating people

motives—thousands of locomotives—and the government expects its suppliers to manufacture most of them inside India. But the Indians also need soft credit to pay for what is imported. Who has more soft credit than the Germans and the Italians? So we have to be a German and an Italian company, we have to be able to build locomotive components there as well as in Switzerland, Sweden, and Austria, since our presence may persuade Bonn and Rome to assist with financing.

We test the borderlines all the time: How far can we push cross-border specialization and scale economies? How effectively can we translate our multi-domestic presence into competitive advantages in third markets?

Is there such a thing as a global manager?

Yes, but we don't have many. One of ABB's biggest priorities is to create more of them; it is a crucial bottleneck for us. On the other hand, a global company does not need thousands of global managers. We need maybe 500 or so out of 15,000 managers to make ABB work well—not more. I have no interest in making managers more "global" than they have to be. We can't have people

across borders, creating mixed-nationality teams to solve problems, and building a culture of trust and communication. The BA leader for power transformers, who is responsible for 25 factories in 16 countries, is a Swede who works out of Mannheim, Germany. The BA leader for instrumentation is British. The BA leader for electric metering is an American based in North Carolina.

Alongside the BA structure sits a country structure. ABB's operations in the developed world are organized as national enterprises with presidents, balance sheets, income statements, and career ladders. In Germany, for example, Asea Brown Boveri Aktiengesellschaft, ABB's national company, employs 36,000 people and generates annual revenues of more than $4 billion. The managing director of ABB Germany, Eberhard von Koerber, plays a role comparable with that of a traditional German CEO. He reports to a supervisory board whose members include German bank representatives and trade union officials. His company produces financial statements comparable with those from any other German company and participates fully in the German apprenticeship program.

The BA structure meets the national structure at the level of ABB's member companies. Percy Barnevik advocates strict decentralization. Wherever possible, ABB creates separate companies to do the work of the 50 business areas in different countries. For example, ABB does not merely sell industrial robots in Norway. Norway has an ABB robotics company charged with manufacturing robots, selling to and servicing domestic customers, and exporting to markets allocated by the BA leader.

There are 1,100 such local companies around the world. Their presidents report to two bosses—the BA leader, who is usually located outside the country, and the president of the national company of which the local company is a subsidiary. At this intersection, ABB's "multidomestic" structure becomes a reality.

abdicating their nationalities, saying, "I am no longer German, I am international." The world doesn't work like that. If you are selling products and services in Germany, you better be German!

That said, we do need a core group of global managers at the top: on our executive committee, on the teams running our business areas (BAs), in other key positions. How are they different? Global managers have exceptionally open minds. They respect how different countries do things, and they have the imagination to appreciate why they do them that way. But they are also incisive, they push the limits of the culture. Global managers don't passively accept it when someone says, "You can't do that in Italy or Spain because of the unions," or "You can't do that in Japan because of the Ministry of Finance." They sort through the debris of cultural excuses and find opportunities to innovate.

Global managers are also generous and patient. They can handle the frustrations of language barriers. As I mentioned earlier, English is the official language of ABB. Every manager with a global role *must* be fluent in English, and anyone with regional management responsibilities must be competent in English. When I write letters to ABB colleagues in Sweden, I write them in

English. It may seem silly for one Swede to write to another in English, but who knows who will need to see that letter a year from now?

We are adamant about the language requirement—and it creates problems. Only 30 percent of our managers speak English as their first language, so there is great potential for misunderstanding, for misjudging people, for mistaking facility with English for intelligence or knowledge. I'm as guilty as anyone. I was rushing through an airport last year and had to return a phone call from one of our managers in Germany. His English wasn't good, and he was speaking slowly and tentatively. I was in a hurry, and finally I insisted, "Can't you speak any faster?" There was complete silence. It was a dumb thing for me to say. Things like that happen every day in this company. Global managers minimize those problems and work to eliminate them.

Where do these new managers come from?

Global managers are made, not born. This is not a natural process. We are herd animals. We like people who are like us. But there are many things you can do. Obviously, you rotate people around the world. There is no substitute for line experience in three or four countries to create a global perspective. You also encourage people to work in mixed-nationality teams. You *force* them to create personal alliances across borders, which means that sometimes you interfere in hiring decisions.

This is why we put so much emphasis on teams in the business areas. If you have 50 business areas and five managers on each BA team, that's 250 people from different parts of the world—people who meet regularly in different places, bring their national perspectives to bear on tough problems, and begin to understand how things are done elsewhere. I experience this every three weeks in our executive committee. When we sit together as Germans, Swiss, Americans, and Swedes, with many of us living, working, and traveling in different places, the insights can be remarkable. But you have to force people into these situations. Mixing nationalities doesn't just happen.

You also have to acknowledge cultural differences without becoming paralyzed by them. We've done some surveys, as have lots of other companies, and we find interesting differences in perception. For example, a Swede may think a Swiss is not completely frank and open, that he doesn't know exactly where he stands. That is a cultural phenomenon. Swiss culture shuns disagreement. A Swiss might say, "Let's come back to that point later, let me review it with my colleagues." A Swede would prefer to confront the issue directly. How do we undo hundreds of years of upbringing and education? We don't, and we shouldn't try to. But we do need to broaden understanding.

Is your goal to develop an "ABB way" of managing that cuts across cultural differences?

Yes and no. Naturally, as CEO, I set the tone for the company's management style. With my Anglo-Saxon education and Swedish upbringing, I have a certain way of doing things. Someone recently asked if my ultimate goal is to create 5,000 little Percy Barneviks, one for each of our profit centers. I laughed for a moment when I thought of the horror of sitting on top of such an organization, then I realized it wasn't a silly question. And the answer is no. We can't have managers who are "un-French" managing in France because 95 percent of them are dealing every day with French customers, French colleagues, French suppliers. That's why global managers also need humility. A global manager respects a formal German manager—Herr Doktor and all that—because that manager may be an outstanding performer in the German context.

Let's talk about the structures of global business. How do you organize a multi-domestic enterprise?

ABB is an organization with three internal contradictions. We want to be global and local, big and small, radically decentralized with centralized reporting and control. If we resolve those contradictions, we create real organizational advantage.

That's where the matrix comes in. The matrix is the framework through which we organize our activities. It allows us to optimize our businesses globally *and* maximize performance in every country in which we operate. Some people resist it. They say the matrix is too rigid, too simplistic. But what choice do you have? To say you don't like a matrix is like saying you don't like factories or you don't like breathing. It's a fact of life. If you deny the formal matrix, you wind up with an informal one—and that's much harder to reckon with. As we learn to master the matrix, we get a truly multidomestic organization.

Can you walk us through how the matrix works?

Look at it first from the point of view of one business area, say, power transformers. The BA manager for power transformers happens to sit in Mannheim, Germany. His charter, however, is worldwide. He runs a business with 25 factories in 16 countries and global revenues of more than $1 billion. He has a small team around him of mixed nationalities—we don't expect superheroes to run our 50 BAs. Together with his colleagues, the BA manager establishes and monitors the trajectory of the business.

The BA leader is a business strategist and global optimizer. He decides which factories are going to make what products, what export markets each factory will serve, how the factories should pool their expertise and research funds for the benefit of the business worldwide. He also tracks talent—the 60 or 70 real standouts around the world. Say we need a plant manager for a new company in Thailand. The BA head should know of three or four people—maybe there's one at our plant in Muncie, Indiana, maybe there's one in Finland—who could help in Thailand. (See sidebar "Power Transformers—The Dynamics of Global Coordination" on page R42.)

It is possible to leave the organization right there, to optimize every business area without regard for ABB's broad collection of activities in specific countries.

Power Transformers—The Dynamics of Global Coordination

ABB is the world's leading manufacturer of power transformers, expensive products used in the transmission of electricity over long distances. The business generates annual revenues of $1 billion, nearly four times the revenues of its nearest competitor. More to the point, ABB's business is consistently and increasingly profitable—a real achievement in an industry that has experienced 15 years of moderate growth and intense price competition.

Power transformers are a case study in Percy Barnevik's approach to global management. Sune Karlsson, a vice president of ABB with a long record in the power transformer field, runs the business area (BA) from Mannheim, Germany. Production takes place in 25 factories in 16 countries. Each of these operations is organized as an independent company with its own president, budget, and balance sheet. Karlsson's job is to optimize the group's strategy and performance independent of national borders—to set the global rules of the game for ABB—while allowing local companies freedom to drive execution.

"We are not a global business," Karlsson says. "We are a collection of local businesses with intense global coordination. This makes us unique. We want our local companies to think small, to worry about their home market and a handful of export markets, and to learn to make money on smaller volumes."

Indeed, ABB has used its global production web to bring a new model of competition to the power transformer industry. Most of ABB's 25 factories are remarkably small by industry standards, with annual sales ranging from as little as $10 million to not more than $150 million, and 70 percent of their output serves their local markets. ABB transformer factories concentrate on slashing throughput times, maximizing design and production flexibility, and focusing tightly on the needs of domestic customers. In short, the company deploys the classic tools of flexible, time-based management in an industry that has traditionally competed on cost and volume.

As with many of its business areas, ABB built its worldwide presence in power transformers through a series of acquisitions. Thus one of Karlsson's jobs is to spread the new model of competition to the local companies ABB acquires.

"Most of the companies we acquired had volume problems, cost problems, quality problems," he says. "We have to convince local managers that they can run smaller operations more efficiently, meet customer needs more flexibly—and make money. Once you've done this ten or 15 times, in several countries, you become confident of the merits of the model."

Karlsson's approach to change is in keeping with the ABB philosophy: show local managers what's been achieved elsewhere, let them drive the change process, make available ABB expertise from around the world, and demand quick results. A turnaround for power transformers takes about 18 months.

In Germany, for example, one of the company's transformer plants had generated red ink for years. It is now a growing, profitable operation, albeit smaller and more focused than before. The work force has been slashed from 520 to 180, throughput time has been cut by one-third, work-in-process inventories have decreased by 80 percent. Annual revenues have fallen $70 million per year to a mere $50 million—but profits are up substantially. Today the German manager who championed this company's changes is in Muncie, Indiana, helping managers of a former Westinghouse plant acquired by ABB to reform their operation.

ABB's global scale also gives it clout with suppliers. The company buys up to $500 million of materials each year—an enormous presence that gives it leverage on price, quality, and delivery schedules. Karlsson has made strategic purchasing a priority. ABB expects zero-defect suppliers, just-in-time deliveries, and price increases lower than 75 percent of inflation—major advantages that it is in a position to win with intelligent coordination.

Sune Karlsson believes these and other "hard" advantages may be less significant, however, than the "soft" advantages of global coordination. "Our most important strength is that we have 25 factories around the world, each with its own president, design manager, marketing manager, and production manager," he says. "These people are working on the same problems and opportunities day after day, year after year, and learning a tremendous amount. We want to create a process of continuous expertise transfer. If we do, that's a source of advantage none of our rivals can match."

Creating these soft advantages requires internal competition and coordination. Every month, the Mannheim headquarters distributes detailed information on how each of the 25 factories is performing on critical parameters, such as failure rates, throughput times, inventories as a percentage of revenues, and receivables as a percentage of revenues. These reports generate competition for outstanding performance within the ABB network—more intense pressure, Karlsson believes, than external competition in the marketplace.

The key, of course, is that this internal competition be constructive, not destructive. Since the creation of ABB, one of Sune Karlsson's most important jobs has been to build a culture of trust and exchange among ABB's power transformer operations around the world and to create forums that facilitate the process of exchange. At least three such forums exist today:

1. The BA's management board resembles the executive committee of an independent company. Karlsson chairs the group, and its members include the presidents of the largest power transformer companies—people from the United States, Canada, Sweden, Norway, Germany, and Brazil. The board meets four to six times a year and shapes the BA's global strategy, monitors performance, and resolves big problems.

2. Karlsson's BA staff in Mannheim is not "staff" in the traditional sense—young professionals rotating through headquarters on their way to a line job. Rather, it is made up of five veteran managers each with worldwide responsibility for activities in critical areas such as purchasing and R&D. They travel constantly, meet with the presidents and top managers of the local companies, and drive the coordination agenda forward.

3. Functional coordination teams meet once or twice a year to exchange information on the details of implementation in production, quality, marketing, and other areas. The teams include managers with functional responsibilities in all the local companies, so they come from around the world. These formal gatherings are important, Karlsson argues, but the real value comes in creating informal exchange throughout the year. The system works when the quality manager in Sweden feels compelled to telephone or fax the quality manager in Brazil with a problem or an idea.

"Sharing expertise does not happen automatically," Karlsson emphasizes. "It takes trust, it takes familiarity. People need to spend time together, to get to know and understand each other. People must also see a payoff for themselves. I never expect our operations to coordinate unless all sides get real benefits. We have to demonstrate that sharing pays—that contributing one idea gets you 24 in return."

—William Taylor

But think about what we lose. We have a power transformer company in Norway that employs 400 people. It builds transformers for the Norwegian market and exports to markets allocated by the BA. But ABB Norway has more than 10,000 other employees in the country. There are tremendous benefits if power transformers coordinates its Norwegian operation with our operations in power generation, switchgear, and process automation: recruiting top people from the universities, building an efficient distribution and service network across product lines, circulating good people among the local companies, maintaining productive relations with top government officials.

So we have a Norwegian company, ABB Norway, with a Norwegian CEO and a headquarters in Oslo, to make these connections. The CEO has the same responsibilities as the CEO of a local Norwegian company for labor negotiations, bank relationships, and high-level contacts with customers. This is no label or gimmick. We *must* be a Norwegian company to work effectively in many businesses. Norway's oil operations in the North Sea are a matter of great national importance and intense national pride. The government wouldn't—and shouldn't—trust some faraway foreign company as a key supplier to those operations.

The opportunities for synergy are clear. So is the potential for tension between the business area structure and the country structure. Can't the matrix pull itself apart?
BA managers, country managers, and presidents of the local companies have very different jobs. They must understand their roles and appreciate that they are *complementing* each other, not competing.

The BA managers are crucial people. They need a strong hand in crafting strategy, evaluating performance around the world, and working with teams made up of different nationalities. We've had to replace some of them—people who lacked vision or cultural sensitivity or the ability to lead without being dictators. You see, BA managers don't own the people working in any business area around the world. They can't order the president of a local company to fire someone or to use a particular strategy in union negotiations. On the other hand, BA managers can't let their role degrade into a statistical coordinator or scorekeeper. There's a natural tendency for this to happen. BA managers don't have a constituency of thousands of direct reports in the same way that country managers do. So it's a difficult balancing act.

Country managers play a different role. They are regional line managers, the equivalent of the CEO of a local company. But country managers must also respect ABB's global objectives. The president of, say, ABB Portugal can't tell the BA manager for low-voltage switchgear or drives to stay out of his hair. He has to cooperate with the BA managers to evaluate and improve what's happening in Portugal in those businesses. He should be able to tell a BA manager, "You may think the plant in Portugal is up to standards, but you're being too loose. Turnover and absenteeism is twice the Portuguese average. There are problems with the union, and it's the managers' fault."

Now, the presidents of our local companies—ABB Transformers in Denmark, say, or ABB Drives in Greece—need a different set of skills. They must be excellent profit center managers. But they must also be able to answer to two bosses effectively. After all, they have two sets of responsibilities. They have a global boss, the BA manager, who creates the rules of the game by which they run their businesses. They also have their country boss, to whom they report in the local setting. I don't want to make too much of this. In all of Germany, where we have 36,000 people, only 50 or so managers have two bosses. But these managers have to handle that ambiguity. They must have the self-confidence not to become paralyzed if they receive conflicting signals and the integrity not to play one boss off against the other.

Isn't all this much easier said than done?
It does require a huge mental change, especially for country managers. Remember, we've built ABB through acquisitions and restructurings. Thirty of the companies we've bought had been around for more than 100 years. Many of them were industry leaders in their countries, national monuments. Now they've got BA managers playing a big role in the direction of their operations. We have to convince country managers that they benefit by being part of this federation, that they gain more than they lose when they give up some autonomy.

What's an example?
Finland has been one of our most spectacular success stories, precisely because the Finns understood how much they could gain. In 1986, Asea acquired Strömberg, the Finnish power and electrical products company. At the time, Strömberg made an unbelievable assortment of products, probably half of what ABB makes today. It built generators, transformers, drives, circuit breakers—all of them for the Finnish market, many of them for export. It was a classic example of a big company in a small country that survived because of a protected market. Not surprisingly, much of what it made was not up to world-class standards, and the company was not very profitable. How can you expect a country with half the population of New Jersey to be profitable in everything from hydropower to circuit breakers?

Strömberg is no longer a stand-alone company. It is part of ABB's global matrix. The company still exists—there is a president of ABB Strömberg—but its charter is different. It is no longer the center of the world for every product it sells. It still manufactures and services many products for the Finnish market. It also sells certain products to allocated markets outside Finland. And it is ABB's worldwide center of excellence for one important group of products, electric drives, in which it had a long history of technology leadership and effective manufacturing.

Strömberg is a hell of a lot stronger because of this. Its total exports from Finland have increased more than 50 percent in three years. ABB Strömberg has become one of the most profitable companies in the whole ABB group, with a return on capital employed of around 30 percent. It is a recognized world leader in drives. Strömberg produces more than 35 percent of all the drives ABB sells, and drives are a billion-dollar business. In four years, Strömberg's exports to Germany and France have increased ten times. Why? Because the company has access to a distribution network it never could have built itself.

This sounds enormously complicated, almost unmanageable. How does the organization avoid getting lost in the complexity?

The only way to structure a complex, global organization is to make it as simple and local as possible. ABB is complicated from where I sit. But on the ground, where the real work gets done, all of our operations must function as closely as possible to stand-alone operations. Our managers need well-defined sets of responsibilities, clear accountability, and maximum degrees of freedom to execute. I don't expect most of our people to have "global mindsets," to do things that hurt their business but are "good for ABB." That's not natural.

Take Strömberg and drives in France. I don't want the drive company president in Finland to think about what's good for France. I want him to think about Finland, about how to sell the hell out of the export markets he has been allocated. Likewise, I don't expect our profit center manager in France to think about Finland. I expect him to do what makes sense for his French customers. If our French salespeople find higher quality drives or more cost-effective drives outside ABB, they are free to sell them in France so long as ABB gets a right of first refusal. Finland has increased its shipments to France because it makes economic sense for both sides. That's the only way to operate.

But how can an organization with 240,000 people all over the world be simple and local?

ABB *is* a huge enterprise. But the work of most of our people is organized in small units with P&L responsibility and meaningful autonomy. Our operations are divided into nearly 1,200 companies with an average of 200 employees. These companies are divided into 4,500 profit centers with an average of 50 employees.

We are fervent believers in decentralization. When we structure local operations, we always push to create separate legal entities. Separate companies allow you to create *real* balance sheets with *real* responsibility for cash flow and dividends. With real balance sheets, managers inherit results from year to year through changes in equity. Separate companies also create more effective tools to recruit and motivate managers. People can aspire to meaningful career ladders in companies small enough to understand and be committed to.

What does that mean for the role of headquarters?

We operate as lean as humanly possible. It's no accident that there are only 100 people at ABB headquarters in Zurich. The closer we get to top management, the tougher we have to be with head count. I believe you can go into any traditionally centralized corporation and cut its headquarters staff by 90 percent in one year. You spin off 30 percent of the staff into freestanding service centers that perform real work—treasury functions, legal services—and charge for it. You decentralize 30 percent of the staff—human resources, for example—by pushing them into the line organization. Then 30 percent disappears through head count reductions.

These are not hypothetical calculations. We bought Combustion Engineering in late 1989. I told the Americans that they had to go from 600 people to 100 in their Stamford, Connecticut headquarters. They didn't believe it was possible. So I told them to go to Finland and take a look. When we bought Strömberg, there were 880 people in headquarters. Today there are 25. I told them to go to Mannheim and take a look at the German operation. In 1988, right after the creation of ABB, there were 1,600 people in headquarters. Today there are 100.

Doesn't such radical decentralization threaten the very advantages that ABB's size creates?

Those are the contradictions again—being simultaneously big and small, decentralized and centralized. To do that, you need a structure at the top that facilitates quick decision making and carefully monitors developments around the world. That's the role of our executive committee. The 13 members of the executive committee are collectively responsible for ABB. But each of us also has responsibility for a business segment, a region, some administrative functions, or more than one of these. Eberhard von Koerber, who is a member of the executive committee located in Mannheim, is responsible for Germany, Austria, Italy, and Eastern Europe. He is also responsible for a worldwide business area, installation materials, and some corporate staff functions. Gerhard Schulmeyer sits in the United States and is responsible for North America. He is also responsible for our global "industry" segment.

Naturally, these 13 executives are busy, stretched people. But think about what happens when we meet every three weeks, which we do for a full day. Sitting in one room are the senior managers collectively responsible for ABB's global strategy and performance. These same managers individually monitor business segments, countries, and staff functions. So when we make a decision—snap, it's covered. The members of the executive committee communicate to their direct reports, the BA managers and the country managers, and the implementation process is under way.

We also have the glue of transparent, centralized reporting through a management information system called Abacus. Every month, Abacus collects performance data on our 4,500 profit centers and compares performance with budgets and forecasts. The data are collected in local currencies but translated into U.S. dollars to allow for analysis across borders. The system also allows you to work with the data. You can aggregate and disaggregate results by business segments, countries, and companies within countries.

What kind of information does the executive committee use to support the fast decision making you need?

We look for early signs that businesses are becoming more or less healthy. On the tenth of every month, for example, I get a binder with information on about 500 different operations—the 50 business areas, all the major countries, and the key companies in key countries. I look at several parameters—new orders, invoicing, margins, cash flows—around the world and in various business segments. Then I stop to study trends that catch my eye.

Let's say the industry segment is behind budget. I look to see which of the five BAs in the segment are behind. I see that process automation is way off. So I look by country and learn that the problem is in the United States and that it's poor margins, not weak revenues. So the answer is obvious—a price war has broken out. That doesn't mean I start giving orders. But I want to have informed dialogues with the appropriate executives.

Let's go back to basics. How do you begin building this kind of global organization?

ABB has grown largely through mergers and strategic investments. For most companies in Europe, this is the right way to cross borders. There is such massive overcapacity in so many European industries and so few companies with the critical mass to hold their own against Japanese and U.S. competitors. My former company, Asea, did fine in the 1980s. Revenues in 1987 were four times greater than in 1980, profits were ten times greater, and our market value was 20 times greater. But the handwriting was on the wall. The European electrical industry was crowded with 20 national competitors. There was up to 50 percent overcapacity, high costs, and little cross-border trade. Half the companies were losing money. The creation of ABB started a painful—but long overdue—process of restructuring.

That same restructuring process will come to other industries: automobiles, telecommunications, steel. But it will come slowly. There have been plenty of articles in the last few years about all the cross-border mergers in Europe. In fact, the more interesting issue is why there have been so *few.* There should be *hundreds* of them, involving *tens of billions* of dollars, in industry after industry. But we're not seeing it. What we're seeing instead are strategic alliances and minority investments. Companies buy 15 percent of each other's shares. Or two rivals agree to cooperate in third markets but not merge their home-market organizations. I worry that many European alliances are poor substitutes for doing what we try to do—complete mergers and cross-border rationalization.

What are the obstacles to such cross-border restructuring?

One obstacle is political. When we decided on the merger between Asea and Brown Boveri, we had no choice but to do it secretly and to do it quickly, with our eyes open about discovering skeletons in the closet. There were no lawyers, no auditors, no environmental investigations, and no due diligence. Sure, we tried to value assets as best we could. But then we had to make the move, with an extremely thin legal document, because we were absolutely convinced of the strategic merits. In fact, the documents from the premerger negotiations are locked away in a Swiss bank and won't be released for 20 years.

Why the secrecy? Think of Sweden. Its industrial jewel, Asea—a 100 year-old company that had built much of the country's infrastructure—was moving its headquarters out of Sweden. The unions were angry: "Decisions will be made in Zurich, we have no influence in Zurich, there is no codetermination in Switzerland."

I remember when we called the press conference in Stockholm on August 10. The news came as a complete surprise. Some journalists didn't even bother to attend; they figured it was an announcement about a new plant in Norway or something. Then came the shock, the fait accompli. That started a communications war of a few weeks where we had to win over shareholders, the public, governments, and unions. But strict confidentiality was our only choice.

Are there obstacles besides politics?

Absolutely. The more powerful the strategic logic behind a merger—the greater the cross-border synergies—the more powerful the human and organizational obstacles. It's hard to tell a competent country manager in Athens or Amsterdam, "You've done a good job for 15 years, but unfortunately this other manager has done a better job and our only choice is to appoint your colleague to run the operation." If you have two plants in the same country running well but you need only one after the merger, it's tough to explain that to employees in the plant to be closed. Restructuring operations creates lots of pain and heartache, so many companies choose not to begin the process, to avoid the pain.

Germany is a case in point. Brown Boveri had operated in Germany for almost 90 years. Its German operation was so big—it had more than 35,000 employees—that there were rivalries with the Swiss parent. BBC Germany was a technology-driven, low-profit organization—a real underperformer. The formation of ABB created the opportunity to tackle problems that had festered for decades.

So what did you do?

We sent in Eberhard von Koerber to lead the effort. He made no secret of our plans. We had to reduce the work force by 10 percent, or 4,000 employees. We had to break up the headquarters, which had grown so big because of all the tensions with Switzerland. We had to rationalize the production overlaps, especially between Switzerland and Germany. We needed lots of new managers, eager people who wanted to be leaders and grow in the business.

The reaction was intense. Von Koerber faced strikes, demonstrations, barricades—real confrontation with the unions. He would turn on the television set and see protesters chanting, "Von Koerber out! Von Koerber out!" After a while, once the unions understood the game plan, the loud protests disappeared and our relationship became very constructive. The silent resistance from managers was more formidable. In fact, much of the union resistance was fed by management. Once the unions got on board, they became allies in our effort to reform management and rationalize operations.

Three years later, the results are in. ABB Germany is a well-structured, dynamic, market-oriented company. Profits are increasing steeply, in line with ABB targets. In 1987, BBC Germany generated revenues of $4 billion. ABB Germany will generate twice that by the end of next year. Three years ago, the management structure in Mannheim was centralized and functional, with few clear responsibilities or accountability. Today there are 30 German companies, each with its own president, manufacturing director, and so on. We can see who the outstanding performers are and apply their talents elsewhere. If we need someone to sort out a problem with circuit breakers in Spain, we know who from Germany can help.

What lessons can other companies learn from the German experience?
To make real change in cross-border mergers, you have to be factual, quick, and neutral. And you have to move boldly. You must avoid the "investigation trap"—you can't postpone tough decisions by studying them to death. You can't permit a "honeymoon" of small changes over a year or two. A long series of small changes just prolongs the pain. Finally, you have to accept a fair share of mistakes. I tell my people that if we make 100 decisions and 70 turn out to be right, that's good enough. I'd rather be roughly right and fast than exactly right and slow. We apply these principles everywhere we go, including in Eastern Europe, where we now have several change programs under way. (See the sidebar "Change Comes to Poland—The Case of ABB Zamech.")

Why emphasize speed at the expense of precision? Because the costs of delay are vastly greater than the costs of an occasional mistake. I won't deny that it was absolutely crazy around here for the first few months after the merger. We *had* to get the matrix in place—we couldn't debate it—and we *had* to figure out which plants would close and which would stay open. We took ten of our best people, the superstars, and gave them six weeks to design the restructuring. We called it the Manhattan Project. I personally interviewed 400 people, virtually day and night, to help select and motivate the people to run our local companies.

Once you've put the global pieces together and have the matrix concept working, what other problems do you have to wrestle with?
Communications. I have no illusions about how hard it is to communicate clearly and quickly to tens of thousands of people around the world. ABB has about 15,000 middle managers prowling around markets all over the world. If we in the executive committee could connect with all of them or even half of them and get them moving in roughly the same direction, we would be unstoppable.

But it's enormously difficult. Last year, for example, we made a big push to squeeze our accounts receivable and free up working capital. We called it the

Change Comes to Poland—The Case of ABB Zamech

L ast May, Zamech, Poland's leading manufacturer of steam turbines, transmission gears, marine equipment, and metal castings began a new life as ABB Zamech—a joint venture of ABB (76 percent ownership), the Polish government (19 percent ownership), and the company's employees (5 percent ownership). ABB Zamech employs 4,300 people in the town of Elblag, outside Gdansk. In September, two more Polish joint ventures became official—ABB Dolmel and Dolmel Drives. These companies manufacture a wide range of generating equipment and electric drives and employ some 2,400 workers.

The joint ventures are noteworthy for their size alone. ABB has become the largest Western investor in Poland. But they are perhaps more significant for their managerial implications, in particular, how ABB is revitalizing these deeply troubled operations. The company intends to demonstrate that the philosophy of business and managerial reform it has applied in places like Mannheim, Germany and Muncie, Indiana can also work in the troubled economies of Eastern Europe. That philosophy has at least four core principles:

1. Immediately reorganize operations into profit centers with well-defined budgets, strict performance targets, and clear lines of authority and accountability.

2. Identify a core group of change agents from local management, give small teams responsibility for championing high-priority programs, and closely monitor results.

3. Transfer ABB expertise from around the world to support the change process, without interfering with it or running it directly.

4. Keep standards high and demand quick results.

Barbara Kux, president of ABB Power Ventures, negotiated the Polish joint ventures and plays a lead role in the turnaround process. "Our goal is to make these companies as productive and profitable as ABB's operations worldwide," she says. "We don't make a 'discount' for Eastern Europe, and we don't expect the change process to take forever. We provide more technical and managerial support than we might to a company in the United States, but we are just as demanding in terms of results."

ABB Zamech has come the furthest to date. The change program began immediately after the creation of the joint venture. For decades, the company had been organized along functional lines, a structure that blurred managerial authority, confused product-line profitability, and slowed decision making. Within four weeks, ABB Zamech was reorganized into discrete profit centers. There are now three business areas (BAs)—the casting foundry, turbines and gears, and marine equipment—as well as a finance and administration department and an in-house service department. Each area has a leadership team that generates the business plans, budgets, and performance targets by which their operations are judged. These teams made final decisions on which employees would stay, which would go, what equipment they would need—tough-minded business choices made for the first time so as to maximize productivity (employee and capital) and business area profitability.

The reorganization was a crucial first step. The second big step was installing ABB's standard finance and control system. For decades, Zamech had been run as a giant overhead machine. Roughly 80 percent of the company's total costs were allocated by central staff accountants rather than traced directly to specific products and services. Managers had no clear idea what their products cost to make and thus no idea which ones made money. Tight financial controls and maximum capital productivity are critical in an economy with interest rates of 40 percent.

Formal reorganization and new control systems, no matter how radical, won't have much of an effect without big changes in who is in charge, however. ABB made two important decisions. First, there would be no "rescue team" from Western Europe. All managerial positions, from the CEO down, would be held by Polish managers from the former Zamech. Second, managers would be selected without regard to rank or seniority; indeed, there would be a premium on young, creative talent. ABB was looking for "hungry wolves"—smart, ambitious change agents who would receive intense training and be the core engine of Zamech's revival.

Most of the new leaders came from the ranks of middle management. The company's top executive, general manager Pawel Olechnowicz, ran the steel castings department prior to the joint venture's creation—a position that put him several layers below the top of the 15-layer management hierarchy. Employees had already elected him general manager shortly before the creation of ABB Zamech, so he looked like a good choice. The marine BA leader had been a production manager in the old Zamech, another low-level position, and the turbines and gears BA manager had been a technical director.

"We put in place a management team that lacked the standard business tools," Kux explains. "They didn't know what cash flow was, they didn't understand much about marketing. But their ambition was incredible. You could feel their hunger to excel. When we began the talent search, we told our Zamech contacts that we wanted to see the 30 people they would take along tomorrow if they were going to open their own business."

Next came the process of developing a detailed agenda for reform. The leadership team settled on 11 priority issues, from reorganizing and retraining the sales force to slashing total cycle times and redesigning the factory layout. Each project was led by a champion—some from top management ranks, some from the other "hungry wolves." A steering committee made up of the general manager, the deputy general manager, the business area managers, and Kux meets monthly to review these critical projects.

To support the change initiatives, ABB created a team of high-level experts from around the world—authorities in functional areas like finance and control and quality, as well as technology specialists and managers with heavy restructuring experience. Team members do not live in Poland. Kux says it is unrealistic to expect top people to spend a year or two in the conditions they would find in Elblag. But they visit frequently and stay updated on progress and problems.

The logistics of expertise transfer are more complicated than they sound. For example, most of the Polish managers spoke little or no Eng-

Cash Race. There are 2,000 people around the world with some role in accounts receivable, so we had to mobilize them to make the program work. Three or four months after the program started—and we made it very visible when it started—I visited an accounts receivable office where 20 people were working. These people hadn't even *heard* of the program, and it should have been their top priority. When you come face-to-face with this lack of communication, this massive inertia, you can get horrified, depressed, almost desperate. Or you can

lish—a serious barrier to effective dialogue. So ABB began intensive language training. "If Polish managers want to draw from the worldwide ABB resource pool, they *must* speak English," Kux emphasizes. "Most communication doesn't happen face-to-face where you can have an interpreter. Last May, I couldn't simply pick up the phone and talk to the general manager. Today we speak in English on the phone almost every day."

Of course, speaking on the telephone in English assumes a working telephone system—a dangerous assumption in the case of Poland. Thus another prerequisite for effective expertise transfer was creating the infrastructure to make it possible. ABB has linked Zamech and Dolmel by satellite to its Zurich headquarters for reliable telephone and fax communications. (It is now easier to communicate between Zamech and Zurich and Dolmel and Zurich than it is between Zamech and Dolmel.) In January, ABB Zamech began electronically transferring three monthly performance reports to Zurich—another big step to make communications more intensive and effective.

Once it created the communications infrastructure, however, ABB had to reckon with a second language barrier—the language of business. To introduce ABB Zamech's "hungry wolves" to basic business concepts and to enable them to transfer these concepts into the ranks, ABB created a "mini MBA program" in Warsaw. The program began in September, covers five key modules (business strategy, marketing, finance, manufacturing, human resources) and is taught by faculty members of INSEAD, the French business school. Sessions run from Thursday evening through Saturday noon, use translated copies of Western business school cases, and closely resemble what goes on in MBA classes everywhere else.

The change program at ABB Zamech has been under way for less than a year, and much remains to be done. But it is already generating results. The company is issuing monthly financial reports that conform to ABB standards—a major achievement in light of the simple systems in place before the joint venture. Cycle times for the production of steam turbines have been cut in half and now meet the ABB worldwide average. A task force is implementing the plan to reduce factory space by 20%—an important step in streamlining the operation. ABB will draw on the Zamech experience as it begins the reform process at Dolmel and Dolmel Drives.

"You *can* change these companies," Kux says. "You *can* make them more competitive and profitable. I can't believe the quality of the reports and presentations these people do today, how at ease they are discussing their strategy and targets. I have worked with many corporate restructurings, but never have I seen so much change so quickly. The energy is incredible. These people really want to learn; they are very ambitious. Basically, ABB Zamech is their business now."

William Taylor

---

concede that this is the way things are, this is how the world works, and commit to doing something about it.

So what do you do?

You don't inform, you *overinform*. That means breaking taboos. There is a strong tendency among European managers to be selective about sharing information.

We faced a huge communications challenge right after the merger. In

January 1988, just days after the birth of ABB, we had a management meeting in Cannes with the top 300 people in the company. At that meeting, we presented our policy bible, a 21-page book that communicates the essential principles by which we run the company. It's no glossy brochure. It's got tough, direct language on the role of BA managers, the role of country managers, the approach to change we just discussed, our commitment to decentralization and strict accountability. I told this group of 300 that they had to reach 30,000 ABB people around the world within 60 days—and that didn't mean just sending out the document. It meant translating it into the local languages, sitting with people for a full day and hashing it out.

Cannes and its aftermath was a small step. Real communication takes time, and top managers must be willing to make the investment. We are the "overhead company." I personally have 2,000 overhead slides and interact with 5,000 people a year in big and small groups. This afternoon, I'll fly up to Lake Constance in Germany, where we have collected 35 managers from around the world. They've been there for three days, and I'll spend three hours with them to end their session. Half the executive committee has already been up there. These are active, working sessions. We talk about how we work in the matrix, how we develop people, about our programs around the world to cut cycle times and raise quality.

I'll give a talk at Lake Constance, but then we'll focus on problems. The manager running high-voltage switchgear in some country may be unhappy about the BA's research priorities. Someone may think we're paying too much attention to Poland. There are lots of tough questions, and my job is to answer on the spot. We'll have 14 such sessions during the course of the year—one every three weeks. That means 400 top managers from all over the world living in close quarters, really communicating about the business and their problems, and meeting with the CEO in an open, honest dialogue.

Let's discuss the politics of global business. For senior executives, the world becomes smaller every day. For most production workers, though, the world is not much different from the way it was 20 years ago, except now their families and communities may depend for jobs on companies with headquarters thousands of miles away. Why shouldn't these workers worry about the loss of local and national control? It's inevitable that a global business will have global decision centers and that for many workers these decision centers will not be located in their community or even their country. The question is, does the company making decisions have a national ax to grind? In our case the answer is no. We have global coordination, but we have no national bias. The 100 professionals who happen to sit in Zurich could just as easily sit in Chicago or Frankfurt. We're not here very much anyway. So what does it mean to have a headquarters in Zurich? It's where my mail arrives before the important letters are faxed to wherever I happen to be. It's where Abacus collects our performance data. Beyond that, I'm not sure if it means much at all.

Of course, saying we have no national ax to grind does not mean there are any guarantees. Workers will often ask if I can guarantee their jobs in Norway or Finland or Portugal. I don't sit like a godfather, allocating jobs. ABB has a global game plan, and the game plan creates opportunities for employment, research, exports. What I guarantee is that every member of the federation has a fair shot at the opportunities.

Let's say you're a production worker at ABB Combustion Engineering in Windsor, Connecticut. Two years ago, you worked for a company that you knew was an "American" company. Today you are part of a "federation" of ABB companies around the world. Should you be happy about that?

You should be happy as hell about it. A production worker in Windsor is probably in the boiler field. He or she doesn't much care what ABB is doing with process automation in Columbus, Ohio, let alone what we're doing with turbines outside Gdansk, Poland. And that's fair. Here's what I would tell that worker: we acquired Combustion Engineering because we believe ABB is a world leader in power plant technology, and we want to extend our lead. We believe that the United States has a great future in power plants both domestically and on an export basis. Combustion represents 80 years of excellence in this technology. Unfortunately, the company sank quite a bit during the 1980s, like many of its U.S. rivals, because of the steep downturn in the industry. It had become a severely weakened organization.

Today, however, the business is coming back, and we have a game plan for the United States. We plan to beef up the Windsor research center to three or four times its current size. We want to tie Windsor's work in new materials, emissions reduction, and pollution control technology with new technologies from our European labs. That will let us respond more effectively to the environmental concerns here. Then we want to combine Combustion's strengths in boilers with ABB's strengths in turbines and generators and Westinghouse's strengths in transmission and distribution to become a broad and unique supplier to the U.S. utility industry. We also have an ambition for Combustion to be much more active in world markets, not with sales agents but through the ABB multidomestic network.

What counts to this production worker is that we deliver, that we are increasing our market share in the United States, raising exports, doing more R&D. That's what makes an American worker's life more secure, not whether the company has its headquarters in the United States.

Don't companies like ABB represent the beginning of a power shift, a transfer of power away from national government to supranational companies?

Are we above governments? No. We answer to governments. We obey the laws in every country in which we operate, and we don't make the laws. However, we do change relations *between* countries. We function as a lubricant for worldwide economic integration.

Think back 15 years ago, when Asea was a Swedish electrical company with 95 percent of its engineers in Sweden. We could complain about high taxes, about how the high cost of living made it difficult to recruit Germans or Americans to come to Sweden. But what could Asea do about it? Not much. Today I can tell the Swedish authorities that they must create a more comprehensive environment for R&D or our research there will decline.

That adjustment process would happen regardless of the creation of ABB. Global companies speed up the adjustment. We don't create the process, but we push it. We make visible the invisible hand of global competition.

MANAGING FOREIGN EXCHANGE RISK PROFITABLY

Ike Mathur

ABSTRACT.   As foreign exchange markets have become increasingly volatile, the importance of the effective management of foreign exchange risk has also grown. This article reports the results of a survey of the foreign exchange practices of US companies.

A multinational firm in its normal, day to day conduct of business is susceptible to potential gains and losses due to changes in the values of its assets and liabilities denominated in foreign currencies. Exporting, importing, and investing abroad expose the firm to foreign exchange risks. Under the 1944 Bretton Woods Agreement, Central Bank interventions in foreign currency markets were frequent, with relatively minor changes in exchange rates. Managers then could afford to ignore foreign exchange exposure. With the demise of the Agreement in 1973, however, exchange rates for major currencies have fluctuated freely, sometimes wildly. Managing foreign exchange risks now constitutes one of the most difficult and persistent problems for financial managers of multinational firms.[*]

The primary goal in foreign exchange risk management is to shelter corporate profits from the negative impact of exchange rate fluctuations. The secondary goal is possibly to profit from exchange exposure management. At a minimum, managing foreign exchange risks implies making profits equal to those possible if the firm did not engage in foreign exchange transactions. Achieving this goal calls for both a corporate structure that fosters accurate assessments of foreign exchange risk exposure and the implementation of successful foreign exchange strategies.

Following a brief description of the foreign exchange system and its risks, this paper reports the results of a survey of the foreign exchange risk management practices of US firms. In particular, the survey examined the organizational and management policies, the forecasting procedures, and the specific foreign exchange techniques that US companies employ.

Foreign Exchange Risks

Diverse factors such as international trade, capital flows for investments, royalty payments, dividends, interest payments, and foreign currency loans contribute to the need for foreign currency transactions. Exchange rates among currencies should reflect the demand for and supply of the currencies. Many theories have

Source: Copyright 1982 *Columbia Journal of World Business* (Winter). Reprinted with permission.

[*] Throughout this paper, we will refer to one variable being related to another one. In all cases, correlation coefficients were computed and tested for statistical significance. All relationships between variables discussed here are statistically significant.

attempted to explain the mechanism that determines exchange rates. Although these theories differ regarding the forces influencing foreign exchange markets, they share one thing in common; they all imply that comparative values of currencies will change over time.

The importance of the foreign exchange (abbreviated as F. E.) market necessitates some system to regulate or oversee the comparative values of currencies. The Bretton Woods Agreement had this purpose. Under this agreement, central banks were expected to intervene in the foreign exchange markets to control moderate fluctuations in exchange rates. If disequilibriums appeared permanent, reflecting supply and demand, then exchange rates were adjusted. Because exchange rates were pegged in a parity band of one percent around par value, there was little change risk in foreign currency transactions. The lag between changes in market conditions and the adjustment of exchange rates made the system inefficient and allowed traders to speculate profitably against the central bankers. The inefficiency of the parity system ultimately led to the demise of the Agreement in 1973. Since then currencies have floated against each other in terms of their exchange rates. With floating exchange rates, currency values fluctuate daily in response to demand and supply.

Exchange risk can be divided into transaction risk and translation risk. When a domestic company buys or sells goods from or to a foreign company, the invoice may be denominated in a foreign currency. Between the date of the agreement and the date of payment, exchange rates may change. This risk is called transaction risk. In contrast, translation risk derives from attempts to value foreign subsidiaries in terms of the balance sheet currency of the parent (or domestic) company. At any point, the accounting value of a multinational corporation is the total value of both the parent firm and its affiliates and floating exchange rates cause changes in currency valuations that affect the reporting of balance sheet and income statement items.

In managing foreign exchange risks, managers can be either risk averters or risk takers. Risk averse managers seek to protect the returns of their primary business operations when engaging in foreign exchange transactions. These managers use risk aversion mechanisms, often called hedging, to eliminate uncertainty. In contrast, risk seekers engage in foreign exchange transactions to profit from their trading activities.

Research Methodology

The study examined the foreign exchange risk management practices of US firms engaged in international trade. A 45 item questionnaire was mailed to the vice presidents of finance of 300 companies. A two-stage sample selection process was utilized. First, a random sample of 300 firms was chosen from the Fortune 500 list of the US industrial firms. Next, *Dun and Bradstreet's Directory of International Companies* was consulted to determine whether it listed the firms selected. Unlisted firms in the *Directory* were replaced with other randomly selected Fortune 500 firms that were listed in the *Directory*.

Eighty-five questionnaires were returned. Sixteen of these were so incomplete that the data provided could not be effectively utilized. Of the remaining 69 responding firms, 14 had foreign sales that were less than 10 percent of their total sales. These firms were eliminated from the statistical sample, primarily to obtain more meaningful insights into the risk management practices of companies extensively engaged in international trade.

Total assets, as a measure of size, for the 55 firms used in the analysis ranged from $70 million to $22.1 billion. The median for total assets for the responding firms was $1.8 billion, while the corresponding median for the Fortune 500 companies generally is $752 million. More responses were received from larger firms than from smaller firms. To examine for possible bias due to size, correlation coefficients were computed between total assets and the remaining variables. Only three variables were found to correlate significantly with total assets. In general, larger firms manufactured or sold their products in more countries than smaller firms. The proportion of foreign sales also tended to be higher for larger than for smaller firms. Finally, larger firms, in general, had higher dollar amounts of foreign exchange transactions with foreign banks than smaller firms. None of these variables was considered crucial for the analyses of risk management practices.

One of the 55 responding firms manufactured or sold its products in 168 countries. On the other end of the scale, one dealt with only two countries. The mean for number of countries with manufacturing and sales operations was 25. Foreign sales as a percentage of total sales varied from 12 percent to 86 percent, with a mean of 31 percent.

Organizational Policies for Managing Foreign Exchange Risks

Written F. E. Policy The treasury functions in a corporation are important and generally complex. Some functions such as asset acquisitions and cash management are directly related to the firm's asset structure. Others such as long term financing and dividends are related to the claims structure. Managing the firm's foreign exchange risks straddles both sides of the balance sheet. Its functional importance calls for a written policy.

As Table 1 indicates, 37 of the 55 respondents had written policies for executing F. E. transactions. A statistically significant relationship existed between a written F. E. management policy and the relative size of foreign sales. Similarly, written policy correlated positively with total assets. This indicates that the more a firm relies on foreign revenues, the more emphasis it places on a written F. E. policy. Also, larger firms have a greater propensity for formalizing F. E. policy.

The survey results show that one-third of the respondents, generally the

TABLE **1** Organizational Policies for Foreign Exchange Transactions*

Item	Positive Number
1. Corporation has written F. E. management policy	37
2. Majority of F. E. transactions are executed at corporate headquarters	39
3. Firm uses reinvoicing center	5

* Total number of respondents = 55.

relatively smaller ones, do not have written F. E. policies. This result is surprising because responding firms are deriving at least ten percent of their revenues from abroad.

The principal advantage of a written F. E. policy is that strategies for risk management can be mapped out *prior* to generating the exposures. Written F. E. policies clarify the operating decisions to be made. At a minimum, firms should have written F. E. risk management policies that cover:

1. Capital structure and liquidity requirements.
2. Foreign exchange forecasting objectives.
3. Foreign exchange exposures due to transactions.
4. Foreign exchange exposures due to translations.
5. Off balance sheet exposures.
6. Reporting requirements for subsidiaries/divisions.
7. Lead and lag strategies.
8. Credit and collection policies.
9. Use of forward market contracts.
10. Use of interest arbitraging.

Centralization of F. E. Transactions Thirty-nine of the 55 firms executed a majority of their F. E. transactions at corporate headquarters. Although many factors such as product, market, and operating characteristics may call for decentralized decision making, centralized exposure management at the policy making strategy, or implementation levels has many benefits.

Policy making only at the headquarters level delegates responsibility for developing and implementing strategies to the operating level. As Table 2 points out, administrative costs are minimal. The operating unit need only report on

TABLE 2   Considerations in Centralizing F. E. Transactions

Degree of Centralization	Advantages	Disadvantages
Policy at HQ; strategy and implementation at operating unit.	Low administrative cost. Low reporting requirements.	External hedging mainly by operating unit. Interdivisional hedging absent.
Policy and strategy at HQ; implementation at operating unit.	Average administrative costs. Better utilization of internal and external hedging.	Average reporting requirements. Operating unit responsibilities become vague.
Policy, strategy, and implementation at HQ.	Full utilization of exposure management techniques.	High reporting requirements. Operational decisions separated from exposure management decisions. High administrative costs.

transactions. The disadvantages, however, are substantial. The operating unit can engage only in external hedging. Interdivisional netting cannot take place.

An intermediate step is to centralize policy and strategy making at headquarters, leaving implementation to operating units. External and internal hedging techniques can be better utilized because of the operating reports required of divisions. Managerial motivation at divisions, however, may be adversely affected because interdivisional netting and pricing will not produce focused pictures of divisional profitability and performance.

The firm can also centralize all three functions at headquarters. This allows the firm to utilize all available exposure management techniques fully. Administrative costs and reporting requirements, however, are high. Centralization affects certain operating decisions such as invoice currency, credit terms, and acquisitions of raw materials because they become part of exposure management decisions.

Reinvoicing Centers Some firms maintain reinvoicing, or autonomous, centralized data centers where "currency invoice" policies are executed. Interdivisional transactions and related exposure positions also can be netted out in reinvoicing centers. Only five of the 55 firms used reinvoicing centers as an exposure management technique (see Table 1). Use of reinvoicing centers was highly positively correlated with percentage of F. E. transactions involving covered interest arbitrage.

The basic strategy in reinvoicing is shown in Table 3. Reinvoicing can prevent a soft currency division from incurring debts in hard currency countries. By invoicing sales divisions in the local currencies, the parent company

TABLE **3**   Currency of Invoicing Strategy

Buyer in/ Seller in	Hard Currency	Soft Currency
Hard Currency	Invoice in buyer's currency	Invoice in buyer's currency or selected third currency
Soft Currency	Invoice in seller's currency	Negotiate third currency invoice

automatically centralizes exposure management. A side benefit of reinvoicing centers is improved tax liability and liquidity management.

F. E. Risk Management Policies

Translation losses affect the balance sheet and are accounting in nature. Transaction losses affect the firm's cash flows. F. E. risk management can focus on minimizing transaction losses, minimizing translation losses, or both. Minimizing transaction losses is not necessarily compatible with minimizing translation losses. For example, hedging operations designed to cover some translation losses cover only paper losses and carry transaction costs.

Fourteen of the 55 responding firms indicated that their corporate F. E. exposure management policy could be best characterized as minimizing F. E. transaction losses (see Table 4). Five firms indicated minimizing translation

TABLE **4**   F. E. Risk Management Policies

Item	Positive Number
1. Corporate F. E. risk management policy can be best characterized as	
a. minimize F. E. transaction losses	14
b. minimize F. E. translation losses	5
c. minimize both	32
d. other	4
2. F. E. management decisions are coordinated with corporate financial management policies related to	
a. capital structure considerations	49
b. cash dividends on common stock	35
c. liquidity management	49

losses, while 32 firms indicated minimizing both. The data also indicated that firms that emphasize minimizing F. E. transaction losses hedge a larger portion of their F. E. transactions with forward market contracts.

The survey results indicated that firms place considerable emphasis on managing translation exposure. A large portion of this emphasis on accounting exposure to risk was possibly related to providing a palatable appearance to financial statements under FASB No. 8. However, if one trusts the efficiency of capital markets in discounting financial information, then "dressing" the financial statements has no material impact on security prices. Perhaps managers should place greater emphasis on actual F. E. risk management rather than managing translation exposure.

Forecasting F. E. Risks

Use of F. E. forecasting depends on whether the firm's managers *believe* that exchange rates can be forecasted. Forty-three of the responding firms forecast their F. E. risk exposure; 12 did not (see Table 3). The managers' belief that exchange rates cannot be forecasted implies that exchange rates fluctuate randomly, or alternatively, that foreign exchange markets are efficient. If foreign exchange markets are efficient, reflecting all existing information, gains and losses from currency fluctuations will tend to offset each other. Hedging strategies will not be consistently effective and will reduce the firm's net cash flows. In this case, the best F. E. risk management strategy is to *not* try to *avoid* risk at all.

Thirty of the 43 firms that forecasted F. E. risk used commercially prepared economic forecasts in estimating the firm's F. E. risks. Thirty-two firms also reported using commercially prepared F. E. forecasts. In the majority of cases, forecasts were prepared on both accounting and cash flow bases. As Table 3 indicates, 38 of the firms were preparing forecasts on an accounting basis. Evidently, translation exposure is of major concern to most firms.

Forecasting can be of three types. The first type involves only a forecast of the direction of exchange rates. That is, only currency devaluations and revaluations are forecasted. The second type involves a forecast of the magnitude as well as the direction of exchange rate changes. This involves forecasting future rates. The third, and most difficult type, involves forecasting the direction, magnitude, and timing of exchange rate fluctuations. A third of the 43 forecasting firms employed only the first type of forecast. Two-thirds of the firms forecast the direction and the magnitude of exchange rate changes. Only one firm attempted the third type of forecast (see Table 5).

All firms forecasted on a currency by currency basis. There was no reliance on forecasting blocks of currencies, such as the European "Snake" or the Middle East "Arcru," as sufficient predictors of rate changes. Thus, firms seemingly desire more precise information so that specific conversion rates can be determined.

TABLE 5   Forecasting Foreign Exchange Risk*

Item	Positive Number
1. Firm forecasts its exposure to F. E. risk (n = 55)	43
2. Uses commercially prepared economic forecasts for forecasting F. E. risk exposure (n = 43)	30
3. Uses commercially prepared F. E. forecasts for forecasting F. E. risk exposure	32
4. F. E. forecasts are on a a. cash flow basis b. accounting basis c. both	5 10 28
5. What is forecasted: a. currency devaluations and revaluations b. future rates in major currencies c. future rates at specific times	14 28 1
6. Forecasts are on a currency by currency basis	43
7. Forecasts are prepared a. monthly b. quarterly	27 13
8. F. E. forecasting procedures used a. regression and trend analysis b. moving average c. subjective d. other	10 5 20 8

*All 55 responses were used for item 1. Twelve respondents did not forecast F. E. risk, and, therefore were excluded from tabulations on the remaining items. Responses to items 2–8 are based on n = 43.

Twenty-seven firms prepared forecasts on a monthly basis, while thirteen did so on a quarterly basis. Two firms reported preparing forecasts on a weekly basis while one reported preparing forecasts annually.

Respondents were asked to indicate the forecasting procedures they used. By far the most prevalent method involved a purely subjective analysis by managers. Twenty employed subjective procedures for forecasting. Regression and trend analysis was used by ten firms and moving averages by another five. Miscellaneous other methods were used by the remaining eight.

From these results it is apparent that, to a large extent, many multinational businesses do not use direct F. E. forecasting. The degree of specialization and sophistication required may necessitate purchase of F. E. information from the outside. Because corporate activity is conducted in monthly or quarterly time-frames, many of the multinational firms are not close enough to daily F. E. activities to warrant internal forecasting and analysis. Banking institutions are actively involved in this area to a much higher degree, and are relied upon as accurate sources of F. E. information.

The evidence on the accuracy of F. E. forecasting is inconclusive. Some studies have shown that F. E. rate changes can be forecasted, while a few studies suggest the contrary. In general, there is agreement on one point: the forecaster with the exclusive forecasting model stands a better chance of forecasting F. E. rate changes. The implication is that it behooves the firm to develop its own forecasting model.

Managing Foreign Exchange Risks for Profits: Strategies and Techniques

The growing importance of managing foreign exchange risk has led multinational firms to devote increasing attention to this topic. As indicated in the previous sections, multinational firms use a variety of organizational, management, and forecasting policies in managing this risk. Our survey indicates that a similar diversity characterizes the specific strategies and foreign exchange techniques that these firms have adopted.

Internal Hedging The most general term used to describe risk avoidance is hedging. Hedging can be defined as strategies pursued by a firm to manage, by elimination or offsetting, potential losses due to changes in the values of its assets and liabilities denominated in foreign currencies.

In a broader sense, hedging includes all actions that the firm takes with the intention of changing its foreign exchange risk exposure due to changes in the relative values of currencies. Hedging can be divided into two categories: internal and external. Internal hedging consists primarily of the shifting of goods or funds within the company to maintain favorable balance sheet positions.

Exposure netting is an internal hedging technique. A firm that has open positions in two or more currencies that balance each other does not need to engage in F. E. transactions in these currencies. Due to parallel movements in some currencies, a short position in one currency can offset a long position in a second.

The procedure of netting transactions between parents and subsidiaries, or between various subsidiaries, was very common with 67 percent and 71 percent of the firms engaging in these activities (see Table 6). Parent-subsidiary and subsidiary-subsidiary netting was highly correlated with leading and lagging intersubsidiary receivables and payables. A negative correlation existed between centralized policy execution and netting of intersubsidiary transfers.

TABLE **6**   Internal Hedging Techniques Utilized[*]

Item	Positive Number
1. Corporation nets currency transactions between:	
a. parent and subsidiaries	37
b. subsidiary and subsidiary	39
2. Following strategies utilized:	
a. speeding up or delaying dividend and fee remittance from subsidiary to parent	45
b. speeding up or delaying remittances from subsidiary to subsidiary	34
c. speeding up or delaying intersubsidiary accounts receivable and payable	38

[*] Total number of respondents = 55

Decentralized firms appear more apt to use subsidiary-subsidiary netting, while centralized firms lean towards parent-subsidiary netting. This behavior is consistent with the notion that centralized firms are in a better position to centralize F. E. exposures. Parent-subsidiary nettings, therefore, are better suited for centralized firms.

Speeding up or delaying dividend payments and fee remittances from subsidiary to parent was used by 82 percent of the responding firms. This variable was positively correlated with recognition of capital structure and dividend payments in F. E. risk management strategies. The evidence suggests that some internal hedging may be undertaken for cash flow rather than for exposure management purposes. Intersubsidiary speeding up or delaying remittances was utilized by 62 percent of the firms and was significantly correlated with intersubsidiary netting. Sixty-nine percent of the firms used speeding up or delaying intersubsidiary accounts receivable and payable as managerial strategies.

Use of internal hedging techniques depends on the extent to which a firm engages in foreign activities. A firm with large foreign sales or many manufacturing subsidiaries can better utilize internal hedging techniques. Table 7 shows hedging strategies for a subsidiary located in a hard currency area. The subsidiary would, for example, delay payments on accounts payable to subsidiaries located in soft currency areas.

External Hedging External hedging techniques generally involve contractual obligations and involvement of parties external to the firm. External hedging includes leading and lagging, adjusting collection and credit terms, currency

TABLE 7   Internal Hedging Strategies for Hard Currency Area Subsidiary

Delay dividend and fee remittances to parent.
Delay remittance to soft currency area subsidiaries.
Delay payments on accounts payable to soft currency area subsidiaries.
Speed up collections on accounts receivable from soft currency area subsidiaries.

loans and deposits, forward market contracts, export credit guarantees, back to back or parallel loans, and interest arbitraging.

Perhaps the simplest of hedging activities is the use of leads and lags. Leads and lags involves the timing of payments and collections in anticipation of changes in relative currency values. Leading and lagging is generally a function of market expectations. Factors influencing lead/lag decisions are trading positions (importing or exporting), relative domestic currency position (soft or hard), and the invoicing currency position. For example, an exporter from a hard currency country, invoicing in a relatively soft foreign currency, would prefer payment to lead.

Sixty-seven percent of the responding firms indicated that they utilized speeding up or delaying collections as a managerial strategy (see Table 8). This variable correlated with the firm's concerns for its capital structure and its dividend payments. This correlation indicates that managers recognize the impact of leads/lags on the firms' cash flows. Speeding up/delaying collections was also positively correlated with forecasting corporate F. E. risk on a currency by currency basis. This is not surprising because leads/lags involve anticipating

TABLE 8   External Hedging Techniques Utilized

Item	Positive Number
1. Speeding up or delaying collections	37
2. Tightening or relaxing credit terms	21
3. Invoicing exports and imports in either local or foreign currency	25
4. Increasing or decreasing local borrowing	49

market changes. Tightening or relaxing credit terms is another lead/lag strategy and was used by 38 percent of the responding firms.

The technique of invoicing in a desirable currency was used by only 46 percent of the firms. This suggests that barriers may limit more extensive use of this technique. The views of the corporations (buyer or seller) and their relative economic powers may constrain the use of favorable invoicing. Invoicing in local or foreign currency correlated positively with inability to convert local currency to dollars. Evidently, invoicing in a favorable currency has helped some firms in avoiding the problems associated with inconvertibility.

Increasing or decreasing local borrowing as a hedging technique was used by 49 of the 55 firms. This practice was negatively correlated with the firm's percentage of foreign sales. Firms that derived a larger percentage of their total sales from abroad were less apt to increase or decrease local borrowing as a hedging strategy. It appears that managers of internationally well-diversified firms feel that adjustments in local currency borrowings will not provide their firms with additional F. E. risk reduction.

Table 9 shows external hedging techniques that could be implemented by a hard currency area subsidiary. The hard currency area subsidiary selling in soft currency areas should be encouraged to relax credit terms for hard currency sales. Exports should be invoiced in the hard currency. The reverse strategies apply for subsidiaries located in soft currency areas.

Forward Market and Other Strategies When asked to indicate the percentage of annual total dollars invested abroad strictly as measures to limit exposure to F. E. risks, 39 firms replied zero percent. The average, though, was 5.5 percent (see Table 10). Most firms apparently make foreign investment decisions based on market and ROI considerations.

Back to back loans involve companies who "swap" loans with each other's subsidiaries. For example, the Germany subsidiary of an American company may borrow deutschmarks from a German company, whose American subsidiary

TABLE **9**   External Hedging Strategies for Hard Currency Area Subsidiary

Speed up collections of receivables in soft currency areas
Relax credit terms for hard currency sales in soft currency areas
Invoice exports in hard currency
Negotiate import invoices in soft currency
Reduce local borrowing
Increase local assets

TABLE **10**   Forward Market and Other Strategies

Item	Response
1. Percent of annual total dollar investments undertaken strictly to limit exposure to F. E. risks (average)	5.5
2. Percent of F. E. transactions covered by back to back swaps	2.3
3. Percent of F. E. transactions that include F. E. adjustment clauses (average)	4.9
4. Percent of foreign sales for most recent year covered by export credit guarantee (average)	7.1
5. Percent of F. E. transactions hedged with forward market contracts (average)	23.1
6. Percent of F. E. transactions involving a. covered interest arbitrage (average) b. uncovered interest arbitrage (average)	0.9 0.6

is lent funds by the American company. On average, swaps covered 2.3 percent of F. E. transactions. Forty-eight of the 55 firms reported no back to back loans. If only the seven firms reporting use of back to back loans are considered, this method accounts for 19 percent of their total dollar amount of F. E. transactions. Thus, the vast majority of firms involved with F. E. transactions do not use such loans, but the few firms using the procedure do so frequently.

Firms can limit their exposure to F. E. risks by including F. E. adjustment clauses in their contracts. Percent of F. E. transactions that included F. E. adjustment clauses ranged from zero percent (reported by 28 firms) to 80 percent with an average of 5 percent. This variable correlated very highly with the dollar amount of back to back swaps. The very nature of back to back loans makes it a natural for adjustment clauses.

On average, 7 percent of sales were covered by export credit guarantees. Sixty-five and one-half percent of the responding firms did not use credit guarantees for their international trading. Those that used credit guarantees did so on average in over 20 percent of transaction volume. Only two firms used credit guarantees for more than half of their transactions. Use of credit guarantees was highly correlated with frequency of occurrences of asset confiscation and nationalization. These two relationships indicate that sovereign risk leads corporate managers to use legal relationships and contracts as methods to manage risk. Use of export credit guarantees correlated negatively with variables such as corporate forecasting of F. E. risk and frequency of forecasts. Firms that rely on export credit guarantees have essentially limited their exposure to F. E. risks and, therefore, forecasting F. E. risk does not carry a high payoff for them.

A common hedging technique, forward exchange, showed a varied degree of usage among the 55 sampled firms. Although it was one of the most utilized methods for insuring against F. E. risk, forward exchange was used sparingly by most firms. The range of use spanned from zero percent (reported by ten firms) to 100 percent with the average being 23 percent. Use of forward markets was significantly correlated with execution level of F. E. management, indicating that centralized firms make greater use of forward exchange. Similarly, correlation results indicated that firms engaged in this form of hedging tend to pursue the objective of minimizing transaction losses. The implication is that the forward exchange is used as a hedge against international trading of goods, rather than as a hedge against changes in the dollar value of foreign investments.

The interesting aspect of forward exchange is that the number of countries within a firm's sphere of operations as well as the volume of its foreign sales affect the degree of hedging use. The survey showed negative correlations between use of forward exchange by a firm and the number of foreign countries in which it had operations and its foreign sales. As firms increase the benefits derived from international diversification, they apparently reduce their dependence on forward exchange for limiting exposure to F. E. risk. As firms become more diverse in their overseas activities, the gains and losses from the various arenas of operations tend to cancel each other, thereby obviating the need for extensive forward market hedging.

Arbitraging may be defined as taking advantage of significant differences in quoted bid and ask prices in foreign exchange markets. Arbitrage may be conducted in the spot or future exchange markets, or in a combination of the two. Interest arbitrage is the investment of short term funds in another currency for the purpose of gaining a higher yield, and it occurs because funds are attracted to the market that provides the highest returns net of interest, discounts, premiums, and covering costs. Typically, interest arbitrage is covered by a swap transaction of spot and forward exchange, with the spot funds invested at the existing interest rate.

A firm can engage in interest arbitrage by shifting funds from one foreign country to another. Interest arbitrage becomes possible when a firm receives a transfer of foreign funds, a transfer of credits, or when it can utilize domestic deposits of foreign currencies. Forty-seven of the 55 firms did not engage at all in covered interest arbitrage. Percent of F. E. transactions involving covered interest arbitraging had an average of 0.9 percent.

Uncovered interest arbitrage involves speculation. The firm will buy or sell currencies as a normal part of business transactions, and, due to market expectations, leave exposure positions unhedged, uncovered, or open. Forty-nine of the 55 firms did not engage in uncovered interest arbitrage. Five firms reported that five percent of their F. E. transactions involved uncovered interest arbitrage and one reported a figure of ten percent.

This result indicates a strong sense of risk aversion among multinational managers. Whereas covered interest arbitrage showed a positive correlation with number of foreign countries in which the firm was operating, the use of uncovered interest arbitrage did not correlate to any of the corporate management dimensions. This supports the notion that multinational firms are not speculative in nature, and engage in foreign funds investment activities only to the degree that the firm is internationally diversified.

Conclusions

As firms expand their overseas operations, foreign currency denominated transactions take on increased significance. Does this necessarily imply, though, that multinational firms should aggressively manage their exposure to F. E. risk? Since recent literature indicates that world securities markets are efficient, or integrated, a logical conclusion might be that investors are perfectly capable of becoming well-diversified in an international sense. However, significant barriers such as taxes and foreign exchange controls prevent investors from achieving international currency diversification. International capital markets integrate not directly through the efforts of investors; rather, integration takes place indirectly through the global diversification efforts of corporations. The implication here is that corporate managers can profit from the proper management of F. E. risks.

The survey results indicate that multinational firms are not placing enough emphasis on centralizing F. E. operations. The survey results basically validate the arguments for centralizing F. E. operations. For example, the results of this study show that centralized firms make more use of forward exchange markets, that decentralized firms do not pay adequate attention to the capital structure/dividends issue, and the centralized firms are more cognizant of lead/lag strategies. Both on conceptual and empirical bases, an argument could be made for centralizing F. E. operations. Multinationals provide their stockholders with valuable international diversification. It is possible that the benefits to stockholders could be enhanced through formalizing and centralizing F. E. risk management operations and through increased emphasis on management of cash flow rather than translation exposure, on improving forecasting procedures, and on greater utilization of interest arbitraging.

EXCHANGE BLOCKAGE RISK: AN INSURANCE OVERVIEW

Francis X. Boylan

ABSTRACT. Investors and exporters doing business overseas are vulnerable to a variety of political and export credit risk loss potentials. For those with existing investments in or selling to the debt-laden nations, the paramount concern is usually exchange blockage (the prevention of the exchange of the local, soft currency into a desired, hard currency and the transfer of that hard currency to a country where it can be used freely).

Exporters may be able to buy insurance against such a risk, but before doing so, they should know more about the attitude of insurers toward the general subject of exchange blockage. To this end, EXPORT TODAY presents a highly technical—yet practical—question and answer interview session with the Managing Vice President of Alexander & Alexander's Foreign Credit Division, Frank Boylan.[1]

Q: In an exchange blockage situation, what are the basic types of risk that may arise from an insurer's viewpoint?

A: In political-risk insurance terminology, an exchange blockage may be expected to give rise either to an "inconvertibility risk" or to a "transfer risk." The term "inconvertibility risk," insofar as it relates to existing investments, is usually associated with the difficulties that may be encountered in some countries in maintaining the historical pattern established for the repatriation by a subsidiary to a parent corporation located in another country of such things as dividends or other distributions of profits, distributions from liquidations of securities, principal and interest payments on loans or advances, royalties and fees, etc. (collectively referred to by many insurers as "scheduled funds").

With inconvertibility-risk situations, the blocked funds are usually owned by the corporation, but are denominated in the local currency of the subsidiary, rather than in the hard currency normally sought by the parent.

By contrast, the term "transfer risk" is usually associated with situations where there is a blockage of local currency that is deposited for the purpose of discharging all or portions of a legally enforceable, hard-currency indebtedness arising out of cross-border sales of products or services to private-sector entities. I might add that the meanings I have suggested for these terms are not necessarily the same as those assigned to these terms by some political risk insurers—especially insurers domiciled outside of the United States.

Source: Reprinted with permission from *Export Today* magazine. To subscribe, call (202) 737-1060 or fax (202) 783-5966. $49/year.

[1] It should be noted that the exchange-fluctuation/currency-devaluation risks associated with an obligation to pay in a soft currency must be borne by the insured-seller, for which there is no known insurance market available for risk transfer. F.B.

Q: Are there different kinds of inconvertibility situations?

A: An inconvertibility situation is normally viewed as "active" where the exchange blockage is a result of the imposition, after the effective date of the insurance, of a law, decree or regulation by the host-country government or exchange authority. By contrast, an inconvertibility situation is normally viewed as "passive" where, after policy inception, inordinate delays by the exchange authority emerge in the approval of applications for conversion or in the authorization of the actual transfer of funds following requisite approval thereof.

Q: Are there significant differences between public-sector insurers and private-sector insurers with respect to the scope of protection against inconvertibility risk?

A: When viewed solely in terms of contractual text, there would appear to be no significant differences among insurers in the scope of protection contemplated. From a practical point of view, however, public-sector insurers, as instruments of governmental policy, are normally able to write coverage on new investments for a substantially greater number of years (usually reflecting the investor's estimate of the time expected to be required to achieve the projected return on his investment) and for repatriations from many developing nations that may not be viewed as financially acceptable to private-sector insurers for this type of risk. Public-sector insurers, unlike private-sector insurers, are usually willing, moreover, to write an inconvertibility cover by itself and not necessarily as a supplement to an expropriation cover. On the other hand, private-sector insurers become the principal markets for this type of insurance only in connection with investments that already exist as of the effective date of the insurance (in contrast to new investments or contemplated expansions of existing investments, where public-sector insurance is normally the principal source of protection for this type of risk).

Q: When a multinational has an existing foreign investment, is there an interrelationship between an "expropriation risk" and an "inconvertibility risk"?

A: "Expropriation risk" usually refers to the possibility that a foreign government will take an asset or enterprise without prompt, adequate and effective compensation. This is usually viewed as a hostile act on the host government's part. An "inconvertibility risk," by contrast, is usually viewed in terms of a financial situation where the foreign government concludes, usually with no noteworthy hostility collectively toward its victims, that it has no realistic alternative but to block the repatriation of the "scheduled funds." I might add by way of clarification that if an asset or enterprise is seized by a foreign government with compensation in the form of a local currency that is blocked, such compensation should *not* be viewed, in my opinion, as "effective" and, therefore, the resulting loss should be treated as an "expropriation risk," rather than as an "inconvertibility risk." At least one private-sector insurer, regrettably, requires that coverage for this type of situation be specifically added to an expropriation policy for an additional premium; I would expect most other political-risk insurers to interpret the expropriation policy in a manner consistent with my opinion without a separate premium requirement.

Q: Returning now to the transfer-risk loss potentials associated with export credits extended to private-sector obligors, will you identify the principal insurers of this type of risk?

A: The principal insurers of this type of risk are the various government-sponsored export credit insurers, such as, in the United States, Foreign Credit Insurance Association (FCIA), which is backed by Export-Import Bank of the United States (Eximbank). While there are a number of private-sector insurers willing to cover defaults by governmental obligors (as political risk insurance), there are relatively few willing to provide comprehensive (political and commercial) cover for defaults by private-sector buyers. The principal private-sector insurers of comprehensive export credit risks (including transfer risk—perhaps with significant limitations for certain countries currently encountering exchange difficulties) are AIG Political Risk Division (AIGPRD), which underwrites in the United States on behalf of National Union Fire Insurance Company of Pittsburgh, Pa., a member of American International Group, Aetna Insurance Company (a member of CIGNA Worldwide) and the newly organized Trade Credit Underwriters, which underwrites these and similar coverages through an agency agreement with The Aetna Casualty and Surety Company.

Q: Is there a need for a separate transfer-risk cover with respect to credits extended to public-sector obligors?

A: Normally, a separate transfer-risk cover is not required where the insurance relates to credits extended to public-sector obligors. Assuming a governmental obligation to pay in hard currency outside of the country, the failure of the public-sector obligor to pay the hard currency as required under the contract of sale (or, as the case may be, under a promissory note or other form of negotiable instrument) should be treated as an insurable "default," whether the obligor's failure to pay was attributable to an exchange-blockage situation or to some other cause, such as an outright repudiation of the indebtedness (unless, of course, the obligor was relieved of his obligation to pay because of an act or omission of the insured seller).

Q: What are the essential elements of FCIA's transfer-risk cover?

A: This question deserves a documented answer! The very substantial volume of default-type losses sustained in a number of debt-laden countries highlights the need for policyholders to understand the benefits and limitations inherent within the scope of coverage afforded under the transfer-risk section of all FCIA policies (as well as under a similar section of the default-type policies issued by other insurers covering credits extended to private-sector obligors). Because of the importance of this subject, it would seem desirable to quote relevant portions of FCIA's transfer risk insuring agreement:

> "The Insurer will indemnify the Insured in United States dollars for the percentage specified in the declarations of the United States dollar equivalent of the currency of the buyer's country deposited *on or before the due date, or within 90 days thereafter,* as payment or part payment of any amount due . . . , which deposit has not been transferred . . . because of *inability to obtain United States dollars* in a lawful market of the buyer's country and *to effect the transfer thereof* to the Insured in the United States, if:
>
> (a) the deposit has been made in a bank in the buyer's country, or with a depository in such country designated by law or administrative regulation for the acquisition and transfer of United States dollars; and
>
> (b) the failure of the appropriate exchange authority to transfer local currency into dollars is not due to the fault of the buyer or any of its agents, including but not limited to: (1) failure to comply with the applicable laws . . . ; and (2) application for dollars at a rate of exchange which is not applicable to the transaction involved." (Emphasis added.)

I stress the phrases "inability to obtain United States dollars" and "to effect the transfer thereof" in order to highlight favorably the fact that FCIA's transfer-risk cover (as well as the transfer-risk cover of some other insurers) extends beyond the mere inability "to effect the transfer" of already-obtained dollars out of a particular country to include also situations where the insured is unable "to obtain United States dollars" that he seeks to transfer.

Q: How important is the phrase "on or before the due date, or within 90 days thereafter" as used in the FCIA transfer-risk insuring agreement?

A: Very! There should be no doubt about the intent of the phrase "on or before the due date, or within 90 days thereafter." In our experience, blocked local-currency deposits made originally more than 90 days after the due date of a U.S.–dollar indebtedness are not treated as insurable under the transfer-risk (one of the political risks) section of the FCIA policy; rather, any ensuing loss arising out of such tardy deposit has been viewed as a commercial credit risk for the purposes of FCIA insurance.

Q: What is the significance of a FCIA policy determination that a particular loss be treated as a commercial credit risk, rather than as a political risk?

A: Under FCIA, commercial credit risk losses, unlike political risk losses, are usually subject to an insured percentage of less than 100 percent, to an annual deductible, and to a lesser limit of liability. Where the insurance relates to sales from a parent to a subsidiary, moreover, most insurers, including FCIA, limit their protection to a "political-only" cover, including the heavily qualified transfer-risk cover we have been discussing, without the complementary commercial credit risk protection needed to cover exchange-blockage losses that do not qualify under the transfer-risk section of the policy.

Because of probable coverage differences and for other reasons, it is normally preferable from the claimant's point of view to secure indemnity for an FCIA-insured loss (whether involving an exchange blockage or another form of governmental action) as a political risk, rather than as a commercial credit risk. This type of difference in the scope of cover makes it essential that any actual or potential holder of an FCIA or private-market policy study carefully the definitions of political risks as set forth in the policy in terms of the exposures the insured is seeking to cover.

Q: Would you explain why the recent Venezuelan trade-debt losses insured under FCIA policies have been treated as commercial credit risks, rather than as political risks?

A: Various elements of the transfer-risk coverage conditions could have been invoked by the insurers, if necessary, as the basis for a denial of coverage under that section of the FCIA policy. First, it is my understanding that Venezuela has not had an official "depository . . . designated by law . . . for the acquisition and transfer of United States dollars."

Second, it is generally conceded that there has not been in Venezuela an "inability to obtain United States dollars in the lawful market . . . ," nor has there been passage of any law, order or decree preventing foreign-debt obligations from being settled in U.S. dollars. Third, and perhaps underlying the other two, many local obligors have tried to avoid the impact of the substantial devaluation of the bolivar by seeking dollars "at a rate of exchange which is not applicable to the transaction involved." It follows, therefore, that to date each of these losses understandably has been treated by FCIA as a "commercial credit risk," rather than as a "political risk." (I might add that we understand that private-sector insurers have applied essentially the same criteria to deny liability under their transfer-risk covers.)

Q: What standards are used by the various insurers when making a determination as to the rate of exchange to be used in settlement of losses arising out of an exchange blockage?

A: Because so many of the debt-laden nations are encountering ongoing devaluations of their local currency, it is extremely important that there be a clear understanding between the policyholder and the insurer as to the rate of exchange to be used in the settlement of loss arising out of an exchange blockage, whether such loss is treated as an "inconvertibility risk" or as a "transfer risk." There is no substitute for a close examination of the terms and conditions of the particular contract of insurance to determine what rate of exchange the specific insurer intends to use. In the case of an inconvertibility risk, for example, Overseas Private Investment Corporation uses a specifically defined term "Reference Rate of Exchange." (OPIC is the principal U.S. government-sponsored insurer of the expropriation/inconvertibility/war risks for new investments or for substantial expansions of existing investments.) Under its current policy forms, OPIC will compensate for blocked currency either at the official exchange rate or, if the official market that corresponds to that rate is not available, at the rate prevailing in normal and legal channels for the type of transaction involved. FCIA, as another example, uses a more succinct standard: "Payment will be made by the Insurer to the Insured based on the rate of exchange applicable to the type of transaction involved existing on the due date or the date of the relevant deposit, whichever is later."

Q: There is widespread concern among exporters regarding potential losses arising from exchange fluctuations or devaluation of currencies when trading abroad. Where do export credit insurers stand with respect to these subjects?

A: Let me pose an even more fundamental question: Does a particular export credit insurance policy cover losses arising out of exchange fluctuations or devaluations of a soft currency in connection with a hard-currency indebtedness created pursuant to an insured transaction?

The following explanation shows that there should be no doubt about the FCIA/Eximbank intent regarding the treatment of losses caused by exchange fluctuations or devaluations of local currencies in connection with U.S.–dollar indebtedness. Regrettably, the policies of at least some of the private-sector insurers on this point are presently in doubt.

CASE. This issue and the misunderstandings associated with this question have been matters of concern to me since 1961. That year, I was representing the interests of those private insurance companies that collectively were about to launch the FCIA program. I was asked by representatives of those insurers to comment on a draft of FCIA's first policy as prepared by Eximbank. The basic construction of that policy called for a precise definition of those "political risks" to be covered by Eximbank, with the understanding that all other risks insurable under the FCIA policies would be treated as "commercial credit risks" to be covered by the private insurers (backed by Eximbank reinsurance).

Like other indemnity-type policies, the contractual format of all FCIA policies calls for a basic grant of cover under the insuring agreements, with qualifications and other restrictions, including specific exclusions, being set forth in the other sections of the policies. One of the exclusions that has remained essentially intact from the beginning reads as follows:

"The Insurers shall not be liable for any loss . . . *under Coverage B–Political Risks* arising out of the exchange fluctuation or devaluation of the currency of the buyer's country occurring on or before the due date or the date of deposit . . . whichever is later;" (Emphasis added.)

In 1961, when this concept was first articulated, I asked Eximbank's counsel to explain why Eximbank required a specific exclusion "under Coverage B–Political Risks" of an event that was not included within the policy definition of "political risks" (in this case, an exchange fluctuation or a devaluation of the currency of the buyer's country). Expressed another way, I was asking why Eximbank considered it necessary to exclude specifically a risk from a particular section of a policy that could not possibly be covered under that section.

In reply, the counsel advised that Eximbank's Board of Directors wanted to provide *added emphasis to the fact that losses arising out of exchange fluctuations or currency devaluations* "occurring on or before the due date or the date of deposit . . . whichever is later," involving a U.S. dollar obligation, *would be treated under all FCIA policies as defaults in the amounts due and insurable as "commercial credit losses,"* rather than as "political losses" (subject to all other terms and conditions of these policies). In the event of a timely deposit of the correct amounts of local currency followed by an exchange blockage covered under the transfer-risk section of the policy, however, any ensuing exchange fluctuation or currency devaluation should not, by itself, reduce the FCIA policyholder's otherwise-attained rights to indemnity. This answer is as valid today as it was then. (We understand, regrettably, that at least some of the private-sector insurers do not necessarily follow this concept.)

While it was probably unnecessary as a matter of drafting to provide for this exclusion in FCIA policies, at least we have the comfort of knowing the historical intent of Eximbank on this point. Unfortunately, the intent of some—but by no means all—of the private insurers that have introduced this exclusion into default policies, regrettably, is far from clear.

FCIA's dual coverage approach calls for separate insuring agreements for political risks and for commercial credit risks, while the private-sector insurers usually employ a unitary approach with one insuring agreement applicable to both types of risks. It follows, therefore, that when this type of exclusion is introduced into private-sector policies without ameliorating qualifications, it is likely to carry with it the unfortunate implication that there is no cover whatever (neither political nor commercial) for losses in connection with hard-currency credit sales where such losses are attributable to an exchange fluctuation or a devaluation of the currency of the buyer's country. We have been disappointed to date with the results of our efforts to prevail upon more private-sector insurers either to eliminate or to qualify this exclusion under policies broadly designed to cover virtually all defaults of hard-currency obligations arising out of eligible shipments not due to the fault of the insured, whether the defaults are attributable to political or commercial causes.

In the event of a claim denial based upon this exclusion under a comprehensive (political and commercial) policy issued by a private-sector insurer, an attorney or broker would probably encourage the policyholder to maintain that the insurer could not possibly have intended the exclusion to operate to deny coverage for otherwise insurable commercial defaults.

Because of the magnitude of the loss potentials associated with exchange fluctuations and devaluation of currencies, the ideal situation would be to attempt to reach agreement with insurers in advance as to the precise intent of this exclusion. (Unfortunately this is not always possible.)

Q: In your responses to the questions regarding the transfer-risk insurance arrangements, you made repeated references to a "hard-currency indebtedness," as distinguished from a "soft-currency indebtedness." Will you summarize your previously expressed views regarding the significance of this distinction?

A: If a foreign buyer assumes an obligation to pay U.S. dollars (or some other hard currency) as of a specified due date for products or services provided by a seller, he thereby becomes obligated to deposit as much local currency as is necessary at the then-current rate of exchange to be able to secure (in the absence of an exchange blockage) the U.S. dollars needed to satisfy the whole of his indebtedness. If a devaluation of the currency of the buyer's country occurs after the delivery of the products/services, but prior to the date of the local-currency deposit, the buyer should be obligated to make good on the "shortfall" by depositing additional local currency in amounts sufficient to produce the dollars needed, at the devalued rate of exchange, to satisfy his debt. The buyer's failure, under such circumstances, to deposit more local currency than initially contemplated should produce a partial default (less-than-antici-pated dollars secured from the exchange). As suggested previously, any such default is likely to be treated by FCIA as a commercial credit risk, rather than as a "political risk," with a likelihood, therefore, of a lesser amount of indemnity.

By contrast, if the sale has been consummated in the local currency of the buyer, the devaluation would not affect the amount of the buyer's contractual obligation to pay. Under such circumstances, the seller would have to bear the devaluation loss potential (or, conversely, to enjoy the financial benefit derived from any revaluation of the currency of the buyer's country).

Q: Do you have any final words of advice to American exporters?

A: As I have stated on innumerable occasions in the past, there is no substitute for a close examination of the particular policy wording. While there is some legal precedent established for the interpretation of the policy provisions we have discussed, my staff and I must rely heavily upon personal discussions with key underwriters to gain insight into their intent vis-a-vis these difficult issues. Each policy and loss circumstance must be evaluated in its unique context. Because of the litigious nature of our society, moreover, I feel compelled to add here a standard caveat to the effect that my answers in this interview are explanatory and illustrative only; they do not control the interpretation of the various policies discussed, nor do they purport to explain the whole of the underwriting attitude of the political/export credit risk insurers toward the subjects discussed.

ARE WE FEELING MORE COMPETITIVE YET? THE EXCHANGE RATE GAMBIT

W. Carl Kester ◆ Timothy A. Luehrman

ABSTRACT. A weak home currency diminishes the future competitiveness of some firms, the authors argue, since foreign competitors use strong currencies to make strategic investments on relatively more favorable terms. Firms that must compete globally in "forward-looking" industries, where heavy investment today is the key to competitiveness tomorrow, are likely to be harmed by a weak home currency. The article concludes that purposeful devaluation of a currency is short sighted and potentially harmful to a country's competitive standing.

At the end of 1987, a Japanese baseball team, the Tokyo Giants, made headlines in many newspapers in the United States. They offered Dave Righetti, a left-handed relief pitcher for the New York Yankees, $8 million to ply his trade in Japan for two years. This sum represented about twice as much as any player in the United States was being paid. A front-page story in the *Boston Globe* called the offer "scary" and noted that it was made possible by the strength of the yen.[1] It was not the first time that the marvelous purchasing power of the yen had been remarked upon; Japanese investors have been making their presence felt in art and real estate markets around the world, as well.

The purchasing power of foreign currencies is cause for concern—though not so much, we think, in the markets for paintings, athletes' services, or even real estate. The same purchasing power is available to foreign investors in manufacturing, and it is potentially far more threatening to domestic firms in that arena. Yet is it precisely in manufacturing that the fall of the dollar has been viewed as a boon to U.S. competitors and the "scariness" of the high yen has been downplayed. While the New York Yankees and the Tokyo Giants may compete to purchase Mr. Righetti's services, they do not thereafter have to compete for the same gate or television revenues. The same cannot be said of manufacturing companies. Many U.S. companies will see their industries transformed by the investments of competitors—investments stimulated at least in part by strong currencies—even as U.S. manufacturers "enjoy," for the moment, a lower dollar.

We do not mean to raise the old shibboleth of "foreigners buying up America"—but a lower dollar does have many effects on U.S. competitiveness. Most discussions about the drawbacks of a cheap currency mention higher U.S. inflation and the potential difficulties of attracting capital to finance U.S. deficits; the list stops there. Other drawbacks are equally troubling, but often

---

[1] *Boston Globe,* 12 December 1987, p. 1.

overlooked. Our focus here is on strategic or "competitive" investment by companies. We argue that competitors' investment behavior has a large role to play in the determination of future competitiveness in the product market, and that this investment activity is affected by changes in currency values. From this perspective, we are led to conclude the following.

- ◆ Some firms will find their future competitiveness diminished rather than enhanced by a weak home currency, as foreign competitors with strong currencies make investments on relatively favorable terms.
- ◆ Managers must develop a more sophisticated appreciation of the foreign exchange exposure of their companies' investment opportunities or "growth options."
- ◆ Public policy regarding exchange rates and competitiveness should be designed to enhance companies' abilities to acquire new growth options, not simply to stimulate current investment per se.
- ◆ Purposeful devaluation of a currency is at best a short sighted, and at worst a seriously flawed, means of promoting competitiveness.
- ◆ The trade deficit reveals little about future competitiveness and should be given a back seat to more relevant gauges of probable product market success.

"Strategic" Investment: The Importance of Growth Options

Our interest in competitiveness is focused on individual firms rather than, say, countries, manufacturing sectors, or labor forces. Although competitiveness may be a national concern, the agents that do the competing are firms, not countries, and this is true even for firms that are state owned or sponsored. Undoubtedly government policies, active and passive, have important implications for firms' competitiveness. But it is still individual managers in individual firms who make the decision to invest or not invest, set a high price or a low one, choose an organizational form, and so on. In short, firms are the competitors.

We also assume that firms are value maximizers. They strive to run their existing businesses to maximize the present (discounted) value of their cash flows, and they seek to invest in new businesses that have positive net present values. Such firms will not compete for market share, for technological leadership, or for edges in quality, *except insofar as they help maximize the value of expected future cash flows.*

What, then, is competitiveness? Firms that maximize value will compete only for value; in other words, for cash flows. In most industries, cash flows are both scarce and contested. A given economic activity generates only so much cash and, within a given span of time, there is typically more than one firm trying to grab that cash for itself. We define competitiveness as a firm's ability, relative to its competitors, to appropriate the scarce, contested cash flows associated with an activity and deliver them to its owners.

Many analyses of competitiveness suffer from two problems. The first is very simple: value-maximizing firms do not necessarily maximize competitiveness. That is, competitiveness is but a means to an end and not the end itself. A lot of what is written about the failings of U.S. managers implies that they are (or should be) trying to maximize competitiveness, but simply are not succeeding. In fact, they may be succeeding at maximizing value.

The analogies from sports that one often hears in discussions of competitiveness are strained for just this reason. The objective in most sports is winning, not maximizing your score—a high score is merely the means to the end of winning. In business the opposite is usually true: "winning" (competitiveness) is a means toward the end of a high score. Most ballplayers would rather win by a score of two to one than lose, fourteen to fifteen. Shareholders, on the other hand, would prefer the fourteen to the two. They would rather lose a high-scoring game than win a low-scoring one.

The second problem is much more serious. Conventional analyses of competitiveness often ignore an important consideration: new investments by firms and their rivals continually change the basis on which future competition will take place. Analyses of exchange rates and competitiveness are a prime example. The usual paradigm posits a simple connection between exchange rates and competitiveness—that a cheaper dollar, for example, promotes U.S. exports and discourages imports, resulting in stronger, more competitive U.S. manufacturers. At best this is only half the story. It focuses on firms and product markets as they currently exist and ignores the role of exchange rates as catalysts in the restructuring of companies and industries. In our view, dramatic shifts in real currency values are not just changing the prices of internationally traded goods; they are also effecting structural changes that will shape the global competition of the future. One of the keys to such structural change (and hence to future competitiveness) is real capital investment.

To highlight the importance of capital investment, it helps to think of companies as undertaking two generic types of activities. On the one hand, they manage existing assets, harvesting the cash flows made possible by previous investments. On the other, they set up future harvests by investing in activities that are expected to yield favorable returns in the future. At any given time, therefore, a company's value has two parts: the present value of cash flows from assets already in place, and the value of future investment opportunities, or *growth options.*

The value of growth options reflects the net present value of cash flows the firm is expected to realize, but for which the necessary investments have not yet been made.[2] These opportunities may be thought of as call options on

---

[2] The significance of growth options has been noted elsewhere, in connection with financing and capital budgeting decisions. See: S.C. Myers, "Determinants of Corporate Borrowing," *Journal of Financial Economics* 5 (November 1977): 147–175; and W.C. Kester, "Today's Options for Tomorrow's Growth," *Harvard Business Review,* March-April 1984, pp. 153–160.

operating assets: the company has the right but not the obligation to undertake a particular investment (in plant and equipment, R & D, etc.) by making the necessary expenditures, in return for which it receives the particular (tangible or intangible) operating assets.

For example, IBM is expected to have access in the future to projects that have positive net present values. This access may arise for various reasons: the company's market position, expected technological developments, and so on. In any case, such access is valuable and makes up part of IBM's current value, regardless of whether the company ultimately exercises a particular option and regardless of how the acquired assets eventually perform. Moreover, a firm like IBM owns many such options, the value of which may depend on each other and, especially, on the order or the combinations in which they are expected to be exercised. There may even be options on options—for example, capacity expansion opportunities following new product development opportunities.

The concept of growth options facilitates an analysis of competitive behavior that goes beyond incremental changes in product prices and quantities. Specifically, it focuses attention on the sort of strategic competition that alters industries dramatically—competition based on new products, new processes, new technologies, and so forth. Two important characteristics of such competition are apparent immediately.

First, strategic investments that could change the structure of an industry are not foregone conclusions. They may or may not be worth making, depending on whether future conditions justify the necessary capital outlays. Until a growth option is exercised, the investment required to put the assets in place is not yet a sunk cost. Instead, it is part of the incremental cash flows associated with the project on which the firm holds the option. An analysis of how an exchange-rate change would affect the company must consider, among other things, effects on the exercise prices of the company's growth options. Doing this is not the same as analyzing the company as a collection of assets already in place and operating, without future investment opportunities.

Second, and more important, growth options play a role in determining future competitiveness that may easily be disproportionate to the amount of value they represent, because individual firms typically do not have exclusive ownership of such options. Major strategic investment opportunities are *shared* among competitors and potential competitors.[3] IBM, for example, owns a share of (some) opportunities to invest in the world computer industry. But so do Digital Equipment Corporation, NEC, and Fujitsu. Which companies will realize a given opportunity when several have the potential to do so is often unclear. So long as an opportunity is unexploited, each of many competitors may claim

---

[3] We find it intuitively appealing to think of options as shared among existing or potential competitors. Alternatively, one may think of firms as having exclusive ownership of an option on a set of operating assets, whose value depends on whether any competitors own either similar assets or options on similar assets.

a piece of its value, and that piece may be small compared to the competitor's existing real assets. But as the opportunity is exploited, its value is consolidated; a few firms—or just one firm—is likely to capture most of it. The value captured by a firm that exploits an option previously shared by many can be substantial compared to its existing assets.

In this sense, companies compete for investments just as they compete in existing product markets. Similarly, there are winners and losers: an option, once it is exercised by a single firm, may expire, greatly decrease in value, or even increase in value for that firm's competitors. In any industry, the *sequence* in which firms are expected to exercise options is critical to determining the value for all firms of both assets in place and growth options.[4] This situation simply acknowledges that competitors' investment decisions are interdependent. Fujitsu's decision to invest in a positive net present value project can be expected to affect the value of IBM—its assets in place, or its opportunities, or both.

Although the sequence in which firms exercise shared growth options is important, being first or preempting competitive investment is not always best. "Winning" the investment competition means appropriating most of a shared option's value, which might well be accomplished by following rather than leading others' investments.

Exchange Rate Changes and Growth Options

Now consider the effects of a hypothetical depreciation of the dollar on the different components of value for a U.S. firm. First note that the change in currency values must be *real* in order to affect the real value of the firm's future operating cash flows. (A "real" change in exchange rates is one that reflects more than a simple difference in inflation rates between two countries.) The effect of a real dollar depreciation on the value of assets in place is fairly straightforward: without having done anything, the firm's managers may suddenly be able to charge higher prices for exports, undercut import prices, or both. Recent experience with a falling dollar has shown that this shift in relative prices is not as automatic nor as large as it was traditionally assumed to be. Still, for assets in place, the familiar paradigm linking a lower dollar to favorable cash flow effects for U.S. producers is an appealing one.

The effect on the value of growth options is more ambiguous. The future cash flows associated with the underlying, unacquired assets are apt to be affected in the same way flows from assets already in place are affected: a dollar depreciation tends to help exports and hurt imports. But if the dollar is less valuable, more dollars may be required to make the investment that will put the assets in place; the (real) exercise price of the option may go up. These two

---

[4] Kester (1984) provides a discussion of some elements of the optimal exercise decision.

effects work in opposite directions, and either may dominate the other under a particular set of circumstances.

A third effect is far more important: changing currency values will affect firms' decisions about whether and when to exercise particular options. As a result, exchange rates help determine *which* competitors (e.g., Japanese or American) will exercise options that are owned *jointly*. This element is critical because typically firms must compete to *invest* before they compete to *sell;* in other words, they must sow before they can harvest. The outcome of the investment competition will affect the terms on which product market competition takes place.

For example, assume that the real future cash inflows associated with investment in a particular new product are only modestly affected by an exchange rate change (perhaps due to a lack of price-based competition early in the product life cycle). However, cash to make the investment is committed in the short run and the amount required may be greatly affected by currency values. A depreciating dollar not only raises the exercise price associated with such new investment for U.S. firms, it simultaneously lowers the exercise price for foreign producers competing to make the same investment. As a result, competitors' *relative* abilities to exercise shared options may change; this affects when and by whom a given investment will be made. In short, it may be true that a lower dollar would enhance the future cash inflows associated with a given option, *but the same lower dollar may keep that option from ever being exercised by a U.S. firm.* Competitors with strong currencies may get such a head start—perhaps even preempting other firms' investments—that the potential diminishment of their future cash flows is inconsequential by comparison.

In summary, an exchange rate shock affects the value of growth options and the value of assets in place very differently. A lower currency value may confer an advantage at the margins of costs and revenues in existing product markets, but it may simultaneously impose a serious *disadvantage* in the competition that restructures the industry.

This argument that a rising home currency can help rather than hurt long-run competitiveness relies on two propositions: that investment plans change when currency values change, and that a rising home currency promotes more, rather than less, investment by home-country firms. While casual observation generally supports this view, the obvious possible exception is investment in new mature-product-market export capacity. Investment by newly industrializing nations in capacity to export products such as steel and textiles may be stimulated by a lower home currency. However, in more highly developed economies, such incidents are the exception rather than the rule; most "new" exports use existing capacity. Ford and Chrysler both announced plans in September 1987 to begin exporting some North American output to Europe. In December 1987, USX made a similar announcement of plans to export steel from the United States. But none of these programs represented investment in new capacity—at most they involved modest investments in local distribution.

Further, the resulting change in the industry is not fundamental and is no more permanent than the level of the exchange rate. As Lee Iacocca remarked in Frankfurt, "If the dollar moves back up to two deutsche marks or three marks, we'll lose our shirts."[5]

Strong Currencies and the Competition to Invest

Generally, this type of export-related activity is swamped by investments made by firms with rising home currencies. These companies use strong currencies to implement strategies aimed at achieving global market dominance or at creating new streams of future cash flows by entering new product markets.

Dainippon Ink and Chemicals (DIC), a Japanese producer of printing inks, is a good example. The printing and graphic arts business has been changing dramatically during the past decade, driven by advances in technologies for digital color imaging. Technological advances are making possible satellite transmission of digital color images, direct digital color proofing, the merging of color and monotone printing systems, and low-cost optical disk data storage. The structure of the industry is changing as the necessary satellite downlinks, workstations, and electronic prepresses are supplied and managed by a few "mega-vendors." The mega-vendors control access to specialized ink, paper, press, computer, data transmission, and process technologies.

By facilitating the completion of a $1-billion acquisition program, the strong yen has helped DIC emerge as the world's leading integrated producer of printing inks and as a dominant mega-vendor. This program began in the late 1970s, when DIC identified the acquisition of the graphic arts division of Sun Chemical as the key to penetrating the U.S. market. Fearing preemption by another foreign company, it initiated negotiations to purchase the division in 1980, when the yen/dollar exchange rate was about ¥250/US$. At first, a gap of $175 million (approximately 30 percent of Sun's asking price) separated buyer and seller. Negotiations stalled, then deadlocked as the yen fell steadily against the dollar through 1984. The yen then began to rise, and by November 1986 reached ¥160/US$, 35 percent higher than in 1980. This new value, and a modest reduction in Sun's asking price, resulted in a deal near the end of 1986. Earlier that year, the same strong yen had facilitated DIC's acquisition of West Germany's Hartmann Group, Europe's third-largest ink producer. Finally, in the summer of 1987, DIC completed a contested takeover of Reichhold Chemicals, a leading U.S. manufacturer of specialty polymers used in inks and paper coatings. At the time many Wall Street observers noted that, because of the strength of the yen, potential rivals in the United States and Europe would have difficult outbidding DIC.

Because it gained control of Reichhold and other major producers, DIC is

---

[5] Quoted in the *Wall Street Journal,* 9 September 1987, p. 7.

now able to consolidate and direct the future exercise of shared growth options in the rapidly changing printing business. This ability is potentially much more valuable than passively investing in U.S. equities or speculating in currencies. DIC managers saw an opportunity to win the strategic investment competition that precedes "tactical" competition in the restructured printing and graphic arts industry. The strong yen helped DIC exploit this opportunity. DIC is now positioned to dominate the industry in the 1990s.

Other Japanese producers are also using the strong yen to their competitive advantage. Japanese automakers not only cut costs following the yen's rise; Honda, Toyota, and Nissan also invested heavily in new product and new dealer networks aimed at the North American and European markets. This activity accelerated as the yen continued to rise through 1986 and 1987. Even companies in industries where growth options are hard to find have been trying to create them through R&D ventures at home and abroad. Nippon Steel has poured cash into ventures with Calgene, Inc., in biotechnology, with GTX Corporation in computer-aided design systems, and with Concurrent Computer Corporation in the development and marketing of super-minicomputers. Other Japanese companies had many growth options before the yen rose and have responded by accelerating their exercise. Toshiba Corporation, for example, has accelerated new product development efforts and predicts that, by 1993, fully half of its products will have been developed within the previous three years. These types of investments are helped rather than hurt by a strong home currency.

Such use of strong currencies in strategic investments is by no means limited to Japanese companies. Many U.S. companies exploited the strong dollar in the early 1980s. Merck & Co., Inc., a leading producer of pharmaceuticals, had a strategic goal of being first or second in each of the world's major prescription drug markets. In Japan, the world's second largest market, Merck ranked thirtieth at the end of 1982. In August 1983 it acquired control of Banyu Pharmaceutical, one of Japan's largest drug companies, while the dollar was at ¥240/US$. The acquisition of Banyu and another smaller Japanese company more than doubled Merck's Japanese market share. More important, it gave Merck control of new distribution channels for a large number of new products about to emerge from its U.S. laboratories. If the exchange rate had been ¥140/US$ instead of ¥240/US$, Merck might still have made the investment. But at ¥240/US$, it had an advantage: it could make the investment more cheaply, in real terms, than German or Swiss competitors. Because opportunities to exploit the Japanese market were limited, this advantage was especially strong.

Merck is an excellent example of a company whose future competitiveness is more closely tied to its growth options than to its positions in existing product markets. Growth options are shared in the pharmaceutical industry—the value of a particular pharmacological discovery can depend very much on whether and when a similar discovery was made elsewhere. Thus, the really decisive competition takes place in laboratories; by the time a new drug reaches the marketplace, the most important battles have already been won or lost. Furthermore, because so much cash must be invested up front in the seven- to ten-year development process, it is nearly inconceivable that a chronically weak currency would aid the cause. Not surprisingly, as the value of the dollar rose between 1980 and 1985, Merck's competitiveness did not collapse. On the contrary, the company became significantly *more* competitive during this period, primarily because of its R&D productivity. The strong relative purchasing power of the dollar helped rather than hurt the strategically crucial R&D program.

Some general observations can be drawn from these examples. First, a rising home currency enhances competitiveness in industries for which substantial investment is the key to future competitiveness. In other words, "sunrise" industries, in which heavy investment in R&D, market development, and new production technology is critical, may derive long-run advantages from a strong currency. In "sunset" industries, however, growth options are less likely to represent a significant fraction of their value. Competitiveness depends not on new investment but on efficient management of existing operations, which may be aided by a falling home currency.

Another important consideration is the degree to which growth options are shared among competitors situated on opposite sides of a given exchange rate. If they are widely shared and if one company's decisions greatly affect others' options, then the benefit of a strong home currency can be considerable even if growth options do not constitute a large fraction of a given company's value.

These effects on investment behavior have more weight if currencies undergo extended periods of over- or undervaluation. A temporarily overvalued currency provides a window for investing at bargain prices. Firms with strong home currencies will make investments that otherwise might not have been made, or will make them on more favorable terms vis-à-vis certain competitors. While it is true, conversely, that a temporarily undervalued currency can increase cash flow from assets in place, most firms have relatively little ability to accelerate these cash flows. Investment plans may be much more easily adjusted. Indeed, the rise of the yen from 1985 to 1988 had surprisingly limited effects on product markets. Dollar prices of many Japanese products, from autos to electronics, did not rise in proportion to the dollar's fall, nor did unit volume fall significantly. Meanwhile, Japanese investment activity in Japan, in Southeast Asia, and in North America has increased dramatically since the beginning of 1986. Japan is now the largest investor in new capacity and technology in Pacific Asia, replacing the United States in that role; it has also become the largest source of new foreign direct investment in the United States.

Moreover, Japanese investors increasingly seek operating control of foreign assets. DIC is only one of the more visible examples of this trend, which includes other foreign companies as well. In 1986, for example, within a year of when the dollar began to slide, a West German investment banker estimated that more than half of Germany's 100 largest companies were actively seeking U.S. properties. Thus an international market for corporate control may develop not because it is always a bargain for strong currency companies to buy weak currency companies—this is only the case if currencies or companies are misvalued—but because shifting currency values provide opportunities for a bidder to acquire a target and then *change* the target's (or its own) investment plans. In this sort of world, exchange rates help determine who are the bidders, who are the targets, and how growth options will ultimately be exercised.

Measuring Changes in Competitiveness

To recapitulate, we have argued that competitiveness is a firm's relative ability to appropriate scarce, contested cash flows and deliver them to its owners. The growth option framework separates these cash flows into those expected from the operation of assets already in place and those expected from discretionary future investments. The distinction between these two components of value is important because some changes in the competitive environment, such as a change in real exchange rates, will affect each component differently—so much so that the combined effects on value and competitiveness may be the reverse of what many have come to expect. A strong currency may help more than hurt. Both components of a company's value should be reflected in the market prices of its securities, which suggests a simple method of measuring changes in competitiveness. Suppose an investor was bullish (or bearish) on a particular industry, but found it difficult to assess which individual companies would perform well and which would not. The investor could avoid intra-industry competitive risk simply by buying (or selling) the entire industry. When investors behave this way, they effectively value the industry as a whole. If the group as a whole is under- or overvalued, they simply buy or sell shares of the group until they feel it is priced correctly.

Inevitably, buy-and-sell decisions with respect to individual stocks result in the distribution of industry value according to the future cash flows each competitor is thought able to realize. If an individual firm is relatively under- or overvalued, an investor can buy (sell) its shares and sell (buy) those of the rest of the group. In this way investors reveal their beliefs about each firm's competitiveness. When new information arrives, investors reassess the value of the industry and redistribute this value among the competitors. Thus, changes in a firm's *relative* value are one measure of changes in its competitiveness.

We refer to a particular firm's value, relative to its industry, as its *value share*. Value share is computed simply as the market value of a given firm divided by the market value of its industry. We propose using changes in value shares to measure changes in competitiveness.[6] Obviously, value shares will be "noisy,"

---

[6] We are not proposing value shares as a way to measure *levels* of competitiveness. To do so is to claim that the largest firm in an industry is the most competitive, which is neither interesting nor convincing. Instead, we want to measure *changes* in competitiveness using *changes* in value shares. How value gets redistributed when the world changes is interesting regardless of different firms' starting points.

partly because they derive from investors' beliefs about the future—beliefs that may prove quite wrong. But unless investors are continually wrong in a systematic way, changes in value shares will contain useful information about changes in shares of expected future cash flows. A company that becomes more competitive, for whatever reason, is expected by investors to earn a larger share of the cash flows available in the business. This change in competitiveness is capitalized as investors bid up the value of the firm relative to its competitors.

Our definition of competitiveness and the value share framework for measuring changes in competitiveness have some distinct advantages. They are forward looking because they focus on expected future cash flows. Many other measures of competitiveness, such as the trade balance, are backward looking, reflecting competitive skirmishes that have already been won or lost. Further, changes in value shares incorporate the capital markets' judgment in the assessment of changes in competitiveness. Even when it is wrong, the judgment of the capital markets is relevant, because it affects the terms on which new investments can be made. The world's increasingly integrated and sophisticated financial markets are a source of data on competition that should not go unexploited.

Value Shares, Competitiveness, and Exchange Rate Surprises

The value share framework for measuring changes in competitiveness can be readily applied to exchange rate changes. If it is true that a given shift in real exchange rates will help some firms and hurt others, we should be able to observe a redistribution of value among competitors following such a shift. A firm made more competitive by an exchange rate shift should experience an increase in its value, relative to its competitors, when all firms' values are measured in the same currency. In other words, its value share should increase.

We have examined the relationship between daily changes in value shares and contemporaneous daily changes in exchange rates for the automobile and pharmaceutical industries during 1985 and 1986.[7] The studies confirm that there is a clear relationship between the two. More important, they show that in both industries, almost without exception, a *depreciation* of a firm's home currency was associated with a *decline* in its value share. This finding is the opposite of what the conventional wisdom would predict, but it is consistent with the ideas outlined above: that a rising home currency can enhance the competitiveness of home-country firms by promoting strategic investment. Table 1 summa-

---

[7] A formal description of the automobile study's methodology and results is available in a working paper: T.A. Luehrman, "Exchange Rates and Intra-Industry Value Redistributions: An Empirical Examination of the World Automobile Industry" (Boston: Harvard Business School, working paper 87-031, July 1987).

TABLE 1   Estimated Responses of Value Shares to a 10 Percent Drop in Home Currency Values

Pharmaceutical Manufacturers
(2 May 1985–28 February 1986)

Portfolio	Value Share 9/20/85	Percent Change in Value Share Associated with 10 Percent Drop in Home-Currency Value versus:		
		US$	¥	DM
North American firms (13)	0.470	—	−1.46%	−2.84%
Japanese firms (8)	0.355	−4.10%	—	−3.46%
European firms (14)	0.175	−3.59%	−1.98%	—

Note: The "home" currency is taken to be DM for the European pharmaceutical portfolio; in regressions for individual firms, natural home currencies were used and produced qualitatively similar results

Automobile Manufacturers
(3 June 1985–31 January 1986)

Portfolio	Value Share 9/20/85	Percent Change in Value Share Associated with 10 Percent Drop in Home-Currency Value versus:		
		US$	¥	European Basket
North American firms (4)	0.413	—	−2.31%	−3.74%
Japanese firms (5)	0.240	−3.87%	—	−3.18%
European firms (10)	0.346	−4.37%	−2.36%	—

Notes: The European Basket consists of deutsche marks, French francs, and Italian lira, weighted according to gross domestic products. Value shares do not add to 1.000 due to rounding.
Reported value share response estimates are derived from regression coefficients, all of which were significant at a level of 0.05

rizes how value shares of automobile- and pharmaceutical-industry members appear to respond to changes in home-currency values.

A concrete example may be helpful. On September 20, 1985 (the midpoint of the sample period), the automobile industry had a total value of $200.187 billion. On that same day four U.S. firms, General Motors, Ford, Chrysler, and American Motors, together had a value share of 0.413. According to Table 1, a 10 percent depreciation of the dollar against the yen was associated with a 2.3

percent decline in value share for these four firms. A 2.3 percent decline would reduce the value share from 0.413 to 0.404, for a loss of about one share point of industry value. One cannot infer precisely the dollar size of the implied value transfer without distinguishing carefully between pre- and post-depreciation dollars. However, the order of magnitude for this hypothetical 10 percent drop against the yen is about $2 billion. This represents value that would be redistributed from these four U.S. firms to their foreign competitors in the global automobile industry.

Within the sample of U.S. pharmaceutical companies, Merck displayed higher-than-average sensitivity to yen/dollar and mark/dollar exchange rates. Merck also had much more of the variability in its value share explained by exchange rate changes than any other U.S. company. Both of these facts are consistent with the description of Merck presented above—its position as an R&D leader and the large fraction of its value accounted for by growth options.

These results do not prove that the positive effect of a strong home currency on growth options outweighs the potential negative effect on assets in place. Even if this were so for some companies in some industries, we would not expect it to be true across the board. Nevertheless, these results and several case studies suggest that the effect of exchange rate changes on the value of shared growth options is an important part of the relationship between currency values and competitiveness.

Implications for Managers and Public Policy

The foregoing analysis leads to some general observations about growth options, exchange rates, and competitiveness. Obviously, managers need to understand better the exposure of their firm's growth options; at least they should recognize that such options exist and are exposed. It seems natural enough that opportunities should change when exchange rates change. Not only do opportunities themselves change, but firms' relative abilities to exploit them change as well.

Despite their complexity, the effects of real exchange rate shocks on assets in place are probably better understood than are their effects on growth options. Many managers have become accustomed to asking themselves what customers, suppliers, and competitors will do in the *product market* when exchange rates shift. (How will prices change? How will sourcing change?) We have introduced another concern: how will industry *investment behavior* change? Will it accelerate? Decelerate? Will it result in different products? Different production techniques? Different investors? Answers to these questions depend on many firm- and industry-specific factors, but more generally on the opportunities facing competitors and the degree to which opportunities are shared by firms situated on opposite sides of a given exchange rate.

It is doubly important to focus managers' attention on investment plans and behavior because, unlike product market responses, capital-spending responses to exchange rate changes are not immediately visible. It may be possible to see a new factory being built, but it is difficult to get a look inside a competitor's laboratory, or to know which new products or technologies are at what stage of development. It is necessary to consider whether an industry will evolve differently if the yen/dollar exchange rate, for example, is at ¥125/US$ rather than at ¥270/US$. By the time one sees the change in the business, it may be too late. The really important competition could be all but over.

The framework outlined above should also be useful in debates over public policy proposals. Dividing firms' activities into "harvesting" and "sowing" (investing), we arrived at a distinction between competition in existing markets and competition that restructures markets. Though perhaps artificial, this distinction points to discretionary investments—their availability and the terms on which they can be made in the future—as a key determinant of competitiveness. While others have cited investment as the key to productivity growth and hence to competitiveness, we go somewhat further here by emphasizing not only investment per se, but the value of *opportunities to invest*. Some public policies will promote the exercise of existing options, which may be good, without helping to create new ones, which would be even better.

Given a vague consensus that investment is good, it is distressing to see a widespread preoccupation with barometers that measure neither investment, nor investment opportunities, nor future competitiveness. A good example is the monthly figures for the U.S. trade deficit. These figures can say almost nothing about future competitiveness; they simply do not contain such information. If they reflect current changes in competitiveness at all, they do so only for some markets and only as those markets are currently configured. What they mainly reflect are the outcomes of decisions made in the 1970s and subsequent economic shocks. Policy makers cannot have an enormous impact on next month's trade deficit. Surely the deficit's stubborn resistance to all manner of pressure applied to date, including protection and devaluation, is sufficient evidence of this. What is at stake instead are the trade figures for the 1990s and beyond.

We do not wish to give the impression that trade deficits are irrelevant. They must be financed, and how this is accomplished may have implications for competitiveness. But policies adopted to "fix" the current deficit problems may fail in that mission and simultaneously cause serious future problems.

This issue brings us around to exchange rates once again. Two popular prescriptions for the ills that have befallen U.S. competitiveness are the protection of U.S. markets and the devaluation of the U.S. dollar. The former is often admitted to be a poor long-term strategy and is most commonly advanced as a temporary measure. Devaluation of the U.S. dollar, in contrast, is viewed by many as necessary, if not sufficient, to ensure the long-run competitiveness of U.S. manufacturing. A low value for the dollar is prominent on many wish lists that accompany proposed national industrial policies. Such purposeful devaluation of the currency may be just as short sighted as protectionism.

At the very least it should be clear that a low dollar is not a universal good—it affects different industries and companies differently. It is important to understand which industries are likely to be helped and which are likely to be hurt. We expect primary beneficiaries to be U.S. participants in mature or declining industries. For industries that are currently net users of cash, or in which future competitiveness hinges on what investments are made today and by whom, a cheaper currency may be a serious handicap. If policy makers wish to tinker with exchange rates in an effort to boost competitiveness, they should ask themselves which type of industry they want to promote. It can hardly be both.

Our arguments always call forth a spate of examples purporting to show the salutary effects of a falling dollar. Newspapers regularly run stories about one or another U.S. company's progress in boosting exports. We do not deny that the stories are true or claim that the incidents are isolated. Indeed, the U.S. trade position seems to have improved. But these gains may have been costly. First, they seem meager in comparison to the plunge that the dollar has taken since 1985—surely we might have expected more from a 50 percent decline in the value of the dollar. Second, they ignore the other part of the story. Japanese and European companies, especially the former, have gone on an investment spree since 1985. Fortuitously (for them) the value of their currencies took off at a time when many of their companies were flush with cash. The typical response in Japan was to increase R&D and redouble efforts to develop new products. A general manager at JVC, a consumer electronics producer, was quoted in the *Financial Times:* "The most important thing for our survival is not the value of the yen, but the development of new technologies. That is where our future lies."[8] Surely there is some truth in what he says, and surely it is no less relevant to competitiveness than a modest upswing in U.S. exports.

---

[8]*Financial Times,* 7 December 1987, sec. 3, p. 1.

INNOVATION IN THE INTERNATIONAL FINANCIAL MARKETS

Gunter Dufey ◆ Ian H. Giddy

ABSTRACT. New financial techniques and instruments are created when both the demand for and the supply of those instruments become sufficiently large. New financial instruments appear almost always to represent new combinations or packages of a relatively small number of financial services. In the international context these packages are designed to cope with controls on international financial transactions and with the peculiar interest and exchange risks faced by international firms and banks. This approach, when applied to a wide range of new international instruments, seems to explain why some have failed and others have succeeded.

Introduction: A Theory of International Financial Innovation

Innovations in international financial markets arise when firms, usually financial institutions, find it profitable to offer or employ a technique or instrument which better fulfills one of the four functions provided by the international financial sector: 1) liquid and standardized instruments for effecting payments in individual currencies; 2) mechanisms for conducting monetary exchange between different currencies; 3) institutions and markets for channeling savings into investments across national boundaries; and 4) mechanisms for allocating, diversifying, and compensating for risk. The objective of this paper is to develop a theory of innovation in financial markets and to focus on factors which determine the creation and likelihood of success of such innovative instruments.

Generation of New Information Innovation of any kind involves, among other things, the production of new information. The conditions for the socially optimal level of information generation and the optimal subsequent pricing of that information have been considered by Arrow [1], Demsetz [19], and Johnson [32], as well as others. While often costly to produce, new information can be used by any number of people without additional cost: it is a public good. The socially optimal price of a public good is zero. Indeed, the more easily new information is disseminated, the more likely its price will quickly fall to zero, thus reducing or eliminating private incentive to produce easily duplicated innovations. This is Arrow's "appropriability problem." [1] Three ways to reconcile this dilemma have been proposed: the government can create the information itself; the government can award prizes[1] to innovating firms in exchange for the right to disseminate the information freely; or private firms

---

Source: *Journal of International Business Studies,* Fall 1981 pp. 33–51. Reprinted with permission.

[1] See [33], pp. 341–343. The value of the prizes would be related to the net present value of the monopoly profits accruing to a patent-protected private innovator, if this value could be reasonably estimated.

may be able to appropriate the returns through the creation of patent-protected temporary monopolies. Where government intervention is absent or patent laws provide poor protection (as is often the case in international business), there is either little incentive for innovation or the market for innovation is internalized and the value of innovations exploited within the firm[2] (hence the existence of large, multinational firms in information-generating industries). In either case there will be welfare losses: in the former case, from inadequate innovation, and in the latter, from the reluctance of monopolistic firms to share the new information they have generated.

Innovative Financial Instruments and Techniques Two strands of thought can be discerned in the meager literature on innovation of financial instruments and techniques.[3] One view holds that the spur to innovation comes mainly from an increased demand; the other view emphasizes changes in supply. To our knowledge, the first consistent framework was supplied by Greenbaum and Haywood [27] who stress rises in nonhuman wealth per capita as the primary, "demand" stimulus to innovation. Extending the Gurley-Shaw [28] hypothesis, Greenbaum and Haywood argue that because of fixed costs involved in portfolio management, increases in individuals' and firms' non-human wealth will result in a greater demand for a wider diversification of financial claims. Supply, in the Greenbaum-Haywood model, is largely a function of improvement in information over time.

In contrast, Ben-Horim and Silber [6] stress supply factors, particularly those associated with external constraints (regulatory or otherwise) imposed on financial intermediaries, and the availability of institutional support. They find some evidence that major U.S. financial innovations (such as negotiable Certificates of Deposit) occur in response to significant increases in the costs of financial constraints on banks. These increases alter the relative costs of various factors in financial service production and so lead to a search for new financial techniques or instruments with a less costly factor mix.

Both studies, then, hold the view that innovations result from changes in the financial environment and from responses aimed at maintaining or increasing profit or income. Although innovations can be "defensive" as well as "aggressive," environmental changes seem to provide the necessary incentive for innovation. (Whether the level and price of financial innovations are socially optimal remains unresolved.) On the other hand, the environment may also act as a disincentive to innovate. In any industry, the incentive for innovation will decline when patent protection is less effective, when the industry is potentially more competitive, and when product imitation is easier. Financial innovations are extremely easy to imitate because the instruments possess a limited number

---

[2] For a detailed discussion of internalized versus patent-protected innovation, see [9], esp. Ch. 2.

[3] In addition to the studies that follow, see [18] and [56].

of attributes,[4] each of which is characterized by degree of risk and expected return. These in turn are functions of maturity, liquidity, the guarantor, and so forth.[5] Thus, we view most financial innovations, except those designed to circumvent regulations, as no more than a change in the combination of features of existing instruments. If this is correct, all an imitating firm need do is observe the particular arrangement of attributes in a competitor's contract and replicate them. Because of the technical ease of imitation and the difficulty of proving any financial contract to be unique rather than a variant of some existing combination, there can be no patent system for financial instruments or techniques.

In light of these environmental disincentives, one might suppose that the innovation rate in financial markets would be relatively low. Yet observations of the U.S. and international markets indicate that new instruments and techniques—successful and unsuccessful—have appeared frequently over the past two decades. To understand why this is the case, and which firms find it possible to retain profits from their financial innovations, a brief excursion into the literature from the advertising field is necessary.

A distinction has been drawn by Nelson [42] between "search" goods and "experience" goods. The qualities of the former are evident on inspection; advertising need only be factual. The qualities of experience goods, on the other hand, can be determined only by consuming them. Physical product innovations are search goods; any firm that can produce them can also sell them. This ease of entry is what makes patent protection necessary in such industries.

Services, however, including complex financial services, are experience goods, at least when first introduced. Because the risks and returns are hard to ascertain, customers will tend to purchase new financial instruments and services only from firms that have a sound reputation. Hence, there is an economic rationale for certain highly reputable financial institutions to specialize in the repeated development, marketing, and support of new financial contracts. These institutions will enjoy a temporary monopoly advantage that enables them to appropriate returns from investment in financial innovation. Even where the imitation lag is zero, innovation will continue, because new entrants with less prestigious names will normally be unable to appropriate the returns from innovation directly. The market for their talents will be internalized; inventive individuals or firms will tend to be absorbed by those who command the most confidence.

---

[4] The attributes, the last two of which are unique to international instruments, include: promised yield, expected rate of return, rate of return risk, liquidity or marketability, maturity or duration, assurance of availability of funds or claims, divisibility, currency of denomination, and country of jurisdiction.

[5] Tobin has suggested that most of the relevant properties of assets can be classified under the headings of "liquidity," "reversibility," "divisibility," "predictability of value," "yield," "return," and "acceptability in exchange." See [27], p. 572.

The higher the costs of introducing financial techniques or instruments, the more strongly this conclusion holds. Silber [52] has observed that, because financial instruments are held for their returns rather than for their direct utility, the ease with which a secondary market can be established strongly affects the likelihood of early success for new financial instruments. In some cases, the innovating firm may have to create the secondary market. The development and maintenance of such support constitutes a fixed cost, creating economies of scale and an obvious "free rider" problem.[6] Only a large firm with an efficient distribution network will be able to reduce such fixed costs, and only one with a reputation-induced temporary monopoly will be able to recover such costs as remain.

Inducements to Financial Innovation Given an institutional mechanism for the continual generation of financial innovations, the theoretical problem remaining is to be able to predict what kind of innovations will appear, under what circumstances. As was observed in the previous section, innovations can be of two kinds: "aggressive" innovations, which are developed by firms specializing in new financial product introduction; and "defensive" innovations, which arise in response to changes in customer needs or in relative costs.[7] The former are presumably random and, in the financial industry, relatively infrequent. The latter, however, should be predictable.

The hypothesis of this paper is that all defensive innovations are of two types: (a) changes aimed at circumventing government regulations of the price or quantity of financial services (either the regulations themselves change, or their effective costs change); or (b) adaptive changes resulting from changes in relative prices or relative risks that give rise to a "gap" in the range of available financial instruments.

The first type has been discussed frequently in the past. (See for example [27].) Silber [52] generalizes the notion to other constraints, including self- and market-imposed constraints. Many such innovations involve altering the jurisdiction or legal form of contracts without changing their riskiness or return.

The second type of defensive innovations, those that arise from newly emerged gaps in the range of financial services offered,[8] usually involves either unbundling or combining existing financial services. Unbundling of various services allows each to be priced and sold on its own merits, whereas combining

---

[6] The thinness of the secondary markets, for example, created a serious barrier to the acceptance of Eurobonds and Eurodollar certificates for deposit.

[7] As with many such distinctions, this one is somewhat arbitrary; but it highlights some contrasts between innovations in stable and in unstable financial environments.

[8] Holland [29] called this category "transcendental innovation" and cites fee-based services and negotiable certificates of deposit as examples. However, he argues that "transcendental innovation has slowed both absolutely and relative to circumventive innovation during the current period of economic difficulty." (p. 163)

services often reduces total transactions costs. Thus one might expect "combining" instruments to emerge in retail markets, and "isolating" instruments to appear in wholesale financial markets. Instruments that serve purely to transfer risk will likely emerge when risk in the financial environment increases.

Financial Innovation in an International Context Some special conditions in the international financial environment have a bearing on financial innovation: (a) the regulatory environment is multinational, (b) the competitive conditions differ, and (c) exchange rate changes constitute an additional risk. Each feature will be considered in turn.

Institutions that have the flexibility to conduct business outside particular national jurisdictions can also design financial contracts that place the legal location of the contracts in favorable jurisdictions. Many international financial innovations, such as Eurobonds, are structured to minimize government interference and to reduce taxes or other regulatory costs. In general, however, it is an oversimplification to claim that international financial transactions are exempt from government regulation and control.

Indeed, the general rule is that controls on transborder transactions—such as, transfer of financial instruments from one jurisdiction to another—are more severe than those on internal transfers. Whether the regulatory environment is more or less restrictive cannot be determined a priori. In some instances, the greater relative freedom has permitted the creation of new instruments, not available domestically; in other cases, greater restriction on international transfers of funds has produced innovations designed solely to circumvent the controls.

In the absence of patent protection, some degree of monopolistic control is necessary for a firm to capture the returns from financial innovation. Because a greater number of large, experienced financial institutions participate aggressively in the international markets than in domestic markets, the degree of competition and the probability of rapid imitation is heightened. The incentive for innovation should accordingly be reduced. Yet, the opposite extreme—the protected, domestic, cartel-like banking system—is not conducive to innovation, either. Arrow [1] has shown that the gains from cost-reducing innovations are smaller to a monopolist than to the competitive firms which can appropriate those gains. This confirms what intuition would suggest: monopolists or oligopolists face less pressure to innovate than do competitive firms. It is not clear, however, whether an innovation is likely to spread faster in a competitive market than in an oligopoly. Whereas competitive firms facing a high elasticity of demand will be forced to copy a cost-reducing innovation quickly, it is also true that oligopolists and cartel members tend to undertake major changes in concert.

These considerations aside, it seems clear that, on balance, the rate of production and spread of financial innovations is greater in international than in domestic markets. One reason is simply the wider range of needs for specialized financial techniques. Another is that the greater variety of institutions and ideas in the international market leads to cross-fertilization of concepts and techniques which can be incorporated in new instruments. More participants also ensure better secondary markets. Most important, however, is the fact that the potential market for cost- or risk-saving techniques is much larger, even if the imitation lag is shorter.

Finally, the international environment involves fluctuating exchange rates, which not only create new risks and new types of transactions, but also require that financial institutions intermediate between entities which have different base currencies and different degrees of access to foreign exchange markets. As exchange rates and other financial variables have become less stable, the risks of international business have increased and the scope for financial innovation has expanded.

International Financial Innovation: A Response to a Riskier Environment

Changes in regulation and changes in the economic environment that produce a different set of risks and returns have been the inducements to defensive innovation in the international context. During the 1960s, rapid economic growth and increasing capital mobility in the industrial countries led governments to establish capital controls to defend their monetary policies and the fixed exchange rate system. The banks quickly responded by implementing techniques designed to circumvent these and other regulatory constraints. This was the decade in which Eurobonds, Eurodollars, and parallel loans were introduced.

By the mid 1970s, in contrast, the regulatory incentives for financial innovation were overshadowed by new economic incentives and changes in the competitive structure of financial markets. Floating exchange rates freed governments from the need to defend misvalued currencies. The financial systems of many major countries became more flexible: interest rate and credit controls had begun to lose their effectiveness. Governments themselves took advantage of the innovations of the previous decade by placing, borrowing, and recycling funds through the Euromarkets.

With greater mobility and flexibility, however, came greater financial interdependence and a period of adjustment to a changed system. Governments, attempting to compensate for the dissipated effects of traditional stabilization policies, increased their intervention in the money and foreign exchange markets; yet all that resulted was a less stable system, evidenced by the increased instability and volatility of exchange rates, interest rates, and inflation rates during the early seventies. The decade of the 1970s produced innovations to cope with exchange and interest rate risks and led to a boom in trading Eurodollars, Eurobonds, and floating rate notes. The remainder of the paper examines these and other innovations, and the reason for their success or failure.

International Financial Instruments: Successes and Failures

The Success Stories This section describes the international financial innovations that must be considered successful, if only by virtue of the magnitude that they have attained. The sequence moves from variations of traditional trade financing techniques to more exotic combinations. Then some examples of techniques and instruments that were not successful will be discussed, and an attempt will be made to draw some conclusions as to the distinguishing factors.

(a) Trade Financing Techniques Recycled The first example illustrates how an age-old technique—export financing through bankers' acceptances—can be successfully adapted to take advantage of new opportunities provided by changes in the external environment. The factors that gave rise to *forfaiting*[9] are closely linked to the activist role played by many governments in the economic development of their countries—particularly, but by no means exclusively, by the socialist countries. There, government-owned enterprises frequently import capital goods, often in the form of turn-key plants, from suppliers in industrialized countries on extended payment terms related to the life of the project. Such maturities, which may range anywhere from 3 to 12 years, cannot be handled through the institutions that traditionally undertake export financing. From the point of view of the exporters who may finance such transactions by borrowing in the markets, this would be costly. More important, technologically oriented capital goods manufacturers feel very uncomfortable with the economic and political risks associated with loans to foreign political entities. Forfaiting solves the exporter's problems, and it is also advantageous to the borrower—that is, the importer.

A typical transaction involves four parties: the exporter and the importer, the importer's bank (which also tends to be a government entity), and the forfaiter, usually a special purpose subsidiary of one of the large Swiss, West German, or Austrian banks which have pioneered this technique.

When the exporter's negotiations with the importing organization are nearly complete, the exporter obtains a commitment for the forfaiter to finance the transaction at a firm interest cost. This cost is the discount at which the forfaiter will purchase at the time the deal is completed. The forfaiter also charges a fee as compensation for the cost of assuring availability of funds, which may require him to borrow funds on a long-term basis and reinvest them on a short-term basis during the commitment period. [43] When the transaction is completed, the importing organization gives the exporter a series of promissory notes with maturities staggered according to the repayment terms, usually in 6-month intervals reflecting the installments. Most important, these promissory notes are endorsed by the importer's bank which becomes the primary obligor in the transactions, just as in the case of a banker's acceptance.

---

[9] The term comes from the French word "a forfait," meaning "without recourse."

The forfaiter will purchase the total bundle from the exporter without recourse, thus assuming the risk of the state-owned bank and, ultimately, of the government of the importer's country. The essence of forfaiting involves shifting the country's risk to an institution that specializes in assessing such risks. But the forfaiter is also an international market specialist. Usually the package of notes is broken up and sold to various investors who prefer different maturities. The forfaiter endorses the notes, thus collecting the risk premium in addition to the difference in yield between the value of the individual note and the discount which he obtained when he bought the package. Thus, the forfaiter exploits both differences in perceived political risk and also, possibly, imperfections in international money markets arising from transactions costs.

While it is fairly obvious why government banks will endorse the notes[10]— they obtain funds which contribute to the economic development of their country—it is not so obvious why they do not borrow directly in international credit markets. Here we encounter another market imperfection: the government banks believe—rightly or wrongly—that the obligations stemming from their endorsements, which are contingent liabilities, will count very little (if at all) against their credit limits in international markets. Because it is next to impossible to set objective credit limits for government borrowers, international lending institutions and their supervisory authorities frequently use arbitrary ratios in lieu of judgment. As the great majority of forfaiting transactions involve East European countries and some Middle Eastern and Latin American governments, forfaiting may represent a device for evading credit rationing in the western banking system.

A different twist on an old trade financing technique is the "domestication" of securities issued by foreign borrowers in national markets. For example, several Brazilian borrowers have gained access to the U.S. commercial paper market by having a domestic bank open a letter of credit on their behalf. [2] From a legal perspective this makes the bank the primary obligor and the paper becomes an acceptable investment for institutional investors which normally face externally or self-imposed restrictions on holdings of foreign securities.

(b) Eurobonds The market for these instruments represents an example of the phenomenon of external markets that coexist and compete with their domestic counterparts. The concept is by now well accepted: an international instrument, identical to the domestic instrument in all respects except location of issue, will be free from certain costs or constraints. In practice, not all such instruments

---

[10] Endorsement of the notes by a government-owned financial institution is very important. First, history has shown that, for a given government, the obligations of its financial institutions tend to have a higher priority than those of its commercial enterprises. Second, and more important, the endorsement (or "aval") makes each note a pure financial instrument, separated from the underlying economic transaction and free from any counterclaims of the importer against the exporter.

succeed, because not all serve a genuinely unsatisfied need in the most efficient fashion. Indeed, the supply of Eurobonds was for a long time inhibited by the high cost of issue and of organizing a secondary market.

The basis of the Eurobond's success is an inconsistency in regulation: governments tend to limit the access of foreign issuers of bonds to their national markets, but have less stringent or noneffective controls on domestic investors who purchase foreign bonds. Internationally active investment banking firms can therefore issue bonds and similar debt instruments in such a way that national restrictions are bypassed. The issues are given the legal form of private placement and/or placement in nonresident investment accounts.[11]

The history of the Eurobond sheds an interesting light on the process of financial innovation. Although the pattern of regulation has been in existence for a long time, the market for Eurobonds did not develop until 1964 when the U.S. balance of payments program, particularly the Interest Equalization Tax (IET), closed the U.S. market to foreign borrowers. Until that time, this market had been reasonably open to all borrowers who were able to comply with SEC accounting and disclosure requirements—largely public entities from developed countries. No doubt a major factor preventing the earlier emergence of the market and contributing to its subsequent erratic growth was the difficulty of developing an organized secondary market for bonds sold in a variety of countries and lacking an integrated mechanism for trading. Substantial sales began only in the mid 1970s, 10 to 15 years after the first Eurobonds were issued. By that time, the volume of bonds outstanding had reached a critical point at which economies of scale in the secondary market came into play. Also, the gradual entry of institutional investors who trade in response to relatively small incentives contributed to the development of an active secondary market.[12] Indeed, when the IET was reduced to zero in January 1974, the Eurobond market continued to flourish, side by side with the revival of the market for foreign bonds in the United States.[13] By this time the instruments developed in the Eurobond market had spawned features distinct from those of the foreign bonds issues in the U.S. market. They are now quite different from bonds issued in any of the national markets.[14]

---

[11] A typical example is a bond issue of a Norwegian municipality, that is managed by an underwriting group based in London, who places a portion of dollar-denominated instruments in the investment accounts that French (or Italian, or Belgian, etc.) investors maintain in Switzerland (or Holland, or the United Kingdom, or Luxembourg).

[12] Eurobond turnover cleared through the two dominant clearing systems, Cedel and Euro-clear, increased more than tenfold during the 1970s: see [7], p. 319.

[13] For data, see OECD, *Capital Market Study—Statistical Annex* (OECD: Paris, periodic); Morgan Guaranty Trust Company, *World Financial Markets,* various issues; and U.S. Federal Reserve Board, *Federal Reserve Bulletin,* various issues.

[14] For a detailed discussion of Eurobond issuing and underwriting techniques, see [23].

(c) **Eurocurrencies** This paper would be incomplete without a brief consideration of the most eminently successful of postwar international financial innovations: the Eurocurrency, or external money market, competes directly with the domestic wholesale money markets of many countries.[15] The necessary condition for the existence of an external money market is that certain regulatory costs affecting both deposits and loans can be avoided by placing time deposits and loans on the books of financial institutions operating in jurisdictions that do not impose costly regulations, such as, reserve requirements, portfolio restrictions. The relaxation of comprehensive exchange controls on both residents and nonresidents has facilitated the international transfer of funds that arises in the course of transactions related to external intermediation.

This innovation has contributed significantly to the ease with which savers' and borrowers' needs can be reconciled, regardless of geographical location. Funds of great magnitude can be intermediated in a context of unrestricted competition, virtually free of administrative credit controls affecting either price or quantity. In essence, the Eurocurrency market has performed an important "unbundling" service by permitting the separation of country of jurisdiction from the currency of denomination of financial instruments.

(d) **Eurodollar Certificates of Deposit** The Eurocurrency market has itself stimulated the development of several new instruments. As occurred in the U.S. money market, a successful market for negotiable certificates of deposit (CDs) has been created in London. These instruments, known as London Dollar CDs or Euro CDs, have been called "the first new negotiable instrument created under English Law since 1896." [58, p. 608] Their function is obvious: they represent Eurodollar deposits with negotiability and potential liquidity. Unlike Eurodollars per se, Euro CDs were created not by regulation, but by the desire of the issuing banks to have assured availability of funds while providing the depositor with the liquidity of an actively traded negotiable instrument. The key to the success of the Euro CD was therefore the development of a viable secondary market in London.

Two financial institutions undertook the initial investment in hopes of gaining a sufficiently high return before competition began to deprive them of the rewards for innovating. With hindsight it can be said that they were disappointed.[16] Other banks quickly began writing similar paper in order to obtain funds at lower rates than were available through deposit taking. Many lenders

---

[15] For recent surveys see [39] and [20].

[16] Citicorp and White, Weld, & Co. were the institutions that introduced the instrument. They spent 15 months in tortuous discussions and legal inquiries; yet the first buyer of a $25,000 London CD was Chemical Bank in London, which promptly began printing its own in blatant imitation! On the other hand, several of the most prominent U.S. banks allowed 7 or 8 years to pass before entering the market. See [59], p. 608.

prefer CDs which provide them with liquidity[17] and are therefore satisfied with a lower yield.

The innovators in the secondary market did not fare much better. Apart from White, Weld, & Co. (whose strength was in the underwriting), the secondary market in Euro CDs was dominated by the British discount houses that began dealing in these instruments as a sideline to their main business in short-dated governments, acceptances, local authority bonds, and so on.

When the volume of CDs outstanding had reached approximately $5 billion, the large U.S.–based money market dealers, using their extensive information and retail networks to good advantage, began outcompeting the London discount houses and—to a lesser extent—the brokers, in both the new issue business and much of the secondary market. [53, p. 422] Today, the U.S. dealers play an important role in the Euro CD market, just as they do in the domestic CD market. At present the liquidity of the Euro CD secondary market is less than that of the U.S. market, largely because of the difference in volume. At the end of 1980 the value of Euro CDs outstanding was approximately one fourth of the volume of the domestic CDs.

(e) Roll-over Credits Domestic banks, as a rule, have a wider range of stable sources of funds, ranging from demand deposits to equity capital. To the extent that these funds are insensitive to interest rate changes, domestic banks can afford to make loans at fixed rates. Eurobanks, in contrast, are specialized wholesale banks that rely on a sole funding source—large external time deposits, mostly from highly interest-sensitive depositors. The Eurobanks' cost of funds therefore varies directly with the level of short-term interest rates. How could they make term loans without facing considerable interest rate risk?

The answer was the roll-over credit, or revolver. Under this arrangement, funds are committed to the borrower for medium-term periods, such as 3 years; but the interest rate changes every 3 or 6 months in direct relation to prevailing short-term rates in the Eurodollar interbank market. Thus the availability of funds could now be assured for longer periods than the interest-commitment period, and medium-term loans could be safely funded by obtaining three- or six-month time deposits.

As interest rates began to fluctuate more widely, the advantage of distinguishing the loan agreement period from the interest rate period became increasingly important to the banks. Customers found these arrangements acceptable, because they were able to avoid the risk of loan nonrenewal.

---

[17] Sometimes this liquidity is illusory, as the issuance of a CD is accompanied by an informal agreement that the CD will not be traded; indeed, the paper is typically held in safekeeping by the issuing bank who will pay a higher rate. The buyer, in turn, can show on his balance sheet dollar assets that are not only safe, but appear to be liquid. Fifty percent of the total volume of Euro-CDs is believed by market observers to consist of "lock-up CDs" see [53], p. 420.

Nonfinancial enterprises are, as a rule, more willing than banks to bear an interest rate risk, especially if their net operating cash flow exhibits some positive correlation with interest rates. Today, the overwhelming majority of Euro-lending is done on a floating-rate basis, as is appropriate for periods in which inflation and interest rates fluctuate widely.

(f) Floating Rate Notes From the revolving loan it was only a small step to the floating rate note (FRN), introduced in 1969. The FRN allowed some corporate borrowers to obtain funds directly from nonbank sources at interest rates that varied with short-term bank rates. These instruments allowed investors greater flexibility to focus on real interest rates in an environment characterized by unprecedented uncertainty about future movements of rates. The growth of FRNs has been impressive. In the first year of issue, the volume was approximately U.S. $15 million; in 1976, the volume was well over $1 billion.[18]

During the "Herstatt Crisis" of 1974, banks learned to appreciate the fact that whereas the overall volume of funds available for deposits may be quite stable, or even expanding, individual institutions are not immune to a funding risk. Hence, the introduction of the bank FRN and the floating rate CD (which differ only in terms of subordination), provided the banks with the same "unbundling" of risks that the "revolver" had provided to their customers.[19] Floating rate CDs enable banks to be assured of the longer-term availability of funds, while allowing the interest rates on their liabilities to vary periodically with market rates. In addition, appropriate placement policies allow the issuing bank to broaden and diversify its sources of funds. As compared with banks, relatively few corporate borrowers use this vehicle, preferring instead revolving loans from banks and the commercial paper market. [49] Interestingly, occasional experiments with more complex clauses—such as, provisions for early redemption at the holder's option at declining discounts from par, or issues with declining spreads over the interbank deposit rate—have not been successful. Investors seem to have a strong preference for instruments which are conceptually simple.[20]

(g) Multicurrency Option Facilities As corporations became aware of the different forms of loans and currencies available in the Eurocurrency market, a

---

[18] For year-by-year data, see *Kredietbank Weekly Bulletin,* 17 June 1977, pp. 6–7.

[19] A further unbundling has been achieved by some syndication managers, who have divided syndicated Eurocredits into negotiable short-term instruments, sometimes called loan participation certificates. They are regarded as a hybrid of Eurocredits and floating rate notes, and are unique to the external markets because issuing them in the United States would subject them to S.E.C. requirements. For an example see [47].

[20] This also holds for a recent "innovation," the drop-lock bond, which starts its life as an FRN. If the Libor Rate falls below a trigger rate, the FRN is automatically and permanently converted into a fixed-rate bond. [35] A similar fate befell an FRN that incorporated a deferred put option which allowed note holders to redeem the note at face value after 3 years. [48]

logical step was to structure loan agreements that would allow them to "draw down" funds on their borrowings in one or more stipulated currencies. The choice tends to be limited to those currencies which are "convertible" and for which external deposit markets[21]—or active forward markets—exist. The pricing is based on the London interbank rate, plus or minus a currency adjustment factor equal to the forward premium or discount prevailing in the foreign exchange market.

Multicurrency option facilities represent just one example of a whole class of instruments that reflect the intimate linkage between interest rates and exchange rates in a multinational market. The instruments differ in how they bundle and unbundle credit and currency transactions, the precise configuration being determined by transactions costs, regulation, and other market imperfections.

(h) Forward and Futures Contracts in Foreign Exchange The basic instrument in foreign exchange is the forward exchange contract, where two parties agree to exchange currencies at a predetermined rate at a specific time in the future.[22] While the forward foreign exchange contract is, of course, not new, there are two variants that warrant notice. The first is the well-publicized futures contract, in effect a standardized forward foreign exchange contract that is negotiable, saleable prior to maturity, and guaranteed to be relatively free of default risk. These features, together with the small denominations in which they are available, make the risks and returns of exchange rate changes accessible to the small investor. Such investors have therefore been willing to pay the higher transactions cost of the organized futures market. Despite such differences, empirical evidence reveals no statistically significant differences between forward and futures prices. [12]

(i) Swaps and Parallel Loans The second variant of interest is the use of a forward exchange contract in conjunction with a credit arrangement which effectively changes the currency of denomination of that deposit or loan. A number of these combinations will be reviewed below; however, the general principle is that the currency of denomination of an asset can be "converted" by contractually selling the future cashflows from that asset for another currency. Similarly, the currency denomination of a liability may be altered by contractually purchasing the foreign currency necessary to liquidate that obligation. The remarkable feature of this use of forward contracts in the Eurocurrency market, for example, is that it enables banks to offer deposits or loans in

---

[21] As bankers have learned to understand the interaction between external and national financial markets, some agreements have given the borrower an additional choice of drawing funds in a chosen currency in either the external or the internal market. Of course, the pricing differs and the agreements become rather complex. See, for example, [8].

[22] If that date is 2 business days or less, the exchange is considered a spot transaction.

any currency for which there is a forward exchange market, even if no external money market exists in that currency. The result is that the Eurodollar is the only full-fledged external money in existence; other Eurocurrencies are often simply Eurodollars linked to forward exchange contracts.

Currency Swaps. While the term swap has come to refer to almost any arrangement that incorporates a forward foreign exchange contract, currency swaps simply denote an agreement to exchange certain amounts of currencies on a spot basis and to reverse the transaction later at a specified time and rate. Currency swaps are used widely by foreign exchange traders who wish to limit their risk over time. When the regulatory environment compels it, corporations sometimes find (long-term) currency swaps useful.

The simultaneous spot purchase and forward sale of a foreign currency serves to lock in any difference between the spot and forward exchange rates. The difference, often referred to as the "swap rate," represents the change in value of funds at two separate points in time, and is therefore the equivalent of an interest rate. Because a currency swap locks in the nominal cost or return of a temporary conversion of funds into a second currency, it can be used to compare the rates of return in two currencies.

Credit Swaps. This instrument explicitly ties together a credit transaction and a forward contract, or their equivalents. A typical transaction would involve a firm in country A providing (hard) currency funds for its affiliate in a weak-currency country. The parent company, for example, would lend dollar funds to an intermediary—a commercial bank, or even the central bank of the weak currency country—which, in turn, lends local currency funds to the foreign affiliate. At a predetermined date in the future, the transaction will be reversed. The cost of the transaction is the interest rate on the dollar funds less the interest rate on the local currency funds, adjusted for the swap rate: the difference between the exchange rates used to convert the parent's funds into, and later out of, the affiliate's currency. Because of these contractual relationships, the intermediary (local or foreign central bank) bears the burden of the exchange risk on the (dollar) principal. The interest on the local currency loan, however, is subject to exchange risk in dollar terms.

Market imperfections provide the rationale for firms and intermediaries undertaking such complex deals instead of simpler alternatives, such as, borrowing in the local money market, or lending dollar funds covered with a forward contract. Neither forward cover nor access to local credit markets may be available at reasonable rates. For the intermediaries, such credit swaps are a means of bolstering their foreign exchange reserves, using the financial needs of captive foreign affiliates to obtain these reserves at a lower cost than might be available through outright borrowing. Moreover, because they are close to the political powers that determine extent and timing of devaluations, they may be able to assess the foreign exchange risk better than private companies. Indeed, the intermediary bank is frequently the central bank itself.

A special form of credit swap is an arrangement whereby a claim is denominated in one currency (say, dollars) but the amount of principal and interest to be paid each period is determined by variations in the dollar exchange rate of another currency (such as, yen). Thus if, one year after the issue of such a bond, the yen has risen by 5 percent, the dollar amount of principal and interest to be paid also rises by 5 percent. The purpose of this instrument, which is effectively a yen-denominated claim, is merely to avoid taxes and restrictions on securities denominated in particular currencies, such as, yen. [60]

Arbi-Loans. This variation of the credit swap occurs when one unit of an integrated firm transfers funds to another unit to take advantage of capital market imperfections. The first affiliate borrows locally, at an advantageous interest rate and passes the funds to the second affiliate for use in the latter's currency. The loan is covered with a forward contract. In effect, the first unit acts as an intermediary, undertaking arbitrage between two financial markets. It is able to do so only if it has both access to cheap local funds and a means to move them out—say, via dividends or other intracompany payments. The funds are cheap in the sense that the difference between the local interest rate and the interest rate in the foreign currency exceeds the swap rate.

Parallel Loans. This is an arrangement under which two corporations (or other institutions) in different countries make loans to each other in their own countries and currencies. The classic example is that of an American firm making a dollar loan to the U.S. subsidiary of a British company, while the British firm simultaneously makes a sterling loan to the British subsidiary of the American firm. Such dollar/sterling parallel loans are concluded at an interest rate differential reflecting the difference between long-term interbank rates.

Each loan serves as collateral for the other and bears an interest rate related to local credit conditions plus the putative cost of a long-term forward exchange contract. Unlike some of the earlier examples, this technique is purely a by-product of regulation; it enables firms to avoid capital (and perhaps also credit) controls.[23] In concept, it is a costly and clumsy arrangement: two parties with matching needs have to be brought together, and the agreement is a combination of three financial contracts (two loans and one implicit forward transaction). Only regulations which constrain credit allocation or prevent free capital flows justify its existence.[24]

Apparent Failures Our contention is that international financial innovations are likely to succeed only if they offer (1) a means of circumventing regulation, (2) an "unbundling" of previously linked financial services, or (3) a combina-

---

[23] Another possible market imperfection is the banks' failure to offer long-term forward contracts at reasonable spreads, perhaps because the market is too "thin." In that case the corporation might as well undertake to find one of the contracting parties directly.

[24] A variant of the parallel loan across currencies involves 2 offsetting transactions in the domestic and the external (Euro-) sector of the credit market in a single currency.

tion of services with relatively low transactions costs. Moreover, even if they fulfill one or more of these conditions, their success is likely to be hindered unless a secondary market or the institutional framework for such a market is already in place.

(a) Currency-Combination Instruments

A prime example of this concept is the "currency-basket Eurobond," much touted by international bankers and officials in past years. The intention was sensible: by offering a bond whose value was linked to a weighted average of several currencies, issuers provided investors with ready-made-currency diversification.[25] Some have even been denominated in Special Drawing Rights (SDRs)–a basket of currencies "backed by the IMF." Yet compared with total Eurobond issues, currency-combination bonds have failed dismally.[26] Why?

Banking practitioners claim that some of these currency baskets have been expensive to administer, and that they included minor currencies in which the investor had no interest; it has also been said that investors simply did not understand them. Although there may be some truth to this, the true reason is probably much simpler: the portfolio of the typical international investor is sufficiently large to allow him to obtain currency diversification tailored to his specific needs at little extra cost—for example, through the purchase of different bonds denominated in single currencies. This contention is supported by the fact that not only did complex, multicurrency formulae fail, but simpler units, based on only a few major currencies, also fared poorly. [11]

(b) Eurocommercial Paper and Euroequities

In the early 1970s, about a dozen U.S. multinational companies were persuaded to issue dollar-denominated commercial paper in London as an alternative to borrowing Eurodollars, largely to comply with U.S. foreign investment restrictions. What the promoters of the "innovation" overlooked was that the spread between deposit rates and borrowing rates is necessarily narrower in the Euromarket than in the domestic banking markets, and therefore the cost of intermediation was very low. Borrowers could save very little by going directly to investors for funds. This fact, together with the cost of issue and distribution, made the advantages of the instrument minimal, and the volume of Eurocommercial paper issued was very small.

Euroequities were an innovation that existed only in the minds of fast-working financial writers, who saw in the success of the Eurobond market the possibility of a similar opportunity for equities. As quickly became apparent, however, only fixed-interest Eurosecurities (for example, Eurobonds) can be sufficiently differentiated from their domestic counterparts to make possible issuing techniques that circumvent those restrictions and tax effects common

---

[25] For an analysis of currency basket formulas, see [50].

[26] For data, see *Kredietbank Weekly Bulletin*, 29 June 1979, p. 5.

to issues in national markets. Euroequities, wherever issued, would give a claim on the residual income of a subsidiary in an integrated corporation and so would not differ from parent-firm equities. Thus, one of the major preconditions for Euroequities—their regulatory advantage over and distinction from national equities—never existed. The few issues were actually either fixed-interest securities with an equity feature, similar to convertible bonds, or internationally distributed shares that were in no way different from those issued in a national market, and the end result was that many drifted back through arbitrage as soon as prices showed the slightest difference.

(c) Index-Linked Financial Instruments During periods of monetary and economic instability, there is an obvious need for financial contracts that allocate equitably among borrowers and lenders windfall gains and losses arising from sizeable, unexpected interest rate movements. Because nominal interest rates are determined largely by expected rates of inflation over the term of the contract, it is tempting to try to insulate financial contracts from unexpected changes in the price level by tying the yield to some index that represents this inflation factor. Yet a survey of the world's financial markets shows that index-linked financial assets are few and far between; even where they have been tried, they were often no more than relatively short-lived experiments. [45] Why have they consistently failed, given that the basic concept appears to be sound?[27]

The fact that we do not find indexation in the unregulated international markets suggests that there must be problems other than governmental opposition. One possible obstacle is that of finding an acceptable index. The usual price indices (consumer-, wholesale-, and GNP deflator) are not universally acceptable; the various goods that make up an index (or the weights assigned to them) may or may not be relevant for particular borrowers, or lenders, or both. Another problem is that the index must be objective and verifiable. Price indices in many countries are often not credible, because they are believed to consist of political numbers manipulated by the government.

Whereas it may be possible to overcome these technical difficulties (though at some cost), there is a more cogent reason why index-linked financial contracts are very rare: there exists a ready alternative, which is to shorten the maturity of the pricing contract. Floating rates capture most of the variation in inflation, and they may have succeeded where index bonds have failed because market interest rates are objective and verifiable.

(d) Commodity-Linked Bonds Even more rare than index-linked bonds are those where the principal (and possibly the interest rate) is tied to the price of a commodity. These instruments, more properly termed commodity equities

---

[27] Stanley Fischer has presented models of the demand for index bonds under several sets of conditions and concludes that "reasons for the nonexistence of indexed bonds in the U.S. economy do not emerge clearly from the analysis." [25], p. 527.

because they are bonds only in the sense of seniority of claims, might provide an issuer with the assurance that his liability would rise or fall in line with his revenues. Thus, this instrument has been suggested as a solution to the debt problems of developing countries that rely for export receipts on one or two commodities.[28]

From the international investor's perspective, commodity equities (if objectively indexed) provide a means of participating in the risks and returns of primary producers.[29] Yet the fact that very few of these instruments have been floated suggests there may be problems on the supply side. First, the issuer is protected only on the revenue side. Should his costs increase by a similar amount, the burden of servicing the increased liability will be considerable. Second, rising prices for the commodity may coincide with a decrease in volume, further affecting net revenues from which the liability must be repaid. From the investor's perspective, changes in the value of his asset (the particular commodity) may not be linked to the cost of his consumption basket. It is not surprising that few of these instruments have actually been issued.

(e) Forward Forwards During the late 1960s a market appeared in London that anticipated the now-thriving interest rate futures market, but itself never took off. A forward forward, or more correctly, a forward Eurodollar CD, is a contract to issue a Eurodollar CD at a fixed interest rate at a given date in the future. Such contracts, in conjunction with the issue of ordinary (spot) CDs, effectively constituted CDs of longer term than were at that time legally permitted in the UK. However, since the same effect can now be achieved as easily by simultaneously buying and selling CDs of different maturities, participants in the Eurodollar market have not employed this technique to any great extent. Whether the introduction of standardized Eurodollar futures contracts traded in organized markets will be able to capture the advantage of unbundling of two financial services (a pure interest rate plus a forward contract) remains to be seen.

(f) Foreign Exchange Options Finally, several authors have pointed out the apparent need for puts and calls in spot foreign exchange. Shapiro and Rutenberg predicted in 1976 that "they will be available soon." [51, p. 53] These contracts involve two parties (a firm and a bank, for example), one of which

---

[28] The most recent discussion of this proposal is in [36]. Mexico has issued five "Petrobonds" between April 1977 and April 1980, and a few (domestic) French issues have been linked to gold. In 1980 a silver mining company issued notes the value of which was linked to the price of silver [54].

[29] An added advantage is the avoidance of the moral hazard problems associated with portfolio investment in markets lacking appropriate disclosure rules and other investor protection laws, which is typical for many LDCs.

has the right to purchase a currency at an agreed-upon exchange rate any time between two given dates. It has been shown that call option prices are tied to interest rates on single-currency and currency-option bonds. [24]

Conceivably, a firm could employ foreign currency options whenever it faces future cash flows that are fixed in amount but of uncertain timing or execution. Standardized contracts could make them accessible even to small investors on the organized futures markets; indeed, commodity options have attracted some investor interest. Such contracts do exist [30, p. 57; 3] but have never attained the status of an established market with publicly known prices. The reason may lie in part in the specialized nature of such instruments and the consequent difficulty of establishing a secondary market. A more persuasive reason, however, is that a bank offering an open options contract exposes itself to considerable risk. Such risks are difficult to offset,[30] and a bank entering into a large number of option contracts would likely face regulatory constraints. In the absence of evidence to the contrary, therefore, we attribute the slow growth of foreign exchange options to government intervention in bank portfolio decisions.

Conclusion: A Rough Taxonomy

Despite the fact that the decade of the 1970s appears to have been demonstrably more conducive than previous decades to the generation and support of international financial innovations, a number of well-publicized innovations have not met their proponents' expectations. The cost and success rates of past innovations are important determinants of the future rate of innovation. In the authors' view, the probability of success can be enhanced by drawing on the lesson of past failures—which is, that in order to succeed the innovation must involve a genuinely new combination of standard financial elements and must bridge a gap arising from some change in the regulatory or economic environment.

Judging the degree of success of a new technique is tricky: demand for some instruments is low merely because they successfully fill a narrow market need; and most innovations with an identifiable likelihood of failure never see the light of day. These reservations notwithstanding, Table 1 summarizes the major innovations and their characteristics. Next to each technique have been identified the major facilitating factors, such as regulatory circumvention and the primary supply constraints or influences.

Several public policy implications emerge from the theory and this survey

---

[30] Feiger and Jacquillat [24] have argued that foreign exchange puts and calls are redundant, in that by using a portfolio of currency option and conventional bonds one can "create" currency puts or calls. This implies that banks could create an offset, given that a sufficiently broad and deep currency option bond market existed.

TABLE 1   International Financial Innovations in the Postwar Era

Instrument or Technique and Date of Introduction	Environmental Factor or Need To Be Filled	Supply Factor	Degree of Success
Swaps (late 1950s)	Currency flexibility in loans, deposits in a single money market	Potentially higher cost than alternative	High
Eurobonds (1958)	Domestic taxes and issue regulations	Severe secondary market difficulties at first	High
Eurodollars (1959)	Domestic bank regulation	Easy to issue	High
Currency basket bond (1961)	Ready-made diversification	Minimal secondary market	Minor
Roll-over credits (early 1960s)	Lenders match assets to liabilities	Transfer of interest rate risk	High
Parallel loans (early 1960s)	Credit and exchange controls	High cost of matching participants' needs	Modest
Currency option bond (1965)	Investor desire for probable gains but not losses from exchange rate changes	Highly risky for borrower	Minor
Dual-currency convertible bonds (mid-1960s)	Issue controls and exchange controls	Thin secondary market	Minor
London dollar CDs (1967)	Liquidity	Secondary market slow to grow at first	Modest
Forward forward CDs (late 1960s)	Transfer of interest rate risk	No secondary market; available in different form	Minor
Forfaiting (late 1960s)	Transfer of country risk to specialist institution	Adaptation of traditional technique	Modest

of financial techniques. Innovation is a public good, and as a rule there is a presumed rationale for the public production of public goods; where, as in the case of financial innovation, it appears that government agencies would be inadequate, there exists a case for patent protection or subsidy of innovators. Patents, however, are impractical for financial contracts, and the government cannot easily determine the appropriate subsidy for a financial contract. One form of subsidy might be in the support of secondary markets; government might commit itself to absorbing part of the losses of market-makers. Whereas

TABLE **1**   (continued)

Instrument or Technique and Date of Introduction	Environmental Factor or Need To Be Filled	Supply Factor	Degree of Success
Floating rate notes (1970)	Transfer of interest rate risk	Small secondary market	Modest
Eurocommercial paper (1971)	None under existing regulatory system	Secondary market difficulties	Minor
Multicurrency option loan	Provides borrower flexibility	Increases risk for banks	Modest
Negotiable Eurocurrency loan participation notes (early 1970s)	Standardization potential liquidity	No assured secondary market	Minor at present
Currency futures (1973)	Standardization, negotiability; transfer of default risk	Institutional framework in place	High
Floating rate CDs (1977)	Transfer of commitment period risk	Small secondary market	Minor so far
Foreign exchange options (1970s)	Hedge currency risk of uncertain cash flows	Regulatory obstacles	Minor
Eurodollar interest futures (introduction under discussion)	Standardization, negotiability; transfer of transfer of default risk	Institutional framework exists	NA
Euroequity (never)	None at present	Secondary market assured	None
Index-linked bonds (rare)	Avoiding risk from unexpected inflation	No objective index available/secondary market difficulties	Minor
Commodity-linked bonds (rare)	Price fluctuation of reference commodity	Unrelated to cash flow of issuer	Minor

this is done to some extent (through the tax system) by governments seeking to develop domestic capital markets, it is difficult to conceive of a mechanism for secondary market support on an international scale.

This leaves the risks and rewards of financial innovation largely in private hands, and especially in the hands of those financial institutions whose reputation allows them to appropriate the returns from financial product development. Whether the rate of innovation that occurs in this fashion is socially optimal or not is impossible to say, although it seems probable that society as a whole would have gained from the earlier development of secondary markets for some instruments such as Eurobonds.

In conclusion, therefore, the public policy implications are primarily negative ones. First, it is contrary to the public interest, at least in this context, to seek to inhibit the risk-taking behavior of resourceful, reputable financial institutions: it is precisely they that have a comparative advantage in gaining a return from investments in new financial ventures. Second, the fewer the regulations that are placed on individuals' or firms' access to the full range of financial contracts, the greater the gain from, and reward to, innovation; the fewer the resources devoted to circumventing regulation; and the more resources allotted to the task of devising contracts that fully match investors' and borrowers' needs.

REFERENCES

Arrow, Kenneth J. "Economic Welfare and the Allocation of Resources for Investment." In *The Rate and Direction of Inventive Activity: Economic and Social Factors,* Princeton: Princeton University Press, 1962. (A Report of the National Bureau of Economic Research.)

"A Way Out for Brazil." *Institutional Investor, International Edition,* December 1980, pp. 96, 97.

Babble, David F. "The Rise and Decline of Currency Options." *Euromoney,* September 1980, pp. 141–149.

"The Back-to-Back Loan: Intercompany Financing Via a Bank Intermediary." *Business International Money Report,* 3 June 1977, pp. 169–170.

"Banks as Borrowers." *The Banker,* January 1977, pp. 61–65.

Ben-Horim, Moshe, and Silber, William L. "Financial Innovation: A Linear Programming Approach." *Journal of Banking and Finance* 1 (1977), pp. 277–296.

Bolusset, Ivan. "Euro-clear et Cedel." *Banque,* March 1981, pp. 313–319.

Business International Money Report, 14 February 1975, p. 3; and 7 March 1975, p. 11.

Casson, Mark. *Alternatives to the Multinational Enterprise.* London: Holmes and Meier, 1979.

"Chicago BofT Developing Futures Pack for 90-Day Eurodollar CDs." *American Banker,* 3 July 1978, p. 1.

"Cocktail Hour in the Euromarkets." *Institutional Investor, International Edition,* December 1980, p. 122.

Cornell, Bradford, and Reinganum, Marc. "Forward and Futures Prices: Evidence from the Foreign Exchange Markets." Graduate School of Management. UCLA, Working Paper 7–80.

Craven, John A. "The Supersonic Rise of the Floating Rate Note." *Euromoney,* October 1976, pp. 80–91.

"The Currency Deals behind the Market's Spree." *Business Week,* 22 May 1978, p. 152.

"Currency Swap Outstrips Parallel Loan as Hedging, Financing Device." *Business International Money Report,* 30 September 1977, pp. 305–306.

"Currency Swapping: Attractive Financing Option for Consenting Firms." *Business International Money Report,* 24 June 1977, pp. 193–194.

Dempsey, James R. "The Mexican Back-to-Back Loan." *Euromoney,* May 1978, pp. 69–75.

Demsetz, Harold. "The Cost of Transacting." *Quarterly Journal of Economics,* February 1968, pp. 33–53.

———. "Information and Efficiency: Another Viewpoint." *Journal of Law and Economics,* 1969, pp. 1–22.

Dufey, Gunter, and Giddy, Ian H. *The International Money Market.* Englewood Cliffs: Prentice-Hall, 1978.

"Eurodollar Contract Puts BOT in World Futures." *Chicago Sun Times,* 21 June 1978.

"Euromarkets: At Last—the Floating Rate CD." *The Banker,* June 1977, pp. 35–37.

Euromoney, various articles, April 1978, pp. 21–121.

Feiger, George, and Jacquillat, Bertrand. "Currency Option bonds, Puts and Calls on Spot Exchange and the Hedging of Contingent Foreign Earnings." *Journal of Finance,* December 1979, pp. 1129–1139.

Fischer, Stanley. "The Demand for Index bonds." *Journal of Political Economy,* June 1975, pp. 509–534.

"Floating Rate Notes, A Novel Investment Formula." *Kredietbank Weekly Bulletin,* 17 June 1977, pp. 1–6.

Greenbaum, Stuart I., and Haywood, Charles F. "Secular Change in the Financial Services Industry," *Journal of Money, Credit and Banking,* May 1971, pp. 571–589.

Gurley, John G., and Shaw, Edward S. "Financial Aspects of Economic Development." *American Economic Review,* September 1955, pp. 515–538.

Holland, Robert C. "Speculation on Future Innovation." In *Financial Innovation,* edited by William L. Silber. Lexington: D. C. Heath, 1976, p. 163.

Hudson, Nigel R. L. *Money and Exchange Dealings in International Banking.* London: Macmillan, 1979.

Hutchins, Warren C. "Problems in Eurocurrency Credits." In *Financial Crisis: Institutions and Markets in a Fragile Environment,* edited by Edward I. Altman. New York: Wiley, 1977, pp. 226–229.

Johnson, Harry G. "The Efficiency and Welfare Implications of the International Corporation." In *The International Corporation,* edited by Charles P. Kindleberger. Cambridge, MA: MIT Press, 1978, pp. 35–56.

Kindleberger, Charles P. "Comment." In *The New International Economic Order,* edited by Jagdish N. Ghagwati. Cambridge, MA: MIT Press, 1977, pp. 341–343.

Lehman Brothers. "Currency Swaps." *Euromoney,* August 1976, pp. 109–111.

———. "Multicurrency Convertibles." *Euromoney,* February 1976, p. 107.

Lessard, Donald R., and Wellons, Philip A. "Financing Development: Innovation in Private Capital Markets." Joint Study on International Industrial Cooperation prepared for United Nations Industrial Development Organization, April 1979.

"London Chooses the Wrong Option." *The Economist,* 25 March 1978, pp. 101–106.

"Market Innovation." *The Banker,* July 1979, p. 121.

McKinnon, Ronald I. "The Eurocurrency Market." *Essays in International Finance,* no. 125, Princeton University.

Mitchell, Richard. "How the Drop-Lock Bond Fits into Place." *Euromoney,* June 1979, pp. 149–151.

"Multinationals Seek Revolving Credits, Combining for Currency, Dollar Lines." *American Banker,* 18 July 1978, p. 1.

Nelson, P. "Information and Consumer Behavior." *Journal of Political Economy* 78, 1970, pp. 311–329.

Neuhaus, Walther. "Quoting for Long Commitment Periods." *Euromoney,* May 1978, pp. 77–84.

"No More." *The Economist,* 25 March 1978, pp. 39–40.

Organization for Economic Cooperation & Development. *Indexation of Financial Assets: Further Material on Problems and Experiences.* Paris: OECD, 1975.

"Parallel Loans and Long Term Currency Swaps." *Multinational Business,* no. 3 (1977) pp. 29–30.

Pearlman, Ellen. "Euronotes Hit The Big Time." *Institutional Investor, International Edition,* February 1981, pp. 29–30.

———. "The Premiere of the Perpetual Put." *Institutional Investor, International Edition,* June 1980, p. 15.

Potter, David R. W. "New Cards and New Players." *The Banker,* January 1978, pp. 61–69.

Robichek, Alexander A., and Eaker, Mark R. "Debt Denomination and Exchange Risk in International Capital Markets." *Financial Management,* Autumn 1976, pp. 11–18.

Shapiro, Alan C., and Rutenberg, David P. "Managing Exchange Risks in a Floating World." *Financial Management,* Summer 1976, p. 53.

Silber, William L. "Towards a Theory of Financial Innovation." In *Financial Innovation,* edited by William L. Silber. Lexington: D. C. Heath, 1976, pp. 53–85.

Stigum, Marcia. *The Money Market: Myth, Reality and Practice.* Homestead, IL: Dow Jones–Irwin, 1978.

"Sunshine Mining Fashions Silver-Backed Certificates to Garner Big Savings." *Business International Money Report,* 21 March 1980, pp. 93, 94.

Teichman, Thomas. "Forfaiting." *The Banker,* March 1977, pp. 41–44.

Tinic, Seha M. "The Economics of Liquidity Services." *Quarterly Journal of Economics,* February 1972, pp. 79–93.

"U.K. Banks Have Free Hand to Develop Imaginative Parallel Loan Deals." *Business International Money Report,* 5 May 1978, pp. 137–138.

"U.K. Portfolio Managers Trigger Second-Generation Currency Swap Deals." *Business International Money Report,* 9 June 1978, pp. 178–179.

von Clemm, Michael. "London Dollar CD: 10th Anniversary." *The Banker,* May 1976, pp. 607–609.

"Yen Issue Comes in Disguise." *Euromoney,* January 1981, pp. 150–151.

READING 9   **ANALYZING POLITICAL RISK**

David A. Schmidt

The decision to establish or maintain a direct investment position abroad necessitates addressing the issue of political turbulence that confronts multinational firms. Various approaches are being adopted that fall into a broad category labeled *political risk analysis.*

If this form of risk analysis is to be a meaningful adjunct to the formulation of any international decision calculus, it is important to understand what constitutes a *political risk*. Once political risks have been defined or identified, international risk managers can posit relationships, gauge risk exposure, and recommend courses of action aimed at alleviating or avoiding the various forms of this peril.

Public Policy as Political Risk

In the examination of any foreign direct investment opportunity, the political environment encompasses numerous areas of concern for the international risk manager, including:

- The role(s) played by political parties, groups, and factions in the political system;
- Prevailing political and economic philosophies; and
- The general atmosphere surrounding business and government relations.

Yet it is the confluence of these elements in the political system that yields the most critical dimension of the political environment, that of the role of government. Public officials are charged with the responsibility of meeting social and economic goals, the desirability of which can be measured or expressed in political terms. Through the exercise of public policy, host governments attempt to influence the behavior of foreign firms in order to shape the domestic environment and meet national objectives.

In making the case for the assessment of government policy in the analysis of political risk, the distinction must be drawn between a *risk event* and a *risk effect*.[1] A *risk event* is some occurrence in the political environment of a host country, with potentially dangerous or detrimental consequences for the invest-

[1] D. W. Bunn and M. M. Mustafaoglu, "Forecasting Political Risk," *Management Studies* 24 (November 1978): 1559.

ment operation. A *risk effect* is the actual occurrence of some action that, in fact, jeopardizes the profitability and/or goals of the foreign investment operation.

For example, a *risk event* would be an increase in the political popularity of fervent nationalism in a host country. One would grant that such a political movement may be an important event. However, what is significant for the investor firm is not so much the movement in and of itself as the *consequences* of that movement for government policies directed toward foreign direct investment.

Empirical evidence supports the position that policy as an effect is more important than any particular political event.[2] Consequently, for political risk analysis to be an integral part of the investment decision process, techniques must be developed by which international risk managers can evaluate the extent to which foreign direct investments may be jeopardized as a result of political— not just financial or economic—considerations. One method is the adoption of a "project risk" approach.

Project Risk

In the course of reviewing foreign market opportunities, it is not unusual to discriminate early on between so-called "safe" countries and the not-so-safe. Initial assessments about the desirability or undesirability of a potential foreign investment site are often based on loosely researched evaluations of a host country's overall business climate. Perceptions that foreign enterprises are not well received quickly relegate a potential host country to the undesirable or not-so-safe category. This kind of thinking is a mistake.

Despite the often ballyhooed actions of the Iranian government in 1978 and 1979, sweeping policy changes targeted against all foreign enterprises, while insidious and dramatic, are less prevalent than more mundane yet restrictive policy actions aimed at selected enterprises. Beyond that, foreign direct investments are often their own source of risk.[3]

---

[2] See, for example, Harold Knudsen, "Explaining the National Propensity to Expropriate: An Ecological Approach," *Journal of International Business Studies* 5 (Spring 1974): 53; Stephen J. Kobrin, "The Environmental Determinants of Foreign Direct Manufacturing Investment: An Ex Post Empirical Analysis," *Journal of International Business Studies* 7 (Fall/Winter 1976): 37–38; and Lars H. Thunell, *Political Risks in International Business* (New York: Praeger, 1977), pp. 4–5.

[3] See J. Frederick Truitt, *Expropriation of Private Investment* (Bloomington: Indiana University Graduate School of Business Division of Research, 1974), pp. 132–34; Brian Hennig, "Political Risk and the Multinational Firm," in *Management in a World Perspective*, ed. Saul J. Berman (Los Angeles: Delmar, 1975), p. 10; Dan Haendel, Gerald T. West, and Robert G. Meadow, *Overseas Investment and Political Risk* (Lexington, MA: Lexington Books, 1975), pp. 15–16, 102–103; Don R. Beeman, "An Empirical Analysis of the Beliefs Held by the International Executives of United States Firms Regarding Political Risk and Risk Reduction Methods in Developing Nations" (Ph.D. diss., Indiana University, 1978), p. 21; and R. J. Rummel and David A. Heenan, "How Multinationals Analyze Political Risks," *Harvard Business Review* 56 (January–February 1978): 68.

Accepting the premise that exposure is a function of operations and organizational attributes, a framework for political risk analysis must concentrate on the relationship of the type of foreign investment project to the application of restrictive host government policies. Project risk analysis is an approach for appraising the political vulnerability of foreign direct investment based upon attributes or characteristics of the investment.

Framework for Analysis

Devising a framework for the analysis of political risk necessitates more than simply defining political risk, which is the dependent variable. It means determining the relevant characteristics that contribute to the distinctive nature of the foreign investment operation, which is the independent variable.

Political risk is defined here as the *application of host government policies that constrain the business operations of a given foreign investment.* With this definition, we can establish criteria that define political risk. The *risk* is a constraint of the business operation, and the *political criteria* that represent or define that constraint are restrictive government policies applied to the foreign investments.

Political risk can be further classified according to a set of typological definitions. Through the pioneering work done on this subject by Franklin Root, political risks can be classified as follows:[4]

- *Transfer Risk.* Risk stemming from government policies that restrict the transfer of capital, payments, products, technology, and persons into or out of the host country.

- *Operational Risk.* Risk arising as a result of host government policies, regulations, and administrative procedures that directly constrain the management and performance of local operations in production, marketing, finance, and other business functions.

- *Ownership-Control Risk.* Risk brought about as a result of host government policies or actions that inhibit ownership and/or control of the local operations of an international company.

Each risk category can be further operationalized.

Transfer Risks

- Tariffs on exports.
- Export restrictions.
- Tariffs on imports.
- Import quotas.

---

[4] See Franklin R. Root, "Analyzing Political Risks in International Business," in *The Multinational Enterprise in Transition,* ed. A. Kapoor and P. Grub (Princeton, N.J.: Darwin Press, 1972), p. 357.

◆ Dividend remittance restrictions.

◆ Capital repatriation restrictions.

◆ Nationality restrictions.

Operational Risks

◆ Price controls.

◆ Increased taxation.

◆ Export commitments.

◆ Local content requirements.

◆ Local sourcing requirements.

◆ Local manufacturing requirements.

◆ Financing restrictions.

Ownership-Control Risks

◆ Geographic limitations on investment.

◆ Economic sector limitations on investment.

◆ Abrogation of proprietary rights.

◆ Foreign ownership limitations.

◆ Pressure for local participation.

◆ Expropriation.

◆ Confiscation.

Another set of variables, depicting the nature of foreign direct investment, can help explain the incidence or occurrence of restrictive policy actions. Foreign direct investment is defined as any long-term private investment in which the business is controlled from abroad, incorporating both ownership and managerial involvement.

The nature of foreign direct investment can be captured in two sets of independent variables. The first set of variables, the *general* nature of investment, is derived from production characteristics of the foreign operation. The second set of variables, the *special* nature of investment, is derived from the following attributes: sector of economic activity, technological sophistication, and pattern of ownership.

The *General* Nature of Foreign Direct Investment: How It Affects Restrictions

Considering the *general* nature of direct investment, through examination of production characteristics only, foreign operations can be categorized according to whether they are conglomerate, vertical, or horizontal investments. These variables are defined in the following way:

- ◆ *Conglomerate Investments.* Production abroad of final goods or services not similar to those produced at home.
- ◆ *Vertical Investments.* Production abroad of raw materials or intermediate goods to be processed into final products.
- ◆ *Horizontal Investments.* Production abroad of the same or similar goods and/or services produced at home.

These investment categories can be ranked according to their priority as potential targets for restrictive host government investment policies.

Conglomerate Investments: The Most Likely Target Conglomerate investments are apt to be perceived by host governments as providing the least benefit to the local economy. Of these three investment categories, they represent the most likely target for government intervention.

Conglomerate investments suffer from an image problem. They are thought to play fast and loose. From a host country perspective, conglomerates take little cognizance of market needs. Rather, when the management of a conglomerate examines corporate activities, it promotes profitable ventures and jettisons those investments with poorer returns. Such corporate actions represent mere opportunistic diversification, seeking profits and/or growth for the parent company.

Conglomerates, often thought to be financially unstable because of this corporate jockeying, provide little or no integrative impact on the economy, lack product and market experience, and bring no proven technology.

Vertical Investments: Symbiosis Host governments are less likely to subject vertical investments to economic restraint by applying policy measures than they are to intervene in conglomerate investments. There are several reasons for this.

1. Vertical investments often offer a substantial inflow of foreign capital during start-up.
2. Vertical investments are frequently export-oriented. In formulating investment policies, host governments are lured by the prospect of large injections of foreign capital. Host governments also have an eye toward increasing export activity as a condition of entry into the host economy.
3. Because of technological sophistication in production and marketing, vertical investments often provide an integrative impact on the economy, creating backward and forward linkages.

Host governments may be tempted to substitute locally available resources or technology in order to gain control over economic activity, but vertically integrated investments are in a strong position with respect to government control measures.

Horizontal Investments: A Helping Hand Host governments view horizontal investments as the least likely candidate for control measures. Horizontal investments are made with an eye toward satisfying host country market demands. As they invest in like or related fields, such operations bring with them proven technologies and expertise.

Managerial and product know-how, as well as marketing know-how in the distribution of the product, make horizontal investments a desirable form of foreign enterprise. Where production arrangements address a market need, the host government will be little inclined to interfere. This is especially the case where investments supply not only the necessary production capacity, but also the marketing capacity to dispose of the product. A strong marketing system is vital in avoiding political risk.

The *Special* Nature of Foreign Direct Investment: How It Affects Restrictions

Turning to the special nature of direct investment, a second set of variables can be elaborated from examining three attributes: sector of economic activity, pattern of ownership, and technological sophistication.

Sector of Economic Activity Sector of economic activity refers to the primary business activity of the foreign direct investment operation.

- ◆ *Primary Sector.* Includes business operations engaged primarily in agricultural production, forestry, mineral exploration, and extraction.
- ◆ *Industrial Sector.* Includes manufacturing operations engaged primarily in the chemical or mechanical processing of raw materials or substances into new products.
- ◆ *Service Sector.* Includes investment operations engaged primarily in transportation, communication, finance, insurance, and related business services.

Technological Sophistication Technological sophistication hinges on the understanding that there is a difference between firms that depend on a single scientific breakthrough and those with a continuous need for sustained high levels of research and development, science, and innovation in order to maintain economic viability. This difference is reflected in the two categories "science-based" and "non-science-based" industries.[5]

---

[5] See *Gaps in Technology*, Analytical Report (Paris: Organization of Economic Cooperation and Development, 1971), pp. 135–37; and *The Multinational Firm, Foreign Direct Investment and Canadian Science Policy* (Ottawa: Science Council of Canada, 1971), pp. 78–91.

- *Science-Based Industry.* Includes manufacturing operations requiring continuous introduction of new products and/or processes.
- *Non-Science-Based Industry.* Includes manufacturing operations not requiring continuous introduction of new products and/or processes.

Pattern of Ownership Pattern of ownership refers to financial control of the foreign investment measured in terms of equity owned by the parent firm.

- *Wholly Owned,* where 100 percent of the equity in the foreign investment is owned by the parent firm.
- *Partially Owned,* where less than 100 percent of the equity in the foreign investment is owned by the parent firm.

Combining Attributes The special nature of foreign investment activity is arrived at by reducing the combination of attributes to a smaller number of investment types. Combining attributes into investment types facilitates categorizing and ranking foreign operations as priority investments for host government action. Schematically, the various combinations of attributes that characterize the operations of a foreign investment are represented in Table 1.

Sector of Economic Activity: Paramount for Political Risk

Perhaps the single most important attribute of any foreign investment operation as it relates to political risk is sector of economic activity. Ownership and technology represent mitigating factors in applying host government policies to foreign direct investment. Yet the overriding consideration in political risk is sector of economic activity. Host governments are genuinely concerned with the prospect of industrial takeover or sectoral domination by foreign investors as well as technological dependence on foreign investors.

Primary Sector: The Most Likely Target Host government policies aimed at controlling or influencing the activities of foreign investors are most frequently applied to primary and service sector operations.

Extractive industries. With respect to primary sector investments, it is hardly surprising to find that extractive operations (petroleum and mining) face a significantly high degree of political risk. Host nations are of the opinion that what is in the ground is dear. Foreign investment engaged in the removal of natural resources is associated not only with the loss of national wealth, but also with the idea that such natural endowments should be exploited for the benefit of the host country population, not for private profit.

The extent of concern for rights accompanying private equity is frequently a matter of little consequence because such investments often become part of

TABLE **1**   The Special Nature of Foreign Direct Investments: Twelve Investment
Combinations

Sector	Technology	Ownership	Combination	Investment Type
Primary	Non-Science Based	Wholly Owned	1	I
		Partially Owned	2	I
	Science Based	Wholly Owned	3	I
		Partially Owned	4	I
Service	Non-Science Based	Wholly Owned	5	II
		Partially Owned	6	II
	Science Based	Wholly Owned	7	II
		Partially Owned	8	II
Industrial	Non-Science Based	Wholly Owned	9	III
		Partially Owned	10	III
	Science Based	Wholly Owned	11	IV
		Partially Owned	12	V

the domain of public sector industry. Technology also becomes increasingly irrelevant as it becomes available on a management contract basis.

Agricultural investments. While extractive industries experience the highest incidence of political risk, the conviction that private foreign investments take advantage of the natural environment, exploit for private profit, and leave nothing behind is an argument also advanced against agricultural investments made by foreigners. The presence of large foreign agricultural enterprises may lead to pressures for land reform, which in turn may force increased government control over both areas of economic activity, extractive and agricultural operations.

Therefore, regardless of ownership patterns of technology, host governments are most likely to apply restrictive policy measures to foreign investments made in the primary sector. Hence, primary sector private foreign investment activity is classified as a Type I investment, highest priority as a target for host government action.

Service Sector: A Sensitive Area It is difficult to separate primary sector investments from service sector investments in terms of their prominence as an object of public attack. Both sectors incorporate certain kinds of business activity that rank high on the list of foreign operations subject to increasing governmental control.

Service sector investments that experience the application of restrictive public policies include banking, insurance, communications, transportation, and utilities. What arguments accompany the exercise of greater control over these service sector investments? Generally they have to do with strategic areas of the economy considered socially or politically sensitive.

Banks and insurance companies are of great concern. Not only do they provide necessary funds for investment, but at the same time they also serve as potential bases of economic influence and control. The communications industry is sensitive because of the potential impact on local culture.

As a result, "abuse of power" by foreign enterprises is ostensibly prevented by government intervention on behalf of the public interest. Service sector investment activity, then, is classified as Type II, second in a rank ordering of private foreign investments in line for some form of increased government control.

Industrial Sector: Where Science-Based Technology Matters Most Because host governments are more apt to aim policy measures at primary and service sector investments, industrial manufacturing operations are lower priorities for government-initiated investment controls. However, firms engaged in manufacturing do not entirely escape host government policy action. Rather, it seems that, for industrial manufacturing operations, the likelihood of government restriction is contingent upon technological sophistication and patterns of ownership.

When reviewing investment opportunities in terms of technology, foreign firms will often appraise not only their own existing technical skills but also the availability of local technology as an incentive to invest. Host governments frequently will seek technologically attractive foreign investments in order to secure the benefits of capital and technological and managerial know-how that transfer to the local economy.

Simultaneously, host governments attempt to avoid the prospect of technological dependence on outsiders. One way to forestall such dependence is to implement investment policies aimed at controlling technologically rich foreign operations. It is precisely on the basis of control and dependence that the following argument can be advanced: the higher the level of technology ("science-based"), the less likely the operation is to be a target of government constraints.

First, on the matter of *control*, host governments will confront industrial manufacturing operations with a higher incidence of political risk if the extent to which the industrial need for sophisticated technological inputs is low. Where an investment is marked by a standardized, noncomplex production process, a country will not require the expertise of the foreign enterprise. The accumulation of capital and indigenous technical or managerial know-how will permit local industry to operate the subsidiary successfully. Thus, indigenous forces will put pressure on the government to reduce the foreign presence.

Second, on the matter of *dependence,* the likely incidence of an industrial manufacturing operation being subject to political risk will be greatly diminished if the investment is marked by a technologically complex production process, especially where the injection of technological improvements is necessary for continued operation. Even when a host government may wish to exert control over certain technical industries, if skills are unavailable or sophisticated research and development capacity is lacking, it is unable to assert itself.

This argument gains considerable force when tailoring risk minimization strategies for foreign direct investment. When a firm can maintain a status of "necessary" in the eyes of the host government, it will reduce the occurrence of political risk. The status of "necessary" is achieved by the continuous inflows of technology, product improvements, and technical and managerial skills. With the success of the foreign investment contingent upon the influx of new products and technology, any effort by the host government to gain control over the operation would result in the parent firm's withholding technical expertise and management skill. The net result would be a decline in productive capacity.

High technology or "science-based" investments, then, are able to exert leverage on the implementation of host government policies. It is often asserted that if a firm transfers technological capacity from the parent to the subsidiary, it loses its competitive edge. However, it might be more accurate to say that locating intangible assets—such as research and development capacity—outside of the host country is done by design to maintain this leverage. Accepting this reasoning, two additional investment types are established relative to the probable incidence of political risk:

◆ *Type III*—"non-science-based" industrial investments; and
◆ *Type IV*—"science-based" industrial investments.

Ownership Counts

Finally, at the core of political risk analysis, the critical question faced by host governments and foreign investors alike is one of control over economic decision making. Patterns of ownership are features of foreign direct investments that contribute to risk exposure. Certainly, corporate strategies for overseas expansion are marked by an overriding desire for control. However, host government policymakers are confronted with a dilemma on the matter of foreign ownership.

On the one hand, it can be argued that, in order to attract capital investment, it would be in the national interest of a host country to allow 100 percent foreign equity in the capital structure of the entering direct investment. Yet, in an increasing number of cases where foreign direct investment is undertaken, such wholly owned operations—and often, even majority positions—are simply not acceptable. Rather, local citizens pressure their governments to demand greater domestic control over foreigners, often through local participation. Wholly owned operations by outsiders tend to foster a sense of dependence or second-class status for the country. The argument for host-country control stresses giving local citizens opportunities to invest. According to this argument, local equity participation will move the foreign firms to act more in accordance with the interests of the nation.

For the investing firm, "going native"—especially in ownership—is a tactic often suggested. "Going native" means selling off equity shares to host nationals and engaging in some form of joint venture with local private or public capital. Adapting the firm's ownership strategy to fit the host country environment can be an effective means to minimize risk. With shared ownership, the investment takes on more of a local image, which in turn reduces public pressure on host governments to undertake unfavorable actions against foreigners in response to antiforeign or nationalistic calls for further domestication.

A fifth type of investment activity, then, is characterized by less political risk exposure than any other type of investment undertaken. Type V applies to "science-based," partially owned, industrial manufacturing operations.

Having developed the variables in the analytical framework, we can diagram the operating mix for assessing risk levels confronting foreign investments. Figure 1 shows the relationship between investment types and risk exposure. The role of international risk managers is to examine this operating mix in light of the type of investment project under consideration.

Managers must go beyond the analysis of conventional perils—war, revolution, and inconvertibility. They need to examine historical policy actions, existing government posture, and attitudes of opposition groups as they affect some segments of the mix. In the process managers will come to grips with the more common policy restrictions applied to foreign investment projects.

FIGURE **1**   Operating Mix for Assessing Political Risk

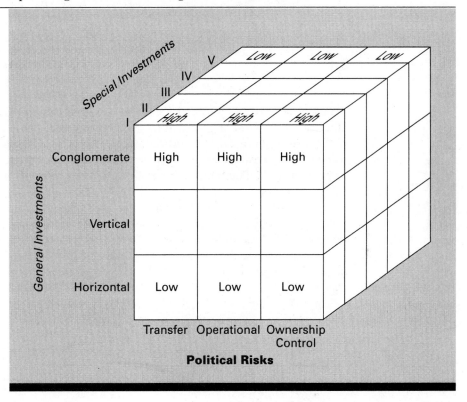

MARKETING BARRIERS IN INTERNATIONAL TRADE

Sak Onkvisit ◆ John J. Shaw

*You cannot exist as an economic entity unto yourself, relying completely on
domestic consumption.*

> —*Bob Petersen, Director of Development
> for the American National Metric Council*

Economists have always advocated free trade because the practice increases
efficiency and economic welfare for all involved. Free trade makes a great deal
of theoretical sense, but it is ignored in practice by virtually all countries. Despite
some obvious advantages, nations are inclined to discourage free trade instead
of promoting it. The temptation to protect one's interests is the cause for this
trade myopia.

Many believe that the United States is the largest promoter of free trade.
Actually, the U.S. by design has many nontariff barriers against foreign goods.
More imported manufactured goods are subject to nontariff barriers here than
in many other nations. As a matter of fact, 34 percent of the products manufactured here are overtly protected.[1] The percentages for selected other countries are:

- Italy, 34 percent.
- France, 32 percent.
- The United Kingdom, 22 percent.
- West Germany, 20 percent.
- Canada, 10 percent.

Surprisingly, only 7 percent of Japan's manufactured goods are protected.

This article catalogs the types and effects of marketing barriers. Once
marketers know and understand these barriers, they should be better able to
cope with them.

Marketing Barriers

Governments in many countries distort trade and welfare arrangements to gain
economic and political advantages or benefits. They use a combination of tariff
and nontariff methods.

It is impossible to list all marketing barriers, because there are simply too

---

Source: Reprinted from *Business Horizons*, (May-June 1988). Copyright 1988 by the Foundation for
the School of Business at Indiana University. Used with permission.

[1] James O'Shea, "U.S. Is Far from Barrier Free," *Chicago Tribune*, January 6, 1983.

many of them. And governments continually create new import restrictions or adjust the ones currently in existence. Trade-distortion practices *can* be grouped into two basic categories: tariffs and nontariff barriers. Figure 1 lists the major barriers in these two categories.

This article will concentrate on nontariff barriers for several reasons. Tariffs, although undesirable, are at least straightforward and obvious. Nontariff barriers are more elusive. Tariffs have declined in importance, while nontariff barriers have become more prominent. Often disguised, the effect of nontariff barriers can be just as devastating as that of tariffs, if not more so. For example, Koreans can be fined if they are found in possession of foreign cigarettes. Nontariff barriers (as cited by Ford) caused the price of the popular Ford Escort to be at least 50 percent more in Japan than in the United States.

The total number of nontariff barriers can be mind-boggling; 850 different types have been identified. These barriers can be grouped into six major categories, and each category can be further broken down into several subcategories.

Government Participation in Trade

The degree of government participation in the actual process of buying and selling may range from simple guidance to state trading. Such practices as subsidies lie between the two extremes.

Administrative Guidance Governments often provide trade consultation, whether it is requested by private companies or not. Japan uses administrative guidance (gyoosei shidoo) to facilitate the implementation of its industrial policies. This systematic cooperation between government and business is labeled, somewhat sarcastically, "Japan, Inc." The MITI (Ministry of International Trade and Industry) is known for its historical role as a caretaker, coordinator, and leader providing guidance, coordination, and arbitration. The government uses a carrot-and-stick approach to achieve conformity by exerting influence through regulations, recommendations, encouragement, discouragement, and prohibition. To achieve its goals, the government uses such tactics as licensing, foreign-exchange allocation, and quotas.

Government Procurement and State Trading In this, the ultimate in government involvement, the government itself is the customer. It engages in commercial operations either directly or indirectly through the agencies under its control. Such business activities are either in place of or in addition to those of private firms. This practice is most common in communist countries, whose governments are responsible for central planning for the whole economy. Thus, the governments of China, the U.S.S.R., and other countries of the Eastern Bloc decide what is purchased, when, where, how, and how much.

The World Bank, the Inter-American Development Bank, and the Asian

FIGURE **1**   Marketing Barriers

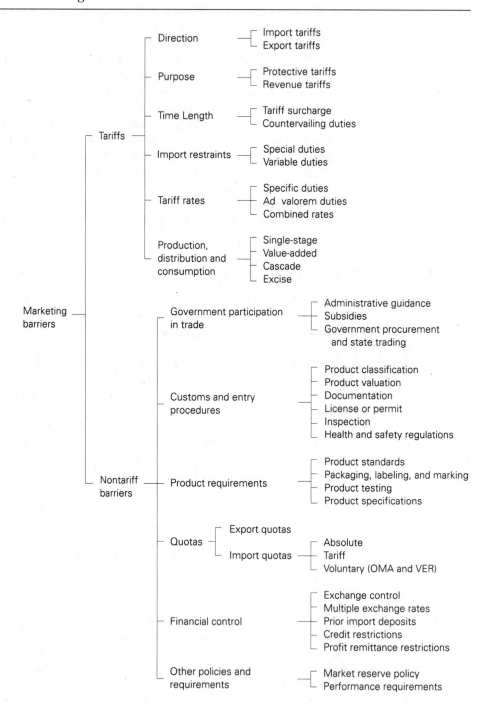

Development Bank seem to encourage a "buy local" policy. They allow a country's procurement system to have a maximum tariff (margin of protection) of 15 percent in favor of local suppliers. The U.S. government, with its many agencies, purchases billions of dollars worth of goods annually. The Buy American Act gives a bidding edge to U.S. suppliers. For foreign suppliers to win a contract from a U.S. government agency, their products must contain at least 50 percent U.S.–made parts, or they must undercut the closest comparable American product by at least 6 percent.

The active involvement of governments in trade, control, and ownership is seemingly universal. State participation is no longer restricted to communist nations and developing countries. The expansion of state-owned companies in Europe is a striking development in the history of capitalism. "The state is no longer limited to its historic function as a regulator, referee, and facilitator of the private market economy."[2] Free trade can easily be affected.

Subsidies Governments can use subsidies to protect local industries or push exports. Subsidies can take many forms: cash, interest rates, value-added tax, corporate income tax, sales tax, freight, insurance, favorable foreign-exchange conversion rate, and infrastructure.

Other kinds of subsidies are not so readily apparent. The building of infrastructure and the training of workers are often used to lure foreign investors, but they are simply subsidies in disguise. Pennsylvania offered Volkswagen a $75 million package of low-cost loans, deferred or minimal taxes, construction of a four-lane highway, and a rail spur. And this figure pales when compared to Illinois' package of tax incentives and direct aid worth $276 million to Chrysler/Mitsubishi.

Sheltered profits form another type of hidden subsidy. A country may allow a corporation to shelter its export profit. The United States, in 1971, allowed companies to form domestic international sales corporations (DISCs). This tax shelter for export profits permitted a company to defer taxes on up to half its export income. More than $3 billion was deferred each year, and the cost to the U.S. Treasury in lost revenue was approximately half that amount. GATT (General Agreements on Tariffs and Trade) eventually ruled that the DISC was an illegal export subsidy. The U.S. government was generous in forgiving $10 billion in deferred taxes when it abolished DISCs. A new law allows companies to form foreign sales corporations (FSCs), which have the same purpose as their predecessors. However, to qualify as a FSC, a firm must meet more stringent requirements of foreign presence and economic substance.

Because all nations practice it, GATT allows subsidies for primary products as long as they do not displace other countries' exports and undercut their

---

prices. These primary products are agricultural products—far, forest, and fishery products—either in their natural forms or that have undergone the processing customarily required to prepare them for transportation and marketing (such as frozen and cured meat). The United States provides subsidies for agricultural exports to the U.S.S.R. and China.

Subsidies are common, but solutions are not, and many issues are ambiguous. It has not been determined, for example, whether foreign government aid to cover operational deficits generated by state-run companies is considered an export subsidy under the U.S. law. Furthermore, proof of displacement, injury, and subsidies are necessary if a suit is to be brought under the U.S. Trade Act. There is also considerable debate over what products should be considered manufactured and so not entitled to any subsidies. According to the United States, the EC's export subsidies for products such as wheat flour and pasta are banned by the international subsidies code. However, the EC responds that its subsidies have not unfairly distorted historical market shares and that pasta and wheat flour are not manufactured products to begin with.

Customs and Entry Procedures

Certain nontariff barriers can be grouped as customs and entry procedures. These restrictions involve classification, valuation, documentation, license, inspection, and health and safety regulations.

Classification The classification of a product can be arbitrary and inconsistent. It is often based on a customs officer's judgment, at least at the time of entry. Product classification is important because the product's category determines its duty status. When Pringles potato chips became popular in Japan, the Japanese customs changed the classification from the processed-foods category, which carried a 15.5 percent import duty, to the confection category and a 35 percent duty.[3]

A company can sometimes take action to affect the classification of its product. For example, Shenandoah Valley Poultry Company was paying a tariff of over 40 percent for shipping frozen poultry into Europe. By seasoning frozen turkey parts, the company had these items re-classified as prepared foods, which were then eligible for a 17 percent duty.[4]

Valuation Regardless of how products are classified, each product must be valued. The value in turn affects the amount of tariff to be levied. A customs appraiser determines the value. The process can be highly subjective, and the valuation of a product can be interpreted in different ways, depending on what

---

[3] "Japan: Why It's a Hard Sell," *Newsweek*, May 15, 1982, p. 112.

[4] Vern Terpstra, *International Dimensions of Marketing* (Boston: Kent, 1982), p. 130.

value is used (foreign, export, import, or manufacturing costs) and how this value is constructed. In Japan, a 15 percent commodity tax is applied to the FOB factory price of Japanese cars. But U.S. cars are valued on the CIF (cost of goods, insurance, and freight) basis, adding $1,000 or more to their retail price.

The United States relies on either the computed or deductive value when transaction value cannot be determined. It also has what is called the American selling price for appraisement of certain products. The American selling price is not an alternative method of value determination. It is used for certain imported articles that are competitive with similar U.S. products (such as benzenoid chemicals, coal-tar products, rubber-soled footwear, canned clams, and knit wool gloves and mittens). This is a controversial method of valuation, and other governments would like to see it abolished.

Documentation The documents governments require can be voluminous and complicated. Japan requires six volumes of standards for each automobile. Without proper documentation, goods may not be cleared through customs. At the very least, complicated and lengthy documents slow down product clearance. France requires customs documentation to be in French. Officials hold up trucks from other European countries for hours to search for instruction manuals not written in French.

Licenses or Permits Not all products can be freely imported. Some require licenses or permits. It is extremely difficult to import foreign beer into Mexico. To get an import license, an importer must be able to prove that domestic demand cannot be met by Mexican brewers. India requires licenses for all imported goods. A product is considered prohibited if not accompanied by a license.[5] In Argentina, in addition to the depositing of funds equivalent to the required duties, an importer of textiles must obtain a certificate attesting that the goods are necessary.

Inspection Inspection is an integral part of product clearance. Goods must be examined to determine quality and quantity. Marketers should be accurate when describing the amount, quality, and type of products. Any deviation from invoices causes further measurements and determination, more delay, and more expenses, all of which must be paid by importers.

Inspection, unfortunately, can be used to discourage imports. Japanese customs agents require imported cars to be partially disassembled to determine whether the serial number on a part matches the number on the shipping document. France requires imported videocassette recorders to go through its

---

[5] *International Trade Reporter: Export Shipping Manual* (Washington, D.C.: The Bureau of International Affairs).

customs office in Poitiers, a small town 200 miles from Paris. That office is properly equipped for the inspection routine.

Health and Safety Regulations Many products are subject to health and safety regulations that protect the public health and environment. Claiming that Japanese snow is different from snow elsewhere, Japan's Consumer Product Safety Association set new standards in 1986 for ski equipment. The special criteria for the dimensions and stiffness of skis and the structure of boots and bindings are supposed to reduce accidents caused by the damper, heavier Japanese snow.[6]

West Germany's health regulations serve to limit beer imports to a mere 1 percent of the beer consumed there. According to the stringent decree, "no other substances but barley, hops and water are used for any type of beer." By banning all artificial additives, West Germany implies that 90 percent of the world's beers are potential health hazards. France's Alsatian Brewery Le Pecheur claims that the German purity standards violate Article 30 of the Common Market treaty, which bans restrictions inside the EC.[7]

Product Requirements

For goods to enter a country, they must meet the product requirements that country sets. Requirements may apply to product standards, packaging, labeling, and marking, testing, and specifications.

Product Standards Each country determines its own product standards to protect its consumers' health and safety. However, such standards may also prevent or slow down importation of foreign goods. Limes, tomatoes, green peppers, and other agricultural commodities coming from Mexico must meet U.S. grade, size, quality, and maturity requirements. Japan is quite notorious for using product standards to limit or exclude imports. Japanese product standards are complex and based on physical characteristics instead of product performance. Such standards make it necessary to repeat the product-approval process when a slight product modification (such as color) occurs, even though the product's performance doesn't change.

Packaging, Labeling, and Marking Many products must be packaged in a certain way for safety and other reasons. The United Kingdom keeps French milk out by requiring it to be sold in pints instead of metric measures. Bottles of distilled spirits and wines are required to be of standard metric sizes to be

---

[6] Katherine Ellison, "Foreign Ski Makers Feel a Chill in Japan," *San Jose Mercury News,* October 4, 1986.

[7] Alice Siegert, "It's Last Call in Europe's Long-Foaming Beer War," *Chicago Tribune,* July 31, 1984.

imported into the United States. In Mexico, product markings must be in metric units. Nigeria wants all imports to carry metric labeling exclusively, since dual markings are no longer permitted. Canada requires imported canned foods to be packed in specific sizes. Furthermore, instructions contained within packages or on them must be in English and French. The Canadian Labeling Act also requires all imported clothing to have labels in both languages.

Product Testing Testing must be done on many products to determine their safety and suitability. This is another area in which the United States runs into trouble in Japan. Although they may have won approval everywhere else for safety and effectiveness, medical equipment and pharmaceuticals must go through elaborate standards testing that can take a few years—just long enough for Japanese companies to develop competing products. The Health and Welfare Ministry sat on Merck's application for new hepatitis vaccine for a year before deciding to test it. In the meantime, two Japanese companies succeeded in developing similar drugs.

Product Specifications Although they appear to be relatively innocent, product specifications can wreak havoc on imports. Specifications can be written to favor local bidders and keep out foreign suppliers. For example, they can be extremely detailed, or they may closely resemble those of domestic products. They can be used to frustrate foreign suppliers who cannot satisfy these specifications without expensive or lengthy modifications. Instead of outlining functional characteristics, NTT (Nippon Telephone and Telegraph Company) specifies physical features—right down to the location of ventilation holes. The details are almost identical to those of Nippon Electric.[8] GATT recently established procedures for setting product standards using performance standards instead of detailed physical specifications.

Quotas

Quotas, also known as quantitative control, protect local firms and conserve foreign currency by limiting the amount of foreign products that can be imported. From a policy standpoint, quotas are not as desirable as tariffs, since quotas generate no revenues for a country.

Absolute Quotas This quota limits absolutely the amount imported during a quota period. Once the amount is reached, further shipments are prohibited. Some quotas are global, but others apply to specific foreign countries. The United States' absolute quotas include milk, ice cream, sugar, and peanuts.

---

[8] "Japan Opens a Door with Built-in Barriers," *Business Week*, November 8, 1982, p. 41.

Tariff Quotas This quota permits the entry of a limited quantity of the product at a reduced duty rate. Quantities in excess of the quota can be imported, but they are subject to a higher duty rate. The primary purpose of tariff quotas is to import what is needed and discourage excessive quantities. The United States' tariff-rate quotas include cattle, whole milk, fish, and potatoes.

Voluntary Quotas A voluntary quota is a formal agreement between nations or between a nation and an industry. Two kinds of voluntary quotas can be distinguished: voluntary export restraint (VER) and orderly marketing agreement (OMA).[9] Whereas an OMA involves a negotiation between two governments, a VER is a direct agreement between an importing nation's government and a foreign exporting industry. If a VER involves private industries, a public disclosure is not necessary. The OMA and VER can be applied in a discriminatory manner. Both enable the importing country to circumvent GATT, which requires the country to reciprocate for the quota received and to impose that market safeguard on a most-favored-nation basis.

The United States has a VER with Europe on steel and an OMA with South Korea and Taiwan on non-rubber footwear. It also has safeguard measures limiting the imports of color TV sets from South Korea and Taiwan and, for all sources of supply, citizens band radios, porcelain-on-steel cookware, high carbon ferro-chromium, industrial fasteners (nuts, bolts, and screws), and spin dryers.[10]

Quotas frequently fail to achieve their objectives. Japanese auto manufacturers, in spite of voluntary quotas, were able to maintain market share and profit in the United States by increasing prices. They shifted their product mix to larger cars and loaded their cars with options. U.S. automakers did not help the matter. After arguing for quotas and price increases so that they could use the resulting profits to improve productivity and competitiveness, they instead paid big bonuses to their executives. Quotas can instill a "damn the consumer" attitude.

Financial Control

Financial regulations can also restrict international trade. They can control capital flow so currencies can be defended and imports can be controlled. To defend the weak Italian lira, Italy instituted a 7 percent tax on the purchase of foreign currencies. There are several forms financial restrictions can take.

Exchange Controls Exchange controls limit the amount of the currency that can be taken abroad. They are usually applied because the local currency is

---

[9] Gerald M. Meier, *International Economics: The Theory of Policy* (New York: Oxford University Press, 1980), p. 108.

[10] Bela Balassa and Carol Balassa, "Industrial Protection in the Developed Countries," *The World Economy,* June 1984, pp. 179–96.

FIGURE 2   Countries with Multiple Exchange Rates, End of 1984[1]

(number of exchange rates)[2]

Afghanistan	3	El Salvador	3	Romania	4
Bahamas	2	Guatemala	3	Sierra Leone	2
Bangladesh	2	Iran	2	Somalia	2
Chile	2	Kuwait	2	Sudan	2
China	2	Lao People's Democratic Republic	4	Syrian Arab Republic	3
Costa Rica	2	Mexico	5	Venezuela	4
Dominican Republic	2	Nicaragua	3	Vietnam	2
Ecuador	3	Paraguay	3		
Egypt	3	Peru	2		

[1]Excluding subsidies, taxes, discounts, and premiums resulting in implicit multiple exchange rates.
[2]Excluding illegal parallel rates that are not officially recognized by the authorities.
Source: IMF Survey, June 24, 1985, p. 197.

overvalued, a condition that encourages imports. Exchange control is thus needed to limit the amount of currency an importer can obtain to pay for the goods he purchases. By the same token, exchange controls also limit the amount of currency an exporter can receive for goods sold and the length of time he can hold it. French exporters, for example, must exchange the foreign currencies for francs within one month.

Multiple Exchange Rates

Multiple exchange rates also regulate exchange. The objectives are twofold: to *encourage* exports and imports of certain goods, and to *discourage* exports and imports of other goods. There is no single rate for all products or industries, so some products and industries will benefit and some will not. Figure 2 lists countries with multiple exchange rates.

Because multiple exchange rates are used to bring in hard currencies through exports while restricting imports, they are condemned by the International Monetary Fund. According to the IMF, any unapproved multiple currency practice is a breach of obligations, and the country may become ineligible to use the fund's resources.[11]

Prior Import Deposits and Credit Restrictions   A government can require prior import deposits that tie up an importer's capital, making imports difficult.

---

[11] Joseph Gold, *SDRs, Currencies, and Gold. Sixth Survey of New Legal Developments* (Washington, D.C.: International Monetary Fund, 1983), pp. 28, 30.

Greece, under its austerity program, requires a pre-import cash deposit of 40 percent or 80 percent of the CIF value of certain goods. The deposit must be left in non-interest bearing accounts for six months. About 63 percent of Greece's total imports are subject to this requirement.[12]

Credit restrictions apply only to imports. Exporters may be able to get loans from the government, usually at very favorable rates, but importers will not be able to receive any government credit or financing. This forces importers to look for loans in the private sector, very likely at significantly higher rates if such loans are even available in the first place.

Profit Remittance Restrictions Many countries regulate the remittance of profits earned in local operations to a parent organization located abroad. In Italy, "dividends, branch profits, and interest not registered as 'productive' are subject to eight percent of the capital investment, while royalties and technical service fees are freely remittable with routine approval and documentation."[13]

To solve this problem, MNCs have looked to legal loopholes. Many employ the following tactics:[14]

1. Switch trading. Goods are sold for credit or for other products which can then be sold later for conversion into the desired currency.

2. Moving up the priority queue. A company can negotiate its way up the government's queue for permission to expatriate profits by bribing officials, refusing to service and repair the products sold, or using other methods of bringing pressure.

3. Currency swaps. This method matches a multinational firm wanting to repatriate its currency with another company that needs that currency and is willing to acquire it at a discount.

4. Netting. A subsidiary's blocked funds are used to cover affiliation costs within a country, such as the legal fees of the parent company.

5. Parallel loans. This variation of netting involves a back-to-back transaction. For example, a British subsidiary of a U.S. corporation lends British pounds to a British multinational firm whose U.S. subsidiary lends the same amount of dollars to the U.S. corporation.

6. Negotiation for a higher value of an investment than its actual worth. In effect, this increases the equity base from which dividend repatriations are calculated. Some techniques are:[15]

---

[12] "Western Europe Highlights," *Business America,* November 25, 1985, p. 16.

[13] *Italy,* Ernst & Whinney International Series, 1983a, p. 1.

[14] "Ways to Beat Exchange Rules," *Business Week,* October 26, 1981, p. 106.

[15] "U.S. Starts to Repatriate Its Cash," *Business Week,* March 31, 1980, pp. 83–84.

- Invoicing—raising the markup on intra-company shipments;
- Royalties—increasing royalties charged to subsidiaries on parts designed in the United States;
- Management fees—charging subsidiaries for the time managers at the parent company spend on international business; and
- Engineering fees—charging subsidiaries for the time engineers spend developing and refining products made overseas.

Other Policies and Requirements

Almost all countries have adopted policies that favor local industries. These policies apply to both public and private projects.

Market-Reserve Policy Many countries reserve specific enterprises and professions for their own citizens. Only Thai nationals are allowed to be barbers in Thailand. In Nigeria, enterprises exclusively reserved for Nigerians include advertising businesses, blending and bottling of alcoholic drinks, bread and cake making, candle manufacturing, casino operations, cinemas, garment manufacturing, hairdressing, taxis, and office cleaning, among others.[16] Brazil's market-reserve policy, sanctioned by the 1984 Informatics Law, prohibits imports of personal computers and reserves the personal-computer market for Brazilian firms. The Brazilian government also systematically reduces MNCs' local market share for all digital technologies. A variation of the market-reserve policy is the market-sharing agreement. The United States, for example, has an agreement with Japan to limit Japanese semiconductor exports.

Performance Requirements An increasing number of governments have required foreign firms to perform specific activities to benefit their countries in exchange for the right to sell there. Requirements include using local content and exporting the host countries' products. Performance requirements do not necessarily cause harm. For example, a construction project in Saudi Arabia requiring local manufacture of goods was not harmful to U.S. trade, because high-bulk/low-value construction items, such as sand and water, would probably have been purchased locally anyway.

The Overseas Private Investment Corporation (OPIC), a U.S. quasi-government agency, has been keeping close watch on performance requirements. Its enabling legislation prohibits OPIC from supporting a project whose performance requirements reduce the trade benefits to the United States. Certain requirements have detrimental effects on U.S. trade and employment because they restrict or displace U.S. exports. U.S. exports are also adversely affected

---

[16] *Nigeria,* Ernst & Whinney International Series, 1983b, p. 6.

when American firms are required by a host country to import that country's products into the United States.[17] OPIC did not assist a leasing project involving transport equipment in Brazil because of a requirement to buy the equipment from local firms even when U.S. equipment was of better price and quality.

A country can choose to open or close its borders to trade. If it adopts the open system, it has a much better chance of fostering economic growth and maximizing consumer welfare. Hong Kong has done well economically by adopting this approach. Albania, in stark contrast, has chosen to discourage almost all forms of contact with the rest of the world. As pointed out by Richard N. Farmer,[18] no nation, the United States included, can accomplish everything by itself. The United States has a choice, and it can choose between the open system of Hong Kong and the closed system of Albania.

The problem facing the world is that most nations, developed and developing, are moving toward Albania's closed system. According to Anjaria, Kirmani, and Petersen, "developed countries actually seem to strengthen their nontariff measures affecting trade."[19] The rise in protectionism is concentrated in sectors where comparative advantage is shifting, and it impairs the functioning of the international price mechanism. The practice undermines trade liberalization. It is in conflict with the principle of comparative advantage—the basis for efficient trade growth. The Multi-Fiber Arrangement, by allowing discriminatory restrictions against LDC exporters, prevents them from fully exploiting their comparative advantages in textile and clothing manufacture. Trade barriers slow specialization, diversification, investment efficiency, and growth. Insufficient political will to resist protectionist and bilateral measures is the major reason for the rise in protectionism. Governments must make concerted and determined efforts to publicize the costs of protectionism. Those who make trade policy must consider such costs.

A government and its corporate citizens should ignore the quick fix for the trade problems. Instead, they need to take a long-term view and adopt an outward-looking strategy. South Korea, for example, has performed well by promoting industries that exhibit superior performance as a result of their export activity. As explained by Westphal, "a pronounced difference in growth performance is associated with a strategy of export promotion as contrasted with one of import substitution."[20]

---

[17] "Understanding Performance Requirements," *Topics*, Spring 1986.

[18] Richard N. Farmer, "Hong Kong or Albania: Which Trade Strategy Should the U.S. Adopt?" *Business Horizons*, November–December 1985, pp. 2–8.

[19] Shailendra J. Anjaria, Naheed Kirmani, and Arne B. Petersen, *Trade Policy Issues and Developments*, Occasional Paper No. 38, International Monetary Fund, 1985.

[20] Larry E. Westphal, "Fostering Technological Mastery by Means of Selective Infant-Industry Protection," in Moshe Syrquin and Simon Teitel, eds., *Trade, Stability, Technology, and Equity in Latin America* (New York: Academic Press, 1982), pp. 225–79.

Regardless of the inappropriateness or injustice of many of these nontariff barriers, they are part of the international marketing game. To participate in this game, one must learn the rules. While nations have used GATT to lessen many of these restrictions, many remain. Since an international marketer has no control over these wide-reaching forces, his best defense is to understand these trade practices. The barriers may be frustrating, but they are not necessarily insurmountable. By understanding them, the marketer can learn what to expect and how to get along. One must always remember that additional problems are often accompanied by additional opportunities—for additional profits.

David B. Yoffie

No U.S. company or industry is immune from the impact of decisions made in Washington. But many corporate executives still act as if politics is an exercise in crisis management—something to worry about after trouble comes.

Ignoring Washington until you need it may have worked 25 years ago. Today it is a prescription for failure. Divisions within the executive branch, the erosion of party discipline on Capitol Hill, and the sprawling power of congressional staffs have rendered obsolete once reliable channels of access and influence. Increased political competition among businesses further complicates the situation. In the early 1960s, fewer than 150 companies maintained Washington offices. Today the number is close to 700. Some 2,500 companies have other forms of Washington representation, and more than 15,000 lobbyists work the halls of Congress and the regulatory agencies.

Executives must bring to politics the same long-term perspectives they apply to marketing and investment decisions. This is especially true for companies or industries whose size and reach don't provide a natural base of influence. Manufacturers of steel, automobiles, or textiles expect a sympathetic hearing in Washington—too many jobs in too many congressional districts are at stake. But politics is very different for smaller industries that don't affect millions of people, don't have employees spread across the country, or can't draw on the clout of national labor unions.

Like a superior business strategy to niche players in a crowded market, intelligent and carefully executed political strategies are crucial for smaller industries to succeed in Washington. The challenge is to create and sustain political advantage—to develop a stable and constructive relationship that makes Washington an ally in the battle for global competitiveness. The process of building political advantage requires high-level executive attention and action. If government is important to an industry's competitive future, political activism must be a business priority.

The political effectiveness of the semiconductor industry shows what it takes to succeed. The design and manufacture of semiconductors is a small industry by any standard. Merchant suppliers (companies that sell chips to other companies) employ fewer than 115,000 U.S. workers and generate revenues of $12 billion—just over 10 percent of the revenues of General Motors. Employment is focused geographically; more than half the industry's work force lives in Arizona, California, and Texas. And most of the top semiconductor companies were founded by self-assured entrepreneurs dedicated to the virtues of small enterprise and corporate self-reliance. For much of their early history, these driven industrialists resisted outside alliances of any sort, especially with Washington. These are hardly the ingredients from which political juggernauts are fashioned.

Yet semiconductor companies have compiled one of the most impressive political performance records of the 1980s. In 1983, the industry established an ambitious agenda for government action: more favorable tax treatment, relaxed antitrust regulation of joint research and development, greater protection of chip designs, and several tough policies to promote fair trade. The industry had realized these objectives and more by the end of 1987. (See the insert, "Big Results for a Small Industry.")

The track record has been most striking on the trade front. The semiconductor industry has nursed serious grievances about Japanese trade practices since the mid-1970s. Once they decided to act, U.S. companies needed less than two years to convince Washington to take aggressive action on their behalf.

The formal campaign began in June 1985, when the Semiconductor Industry Association (SIA) filed for relief under Section 301 of the Trade Act of 1974. Section 301 authorizes the president to penalize countries that deny U.S. products fair access to their markets. Fourteen months later, the United States and Japan signed an accord that gave the industry the assistance it sought. The Japanese agreed to open their markets to foreign semiconductors and to stop selling chips below cost. In April 1987, concluding that Japan was violating the accord, the Reagan administration approved $300 million in punitive sanctions—the first such penalties against Japan since World War II. This series of measures is unprecedented for its swiftness, severity, and agreement with industry recommendations.

Why have semiconductor companies succeeded in Washington when other industries of comparable and greater size (telecommunications equipment, footwear, automobile parts) have not? There are no magic formulas for influencing government. Political environments change, public officials come and go, opponents and allies shift overnight. But the semiconductor industry's experiences illuminate four general principles for making things happen in Washington:

1. *Companies need a united front.* Small industries must develop and maintain alliances among competitors, suppliers, and customers. Such ties expand the range of affected constituencies, increase the resources available for political action, and defuse potential sources of opposition.

2. *Government allies are essential.* Friends inside the government are as important as corporate allies. An industry should identify and cultivate executive branch agencies and members of Congress with stakes in its agenda. This means crafting positions that will appeal to targeted officials and factoring their interests and agendas into the industry's

own political calculations. An industry should also identify potential adversaries in government and take steps to minimize their impact.

3. *CEOs have a special role to play.* A visible, persuasive, accessible CEO is often more effective than dozens of hired political guns. Top executives can overcome "barriers to entry" in Washington. In the early stages of political activism, gaining access to public officials and raising industry visibility can be especially difficult. Lobbyists often struggle to get time with a senator or a cabinet member. Business leaders can get to them more easily. When CEOs make promises, they can deliver; lobbyists are only messengers. Politicians know this.

4. *Political action by company executives is more effective than trade association efforts.* Trade associations can play important roles in setting agendas, monitoring political developments, and establishing contacts in Washington. But company managers—senior executives, middle managers, plant supervisors—should be on the front lines. Managers understand the details and subtleties of their industry; it's their livelihood. And precisely because it's their livelihood, they may be more driven to get results.

The modern semiconductor industry was born in 1959 with the invention of the integrated circuit. The industry has experienced three phases of political engagement. The first 15 years were marked by an arm's-length relationship with government. U.S. companies were global technology leaders in all segments of the chip market, industry revenues exploded, and many millionaires were born. During this expansion period, NASA and the Pentagon were important customers, but chip makers wanted the government's business—not its meddling.

This attitude began to change in the mid-1970s with the first stirrings of foreign competition. During the 1975 recession, U.S. semiconductor companies scaled back plans to add production capacity much as they had in previous recessions. Then, when the economy rallied, they were caught short of capacity. This time the Japanese rushed in to meet excess demand. When Japanese success in commodity chips threatened to put certain U.S. producers out of business, a few of them turned to Washington for help. But their proposals for government intervention fell on deaf ears.

Gradually, as Japanese competition seemed to verge on domination, more chip makers began to look to Washington. U.S. companies accounted for 55 percent of world semiconductor production in 1978; by 1987, their share had dropped to 44 percent. During this same period, Japanese market share rose from 28 percent to 50 percent. Alarmed by these trends, semiconductor companies made political activism a priority.

Trade policy has been an issue of particular urgency. Its importance was rooted in one of the industry's most striking characteristics—that production costs for most products declined by 30 percent for every doubling of cumulative volume. This is because semiconductor manufacturing lines frequently turned out more defective than sound chips. With new products, yields were often as low as 25 percent, even for the best companies. As products matured, however, yields would run as high as 90 percent.

The need to raise yields led companies to manufacture high-volume products that could act as "technology drivers." It was generally believed that skills learned in manufacturing large quantities of a simple product could be transferred to more complicated, higher value-added devices and help "drive" the company down a steep learning curve. Dynamic random access memory (DRAM) chips, a 1971 American invention, were the most widely used technology driver for many years. Other technology drivers included static random access memory (SRAM) chips and erasable programmable read only memory (EPROM) chips.

During the past ten years, however, U.S. companies have lost market share in each of these critical products. In 1975, for example, U.S. companies accounted for 90 percent of world DRAM shipments. By 1987, their share was just over 20 percent, an erosion suffered almost exclusively at the hands of the Japanese.

U.S. merchant producers have articulated two basic objections to Japanese practices. First, for decades U.S. companies have been unable to increase their 10 percent share of the Japanese market, despite wide swings in the dollar's value and their consistent success in Europe against the Japanese. De facto exclusion from Japan, which by 1986 had become the world's largest market for semiconductors, put American manufacturers at a serious competitive disadvantage in technology drivers. Second, U.S. companies claimed that the Japanese were selling commodity chips in the United States below production costs. This alleged dumping not only cost U.S. companies market share, it also put tremendous pressure on industry profits. U.S. merchant producers lost a staggering $2 billion in 1985 and 1986. This dismal outcome was largely the result of a global industry downturn (Japanese producers also lost $2 billion), but dumping in the U.S. market made a bad situation worse.

It's easy to see why most semiconductor executives eventually agreed that the trade situation and their collective market position would deteriorate further without aggressive intervention from Washington. The challenge became translating the goal of fair trade into the reality of government policy.

Stand United

A crucial choice for executives trying to build political advantage is whether to advance the interests of their own companies or to support industrywide initiatives. Political activism is expensive, so only big corporations can consider a company-based agenda. The startup investment for a bare-bones Washington operation—an office, a secretary, and a full-time lobbyist—typically runs about $1 million.

Even for large companies, industrywide campaigns are often preferable for

Big Results for a Small Industry

The performance of the semiconductor industry in Washington during the past five years compares favorably with the recent political success of any domestic industry, regardless of size. Here is a selective catalog of legislation and executive actions adopted since 1983 that bolstered the competitive position of U.S. semiconductor manufacturers.

October 1984. President Reagan signs the National Cooperative Research Act after the House and Senate approve it unanimously. The law, clearing a legal path for the industry's Sematech research consortium, eases antitrust restrictions against joint research and development.

October 1984. The Trade and Tariff Act of 1984 becomes law. An important provision of this omnibus trade statute clarifies that denial of "fair and equitable market access" is a basis to petition for relief under Section 301 of the Trade Act of 1974. The law also instructs the president to negotiate reductions in barriers to trade in services and high-technology products, and it specifically authorizes lower tariffs on semiconductors.

November 1984, President Reagan signs the Semiconductor Chip Protection Act. For the first time, semiconductor companies get statutory protection against duplication of their chip designs. Enforcement of the act is potentially worth millions of dollars in additional profits to U.S. companies, which have been fighting low-priced competition from foreign-made chips.

March 1985. The United States and Japan eliminate tariffs on imported semiconductors. This agreement took two years to negotiate, even though tariffs were so modest that their elimination was not expected to affect chip prices. The biggest impact was improved profits for U.S. producers, which were paying a duty on chips sent abroad for final assembly and then shipped back for sale in the U.S. market, and lower overhead associated with these shipments.

August 1986. The United States and Japan sign a landmark agreement on trade in semiconductors that reflects virtually all the Semiconductor Industry Association's demands. The Japanese pledge to lift their purchases of foreign-made chips to slightly more than 20 percent of their market over a five-year period, effectively doubling U.S. sales to Japan. In addition, the U.S. Commerce Department establishes a system to monitor production costs and prices for Japanese chips and to set fair market values. The Japanese agree not to sell chips outside their home market below these levels.

April 1987. President Reagan imposes $300 million in sanctions on Japanese products in response to alleged violations of the semiconductor accord. He raises duties on a number of products—including portable computers, selected power hand tools, and some color television sets—to 100 percent of their value. In June and November, after determining that the Japanese were no longer dumping chips, the president lifts some of the sanctions. Other sanctions remain in place to signal continued U.S. displeasure with the slow improvement in U.S. access to the Japanese semiconductor market.

November 1987. Congress includes $100 million in the fiscal 1988 defense appropriations bill to help underwrite the Sematech research consortium. Sematech's Austin, Texas facilities focus on reestablishing U.S. leadership in semiconductor chip manufacture. The goal is to develop leading-edge chip-making techniques, based exclusively on U.S. materials and technology, by 1993.

issues where rivals share common political interests. For small companies, forging common political ground is a necessity (see sidebar on page R148). A politician evaluating a proposal from business usually searches for answers to several basic questions: What will the proposal cost? What sectors of the economy benefit? What sectors lose? No politician wants to help one industry if it means antagonizing three others. That's why coalitions are so important from a strategic perspective. Just as powerful suppliers and customers squeeze profit margins in the marketplace, unrestrained political competition among rivals, suppliers, and customers usually reduces everyone's influence.

The defeat of several early proposals for government assistance taught semiconductor industry leaders the importance of building coalitions. During the first 20 years of the industry's existence, it had no organization to represent its interests in Washington. Some companies belonged to large electronics trade associations, but these groups' agendas did not reflect semiconductor industry priorities. So in 1977, five leading merchant producers of high-volume chips— Advanced Micro Devices (AMD), Fairchild, Intel, Motorola, and National Semiconductor—founded the Semiconductor Industry Association.

The SIA and individual companies floated several initiatives against Japan during the late 1970s, and political leaders did what political leaders invariably do. They sought the reactions of other players in the industry as well as outside constituencies. In this case, the key outside constituency was the biggest buyers of chips—giant computer builders like Hewlett-Packard and Digital Equipment. The users' primary concern was maintaining reasonable prices and flexible supplies. Invariably, they opposed SIA initiatives, which effectively doomed the proposals. A string of defeats convinced semiconductor leaders that they had to expand their base of business support.

The process of building coalitions took two forms. Merchant producers cultivated active support from companies and industry associations that had opposed previous SIA initiatives. They also worked to discourage active opposition. If a company or association could not endorse a semiconductor proposal, it might be persuaded at least not to undermine it.

One important step in the coalition-building process was expanding the industry's trade association membership. SIA leaders had been working to increase membership since 1977, but in the early 1980s they made a particular effort to enroll the large captive producers of chips. (Captive producers build chips primarily for use in their own products.) IBM joined the SIA in December 1980, and during the next few years, so did other big captive producers. By 1985, the SIA had 48 members with combined revenues of more than $100 billion. The organization included some large merchant producers like Texas Instruments that had initially resisted joining the group, smaller companies building custom chips, major chip buyers like Control Data and NCR (most of which also produced their own chips), and giant captive producers like IBM and Digital Equipment.

The most important new member, of course, was IBM, the world's largest manufacturer and consumer of semiconductors. IBM never played a leadership role on trade issues, but the company's envoy convoyed to the SIA what positions IBM could and could not live with. Moreover, IBM's membership gave the SIA a level of credibility and visibility in Washington that it had never before enjoyed.

Collecting in one organization large and small merchant producers, captive producers, and important users also created a means by which each industry segment could develop a better understanding of other segments' interests and priorities. Debates within the SIA were, in effect, a negotiating process that produced consensus on particular initiatives. Even if a member company was unenthusiastic about a final SIA proposal, it was unlikely to sabotage the initiative in Washington. It had participated in the internal debates and understood how and why the SIA had reached the position.

The evolution of the Section 301 petition is a case in point. Agreement on the terms of the complaint took three years of bargaining among SIA members. A critical issue was whether trade sanctions should be proposed and, if so, how severe they should be. Some large merchant companies favored an outright embargo on certain commodity chips, or at least the imposition of high tariffs and stiff fines, unless Japan met a timetable for increased U.S. access to its markets. Large users like IBM and Hewlett-Packard rejected this proposal outright. Merchant suppliers realized that user opposition would pose huge political obstacles, as it had with previous initiatives, so IBM's and other companies' objections carried great weight in the SIA.

The petition filed in June 1985 did not advocate punitive embargoes, tariffs, or other restrictions on chip supplies. It proposed two tough but constructive policies. First, it demanded a commitment that by the early 1990s the U.S. share of the Japanese semiconductor market increase commensurately with the U.S. position in the rest of the world. Penalties for noncompliance were left vague, although the SIA made it clear that it expected penalties if negotiations failed. Second, the petition suggested a monitoring system to ensure that Japanese companies were not selling chips below cost in the United States or elsewhere. All SIA members could live with these positions.

The process of building coalitions—or at least of neutralizing potential opposition—extended beyond industry borders. George Scalise, chief administrative officer of AMD and chairman of the SIA's public policy committee, worked hard to secure an endorsement of the 301 suit from the American Electronics Association. The AEA, which has been a Washington presence for decades, represents some 2,800 companies with $305 billion in global sales. Scalise understood that strong opposition from the electronics group might doom the 301 action.

The AEA never fully embraced the SIA position, but it did issue a letter supporting the objectives of the trade case. Coordination with the AEA was also important after adoption of the August 1986 trade agreement. Prices for certain DRAMs quickly skyrocketed, which shook up small chip buyers. The SIA established a subcommittee within the AEA to address user concerns and dampen possible calls for repeal of the agreement.

Target Government Allies

A sound marketing strategy balances product positioning, distribution channels, and reasonable prices. A sound political strategy has similar balances. An industry must position a proposed course of action so as to appeal to the customer (White House officials, regulators, or members of Congress), target the most effective channels of influence (congressional committees, executive agencies, or the courts), and impose reasonable costs on taxpayers and other constituencies. Pushing the right buttons, identifying government allies, and working hard not to antagonize potential adversaries are all essential. Failure in any area usually dooms the entire initiative.

The semiconductor industry paid close attention to all three areas. The 301 complaint's primary objective was opening foreign markets rather than closing U.S. doors. This positioning meant the trade action appealed simultaneously to "Japan bashers" and free traders. It certainly satisfied the White House, which liked the idea of appeasing protectionist sentiment on Capitol Hill by supporting a trade initiative that rejected quotas and tariffs. Representatives and senators with protectionist leanings were also satisfied. Even legislators whose districts included no semiconductor employment were attracted to the cause. They could go home and tell voters they were being tough on Japan, and not antagonize other corporate interests. In short, virtually every set of actors in Washington had something to gain by supporting the skillfully crafted industry position, and few had anything to lose.

As for distribution, the industry used a number of complementary political channels. A common strategy of smaller industries is to avoid "politicized" channels (Congress and the White House), where votes matter, and pursue "administrative" channels (the courts and regulatory agencies), where cases are won or lost on their merits. When the data are clear and convincing and the issue is a one-time problem, administrative remedies are usually adequate. If the objective is to make government an ongoing ally, however, companies and industries must tap political channels and find ways to build alliances with public officials.

A Section 301 petition is one of the more politicized avenues for relief under the trade laws. The U.S. trade representative rules on the merits of the case, and the president determines appropriate sanctions. But the law leaves much room for maneuver. The trade representative can postpone the decision for up to one year, and the president can choose not to act even in the face of a favorable ruling. So the semiconductor industry took steps to heighten the visibility of its trade complaint and the costs of complacency.

One tactic was for companies to file their own trade actions, even without SIA endorsement. Days after the SIA filed the 301, Micron Technology charged that Japanese companies were dumping 64K DRAMs. A few months later, three industry leaders (Intel, AMD, and National Semiconductor) accused the Japanese of dumping EPROMs. Even the Commerce Department, anxious to get tough with the Japanese, initiated its own dumping complaint on 256K and higher DRAMs in December. By the end of 1985, the U.S. government faced four separate complaints on unfair semiconductor trade practices, which put even more pressure on the administration and the Japanese to reach an accommodation.

Capitol Hill was another focus. Congress has no direct role in complaints filed under the trade laws, but the SIA approached representatives and senators to support the 301 petition by lobbying the administration and drawing media attention to the issue of unfair trade practices. The association set a very specific objective: develop legislative support that was bipartisan, bicameral, and as geographically broad as possible. The result was the Congressional Support Group, a caucus composed of ten representatives and ten senators, ten Democrats and ten Republicans, from states including California, Missouri, Florida, and Pennsylvania. The legislators applied pressure on the White House by making telephone calls, lobbying members of the cabinet, and pushing the trade representative to become more involved in the trade dispute.

The SIA also persuaded 180 representatives and senators—including the entire delegations from several states with heavy semiconductor employment—to send letters (drafted by the SIA's general counsel) to the administration. Meanwhile, the California delegation met with the Japanese ambassador to the United States to emphasize the gravity of the issue. By the time the White House decided to negotiate a semiconductor agreement, the SIA had made as many allies inside the government as it had developed among suppliers and customers.

Many political observers believe that the Pentagon figured prominently in the semiconductor dispute. They argue that microelectronics is so important to high-technology weapons and communications systems that the Defense Department must have been the natural ally of U.S. chip producers. How could the Pentagon tolerate Japanese domination of a commodity dubbed the "oil of the 1980s"?

The truth is, the Defense Department never weighed in strongly on semiconductor trade policy. One of the department's long-standing priorities was to persuade Japan to increase its military spending; trade disputes wouldn't advance this goal. The SIA understood this and kept its distance from the defense establishment until after trade issues were settled. Later, when it was looking for funding for its Sematech research consortium, the industry enlisted the Pentagon's support. The fiscal 1988 defense appropriations bill included $100 million for Sematech.

Get CEOs Involved

Broad membership in an association or informal coalition helps build legitimacy in Washington. Effective political targeting further improves the odds of success. But who does the work?

Here again, semiconductor companies made the right moves at the right times. Even before they had forged an industry consensus on trade policy, they

TABLE **1**   Japan sells more chips . . . *(percent share of world DRAM shipments)*

	United States	Japan	Europe
1980	57 percent	41 percent	2 percent
1982	53	43	4
1984	38	56	6
1986	18	75	3
1987	22	65	3

Source: Dataquest Inc., February 1988. Figures refer to units shipped, not revenues. Some years do not add up to 100 percent because of shipments from other regions.

had worked hard to establish a beachhead in Washington. Like companies in so many other industries, chip makers turned to political activism only after troubling market trends had surfaced. Like the marketplace, however, politics usually rewards early movers. The first companies that enter political life make the campaign contributions, build the key congressional ties, and establish the reputations that translate into access and influence. Latecomers can find themselves at the end of a very long line.

The semiconductor industry recognized it needed a distinct approach. So it called on the charisma and persuasiveness of its senior executives, who proved to be a very valuable resource. Their technical achievements and business

TABLE **2**   . . . and buys more too *(semiconductor consumption in millions of dollars)*

	N. America	Japan	Europe
1980	$ 6,053	$ 3,383	$3,686
1982	6,970	4,082	3,167
1984	13,139	8,845	4,805
1986	10,201	12,356	5,532
1987*	11,743	14,239	6,780

* Estimated
Source: Dataquest Inc., August 1987.

celebrity gave them great visibility on Capitol Hill. Chairmen, presidents, and other high-ranking executives traveled to Washington to meet with cabinet secretaries, senators, and members of Congress and to testify before congressional committees. Especially prominent from 1979 through 1981 were Robert Noyce, vice chairman of Intel, Charles Sporck, CEO of National Semiconductor, W. Jerry Sanders III, chairman of Advanced Micro Devices, and Motorola Chairman Robert Galvin.

These men opened many doors that might have been closed to lobbyists or lower ranking businesspeople. Noyce, for example, is something of a legend in the electronics world. A multimillionaire, coinventor of the integrated circuit, he was general manager of Fairchild Semiconductor during its rise in the 1960s and one of the founders of Intel. The Washington establishment wanted to get to know him as much as he wanted to develop political contacts. Noyce spent 20 percent of his time during the early 1980s on political action. He and his colleagues in effect softened up Washington for the formal campaign that began in 1985.

Politically engaged CEOs are an effective weapon against the ever-increasing Washington barriers to entry. They are also important for maintaining political ties. Even the most loyal customers need periodic attention from top brass; so do politicians. Noyce and his industry peers still visit Washington a few times a year, every year, to stay close to the players.

Put Managers on Front Lines

Of course, top executives can't do the whole job. Over the long term, companies face another critical choice: whether to rely on their trade association's staff and paid lobbyists or to involve other corporate managers. The nature of the agenda determines the right answer.

When an industry is involved in maintaining the political status quo—staying in touch with Capitol Hill, conducting routine public relations, monitoring the regulatory agencies—the best strategy is to use trade association professionals. Large groups like the National Association of Manufacturers and the Food Marketing Institute exist mainly to keep tabs on Washington and influence technical regulations and bills. It makes sense for large association staffs to run these activities. As the issues become more urgent, however, and the political agenda moves from reacting to initiating new policies, managers should become involved directly. The more consequential the issue, the higher the level of manager needed.

The semiconductor industry never had the luxury of maintaining the political status quo. By the time it turned its attention to Washington, the trade situation was urgent. So the companies agreed to dedicate money and some of their own people to government relations. Time and again, managers from the large manufacturers came to Washington to support the trade initiative. Chip producers and users, including AMD, Digital Equipment, General Instruments, Harris Corporation, Intel, International Rectifier, Motorola, National Semiconductor, Rockwell International, and Texas Instruments committed executives to help build congressional support, visit trade officials, generate press releases, and for other work to build political bridges. AMD's George Scalise devoted 25 percent of his time to managing the trade case.

Washington lawyer Alan Wolff, a former deputy special trade representative, supplemented these industry lobbying efforts. The combination of experienced outside counsel and hands-on executive involvement proved powerful. Wolff provided the SIA with government contacts and a good feel for what agencies would be open to what positions. But many of the foot soldiers in the campaign were company managers whose expertise and commitment made them very persuasive with public officials.

This pattern of direct executive action explains why the SIA has remained such a lean organization. Despite its ambitious political agenda, the SIA employs only six professionals and two government affairs executives. Its annual budget runs less than $1 million, and the association doesn't have a Washington office. The Japanese, on the other hand, reportedly spent between $30 and $50 million lobbying against the trade initiatives.

In less than a decade, the semiconductor industry has built a constructive and nonadversarial relationship with Congress and the executive branch. These ties have produced a series of policy initiatives which, while not ideal, have had overwhelmingly positive consequences for the industry. U.S. semiconductor companies still have serious competitive problems, including quality and manufacturing costs. But government intervention has improved short-term profitability and cash flows and long-term profitability and cash flows and long-term prospects for research and development.

The work of the semiconductor industry in Washington is not over. For government to be a reliable ally and partner, the relationship must be stable and on-going. A shotgun approach to politics—get what you want and don't return until you need something else—simply won't suffice. So the industry remains mobilized. The SIA and member companies continue to monitor Japanese chip prices and foreign access to the Japanese market and to supply the data to Washington. This vigilance helps explain why the Reagan administration imposed the sanctions in April 1987. Literally hundreds of violations of similar agreements have occurred over the past 30 years, but no administration has taken action as severe as the semiconductor sanctions.

Most American companies continue to have an adversarial relationship with Washington. Business leaders complain about government bureaucracy and inefficiencies. Public officials complain about special interest groups maneuvering for their own side deals, making it impossible to fashion coherent national policy. Even in the semiconductor case, business-government relations have not always been smooth. Some companies have worked to undermine SIA proposals; certain government officials have tried to obstruct semiconductor policies.

We must build more constructive business-government relationships in the United States, which means not always assuming that government is the enemy.

Many public officials are eager to help business in the battle for global competitiveness, especially when business frames its proposals in a way that appeals to the officials' own agendas and priorities. The process of building political advantage may be especially challenging for smaller companies and industries, but it is far from impossible, especially if they focus their efforts. Semiconductor companies did not try to shape the entire range of policies affecting them. They targeted certain issues that were central to their future and where their case was strongest.

Not every industry can expect to duplicate the semiconductor producers' success in Washington. But if U.S. companies are serious about regaining world competitiveness, the semiconductor experience must become the rule, not the exception.

READING 12 **POLITICAL RISK ANALYSIS AND DIRECT FOREIGN INVESTMENT: SOME PROBLEMS OF DEFINITION AND MEASUREMENT**

S. Prakash Sethi ◆ K. A. N. Luther

One of the major uncertainties and risks associated with foreign investments—portfolio, direct, or loan—involves the political developments occurring in the international arena and in both the host and home countries of multinational business operations. The impact of these political developments on the safety and profitability of foreign investments is quite often far greater than the normal uncertainties and risks associated with overseas developments, for example:

◆ In the international organizations, less-developed countries (LDCs) have become more strident in their demands for shifts in economic resources from the developed countries under the rubric of the "New International Economic Order," or the North-South conflict.

◆ Private lenders have substantially increased their loans to both the LDCs and socialist countries in the Eastern Bloc. The interest payments of these loans are absorbing a large portion of these countries' foreign exchange resources and more loans are being advanced just to meet the interest payments.

◆ The oil-rich countries of the Middle East are displaying increasing instability while at the same time creating greater trade and investment links and dependencies with the developing countries.

◆ Protectionist sentiments in the economies of the West have made them more reluctant to open their doors to exports from LDCs.

◆ The combined population pressures, the lack of economic growth, and the totalitarian and often inefficient political orders and governmental bureaucracies create a need for dependence and foreign aid. However, international lending institutions (e.g., the World Bank) are tightening their lending criteria, and developed countries led by the United Stares are pulling back on their government-to-government direct aid.

All these factors, along with the happenings in Iran, El Salvador, and Nicaragua, highlight the importance of political events to business decision making. It is, therefore, no wonder that corporations and lending institutions have been paying more attention to the analysis of the impact of political risk on their current and potential foreign investment decisions.

Source: Copyright 1986 by The Regents of the University of California. Reprinted from the *California Management Review*, Vol. 28, No. 2, Winter 1986. By permission of The Regents.

Political Risk Analysis—The State of the Art

A survey of current scholarly and professional literature would also indicate a significant increase in the research and analysis of political risk. The current state of research, however, is faced with a number of problems that are likely to limit severely the relevance of the concept both as an analytical tool and as a practical guide to business decision making. These problems are broadly those of definition and measurement.

Without quite specifying it, most writers tend to use "political risk" as a catchall term for the risk dimensions of political events which have an impact on business decisions. As such, it is replete with definitional incongruities. Political risk is generally equated with political instability and is analyzed along those lines. However, political risk, as it affects business investment decisions, cannot be equated simply with political instability such as a change in government. Furthermore, political instability has different connotations in different sociocultural frameworks. Thus, any measure of political risk based on some index of political instability would most likely lead to erroneous findings of dubious practical value.

Consider, for example, the case of Italy and the United Kingdom. If one were to measure changes in government as proxy for political instability, ten changes in Italy would not mean the same thing as ten changes in the government of the United Kingdom during the same period; yet the index would not be able to differentiate between the two conditions. Similarly, there may be frequent changes in the military strong men running a government; but so long as the government is controlled by the army, the changes in government would have little practical impact on economic activity. Also, it is not certain that the process of economic development, which leads to environmental changes, is the cause of political instability—as argued in some studies.[1] Political stability can be found in some of the fast-growing nations (such as South Korea, Malaysia, and Taiwan) and in some of the low achievers (like Cuba, Zaire, Kenya, and Tanzania).

It seems that in much of the research effort on political risk, not enough attention has been paid to the development of concepts and definitions that capture the breadth of the problem. Unless the definitions are clear, other methodological issues are not likely to be resolved. The penchant is for quantification. The process has led to unrealistic expectations about the usefulness of the results. Given the poor definitions of the concept to begin with, the

---

[1] Robert T. Green, *Political Instability as a Determinant of U.S. Foreign Investments*, Studies in Marketing, No. 17, Bureau of Business Research, Graduate School of Business, University of Texas at Austin, 1972; Lee C. Nehrt, "The Political Climate for Private Investment, Analysis Will Reduce Uncertainty," *Business Horizons* (June 1972), pp. 51–58; Franklin R. Root, "Analyzing Political Risks in International Business," in Ashok Kapoor and Phillip D. Grub, eds., *The Multinational Enterprise in Transition* (Princeton, NJ: The Darwin Press, 1972); A. Van Agtmael, "How Business Has Dealt with Political Risk," *Financial Executive* (January 1976), pp. 26–30.

results provide the wrong answers. The problems are compounded by inconsistent interpretations, limitations in technical skills, and, given the lack of a "real feel" for the country being analyzed, misperceptions of possible uses of the data.

Questions of definition and measurement are fundamental to the use of effective political risk analysis by business entities. There is a tendency to proceed with the analysis as if a commonly agreed upon definition of the phenomenon existed. The result is that while there may be a great deal of dialogue or "noise," there is little understanding of the problem. A fuzziness in the definition invariably leads to the wrong selection of data, the inappropriate choice of analytical tools, and the interpretation of findings and solutions that have little, if anything, to do with the original problem.

Professor Kobrin has stated this impasse in his review essay on the subject:

> We need better definitions of the phenomena, a conceptual structure relating politics to the firm, and a great deal of information about the impact of the political environment. The three are, of course, related.[2]

The first objective of this article is to develop a structure of political risk such that it would lend itself to systematic analysis of its various dimensions in terms of degree and type of risk and the modes of containment measures that can be undertaken by the investors. The second objective is to identify certain approaches for the measurement and interpretation of data pertaining to different categories of risk.

Problems of Definition

The term "political risk" has had various interpretations in the literature. Most studies define it as unanticipated government actions that have an impact on business operations.[3] National governments by their actions might prevent business transactions, change terms of agreements, or even expropriate business units. Other studies have defined political risk on the basis of environmental changes due to political developments (like acts of violence, instability, riots, and so on) that have repercussions on business activity.[4] These two distinct

---

[2] Stephen Kobrin, "Political Risk: A Review and Reconsideration," *Journal of International Business Studies,* Vol. X, No. 1 (Spring/Summer 1979):77.

[3] John Fayweather, "Nationalism and the Multinational Firm," in Ashok Kapoor and Phillip D. Grub, eds., op cit.; Robert T. Green, "Political Structure as a Predictor of Radical Political Change," *Columbia Journal of World Business,* Vol. IX, No. 1 (Spring 1974):28–36; Stephen Kobrin, "Political Assessment by International Firms: Models or Methodologies," *Journal of Policy Modeling* 3/2 (1981):251–270; I. C. MacMillan, "Business Strategies for Political Action," *Journal of General Management* (Autumn 1974).

[4] Robert T. Green, op. cit., (1972); Robert T. Green, op. cit., (1974); Robert T. Green and Christopher M. Korth, "Political Instability and the Foreign Investor," *California Management Review* (Fall 1974), pp. 23–31; A. Van Agtmael, op. cit.

definitions of political risk—one deliberative and the other environmental—are interdependent. Environmental changes can prompt government actions as much as government activity can provoke environmental developments.

An operational definition of political risk such as that offered by Robock (who refers to it as being "discontinuities in the business environment" and "difficult to anticipate"[5]) is, of course, correct but not very useful. A business entity needs to have an understanding of the sources of risk to take a proactive stand against such risks or initiate measures to contain them. Adequate responses from corporations require an understanding of the total environment of political risk.

It is clear that political risks emanate from different sources and have an impact on a business entity in a manner different from pure market developments. They threaten both profitability and satisfactory repatriation of profits of a foreign direct investment. The risk potential faced by a business is influenced by: entry conditions in terms of magnitude and types of investment; ownership patterns, in as much as expatriate versus local participation is a factor; type of product lines and operations, where the relative technological and human skills sophistication of production processes and final products play a part; and government instruments and directives both of host and parent countries that would insure or hinder freedom and safety of operations. This means that country, industry, and firm characteristics all influence the potential vulnerability and intensity of political risk for a business firm.[6]

The difficulty of political risk assessment is further compounded by distinctions between macro dimensions (which affect all business enterprises in general) and micro political risks (which selectively affect specific business activities).[7] Political instabilities, government actions, or other factors might translate into either one of these two types of risks and it is not possible *a priori* to identify outcomes.

These considerations, therefore, warrant a more extensive classification of political risks than prevalent in the literature. But if the term political risk is not going to be "overly constrained from both an analytical and operational viewpoint," we need to be concerned with not political events "but their potential manifestations as constraints upon foreign investors."[8] This again requires an understanding of the sources of political risk. It is this concern that leads us to argue for a more encompassing identification of the types of risks that are generated by events that have political dimensions.

---

[5] S. Robock, "Political Risk: Identification and Assessment," *Columbia Journal of World Business* (July/August 1971), p. 7.

[6] Ibid.; Franklin R. Root, op. cit., (1972); F. Root, "U.S. Business Abroad and Political Risks," *MSU Business Topics* (Winter 1968), pp. 73–80.

[7] Robock, op. cit.

[8] Kobrin, op. cit., (1979), p. 71

In Figure 1, various dimensions of political risk are identified along with different avenues of containment. Such a matrix helps in the task of political risk assessment by making explicit the multidimensional nature of the political risk problem. Possible strategies can then be identified for a business unit, particularly if it is going to be proactive rather than reactive in making decisions pertaining to foreign direct investment.

In the matrix, risk to foreign enterprises is viewed as a combination of three interrelated factors: political, economic, and sociocultural.

FIGURE 1   Matrix of Risk and Containment

Sources of Political Risk	Methods of Containment		
	International	Home Country	Host Country
Host Country Conditions			
Political	Insurance Against Political Risk	Foreign Aid Military Aid	Joint Ownership Shorter Payback Period
Economic	International/Multilateral Agreements	Foreign Aid Restrictions on Technology Transfer Bilateral Agreements	Higher ROI Restrictions on Technology Transfer
Sociocultural	Changes in Public Opinion	Maintain a Low Profile Posture of Non-Involvement	Change in Product Design
Home Country Conditions			
Political	Use of International Organizations Pressure from Other Countries	Lobbying for Change in Laws and Government Policy Threat of International Reparations	Insulate Local Subsidiaries from Home Country Laws Be a Good Corporate Citizen
Economic	International/Multilateral Agreements	Coalition of Businesses with Common Interests	Increase economic Benefits and Host Country Dependence on Foreign Enterprise
Sociocultural	International Public Opinion	Create Positive Public Opinion Towards Needs and Aspirations of People in the Host Country	Be a Good Corporate Citizen Maintain a Low Profile

◆ The *political* dimension refers to events that arise from power or authority relationships, which can stem from many different sources. Political instability can refer to cataclysmic events such as violent changes in government, assassinations, and riots. It can also refer to gradual events that have implications for business decisions, such as the effect of growing national pride on the ownership of business entities or the gradual undermining of the power base of the current leadership by ideological and institutional developments.

◆ *Economic* factors also play a role in bringing about political risks. As has been noticed in the literature, the distinction between purely political and economic risks breaks down at the operational level because of the interdependence of economic and political phenomena.[9] However, the distinction is useful insofar as it identifies the root cause of the problem being tied to economic conditions (such as poor economic management, low employment, high inflation rates, balance of payments problems, and inequities in income and wealth distributions). Furthermore, to the extent to which national governments modify economic arrangements to accommodate political pressure (as in the case of protectionism and foreign exchange controls), political risk dimensions are accentuated in business decision making. Because they engage in the import and export of finished products, foreign direct investment units are vulnerable to trade-related disruptions caused by the political influence of pressure groups.

◆ Finally, political risk dimensions may also result from *sociocultural* developments. The Iranian experience is a case in point: the rapid pace of Westernization created social tensions and cultural conflicts which resulted in the fundamentalist revolution.

In general, the risks posed by host-country developments are adequately covered in the political risk literature, but risks emanating from parent or home-country policies are ignored. For example, export controls have become increasingly important as instruments of foreign policy. Other examples of economic alternatives that are used by parent countries to bolster political influence include trade embargoes, sanctions, and controls on the transfer of technology and goods to unfriendly nations. Foreign entities of domestic enterprises are affected by these restrictions since they infringe on the free flow of goods and services from the headquarters to the foreign subsidiary.

Two examples illustrate the interdependence of international, home-country, and host-country government policies on the one hand, and political, economic, and sociocultural factors on the other hand. The cases in point are

---

[9] Root, op. cit., (1972).

investments in South Africa and the sale and marketing of infant formula in less-developed countries. There are conflicting crosscurrents between the policies of various U.S. administrations in terms of the degree of compliance with various U.N. resolutions on these issues. There are also different types of pressures by vested interest groups, especially religious groups, on U.S. corporations both to refrain from investing in South Africa and to comply with the WHO code on marketing practices for the sale of infant formula in less-developed countries. The response of U.S. multinationals in both these cases is invariably complicated by their vulnerability to U.S. domestic pressures; pressures from other countries, where they have operations; their global market shares and international production strategy; and their relative investment exposure in South Africa and third-world countries. It should, therefore, be clear that any analysis of risk that ignores these interdependencies is likely to have little practical value for MNCs in assessing relative investment or operational risks in their overseas operations.

The analysis can be further extended by considering possible avenues of containment for political risk problems. Each of the risks mentioned can involve a composite of responses for containment. International treaties, concessions, and pacts can safeguard against some aspects of risk. Parent countries can choose less interventionist measures to influence foreign policy objectives or respond by withholding foreign aid or arms if the risk emanates from the host country. Considerable responsibility for reducing political risk for business might be in the hands of the host country, which has to guarantee a favorable business climate despite political and socio-cultural pressures that potentially may be destabilizing.

Corporate response to these pressures is also important. By anticipating possible sources of conflict, corporations can make adjustments in their business practices and ownership patterns (such as permitting greater local participation) and, hence, can take a proactive stance. The common reactive stance seems to occur because assessment resources are limited and therefore are used sparingly. A proactive stance would entail anticipating the political risk problem well in advance and taking measures to lessen social conflict. Quite apart from "self insurance" through a shorter payback period or higher rate of return, an activist strategy can diffuse potential sources of conflict for corporate management.

Although not all of the cells of the matrix are of relevance for every strategy of containment, the schema enables decision makers to have a sense of the alternatives involved. Careful identification of the sources of risks will go a long way in suggesting possible strategies of containment against political risks. Definitions that do not take into account the broad spectrum of the political risk problem are not likely to be useful for formulating responses. To focus upon just political instability defined in a narrow manner leads either to empirical studies that show political factors as not being a major determinant for foreign direct investment or to assessments which claim that "political instability is neither a necessary nor a sufficient condition for changes in policy relevant to foreign investment."[10]

Problems of Measurement

Political risk assessment, besides requiring comprehensive definitions, demands reconciliation of numerous problems of measurement. These range from problems with data (in terms of collection and quality) to problems of analysis and interpretation of findings.

General Problems of Data Collection

It is well known that problems of data severely limit the predictability of models of political risk. Data deficiencies exist for even the simplest of tests, leave alone sophisticated assessment techniques like Delphi, time series analysis, and regression models. Data collection of a political nature is not only difficult and time-consuming but is likely to be biased as the local people respond guardedly to sensitive questioning. Problems are further compounded by censorship of published sources and records. Whatever data are available are likely to be haphazard and not in a format readily usable by a multinational corporation. The risk-averse proclivities of the bureaucrats who gather information lead to "bad" information being hidden. Official data-gathering agencies like the United Nations and the State Department might be susceptible to a great deal of "doctoring" of data that have been supplied voluntarily by country bureaucrats to create positive, as opposed to truthful, country images.

More fundamentally, however, it could be argued that the data that are available for political risk assessment suffer because they are not collected with respect to a specific strategic position of a business entity. The decision-related dimension of political risk assessment does not feature in the collection stage. Pursuance of a particular strategy generates its own unique risk exposure, and correct evaluation of this risk requires not just general or broad data, but rather strategy-specific information. Furthermore, data have to be somewhat firm- and industry-specific. The issue of data collection, therefore, is ultimately tied to strategic containment avenues that are contemplated by a business. An emphasis on collecting data that are strategy-specific and micro-oriented should yield more focused information gathering and eliminate some of the problems outlined above.

Problems of Analysis and Interpretation

Quite apart from data problems, there are problems of analysis and interpretation once the data have been collected. Until recently, impressionistic and qualitative assessments of political

---

[10] Kobrin, op. cit., (1979), p. 74.

risk were made. But now, more and more sophisticated and quantitatively oriented techniques are being used. In the literature, models range from subjective assessments (such as the Delphi method with its reliance on expert opinions) to those that use quantitative indicators of political and environmental instability. Models have been employed both to gauge the extent of political risks and to forecast the likelihood of these risks.

Haner has constructed indices of instability on the basis of expert opinions and assigning of probabilistic weights to a number of variables to arrive at the prospect for political risk.[11] The technique provides a collective impressionistic assessment by a panel of experts. But the multidimensionality of the risk function is glossed over in the aggregation process, which attempts at generating a single scale of potential risk.

A more sophisticated version is provided by Rummel and Heenan, who break up the risk dimension into components (domestic instability, foreign conflict, political and economic climate) and assign probability values based on insight and intuition for each of them.[12] Although this is an improvement in terms of having a broader focus on risks and a finer distillation of information, it still suffers from too much aggregation.

Researchers have also attempted to compute political instability indices for different national environments. Variables (such as number of years of independence, number of changes in government, and number of deaths by political violence) are used to arrive at an index of instability. Weights are also ascribed to variables to convey intensity. Cluster analyses are used to enable grouping of countries so as to generate experience from one country to another in light of poor data availability.[13] This approach is most helpful in enabling a generalization of characteristics in a particular country across a cluster of countries that are similar and where data and operational and other difficulties do not permit a country by country analysis. The technique offers an effective method of getting around data limitations with respect to political risk assessment. However, problems of definition of variables, limited applicability of an extrapolation of the past into the future in dynamic environments, and a lack of consensus on what variables constitute political instability restrict the usefulness of these approaches.

---

[11] F. T. Haner, "Business Environmental Risk Index," *Best's Review* (Property Liability ed.) (July 1975).

[12] R.J. Rummell and D.A. Heenan, "How Multinationals Analyze Political Risk," *Harvard Business Review* (January/February 1978), pp. 67–76.

[13] S. Prakash Sethi, "Comparative Cluster Analysis of World Markets," *Journal of Marketing Research* (August 1971); S. Prakash Sethi and David L. Curry, "Variable and Object Clustering of Cross-Cultural Data: Some Implications for Comparative Research and Policy Formulation," *Journal of Comparative Political Studies* (October 1972); S. Prakash Sethi and Richard H. Holton, "Country Typologies for the Multinational Corporation: A New Basic Approach," *California Management Review* (Spring 1973).

More sophisticated techniques are suggested by Stobaugh, who deals with a range of estimates and methods for risk exposure.[14] Political risks are accounted for by adjusting "the present value of expected cash flows, or the internal rate of return from the investment project under consideration" so as to "reflect the timing and magnitude of risk probabilities." Further extensions of this approach involve adjusting incremental cash flows to allow for the political uncertainty faced on a per period basis. But as suggested by Kobrin, these judgements on adjustments of cash flows or discount rates are "determined by one's judgements to (1) the applicability of the Capital Asset Pricing Model and (2) whether the risk is systematic or not."[15] There are also immense problems of data availability and estimation of various probabilities. The real danger is that a sophisticated approach for political risk assessment would be used by corporate managements as a "black box," giving interpretations that are questionable and based on data that are very dubious to begin with.

Inasmuch as formal models of the political risk process enable corporate planners to state some of the subjective probabilities that are associated with corporate decisions, these models are useful. They demand a formal accounting of dimensions which otherwise might have been ignored with qualitative assessments. However, there is also the danger that an elaborate and complex model would be treated as a substitute for reality. The political risk assessment process could be seriously misleading if "mechanistic" reliance is placed on mathematical models.

Empirical research has shown that few companies use these sophisticated techniques regularly.[16] The organization of the political assessment function appears to be quite varied, ranging from informal assessment by top management to a formal "unit with five or more professionals, who are charged with developing and implementing an assessment methodology."[17] When scanning the external environment, managers tend to rely heavily on interpersonal contact for their information sources.[18] The integration of the assessment of

---

[14] R. Stobaugh, "How to Analyze Foreign Investment Climates," *Harvard Business Review* (September/October 1969), pp. 100–107.

[15] Kobrin, op. cit., (1979), p. 72.

[16] J. LaPalombara and S. Blank, *Multinational Corporations in Comparative Perspective* (New York, NY: The Conference Board, 1977); F. Root, op. cit., (1968).

[17] Stephen J. Kobrin, "The Environmental Determinants of Foreign Direct Manufacturing Investment: An ExPost Empirical Analysis," *Journal of International Business Studies*, Vol. 7, No. 2 (Fall/Winter 1976):35.

[18] F.J. Aguilar, *Scanning the Business Environment* (New York, NY: MacMillan, 1967); W. Keegan, "Multinational Scanning: A Study of Information Sources Used by Headquarters Executives in Multinational Companies," *Administrative Science Quarterly* (September 1974), pp. 411–421.

political risk into the decision-making process, therefore, tends to be informal and unsystematic.[19]

In general, narrow definitions of the political risk concept have led to techniques that can help operationalize the political risk issue. But the very process of simplification demanded by formal models makes the exercise less beneficial, since the complexity of the problem is assumed away. These models, based on limited definitions, assume deterministic relationships between, for example, political instability and political risk. In reality, the causation is a result of numerous sources of risk—and not at all determinable in the fashion demanded by the formal techniques.

Conclusions

Notwithstanding the problems of definition, measurement, analysis, and interpretation, multinational corporations must cope with the evaluation of political risks involved in their overseas investments. Some of these issues could be solved with further research. For multinationals, a five-step approach is suggested here to deal with political risk assessment:

◆ Broad measures of political risk, based on secondary data, should be used, but only as a first step in political risk assessment. Since the quality of these data is likely to be highly inconsistent, any conclusions derived from these measures should be taken with a large dose of skepticism.

◆ To the extent that global or regional scales of political risk are developed, emphasis should be placed on ensuring that the data are consistent across countries, not only in terms of inputs (i.e., number of changes in governments, number of assassinations, etc.), but also, more importantly, in terms of measures of output (i.e., degree of political instability, internal turmoil, etc.).

◆ These global-regional measures must be supplemented with current analysis or country-specific information for both the host countries and home country of the MNC parent.

◆ Global-regional and country-specific information must be evaluated in terms of a company's strengths and weaknesses in dealing with a particular type of political risk emanating from one or more of the three sources. Each company's potential for political risk absorption would be different based on its global investment strategy, technological lead, and market position.

---

[19] S. Kobrin, J. Basek, S. Blank, and J. LaPalombara, "The Assessment and Evaluation of Non-Economic Environments by American Firms: A Preliminary Report," *Journal of International Business Studies* (Spring/Summer 1980).

◆ Individual investment strategies would depend on a careful analysis of the sources of political risk, avenues of containment available to the MNC, and the MNC's bargaining and negotiating skills.

There is no substitute for solid experience, deep familiarity with the economic, social, and political environment (as well as the political leadership) of the countries involved, a willingness to look at the long-term prospects of direct foreign investments, and an appreciation of the legitimate needs and aspirations of the host-country governments and people.

Businesses need to devote greater effort to trying to work out their differences with host governments and anticipate home-country and international developments. The proactive approach entails a strategy formulation in advance of political risk problems. Thus, collection of information for an assessment of risk exposure is done with respect to a particular strategy of containment.

Research activity in the area of political risk needs to move towards an evaluation of both the substantive and symbolic relationships between governments and multinational companies. Such a move would be desirable because the complexity of the phenomena tends to undermine existing approaches to the problem and because of the firm-specific nature of the political risk question. Creative conflict-management activity seems to be the desired area of extension for political risk analysts.

READING 13 THE SILENT LANGUAGE IN OVERSEAS BUSINESS

Edward T. Hall

With few exceptions, Americans are relative newcomers on the international business scene. Today, as in Mark Twain's time, we are all too often "innocents abroad," in an era when naiveté and blundering in foreign business dealings may have serious political repercussions.

When the American executive travels abroad to do business, he is frequently shocked to discover to what extent the many variables of foreign behavior and custom complicate his efforts. Although the American has recognized, certainly, that even the man next door has many minor traits which make him somewhat peculiar, for some reason he has failed to appreciate how different foreign businessmen and their practices will seem to him.

He should understand that the various peoples around the world have worked out and integrated into their subconscious literally thousands of behavior patterns that they take for granted in each other.[1] Then, when the stranger enters, and behaves differently from the local norm, he often quite unintentionally insults, annoys, or amuses the native with whom he is attempting to do business. For example:

> In the United States, a corporation executive knows what is meant when a client lets a month go by before replying to a business proposal. On the other hand, he senses an eagerness to do business if he is immediately ushered into the client's office. In both instances, he is reacting to subtle cues in the timing of interaction, cues which he depends on to chart his course of action.
>
> Abroad, however, all this changes. The American executive learns that the Latin Americans are casual about time and that if he waits an hour in the outer office before seeing the Deputy Minister of Finance, it does not necessarily mean he is not getting anywhere. There people are so important that nobody can bear to tear himself away; because of the resultant interruptions and conversational detours, everybody is constantly getting behind. What the American does not know is the point at which the waiting becomes significant.
>
> In another instance, after traveling 7,000 miles an American walks into the office of a highly recommended Arab businessman on whom he will have to depend completely. What he sees does not breed confidence. The office is reached by walking through a suspicious-looking coffee-house in an odd, dilapidated building situated in a crowded non-Euro-

---

Source: Reprinted by permission of *Harvard Business Review.* "The SILENT LANGUAGE in Overseas Business" by Edward T. Hall, May-June 1960. Copyright © 1960 by the President and Fellows of Harvard College; all rights reserved.

[1] For details, see my book, *The Silent Language* (New York, Doubleday & Company, Inc., 1959).

pean section of town. The elevator, rising from dark, smelly corridors, is rickety and equally foul. When he gets to the office itself, he is shocked to find it small, crowded, and confused. Papers are stacked all over the desk and table tops—even scattered on the floor in irregular piles.

The Arab merchant he has come to see had met him at the airport the night before and sent his driver to the hotel this morning to pick him up. But now, after the American's rush, the Arab is tied up with something else. Even when they finally start talking business, there are constant interruptions. If the American is at all sensitive to his environment, everything around him signals, "What am I getting into?"

Before leaving home he was told that things would be different, but how different? The hotel is modern enough. The shops in the new part of town have many more American and European trade goods than he had anticipated. His first impression was that doing business in the Middle East would not present any new problems. Now he is beginning to have doubts. One minute everything looks familiar and he is on firm ground; the next, familiar landmarks are gone. His greatest problem is that so much assails his senses all at once that he does not know where to start looking for something that will tell him where he stands. He needs a frame of reference—a way of sorting out what is significant and relevant.

That is why it is so important for American businessmen to have a real understanding of the various social, cultural, and economic differences they will face when they attempt to do business in foreign countries. To help give some frame of reference, this article will map out a few areas of human activity that have largely been unstudied.

The topics I will discuss are certainly not presented as the last word on the subject, but they have proved to be highly reliable points at which to begin to gain an understanding of foreign cultures. While additional research will undoubtedly turn up other items just as relevant, at present I think the businessman can do well to begin by appreciating cultural differences in matters concerning the language of time, of space, of material possessions, of friendship patterns, and of agreements.

Language of Time

Everywhere in the world people use time to communicate with each other. There are different languages of time just as there are different spoken languages. The unspoken languages are informal; yet the rules governing their interpretation are surprisingly *ironbound*.

In the United States, a delay in answering a communication can result from a large volume of business causing the request to be postponed until the backlog is cleared away, from poor organization, or possibly from technical complexity requiring deep analysis. But if the person awaiting the answer or decision rules out these reasons, then the delay means to him that the matter has low priority on the part of the other person—lack of interest. On the other hand, a similar delay in a foreign country may mean something altogether different. Thus:

> In Ethiopia, the time required for a decision is directly proportional to its importance. This is so much the case that low-level bureaucrats there have a way of trying to elevate the prestige of their work by taking a long time to make up their minds. (Americans in that part of the world are innocently prone to downgrade their work in the local people's eyes by trying to speed things up.)
>
> In the Arab East, time does not generally include schedules as Americans know and use them. The time required to get something accomplished depends on the relationship. More important people get fast service from less important people, and conversely. Close relatives take absolute priority; nonrelatives are kept waiting.

In the United States, giving a person a deadline is a way of indicating the degree of urgency or relative importance of the work. But in the Middle East, the American runs into a cultural trap the minute he opens his mouth. "Mr. Aziz will have to make up his mind in a hurry because my board meets next week and I have to have an answer by then," is taken as indicating the American is overly demanding and is exerting undue pressure. "I am going to Damascus tomorrow morning and will have to have my car tonight," is a sure way to get the mechanic to stop work, because to give another person a deadline in this part of the world is to be rude, pushy, and demanding.

An Arab's evasiveness as to when something is going to happen does not mean he does not want to do business; it only means he is avoiding unpleasantness and is side-stepping possible commitments which he takes more seriously than we do. For example:

> The Arabs themselves at times find it impossible to communicate even to each other that some processes cannot be hurried, and are controlled by built-in schedules. This is obvious enough to the Westerner but not to the Arab. A highly placed public official in Baghdad precipitated a bitter family dispute because his nephew, a biochemist, could not speed up the complete analysis of the uncle's blood. He accused the nephew of putting other less important people before him and of not caring. Nothing could sway the uncle, who could not grasp the fact that there is such a thing as an *inherent* schedule.

With us the more important an event is, the further ahead we schedule it, which is why we find it insulting to be asked to a party at the last minute. In planning future events with Arabs, it pays to hold the lead time to a week or less because other factors may intervene or take precedence.

Again, time spent waiting in an American's outer office is a sure indicator of what one person thinks of another or how important he feels the other's business to be. This is so much the case that most Americans cannot help getting angry after waiting 30 minutes; one may even feel such a delay is an insult, and will walk out. In Latin America, on the other hand, one learns that it does not mean anything to wait in an outer office. An American businessman with years of experience in Mexico once told me, "You know, I have spent two hours cooling my heels in an executive's outer office. It took me a long time to learn to keep my blood pressure down. Even now, I find it hard to convince myself they are still interested when they keep me waiting."

The Japanese handle time in ways which are almost inexplicable to the Western European and particularly the American. A delay of years with them does not mean that they have lost interest. It only means that they are building up to something. They have learned that Americans are vulnerable to long waits. One of them expressed it, "You Americans have one terrible weakness. If we make you wait long enough, you will agree to anything."

Indians of South Asia have an elastic view of time as compared to our own. Delays do not, therefore, have the same meaning to them. Nor does indefiniteness in pinpointing appointments mean that they are evasive. Two Americans meeting will say, "We should get together sometime," thereby setting a low priority on the meeting. The Indian who says, "Come over and see me, see me anytime," means just that.

Americans make a place at the table which may or may not mean a place made in the heart. But when the Indian makes a place in his time, it is yours to fill in every sense of the word if you realize that by so doing you have crossed a boundary and are now friends with him. The point of all this is that time communicates just as surely as do words and that the vocabulary of time is different around the world. The principle to be remembered is that time has different meanings in each country.

Language of Space

Like time, the language of space is different wherever one goes. The American businessman, familiar with the pattern of American corporate life, has no difficulty in appraising the relative importance of someone else, simply by noting the size of his office in relation to other offices around him:

> Our pattern calls for the president or the chairman of the board to have the biggest office. The executive vice president will have the next largest, and so on down the line until you end up in the "bull pen." More important offices are usually located at the corners of buildings and on the upper floors. Executive suites will be on the top floor. The relative rank of vice presidents will be reflected in where they are placed along "Executive Row."

The French, on the other hand, are much more likely to lay out space as a network of connecting points of influence, activity, or interest. The French supervisor will ordinarily be found in the middle of his subordinates where he can control them.

Americans who are crowded will often feel that their status in the organization is suffering. As one would expect in the Arab world, the location of an office and its size constitute a poor index of the importance of the man who occupies it. What we experience as crowded, the Arab will often regard as spacious. The same is true in Spanish cultures. A Latin American official illustrated the Spanish view of this point while showing me around a plant. Opening the door to an 18-by-20-foot office in which seventeen clerks and their desks were placed, he said, "See, we have nice spacious offices. Lots of space for everyone."

The American will look at a Japanese room and remark how bare it is. Similarly, the Japanese look at our rooms and comment, "How bare!" Furniture in the American home tends to be placed along the walls (around the edge). Japanese have their charcoal pit where the family gathers in the *middle* of the room. The top floor of Japanese department stores is not reserved for the chief executive—it is the bargain roof!

In the Middle East and Latin America, the businessman is likely to feel left out in time and overcrowded in space. People get too close to him, lay their hands on him, and generally crowd his physical being. In Scandinavia and Germany, he feels more at home, but at the same time the people are a little cold and distant. It is space itself that conveys this feeling.

In the United States, because of our tendency to zone activities, nearness carries rights of familiarity so that the neighbor can borrow material possessions and invade time. This is not true in England. Propinquity entitles you to nothing. American Air Force personnel stationed there complain because they have to make an appointment for their children to play with the neighbor's child next door.

Conversation distance between two people is learned early in life by copying elders. Its controlling patterns operate almost totally unconsciously. In the United States, in contrast to many foreign countries, men avoid excessive touching. Regular business is conducted at distances such as 5 feet to 8 feet; highly personal business, 18 inches to 3 feet—not 2 or 3 inches.

In the United States, it is perfectly possible for an experienced executive to schedule the steps of negotiation in time and space so that most people feel comfortable about what is happening. Business transactions progress in stages from across the desk to beside the desk, to the coffee table, then on to the conference table, the luncheon table, or the golf course, or even into the home —all according to a complex set of hidden rules which we obey instinctively.

Even in the United States, however, an executive may slip when he moves into new and unfamiliar realms, when dealing with a new group, doing business with a new company, or moving to a new place in the industrial hierarchy. In a new country the danger is magnified. For example, in India it is considered improper to discuss business in the home on social occasions. One never invites a business acquaintance to the home for the purpose of furthering business aims. That would be a violation of sacred hospitality rules.

Language of Things

Americans are often contrasted with the rest of the world in terms of material possessions. We are accused of being materialistic, gadget-crazy. And, as a matter of fact, we have developed material things for some very interesting reasons. Lacking a fixed class system and having an extremely mobile population, Americans have become highly sensitive to how others make use of material possessions. We use everything from clothes to houses as a highly evolved and complex means of ascertaining each other's status. Ours is a rapidly shifting system in which both styles and people move up or down. For example:

> The Cadillac ad men feel that not only is it natural but quite insightful of them to show a picture of a Cadillac and a well-turned out gentleman in his early fifties opening the door. The caption underneath reads, "You already know a great deal about this man."
>
> Following this same pattern, the head of a big union spends in excess of $100,000 furnishing his office so that the president of United States Steel cannot look down on him. Good materials, large space, and the proper surroundings signify that the people who occupy the premises are solid citizens, that they are dependable and successful.

The French, the English, and the Germans have entirely different ways of using their material possessions. What stands for the height of dependability and respectability with the English would be old-fashioned and backward to us. The Japanese take pride in often inexpensive but tasteful arrangements that are used to produce the proper emotional setting.

Middle East businessmen look for something else—family, connections, friendship. They do not use the furnishings of their office as part of their status system; nor do they expect to impress a client by these means or to fool a banker into lending more money than he should. They like good things, too, but feel that they, as persons, should be known and not judged solely by what the public sees.

One of the most common criticisms of American relations abroad, both commercial and governmental, is that we usually think in terms of material things. "Money talks," says the American, who goes on talking the language of money abroad, in the belief that money talks the *same* language all over the world. A common practice in the United States is to try to buy loyalty with high salaries. In foreign countries, this maneuver almost never works, for money and material possessions stand for something different there than they do in America.

Language of Friendship

The American finds his friends next door and among those with whom he works. It has been noted that we take people up quickly and drop them just as quickly. Occasionally a friendship formed during schooldays will persist, but this is rare. For us there are few well-defined rules governing the obligations of friendship. It is difficult to say at which point our friendship gives way to business opportunism or pressure from above. In this we differ from many other people in the world. As a general rule in foreign countries friendships are not formed as quickly as in the United States but go much deeper, last longer, and involve real obligations. For example:

> It is important to stress that in the Middle East and Latin America your "friends" will not let you down. The fact that they personally are feeling the pinch is never an excuse for failing their friends. They are supposed to look out for your interests.

Friends and family around the world represent a sort of social insurance that would be difficult to find in the United States. We do not use our friends to help us out in disaster as much as we do as a means of getting ahead—or, at least, of getting the job done. The United States systems work by means of a series of closely tabulated favors and obligations carefully doled out where they will do the most good. And the least that we expect in exchange for a favor is gratitude.

The opposite is the case in India, where the friend's role is to "sense" a person's need and do something about it. The idea of reciprocity as we know it is unheard of. An American in India will have difficulty if he attempts to follow American friendship patterns. He gains nothing by extending himself in behalf of others, least of all gratitude, because the Indian assumes that what he does for others he does for the good of his own psyche. He will find it impossible to make friends quickly and is unlikely to allow sufficient time for friendships to ripen. He will also note that as he gets to know people better, they may become more critical of him, a fact that he finds hard to take. What he does not know is that one sign of friendship in India is speaking one's mind.

Language of Agreements

While it is important for American businessmen abroad to understand the symbolic meanings of friendship rules, time, space, and material possessions, it is just as important for executives to know the rules for negotiating agreements in various countries. Even if they cannot be expected to know the details of each nation's commercial legal practices, just the awareness of and the expectation of the existence of differences will eliminate much complication.

Actually, no society can exist on a high commercial level without a highly developed working base on which agreements can rest. This base may be one or a combination of three types:

1. Rules that are spelled out technically as law or regulation.
2. Moral practices mutually agreed on and taught to the young as a set of principles.
3. Informal customs to which everyone conforms without being able to state the exact rules.

Some societies favor one, some another. Ours, particularly in the business world, lays heavy emphasis on the first variety. Few Americans will conduct any business nowadays without some written agreement or contract.

Varying from culture to culture will be the circumstances under which such rules apply. Americans consider that negotiations have more or less ceased when the contract is signed. With the Greeks, on the other hand, the contract is seen as a sort of way station on the route to negotiation that will cease only when the work is completed. The contract is nothing more than a charter for serious negotiations. In the Arab world, once a man's word is given in a particular kind of way, it is just as binding, if not more so, than most of our written contracts. The written contract, therefore, violates the Moslem's sensitivities and reflects on his honor. Unfortunately, the situation is now so hopelessly confused that neither system can be counted on to prevail consistently.

Informal patterns and unstated agreements often lead to untold difficulty in the cross-cultural situation. Take the case of the before-and-after patterns where there is a wide discrepancy between the American's expectations and those of the Arab:

In the United States, when you engage a specialist such as a lawyer or a doctor, require any standard service, or even take a taxi, you make several assumptions: (1) the charge will be fair; (b) it will be in proportion to the services rendered; and (c) it will bear a close relationship to the "going rate."

You wait until after the services are performed before asking what the tab will be. If the charge is too high in the light of the above assumptions, you feel you have been cheated. You can complain, or can say nothing, pay up, and take your business elsewhere the next time.

As one would expect in the Middle East, basic differences emerge which lead to difficulty if not understood. For instance, when taking a cab in Beirut it is well to know the going rate as a point around which to bargain and for settling the charge, which must be fixed before engaging the cab.

If you have not fixed the rate *in advance*, there is a complete change and an entirely different set of rules will apply. According to these rules, the going rate plays no part whatsoever. The whole relationship is altered. The sky is the limit, and the customer has no kick coming. I have seen taxi drivers shouting at the top of their lungs, waving their arms, following a redfaced American with his head pulled down between his shoulders, demanding for a two-pound ride ten Lebanese pounds which the American eventually had to pay.

It is difficult for the American to accommodate his frame of reference to the fact that what constitutes one thing to him, namely, a taxi ride, is to the Arab two very different operations involving two different sets of relationships and two sets of rules. The crucial factor is whether the bargaining is done at the beginning or the end of the ride! As a matter of fact, you cannot bargain at the end. What the driver asks for he is entitled to!

One of the greatest difficulties Americans have abroad stems from the fact that we often think we have a commitment when we do not. The second complication on this same topic is the other side of the coin, i.e., when others think we have agreed to things that we have not. Our own failure to recognize binding obligations, plus our custom of setting organizational goals ahead of everything else, has put us in hot water far too often.

People sometimes do not keep agreements with us because we do not keep agreements with them. As a general rule, the American treats the agreement as something he may eventually have to break. Here are two examples:

> Once while I was visiting an American post in Latin America, the Ambassador sent the Spanish version of a trade treaty down to his language officer with instructions to write in some "weasel words." To his dismay, he was told, "There are no weasel words in Spanish."

> A personnel officer of a large corporation in Iran made an agreement with local employees that American employees would not receive preferential treatment. When the first American employee arrived, it was learned quickly that in the United States he had been covered by a variety of health plans that were not available to Iranians. And this led to immediate protests from the Iranians which were never satisfied. The personnel officer never really grasped the fact that he had violated an iron-bound contract.

Certainly, this is the most important generalization to be drawn by American businessmen from this discussion of agreements: there are many times when we are vulnerable *even when judged by our own standards*. Many instances of actual sharp practices by American companies are well known abroad and are giving

American business a bad name. The cure for such questionable behavior is simple. The companies concerned usually have it within their power to discharge offenders and to foster within their organization an atmosphere in which only honesty and fairness can thrive.

But the cure for ignorance of the social and legal rules which underlie business agreements is not so easy. This is because:

◆ The subject is complex.

◆ Little research has been conducted to determine the culturally different concepts of what is an agreement.

◆ The people of each country think that their own code is the only one, and that everything else is dishonest.

◆ Each code is different from our own; and the farther away one is traveling from Western Europe, the greater the difference is.

But the little that has already been learned about this subject indicates that as a problem it is not insoluble and will yield to research. Since it is probably one of the more relevant and immediately applicable areas of interest to modern business, it would certainly be advisable for companies with large foreign operations to sponsor some serious research in this vital field.

A Case in Point

Thus far, I have been concerned with developing the five check points around which a real understanding of foreign cultures can begin. But the problems that arise from a faulty understanding of the silent language of foreign custom are human problems and perhaps can best be dramatized by an actual case.

A Latin American republic had decided to modernize one of its communication networks to the tune of several million dollars. Because of its reputation for quality and price, the inside track was quickly taken by American company "Y."

The company, having been sounded out informally, considered the size of the order and decided to bypass its regular Latin American representative and send instead its sales manager. The following describes what took place.

The sales manager arrived and checked in at the leading hotel. He immediately had some difficulty pinning down just who it was he had to see about his business. After several days without results, he called at the American Embassy where he found that the commercial attaché had the up-to-the-minute information he needed. The commercial attaché listened to his story. Realizing that the sales manager had already made a number of mistakes, but figuring that the Latins were used to American blundering, the attache reasoned that all was not lost. He informed the sales manager that the Minister of Communications was the key man and that whoever got the nod from him would get the contract. He also briefed the sales manager on methods of conducting business in Latin America and offered some pointers about dealing with the minister. The attaché's advice ran somewhat as follows:

1. "You don't do business here the way you do in the States; it is necessary to spend much more time. You have to get to know your man and vice versa.

2. "You must meet with him *several times* before you talk business. I will tell you at what point you can bring up the subject. Take your cues from me. [Our American sales manager at this point made a few observations to himself about "cookie pushers" and wondered how many payrolls had been met by the commercial attaché.]

3. "Take that price list and put it in your pocket. Don't get it out until I tell you to. Down here price is only one of the many things taken into account before closing a deal. In the United States, your past experience will prompt you to act according to a certain set of principles, but many of these principles will *not* work here. Every time you feel the urge to act or to say something, look at me. Suppress the urge and take your cues from me. This is very important.

4. "Down here people like to do business with men who *are* somebody. In order to be somebody, it is well to have written a book, to have lectured at a university, or to have developed your intellect in some way. The man you are going to see is a poet. He has published several volumes of poetry. Like many Latin Americans, he prizes poetry highly. You will find that he will spend a good deal of business time quoting his poetry to you, and he will take great pleasure in this.

5. "You will also note that the people here are very proud of their past and of their Spanish blood, but they are also exceedingly proud of their liberation from Spain and their independence. The fact that they are a democracy, that they are free, and also that they are no longer a colony is very, very important to them. They are warm and friendly and enthusiastic if they like you. If they don't, they are cold and withdrawn.

6. "And another thing, time down here means something different. It works in a different way. You know how it is back in the States when a certain type blurts out whatever is on his mind without waiting to see if the situation is right. He is considered an impatient bore and somewhat egocentric. Well, down here, you have to wait much, much longer, and I really mean *much, much* longer, before you can begin to talk about the reason for your visit.

7. There is another point I want to caution you about. At home, the man who sells takes the initiative. Here, *they* tell you when they are

ready to do business. But, most of all, don't discuss price until you are asked and don't rush things."

The Pitch The next day the commercial attaché introduced the sales manager to the Minister of Communications. First, there was a long wait in the outer office while people kept coming in and out. The sales manager looked at his watch, fidgeted, and finally asked whether the minister was really expecting him. The reply he received was scarcely reassuring, "Oh yes, he is expecting you but several things have come up that require his attention. Besides, one gets used to waiting down here." The sales manager irritably replied, "But doesn't he know I flew all the way down here from the United States to see him, and I have spent over a week already of my valuable time trying to find him?" "Yes, I know," was the answer, "but things just move much more slowly here."

At the end of about 30 minutes, the minister emerged from the office, greeted the commercial attaché with a *doble abrazo,* throwing his arms around him and patting him on the back as though they were long-lost brothers. Now, turning and smiling, the minister extended his hand to the sales manager, who, by this time, was feeling rather miffed because he had been kept in the outer office so long.

After what seemed to be an all too short chat, the minister rose, suggesting a well-known café where they might meet for dinner the next evening. The sales manager expected, of course, that, considering the nature of their business and the size of the order, he might be taken to the minister's home, not realizing that the Latin home is reserved for family and very close friends.

Until now, nothing at all had been said about the reason for the sales manager's visit, a fact which bothered him somewhat. The whole set-up seemed wrong; neither did he like the idea of wasting another day in town. He told the home office before he left that he would be gone for a week or ten days at most, and made a mental note that he would clean this order up in three days and enjoy a few days in Acapulco or Mexico City. Now the week had already gone and he would be lucky if he made it home in ten days.

Voicing his misgivings to the commercial attaché, he wanted to know if the minister really meant business, and, if he did, why could they not get together and talk about it? The commercial attaché by now was beginning to show the strain of constantly having to reassure the sales manager. Nevertheless, he tried again:

> What you don't realize is that part of the time we were waiting, the minister was rearranging a very tight schedule so that he could spend tomorrow night with you. You see, down here they don't delegate responsibility the way we do in the States. They exercise much tighter control than we do. As a consequence, this man spends up to 15 hours a day at his desk. It may not look like it to you, but I assure you he really means business. He wants to give your company the order; if you play your cards right, you will get it.

The next evening provided more of the same. Much conversation about food and music, about many people the sales manager had never heard of. They went to a night club, where the sales manager brightened up and began to think that perhaps he and the minister might have something in common after all. It bothered him, however, that the principal reason for his visit was not even alluded to tangentially. But every time he started to talk about electronics, the commercial attaché would nudge him and proceed to change the subject.

The next meeting was for morning coffee at a café. By now the sales manager was having difficulty hiding his impatience. To make matters worse, the minister had a mannerism which he did not like. When they talked, he was likely to put his hand on him; he would take hold of his arm and get so close that he almost "spat" in his face. As a consequence, the sales manager was kept busy trying to dodge and back up.

Following coffee, there was a walk in a nearby park. The minister expounded on the shrubs, the birds, and the beauties of nature, and at one spot he stopped to point at a statue and said: "There is a statue of the world's greatest hero, the liberator of mankind!" At this point, the worst happened, for the sales manager asked who the statue was of and, being given the name of a famous Latin American patriot, said, "I never heard of him," and walked on.

The Failure It is quite clear from this that the sales manager did not get the order, which went to a Swedish concern. The American, moreover, was never able to see the minister again. Why did the minister feel the way he did? His reasoning went somewhat as follows:

> I like the American's equipment and it makes sense to deal with North Americans who are near us and whose price is right. But I could never be friends with this man. He is not my kind of human being and we have nothing in common. He is not *simpatico*. If I can't be friends and he is not *simpatico*, I can't depend on him to treat me right. I tried everything, every conceivable situation, and only once did we seem to understand each other. If we could be friends, he would feel obligated to me and this obligation would give me some control. Without control, how do I know he will deliver what he says he will at the price he quotes?

Of course, what the minister did not know was that the price was quite firm, and that quality control was a matter of company policy. He did not realize that the sales manager was a member of an organization, and that the man is always subordinate to the organization in the United States. Next year maybe the sales manager would not even be representing the company, but would be replaced. Further, if he wanted someone to depend on, his best bet would be to hire a good American lawyer to represent him and write a binding contract.

In this instance, both sides suffered. The American felt he was being slighted and put off, and did not see how there could possibly be any connection between poetry and doing business or why it should all take so long. He interpreted the delay as a form of polite brushoff. Even if things had gone differently and there had been a contract, it is doubtful that the minister would have trusted the contract as much as he would a man whom he considered his friend. Throughout Latin America, the law is made livable and contracts workable by having friends and relatives operating from the inside. Lacking a friend, someone who would look out for his interests, the minister did not want to take a chance. He stated this simply and directly.

Conclusion

The case just described has of necessity been oversimplified. The danger is that the reader will say, "Oh, I see. All you really have to do is be friends." At which point the expert will step in and reply:

> Yes, of course, but what you don't realize is that in Latin America being a friend involves much more than it does in the United States and is an entirely different proposition. A friendship implies obligations. You go about it differently. It involves much more than being nice, visiting, and playing golf. You would not want to enter into friendship lightly.

The point is simply this. It takes years and years to develop a sound foundation for doing business in a given country. Much that is done seems silly or strange to the home office. Indeed, the most common error made by home offices, once they have found representatives who can get results, is failure to take their advice and allow sufficient time for representatives to develop the proper contacts.

The second most common error, if that is what it can be called, is ignorance of the secret and hidden language of foreign cultures. In this article I have tried to show how five key topics—time, space, material possessions, friendship patterns, and business agreements—offer a starting point from which companies can begin to acquire the understanding necessary to do business in foreign countries.

Our present knowledge is meager, and much more research is needed before the businessman of the future can go abroad fully equipped for his work. Not only will he need to be well versed in the economics, law, and politics of the area, but he will have to understand, if not speak, the silent languages of other cultures.

SOCIAL TIME: THE HEARTBEAT OF CULTURE

Robert Levine with Ellen Wolff

"If a man does not keep pace with his companions, perhaps it is because he hears a different drummer." This thought by Thoreau strikes a chord in so many people that it has become part of our language. We use the phrase "the beat of a different drummer" to explain any pace of life unlike our own. Such colorful vagueness reveals how informal our rules of time really are. The world over, children simply "pick up" their society's time concepts as they mature. No dictionary clearly defines the meaning of "early" or "late" for them or for strangers who stumble over the maddening incongruities between the time sense they bring with them and the one they face in a new land.

I learned this firsthand, a few years ago, and the resulting culture shock led me halfway around the world to find answers. It seemed clear that time "talks." But what is it telling us?

My journey started shortly after I accepted an appointment as visiting professor of psychology at the federal university in Niteroi, Brazil, a midsized city across the bay from Rio de Janeiro. As I left home for my first day of class, I asked someone the time. It was 9:05 a.m., which allowed me time to relax and look around the campus before my 10 o'clock lecture. After what I judged to be half an hour, I glanced at a clock I was passing. It said 10:20! In panic, I broke for the classroom, followed by gentle calls of "Hola, professor" and "Tudo bem, professor?" from unhurried students, many of whom, I later realized, were my own. I arrived breathless to find an empty room.

Frantically, I asked a passerby the time. "Nine forty-five" was the answer. No, that couldn't be. I asked someone else. "Nine fifty-five." Another said: "Exactly 9:43." The clock in a nearby office read 3:15. I had learned my first lesson about Brazilians: Their timepieces are consistently inaccurate. And nobody minds.

My class was scheduled from 10 until noon. Many students came late, some very late. Several arrived after 10:30. A few showed up closer to 11. Two came after that. All of the late-comers wore the relaxed smiles that I came, later, to enjoy. Each one said hello, and although a few apologized briefly, none seemed terribly concerned about lateness. They assumed that I understood.

The idea of Brazilians arriving late was not a great shock. I had heard about "manha," the Portuguese equivalent of "mañana" in Spanish. This term, meaning "tomorrow" or "the morning," stereotypes the Brazilian who puts off the business of today until tomorrow. The real surprise came at noon that first day, when the end of class arrived.

Back home in California, I never need to look at a clock to know when the class hour is ending. The shuffling of books is accompanied by strained expressions that say plaintively, "I'm starving. . . . I've got to go to the bathroom. . . . I'm going to suffocate if you keep us one more second." (The pain usually

Source: from *Psychology Today,* March 1985. Reprinted with permission.

becomes unbearable at two minutes to the hour in undergraduate classes and five minutes before the close of graduate classes.)

When noon arrived in my first Brazilian class, only a few students left immediately. Others slowly drifted out during the next 15 minutes, and some continued asking me questions long after that. When several remaining students kicked off their shoes at 12:30, I went into my own "starving/bathroom/suffocation" routine.

I could not, in all honesty, attribute their lingering to my superb teaching style. I had just spent two hours lecturing on statistics in halting Portuguese. Apparently, for many of my students, staying late was simply of no more importance than arriving late in the first place. As I observed this casual approach in infinite variations during the year, I learned that the "mañha" stereotype oversimplified the real Anglo/Brazilian differences in conceptions of time. Research revealed a more complex picture.

With the assistance of colleagues Laurie West and Harry Reis, I compared the time sense of 91 male and female students in Niteroi with that of 107 similar students at California State University in Fresno. The universities are similar in academic quality and size, and the cities are both secondary metropolitan centers with populations of about 350,000.

We asked students about their perceptions of time in several situations, such as what they would consider late or early for a hypothetical lunch appointment with a friend. The average Brazilian student defined lateness for lunch as $33\frac{1}{2}$ minutes after the scheduled time, compared to only 19 minutes for the Fresno students. But Brazilians also allowed an average of about 54 minutes before they'd consider someone early, while the Fresno students drew the line at 24.

Are Brazilians simply more flexible in their concepts of time and punctuality? And how does this relate to the stereotype of the apathetic, fatalistic and irresponsible Latin temperament? When we asked students to give typical reasons for lateness, the Brazilians were less likely to attribute it to a lack of caring than the North Americans were. Instead, they pointed to unforeseen circumstances that the person couldn't control. Because they seemed less inclined to feel personally responsible for being late, they also expressed less regret for their own lateness and blamed others less when they were late.

We found similar differences in how students from the two countries characterized people who were late for appointments. Unlike their North American counterparts, the Brazilian students believed that a person who is consistently late is probably more successful than one who is consistently on time. They seemed to accept the idea that someone of status is expected to arrive late. Lack of punctuality is a badge of success.

Even within our own country, of course, ideas of time and punctuality vary considerably from place to place. Different regions and even cities have their own distinct rhythms and rules. Seemingly simple words like "now," snapped out by an impatient New Yorker, and "later," said by a relaxed Californian, suggest a world of difference. Despite our familiarity with these homegrown differences in tempo, problems with time present a major stumbling block to Americans abroad. Peace Corps volunteers told researchers James Spradley of Macalester College and Mark Phillips of the University of Washington that their greatest difficulties with other people, after language problems, were the general pace of life and the punctuality of others. Formal "clock time" may be a standard on which the world agrees, but "social time," the heartbeat of society, is something else again.

How a country paces its social life is a mystery to most outsiders, one that we're just beginning to unravel. Twenty-six years ago, anthropologist Edward Hall noted in *The Silent Language* that informal patterns of time "are seldom, if ever, made explicit. They exist in the air around us. They are either familiar and comfortable, or unfamiliar and wrong." When we realize we are out of step, we often blame the people around us to make ourselves feel better.

Appreciating cultural differences in time sense becomes increasingly important as modern communications put more and more people in daily contact. If we are to avoid misreading issues that involve time perceptions, we need to understand better our own cultural biases and those of others.

When people of different cultures interact, the potential for misunderstanding exists on many levels. For example, members of Arab and Latin cultures usually stand much closer when they are speaking to people than we usually do in the United States, a fact we frequently misinterpret as aggression or disrespect. Similarly, we assign personality traits to groups with a pace of life that is markedly faster or slower than our own. We build ideas of national character, for example, around the traditional Swiss and German ability to "make the trains run on time." Westerners like ourselves define punctuality using precise measures of time: 5 minutes, 15 minutes, an hour. But according to Hall, in many Mediterranean Arab cultures there are only three sets of time: no time at all, now (which is of varying duration) and forever (too long). Because of this, Americans often find difficulty in getting Arabs to distinguish between waiting a long time and a very long time.

According to historian Will Durant, "No man in a hurry is quite civilized." What do our time judgments say about our attitude toward life? How can a North American, coming from a land of digital precision, relate to a North African who may consider a clock "the devil's mill"?

Each language has a vocabulary of time that does not always survive translation. When we translated our questionnaires into Portuguese for my Brazilian students, we found that English distinctions of time were not readily articulated in their language. Several of our questions concerned how long the respondent would wait for someone to arrive, as compared with when they hoped for arrival or actually expected the person would come. In Portuguese, the verbs "to wait for," "to hope for" and "to expect" are all translated as "esperar." We had to add further words of explanation to make the distinction clear to the Brazilian students.

To avoid these language problems, my Fresno colleague Kathy Bartlett and

I decided to clock the pace of life in other countries by using as little language as possible. We looked directly at three basic indicators of time: the accuracy of a country's bank clocks, the speed at which pedestrians walked and the average time it took a postal clerk to sell us a single stamp. In six countries on three continents, we made observations in both the nation's largest urban area and a medium-sized city: Japan (Tokyo and Sendai), Taiwan (Taipei and Tainan), Indonesia (Jakarta and Solo), Italy (Rome and Florence), England (London and Bristol) and the United States (New York City and Rochester).

What we wanted to know was: Can we speak of a unitary concept called "pace of life"? What we've learned suggests that we can. There appears to be a very strong relationship (see Table 1) between the accuracy of clock time, walking speed and postal efficiency across the countries we studied.

We checked 15 clocks in each city, selecting them at random in downtown banks and comparing the time they showed with that reported by the local telephone company. In Japan, which leads the way in accuracy, the clocks averaged just over half a minute early or late. Indonesian clocks, the least accurate, were more than three minutes off the mark.

I will be interested to see how the digital-information age will affect our perceptions of time. In the United States today, we are reminded of the exact hour of the day more than ever, through little symphonies of beeps emanating from people's digital watches. As they become the norm, I fear our sense of precision may take an absurd twist. The other day, when I asked for the time, a student looked at his watch and replied, "Three twelve and eighteen seconds."

TABLE **1**   The Pace of Life in Six Countries

	Accuracy of Bank Clocks	Walking Speed	Post Office Speed
Japan	1*	1	1
United States	2	3	2
England	4	2	3
Italy	5	4	6
Taiwan	3	5	4
Indonesia	6	6	5

* Numbers (1 is the top value) indicate the comparative rankings of each country for each indicator of time sense.

'Will you walk a little faster?' said a whiting to a snail. 'There's a porpoise close behind us, and he's treading on my tail.'

So goes the rhyme from *Alice in Wonderland*, which also gave us that famous symbol of haste, the White Rabbit. He came to mind often as we measured the walking speeds in our experimental cities. We clocked how long it took pedestrians to walk 100 feet along a main downtown street during business hours on clear days. To eliminate the effects of socializing, we observed only people walking alone, timing at least 100 in each city. We found, once again, that the Japanese led the way, averaging just 20.7 seconds to cover the distance. The English nosed out the Americans for second place—21.6 to 22.5 seconds—and the Indonesians again trailed the pack, sauntering along at 27.2 seconds. As you might guess, speed was greater in the larger city of each nation than in its smaller one.

Our final measurement, the average time it took postal clerks to sell one stamp, turned out to be less straightforward than we expected. In each city, including those in the United States, we presented clerks with a note in the native language requesting a common-priced stamp—a 20-center in the United States, for example. They were also handed paper money, the equivalent of a $5 bill. In Indonesia, this procedure led to more than we bargained for.

At the large central post office in Jakarta, I asked for the line to buy stamps and was directed to a group of private vendors sitting outside. Each of them hustled for my business: "Hey, good stamps, mister!" "Best stamps here!" In the smaller city of Solo, I found a volleyball game in progress when I arrived at the main post office on Friday afternoon. Business hours, I was told, were over. When I finally did get there during business hours, the clerk was more interested in discussing relatives in America. Would I like to meet his uncle in Cincinnati? Which did I like better: California or the United States? Five people behind me in line waited patiently. Instead of complaining, they began paying attention to our conversation.

When it came to efficiency of service, however, the Indonesians were not the slowest, although they did place far behind the Japanese postal clerks, who averaged 25 seconds. That distinction went to the Italians, whose infamous postal service took 47 seconds on the average.

A man who wastes one hour of time has not discovered the meaning of life. . . .

That was Charles Darwin's belief, and many share it, perhaps at the cost of their health. My colleagues and I have recently begun studying the relationship between pace of life and well-being. Other researchers have demonstrated that a chronic sense of urgency is a basic component of the Type A, coronary-prone personality. We expect that future research will demonstrate that pace of life is related to rate of heart disease, hypertension, ulcers, suicide, alcoholism, divorce and other indicators of general psychological and physical well-being.

As you envision tomorrow's international society, do you wonder who will set the pace? Americans eye Japan carefully, because the Japanese are obviously "ahead of us" in measurable ways. In both countries, speed is frequently confused with progress. Perhaps looking carefully at the different paces of life around the world will help us distinguish more accurately between the two qualities. Clues are everywhere but sometimes hard to distinguish. You have to listen carefully to hear the beat of even your own drummer.

THE CUSTOMER IS ALWAYS WRONG: A LOOK AT THE SOCIO-CULTURAL IMPEDIMENTS TO THE GROWTH OF CONSUMER ORIENTATION IN INDIA

Hari Das ◆ Mallika Das

ABSTRACT. Widespread poverty, low rates of economic growth, low levels of per-capita income, illiteracy, poor economic and social infrastructure, etc., pose special problems to the marketing managers operating in the developing world. Past research studies have looked at several of these variables which influence marketing practices in developing settings. However, a critical variable, namely, the cultural history of the focal society is often ignored. The present paper looks at the cultural history of one developing country (namely, India) and examines how traditional social norms and stratification methods have affected the emergence of a western marketing orientation in it. A model outlining the impact of these variables on marketing practices is suggested to facilitate further research in the area.

◆ Place: Ahmedabad, North India; time: November 1985, 7:00 p.m.

The customer who entered the shop was in a hurry. The three sales assistants in the store who were busy discussing the previous day's film took no notice of the customer. The owner who was on the phone, briefly glanced at the customer but continued his conversation apparently ignoring him. Finally, one of the assistants came to the customer, and after listening to the customer referred him to a second assistant. The second assistant looked at the customer indifferently and started to pick items out of the shelf.

◆ Place: Madras, South India; time: February 1986, 9:25 a.m.

The customer heaved a sigh of relief when he saw four taxi cabs in the stand. Thank God! Now he is sure to make his important 10:00 a.m. appointment. His ebullience ended when he saw that there were no drivers in three of the four taxis. The fourth one in which a driver sat reading a newspaper told the customer in an indifferent tone that he can not take him. No particular reason was offered.

◆ A customer of Life Insurance Corporation of India (LIC) who had two separate policies with the company received a letter from the corporation saying that the cheque he had sent for the payment of the premium six months back had been lost by LIC's bank in transit. He was asked to issue another cheque along with a penalty for the delay in payment. This was in spite of the fact that on his other policy he had made an overpayment of Rs.450.00 and it had taken the company six months to refund his money—with, of course, no interest on his funds! It seemed that LIC's policy was simply: when the customer is to blame, punish the customer;

Source: *Journal of International Consumer Marketing*, Vol.1(1) 1988. Copyright © 1989 by The Haworth Press, Inc., 10 Alice Street, Binghamton, NY 13904. All rights reserved. Reprinted with permission.

when the customer is not to blame, punish the customer; when the company is to blame, punish the customer! (Sarin & Avasthi, 1980)

To even a casual observer, Indian firms would appear to be less customer oriented than organizations in developed countries. This paper is an attempt to identify some socio-cultural reasons for the lack of consumer orientation of Indian businesses. To begin with, a brief discussion of the Indian marketing system and the traditional explanations for the lack of consumer orientation among Indian marketers is provided. This is followed by a model highlighting the effects of socio-cultural variables on Indian marketers and a discussion of these variables.

The Indian Marketing System

As most people have found, it is hard to generalize about any aspect of India. As in many other developing countries, vast differences in key aspects of life including marketing systems, exist within the country. Added to this is the absence of any systematically collected, hard data on Indian marketing practices in general and individual seller behavior in particular. In general, the Indian market is characterized by the presence of many small producers and retailers, small capital investments with production still being seen as the major function. Marketing does not mean much more than selling. This is similar to the situation found in many other developing countries. Thus the Indian marketing system can be said to be in the fourth stage of development as discussed by Stanton (1964) i.e., some division of labor may exist and small scale production of goods has begun, central markets and middlemen are present, but production is still the main focus of businesses. In the rural and smaller communities of the country, the marketing system may even be in stage three i.e., home handicrafts are slowly being replaced by small firms. Following Kaynak and Samli (1984) the average individual firm in India can be said to be in stage 1 or 2 of marketing development (characterised in most instances, with little or no division of labor with marketing being considered as just selling). The larger organizations have a formalized marketing department but only in a few rare instances is the marketing manager in charge of all the marketing activities in a fully integrated way. Thus even these firms are probably still primarily in the third stage of marketing development with a few having entered the fourth stage. (For a complete description of the stages, please see Kaynak and Hudanah, 1987.)

The few available studies on the state of marketing in India (e.g., Bhatt, 1985; Mehta, 1980; Sarin and Avasthi, 1980; J. D. Singh, 1983, 1984; L. P. Singh, 1978) by and large point out the lack of marketing and customer orientation on the part of Indian organizations. Bhatt (1984), for example, found that Indian consumers are exploited in a variety of ways such as sale of products that are of inferior quality and at times hazardous, creation of artificial scarcity of essential products through hoarding, improper or rude behavior toward customers, etc. Singh (1978), Mehta (1980) and Sarin and Avasthi (1980) report data supporting the conclusions of Bhatt. For example, in a survey of 350 consumers, Mehta found that as many as 76 percent of the respondents believed that most shortages were artificially created by retailers through hoarding. As many as 67% of the respondents felt that "retailers took little interest in customers and the service provided by them was poor. Rating on courtesy extended to customers, assistance provided in making a brand choice and handling of complaints was extremely poor" (p. 41). Sarin and Avasthi (p. 96) after a study of 103 housewives concluded that "there is complete alienation between the consumer and the marketing system."

Even large companies and subsidiaries of multinationals (with head offices in North America and Europe) may not be beyond this criticism. In one study, the Consumer Guidance Society of India (CGSI) tested twenty-two units of pressure stoves belonging to eleven major brands. Of the ones tested, eighteen were found to be substandard and even unsafe. In another testing by CGSI, only five out of a dozen electric irons tested were found to be safe (Ninan and Singh, 1984).

What led to this state of affairs? Obviously, no simple answer would suffice. Several past studies (see, for example, Collins, 1963; Preston, 1968; Soloman, 1948) have attempted to answer this question. Indeed, since Drucker's (1958) classic article stating that marketing plays a critical role in economic growth, a large number of researchers have attempted to link marketing and economic variables (e.g., Cundiff and Hilger, 1980; Dholakia and Dholakia, 1982; El-Sherbini, 1980; Hilger, 1978; McCarthy, 1963; Moyer and Hollander, 1968; Shapiro, 1965). The exact relationship between the two has, however, been a subject of some controversy. While some writers have indicated that effective marketing institutions lead to economic progress (e.g., McCarthy, 1963), other writers have suggested that the relationship between these variables is much more complex and may even be in the opposite direction (e.g., Moyer and Hollander, 1968). Since all developing countries are very poor and often primitive in a variety of sectors and technology, competition in the market is often atomistic or absent. For most products, there will be only one or two key producers thus leading to the emergence of a seller's market. Also, as Wadinambiarachi (1965) found, the marketing institutions, the channel structures and the economic conditions of a country may be intricately related to each other. In several of the developing countries which face recurring shortage of key materials, services and other infrastructural facilities, the consumer is often helpless and virtually under the control of sellers (Kaynak, 1982). In a similar vein, Arndt (1972) who studied retailing in sixteen different countries relatively homogeneous in terms of socio-political characteristics concluded that retailing is a function of specific environmental factors.

Because of the low per capita income, consumers in developing countries may be unable or unwilling to pay any extra for the services provided by the improved marketing system. Further, underdeveloped countries are more interested in raising production levels of physical goods rather than improving intangible marketing services. Inefficient marketing systems in developing countries also absorb extra manpower and can disguise unemployment (Collins and Holton, 1963).

We do not question the position that economic variables play a key role in the development of a marketing orientation in any society. What is asserted here is that economic factors alone do not in many instances provide a sufficient explanation of the prevailing state of affairs. For example, in the case of India, how does one account for the fact that all competing shops in an area often provide bad service to the customer even when they are selling nonessential and nonscarce goods? Why do taxi drivers who have not made even their minimum daily earnings refuse and ill-treat their customers? Why do even large professionally managed organizations that exist in highly competitive industries show utter disregard for their customers?

A Model of the Behavior of Indian Marketers

It is suggested here that a partial answer may lie in the history of India and its people. This is consistent with the position taken by some past writers that the history of a society has nontrivial impact on the evolving systems (Darian, 1985; Dholakia and Lee, 1985; Kapp, 1963; Mishra, 1962). The Hindu religion, the caste based social stratification, and the emergent Indian personality—all these influence and shape the behaviors of an individual in the presence of others. A model highlighting the effects of some of these variables on Indian marketers and consumers' orientation is shown in Figure 1.

In the model presented, box 1 is self-explanatory and needs little elaboration. Past studies have highlighted how factors such as lack of capital, the presence of unsophisticated capital goods industry (with limited technological capabilities), the existence of a large pool of unskilled labour and the small size of middle and upper class in the society affect the emergence of specific marketing strategies and tactics (Baker, 1965; Goldman, 1974; Kaynak, 1978, 1982; Preston, 1968; Samli and Kaynak, 1984; Yavas, Kaynak, and Borak, 1981). Kaynak (1982) provides a good discussion on several of the economic factors that affect marketing systems in the developing world. In general, most of these conditions tend to increase the power of the seller over the consumer.

Several external factors (box 3) that are unique to the developing world also increase the power of the seller vis-à-vis the customer. Ignorance and illiteracy on the part of the consumers, lack of any organized efforts on the part of the consumers to represent their interests, the absence of laws effectively protecting the rights of consumers, lack of effective information transmission systems, presence of corruption, black money and even a parallel economy in many instances—all go to make the consumer very vulnerable and the sellers powerful. All these factors also contribute to lack of consumer orientation (box 7).

FIGURE 1   Social and economic antecedents of prevailing marketing practices in India.

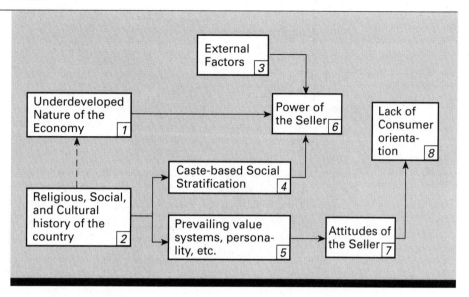

The main theme of this reading, however, is on how India's religious, social and cultural history affects the emergence of a Western marketing orientation in the country (boxes 2, 4 and 5 of Figure 1). In the remainder of this reading, an attempt will be made to elaborate on this thesis. Before that, a brief summary of past research studies on the effects of religious and socio-cultural factors on buyers and sellers is provided.

Impact of Religious and Socio-Cultural Variables

Several authors have attempted to study the effects of religion, culture and social systems on businesses and the individuals working in them. Most of these studies have been in the field of cross-cultural management. Research has indicated that cultural differences exist in various aspects of business and managerial practices. For excellent summaries and evaluations of the past work in this area, please refer to Adler (1983), England and Harpaz (1983), Negandhi (1983), and Sekaran (1983). Of more interest to marketers are studies indicating that culture affects, among other things, ethical beliefs of marketing managers (Lee, 1981), marketing strategy (O'Shaughnessy, 1985), complaint behavior of customers (Vilarreal-Camacho, 1983) and household purchasing decisions (Green, 1981).

Research on the effects of culture on business practices is especially difficult due to the problems associated with defining culture. As Ajiferuke and Bodewyn (1970) state, "Culture is one of those terms that defy a single all purpose definition and there are almost as many measurings of culture as people using the term" (p. 54). As Negandhi (1983) points out, culture has often been treated as a residual variable rather than an independent or intervening variable. Also, as long as the concept of culture is not well defined and operationalized, most cross cultural studies really end up as being cross national ones. Similar issues have been raised by other authors—see for example, Adler (1983), England and Harpaz (1983), Hofstede (1983), and Sekaran (1983). Thus, any finding on the effects of culture has to be examined carefully before being accepted.

Studies on religion and its impact on consumer behavior and marketing have been relatively few in number. As Hirschman (1983) states, the lack of attention to religion as a causal variable may stem from three sources: lack of awareness among marketers of the evidence linking religion and consumption, the existence of an implicit normative sanction against the study of religion as a causal variable in consumer research and the feeling that religion is too ubiquitous a concept influencing all aspects of one's life and hence a difficult one to study. Researchers in other fields have examined the relationship between religion and other variables of interest to marketers like consumption values, expectations and beliefs, personality characteristics, etc., and found evidence linking them (Hirschman, 1983).

Hirschman (1983), in one of the few studies in marketing on the topic, looked at religious affiliations as cognitive systems that affect values, beliefs and behavioral tendencies. These, in turn, affect problem solving behavior and consumption. It was found that people of Jewish, Catholic and Protestant religious affiliations differed in their problem solving criteria and solutions in four consumption situations—entertainment, housing, transportation and choice of family pets. The same author had also previously found that religious affiliation may affect a consumer's information processing activities (Hirschman, 1982). In another study, Wilkes, Burnett and Howell (1986) found that religiosity correlated with life-style variables and opinion leadership.

Thus, there is evidence that religious and socio-cultural factors affect both managerial practices and attitudes and consumer behavior. This paper attempts to identify the impact that Hinduism (the most popular religion in India) and India's socio-cultural heritage have on Indian marketers and their level of customer orientation. Due to space constraints, the following discussion will be restricted to the retailer level. However, the same effects may be found at other levels and other marketing activities with minor changes.

Religious and Socio-Cultural Impediments to Marketing Development in India

In this section, boxes 4 and 5 of the model in Figure 1 will be elaborated upon. The impact of these variables on marketers in India is also provided.

Caste in India In the past, several scholars have written books and elaborate treatises on the caste system in India (Blunt, 1931; Ghurye, 1952; Kapp, 1963; Karve, 1961; Kosambi, 1956; Mishra, 1962; Srinivas, 1962). Hence, a detailed discussion on the ancient caste system in India and its effects on the larger society is not attempted here. What follows is a brief description of some key aspects of the caste system to familiarize the readers to its key dimensions to help them appreciate its impact on the marketing system.

Castes in India could be thought of as "exclusive social groupings practicing endogamy and following their own customs regarding food and dress" (Kapp, 1963; p. 24). Castes generally have traditional behavior patterns (which in the past was enforced by a Caste Council in many instances) and do not mingle with other castes except on special occasions (Karve, 1961). Following the writings of Kapp (1963) and Karve (1961), the major characteristics of Indian caste system can be summarized as: (1) Marrying outside one's caste is prohibited; (2) partaking of food with lower caste members is also prohibited; (3) hereditary occupations for each caste exist and choosing other occupations is not allowed; (4) a hierarchy of castes exists; and (5) a person's birth determines his/her caste; movement from one caste to another is not possible.

The belief that pollution can be communicated by some castes to members of higher castes was widely prevalent in many parts of India until recently. This was especially so in the provinces of Gujarat, Tamil Nadu and Kerala. According to Ghurye (1952), the toddy tapper in Tamil Nadu contaminates a brahmin if he approaches the latter within twenty-four paces. The same way a Tiyyan of Kerala was expected to keep a distance of thirty-six steps from a brahmin; a pulayan was not allowed to approach a brahmin within ninety-six paces. Most of the servants who belonged to the shudra and lower castes were thus expected to keep a distance from the merchants (who belonged to a higher vaisya caste). Indeed, it is possible that the disdain for customers had its origin in the inferior position that several buyers occupied in the social hierarchy. The merchant class was in a very peculiar position. They had their origin in the indigenous, peasant non-Aryan class. Most of them were chosen by the ruling elite (brahmins) who were of Aryan origin to do the "wretched" job of selling goods for a profit (Tadpatrikar, 1945). To the brahmins, engaging in such worldly activities as money lending, trading, etc. was quite detestable. Indeed, most of the dealings with the vaishyas were done by brahmins through their servants, shudras or other slave labor. In ancient India the brahmins probably never had to go to the village shop in person for making their purchases. Either they sent their servants and got the items or the merchants delivered the goods to the brahmin's house. Thus, the merchant probably never had to show respect to the person who came to his shop as the latter belonged to a social class lower than himself. Nor did they socially interact or form friendships with their customers in any extensive manner. Over a period of time, the merchant or Vaisya caste became affluent and hence socially powerful. However, their upward social mobility was blocked by the social caste system. One author suggests that faced with this status inconsistency many of the vaisyas adopted a new ideology and religion as dissonance reduction mechanisms (Darian, 1985). Whatever may be the real case, as the affluence and prestige of the seller grew over the time, the gap between the seller and the buyer increasingly widened.

The caste system also had another direct impact on the buyer-seller relationship. As mentioned earlier, generally, each caste or group of castes considered some of the callings as its hereditary occupation. It was considered to be morally wrong to abandon its hereditary occupation in pursuit of another however lucrative the latter might be. Thus, "it is conceived to be far better to perform imperfectly one's duties as prescribed by one's caste than to perform the dharma of another caste perfectly . . . the performance of one's duty in accordance with one's inherited occupation or status leads to spiritual progress . . ." (Kapp, 1963, p. 27). This essentially limited the degree of competition in any particular trade or profession as there was no provision for changing one's caste and hence one's career. Kapp (1963; p. 44) notes the effects of this on individual motivation and aspiration level:

> If perfection can be reached by obedience to dharma, i.e., by fulfilling one's ascribed and inherited duties, the level of aspiration and motivation however high or low, tends to be confined to the field of one's prescribed traditional activities. That is to say, the desire for change, mobility and improvement must be seriously curbed.

It is possible that the prevalence of a rigid caste based social stratification system led to the placing of a premium on following traditional occupations thus retarding individual initiative and freedom. Since an individual's social relations and even eating habits are prescribed by the caste, ". . . caste may thus be said to achieve what western advertising aims at: it differentiates" (Kapp, 1963; p. 47). A probable outcome of this was lower felt need for product packaging, customer service, advertising and sales force training.

While the effects of caste may be less visible now, it still is a fairly significant factor in the lives of Indians (e.g., consider the importance given to caste in Indian matrimonial ads). Also, while the overt discriminations based on caste may be diminishing, the unconscious effects of years of social stratification may take many more years to disappear.

Hindu Value Systems and Personality Closely intertwined with the ancient caste system was the Hindu religion itself. Often, it becomes impossible to distinguish the sphere of the sacred from that of the social. As Kapp (1963, p. 10) points out:

> Indeed, the relation between the sexes, birth, death, the roles of sons and daughters, occupation, the attitude toward work and its fruits, the meaning of freedom and "salvation," a man's relation to the physical world including animals

and particularly the cow, are all mediated by and integrated into an essentially religious system of vast cosmological proportions and regularities . . .

Hindu cultural values have traditionally shaped the thought and action patterns of most Indians (in many cases even non-Hindus).

In this section, a few key values in Indian society are discussed.

Focus on Group. A key element in this culture has been the focus on group as the unit of action and the source of aspiration (Kapp, 1963). These group aspirations, in turn, are moulded by the traditional patterns of behavior and religious prescriptions. Tradition-determined actions, thus get preference over voluntaristic individual actions. Initiative, creativity, entrepreneurship etc., were not rewarded as much as consistency with past actions—a factor that may have stood in the way of customer oriented innovative marketing approaches. Added to this, the cyclical concepts of time and history as returning upon themselves result in the metaphysical notion of cosmic causation and belief in one's fate—both possibly encouraging inaction and definitely retarding innovation.

Perception of Life. Added to this is the Hindu notion of life as illusory and transitory. Renunciation, sacrifice and austerity have continued to command the highest respect of most Hindus (Kapp, 1963). Lord Krishna's prescriptions on good life as spelt out in Bhagavadgita (Radhakrishnan, 1948; p. 138) point out:

> To action alone hast thou a right and never at all to its fruits; let not the fruits of action be thy motive; neither let there be any attachment to inaction . . . Therefore, without attachment, perform always the work that has to be done for man attains to the highest by doing work without attachment . . .

Kapp (1963; p. 44) points out how the nonattachment to the fruits of one's actions

> deprives man of the necessary motivation and involvement needed to act purposely and productively either in the economic or other spheres. For such a doctrine may not only promote lack of interest in the formulation of proper plans of action but may ultimately lead to indifference to the results of one's action altogether.

It also makes individuals passively accept the happenings around them. Further, "the knowledge that the course of life has already been determined by past actions and that the only scope is for bettering one's next life would in most people generate no incentive (and indeed would generate a disincentive) to better material conditions" (Mishra, 1962; p. 202).

What then are the implications of these values for emergence of sound marketing practices? On the buyer's side, this may lead to a noninsistence on new and better quality products or a lack of motivation to find good alternatives for one's needs. The sellers, in turn, are likely to become disinterested in their jobs and may not try to improve their performance as they are less concerned with matters of immediate concern. Hinduism, through its laws and concept of ritual pollution did discourage trade and industry and stood in the way of any psychological bond developing between the buyer and seller. Indeed, the available evidence indicates that the position of the trader was often an unenviable one beset with status inconsistency and general alienation from existing value systems (Darian, 1985). The existing religious and social values may also lead a seller to feel that any (business) failure was "pre-ordained" and hence he/she may not try to analyze the situation and take corrective action. Finally, "the levels of aspiration are dictated by the group and hence are as static or dynamic as group tradition permits them to be but the failure to reach traditional goals need not be experienced as a source of individual frustration" (Kapp, 1963; p. 11). There is hence very little to motivate an individual to pioneer and change; to influence and build the cornerstones of modern marketing.

The Joint Family System. The joint family system which was a by-product of the Hindu social organization also reduced spatial mobility of people thus reducing competition in the market place. It also led to the emergence of a dependency complex among its members (Kapp, 1963). Developing an impersonal work discipline and commitment to an organization or profession may hence become very difficult for its members. As Kapp (1963; p. 60) noted, "indeed, discipline, orderliness, precision and punctuality for the sake of such an impersonal organization, may be rejected as pedantic, tyrannical and intolerable."

In a more recent article, Garg and Parikh (1986) state that the major problems faced by Indian organizations regardless of their size can be traced to the joint family system. The above authors found that Indian organizations, in general, faced problems of apathy and lack of initiative among middle and senior managers. According to the authors,

> Indian organizations in their operationalization of management and organizational processes—irrespective of size, technology, complexity, structures and task—converge on structural prototypes that are anchored in the joint family system. The basic characteristics of the joint family is that of a role bounded structure. Families, like organizations, have a mechanical and sequential technology and a departmentalized structure. Authority is centralized . . . there is tolerance of invisible waste and low efficiency. . . . The emphasis and expectation of employees is that of loyalty, obedience and conformity (p. 52).

Similar statements are made by Sekaran (1983) who finds that the ideals of duty, devotion, deference and obedience to parents, teachers and elders are the traits that are developed by the joint family system and the Indian society.

Thus, the traits that are emphasized and rewarded by the joint family system that is still prevalent in most parts of India are not conducive to the development of efficient organizations. The system does not encourage individual initiative. As long as one is loyal to the family and the family owned enterprise, one is assured of a position within the organization.

Conclusion

In the preceding pages, we have attempted to briefly outline how traditional Hindu organization and cultural values have stood in the way of the emergence of customer orientation in India. It was argued that the ancient caste system, the traditional Hindu notions of Dharma (doing one's assigned duty) and the joint family system are instrumental in creating a set of conditions that hamper the growth of marketing orientation in India. A summary of these is provided in Figure 2.

What are the implications of these factors for marketers? While this paper has looked at the impact of religion and sociocultural factors on marketing in one country, i.e., India, it is felt the issues identified here can be of interest to marketers who are involved in international marketing. These implications are discussed in the following:

1. Religion and culture would seem to have a greater impact on marketing practices than hitherto given credit for. Before transplanting a marketing strategy or program from another culture the conditions and constraints under which they were successfully implemented have to be identified. These need to be compared with the conditions that exist in the host country or culture to evaluate the appropriateness of the strategy/program under consideration.

2. When dealing with countries such as India, which have culture and value systems dating back centuries (if not more), special problems posed by the prevailing cultural values are to be recognized. It is but a truism that strong culture requires strong intervention strategies to bring about changes. But what is perhaps not so obvious is that a culture (such as the one in India) which has faced successful onslaughts by other cultures and value systems (as exemplified by the number of foreign invaders who attempted to conquer India) may have some built-in elasticity to absorb new ideas—but still remain predominantly old in all key aspects. Changes will happen even in such settings; but they will be slow and often unpredictable.

3. An MNC trying to do business in such a culture has some advantages and problems. Since most Indian organizations are not marketing oriented, by having a customer oriented strategy, one could capture a significant market share. Consumers' awareness of their rights is a

FIGURE 2   Conditions for the Emergence of Professional Marketing versus Actual
Social Conditions Created by Indian Social System

Dimension	Required conditions for the emergence of professional marketing practices*	Actual social conditions created by Indian social system and Hindu values
1. Goals of marketing	Maximize consumption, consumer satisfaction, consumer choice and/or quality of life	Active pursuit of any of the marketing goals is absent and may even be considered immoral under specific conditions. Performing one's duty irrespective of the associated outcomes is the guiding principle.
2. Goals of the participants a) the buyer	Get good quality products at reasonable price	Given the Hindu values, maximizing own utility may not be emphasized; social roles play key roles in deciding consumption patterns.
b) the seller	Develop and change marketing mix variables to attain own goals and those of the organization	To continue to practice one's traditional occupation; neither concerned with the outcomes of one's efforts nor a conscious effort to improve it always visible.
c) the citizen	Ensuring safety of the public; ensuring social goals are not sacrificed while marketing products	Ritual purity, fear of pollution and caste based stratification stand in the way of any organized social action and mobilization of human energies for common social causes.
3. Economic system	Freedom to move in and out of markets; freedom to produce and innovate.	No mobility across caste, sector or occupation; in turn this prevents competition and innovation.
4. Demand patterns	Apparent or at least latent demand for a variety of products and services.	Caste and family decide the consumption patterns. No demand or even negative demand for some products.
5. Overall philosophy underlying marketing	The marketing concept of determining needs of target consumers; delivering satisfaction more effectively than one's competitors.	The dharma concept of doing one's traditional duty with the ultimate goal of salvation; attempts to master the problems of this world are not only considered unimportant but also illusory.
6. Personality traits	Analytical ability, creativity, entrepreneurship, risk-taking, need to achieve, rational response to problems, etc.	Dependency on others; past orientation; emotional responses to decision situations, etc.

*Some of these items are adapted from Kotler, P. *Principles of Marketing*, Englewood Cliffs, New Jersey: Prentice Hall, 1983.

relatively new phenomenon in such cultures and this may provide opportunities to organizations entering such nations. Consumer education programs and campaigns may be very effective in such situations in creating a good image for the company. On the negative side, trained sales persons may be hard to locate. True enough, there are skilled men and women available in the country—but they may not be customer oriented. Sales force training may thus play a major role in MNCs entering such cultures.

Marketing practices in India are undergoing turbulent changes at the present time. Most of these have occurred due to changes in the economic conditions (e.g., higher disposable income for consumers, especially in the middle class, relaxing of governmental controls on private industry, impact of foreign technology and marketing practices, etc.). Indeed, the newer generation of consumers seems to exhibit behaviors and preferences that are different from those of their parents (Dholakia, 1984) with serious implications for marketers in India. However, these changes have mostly occurred in cities and in large, professionally managed organizations. To the small trader or the cashier in the village bank, tradition and remnants of caste system still seem to largely guide their behaviors. This is not to discount the effects of economic factors on emerging marketing practices; rather we believe that the economic orientation itself is significantly influenced by these historical and socio-cultural factors. Hard empirical data supporting this position is yet to emerge; we welcome our fellow researchers to join this promising area of inquiry.

REFERENCES

Adler, N. (1983), Typology of Management Studies Involving Culture, *Journal of International Business Studies,* Vol. XIV, No. 2 (fall), 29–49.

Ajiferuke, M. and Bodewyn, J. (1970), Socio-economic Indicators in Comparative Management, *Administrative Science Quarterly,* December, 453–458.

Arndt, Johan (1972), Temporal Lags in Comparative Retailing, *Journal of Marketing,* 36 (October), 40–45.

Baker, Raymond W. (1965), Marketing in Nigeria, *Journal of Marketing,* 29 (July), 40–48.

Bhatt, G.R. (1985), Consumerism: Concept and Its Need for Our Era, *Indian Journal of Marketing,* 15 (12, August), 3–8.

Blunt, E.A. (1931), *The Caste System of Northern India,* London: Oxford.

Collins, N.L. (1963), Impact of Economic Growth upon the Structure of the Italian Distributive Sector, *Economia Internazionale,* 16 (May), 325–340.

Collins, N.R. and Holton, R.H. (1963), Programming Changes in Marketing in Planned Economic Development, *Kyklos,* 16 (January), 123–135.

Cundiff, Edward W. and Marye T. Hilger (1980), Marketing and the Production-Consumption Thesis in Economic Development, in *Macromarketing: Evolution of Thought,* George Fisk, Robert Nason and Phillip D. White, eds., Boulder: Graduate School of Business Administration, University of Colorado.

Darian, Jean C. (1985), Marketing and Economic Development: A Case Study from Classical India, *Journal of Macromarketing,* 5 (spring), 14–26.

Dholakia, Ruby R. (1984), Intergeneration Differences in Consumer Behaviour: Some Evidence from a Developing Country, *Journal of Business Research,* 12 (March), 19–34.

Dholakia, Nikilesh and Ruby R. Dholakia (1982), Marketing in an Emerging World Order, *Journal of Macromarketing,* 2 (spring), 47–56.

Dholakia, Nikilesh and K.H. Lee (1985), Marketing Development in Asia: A Comparative Study of Japan, China and India in 1700–1950, Unpublished manuscript, Hongkong: Department of Marketing and International Business, The Chinese University of Hongkong.

Drucker, Peter F. (1958), Marketing and Economic Development, *Journal of Marketing,* 5 (February), 29–33.

El-Sherbini, A.A. (1980), Behavioural Adjustments as Marketing Constraints on Economic Development, in *Macromarketing: Evolution of Thought,* George Fisk, Robert Nason and Phillip D. White, eds., Boulder: Graduate School of Business Administration, University of Colorado.

England, G.W., and Harpaz, I. (1983), Some Methodological and Analytical Considerations in Cross-cultural Comparative Research, *Journal of International Business Studies,* Vol. XIV, No. 2 (fall), 49–69.

Garg, P.J. and Parick, I.J. (1986), Managers and Corporate Cultures: The Case of Indian Organizations, *Management International Review,* Vol. 26, 3, 50–66.

Ghurye, G.S. (1952), *Caste and Class in India,* Bombay: Popular Books.

Goldman, A. (1974), Outreach of Consumers and the Modernization of Urban Food Retailing in Developing Countries, *Journal of Marketing,* 38 (October), 11–12.

Green, R.W. (1973), *Protestantism, Capitalism and Social Science,* Lexington, MA: Heath.

Hilger, Marye T. (1978), Theories of the Relationship Between Marketing and Economic Development: Public Policy Implications, in *Macromarketing: Distributive Process from a Societal Perspective—an Elaboration of Issues,* Charles C. Slater, ed., Boulder: Graduate School of Business Administration, University of Colorado.

Hirschmann, E.C. (1980), Ethnic Variation in Leisure Activities and Motives. Proceedings of the American Marketing Association Educator's Conference, Chicago, AMA.

Hirschmann, E.C. (1983), Religious Affiliation and Consumption Processes: An Initial Paradigm, *Research in Marketing,* Sheth, ed., Vol. 6, 131–170, Jai Press.

Hofstede, G. (1980), *Culture's Consequences: International Differences in Work Related Values,* Beverly Hills/London: Sage Publications.

——— (1983), The Cultural Relativity of Organizational Practices & Theories, *Journal of International Business Studies,* Vol. XIV, No. 2 (fall) 75–91.

Kapp, K.W. (1963), *Hindu Culture, Economic Development and Economic Planning in India,* Bombay: Asia Publishing House.

Karve, I. (1961), *Hindu Society: An Interpretation,* Poona: Deccan College & Sangram Press.

Kaynak, E. (1978), Difficulties of Undertaking Marketing Research in the Developing Countries, *European Research,* 6 (November), 251–259.

——— (1982), *Marketing in the Third World,* New York: Praeger.

Kaynak, E. and Samli, A.C. (1984), Marketing Practices in Less Developed Countries, *Journal of Business Research,* (Fall), 55–64.

Kaynak, E. and Hudanah, B.I. (1987), Operationalizing the Relationship Between Marketing & Economic Development: Some Insights from Less Developed Countries, *European Journal of Marketing,* 21, 48–65.

Kosambi, D.D. (1956), *Introduction to the Study of Indian History,* Bombay: Popular Prakashan.

Lee, K.H. (1981), Ethical Beliefs in Marketing Management: A Cross Cultural Study, *European Journal of Marketing,* 15, 58–67.

McCarthy, E.J. (1963), Effective Marketing Institutions for Economic Development, in *Towards Scientific Marketing,* Stephen A. Greyser, ed., Chicago: American Marketing Association, 393–404.

Mehta, S.C. (1980), The Consumer's View of Marketing in India, in *Marketing: Environment, Concepts and Cases,* S.C. Mehta and K. Prasad, eds., New Delhi: Tata McGraw-Hill.

Mishra, V. (1962), *Hinduism and Economic Growth,* London: Oxford University Press.

Moyer, R., and S. Hollander (1968), *Markets and Marketing in Developing Economies,* Homewood, IL: Richard D. Irwin.

Negandhi, A.R., (1983), Cross Cultural Management Research: Trends and Future Directions, *Journal of International Business Studies,* XIV, 2, 17–29.

Ninan, T.N. and C.U. Singh (1984), The Consumer Boom, *India Today,* February 15, 82–90.

O'Shaughnessy, W. (1985), Strategy and U.S. Cultural Bias, *European Journal of Marketing,* Vol. 19(4), 23–32.

Preston, L.E. (1968), *Consumer Goods Marketing in a Developing Economy, Research Monograph No. 19,* Athens, Greece: Center of Planning and Economic Research.

Radhakrishnan, S. (1948), *The Bhagavadgita,* London: George Allen & Unwin Ltd.

Samli, Coskun A. and Erdener Kaynak (1984), Marketing Practices in Less Developed Countries, *Journal of Business Research,* 12, 5–18.

Sarin, S. and P. Avasthi (1980), The Alienated Indian Consumer and the Role of Consumer Education, *Vikalpa,* 5(2) (April), 95–105.

Sekaran, U. (1983), Methodological and Theoretical Issues and Advancements in Cross Cultural Research, *Journal of International Business Studies,* XIV, 2.

Shapiro, S.J. (1965), Comparative Marketing and Economic Development, in *Science in Marketing*, George Schwartz, ed., New York: John Wiley & Sons, 398–429.

Singh, J.D. (1983), Marketing Management in Indian Public Enterprises, *Institute of Public Enterprise Journal*, 6(1), 1–17.

——— (1984), Marketing Management in India: the State of Art, *ASCI Journal of Management*, 13(2), 206–225.

——— (1978), Consumers' Problems in India, *Indian Journal of Commerce*, 31 (115), 45–50.

Soloman, M.R. (1948), The Structure of the Market in Underdeveloped Economies, *Quarterly Journal of Economics*, August, 519–541.

Srinivas, M.N. (1962), *Caste in Modern India*, Bombay: Meia Promoters and Publishers Ltd.

Srinivasan, B. (1986), Vagaries of Telephones, *The Hindu*, January 27, p.8.

Stanton, W.J. (1964), *Fundamentals of Marketing*, New York: McGraw Hill, 12–18.

Tadpatrikar, S. (1945), Vaishyas and the Social Order, Annals of the Bhandarkar Oriental Research Institute, 26, 301–306.

Vilarreal-Camacho, R. (1983), Consumer Complaining Behaviour: A Cross Cultural Comparison, Proceedings of the Educators' Conference, 49, 68–77.

Wadinambiaratchi, George (1965), Channels of Distribution in Developing Economies, *Business Quarterly*, 30 (Winter), 74–82.

Wilkes, Burnett, and Howell (1986), On the Meaning and Measurement of Religiosity in Consumer Research, *Journal of the Academy of Marketing Science*, Vol. 14(1), (Spring), 47–56.

Yavas, Ugur, Kaynak, Erdener and E. Borak (1981), Retail Institutions in Developing Countries: Determinants of Super Market Patronage in Istanbul, Turkey, *Journal of Business Research*, (December), 367–379.

THE IMPACT OF CULTURE UPON PACKAGE PERCEPTION: AN EXPERIMENT IN HONG KONG AND THE UNITED STATES

John Knutsen ◆ Steven Thrasher ◆ Yunus Kathawala

ABSTRACT. An experimental study of the package and product perception of toilet soap manufacturers in the Peoples Republic of China was conducted in Hong Kong and the United States. Although it was found that there were greater similarities than dissimilarities in the two cultural samples in evaluating the soap packages and in implying product quality from those packages, the dissimilarities deserve attention. Certain package design and material have differing connotations among these two distinct cultures, thus causing differing buying behaviors. Certain visual package designs were instrumental in positioning the soaps differently by the different sample groups.

As dependence upon international markets for corporate growth increases, firms find themselves having to decide whether or not to market their products in essentially the same manner as their domestic market. While the benefits of standardization can be considerable, such standardization can also limit value-enhancing product differences which become apparent when recognizing the differences in non-domestic markets pertaining to consumer perceptions and needs. Packaging, for example, may be standardized in such aspects as shape, size, material, design, and use of the color. Changes in some packaging attributes, as will be shown in this manuscript, could make a difference in how the package is perceived. Some changes in packaging attributes cost more to modify than others and should be considered against the gain expected from such a change.[1] This is especially true if the packaging form demands new capital equipment.

The packaging of a product helps to identify the product to the purchaser in his attempt to fit the product to what is sought either for himself or others, in the case of a gift or shared product. Especially for new purchases, the packaging identification may be symbolic of the physical qualities or what is to be found inside, the performance or experience from product use and type of people using the product. This is especially true for self-service products:

> The package must now do much of the work that the retail salesman did. As such, the package must attract the consumer to the product; explain product benefits; create an image of product quality; outline how to use the product; give a price; announce about the weight, contents, and the producer of the product and offer some incentive to close the sale.[2]

Source: *International Journal of Management* Vol. 5, No. 2, June 1988, pp. 117–124. Reprinted with permission.

[1] Terpstra, V., *International Marketing* (2nd Ed.), The Dryden Press, 1978, p. 235.

[2] Nickels, W. G., *Marketing Communications and Promotion*, Columbus, Ohio: Grid, Inc., 1976, pp. 146–47.

In Twedt's research on the question of "How Much Value Can Be Added Through Packaging?" he summarizes the impact on the emotional appeal of packages and the dimensions which could be measured as follows:

> Packages, like people, have definite personalities. Various combinations of design element such as shape, color, typography, illustration, packaging materials—all contribute to the 'package Gestalt.' A package may be 'expensive' or 'inexpensive'; 'old fashioned' or 'modern'; 'for young people' or 'for old people'; in fact, the dimensions along which packages may be located are almost limitless.[3]

Moreover, consumers attempt to find consistency in a product's image, considering its packaging but one aspect of the "product Gestalt":

> That stimuli are viewed as a total configuration suggests that a brand must be considered as an organized whole. Thus, the alteration of a single component may indeed affect the total configuration. In terms of a perceptual map . . . we might see that there are interactions among the various dimensions; that is, it is not possible to operate on one independently of the others. If one dimension is affected or a new dimension added, the perception of the brand along the others may change radically to consumers, as may the relative importance of the various dimensions (or product attributes).[4]

Packages provide verbal and non-verbal symbols that inform potential buyers about the product's content, features, uses, advantages, and (implied) marketing position. The firm can create desirable images and associations for one culture by using certain colors, designs, shapes, textures, and materials. The problem we are all aware of is in transmitting the package to another culture where the "images" and "associations" may be undesirable at the worst to "not helpful" at the best.

Package design helps to position a product by aiding in differentiating it from its competition, by focusing its appeal on a specific consumer segment, and by communicating its personality and performance claims. The continuing difficulty in cross cultural marketing is that the package may detract from attempts at differentiation, attempts to target toward a specific segment, or be a different "personality" in the "different" culture. For example, the product package that is defined by culture "A" as old fashioned may be defined in culture "B" as modern.

One of the major assumptions which could be made by managers is that the person in one culture "sees" a given package in very much the same way as

---

[3] Twedt, D. W., "How Much Value Can Be Added Through Packaging." *Journal of Marketing*, January, 1968 (vol. 32, no. 1), p. 60, (article, pp. 58–61).

[4] Aaker, D. A. and J. G. Myers, *Advertising Management*, Englewood Cliffs, N.J.: Prentice Hall, Inc., 1982, p. 251.

a person in another culture. The issue is obviously open to an experimental setting. This type of research is important for two major marketing groups: first, for manufacturers located outside of a domestic market and interested in selling a "package" into the other market without package change, and secondly for package designers creating a totally new package form in a developing economy. In such an economy, it is likely that the protection/containment aspects of a product's package will be emphasized, while the promotional/product image will be overlooked. The firm in the developing country making its packaging decisions may lack appreciation for the important point-of-purchase selling influence of a package.

The critical issue for international marketers is to either adjust or choose not to adjust marketing strategies (i.e. packaging strategies) to the world market by taking into account the factors such as language, customs, living standards (i.e. package size), religion, and cultural tradition. It is very logical that cross cultural package perception studies can assist a marketer in the process of making the decision to change a package for another nation's market or not change the package and use his/her resources in another marketing area.

Hypothesis

1. The package will cause the respondent to evaluate the quality of the "bare soap" differently than respondents viewing the bare soap alone.

2. The two groups of respondents will evaluate the marketing issues of product use, package, user targets, channel, and price in a different light because they perceived the package differently.

Methodology

The experiment was designed to evaluate the perceptions of six branded packages of toilet soap from the Peoples Republic of China (PRC) on 210 students at a Hong Kong university and 159 students from a university in the United States. All students were majoring in Business Administration. The study was conducted simultaneously in both countries.

At the time of the study there were twelve brands of PRC soaps available in Hong Kong. The six chosen were judged to range from the best to the poorest of packaging materials and techniques in a pre-test by Hong Kong students. Only one PRC soap brand had been seen in the Northwestern U.S. at the time of the study (Bee and Flower Brand). The six brands of soap that were used were Jasmine, Fortune, Bee and Flower Brand, Magnolia, Jaili, and Maxam.

Bar shaped soaps (toilet soaps) were chosen to be the studied packaged product because such products are widely available and used in both test cultures. Also bar soaps are low priced and purchased relatively frequently as well as being highly visible at counters or displayed on shelves. Packaging, especially its promotional aspects, is usually found to be a more critical element of the marketing mix for convenience goods sold on a self-service basis.[5] Moreover, bar soaps have the potential for consumers both to express a high degree of personal choice in their selection of one brand over another and to risk personal dissatisfaction because of smell and harshness to the skin. In other words, bar soaps were thought to invoke a high degree of personal preference rather than indifference when choosing among alternatives.

The questionnaire was comprised of two major sections. The first dealt with the respondent's judgement on the product itself. Six dimensions of soap quality (cleaning power, lather, durability, smoothness, effect on skin, and likely scent) were measured in addition to an overall quality measure. The second section of the questionnaire asked respondents to rate likely users of the product, the "mechanical" features of the package, who the product was for, likely price (implied by package) and likely channel of sale (implied by package). The first and second sections both consisted of having respondents rate the soap packages on a seven point semantic differential scale which is a series of attitude scales consisting of bipolar adjectives, such as "good" and "bad."

Students were randomly assigned to one control group and six experimental groups. The control group was shown a "bare soap" and asked to rate the soap against seven quality dimensions. Each of the other six groups was asked to rate the same bare soap and what was purported to be the package for the bare soap. It should be noted that all groups saw the same bare soap, and in reality the bare soap was another PRC soap (translated brand is Jade Leaf or Green Leaf, manufactured by the Shanghai Soap Manufacturing Production Co.).

After this first evaluation, all groups were asked to evaluate, through the use of the questionnaire, each soap package when all six soaps were placed in front of the subject on the table. The respondents were not allowed to touch or smell the bare soap or any of the packaged soaps from the end of the experiment. Also, no subjects were told that the soaps were manufactured in the PRC. (Although many Hong Kong students knew some of the soaps were from PRC.)

Results

The respondents' evaluations of the soaps along the six dimensions of soap quality (cleaning power, lather, durability, smoothness, effect on skin, likely scent) were summed to arrive at a "qualscore" and the only "overall quality" of the package with bare soap, versus bare soap only, the following statistically significant findings were discovered using an F test of means. These results are depicted in Table 1.

---

[5] Rewoldt, S. H., J. D. Scott, and M. R. Washaw, *Introduction to Marketing Management,* Homewood, Illinois: Richard D. Irwin, 1981, p. 281.

TABLE 1   Comparing Product Perception With and Without Package

		U.S.	Hong Kong
Jasmine package vs. Bare	Qualscore overall quality	N.S. N.S.	N.S. N.S.
Fortune package vs. Bare	Qualscore overall quality	N.S. N.S.	N.S. N.S.
Bee and Flower package vs. Bare	Qualscore overall quality	N.S. sig .95	N.S. N.S.
Magnolia package vs. Bare	Qualscore overall quality	N.S. sig .95	N.S. N.S.
Jaili package vs. Bare	Qualscore overall quality	N.S. N.S.	N.S. N.S.
Maxam package vs. Bare	Qualscore overall quality	N.S. N.S.	N.S. N.S.

As can be seen, the first hypothesis was soundly rejected. In both the United States and in Hong Kong, respondents who were shown a bare soap tended to rate the soap comparable to the respondents in each culture which saw both the (same) bare soap plus one of the branded packaged soaps.

Depicted in Table 2 is the comparison of the actual mean scores for the question "overall quality of soap is good/bad" (+3 to −3). On the average of all the soaps, the mean difference equal to .753 was significant at the .99 level; i.e. the two cultural groups looking at the same bare soap with a package saw different implications of quality based upon the package. An even greater difference was seen in bare soap alone.

The first choice by Hong Kong and the United States respondents when evaluating all six soaps along the individual attribute dimensions are shown in Table 3.

Of twenty areas for choice among the six soaps, fifteen were identified as having the same perception, and only five attributes were different. Interesting to contemplate is the finding of complete agreement in evaluation of the mechanical package factor, in the channel and user target categories of analysis.

Although the mean scores were consistently significantly different, the rank order for these many dimensions was very similar.

Thus, looking at the aggregate level of agreement, particularly in the many package factors, of what is the most attractive or most modern package etc., we have to conclude that the similarities of package perception at the extreme is much greater than the differences between the two cultures.

TABLE **2**   Comparing Mean Scores—Overall Quality U.S. and Hong Kong

				H.K.	U.S.	Diff.
Control (saw bare soap only)						
	Rank	H.K.	U.S.			
Jasmine		4	5	-.63	0.0	.63
Fortune		2	3	+.10	+0.40	.30
Bee & Flower	High	1	1	+.17	+0.93	.76
Magnolia		4	6	−.63	−0.08	.55
Jaili		6	2	−.70	+0.52	1.22
Maxim		3	4	−.43	+0.29	.72
						x = .753

A review of the data also revealed that the three floral design single wrapper soap packages tended to be evaluated closely together by both the Hong Kong respondents and United States respondents. To more easily spot the overall patterns and cultural evaluative differences, the scores for Jasmine, Magnolia, and Jaili were combined to form Table 4. From this table, it can be seen that floral design, single wrapper packages were judged by Hong Kong respondents as rather old fashioned and not very distinctive or attractive in design. The packaging material and technique were down-rated. Consistent with these judgements, the Hong Kong respondents evaluated such packages as housing a low priced product which is inappropriate for gift giving.

United States respondents were more neutral about such single wrapper, floral design packages as to modernity, distinctiveness, and package construction. They, however, judged such packaging as more feminine and housing soaps more suitable for body or facial use than the Hong Kong respondents. Such packages were viewed as supermarket soaps and not especially appropriate for gift giving.

In sharp contrast with the single wrapper, floral design soaps were the boxed soaps, Fortune and the Bee and Flower Brand, a soap with a multi-brand wrapper and gold seal. These packaged products were considered by respondent groups in both settings to be more distinctive, with a higher quality of both package material and packaging technique. Both groups judged these "higher quality" packaged soaps to be very appropriate for sale at department stores and at a high price level. Curiously, however, the Hong Kong respondents were more accepting of such soaps as supermarket items. In the United States, the boxed

TABLE 3   Comparison by Individual Attribute Dimensions

The Use Factors	HK	HK x score	US x score	US
For washing hands	Jasmine	0.84	0.66	Magnolia
For washing face	Fortune	0.86	0.99	Magnolia
For washing body	Fortune and Maxam	0.98	0.90	Magnolia
For everyday use	Maxam	−0.85	−1.64	Maxam
For use as gift	Fortune	−0.01	1.70	Fortune
The Package Factors Distinctive packaging	Fortune	1.31	1.87	Fortune
Attractive package color	Fortune	0.66	1.15	Fortune
Attractive graphic design	Fortune	0.43	1.05	Fortune
Quality of packaging design	Fortune	0.99	2.01	Fortune
Packaging technique is good	Fortune	0.74	1.66	Fortune
Overall package is modern	Fortune	0.66	1.56	Fortune
The User Target A masculine soap	Fortune	0.05	2.26	Fortune
A feminine soap	Magnolia	−1.01	−1.70	Magnolia
Soap for adults	Fortune	−1.22	−2.11	Fortune
Soap for children	Maxam	0.10	0.07	Maxam
The Channel Likely to be sold in supermarkets	Maxam	0.80	2.09	Maxam
Likely to be sold in department stores	Fortune	1.10	1.98	Fortune
The Price Price is high (est.)	Fortune	1.06	2.18	Fortune
Price is low (est.)	Jasmine	−1.62	−0.82	Maxam

TABLE **4**   Combined Comparisons—Three Floral Designs

	Hong Kong	United States
For hands	+2.21	+1.75
For face	−1.44	+2.68
For body	+0.80	+2.40
Distinctive	−4.27	−1.12
Package color	−2.97	+1.25
Graphic design	−3.00	+0.91
Qual package material	−2.96	−0.79
Pqual package technique	−2.96	+0.44
Mod/	−4.04	−0.42
Overall impress	−2.46	+0.58
Miscellaneous	−2.46	−4.75
Adults−/child+	−1.04	−1.28
Supermarket	−0.86	+4.50
Department store	−0.73	−1.10
Not everyday	−2.21	−2.43
High-priced	−3.77	−0.48
Gift	−5.20	−2.51

or fancily wrapped soaps were judged to be appropriate for gifts, while this estimation was not shared by Hong Kong respondents.

Limitations

Among the limitations faced in this study was a slight bias in the sex mix of the two groups with slightly more women (41 percent versus 29 percent) in the U.S. sample.

To avoid the limitation of the language barrier, the study was conducted with Chinese students in Hong Kong who were very highly skilled in English.

This advantage allowed us not to concern ourselves with the loss of the associative value of the English language through translation.

Conclusions

The package perception experiment between respondent groups in both the United States and Hong Kong provided evidence of both cultural perception similarities and differences. In common, in each perspective area, respondents did not especially tend to attribute product qualities with soap from different soap packages (they did not "judge the book by the cover"). Also, to a high degree of agreement, respondents in both cultural settings chose a common packaging design across numerous evaluative criteria. In other words, there was agreement between the two groups as to which soap package designs they most preferred, for whom the package was intended and the outlet type through which the product was best distributed.

Respondents' views of the various soap products were, however, different in other ways of importance to the marketer of such products. In Hong Kong, for example, the floral design element of soap packages apparently is not value-enhancing and tends to cause respondents to categorize such packaged products rather lowly. In the United States, floral designs were neutral in value-enhancement but strongly identified as feminine. Soaps in boxes or fancy wrappers were judged as an acceptable gift product in the United States unlike in Hong Kong.

The authors feel that these differences may be due to differing aspects in the two cultures' social systems. There are passages in the literature, for example, that cite differences in the connotations associated with different colors among different cultures. This would lead one to believe that such a thing as an entire package, of which color is only one attribute, could be perceived differently by consumers from two different cultures.

Implications Findings such as these allow the marketer to better attune his product offering to the intended markets. At risk if the marketer does not understand how a non-domestic market perceives a given package design is the consistency of the overall marketing campaign. A television advertisement targeted at a non-domestic market may, for example, be suggesting "everyday use" of the product when the package design, as perceived by the same target market, says "special occasion" product. Such incongruence is likely to send different, hence confusing, signals to the intended consumers. Such confusion may thwart product preference and purchase. Wise, then is the international marketer who embraces the age-old advice to "know your market." The authors are planning future studies using culture as a variable in different countries and for different products.

THE PRODUCT DEVELOPMENT PROCESS IN NIC MULTINATIONALS

Wenlee Ting

ABSTRACT. Firms in the newly industrializing countries (NICs) of Asia are rapidly adapting their products to changing markets and adopting more innovative product strategies. An early awareness of these NIC multinationals would help US as well as world businessmen anticipate and understand both the challenges and opportunities posed by these emerging mini-Japans of the future in an increasingly competitive and intense world market place.

In the late 1970s, a number of Asian-Pacific countries began rapidly to industrialize. Newly industrializing countries (NICs)[1] like Korea, Taiwan, Singapore and Hong Kong were attaining phenomenal growth rates; and together with Japan and China, these NICs are helping to establish the Asia-Pacific as a region of surging growth, possibly well into the 21st century.

A notable part of this phenomenon was the rise of a new class of multinationals in these countries which helped to spearhead the process of growth and industrialization. One of the main formulas of success for the NICs has been a heavy reliance on a production for export strategy based on low cost competition to gain market success. NIC firms have been very capable in producing imitation of standardized mature items based on low labor cost in these countries.

Recently however, these firms have been facing radical changes in the business environment. Energy and material shortages coupled with increasingly intense competition in both their domestic and world markets mean that these countries can no longer rely on the old formula which has been so successful in the past. Also with their own rising standard of living, wages there are no longer competitive with those of other developing nations.

Thus, with the quickening pace of industrialization, a more dynamic marketing environment and competition from other developing countries, NIC firms are impelled to respond by adopting a more marketing oriented stance through designing effective marketing mix strategies. Specifically, these firms may have to abandon the low labor cost and production oriented formula and commence to develop more innovative product objectives and policies. They also may be impelled to move into higher technology products and industries

---

Source: Copyright 1982 *Columbia Journal of World Business* (Spring). Reprinted with permission.

[1] The term "NICs" highlights the special characteristics of a group of rapidly industrializing countries which sets them apart from the rest of the LDCs. See David A. Heenan and Warren J. Keegan, "The Rise of Third World Multinationals," *Harvard Business Review,* January-February, 1979, pp. 101–109.

and even begin to compete with advanced countries' multinationals in the world market place.

Objectives of the Study

This paper examines top management's motivations and strategies underlying product development, the organizational structure, process and functions designed for it and the results of these activities. The paper will also highlight the past and present product strategies in order to project the future product development scenario for NIC firms. Moreover, the intention is to identify and clarify the potential role NIC firms will play in the increasingly competitive and intense world market place. Since it is the declared policy of NICs like Taiwan and Singapore to move into higher technology markets, their potential role in these product areas would also be of interest in terms of the ever shifting cycles of dynamic comparative advantages.[2] Any light shed on this issue may help world businessmen to better understand the challenge and opportunities posed by these increasingly active NIC multinationals in the decades ahead.[3]

Methodology and Framework of Analysis

This article draws on the author's research and consulting with firms in Taiwan and Singapore, with data on South Korea and Hong Kong from secondary sources. Overall, we were able to take a closeup look at some of the product development strategies and practices of NIC firms and the underlying management motivations. The experiences and activities of these firms are still in the early stages of marketing development. Yet they form a collective picture which suggests that the imperatives of market dynamics are causing NIC firms to take a hard look at their market and product strategies. The marketing dynamics facing NIC firms may best be captured by an analytical framework outlined below.

A useful way of examining the nature of a company's product development process is to assess where the company stands along a continuum of product innovation.[4] Figure 1 shows the continuum of four major identifiable stages. Multiproduct as well as single product line companies could conceivably occupy several positions along the continuum at any one time. For instance, IBM and other major computer makers may be the innovators and market leaders for

---

[2] For a more detailed statement on the technology policies of Taiwan, see "New Opportunities for US-ROC Business Partnership," *The Economic News,* (Taiwan), June 4, 1979. For Singapore, see "Singapore: Trying for a Second Industrial Revolution," *Business Week,* May 25, 1981, p. 75.

[3] "Make Way for New Japans," *Fortune,* August 10, 1981, p. 176.

[4] William J. Abernathy and J. M. Utterback, "A Dynamic Model of Process and Product Innovations," *Omega,* Vol. 3, No. 6, 1975, p. 639.

FIGURE 1   The Product Innovation Continuum for NIC Firms

(1) Existing products (Imitator)	(2) Modified products (Modifier)	(3) Improved products (Improver)	(4) New products (Innovator)
Market follower			
		Barriers: R&D, marketing, finance, etc.	
		Market leader	
Firm's objectives • Short-run • Profit	Short run profit, Market presence	Market development Sales expansion Medium term profit	Market penetration Sales maximization Long-run profit
Brand policy • Major outside • brand (e.g., Sears, J.C. Penney)	Multiple outside brands	Outside and own brand	Own brands only

top of the line mainframe computer units, but may be content to be market followers for "me too" products such as minicomputers further down the product line. This is usually done as a conscious strategic move to preserve their overall market position. By maintaining a presence with a "me too" product at the lower end of the line, the mainframe makers hope to preempt potential competition from small computer makers who may aspire eventually to trade up. A company may also span the continuum because of diversification into industries of different technological level. A diversified conglomerate's portfolio of companies could then range across the spectrum, from companies with mature technologies to highly innovative ones.

NIC firms also occupy multiple positions along the innovation spectrum for other reasons. Instead of "trading down," many of them are "trading up." Most NIC manufacturing firms began life as market followers producing imitations of existing products.[5] However, with the impetus of industrialization and the dynamics of a more demanding market, these firms are striving to trade up the innovation spectrum through in-house development as well as through conglomeration and vertical integration.

---

[5] Louis T. Wells, Jr., "Foreign Investment from the Third World: The Experience of Chinese Firms From Hong Kong," *Columbia Journal of World Business*, Spring, 1978.

In the process of doing so, it may have to surmount barriers created by the formidable levels of financial, manufacturing, marketing and R&D resources required. Specifically, these firms may lack the necessary marketing experience and technological capability to be successfully innovative in the development of certain technology-intensive products. For these products, generally, the NIC firms may have to remain imitators at least for the present. However, for products specific to the local markets such as intermediate and lower technology items, NIC firms do exhibit a certain degree of product leadership.

Past Product Strategies

Leading industrial corporations in the NICs are usually multidivisional companies that market products ranging from consumer household appliances, to industrial items that include telecommunications equipment, machine tools, chemicals, and including even financial services. For instance, the Lucky and Samsung Groups of companies of Korea resemble Japanese trading conglomerates in their multifaceted activities ranging from consumer products, to heavy industrial equipment, banking and insurance, shipbuilding and construction. Likewise, some Taiwanese multinationals are diversified conglomerates with interests ranging across a wide spectrum of product lines.

NIC multinationals are attempting to model themselves on the successful examples of Japanese trading/manufacturing/banking conglomerates.

Most of the NIC firms' entry into international business followed the classic pattern of development and is closely linked to the results of their product strategies. In the early and late 1960s, they were the recipients of technological knowhow from the United States, Japan, and Europe through licensing agreements and technical assistance programs for a wide range of consumer products. Initially, the output from these ventures were "off-shore" production intended for exports back to the source countries. Thus, for example, US retail chains like J.C. Penney and Sears took advantage of the low labor costs and the willingness of the local suppliers to engage in product imitation for exports. Referring back to Figure 1, the major objective of many of the local NIC producers associated with the foreign multinationals was basically to reap short run profits from products using others' brand names. Thus, NIC exports were widely marketed in the United States and Europe under well known foreign brands. There was no desire then to establish their own brands, even though many of these products, ranging from clothing to calculators, were of superior quality.

Domestically, portions of the offshore products began to trickle into local markets and then later became entrenched enough in domestic markets to set off changes in consumption patterns in the NICs themselves.

Local firms began full scale manufacturing and marketing of imitations domestically, and later, after domestic success, began their exports to other markets independent of the original US and European multinationals Their own successful efforts at exports subsequently led NIC firms into foreign technical cooperation and the licensing of technical knowhow to companies in other countries, and eventually into direct investment in manufacturing subsidiaries. For instance, Taiwan's Tatung Company subsidiaries in Japan, Singapore and the United States primarily manufacture and assemble products such as household appliances and electronic items—products that have been domestic successes and whose initial technology originated in the United States and Japan. Since these products have gone "full circle," the original producers in NIC countries are now exporting and even investing in advanced markets which innovated and transferred the product technology in the first place. This is a classic illustration of the unfolding of the international product life cycle phenomenon.[6]

The marketplace abounds with many examples of products which have gone full circle, i.e., products whose exporting and investments now rest primarily with firms of NICs like Taiwan, Korea and Singapore. The surge of made-in-Taiwan or Korea or Singapore electronics, clothing, furniture and other consumer items in the US and European markets are cases in point. At this stage of the dynamic cycle of trade and investment, the NIC producers are already capable of manufacturing improved versions of the original imitated products. Thus, as the technological contents of NIC exports increased in such products as Hong Kong wristwatches, Taiwanese calculators and Korean automobiles, the tendency towards longer term market objectives also strengthened. As Figure 1 indicates, NIC firms in the improvement stage of the product continuum envision a longer term perspective, experiment with their own brands and commit resources for sales expansion and preliminary market development.

Besides licensing of manufacturing know how and the purchasing activities of the multinational retail chains, direct investment by US and other advanced countries also constitutes sources of product ideas. Direct investment by these multinationals spreads its effect on product development in two ways: (1) Competitive imitation; (2) Supplier and vendor development.

The experience of two Fortune 500 companies operating in Taiwan illustrates these processes. The subsidiary of one leading US chemical company there faces imitation by local firms of all its product lines in plastics, animal feed activities and agricultural chemicals with the possible exception of silicon waffles which are at present technologically beyond the capability of local firms. The other top US pharmaceutical company also has to contend with local imitation of its medical drugs, which are within easy technological reach of many of the local firms.

On the vendor side, local suppliers developed manufacturing expertise in providing semi-fabricated and processed items or even finished products to the US multinationals. Later, many of these firms developed new customers domes-

---

[6] Louis T. Wells Jr., "Test of the Product Life Cycle Model of International Trade," *Quarterly Journal of Economics*, February, 1969, pp. 152–62.

tically and abroad, and some even integrated forward . . . to become competitors of the multinationals who were their original customers.

Thus, the supplier-multinational company linkage and competitive imitation are additional springboards on which NIC firms initiated their product strategy. It was a time when, lacking any R&D capability of their own, they could only assimilate product ideas originated by the multinationals which were transferring and, recently, marketing these technologies abroad.[7]

Of late however, with the realization that an imitative strategy would be self defeating in the face of rapid industrialization and more intense worldwide competition, many NIC firms are now prompted to adopt more aggressive product strategies that are commensurate with present market realities.

Transition

The path taken by NIC multinationals toward more activist product strategies proceeds along the technological spectrum. NIC firms are constantly trading up technologically as they are caught up by and compete for evolving comparative advantages. For example, what Japan did to the United States and the other advanced countries in the way of product imitation and improvement, Hong Kong is now doing to Japan. Hong Kong watch manufacturers are taking Japanese made models and improving on them. Hong Kong in turn, is being driven out of the market for finished textile and apparel products by countries like China, Thailand and Macau. NICs are, therefore, actively caught up in the process of dynamically shifting comparative advantages.

Not content with merely adding low cost labor, NIC firms are now venturing into product modification strategies, albeit in light consumer product items like TV, calculators, pens and lighters. In the realm of heavy industrial products, Korean, Taiwan and Singapore firms are also gradually establishing footholds in competition with industrialized countries. Korean construction firms are active in worldwide infrastructure projects. Singapore shipbuilding firms, likewise, have a global reach in manufacturing and marketing. Singapore has, for instance, a 25 percent share of the global market for oil rigs.

With this change in market perspective, the NIC firms' objectives also changed in the direction of greater market and brand image development. The world markets are seeing more in-company brands for NIC products than ever before.

Present Product Strategies

Although an innovative product strategy is the ultimate goal, many NIC firms are constrained by inadequate resources and technological capability and are

---

[7] Peter Killing, "Technology Acquisition: License Agreement or Joint Venture," *Columbia Journal of World Business,* Fall, 1980, p. 38.

FIGURE 2   Selected Products of NIC Firms on the Innovation Continuum

Products	Continuum Position	Innovating source
Avionics	Imitator	US
Stereo hi-fi	Imitator	Japan
Television	Imitator/modifier	US, Japan, Europe
Refrigerator	Modifier	US, Japan
Washer	Modifier	Japan
Electric fan	Product leader/innovator	Domestic
Cooking appliance (electric cooker)	Product leader/innovator	Domestic
Calculators	Product leader/innovator	Domestic

therefore still confined to product imitation and in some instances have more advanced adaptive and modification R&D capability.

Thus, whether by design, circumstantial constraints, or past opportunities, NIC firms' product strategies reflect a pattern which spans the product innovation continuum, as shown in Figure 2. Thus, the specific product development strategies depend on the product's position along the innovation continuum. As Figure 2 shows, in consumer electronic products like stereo and television, NIC firms remain basically imitators of similar products from the advanced industrialized countries. But even here market dynamics are in active interplay. For example, some Taiwan and Korean firms have begun to market in the United States innovative television designs with better performing acoustic and visual systems.

Product Modification

Because of the realization that an imitative strategy has limited growth possibilities and in order to pursue more flexible product strategies that will enable them to adjust effectively to market changes, NIC firms are moving into selective product modification. Pursuing a product modification strategy would allow medium size NIC firms with limited resources to adapt their products to market needs without substantial and expensive investment in capital and R&D. For instance, for refrigerators, washers, and television, firms in Taiwan and Singapore have adapted the original foreign designs to the special characteristics of their domestic markets. They have also modified some of the product features of various electronic exports to the United States and Europe and to other LDCs.

Generally, the modification process would involve minor changes in the design and features of the product.[8] Design changes usually occur through scaling up or scaling down.

Scaling up basically involves adding quantitatively more features or qualitatively more complex or sophisticated features. Scaling down is the reverse, i.e., deleting features from the product or qualitatively simplifying some of the features. A scaling up strategy is used to adapt products to more sophisticated market needs. For instance, most NIC exports destined for the United States and Europe are rendered more sophisticated, or scaled up. The technically more superior buyers from the advanced markets are able to transmit the product specifications accurately and can transfer a degree of technological skill to the NIC company's design and engineering personnel.

Scaling down usually presents more problems because it is applied to less sophisticated markets where it is necessary to reduce the features or simplify the products. A reduction of features is more inexact in terms of consumer needs when compared to scaling up. Often the product may be scaled down too radically because of misinterpretation of the customer's specifications. Most NIC firms found that customers from less advanced markets may lack the technical competence to provide detailed or exact specifications to the design and engineering personnel. As a result, the delivered product may be different from what the customer had in mind.

Product Leadership

A modification strategy is essentially a market follower position. The drawbacks are obvious. The NIC firm would still be reacting to market conditions rather than anticipating evolving consumer needs. It is imperative that more innovative product strategies would be required for the firm's long term growth and viability through anticipating changing market needs, especially in view of the threats and opportunities inherent in the spiral of dynamic comparative advantages.

An innovative product strategy would require the creation of a product with better performance to serve existing needs or new products serving new needs. In this vein, many NIC firms have attempted to initiate the innovation process for products like electric fans and cookers. For products with a simpler technology such as these, NIC firms have been able to effect significant changes in the product's technology and thereby create a favorable change in the consumer's perception of the product's performance. The major stimulus for NIC firms' product leadership stems from the domestic market where such products as electric fans and cookers are important local products. Thus, domestic competition and heightened consumer awareness may have spurred innovative behavior

---

[8] John B. Stewart, "Functional Features in Product Strategy," *Harvard Business Review*, March-April, 1959, pp. 65–78.

regarding these products. In the case of one Taiwanese multinational, acknowledged leadership in these products is the main motivating force behind internationalizing the production and marketing of its electric fan abroad, including in the United States, where a manufacturing subsidiary has been established.[9]

In summary, it is observed that although NIC firms' products span the entire spectrum of the product innovation continuum, their forte remains a modification strategy in which their adaptive capability permits them to attune themselves to market conditions. The same general pattern of product modification appears to prevail for most NIC firms because modification is a technologically attainable way to be effectively consumer oriented without the necessity of committing huge capital and R&D resources.

The Process of Decision Making and Structure

In most firms, the product development process opens itself to decision inputs from a variety of sources ranging from marketing, production, design and engineering to purchasing and even customer's inputs. In the NIC firms observed, a situation of multiple influences also prevails. From the early stage of generation of product ideas to testing of the product prototypes, contributions to the development process emanate from various sources. The relative degree of the contribution from the various sources seems to depend on whether the firm's position is one of product leader, modifier or imitator. Figure 3 shows how the relative importance or decision inputs from different sources is related to the products' position on the innovation continuum during the idea generation and testing stages.

1. *Imitation.* As the chart shows, for a product such as stereo for which NIC producers are usually imitators, all sources contribute equally important inputs to product ideas and design, with the exception of marketing. The design and engineering personnel exert considerable influence in "trouble shooting" for a product technology that is relatively unfamiliar to the company personnel. Also, because of uncertain mastery of the technology, production personnel frequently contribute ideas about changes in product design, especially during the test run stages. The availability of components also confers on purchasing potential power in the decision process. Not surprisingly, customers and dealers, especially foreign ones, have a heavy influence in design changes. Ideas from trade customers are given considerable weight in order to avoid rejection of shipments not meeting their specifications.

---

[9] Wenlee Ting, "New Wave Multinationals—Case Study of a Growing Taiwanese Firm," *Marketing News*, October 17, 1980, p. 12.

FIGURE 3   Relative Importance of Decision Inputs During Idea Generation, Design and Testing of Selected NIC Products

Decision sources	Leader (fan, cooker)	Modifier (washer, refrigerator)	Imitator (stereo)
Marketing	H	M	L
Design/engineering	H	H	H
Production	L	H	H
Purchasing	L	L	H
Customers/dealers	L	M	H

Key: Relative importance of decision inputs
    H—High
    M—Moderate
    L—Low

Thus when a product technology has not yet been mastered by the NIC firm, decisional influences are equally distributed among the various parties. The resulting organizational structure is usually a loose and informal production-design-marketing interface mechanism. In some of the periodic meetings of this interface mechanism observed by the author, discussions were dominated by design and production scheduling problems with differences frequently remaining unresolved.

2. *Modification.* In the case of NIC firms producing washers and refrigerators, the product modification process involves adaptive R&D capability. As such, the locus of decision making is in the design and production departments. The technical nature of the modification process permits the two departments to exert a major influence in the development process, while other departments have a moderate to low influence. The customers retain moderate influence by contributing ideas which render the products more consumer oriented. The marketing department has only low to moderate influence and its role is confined to order processing and other facilitating functions.

The organizational unit established for the development of these products is somewhat more structured and formal than that for product imitation. Normally, for most of the NIC firms observed, a regularly functioning product development committee exists and the relative dominance of design and production in this committee ensures a fairly smooth decision followed by effective implementation.

3. *Product Leadership.* In the case of electric fans and cookers, where some NIC companies are recognized product leaders domestically and also abroad, there is a clear dominance in the generation of ideas and product testing stages by marketing and design. The marketing personnel in the NIC firms conducted relatively sophisticated market research such as questionnaire surveys, and focus group interviews in eliciting consumer input for the development process. Thus the more ambiguous and conflicting decision making process found in the development of imitative products like stereo and television is being replaced by a classically consumer oriented approach for products in which a company is a product leader.

The organizational mechanism established for the development process for these products is, in many cases, a smoothly functioning new product development unit. The decision process is characterized by discussion of substantive issues. Even the concern of production and purchasing is now directed to the more consumer oriented areas of quality control and servicing. Thus, overall, the product development process reflects the company's position as a product leader.

Conclusion and Implications

Firms in newly industrializing countries are beginning to enter into a more marketing oriented era. Although still pursuing a product imitation strategy in many cases, NIC firms are abandoning cheap labor items and are venturing into more innovative product strategies. As a result, NIC products have increasingly more technological content compared to their previous high labor content. Firms in Taiwan, South Korea, Singapore, and Hong Kong are replaying the early experience of Japan and are showing signs of progressing through the successive stages of becoming product leaders and innovators. Although the phenomenon is still in its infancy, the US and Western business in general may do well to heed these signs of vigorous competition from the potential "Japans" of the future. Already US, European, and Japanese multinationals are competing head on as well as cooperating with many firms from these emerging economic dynamos.

KEY DECISIONS IN INTERNATIONAL MARKETING: INTRODUCING NEW PRODUCTS ABROAD

William H. Davidson ◆ Richard Harrigan

ABSTRACT. This material is based upon research supported by the National Science Foundation under Grant Number PRA76-11108.

Any opinions, findings and conclusions or recommendations expressed in this publication are those of the authors and do not necessarily reflect the views of the National Science Foundation.

Marketing executives have found their domain expanding along two critical dimensions—the number of national markets in which they are active and the range of products which they manage.

The extensive penetration of foreign markets by U.S. companies is well documented. As one indication of the size of this trend, a large sample of U.S. companies showed more than sevenfold expansion in foreign manufacturing and sales subsidiaries between 1950 and 1976.[1]

New products have played an increasingly important role in the product lines of many companies. One survey of a broad sample of machinery firms showed the percentage of sales accounted for by new products (those less than four years old) virtually doubling between 1960 and 1970.[2] A similar survey in the consumer sector showed the percentage of sales attributed to new products more than doubling in the same period.[3]

The introduction of new products and expansion into foreign markets have been stimulated by managers' broadening perception of marketing opportunities. This paper will describe and analyze one aspect of the managerial response to these opportunities—the introduction of new products into foreign markets.

In introducing new products into foreign markets, there are several key decisions facing the international marketing manager. Which new products does the firm introduce overseas? In what markets? In what sequence? When should a product be introduced overseas? To address these questions, the experience of a sample of U.S.–based multinational firms was examined.

The Sample

A sample of 44 large U.S. firms was selected on the criterion of broad representation across product sectors. On the basis of extensive library research and

Source: Copyright 1977 *Columbia Journal of World Business* (Winter). Reprinted with permission.

[1] Curhan, J.P., W.H. Davidson and Rajan Suri, *Tracing The Multinationals: A Sourcebook on U.S.-Based Enterprises,* Cambridge, Mass., Ballinger, 1977.

[2] *Business Week,* May 13, 1973, 67.

[3] *Ibid.*

in-depth interviews with company executives, a list was developed of new products introduced by each company between 1945 and 1976. These products were then screened for commercial and technical significance. Only those with cumulative sales in excess of ten million dollars were included. In addition, knowledgeable persons were asked to categorize new products in terms of technical significance.

Each product was then traced from its initial introduction in the United States to all foreign markets in which the product had achieved sufficient sales volume to warrant the establishment of local manufacturing, assembly, packaging or distribution operations through a licensing arrangement or direct investment. This criterion serves as a proxy for sales volume by country, for which data are not available. It is an attempt to establish a threshold for significance of sales volume in foreign markets. The limitations of this approach, however, are such that it may omit genuine cases of significant export penetration of a foreign market.

The markets which are included under this format generally represent areas of major market penetration and activity. These are areas where a major investment has been made, and this is the critical marketing decision we are attempting to capture.

The Spread of U.S. Innovations

Industry There were 733 commercially significant new products introduced since 1945 by the 44 firms in our sample. Of these 733 new products, 532, or 71.5 percent, have also been produced for the local market in at least one foreign country.

A breakdown of these new products by industry is shown in Figure 1. Several important generalizations emerge. Although industries such as chemicals and machinery have introduced the largest number of new products, all industrial sectors have witnessed the introduction of significant new products.

The frequency of foreign introduction of new products varies significantly by industry. Office machines, computers and instrument innovations are introduced abroad in less than half the cases. Textiles, paper, and fabricated metal innovations are introduced abroad in 85 percent of the cases.

Part of the variance across industries is explained by the more recent introduction of new products in some industries relative to others. However, if this factor is controlled, significant differences in rate of foreign introduction remain.

These major differences in frequency of foreign introduction suggest an important avenue for research. Examination of industrial characteristics may explain these variances.

For example, some industries with high rates of foreign spread, notably paper, chemicals and fabricated metal, are distinguished by relatively low value

FIGURE 1   Number of U.S. Innovations and Frequency of Foreign
             Introduction by Industry, 1945–1976

SIC	Industry	Number of Innovations	Number Introduced Abroad	Percent Introduced Abroad
22	Textiles	18	16	88.8%
26	Paper	22	19	86.3%
281	Industrial chemicals	12	12	100.0%
282	Plastics and synthetics	81	62	76.5%
285–9	Other chemicals	64	52	81.2%
30	Tires and fabricated plastics	49	38	77.5%
32	Abrasives, ceramics, glass	44	34	77.3%
34	Fabricated metal	47	40	85.1%
352	Farm machinery	35	23	65.7%
353	Construction machinery	58	46	79.3%
355–56	Industrial machinery	57	40	70.2%
357	Office machines and computers	43	19	44.2%
365–9	Electronics	52	46	88.5%
37	Transportation	47	26	55.3%
38	Instruments and precision goods	42	19	45.2%
	Other and miscellaneous	62	40	64.5%
TOTAL		733	532	71.5%

per weight or volume ratios. In such industries, local production may be required for markets of substantial volume. Subsequent research will develop additional hypotheses relating industry characteristics to frequency of foreign introduction.

Recipient Country Another important set of research issues focuses on the countries in which new products are introduced. Several hypotheses regarding corporate behavior in entering foreign markets can be addressed.

One hypothesis to be examined is that first proposed by Linder.[4] He held

---

[4] Linder, S.B., *An Essay on Trade and Transformation*, New York, John Wiley, 1961.

FIGURE 2   Number of First Foreign Introductions by Country Category, 1945–1976

Country Category	Number of first Foreign Introductions*	Percentage of Total Sample
English-speaking	301	46.4%
Other developed	241	37.1%
Developing	107	16.5%

* Of the 532 innovations introduced in a foreign market, 63 were introduced in more than one market simultaneously, resulting in a total number of first foreign introductions in excess of the total number of innovations.

that companies tend to market their goods to countries of similar cultures and economic conditions before venturing into less similar territories.

We examined this hypothesis by analyzing where innovations were initially marketed overseas. Figure 2 shows that innovations are very frequently first introduced in markets which are culturally similar to the United States. The English-speaking markets of Great Britain, Canada and Australia accounted for almost half of the initial introductions of U.S. innovations in foreign markets.

There are a number of country-market characteristics which can influence the decision to introduce a product abroad. Numerous researchers have identified the proximity, size and rate of growth of a market as important variables.[5] Income levels have also been isolated as an important factor.[6] These effects and others are implicit in the data below which reflect decisions made by marketing managers to establish a product in a foreign market. Isolation of the effect of individual factors is a principal research goal.

There is a distinct difference between the foreign markets where new products are first introduced and the markets they eventually reach, as Figure 3 shows. During the first post-war decade, the United Kingdom and Canada accounted for 40 percent of all post-war U.S. product innovations introduced abroad. When the rest of Europe, Japan, and Australia are added to the list, the proportion rises to 76.2 percent. The second post-war decade witnessed a dramatic increase in the absolute number of products introduced in foreign markets. The number of new product introductions rises from 160 in the

---

[5] Knickerbocker, F. T., *Oligopolistic Reaction and Multinational Enterprise*, Boston, Mass., Division of Research, Harvard Business School, 1973.
Stobaugh, R. B., "How to Analyze Foreign Investment Climates," *Harvard Business Review*, Vol. 47, No. 5, (September-October 1969), 100–108.

[6] Wells, L. T., Jr. (ed.), *The Product Life Cycle and International Trade*, Boston, Mass., Division of Research, Harvard Business School, 1972.

FIGURE 3   Foreign Introductions of U.S. Innovations by Period and Country

Country	Period 1945–55	Per-cent*	Period 1956–65	Per-cent*	Net change from previous period	Period 1966–75	Per-cent*	Net change from previous period
	42	26.2	111	14.4	164.0	74	6.5	-33.0
United Kingdom	22	13.8	111	14.4	404.0	112	9.9	0.9
France	16	10.0	72	9.4	350.0	83	7.3	15.2
West Germany	11	6.9	38	4.9	245.0	81	7.1	113.2
Italy	2	1.2	43	5.6	2,050.0	55	4.8	28.1
Belgium	7	4.4	16	2.0	128.0	45	3.9	181.1
Netherlands	0	0.0	35	4.5	—	35	3.1	0.0
Sweden	0	0.0	6	0.8	—	16	1.4	166.6
Other Europe	6	3.8	28	3.6	367.0	57	5.0	103.6
Japan	5	3.1	79	10.2	1,480.0	103	9.0	30.4
Australia	11	6.9	54	7.0	391.0	92	8.1	70.4
South Africa	6	3.7	18	2.3	200.0	44	3.9	144.4
Eastern Bloc	0	0.0	0	0.0	0.0	13	1.1	—
Mexico	10	6.2	47	6.1	370.0	67	5.9	42.6
Brazil	11	6.9	29	3.7	163.0	80	7.0	175.9
Argentina	5	3.1	28	3.6	460.0	34	3.0	21.4
Colombia	0	0.0	14	1.8	—	19	1.7	35.7
Other Latin America	3	1.9	8	1.0	167.0	38	3.3	375.0
Taiwan	1	0.6	1	0.1	0.0	21	1.8	—
Hong Kong	0	0.0	1	0.1	—	3	.3	200.0
Thailand	0	0.0	1	0.1	—	4	.4	300.0
Other Asia	0	0.0	8	1.0	—	38	3.3	375.0
Africa	0	0.0	1	0.1	—	4	.4	
Middle East	0	0.0	2	0.2	—	12	1.1	500.0
India	2	1.2	19	2.5	850.0	7	.6	−63.1
TOTAL	160		770		381.0%	1,137		148.0%

* Country's percentage of total new product introductions for period.

FIGURE 4   Frequency of First Foreign Introduction Within 1 and 5 Years of U.S. Introduction: By Period of U.S. Innovation

Period of U.S. Innovation	Number of Innovations	Percent introduced in foreign markets:	
		Within 1 year of U.S. Introduction	Within 5 years of U.S. Introduction
1945–1950	161	5.6%	22.0%
1951–1955	115	2.6%	29.6%
1956–1960	134	10.4%	36.6%
1961–1965	133	24.1%	55.6%
1966–1970	115	37.4%	60.1%
1971–1975	75	38.7%	64.0%

1945–1955 period to 770 in the 1955–1965 period. The number then increases to 1137 new product introductions in the 1965–1975 period.

There are also changes in the distribution of new product introductions in world markets. The combined share of Canada and Great Britain declines from 40 percent in 1945–1955 to 28.8 percent in 1955–1965 and 16.4 percent in 1965–1975. The percent of new product introductions in other developed countries increases from 40 percent in 1945–1955 to 50.3 percent in 1955–1965, and then to 53.6 percent in 1965–1975. The developing countries' share of these new product introductions has also risen from 19.9 percent in the first decade and 20.3 percent in the second decade, and 28.8 percent in 1965–1975.

There is the suggestion of a hierarchical roll-over in these data. Figure 3 suggests an initial focus of marketing managers on the English speaking markets, followed by other developed industrial markets and finally the less developed countries as suggested by Vernon.[7] Examination of this proposition represents a major avenue for research.

"Timing" Another key question facing the international marketing manager is the timing of new product introduction overseas. Figure 4 summarizes the length of time that has elapsed between the introduction of a product in the United States and initial production overseas. This table shows a dramatic trend in the length of time from U.S. introduction to first foreign introduction.

---

[7] Vernon, Raymond, *Storm Over the Multinationals,* Cambridge, Mass., Harvard University Press, 1977.

Multinational managers are marketing new products in foreign markets more rapidly than ever before. Note that the percentage of innovations introduced in a foreign market within one year of U.S. introduction rises from 5.6 percent of all innovations introduced between 1945–1950 to 38.7 percent of those innovations introduced between 1971–1975. This dramatic trend indicates the increasing responsiveness of marketing managers to foreign market opportunities.

One aspect of Figure 4 deserves special mention. This table includes foreign introductions both by independent licensees of the innovator and by its foreign affiliates and subsidiaries. By breaking out these categories, we can examine the use of licensing versus direct investment as a means of introducing a new product in a foreign market. Figure 5 distinguishes between these two methods of initially introducing a new product abroad. Note that for innovations introduced in the United States between 1945–50, licensing was used at roughly the same rate as direct investment in initially introducing new products abroad. The use of direct investment relative to independent licensing expands dramatically in subsequent periods, although this trend peaks by the 1970's.

The data in Figures 4 and 5 emphasize two important trends in international marketing. New products are being introduced in foreign markets at an increasing pace, and they are being introduced by foreign affiliates of the domestic innovator to an increasing extent. Marketing managers are becoming more aware of foreign market opportunities, and they are becoming increasingly comfortable in foreign markets.

How is it that multinational corporations have developed the ability to monitor foreign markets, and to exploit the potentials of these markets so quickly and adroitly?

Part of the answer may lie in the fact that U.S. firms have acquired substantial knowledge of foreign markets through the operations of their foreign subsidiaries. With the existence of a subsidiary in a foreign market comes a lower and more certain cost of new product introduction. The presence of a

FIGURE 5   Percentage of First Foreign Introductions by Method of Introduction

Method of Introduction	Percent of Total First Foreign Introductions by Period of U.S. Innovation					
	1945–50	1951–55	1956–60	1961–65	1966–70	1971–75
By affiliates or subsidiaries	53.6%	79.4%	85.5%	88.0%	86.5%	79.2%
By independent licensees	46.4%	20.6%	14.5%	12.0%	13.5%	20.8%
	100.0%	100.0%	100.0%	100.0%	100.0%	100.0%

learning curve and scale effect complements the additional information available to the firm and may make the introduction of new products in foreign markets more attractive to firms with foreign subsidiaries. This suggests a different type of behavior towards foreign marketing by firms which are already established in foreign markets.

Part of the answer may also be a function of increasing strategic emphasis on international marketing. This may be best reflected in the evolving organizational structure of the firm.

Evolution of the International Marketing Function

An American firm which has successfully introduced a new product in the U.S. market can react in several ways to foreign market opportunities. The firm which has not been extensively involved in foreign markets is likely to respond quite differently from one with substantial previous experience in foreign marketing. A firm's approach to international marketing typically passes through several evolutionary stages.

Early Stage Companies in the first stage rarely engage in the active pursuit of foreign markets for their new products. Their initial involvement in foreign markets arises through unsolicited export orders or requests by local customers for foreign shipment. As such requests are repeated, the company may secure formal distribution arrangements in these foreign markets.[8]

As export business grows, the typical firm creates a slot within the marketing organization for an export manager. Now a segment of the marketing organization has a vested interest in continuing and expanding foreign markets. As export volume increases, distribution and sales arrangements for the product are developed.[9]

The firm may establish sales and service offices for foreign markets. If volume warrants, the firm might enter a licensing arrangement with a foreign producer, or it may invest directly in its own foreign assembly or production facilities. This process has been explored by Vernon in the product lifecycle model.[10] According to Vernon's model, the timing of this process depends primarily on the size and rate of growth in export markets and the threat from actual or potential local competition in foreign markets.

Under this framework an innovating firm would tend to serve foreign markets with exports until local competition forces the firm to establish facilities

---

[8] Suzman, C. L., "The Changing Export Activities of U. S. Firms With Foreign Manufacturing Affiliates," unpublished D.B.A. thesis, Harvard Business School, 1969.

[9] Vernon, Raymond, *Sovereignty at Bay*, New York, Basic Books, 1971.

[10] Vernon, Raymond, "International Investment and International Trade in the Product Life Cycle," *Quarterly Journal of Economics*, Vol. 80, No. 2, (May, 1966), 190–207.

in its principal foreign markets. There are several reasons for a firm's reluctance to produce in a foreign market until forced to do so. The establishment of foreign facilities duplicates overhead, reduces scale benefits in manufacturing, and increases communication and information requirements. The firm may also be averse to the risks associated with operation in an unfamiliar, uncertain foreign environment.

Intermediate Stage As the firm becomes more involved in international markets, its organization will probably undergo changes. The international marketing function may be centralized in an international division, which administers U.S. exports, corporate offices and facilities in foreign countries, and distribution and licensing arrangements. The development of the organization and its presence in foreign markets will result in a different pattern of marketing new products abroad.

When an innovation is introduced in the United States, there is now an organizational unit whose sole interest in the new product is its potential in foreign markets. The international division will probably have second priority in overall corporate marketing strategy for the product, but the international managers will be prepared to promote the new product in foreign markets. The development of foreign markets will be likely to occur at a more rapid rate.

As foreign operations assume a greater role in overall corporate activities, the focus of corporate policy will shift to global strategies for the company. Once the firm begins to see itself as a global corporation, and a global policy is formulated, the organization of the firm will evolve into a global structure.

The most common global structure is the worldwide product division organization. This organization makes managers of a product line responsive to all world markets. An innovation introduced in the United States will be marketed by the division globally.

The speed with which the division introduces the product abroad may depend on its sales level abroad prior to the innovation. If the division has extensive foreign production, distribution and marketing operations, it may be more aggressive in introducing the product abroad. For narrow product line firms, this scenario also holds, although organization is likely to be on a geographic or functional basis.

Advanced Stage For firms with multiple product lines and activity in many markets, the international marketing problem becomes more complex. If the firm has ten product groups, and is active in twenty foreign markets, there may be up to two hundred alternative new product-market opportunities to pursue. How can the firm organize to effectively assess these opportunities?

One company with an interesting approach to this problem is the 3M Company. It has nine major product divisions which operate on a global basis. These divisions are responsible for the introduction of new products into foreign markets.

The divisions provide new products and support services to 3M's subsidiaries in 48 countries. Each division is represented by a marketing executive in each of the 48 countries. These executives monitor local markets and assess opportunities for the division's products. Their assessments are communicated to divisional headquarters where a central staff evaluates the set of divisional opportunities across all markets.

The decision to introduce a new product in a foreign market is not made solely at the divisional level. In each subsidiary, top management evaluates opportunities for new business across all product lines and determines priorities. The subsidiary managers then consult with the product divisions to coordinate the introduction of new products. This process results in a balancing of divisional priorities with the priorities of area managers to promote an efficient allocation of company resources.

The approach used by 3M represents a sophisticated means of monitoring product-market opportunities and selecting those with greatest relative merit. The company's close ties to foreign markets through its subsidiaries result in a global marketing strategy which maximizes 3M's return on its investment in new product research and development. The marketing strategy for a new product is global, but it is also based on recognition of the opportunity costs associated with a given product line or with subsidiary resources. Global marketing opportunities are assessed at an early stage in a product's development, and aggressive action is taken to pursue new product-market combinations which are perceived to have high potential.

Organizing For International Markets

Does organizational structure imply a different ability to respond to foreign market opportunities? Although there are many other variables which affect this ability, Figure 6 suggests a general trend toward faster response for firms in certain organizational modes. The results of this sample are by no means conclusive, but do reveal important tendencies.

The exhibit indicates that firms with international divisions introduce new products abroad more quickly than similar firms without international divisions. In the case of functionally organized firms, 40 percent of the innovations from firms with international divisions went abroad in two years or less. Contrast this with 6 percent of innovations that went abroad in functionally organized firms without an international division. Analogous figures for firms organized along product lines are 33 percent for firms with international divisions and only 18 percent for those firms having no international division. When globally integrated organizations are considered, about 80 percent of all products introduced in such organizations go abroad in two years or less, and every innovation in our sample was introduced abroad in five years or less. This exhibit reveals the effect of changes in corporate strategy as much as changes in formal structure.

FIGURE 6   Years to First Foreign Introduction by Organizational Stage of Innovator

Organizational stage at the time of innovation*	Total number of innovations	Years to first foreign introduction					
		0	1	2	3–5	6–10	More than 10
Domestic function divisions	104	4	6	5	11	27	51
a. Without international division	79	1	3	1	7	21	46
b. With international division	25	3	3	4	4	6	5
Domestic product divisions	242	21	18	27	62	66	48
a. Without international division	95	5	3	9	26	27	25
b. With international division	147	16	15	18	36	39	23
Global product division	18	6	6	4	2	0	0
Global area divisions	6	2	1	1	2	0	0
Global matrix	19	5	7	2	5	0	0

* The sample used in this Table is limited to those parent firms for which historical data exist on successive organizational stages and years of organizational transition. Innovations are tabulated according to the organizational stage of the firm at the time the innovation was introduced in the United States. For definition of organizational stages, see Stopford, J.M. and Wells, L.T., Jr., *Managing the Multinational Enterprise: Organization of the Firm and Ownership of the Subsidiaries* (New York: Basic Books, 1972).

The Future

The 3M model depicts how a company can effectively market new products on a global scale. The next stage of corporate evolution may focus on the product development process. Currently, most innovations by U.S. firms appear to be keyed to the domestic market.[11] Although products are frequently adapted to local market conditions, little significant product innovation is done with foreign markets in mind. The distinguishing feature of the next stage may be coordinated interaction between the firm's global scanning function and its research and development function. The result of such interaction would be innovational activity on a global basis. New products would be developed primarily to serve foreign markets. There is some evidence that this type of capability has been developed by Japanese trading firms.[12] Global innovation

---

[11] Vernon, Raymond, *Storm Over the Multinationals. op. cit.*

[12] Vernon, Raymond and L. T. Wells, Jr., *Manager in the International Economy,* Englewood Cliffs, N.J., Prentice-Hall, 1976.

efforts may also appear in firms with extensive foreign R & D facilities such as IBM. Here the marketing function may be further complicated by multiple intra-system sources of new products.

Management Implications

Many authors have suggested that the principal success factor for a business is the initial selection of its products and markets.[13] For the international marketer—who is facing a geometric expansion in product-market possibilities—this decision is critical. How can the marketing manager assess these opportunities in order to maximize chances of success?

The first concern of the manager must be market awareness. An effective system for monitoring foreign markets is necessary. This system should provide managers with information on both consumer-related variables and key environmental variables for individual markets. A global scanning capability is the goal.

The firm's ability to achieve this goal is crucially affected by its organizational structure. Key issues are—how are different product-market opportunities currently assessed and ranked in the organization? Who performs this function? How are interdivisional priorities assigned? Is there a formal decision-making process? Do the appropriate organizational units exist to undertake the information-gathering, evaluation and decision-making? Formalization of these processes may result in better performance.

Research Issues

This article raises several important research issues. What characteristics of firms, products, markets and industries influence the introduction of new products in foreign markets? Several hypotheses were stated about each broad set of variables. Much additional work remains.

In particular, there is need to investigate how the presence of an existing operation in a foreign market affects the decisions to introduce new products in that market.

What factors influence the choice of licensing versus investment as a means of introducing new products? Investment can also be broken into categories of wholly-owned operation, majority-owned, co-owned, and minority-owned joint ventures.

Additional research is also needed on how the company characteristics of size, product diversity, and leader-follower orientation affect new product introduction decisions. The effect of product characteristics such as sector (consumer, intermediate, industrial), industry and perceived advantage (factor-saving, convenience, novelty) must also be explored.

---

[13] Kotler, Philip, *Marketing Management: Analysis, Planning and Control,* Englewood Cliffs, N.J., Prentice-Hall, 1972.

READING 19 **EFFECTS OF URBANIZATION ON MULTINATIONAL PRODUCT PLANNING: MARKETS IN LESSER-DEVELOPED COUNTRIES**

John S. Hill ◆ Richard R. Still

ABSTRACT. Differences in the relative urbanization of target markets in lesser-developed countries influence the product strategies used by multinational corporations. Products targeted to urban markets in lesser-developed countries need only minimal changes from those marketed in developed countries. Products targeted for both semi-urban and urban markets require more changes, and those targeted for national markets undergo further adaptions to accommodate the requirements of culturally-diverse rural populations.

Formulation of product strategies for markets in lesser-developed countries (LDCs) is influenced importantly by the relative urbanization of target markets.[1] At one extreme, heavily urbanized markets in LDCs contain sizable pockets of high-income consumers as sophisticated as their counterparts in developed countries. At the other extreme rural areas in LDCs contain substantial populations with largely provincial tastes, some groups living entirely outside the monetarized sector.

Industrialization in LDCs occurs around major cities like Sao Paulo and Rio de Janeiro in Brazil and Buenos Aires in Argentina. Multinational corporations (MNCs) locate there to take advantage of transportation and communications amenities, and to be near economically-significant consumers holding jobs in government and commerce. The presence of industry creates demand for labor, and some rural inhabitants migrate to cities to find employment. Meanwhile, lifestyles of the remaining rural inhabitants are barely touched, and the increasing urbanization leads to numerous cultural and economic gaps between cities, on one hand, and villages or rural areas, on the other hand.[2] This industrialization process produces consumers with widely varying exposures to and experience of modern lifestyles in LDCs.

This consumer diversity becomes perplexing when MNCs transfer home-country products from modern economies like the United States/United Kingdom and try to modify them to fit LDC market needs. Modern products usually fit right into the lifestyles of urban consumers with high incomes. Unfortunately, 80 percent of most LDC populations live outside of cities in semi-urban areas

[1] Richard D. Robinson, *International Business Management,* (Hinsdale, IL, The Dryden Press, 1978), p. 55 and Vern Terpstra, *International Marketing,* (Hinsdale, IL, The Dryden Press, 1978), pp. 77–79.

[2] Terpstra, p. 77.

(where migrant populations reside)[3] and in rural areas. Rural inhabitants have meager incomes—often from sales of local handicrafts, surplus crops or through labor on farms—and have few resources to purchase products. Rural migrants working around cities earn consistent wages and become frequent users of goods and services. Perceptive managers know that as they expand product distribution outside cities, they deal with increasingly less experienced and less sophisticated consumers. The question is, do marketing strategies differ when products are rolled out over areas with lesser degrees of urbanization and to consumers with less purchasing experience and sophistication?

The purpose of the research reported here was to determine if product adaption strategies of MNCs differ with the degree of urbanization present in LDC target markets.

Details of Study

Information was obtained on strategies used in LDC markets by 61 subsidiaries of 19 cooperating MNCs. Collectively, these subsidiaries operated in 22 LDCs. Product adaption strategies for 173 consumer nondurables were studied. The respondents were international marketing vice presidents, marketing managers, and executives in international divisions.

Each respondent selected three consumer nondurables transferred from home markets (either the United States or United Kingdom) to LDC markets. Data were provided on the type of target market in the LDC: national (urban/semi-urban/rural) market, urban/semi-urban market, or urban market. Of 174 products reported, 74 were marketed nationally, 78 in urban/semi-urban markets, 21 in urban markets, and one exclusively in a rural market. In each case, respondents reported on adaptions made to each of nine individual product components:

- ◆ Brand name.
- ◆ Packaging protection.
- ◆ Packaging aesthetics.
- ◆ Measurement units.
- ◆ Product features.
- ◆ Usage instructions.
- ◆ Labeling.

---

[3] The term "semi-urban" consumers refer to inhabitants living 10–15 miles outside of major urban areas. Usually they are migrants from rural communities that are employed in unskilled or semi-skilled capacities in industrializing cities. The term was first used by Y. S. Verma "Marketing in Rural India" *Management International Review* (1980) Vol. 20, No. 4, pp. 47–52.

TABLE **1**   Total Number of Adaptions Per Product

Target Market	0	1	2	3	4	5	6	7	8	9	Total
National Market (Urban/semi-urban/rural Market)	2	7	6	3	10	16	13	9	3	5	74
Urban/semi-urban Market	13	14	8	0	5	3	22	13	0	0	78
Urban Market	0	6	1	6	2	2	4	0	0	0	21
TOTALS	15	27	15	9	17	21	39	22	3	5	173

◆ Constituents.

◆ Sizing.

Extent of Product Adaption by Degree of Urbanization

To determine the relationship of product-component adaptions and the relative urbanization of target markets, the cross-tabulation in Table 1 was made. A contingency table test revealed that adaption practices varied significantly (at the 0.001 level) among target markets. In order to bring these differences into sharper focus, the mean number of product adaptions for each target-market type was computed (see Table 2). An F-ratio test indicated significant differences among the means. Pairwise comparisons by the Scheffe method showed that the mean number of adaptions per product were significantly different (at the 0.001 level) for urban-targeted products and nationally-marketed products, and (at the 0.05 level) for urban/semi-urban targeted products and nationally-

TABLE **2**   Mean Number of Product Adaptions in Each Market Type

Market Type	Mean Number Adaptions/Product	Sample Size
National (Urban/semi-urban/rural)	4.83	74
Urban/semi-urban	3.69	78
Urban	3.23	21
TOTALS	4.12	173

marketed products. This means that as modern products are distributed over less urbanized markets to less experienced consumers, more adaptions are needed. This is especially true when products are rolled out beyond semi-urban into rural areas, where significantly more adaptions are needed to ensure product acceptability in the less-advanced parts of LDCs.

Nationally-Marketed Products Versus Products Targeted for Urban/Semi-urban, or Urban Markets

Comparing nationally-marketed and urban/semi-urban–marketed products emphasizes how urbanization affects product-adaption strategies. Products sold only in LDC urban and semi-urban markets require significantly fewer adaptions than nationally-marketed products. One reason is that the nationally-marketed product must appeal not only to urban sophisticates, at one extreme, but to culturally-diverse rural residents, at the opposite extreme. If a consumer nondurable lacks near-universal appeal in an LDC, time and effort are wasted trying to market it nationally. Rural populations in LDCs are extremely provincial and have traditional lifestyles, often living in small self-contained communities which preserve cultural identities and idiosyncracies. Nationally-marketed products in LDCs must be congruent with both advanced and traditional lifestyles. But because rural peoples know little about modern lifestyles while most urban/semi-urban dwellers have kinship ties and ancestral roots in traditional societies, marketers can give products rural orientations without alienating consumers in urbanized areas.

Marketers targeting their products for urban/semi-urban markets are appealing to consumers who have been or are being acculturalized out of traditional and into modern lifestyles.[4] The urbanization process brings together culturally-diverse consumers. Continuous exposures of these groups to modern production methods, mass media and consumption-oriented lifestyles inculcate new consumption standards allowing acceptance of consumer products resembling those sold in the developed world.

Although LDC urban and semi-urban consumers live and work in areas with urban amenities, the two groups share fewer similarities than in the developed world. The great bulk of peoples living on the outskirts of cities are migrants or migrants' descendants who left traditional rural lifestyles to become part of industrializing society. Because of lingering provincial manners and lack of

---

[4] "Acculturation is . . . what happens when individuals and groups from different cultures come into first-hand contact and modifications in the original cultural patterns of either or both occur." See Thomas N. Gladwin, "Technology and Material Culture," in Vern Terpstra (Ed.) *The Cultural Environment of International Business* (Cincinnati, Ohio: South-Western Publishing Co., 1978), pp. 200–01. In this case, the influence of traditional ways erodes, and modern lifestyles are substituted. Programmed efficiency of factories replaces the leisurely pace of village production. Economic rewards are based on personal efforts. Occupational and social mobility increases, and so on. For further details on the cultural effects of urbanization, see John S. Hill and Richard R. Still, "Cultural Effects of Technology Transfer by Multinational Corporations on Lesser-Developed Countries," *Columbia Journal of World Business,* Vol. 15 (Summer 1980), pp. 40–51.

training, most migrants in semi-urban areas accept unskilled jobs at low pay or else join the hordes of unemployed, barely subsisting and living in shanty towns or on the streets.[5] But some migrants or their offspring eventually earn above-subsistence incomes and, for these, opportunities open up to gain more experience and sophistication in consumption. Migrant tastes, therefore, are a mixture of the new and the old. Frequent exposure to urban and modern lifestyles provides semi-urban consumers with reference points to guide consumption aspirations.

The difference in product-adaption strategies between target markets, as indicated earlier, is most significant between products distributed exclusively in urban markets and those marketed nationally. MNCs concentrating on LDC urban markets need to make few changes in their products except, of course, for mandatory adaptions stipulated by law. Upper income and upper middle income classes in LDC urban areas are predominantly prosperous LDC nationals and expatriates. Other LDC urban middle income groups are made up of white collar and skilled workers, small business owners and in some cases, as in Brazil and Peru, recent arrivals from Europe and Asia. Numerous LDC urban areas, too, are tourist centers frequented by large numbers of foreign visitors. Mexico City, Sao Paulo, and Buenos Aires are representative of large cities in LDCs where all or most of the modern conveniences—and consumer products—common to urbanized areas of developed countries are available.

The fact that significant differences in the mean number of adaptions for urban- and urban/semi-urban–targeted products are lacking reflects the strength of the "demonstration effect" in LDCs. The power of mass communications media and continual exposure to modern lifestyles causes semi-urban migrants in LDCs to work toward emulating their urban compatriots. This is evident in the disinterest LDC migrants show in products obviously dissimilar to those bought by the urban *beau monde*. In adapting a product too closely to the rural traditions of semi-urban migrants, a marketer may "over-localize" it, causing its rejection by intended buyers as being inferior.[6]

There are two implications for marketing management. The first is that modern consumer products marketed in LDCs should be first introduced in urbanized areas. Then, they should be rolled out regionally and their suitability for the rural markets reappraised when coverage expands beyond LDC semi-

---

[5] The sprawling semi-urban ghetto-like areas around Bogota (Colombia), Djakarta (Indonesia), and Tehran (Iran) are good examples. Such ghettos are often crime-ridden and present national governments with numerous other problems. Recently, the Indonesian government has been stepping up its efforts to relocate people from the suburban slums surrounding Djakarta and other cities to remote locations in low-density outlying islands. Families receive free air transport to the new locations, are granted tracts of free land, and receive assistance in erecting dwellings and clearing the land.

[6] Bantus in South Africa rejected products that were too locally-oriented, but trusted western brands, presumably because they had been on the market longer. See Hans B. Thorelli, "South Africa: Its Multi-Cultural Marketing System," *Journal of Marketing,* Vol. 32 (1968), pp. 40–48.

urban markets. The second implication is that products launched nationally in an LDC without the needed adaptions are headed for rejection in all or part of the market and at best can achieve limited marketing success.

Market Adaption Profiles and Comparisons

To determine the relative sensitivity to change of each of the nine product components by type of target market, individual market-adaption profiles were examined. Profiles were constructed from data contained in Table 3. Profiles for the different target markets were then contrasted.

National Versus Urban/Semi-urban Targeted Products Adaption profiles for products targeted for national markets and for urban/semi-urban markets are contrasted in Figure 1.

FIGURE 1   Contrast of Adaption Profiles: Products Marketed Nationally Versus Products Targeted to Urban/Semi-urban Markets

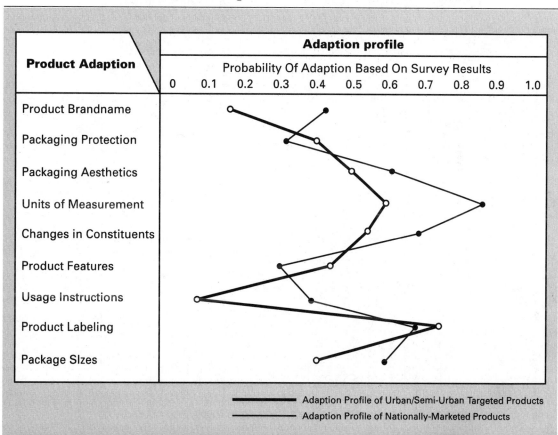

TABLE 3 Adaptions Made in Product Components by Type of Target Market

A = Adapted   N = Nonadapted

Target market	Product Brand Name		Packaging Protection		Packaging Aesthetics		Measurement Units		Product Constituents		Product Features		Usage Instructions		Labeling		Size Package	
	A	N	A	N	A	N	A	N	A	N	A	N	A	N	A	N	A	N
National (Urban/semi-urban/rural)	31	42	23	50	44	26	65	9	51	23	21	52	26	44	48	22	43	30
Probability of adaption/nonadaption	0.43	0.57	0.32	0.68	0.63	0.37	0.88	0.12	0.69	0.31	0.29	0.71	0.37	0.63	0.69	0.31	0.59	0.41
Urban/semi-urban	11	64	32	46	39	39	46	32	40	35	33	41	2	51	42	10	30	44
Probability of adaption/nonadaption	0.15	0.85	0.41	0.59	0.50	0.50	0.59	0.41	0.53	0.47	0.45	0.55	0.04	0.96	0.81	0.19	0.41	0.59
Urban	9	12	4	17	9	12	11	10	8	13	1	20	3	18	10	11	16	5
Probability of adaption/nonadaption	0.43	0.57	0.19	0.81	0.43	0.57	0.52	0.48	0.38	0.62	0.05	0.95	0.14	0.86	0.48	0.52	0.76	0.24
Totals	51	118	59	113	92	77	122	51	99	71	55	113	31	113	100	43	89	79
Probability of adaption/nonadaption	0.31	0.69	0.35	0.65	0.54	0.46	0.70	0.30	0.58	0.42	0.33	0.67	0.22	0.78	0.69	0.31	0.53	0.47
Contingency Table Test for differences among target markets	Significant at 0.001 level		Not Significant		Not Significant		Significant at 0.001 level		Significant at 0.05 level		Significant at 0.001 level		Significant at 0.001 level		Significant at 0.05 level		Significant at 0.05 level	

The statistically-significant difference in the number of changes made to nationally-targeted products and those marketed in urban/semi-urban markets suggests that highly-standardized (i.e., "international") products are best targeted for LDC large city markets. Adaptions of six of the nine components are less likely when products are targeted for urban/semi-urban markets than when products are marketed nationally. Regular exposure to modern lifestyles and communications media sharpens the awareness of migrant consumers to imported brand names and lessens the need for change in usage instructions.[7]

Furthermore, when products are sold only in urban and semi-urban markets and not in rural areas, there is no need to adapt in order to conform to rural aesthetic tastes, provincial weights and measures, and locally-favored constituents. These three product components—packaging aesthetics, measurement units, and product constituents—are all adapted with less frequency for urban/suburban markets than for nationally-marketed products.[8]

Similarly, because urban/semi-urban consumers possess more purchasing power than rural consumers, pack sizes of urban/semi-urban-targeted products are apt to be those sold in home country markets. The smaller size packs used for nationally-marketed products reflect the lower purchasing power of rural consumers.

Urban/Semi-urban Versus Urban-Targeted Products Figure 2 shows the contrast of urban with urban/semi-urban-targeted products. Although, as brought out earlier, substantial differences exist between LDC urban and semi-urban consumers, no statistically-significant differences are present in the contrast of product-adaption profiles. While six of the nine product components are adapted less frequently for urban-targeted products than for urban/semi-urban-targeted products, only in the cases of packaging protection, product features, and labeling are the differences large.[9]

The increase in packaging-protection adaptions made for products marketed outside of urban areas suggests that LDC semi-urban areas have inferior storage conditions, and more primitive distribution and handling facilities. Extra packaging protection is necessary to prevent breakage and product spoilage, to give longer shelf life, and to survive the machinations of inexperienced retailers. Urbanization stimulates development of improved distribution systems,

---

[7] Brand name and usage instruction have less probability of adaption in urban/suburban markets (0.15 and 0.04) than in total market situations (0.43 and 0.37).

[8] Packaging aesthetics, measurement units, and product constituents are adapted 0.13 (0.63–0.50), 0.29 (0.88–0.49), and 0.16 (0.69–0.53) less often in urban/suburban areas.

[9] Packaging protection, product features, and labeling are adapted 0.22 (0.41–0.19), 0.40 (0.45–0.05), and 0.33 (0.81–0.48) less in urban than in urban/semi-urban areas. Packaging aesthetics, measurement units, and other constituent changes are adapted more in urban/semi-urban than in urban areas by 0.07 (0.50–0.43), 0.07 (0.59–0.52), and 0.15 (0.53–0.38) respectively.

FIGURE 2   Comparison of Adaption Profiles: Urban-Targeted Products
Versus Urban/Semi-Urban-Targeted Products

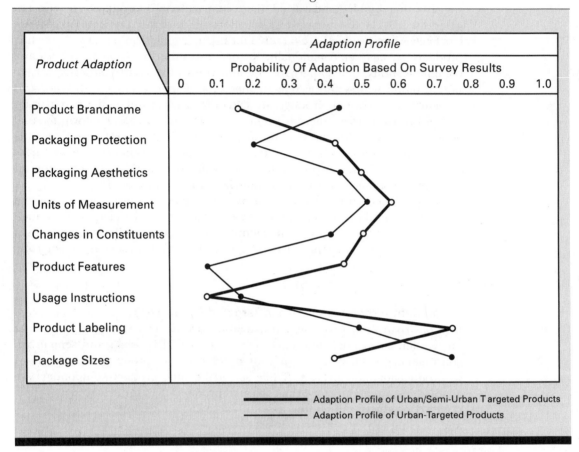

allowing MNCs to use cost-efficient packaging which, in turn, brings fresher and lower-priced products to store shelves.

There is less need to change product features for products targeted to LDC urban markets because of similarities in consumption patterns between LDC urban markets and markets in developed countries. Consumers in both cases exhibit substantially similar reactions to modern product features. By contrast, the mixture of old and new lifestyles on the outskirts of LDC cities forces closer adjustments to the traditional culture. The urbanized market provides a favorable setting for applying the mass-marketing techniques that go along with standardized product features. But when product distribution expands to semi-urban areas, such techniques as standardized advertising messages become unfeasible because of the existence of multiple dialects and in some cases even multiple languages. With minimum opportunity for capitalizing upon advertising scale economies, both product features and product advertisements are adapted to accommodate the semi-sophisticated tastes of semi-urban migrants.

Labeling adaptions are also less common for products aimed for urban markets than for those targeted to both urban and semi-urban markets. This is because LDC legal systems generally require that the content of manufacturers' product labels be clearly marked and comprehensible to all potential consumers. Label content includes the producer's name and address, the ingredients inside the package, usage instructions, and the like. As product distribution rolls out from urban areas, label content is adapted to meet the requirements of semi-sophisticated semi-urban consumers, people with different dialects, and multilingual market segments.

Inasmuch as many transferred US/UK consumer products are launched initially in LDC urban markets, early adaptions are made mainly to qualify the products for market entry. Brand names, for instance, sometimes are changed to meet LDC legal requirements. Similarly, changes in package sizes occasionally are dictated by LDC consumer buying preferences or purchasing power. Changes in package sizes, though not legally required, often help to increase the chances of successful market entry.

Conclusion

MNCs marketing consumer packaged goods in LDCs find that a semblance of an international market segment exists when they target distribution exclusively to urban markets. Such products targeted exclusively to LDC urban markets need minimal adapting, just enough to meet market entry requirements. Those targeted for both semi-urban and urban markets need additional adaptions to fit the semi-sophisticated tastes of the migrants who form a bridge between urban sophistication and rural provincialism. Products targeted for LDC national markets require still further adaptions to match more closely the provincial expectations and narrow consumption experiences of the rural population.

An interesting by-product of the research is that contrary to popular belief, MNCs do not usually enter LDC markets with the expectation of serving only affluent urban target markets. If our sample is typical, then most products are aimed at semi-urban and rural consumers. Only 21 out of 173 ex-US/UK products (just over 12 percent) were targeted just to city consumers. Clearly, most MNCs recognize the importance of semi-urban and rural consumers in their marketing plans, and do not shrink away from making appropriate adjustments to product strategies to reach the bulk of LDC consumers.

JAPANESE CONSUMERS: INTRODUCING FOREIGN PRODUCTS/BRANDS INTO THE JAPANESE MARKET

Sadafumi Nishina

Japanese enterprises are approaching business and marketing activities through an international perspective. The internationalized conditions of this environment have made consumers more receptive to foreign products. Foreign products in the Japanese market are beneficiaries of such factors as the trade surplus, the yen's appreciation, the expansion of domestic demand, and the market's maturity.

This report will present the results of our research on foreign products from the following four points:

1. The attitude of consumers toward foreign countries and products: to Japanese consumers "foreign product" means something more than its function and quality.

2. The consumer sector that prefers foreign products: there is a segment of Japanese consumers who are very receptive to foreign markets.

3. The image positioning of foreign brands: foreign brands can be divided into four categories from the standpoint of consumers' attitudes.

4. The expressions used in advertising foreign products: the advertising expressions can also be classified according to the images of the originating countries and internationality.

When marketing a product in Japan, it is necessary to "localize" for consumers. This does not mean merely modifying products and advertisements to reflect Japanese tone; it requires an aggressive image-creating strategy to meet the expectations that Japanese consumers have for foreign countries and products.

Conditions Affecting Foreign Products

Trends in the Economic Environment

Stimulation of Imports for a Continued Trade Surplus. Japan's balance-of-trade has been showing a surplus every year since 1981, and it registered an unprecedented high of U.S. $82.7 billion in 1986. Amidst growing criticism from foreign countries to open its markets, the Japanese government assumed international responsibility to diminish the trade surplus by expanding domestic demand and by executing various measures such as elimination or lowering of tariffs, easing

Source: Reprinted with permission from *Journal of Advertising Research,* April-May 1990, pp. 35–45.

import restrictions, and improvement of the import inspection process. As a result, imports for fiscal 1987 totaled U.S. $149,515 million, a remarkable increase from U.S. $126,408 million of the previous year. This trend of rising imports continues.

Declines in Import Prices Due to Appreciated Yen. The exchange rate of the yen against the dollar bottomed-out in February 1985 at 263.4 yen per U.S. dollar. Triggered by the G5 meeting of September 1985, the yen's appreciation began rapidly and continued thereafter. It reached 130 yen against the dollar in January 1988. The appreciation of the yen decreased the prices of imported goods in the Japanese market and worked to the advantage of foreign products.

Business Trends

Foreign Products for New-Product Development and Corporate Diversification. As many of the domestic markets became saturated, the products became equal in technological standards and difficult to distinguish, and competition among businesses intensified. The introduction of easily recognized foreign brands functions as an effective solution to a serious dilemma. Utilizing foreign ideas is also essential as a countermeasure against the shortened lifespan of products and for development of new products in a mature market where diverse products are produced in small lots. As a vehicle for diversification, which is the mainstay of corporate strategies, introduction of knowledge from abroad or acquisition of technology and products by marketing and advertising is increasing.

Increases in Overseas Production and Development. Because of the yen's appreciation and wage increases, production costs in Japan have become relatively high by international comparison. In addition to importing low-cost materials, production of low added-value items in low-cost Asian countries is becoming common. One such example is the electric appliance industry. This has resulted in a phenomenon in which "overseas-produced Japanese products" are flowing back into the domestic market.

Significance of the Japanese Market for Foreign Enterprises. The Japanese market is most attractive to foreign businesses because of scale (120 million people) and quality (high standard of income). More and more foreign industries are researching ways to enter the Japanese market. This has resulted in the development of unique products, new distribution routes developed in partnership with Japanese companies, investment in advertising, and the development of after-sales and support services.

Growth of Asian Newly Industrialized Countries (NICs). Coupled with the strong yen and weak dollar, the currencies of NICs are undervalued. This has made the products of NICs competitive in the Japanese market and their imports into Japan are increasing markedly.

Trends in Consumers The number of Japanese who travel abroad increases year by year and reached 6.83 million in 1987, an increase of 124 percent from the previous year. The increase of those who have overseas experience means increased opportunities for the Japanese to become acquainted with authentic foreign products and to cultivate an appreciation for them. This is also creating a demand as travelers seek foreign products in Japan after they return home.

Not only have lifestyles become more western but also the flow of people, products, and information has become international. This has enhanced the consumers' interest in foreign countries even more and at the same time made them receptive to foreign products. At present, the consumers' demands show orientation toward "authenticity," "individuality," "sensuality," and polarization between "high quality" and "economy." These demands seem to coincide with the appeal of foreign products.

Marketing Foreign Products

Roles Played by Foreign Corporations and Japanese Counterparts The history of imported products reflected the influx of foreign corporations into Japan: importation of completed products, that is, the importation of parts, and the local production in Japan. As Japanese corporations gained strength as partners, however, they have begun to import foreign elements (design, technology, and brand) aggressively and to develop foreign products that appeal to the Japanese market.

Foreign elements in foreign products have expanded from "hardware" such as completed products and parts to "software" such as production systems, technology, ideas, designs, and brand names. Recently, importation of "hardware" became the center of attention again as imports of overseas-developed products increased (see Figure 1).

Promoting Foreign Products through a "Product-based Approach." For foreign products imported or produced with a license, the product-based approach is adopted, using foreign products as prototypes and then adjusting the products to the Japanese market. The issues to be discussed in this case include comparison of the Japanese market with different markets in the country of origin, "localization" of products, and development of marketing plans targeted at Japanese markets (see Figure 2).

Promoting Foreign Products through a "Market-based Approach." For foreign products jointly developed by Japanese and foreign corporations and those products planned by Japanese enterprises and produced overseas, the

FIGURE **1**   Changes of Foreign Product Marketing

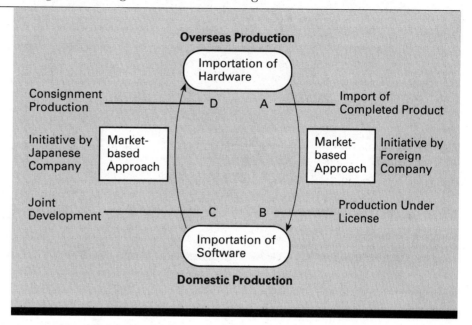

FIGURE **2**   Product-based Approach

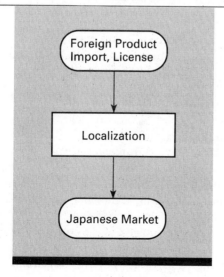

FIGURE **3**   Market-based Approach

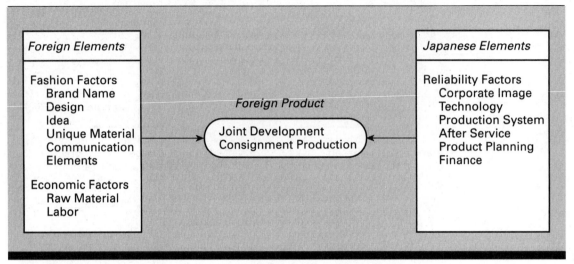

combination of domestic and foreign elements is the key point to developing a competitive product in the Japanese market, and a market-based approach is adopted. The conventional idea of integrated production within Japan is already outgrown by the idea of "the right elements from the right country" (see Figure 3).

Attitudes Toward Foreign Countries and Products

We first examined Japanese consumers' perception of foreign countries and products based on two surveys. Survey A was conducted in Tokyo and Osaka in 1986 on 1,420 men and women between the ages of 15 and 49. Survey B was conducted in Tokyo in 1987 on 700 women between 18 and 49 years of age.

Image of Countries or Regions   The amount of consumer association depends on the particular countries or regions. Paris, France, and America, all familiar to the Japanese, brought up an average 1.7 items of association, while Eastern Europe and Poland produced only 0.5 items.

As for the content, "America" was associated with "President Reagan," "great power/strong nation," etc. It was associated with such products as "cars, beef, oranges, wheat, and corn." However, California, New York, and Los Angeles recalled different associations, as shown in Table 1.

As Table 2 shows, Japanese images of 32 countries were estimated by 8 characteristics. According to this examination, countries can be divided into seven stereotypes including "a pastoral-type" and "an urban-type."

TABLE **1**   Contents of Associations by Countries or Regions (Survey A)

Associations	America	California	Los Angeles	New York	Canada
Associated words	Reagan great power Statue of Liberty large and wide	oranges fruit sunshine ocean	Disneyland metropolis skyscrapers Olympics	Skyscrapers Statue of Liberty Manhattan metropolis	forests nature timber mountains
Associated products	cars beef oranges wheat corn	oranges fruit grapefruit raisins wine	cars oranges fruit grapefruit clothes	clothes cars accessories fashion	lumber salmon furs wheat cardigan

Evaluation of Foreign Products A general comparison with domestic products shows that foreign products are thought to be appealing in terms of design and individuality. However, their function and quality are not necessarily rated as reliable. The evaluation is especially low among those who are potential targets (High-Hype, HH) for foreign products (see Table 3).

In a comparison of separate goods in terms of "quality, design, and price," foreign furniture, sports/leisure goods, and accessories are highly evaluated both in terms of quality and design, but their prices are thought to be relatively expensive (see Table 4).

Foreign products are often used as gifts in Japan. Of the people surveyed, 27 percent had received whiskey, 17 percent had received cosmetics or toiletries, and 15 percent had received tea.

There is a relationship between those who favor (like or want to visit) a country or region and the purchase of foreign products from there. New York "fans" often buy foreign beer, while "fans" of Spain and Germany are more likely to buy foreign wines than French "fans" (see Table 5).

Targets of Foreign Products

Development of Foreign Interest Scale So far, foreign products have been targeted at (1) the younger generation, (2) those in the high income bracket, or (3) those who have made purchases in the past. However, the idea that "foreign products fit the young" is too simple. Also, if a product is targeted only at past consumers, marketing opportunities will be restricted. Therefore, we searched for a new segment scale which is more closely connected with consumption of foreign products. In a comparison among the following four

TABLE 2 Image of Countries and Regions (Survey B)

Stereotypes		Countries or regions	Image 1[1] (%)	2 (%)	3 (%)	4 (%)	5 (%)	6 (%)	7 (%)	8 (%)
Pastoral type	A[2]	Switzerland	12	78	22	11	14	21	6	10
		Mediterranean Sea	16	63	13	16	1	1	2	1
		Sweden	13	62	22	11	7	7	9	3
		Northern Europe	27	55	20	14	7	5	11	5
		Canada	7	74	7	30	10	5	4	1
		Australia	5	81	7	44	3	2	3	2
		New Zealand	5	71	8	39	1	2	1	1
		Holland	17	55	52	32	1	1	1	0
		Eastern Europe	22	31	22	19	11	4	3	1
	B	California	3	51	5	65	3	0	3	2
		Brazil	8	50	41	59	4	2	0	1
	C	Spain	28	17	71	9	1	1	2	1
		Mexico	18	25	66	17	1	1	1	0
		India	38	25	61	16	1	0	1	1
		R.O.K.	21	9	55	13	11	2	0	0
		Hong Kong	7	6	25	6	6	4	5	9
		Taiwan	12	14	38	27	7	3	0	1
		Scotland	39	41	47	7	3	4	7	6
		Poland	22	21	36	16	6	1	1	1
	D	Greece	74	29	29	6	1	1	1	1
		China	66	43	45	31	5	3	0	1
		U.S.S.R.	35	23	31	23	23	4	1	1
Urban type	E	U.S.A.	13	24	9	37	56	24	22	9
		L.A.	4	7	5	6	24	12	19	13
		Germany	47	16	13	5	53	40	7	12
	F	France	41	10	8	11	3	15	73	63
		Paris	43	5	3	3	3	17	77	70
		Italy	36	11	29	9	5	11	35	22
		N.Y.	4	1	4	1	32	17	39	33
	G	U.K.	80	10	10	1	15	15	24	38

[1] 1. Long history and tradition 2. Rich nature 3. Rich ethnicity 4. Plentiful agricultural products 5. Advanced industrial technology 6. Products of high function and quality 7. Good sense of design 8. Abundant high-class products.

[2] A. Nature type B. Agricultural type C. Ethnic type D. Traditional type E. High-tech type F. High-quality type G. Historical type.

TABLE 3   Attitude toward Foreign Products (Survey B)

Attitude	Total (%)	HH (%)
Foreign products are better in design than domestic ones.	70	78
Foreign products have attributes different from domestic ones.	69	83
I buy foreign products if I can afford them.	61	70
I buy foreign products if the function and price are the same as domestic ones.	51	58
I feel good when I have foreign products with me.	50	49
I like foreign products.	42	49
Foreign products are more economical in the long term than domestic ones.	42	42
Foreign products are better in function and quality than domestic ones.	32	20

(These figures are the totals for those who are "very positive" and "quite positive.")

TABLE 4   Comparison between Foreign and Domestic Products (Survey A)

Products	Quality			Design			Economy		
	F* (%)	N (%)	D (%)	F (%)	N (%)	D (%)	F (%)	N (%)	D (%)
Foods	9	38	53	24	41	35	10	30	60
Clothes	20	38	42	34	36	30	11	29	60
Furniture	34	36	30	40	36	24	13	34	53
Household goods	15	35	50	24	43	33	8	34	58
Sports goods	33	39	28	34	41	25	12	36	52
Cars	10	25	65	28	34	38	5	26	69
Accessories	37	41	22	41	41	18	16	40	44

* F = foreign, N = neutral, D = domestic

TABLE **5**   Purchase Rate of Foreign Products by Country Preference (Survey B)

Country	Purchase rate of foreign beer (6 months) (%)
Total	25
U.S.-fan	31
U.K.-fan	29
F.D.R.-fan	35
N.Y.-fan	40

Country	Purchase rate of foreign wine (6 months) (%)
Total	14
France-fan	13
F.D.R.-fan	20
Spain-fan	22

Country	Purchase rate of foreign tea (6 months) (%)
Total	23
U.K.-fan	26
India-fan	32
U.S.-fan	21

Country	Purchase rate of foreign cars (including purchase intention rate) (%)
Total	16
F.D.R.-fan	21
U.S.-fan	19
U.K.-fan	22
R.O.K.-fan	24

proposed scales based on survey data, the "Foreign Interest Scale" was the most effective:

- ◆ Foreign Interest Scale (degree of interest in foreign countries)
- ◆ Foreign Products Preference Scale (degree of preference toward foreign products in general)
- ◆ Degree of Favorable Perceptions of Foreign Products (total degree of positive impressions of foreign products)
- ◆ Evaluation Style of Foreign Products (which attributes of foreign products were ranked highly)

In choosing the questions which comprise the Foreign Interest Scale, no direct questions about the consumption of foreign products were included. Rather, the questions in the scale are concerned with experiences and conditions which lie behind consumer action, namely, foreign language skills, interest in overseas information, overseas experience, overseas personal contacts, etc. (see Tables 6 to 8).

TABLE 6   Constituent Items of Foreign Interest Scale and the Response (Survey B)

Constituent items of foreign interest scale	Total (%)	HH (%)
Foreign language skill 1. I would like to learn English.	62	88
2. I have spoken to foreigners in the past year.	20	85
3. I can manage daily conversation in English.	12	73
Interest in overseas information. 4. I am interested in the foreign news in newspapers.	42	92
5. I am interested in magazine articles about foreign cultures and sites.	41	95
6. I have read newspapers, magazines, or books in a foreign language.	18	85
Overseas experience 7. I have traveled abroad.	40	95
8. I have stayed abroad for more than two weeks.	13	70
Overseas personal contacts 9. I have family or close friends who often go abroad.	34	84
10. My family or my Japanese friends live in foreign countries.	28	81
11. I have foreign friends.	14	71

TABLE **7**   Distribution of Degree of Foreign Interest (Survey B)

HH	High	Middle	Low	LL
8	20	39	19	14

TABLE **8**   Features of Those Who Ranked HH in Degree of Foreign Interest (Survey B)

| | Age | | | | Marital status | | Education | Household income (million Yen) | | | |
Rank	18–24	25–34	35–44	45–49	Single	Married	College or university	~–4.99	5.00–5.99	6.00–9.99	10.00–~
HH	22	34	34	10	35	65	68	30	26	29	14
Total	20	30	36	14	25	75	32	33	36	23	8

Marks of individuals were calculated by just totaling the number of items with positive responses. The marks were spread between the values of 0 and 11 and, for the convenience of simplicity, were divided into 5 categories: HH (high/high), high, middle, low, and LL (low/low).

We calculated a correlation coefficient between the standard variables (purchasing action of foreign products and brands) and each of those scales. The result showed that the Foreign Interest Scale has a stronger relationship with consumption of foreign products than other scales.

Validity of Foreign Interest Scale   As Figure 4 shows, the Foreign Interest Scale is more closely related with the consumption of foreign products than with the age scale. The HH group shows the highest action rates in purchase of goods and brands. The low groups tend to have lower action rates in order. No such orderly tendency is found in the age scale.

As shown in Table 8, this HH group in the Foreign Interest Scale is not represented by any particular age group or income group, but they tend to have a high level of education. As Table 9 shows, the HH group members imagine themselves as "sensuous, intelligent, individualistic." In shopping, they use mail order and credit cards relatively frequently. Also, when they choose an item, they do not care what others say about it; they are concerned with its "design and atmosphere."

FIGURE 4   Foreign Interest Scale Versus Age Scale (Survey B)

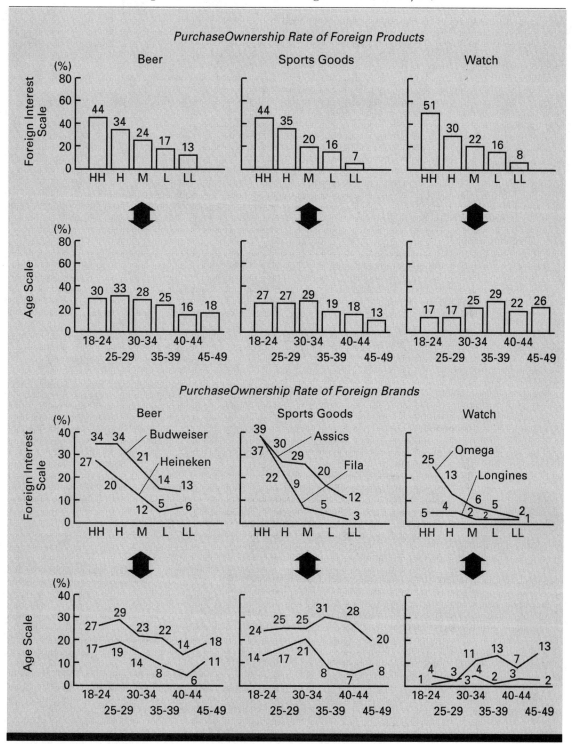

TABLE **9**   Characteristics of the HH Group in the Foreign Interest Scale (Survey B)

Characteristics	HH	Total
Self image Sensuous	3.68	3.22
Intelligent	3.24	2.84
Individualistic	3.44	2.78
Luxurious	3.40	2.68
Sophisticated	2.86	2.40
Consumption attitude I based my selection on feeling and intuition.	3.94	3.20
I try to use or match products in my own way.	4.38	3.90
I try to look for unique items that no one has.	3.58	3.32
I would like to use mail-order more.	2.84	2.12
I would like to use credit cards more.	1.82	0.98
Criteria for product selection Good design	81	73
Reputation	20	32
"Atmoshpere"	34	28
Sense of high quality	34	26

For self-image and consumer attitude, figures are average of the 5-point scale.

Image Positioning of Foreign Brands

Measurement of Images of Foreign Brands From the "attitude toward foreign products in general," four viewpoints, namely "function/quality," "atmosphere," "scarcity value," and "reputation," were chosen as items to measure the image of separate brands. Since the image of being international and the image of the country-of-origin are important to foreign products, such viewpoints as "internationality," "domestic-ness," "European-ness," and "Americanness," were added. The survey was done on 160 major foreign brands. Figure 5 shows part of the result.

As for specific images, "atmosphere" was the strongest in luxury goods such

FIGURE **5**   Image Positioning of Foreign Brands (Survey A)

			S		
	BASF Apple	AGFA Santana	Wrigley Miller	Camel Wedgwood	
Scotch Marantz	Omega Longines	BMW Swatch Mercedes Benz Amex	Rosenthal Sears	Marlboro Lark	
Gillette	Olivetti CHeerr L'Oreal	Borden Max Factor Old Spice	Cutty Sark Budweiser Heineken	Denny's	Royal Host Skylark
IBM	Polaroid Wrangler Wella	Coca-Cola Ivory Big John	Seven Eleven White Horse	McDonald's Kentucky Fried Chicken	
Kodack Xerox	Twinings Exxon	Lipton VISA	Johnnie Walker	Johnnie Walker	
Dunlop	Levis				

F ... A

R

Vertical axis = Scarcity versus Reputation
Horizontal axis = Function versus Atmospheric

as tobacco, wine, beer, and liquors. The image of "function/quality" was strong in brands of miscellaneous goods and medicine such as Kleenex, Band-aids, or business machines such as Xerox. Food was rather on the "function/quality" side. The image of cars is more on the "atmosphere" side than any other kind of machine. The "international" image is strong in foreign cars like Mercedes Benz and BMW and traditional imported goods such as liquor and watches. The "European" image is represented by traditional goods like Rosenthal and Wedgwood and the "American" image by cola, jeans, cigarettes, and chain restaurants.

Indeed, there is a difference among brands even within a single product. American Express has a strong image of "scarcity" while VISA has one of "reputation." Heineken and Lowenbrau have clear images of "European" while Budweiser has an "American" image, and Miller has not yet established an image of country-of-origin. Products such as beer, which are manufactured under license, and those products modified for the domestic market, such as LASER automobiles produced by Mazda and sold by Ford, are still perceived as foreign products as far as image is concerned.

Figure 6 shows that an image of "scarcity value" is strongest among those in "total" but shifts toward one of "reputation" among "those who know" and "those who use." Hence, the distinction between "function/quality" type and "atmosphere" type products becomes clear. The more contact there is with foreign products, the more clearly the feature of the products is understood.

FIGURE 6   Change of Image Among Those Who Know or Use a Product
(Survey A)

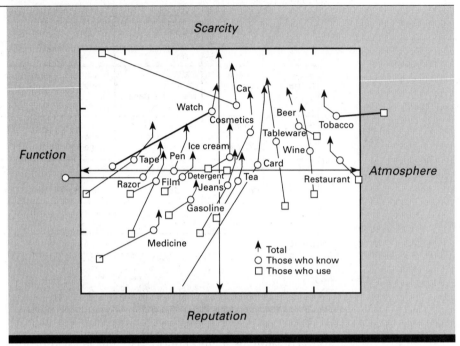

Image Clusters in Foreign Products and Brands As a result of a cluster analysis based on the eight items of image data, four types or clusters were recognized (see Table 10).

1. *Brands with Images Based on Internationality.* The highest class brands represented by Mercedes Benz, Omega, etc., and the brands mainly aimed at universal service such as credit cards and computers are in this cluster.

2. *Brands with Images Based on Countries-of-Origin.* This group produces clear images of countries-of-origin. Popular ones are Scotch whiskey, British tea, German beer, American cigarettes, fast-food outlets, and jeans.

3. *Brands with Images Based on Country-of-Entry.* This group includes the foreign products localized in Japan for a long time and those produced domestically but sold as if they are foreign products.

4. *Brands with Images Based on Function/Quality.* The products which have stronger reputations for quality than foreign image belong to this

TABLE 10 Image Cluster in Foreign Brands (Survey A)

Image*		1	2	3	4	5	6	7	8	Typical brands
① (12%)	High–class import type	XX		XX			XX		XX	Mercedes Benz, BMW, Omega, Wedgwood
	International service type	XX			X			X	XX	Rosenthal, Amex, Diners, Apple
② (32%)	European image type	X		XX			X			Twinings, Swatch, Heineken, Löwenbrau, Burberry
	American image type				XX		X	X		Marlboro, Lark, Coca-Cola, Max Factor, McDonald's, Kentucky Fried Chicken
③ (6%)	Domestic type		XX							Brother, Onward, House, Kanebo, Noritake, Cosmo, Pilot
④ (49%)	Functional image type					XX	XX			Schick, Kleenex, Xerox, Contac, Kodak, IBM, Band-aids
	Popular image type									Olivetti, Polaroid, Maggie, Del Monte, Nabisco, Abon, Borden

* Image types: ① International image type ② Country-of-origin type ③ Country-of-entry type ④ Function/quality type
Image clusters: 1. International 2. Domestic 3. European 4. American 5. Function/quality 6. Atmosphere 7. Reputation 8. Scarcity

group. This includes razors, tissues, cosmetics, and foods which compete with domestic counterparts and have substantial merchandising power.

Advertising Expressions of Foreign Products

As discussed before, the foreign attributes of foreign products have a positive meaning to Japanese consumers. Therefore, "localization" in an advertising expression involves not just adding a Japanese element but expressing emphatically the international image or the image of the country-of-origin according to the Japanese perception of foreign countries, especially those of Western orientation.

It turned out that advertising copy for foreign products used in Japan can be classified into basically the same categories as the four groups of brands presented earlier. Expressions could be classified with subcategories as follows.

Expressions Based on International Images

- International-reputation type: an expression which appeals to its being a product of world-wide reputation
- International-sense type: an expression which emphasizes elements appealing to the consumers' international sense, namely their vague liking for international or exotic images

Expressions Based on Countries-of-Origin

- Country-of-origin's reputation type: products which have established reputations related to the countries-of-origin such as Scotch whiskey, French cognac, or German wine
- Country-of-origin's image type: an expression which uses a positive image of the country such as the traditions of Britain, mechanical precision from Switzerland, and chic fashions from France
- Country-of-origin's "climate" and culture type: the characteristic culture, manner, and "climate" of a country are used as elements of expression to add a unique image and "taste" to the product, for example, cowboys from the United States, Mother Nature from Canada, tartans from Britain, etc.

Expressions Based on Country-of-Entry-Image

- Country-of-entry's reputation type: an expression which appeals through the product's history and reputation in Japan
- Adjustment-to-country-of-entry type: an expression which stresses that the product was reformed or remodeled to match Japanese situations
- Mismatch type: an expression which uses an amusing combination of foreign and Japanese elements
- Assimilation-to-country-of-entry type: an expression which does not distinguish the foreign product from domestic counterparts

Expressions Based on Images of Function/Quality

- Explanation-of-product type: an expression explaining the function and qualities unique to the brand. In a visual expression, the picture of the product is prominent.

♦ Brand-image type: an expression which appeals through the "atmosphere" of the brand, not through an explanation. This method can be used only with products of established reputation or with established brand names. Many of the ads of this type use a standard universal format, shared by all nations.

Ads for whiskey exemplify this universal format. White Horse Mild has an international image. This ad features a western man and woman, reminding the viewer of a modern lifestyle of the "mild" sense. Vague internationality is stressed without suggesting any specific country. Burberry Whiskey has an image based on country-of-origin. This stresses an element of the country-of-origin through the "English gentleman" and Burberry coats. It is aimed at adding an authentic image to the product. White Horse Extra Fine has an image based on country-of-entry. This stresses a Japanese element with a *kimono* and a *hikido* (Japanese sliding door). It is targeted for the Japanese gift market. Johnnie Walker has an image based on function and quality. This ad consists of almost minimal elements such as a photo, the name of the product, and a price. It describes Johnnie Walker as the highest class product among brand names.

For foreign products whose images are based on function/quality, comparative advertisements with famous domestic brands are thought to be the most appealing and effective approach. In 1987, the Japan Fair Trade Commission provided guidelines that show their approval of such comparative advertising expressions.

SOME ASPECTS OF INTERNATIONAL PRICING: A NEGLECTED AREA OF MANAGEMENT POLICY

James C. Baker ◆ John K. Ryans, Jr.

Much attention has been focused recently on the increased overseas business of U.S. corporations, the growth of the multinational firm and similar international developments. Understandably, this has attracted marketers' interest in management policies and practices relating to overseas advertising, distribution channels, and product planning.[1]

Pricing, however, has been one tool of the marketer that has received much less attention in this examination of the non-domestic marketing management strategy of U.S. firms. Remaining generally unanswered—except in the traditional textbook sense—have been basic questions concerning the relative importance of price in overseas markets and how international marketing management has approached this critical area of decision-making. The purpose of the study reported here is to offer some answers to these and similar concerns, regarding international pricing, i.e., the price or prices at which their goods are offered for sale in the various overseas markets.

Specifically, this project sought to determine: (1) at what level in U.S. multinational firms are basic international pricing policy decisions made and who makes these decisions; (2) the principal considerations of international pricing policy decision-makers; (3) the most important factors in setting *overseas* prices according to the executives; and (4) the most serious problem areas facing international marketing managers in pricing products to be marketed internationally. Each of these topics will be explored in the following sections.

Methodology

In seeking answers to the pricing concerns noted above, a mail questionnaire, utilizing both highly structured and open-end questions, was sent to the inter-

---

Source: *Management Decision,* (Summer 1973 Vol. 11). MCB University Press. Reprinted with permission.

[1] See Donnelly, James H., Jr., and Ryans, John K., Jr., "The Role of Culture in Organizing Overseas Operations: The Advertising Experience", *University of Washington Business Review,* Vol. XXIX (Autumn 1969), pp. 35–41; Donnelly, J. H., and Ryans, J. K. "How American Companies Advertise Overseas", *European Business,* No. 24 (January 1970), pp. 58–61; Goldstucker, Jac. L., "The Influence of Culture on Channels of Distribution", in *Marketing and the New Science of Planning,* Robert L. King, editor (Chicago, Ill.: American Marketing Association, Fall, 1968), pp. 468–473; Keegan, Warren J., "Multinational Product Planning: Strategic Alternatives", *Journal of Marketing,* Vol. 33 (January 1969), pp. 58–62; and Wortzel, Laurence H., "Product Policy and the United States Multinational Corporation: Some Emerging Generalizations", in *Marketing and the New Science of Planning,* Robert L. King, ed. (Chicago, Ill.: American Marketing Association, Fall, 1968), pp. 474–8.

national marketing division director, the international marketing manager, or the international marketing vice-president of the 76 U.S. companies in the consumer goods fields that appear to have the most extensive international operations. (It should be noted that there is no truly definitive listing of such U.S. concerns.) Firms were selected primarily from among those ranked at the top of *Fortune's* 500 largest industrials, which were also listed in the Angel *Directory of American Firms Operating in Foreign Countries*. Responses were received from 51 companies and 42 of these firms co-operated completely by answering all portions of the questionnaire. Eight companies returned the instrument unanswered. Thus, 67 percent of the universe responded and 82 percent of these respondents furnished meaningful information regarding their firm's pricing policies and practices. Among the techniques employed in the study were open-end questions, rankings, and rating scales.

Profile of Firm's Pricing Function in International Operations Since so little is currently known about the pricing practices and policies of these multinational giants, information was first sought on two questions central to any discussion of marketing policies and practices: who makes such decisions in the firm and are such decisions centralized (made in the home office) or decentralized (made by executives in the various overseas locations)? The study revealed that pricing decisions in most of the firms are made at executive levels *lower* than top management. In fact, individual product managers or middle management personnel make the international pricing decision in 56 percent of the responding companies while in only 44 percent are such decisions made by top management. Considering the importance historically attributed to domestic price decision-making in the firm, the locus of this decision area for international pricing is especially revealing and will be explored more fully later.

In contrast, the companies almost equally divided as to whether their international pricing decisions were made at the U.S. home office or in the various overseas bases of operation. International pricing decisions were reported to be decentralized in 21 of the companies and centralized in 20. However, decentralization occurs in roughly the *same* percentage of firms in which pricing decisions are made at top management levels, as in firms in which such decisions are made by lower management executives. Thus, there is no correlation between level of international pricing decisions and geographical locus of such decisions in these major multinational firms.

Relative Importance of Pricing

Next, an effort was made to determine the relative importance of price as an international marketing strategy element to the firms participating in the study. These marketing executives—all employed by firms heavily engaged in multinational corporate operations—were asked to rank six traditional elements of marketing strategy (advertising, product policy, channel, credit, packaging and price) in terms of their importance in *non-domestic* markets.[2]

A heavy majority of the executives felt that the quality of the product was the single most important marketing strategy factor. In fact, two-thirds of the respondents ranked it *most important.* However, pricing was considered to be most important by another 45 percent of the respondents. Thus, pricing ranks as a key marketing tool overseas—as in the U.S. market—even though the non-domestic pricing decisions are made at middle management level in a majority of the firms.

Considerations of International Pricing Decision-Making To get a better understanding of the pricing practices and policies of these major U.S.–based multinationals, it was necessary to determine which potential price considerations, such as production costs, tariffs, and consumer demand, etc. they feel to be most relevant in their overseas pricing strategy. The marketing executives participating in the study were asked to rate on a seven-point scale some eight different considerations—each generally felt to be important concerns when pricing in overseas markets. (These executives rated each factor on a scale ranging from zero (no importance) to plus-six (very important).)

As shown by Table 1, production costs and the international competitor's (typically another multinational firm) prices received equally high *mean* ratings from the executives. However, production costs did receive more "plus-six" ratings from executives than did international competitors' prices and on this basis would be considered slightly more important. Rated third in importance among the price considerations was domestic competitor's prices, i.e., the prices of "local" competition in the particular overseas market itself.

The cost orientation and competitive concerns of these executives were even more strongly reflected by the fact that consumer demand was rated only fourth in importance by the total group. Such a finding may be somewhat surprising to marketers who are mainly concerned with U.S. domestic markets where the "consumer king concept" pervades and where much attention is centered on determining consumers' desires. However, in the aggressive markets in Europe where the multinational is often the outsider, such an orientation often reflects a "survival goal" for many firms.

Tariffs and various other "taxes" such as border taxes, apparently receive relatively little pricing consideration from the marketing executives participating in the study. Only four executives rated this consideration to be plus-six in importance and it had a mean rating score below all other considerations except advertising and promotion. Since so many multinational firms have branches

---

[2] Based on the response of the study, the general ranking of the strategies was: (a) quality of product, (b) pricing, (c) type of outlet in which the product is sold, (d) credit policy, (e) packaging, and (f) advertising.

TABLE 1   International Marketing Managers' Ratings of Potential
               Price Considerations

Overall ranking (based on mean rating)	Price consideration	Mean rating score (0 – +6 scale)	No. of firms ranking +6 (very imp.)
1	Production costs	4·92	22
1	International competitors' prices	4·92	20
3	Domestic competitors' prices	4·30	15
4	Consumer demand	4·24	12
5	Transportation costs	3·58	7
6	Markup required by middlemen (both domestic and international)	3·17	4
7	Tariffs and various taxes	3·10	4
8	Amount of advertising and promotion used	1·97	1

or subsidiaries in key overseas locations, tariffs and other trade barriers become important only in areas where they are exporting and even then common market or preferential status may obviate the concern.

Decentralized Decision-Making While "production costs" and "international competitors' prices" were rated equally important in terms of the total group of study respondents, a more careful analysis of the findings indicates that production costs are considered a less important factor by those firms in which price decisions are decentralized (price decisions made in the various local markets). In firms where price decisions are made in the home office (centralized) production costs are clearly felt to be the single most important consideration. On the other hand, competitors' pricing actions—whether by international competitors or by nationals in the marketplace itself—are rated most important by respondents in decentralized price decision-making firms. Since the likelihood is perhaps greater that some or all of the centralized firm's products are exported from the United States, a greater concern for costs might appear obvious. However, this view could just as readily be related to the proximity of the decentralized decision-maker to the day-to-day struggle in heavily competitive markets.

Further, the decentralized decision-making group considered markup to be of much greater concern than did the respondents in firms with centralized decision-making, perhaps a result of working more closely with distributors. It is especially worth noting that both groups rated consumer demand about equally low as a price consideration; one because of a pre-occupation with costs and the other due to an overwhelming concern for their competitive battles. Whether either would fair better with a true "consumer" orientation is an area of potential debate and research.

In addition, the respondents were asked to *rank* eight selected factors according to their *relative importance* in overseas pricing. These eight factors, including "your total costs" and "competitors' pricing policies" were somewhat similar to the considerations rated (0 to 6) by the respondents (above). Such a ranking furnished a more definitive *hierarchy of pricing factors* or *considerations* than could be obtained from the scale ratings, and also provided a means of checking the consistency of the respondents' views.

As shown in Table 2, the respondents as a whole felt total costs to be the most important factor in overseas pricing. In fact, some 16 of the international marketing executives (40 percent) ranked total costs as being most important to their firm, while only 12 executives (30 percent) ranked competitors' pricing policies first.

TABLE 2   Overall rankings of overseas pricing factors by international marketing managers and cross tabulation of these rankings according to locus of international price decision-making in managers' firm, i.e., centralized or decentralized.

	Overall rank	Rank by centralized	Rank by decentralized
Your total costs	1	1	2
Competitors' pricing policies	2	3	1
Your "out of pocket" costs	3	4	3
Your return on investment policy	4	2	5
What you feel the customer will pay	5	5	4
Extra charge or margins paid to distributors	6	6	6
Amount of tariffs and taxes	7	6	7
Susceptibility of the market to promotion	8	8	8

In general, the overall response pattern in the rankings was much like the rating results. Further, as with the ratings, the centralized/home office decision firms placed greater importance on total costs and indicated a much different response pattern from the executives in firms in which price decisions are decentralized.

Problem Areas in International Pricing Finally, when asked the "biggest" international pricing problem area facing their firm, the marketing executives tended to cite their troubles in meeting competition and their cost situation. Whether they felt their overseas competitors had an advantage in a given market or that reliable information about competitors' operations was unavailable or that they were simply being priced out of markets by high costs (those exporting their goods), the respondents clearly indicated that overseas markets can provide considerable "challenge" to the international markets.

Generally, as shown in Table 3, the responses to this critical open-end question could be roughly grouped into five problem areas. Nearly one-half of the international marketing executives felt that either meeting competition or

TABLE **3**   Major problem areas perceived by international marketing managers and a cross tabulation of these views, according to the locus of international price decision-making in the managers' firm, i.e., centralized or decentralized

Problem area (1)*	Total respondents (2)		Firms with centralized Price decision-making (3)		Firms with decentralized price decision-making (4)	
Meeting competition	32·5%	13	26·3%	5	38·1%	8
Cost, ROI, price list financing	30·0	12	31·6	6	28·6	6
Lack of competitive information	15·0	6	5·3	1	23·9	5
Distribution and channel factors	12·5	5	21·0	4	4·7	1
Government barriers	10·0	4	15·8	3	4·7	1
Total	100·0%	40	100·0%	19	100·0%	21

* (1) The respondents were *not* presented with a list of problem areas. The areas indicated represent a collation of similar problem themes.
(2) Percentage; N = 40
(3) Percentage; N = 19
(4) Percentage; N = 21

lack of competitive information was their greatest source of pricing difficulty. Cost or cost/profit-related problems were considered most serious by roughly one-third of the remaining respondents.

Centralized More Cost Concerned The respondents representing companies which have centralized the pricing function were somewhat divided as to what they perceived their major overseas pricing problem to be. About one-third felt that cost and ROI factors were their most serious problems, while the remainder were split among other problem areas.

On the other hand, the decentralized price decision-making group (executives in firms with decentralized pricing decision-making) were more solidly in agreement that competitive concerns were most troublesome. In fact, some 60 plus percent of the latter groups indicated meeting competition or lack of competitive information to be their biggest problem.

Conclusions

Two closely related conclusions are especially apparent from the findings of this study. First, it is quite clear that most of the responding international marketing managers do *not* take a "marketing orientated" approach to pricing abroad, either in their policies or practices. Domestically, the chief concern of marketing managers is consumer demand and much attention is given to the consumer in the manager's marketing strategy. This is simply not the case abroad.

Second, the international marketing managers in firms that make their overseas price decisions in the home office (domestic) are more "cost concerned" in their pricing policies and practices than those in firms in which such decisions are made in the individual local overseas markets. Clearly, in many markets this problem for the former group is *real*, especially if they are exporting from the United States or from locations that do not have common market or preferential status in the areas to which their goods are being sent. This latter group is most concerned about their competition and competitive situations. This concern, in fact, may be a *reflection* of their presence in these local markets or it may *explain* their presence there. Although there seems to be obvious differences in opinion based on the locus of their price decisions, neither group seems overly concerned about consumer demand.

LIVING WITH PRICE CONTROL ABROAD

Victor H. Frank, Jr.

ABSTRACT.   When inflation becomes rampant in a country, its ruling party may decide to impose price controls to try to put the economy back into equilibrium. This, of course, often works hardship on many organizations (as well as on individuals) that make up the economy, including makers and sellers of goods. CPC International has had long experience in dealing with price controls and has spent much time trying to convince officials in the many nations where it operates that price controls are not in the particular country's long-term interests, as well as CPC's. Here a CPC officer gives guidance for dealing with government agencies and for marshaling arguments favoring reduction if not lifting of controls.

Rapidly escalating prices constitute one of the most dangerous problems for governments. In response, a government will often invoke price controls and wage controls or an incomes policy. But sooner or later the government will become disenchanted with controls and terminate them or at least reduce their scope.

Similarly, price controls are one of the most serious problems for a multinational company. Once under price controls in a certain country, the company's division there is virtually operating in a regulated industry. Dealing with regulations and regulators consumes a vast amount of time. And if management cannot handle the situation, hardship is certain.

Inasmuch as it markets its products around the world and operates 107 plants in 45 countries (including 4 plants through joint ventures), CPC International has had wide experience since 1945 with price controls on raw materials and on its products. In this article I pass on some lessons from that experience, while noting that the rules, though fraught with problems, must be obeyed and that action, which may be desirable in order to live with price controls, may be impossible due to competitive conditions. While, of course, I'm writing about foodstuffs and processed food exclusively, my account should apply to producers and sellers of many types of goods.

Along the way I outline the problems that management faces under price controls and the choices it must make, and I discuss the effects of these restraints on local economies. I also refer to theories about price controls, pro and con, and the experience governments have had with price controls as set forth in the insert to the article. These arguments are important because it is good policy to try to convince government policymakers, government regulators, and government's own employees that the best policy is to let prices be set by, or allowed to equal what they would be in, a free market.

Source: Reprinted by permission of *Harvard Business Review.* "Living with Price Control Abroad," by Victor H. Frank, Jr., March-April 1984. Copyright © 1984 by the President and Fellows of Harvard College; all rights reserved.

Operating Under Controls

The term *price control* has many meanings. Generally I have defined it as the setting of maximum not minimum (or support) prices. In some cases of so-called price control the government merely requires the filing of information about a price rise for information or comment; or control really means "jaw-boning" by an agency, but not as a preliminary to disallowance. This was the case in early 1983 for certain foodstuffs in Italy.

Controls may involve a freeze on prices for a certain amount of time. Freezes have been imposed in recent years in the United States, Belgium, France, Greece, Portugal, Sweden, and New Zealand. And back in 1974 Argentina went so far as to decree a six-month rollback. Even under a freeze there may be questions as to whether a particular product is in the sector or group coming under the restrictions.

Price freezes, however, are seldom absolute. On petitions citing unusual circumstances, increases are usually authorized or at least countenanced. Unusual circumstances include those in the case of the vegetable dehydrators who were freed from the recent freeze in France when they demonstrated that competitors selling fresh vegetables had not had their prices restrained and that the dehydrators' energy costs were beyond their control. And one Asian country some years ago allowed CPC to raise its corn syrup price above the freeze maximum when the company showed that the restriction had come at a time when it was selling its corn syrup at a very low price in order to raise cash to service a debt.

But price control usually means not a freeze but fixed prices which the government periodically adjusts in many cases, either arbitrarily or in accordance with some percentage or index irrespective of actual costs or margins. This was the case in Brazil in 1983, when the country's government allowed increases periodically throughout the year equal to a certain percentage of a monetary correction that revalued the principal of treasury bonds and certain other accounts.

There are other examples of price increases based on theoretical, rather than actual, increases of certain costs. Formerly in Brazil, some price increases were allowed based not on the actual labor cost increase but on labor cost increases decreed by a labor court. Under its 1981 controls, Belgium allowed only a 1 percent increment to offset wage increases, whatever the actual wage increases were. Holland recently permitted no price increase to offset rising labor costs.

If the cost to the producer involves imported ingredients, these items may be adjusted automatically (though perhaps not fully) for official movements in exchange rates. Even under controls based on theoretical costs, however, a company that is sorely hurt should present its case based on true costs.

Standard types The usual policy is to grant price increases according to actual cost rises. A higher actual cost of working capital presents a particularly difficult problem. Many countries do not view higher interest rates as justification for a price boost. Yet the cost of carrying working capital is significant and that of fixed assets may be even greater.

Under the rules in some countries, the company may have its supplier carry the inventory until the time of use, thus making the price of the inventory reflect the carrying cost. The supplier whose own prices are controlled, however, may be unable to do this.

Where otherwise allowed price increases are reduced in whole or in part because of presumed productivity increases—as they were for the industry average productivity gains under Phase II of controls in the United States in the early 1970s—the company may well raise questions concerning the fairness of the percentage and the applicability of the productivity factor to itself, given certain labor and other restrictions. CPC, by the way, had little success on this point with the U.S. Council on Wage and Price Stability.

Where price boosts are subject to gross or net margin limitations, the company should ascertain whether the absolute currency margins ($10 – $7 = an allowable margin of $3) or the percentage margins (30 percent) apply. Controls based on the allowance of a percentage margin in many cases encourage the purchase of high-cost raw materials in time of inflation, since a higher percentage margin will allow a larger absolute margin ($15 × 30% = $4.50).

Similarly, controls based on the allowance of an absolute currency margin often make choosing the cheapest raw material almost irrelevant when costs are falling, since the same absolute margin is permitted irrespective of the cost. Moreover, if net margins are restricted, the company should ascertain how general and administrative costs, as well as financing costs, are to be allocated among products.

Price controls often prescribe accounting rules, and the company should be alert to make sure these rules do not treat it inequitably. For example, by-products from the same raw material generally do not reflect all the costs of their production since head or principal products therefrom bear all of such costs. In a presentation for price relief for by-products, under a system allowing relief for increased costs, by-products should reflect all costs.

Where price control includes a limitation on profits, the company should seek to have carryover or carryback losses, if any, taken into consideration.

Almost all forms of price control refer to a base period. When election of the base period is prohibited, the company should offer any valid arguments as to why the designated period is unfair.

All forms of price control have rules governing the grouping of products or businesses within a company. At one extreme, one or more product lines may be subject to separate restraints. In France, for example, and formerly in Argentina, the industry sector or a product line such as mayonnaise is regulated. In CPC's experience, vegetable oils often are initially treated as one sector. The rules make little distinction between Mazola oil, which is based on corn oil, and vegetable oils based on the normally cheaper soybean or sunflower oils. Eventually the government agency usually permits a price difference based on these cost differences, as the Puerto Rican authorities did.

At the other extreme of government policy, all the businesses of the company in a particular country, unrelated or not, may be subject to control as a group. The point is that the company should seek the most reasonable grouping permissible and spread an allowable increase accordingly. Under the controls in the United States a decade ago, the broadest grouping was the most advantageous one for CPC.

Dealing with Administrators

Most of the time a company will be dealing not with the country's policymakers but with the agency administrators. These administrators, in my view, must be convinced that price relief is not only fair for the company but also in the best interest of their country.

To convince them the company should demonstrate, if such is the case, that it is getting an unacceptable (perhaps even zero) ROI, and that without an acceptable profit opportunity, future investments will not be made and even production perhaps will be stopped. While such a statement sounds like a threat, it can represent reality. Cadbury Schweppes sold its plant in Kenya in April 1982 because price control made its operation unprofitable. In Mexico in early 1983, Coca-Cola and PepsiCo withdrew their products from the shelves until they received a price hike. Pakistani milk producers terminated their business when they could not raise prices, and Glaxo, a pharmaceutical manufacturer, is reported to have cancelled its expansion plans in Pakistan because of price controls.

Companies naturally will invest only where the prospect of return is attractive. In this connection it might be useful to show that the company could make more by investing in the relatively safe local bond market! The corporate representatives could indicate the consequences to the local economy of curtailment of the company's investment. These would include a possible decline in employment and cuts in the company's demand for goods and services from local suppliers.

To present its case the company should generally use a person such as the internal lawyer or internal accountant who is familiar with the company's business and with the local rules and, more particularly, the administrative practices and interpretation. Familiarity with such practices and interpretations is especially important where the regulating body has much discretion.

A troublesome question is how to handle delays imposed under the regulations arbitrarily. It is not unusual for a company to wait 30 days (as in Sweden) or 45 days (as in Brazil) before receiving merely an answer to a price increase petition. Generally a company should appear before the agency as many times as it has a legitimate reason to—and no more. The company will want to emphasize any significant unfairness to it and to request early relief. The relief could be based on costs reflected in a forward purchase commitment or on higher replacement values.

If the authorities seem amenable, the company may want to seek a rule allowing automatic price changes based on moves in the costs of raw materials and other items.

Another troublesome question is where the right of the government agency to know starts and the right of the company to maintain confidentiality about its business ends. A company's product recipe, which is sometimes reflected in certain item costs, and the profitability of product lines are not items a company wishes to reveal to its rivals. The company can never be certain that the agency or one of its employees, especially one who leaves it, will not give such information to competitors. There is no easy answer to this question. Agencies usually demand only categories of costs. The company can only stamp each document "confidential property of the company" and hope.

Arguing Against Controls

When a government believes it must introduce price controls or make changes in existing controls, management has a choice: it can sit idly by or present its view on the law, on the regulations, and on the economic and political policies underlying price restrictions. Management's views on the wisdom of controls are probably best presented through an association such as the chamber of commerce in the country. The view of such an association, joining many different companies, usually is considered more persuasive than that of one corporation.

The representative should try to persuade the administrators and policy-makers not only that price controls will hurt the country in the long run, but also that price control is not the way to solve the country's inflation difficulties. This argument reportedly was a factor in the decision of Puerto Rico's Department of Consumer Affairs to decontrol vegetable oil as well as other products.

There are, of course, many arguments for price control. These center on claims that it stops inflation and the accelerating wage-price spiral and that consumers want controls in order to slow inflation. Supporters of controls also maintain that they raise the income of the poor; that when coupled with rationing they are the fair way to allocate a short supply; that there is no really free market anyway; and that investment, and thus employment, will still get encouragement because of government deficit spending and increases in the money supply.

These arguments generally receive more political support shortly before an election. The party in power hopes to demonstrate to its citizens the benefits of halting price increases without (in the short term) causing greater unemployment or sharp devaluations.

Many reputable scholars not in the employ of business, however, say it is

Controls on foodstuffs since 1945

T he three countries that almost never have imposed mandatory price controls on foodstuffs, West Germany, Hong Kong, and Japan, have generally had buoyant, expansive economies. West Germany abandoned controls in 1951 and Hong Kong controlled the price of rice briefly in 1974. The Japanese government buys certain commodities at a support price and resells them, often at a loss—but this is not price control as defined in this article.

Admittedly, many countries that have dropped price controls in the recent past have reactivated them under continuing or new authority. These include France, Denmark, Finland, Greece, the Philippines, Brazil, Venezuela, and Argentina. The point is that at one time or another these countries terminated price controls.

Argentina may eventually find its decision to be an unhappy one. According to two economists at the International Monetary Fund, a decade of price controls (1963–1973) aggravated Argentinian inflation because the government subsidized businesses that lost money. This program increased the amount of credit outstanding and made it difficult for the government to defend its price targets.*

Moreover, most countries that now have price restraints on foodstuffs confine them to what they consider to be essentials. To name a few, such is the case in Italy (sugar, bread, some meats, pasta), Spain (basic foodstuffs), Switzerland (milk, eggs, and a few other items), Honduras (basic foods), Peru (essential foodstuffs), Malaysia (rice, milk, sugar, and flour), and the Philippines (rice, repacked sugar, canned or evaporated milk, chicken and pork).

But more impressively, many countries have abandoned mandatory price controls in recent years. They include the United States, Canada (though it did institute controls on certain public industries in June 1982), the United Kingdom (except for milk), Sweden recently (except for a few agricultural products), Turkey (except for cereals), South Africa, Colombia, Chile, and Korea.

* See Ke-Young Chu and Andrew Feltenstein, "Extraordinary inflation: The Argentine Experience," *Finance and Development*, June 1979, p. 32.

not in a country's economic interest to invoke price control. Their reasoning is based mainly on the need for a relatively free market.

I say *relatively* because it is not necessary for corporate executives to support (although they may believe in) a completely free worldwide market with no tariffs or protectionism. The company need not be against control of the currency, of the exchange rate, or of public utilities or against food subsidies to the poor. What the company can unabashedly contend is that within the country no maximum prices should be set and that if a relatively free market, not a monopoly, exists within a country, it should be the deciding force in setting prices. Admittedly, the question of what constitutes the market is a hard one. But certainly a market is not just corn oil but all vegetable oils from the viewpoint of the government, which should be concerned with functional substitutes. And even if the company predominates in that market, it does not abuse its pricing power if it determines the product's selling price by reference to a price determined in a free market in another, similar country where there are many competitors.

A relatively free market is the most efficient way to attack escalating prices, since higher prices indicate to potential market entrants the possibility of healthy margins. Their investment leads to more products (and more employment) and thus lower prices. This is classic wisdom, but it is true. A relatively free market is the best allocator of products in short supply and the best inducement to the right investment. An investment decision based on artificial market conditions would be a mistake.

Tough consequences The effort to put a lid on prices often diverts a government's attention from the money supply level, which often is a material cause of inflation. To focus the government's attention on the problems of controls as well as the possibilities, company representatives can cite these consequences:

◆ The maximum price often becomes the minimum price because if a sector is allowed a price increase, all businesses in the sector will take it regardless of cost justification.

◆ The wage-price spiral advances vigorously in anticipation of controls—and after, since they invariably end.

◆ Labor often turns against restrictions because they are usually accompanied by an incomes policy or wage restrictions (e.g., the United States, France, Portugal, and the United Kingdom).

◆ Noninflationary wage hikes are forestalled.

◆ Government control not only creates a costly regulatory body, but control is also difficult to enforce. In Mexico, for instance, the ceiling price of milk in grocery stores could not be maintained when the milk was sold by route salesmen. And even though refined sugar is controlled in India and Pakistan, farmers boil their own raw sugar and sell the refined product at prices and in transactions that their governments cannot curb.

◆ Under price control the authorities raise less in taxes because less money is made.

◆ A government may have to bail out many companies with cheap loans (as in Argentina) or make grants to prevent bankruptcies and unemployment.

And what of the effects on business? Apart from those I have mentioned, there are the inequities when competitors are treated differently, which have differently costed inventories at the time that price control takes effect. Or they may have different costs of money or different equity capital, which becomes a factor when the controls include an allowable return on equity, as in Portugal. In agribusiness there is the inequity that price controls may not be imposed uniformly on growers and processors. In Brazil, for instance, corn costs are not controlled but the price of packaged cornstarch is. The result is a constant squeeze on gross margins. Finally, restrictions on the large companies in a sector

'Durable' Third World development

Many advocates of appropriate technology in the developing world do not necessarily see it as a stepping stone to Northern-style industrialization. They see technical cooperation among developing countries as the way in which poor nations can gain the economic independence and self confidence to be able to produce their own form of economy and industry rather than importing foreign systems.

"The developing countries must break a psychological and attitudinal barrier," Shridath S. Ramphal, secretary general of the British Commonwealth and a former minister of the Guyana Government, said at [a] Buenos Aires conference.

"For too long we have been brainwashed into believing that the best education, the best technology, the best services, the best intellects, the best anything you can think of, comes from the so-called developed world—'All that is rural is bad. All that is urban is better. All that is foreign is best.' Despite all our intellectualizing to the contrary, these notions retain a stranglehold on the development process, which continues to be confused with Westernization."

Mr. Ramphal said durable development was a more complex process than the simple adoption of Western ways. "Its touchstone," he said, "is the growth of a feeling of self-confidence in a society that can solve its own problems and devise its own solutions, relying largely on its own capability. It can neither be bought nor taught.

"The task of development is not simply one of making a technological jump, but of creating and nurturing an internal innovative capability."

That philosophy, of course, is not far from one that nurtured the United States when, two centuries ago, it was also a developing country. The concept has even become a part of the national folklore as "Yankee ingenuity."

From the *New York Times*, by Boyce Rensberger, in the Tuesday, April 10, 1979 issue. Copyright © 1979 by the New York Times Company. Reprinted by permission.

---

mean that small businesses in that sector, even if unregulated, cannot sell above the price ceiling because of competitive pressures.

Not only are there valid economic policy reasons for not invoking price controls in the interests of the country, but also the experience which countries have had with such regulation indicates that governments are generally moving away from it toward freer markets (see the sidebar on page R276 for a brief account of controls on foodstuffs).

Difficult for Both Sides

Rapidly escalating prices are not just a serious government problem; they are a serious management problem. Corporate management or representatives of companies should work with governments in establishing an economic policy centered around a relatively free market in order to ameliorate this problem without price control. Clearly, once price control is invoked, management will have to devote much time to resolving the many difficulties that controls present.

REFERENCES

Here are some publications on the topic of price controls, listed in order of helpfulness toward understanding.

"Investment, Licensing & Trading Conditions Abroad" (New York: Business International Corporation). These are looseleaf books, kept fairly current, on various countries. Section 5 with respect to each country deals with price control.

Comptroller General of the General Accounting Office: "Report to the Congress of the United States on the Voluntary Pay and Price Standards" (1980), and "Report to the Chairman of the Joint Economic Committee," which includes the response of President Alfred E. Kahn of the Council on Wage and Price Stability to the report (1980).

Paul D. Staudohar, "Effects of Wage and Price Controls in Canada, 1975–1978," *Relations Industrielles,* vol. 34, no. 4, 1979, p. 674.

Arthur M. Okun, *Prices and Quantities, A Macroeconomic Analysis* (Washington, D.C.: Brookings Institution, 1980), especially pp. 342–348.

Robert Schuettinger and Eamonn Butler, *Forty Centuries of Wage and Price Controls,* (Washington, D.C.: The Heritage Foundation, 1979). A partisan advocacy against price control as a means of fighting inflation.

UNRAVELING THE MYSTIQUE OF EXPORT PRICING

S. Tamer Cavusgil

In recent years, hundreds of U.S. companies have become involved in international business. The initial foreign activity is typically exporting. Perhaps the most puzzling part of international business for these firms is making pricing decisions.

What role should pricing play in the exporting company's marketing efforts? Can pricing be used as an effective marketing tool? Or would that practice expose the firm to unnecessary risks? What considerations affect the choice between incremental and full-cost pricing strategies? What approach should management take when setting export prices? How can the firm cope with escalations in international prices? What strategies are appropriate when a strong currency impairs overseas competitiveness? These are only a few of the many questions international marketing managers must answer.

Export pricing is a complex issue, and simple decision rules are often inadequate. The complexity lies in the large number of variables that affect international pricing decisions and the uncertainty surrounding them. These variables can be classified as either internal or external to the organization. The internal group includes corporate goals, desire for control over prices, approach to costing, and degree of company internationalization. The external group includes competitive pressures, demand levels, legal and government regulations, general economic conditions, and exchange rates.

Despite export pricing's importance and complexity, very little empirical research has been conducted that might give managers norms to follow.[1] This article attempts to illuminate this important area of international marketing management. The overall purpose is to provide a better understanding of export pricing issues and to identify propositions that can be tested by more definitive, large-scale surveys, as well as to generate findings and implications useful to export managers.

Personal interviews, two to three hours in length, were conducted with one or more executives at each of 24 firms. Most of the firms studied were exporters of industrial or specialized products. The typical firm employed about 500 persons. Background information about each firm was collected with the use of a structured questionnaire either prior to or during the interview. All firms were located in the Midwestern United States.

Source: Reprinted from *Business Horizons,* May-June 1988. Copyright 1988 by the Foundation for the School of Business at Indiana University. Used with permission.

[1] Vern Terpstra, "Suggestions for Research Themes and Publications," *Journal of International Business Studies,* Spring/Summer 1983, pp. 9–10.

Pricing Literature

Price is the only marketing variable that generates revenue. Top marketing executives call pricing the most critical pressure point of the 1980s.[2] Recently, with accelerating technological advances, shorter product life cycles, and increasing input costs, price changes have become more common. Despite these developments, academic research on pricing has been modest at best.[3]

The neglect of international pricing is even more serious.[4] Intracorporate (transfer) pricing issues received attention during the 1970s, when study of multinational corporations (MNCs) was intense, but other pricing topics remain relatively unexplored.[5]

Other studies have focused on pricing practices under floating exchange rates,[6] location of pricing authority within MNCs,[7] price leadership of MNCs,[8] multinational pricing in developing countries,[9] and uniform pricing.[10] Several studies have had a regional/industry focus. One found a relatively high degree of export price discrimination among industrial firms in Northern England.[11] Another compared the pricing practices of chemical and construction industries

---

[2] "Pricing Competition is Shaping Up as 84's Top Marketing Pressure Point," *Marketing News,* November 11, 1983, p. 1.

[3] Vithala R. Rao, "Pricing Research in Marketing: The State of the Art," *Journal of Business,* January 1984, pp. 539–559.

[4] See: James C. Baker and John K. Ryans, Jr., "Some Aspects of International Pricing: A Neglected Area of Management Policy," *Management Decision,* Summer 1973, pp. 177–182; S. Tamer Cavusgil and John R. Nevin, "State-of-the-Art in International Marketing: An Assessment," in B. M. Enis and K. J. Roering, eds., *Review of Marketing 1981* (Chicago: American Marketing Association), pp. 195–216; and Terpstra, pp. 9–10.

[5] See: Jeffrey S. Arpan, "Multinational Firm Pricing in International Markets," *Sloan Management Review,* Winter 1973, pp. 1–9; M. Edgar Barrett, "Case of the Tangled Transfer Price," *Harvard Business Review,* May–June 1977, p. 21; Seung H. Kim and Stephen W. Miller, "Constituents of the International Transfer Pricing Decision," *Columbia Journal of World Business,* Spring 1979, pp. 69–77.

[6] Llewellyn Clague and Rena Grossfield, "Exporting Pricing in a Floating Rate World," *Columbia Journal of World Business,* Winter 1974, pp. 17–22.

[7] Baker and Ryans, pp. 177–182.

[8] Donald J. Lecraw, "Pricing Strategies of Transnational Corporations," *Asia Pacific Journal of Management,* January 1984, pp. 112–119.

[9] Nathaniel H. Left, "Multinational Corporate Pricing Strategy in Developing Countries," *Journal of International Business Studies,* Fall 1975, pp. 55–64.

[10] Peter R. Kressler, "Is Uniform Pricing Desirable in Multinational Markets?" *Akron Business and Economic Review,* Winter 1971.

[11] Nigel Piercy, "British Export Market Selection and Pricing," *Industrial Marketing Management,* October 1981, pp. 287–297.

in South Africa.[12] A third, on the other hand, studied price-setting processes among industrial firms in the French market.[13]

This last study is particularly important, because it represents an effort to systematically describe and compare the processes used by firms to set prices. Through in-depth analyses of price decisions made by companies, the authors were able to develop flowcharts as well as indices of similarity, participation, and activity. They contend that decision-process methodology can help people gain insights into the dynamic activities of firms. The decision-making model for export pricing discussed in this article employs a similar approach.

The discussion here focuses on three major issues. First, those factors which have a bearing on export pricing are examined, and each factor's relevance is illustrated with company examples. The next section reveals that companies appear to follow one of three export pricing strategies. Finally, a decision framework for export pricing is offered.

Factors in Export Pricing

Export pricing is not a topic that lends itself easily to generalization. As with domestic pricing, any consideration of policies for setting export prices must first address the unique nature of the individual firm. Company philosophy, corporate culture, product offerings, and operating environment all have a significant impact on the creation of pricing policy. In addition, export marketers face unique constraints in each market destination.

The interaction of the internal and external environments gives rise to distinct—yet predictable—pricing constraints in different markets. These to a large extent determine export price strategy. For example, negotiation is normally required in the Middle East, so Regal Ware, a producer of kitchen appliances and cookware, uses a higher list price in such markets to leave a margin for discretion. But D. W. Witter, a manufacturer of grain storage and handling equipment, doesn't make price concessions in the Middle East. Witter is convinced that once a price becomes negotiable, the Middle Eastern buyer will expect and demand future concessions, making future negotiations interminable.

In Algeria, the interest rate is limited by the government. To counter this one company, a manufacturer of mining and construction equipment, builds the additional cost of capital into the price.

Six variables have important influences on export pricing. They are:

1. Nature of the product/industry;

2. Location of the production facility;

---

[12] Russell Abratt and Leyland F. Pitt, "Pricing Practices in Two Industries," *Industrial Marketing Management*, 14: 301–306.

[13] John U. Farley, James M. Hulbert and David Weistein, "Price Setting and Volume Planning by Two European Industrial Companies: A Study and Comparison of Decision Processes," *Journal of Marketing*, Winter 1980, pp. 46–54.

3. Chosen system of distribution;

4. Location and environment of the foreign market;

5. U.S. government regulations; and

6. Attitude of the firm's management.

A brief discussion of each factor is presented below.

Nature of the Product/Industry

A specialized product, or one with a technological edge, gives the firm flexibility. There are few competitors in such cases. In many markets there is no local production of the product, government-imposed import barriers are minimal, and importing firms all face similar price-escalation factors. Under such circumstances, firms are able to remain competitive with little adjustment in price strategy. Firms with a technological edge, such as the Burdick Corporation (hospital equipment) and Nicolet Instruments (scientific instruments), enjoy similar advantages, but both experience greater service requirements and longer production and sales lead times.

A relatively low level of price competition usually leads to administered prices and a static role for pricing in the export marketing mix. Over the years, however, as price competition evolves and technological advantages shrink, specialized and highly technical firms must make more market-based exceptions to their uniform export pricing strategies.

Many firms' export pricing strategies are also influenced by industry-specific factors, such as drastic fluctuations in the price of raw materials and predatory pricing practices by foreign competitors (most notably the Japanese). The presence of such factors demands greater flexibility in export pricing at some companies: Ray-O-Vac adjusts export prices frequently according to current silver prices. Other companies negotiate fixed-price agreements with suppliers prior to making a contract bid.

Location of Production Facility

Many U.S. companies produce exported products only in the United States. These U.S. exporters are unable to shift manufacturing to locations that make economic sense. Purely domestic companies are tied to conditions prevailing in the home market, in this case the United States.

Those companies with production or assembly facilities abroad, often closer to foreign customers, have additional flexibility in overseas markets. These companies find it easier to respond to fluctuations in foreign exchange. Cummins Engine, for example, supplies Latin American customers with U.S. production when the U.S. dollar is weak. When the dollar is relatively strong, U.K. plants assume greater importance.

A number of factors may have impeded the global competitiveness of U.S. manufacturers in recent years. These include lagging productivity in many sectors of the economy and, until recently, reluctance to seek global sources of supply for materials, parts, and components. Also, strong unions and a high standard of living in the United States have contributed to higher labor costs. Naturally, these comparative disadvantages are reflected in the quotations submitted to overseas buyers.

Chosen System of Distribution The channels of export distribution a company uses dictate much in export pricing. For example, subsidiary relationships offer greater control over final prices, first-hand knowledge of market conditions, and the ability to adjust prices rapidly. With independent distributors, control usually extends only to the landed price received by the exporter. As one might expect, many of the executives interviewed spoke of the difficulty of maintaining price levels. These firms report that distributors may mark up prices substantially—up to 200 percent in some cases.

When a firm initiates exporting through independent distributors, many new pricing considerations arise. Significant administrative costs stem from the selection of foreign distributors and the maintenance of harmonious relationships. Discount policies for intermediaries must be established. Also, the costs of exporting (promotion, freight service, and so forth) must be assigned to either the intermediaries or the manufacturer. To minimize the administrative, research, and travel expenses involved in switching to direct exporting, most firms use a relatively uniform export pricing strategy across different markets. Gross margins are then increased to account for additional levels of distribution. In other cases, companies establish prices on a case-by-case basis.

The use of manufacturers' representatives offers greater price control to the exporter, but this method is used less frequently. Finally, sales to end users may involve negotiation or, in the case of selling to governmental agencies, protracted purchasing decisions. List prices are not used in these circumstances.

Firms often attempt to establish more direct channels of distribution to reach their customers in overseas markets. By reducing the number of intermediaries between the manufacturer and the customer, they offset the adverse effects of *international price escalation*. Excessive escalation of prices is a problem encountered by most exporters. Aside from shorter distribution channels, the firms studied had developed other strategies to cope with price escalation. These alternatives are listed in Figure 1.

Location and Environment of the Foreign Market The climatic conditions of a market may necessitate product modification. For example, a producer of soft-drink equipment must treat its products against rust corrosion in tropical markets. Another company, an agri-business concern, must take into account climate, soil conditions, and the country's infrastructure before making any bid. Economic factors, such as inflation, exchange-rate fluctuations, and price controls, may hinder market entry and effectiveness.[14] These factors, especially the

---

[14] Victor H. Frank, Jr., "Living with Price Controls Abroad," *Harvard Business Review*, March-April 1984, pp. 137–142.

FIGURE 1   Strategic Options to Deal with Price Escalation

Shortening channels of distribution by reducing number of intermediaries or engaging in company-sponsored distribution. Fewer intermediaries would also have the effect of minimizing value added taxes.

Reducing cost to overseas customers by eliminating costly features from the product, lowering overall product quality, or offering a stripped-down model.

Shipping and assembling components in foreign markets. Popularity of the Free Trade Zones in Hong Kong, Panama or the Caribbean Basin is due to companies' desire to minimize price escalation.

Modifying the product to bring it into a different, lower-tariff classification. The Microbattery division of Ray-O-Vac Corporation, for example, ships bulk to foreign marketing companies who then repackage. Another company, through consultations with local distributors, places products in "proper" import classifications. Proper wording is used for initial import registration to qualify for lower duties.

Lowering the new price (landed price) to reduce tariffs and other charges by the importing country. This can be accomplished through the application of marginal cost pricing or by allowing discounts to distributors. Nicolet Instruments, a producer of scientific instruments, for example, compensates its distributors for the cost of installation and service. Western Publishing Company compensates its distributors for the differences in import duties between book and nonbook exports.

Going into overseas production and sourcing in order to remain competitive in the foreign markets. Dairy Equipment Company located in Wisconsin, for example, supplies the European market with bulk coolers made at its Danish plant as a way of reducing freight costs.

firms interviewed. Consequently, several companies have introduced temporary compensating adjustments as part of their pricing strategies. The unusually strong value of the U.S. dollar during the first half of the 1980s was a significant factor in pricing strategy.

Since currency fluctuations are cyclical, exporters who find themselves blessed with a price advantage when their currency is undervalued must carry an extra burden when their currency is overvalued. Committed exporters must be creative, pursuing different strategies during different periods. Appropriate strategies practiced by the firms studied are outlined in Figure 2.

It must be noted that, while exporters can implement some of these strategies quickly, others require a long-term response. For example, the decision to manufacture overseas is often a part of a deliberate and long-term plan for most companies. And while some strategies can be used by any exporter, others, such as countertrade and speculative currency trading, are limited to use by the larger, more experienced exporters. In fact, most managers inter-

FIGURE **2**   Exporter Strategies under Varying Currency Conditions

When domestic currency is WEAK. . . .	When domestic currency is STRONG. . . .
Stress price benefits.	Engage in nonprice competition by improving quality, delivery and aftersale service.
Expand product line and add more costly features.	Improve productivity and engage in vigorous cost reduction.
Shift sourcing and manufacturing to domestic market.	Shift sourcing and manufacturing overseas.
Exploit export opportunities in all markets.	Give priority to exports to relatively strong-currency countries.
Conduct conventional cash-for-goods trade.	Deal in countertrade with weak-currency countries.
Use full-costing approach, but use marginal-cost pricing to penetrate new/competitive markets.	Trim profit margins and use marginal-cost pricing.
Speed repatriation of foreign-earned income and collections.	Keep the foreign-earned income in host country, slow collections.
Minimize expenditures in local, host country currency.	Maximize expenditures in local, host country currency.
Buy needed services (advertising, insurance, transportation, etc.) in domestic market.	Buy needed services abroad and pay for them in local currencies.
Minimize local borrowing.	Borrow money needed for expansion in local market.
Bill foreign customers in domestic currency.	Bill foreign customers in their own currency.

viewed said that high-risk propositions such as countertrade deals should be used only by multinational companies.

The cultural environment and business practices of the foreign market also play a large role in export pricing. Some countries abhor negotiation, others expect it. As previously noted, D. W. Witter has successfully overcome the expectation of price negotiation in the Middle East market. In some markets, a subtle barrier to foreign imports is erected in the form of procurement practices which favor domestic companies.

U.S. Government Regulations Government policy also affects export pricing strategy. While the majority of the firms interviewed are not directly affected by U.S. pricing regulations, they feel that U.S. regulations such as the Foreign Corrupt Practices Act put them at a significant competitive disadvantage. One company often receives "requests" by overseas customers to add over $100,000 to the contract price and make appropriate arrangements to transfer the money to private accounts abroad. Interestingly, such requests are sometimes openly made. Submission to demands for "grease payments" appears to be the only option if businesses want to compete in certain countries.

Attitude of the Firm's Management Many U.S. firms still view exporting as an extension of the domestic sales effort, and export pricing policy is established accordingly. Smaller companies whose top management concerns itself mostly with domestic matters have major problems setting export prices. Price determination of export sales is often based on a full-costing approach. The preference for cost-based pricing over market-oriented pricing reflects the relative importance given to profits and market share. This is particularly notable with firms that are unconcerned with market share and require that every quote meet their profit expectations. Other companies are more concerned with selling one product line at any price, even below cost, and reap longer-term benefits from the sale of follow-up consumables and spare parts. Producers of expensive industrial equipment, scientific instruments, and medical equipment fall into this category.

Alternative Approaches to Pricing

Firms typically choose one of three approaches to pricing. These can be called the rigid cost-plus, flexible cost-plus, and dynamic incremental pricing strategies.

Rigid Cost-Plus Strategy The complexity of export pricing has caused many managers to cling to a rigid cost-plus pricing strategy in an effort to secure profitability. This strategy establishes the foreign list price by adding international customer costs and a gross margin to domestic manufacturing costs. The final cost to the customer includes administrative and R&D overhead costs, transportation, insurance, packaging, marketing, documentation, and customs charges, as well as the profit margins for both the distributor and the manufacturer. Although this type of pricing ensures margins, the final price may be so high that it keeps the firm from being competitive in major foreign markets.

Nevertheless, cost-plus pricing appears to be the most dominant strategy among American firms. Approximately 70 percent of the sampled firms used this strategy. Over half of the firms using a cost-plus strategy adhered to it rigidly, with no exceptions. This approach may be typical of other exporting firms in the United States. The following company examples illustrate the popularity of the rigid cost-plus pricing approach.

Autotrol is a Wisconsin manufacturer of water treatment and control equipment. The firm employs about 80 people, and exports account for about 60 percent of its estimated $14 million annual sales. Principal markets include Western Europe, Japan, Australia, New Zealand, and Venezuela. Autotrol sets export prices 3 percent to 4 percent higher than domestic prices to cover the additional costs. Such costs include foreign advertising, foreign travel, and all costs incurred when shipping the product from the factory to the foreign distributor. The firm has successfully exported for the past 15 years by using a rigid cost-plus strategy.

Chillicothe Metal Co. is a solely owned manufacturer of generator sets, pump packages, engine enclosures, controls, and spare parts. The firm has recently lost a significant portion of its foreign business. Sales dropped from $5 million in 1982 to $3 million in 1984, and the current employment of 40 is down from its 1982 high of 100. The company had successfully exported for more than 15 years, but current exports are down 40 percent from the 1982 level. Principal foreign markets are the Middle East, North Africa, and the Far East. The company adheres to a rigid cost-plus pricing strategy that includes a built-in margin ranging from 5 percent to 15 percent. However, the president has recently taken efforts to control costs, extend credit, and reduce margins for cash-in-advance customers in an attempt to counter the effects of the slow business cycle.

Dairy Equipment Co. produces milk machines, bulk coolers, and other high-quality equipment for the dairy industry. The company's annual sales are about $40 million, with current employment at 400. Although the company has exported continuously over the past decade, export earnings have become negligible. This has been caused by a significant drop in sales in the company's primary foreign market—West Germany. Gross profit has remained the company's primary export goal, but the rigid cost-plus pricing strategy has not yet proved to be effective. The company has always sought equal profitability from foreign sales, although fierce competition in some markets has forced it to consider lower profit margins. The company's export pricing policy remains a static element of the marketing mix.

These examples demonstrate that a rigid cost-plus pricing strategy may or may not be effective. They also imply that just because a strategy has been successful in the past, there is no guarantee that it will be successful in the future. Competitive pressures often force firms to reevaluate their pricing decisions and consider new alternatives.

Flexible Cost-Plus Strategy One such alternative is a flexible cost-plus strategy. This is also the most logical strategy for companies that are in the process of moving away from their traditionally rigid pricing policies.

Flexible cost-plus price strategy is identical to the rigid strategy in establishing list prices. Flexible strategy, however, allows for price variations in special circumstances. For example, discounts may be granted, depending on the customer, the size of the order, or the intensity of competition. Although discounts occasionally are granted on a case-by-case basis, the primary objective of flexible cost-plus pricing is profit. Thus, pricing is still a static element of the marketing mix. The following cases are good examples of companies that use a flexible cost-plus pricing strategy.

Baughman, a division of Fuqua Industries, manufactures steel grain-storage silos and related equipment. The company currently employs about 125 people, and annual sales are around $6 million. The company has traditionally exported about 30 percent of its sales over the past ten years, but recently exports have grown to over 50 percent of annual sales. Baughman's products are of high quality, and pricing has not often been an active element in the marketing mix. The firm's export sales terms consist of an irrevocable confirmed letter of credit in U.S. currency with no provisions for fluctuating exchange rates. Export and domestic prices are identical before exporting costs are added. However, Baughman will make concessions to this policy to secure strategically important sales.

Nicolet Instrument Corporation designs, manufactures, and markets electronic instruments that are used in science, medicine, industry, and engineering. The firm employs more than 500 people and has annual sales of over $85 million. Exports account for about 42 percent of total sales, and the firm has been exporting for the past ten years. Major foreign markets include Japan, West Germany, France, Canada, England, Mexico, Sweden, and the Netherlands. Foreign and domestic prices are calculated according to full cost. Since Nicolet has held a technological edge, it has not been affected by competition in foreign markets. However, the competitive gap has been slowly closing, and the company now varies from administered prices more frequently.

Badger Meter manufactures and sells industrial liquid meters. The company employs 700 people, and its annual sales are estimated at $60 million. The company has sold internationally for more than 50 years, but export sales only account for 9 percent of total sales. Major markets include Europe, Canada, Taiwan, and the Philippines. The company owns a production facility in Mexico and has licensees in Ecuador and Peru. Cost-based list prices are used for both domestic and foreign markets. Although prices usually remain fixed, the company has, at times, offered special discounts to regain market share or to offset unfavorable exchange rates.

Flexible pricing strategies are useful to counter competitive pressures or exchange-rate fluctuations. They help firms stay competitive in certain markets without disrupting the entire pricing strategy. However, if competitive pressures persist and technology gaps continue to close, the company could face losing its export market. This is when a company may consider the third alternative.

Dynamic Incremental Strategy The dynamic incremental pricing strategy was used by approximately 30 percent of the firms studied. Most firms using this strategy had sales well over $50 million with exports ranging from 20 to 65 percent of total sales. In the dynamic incremental strategy, prices are set by subtracting fixed costs for plants, R&D, and domestic overhead from cost-plus figures. In addition, domestic marketing and promotion costs are also disregarded.

This strategy is based on the assumption that fixed and variable domestic costs are incurred regardless of export sales. Therefore, only variable and international customer costs need to be recovered on exported products. This makes it possible for a company to maintain profit margins while selling its exported products at prices below U.S. list. It is also assumed that unused production capacity exists and that the exported products could not be otherwise sold at full cost. Companies can thus lower their prices and be competitive in markets that may otherwise be prohibitive to enter or penetrate. The following examples illustrate this strategy.

Flo-Con Systems, a subsidiary of Masco Inc., manufactures high-quality and sophisticated flow-control valves for molten-steel-pouring applications. The company employs 500 people and has sales between $50 and $60 million, of which 25 percent result from exports. A plant located in Canada produces final products, and an additional plant in Mexico is being considered. Flo-Con finds the nature of its markets very competitive. The firm's export prices are based on competitive prices in the local market. Management is often forced to temporarily overlook costs and margins to remain competitive and secure orders.

Ray-O-Vac, a producer of batteries and other consumer goods, has been exporting successfully for over 30 years. Its Micro Power Division employs 250 and has estimated annual sales of $100 million. The major products in this division include batteries for hearing aids and watches. Exports account for 20 percent of total business, and major markets include Europe, Far East, and Japan. These markets are entered through wholly-owned subsidiaries strategically located around the world. Each subsidiary may be treated as a cost or profit center depending upon the market circumstances. Competitive pressures demand flexible pricing, and discounts are often granted to gain market share or secure OEM business. Branch managers may adjust prices on a day-to-day basis to counter exchange-rate fluctuations. Export pricing is a very active ingredient in the firm's marketing mix.

Econ-O-Cloth is an independent manufacturer of optical polishing cloths and a wholesaler of related goods. Although the company has traditionally exported around 25 percent of its sales volume, this figure has slipped to around 5 percent over the past five years. Major markets include Canada, Mexico, and Western Europe. Econ-O-Cloth reduced export margins to compensate for the strong dollar in the early 1980s, and it considers pricing an active instrument for achieving marketing objectives. The firm continually monitors the foreign environment and at times modifies its prices and products to blend with foreign consumer demands. Econ-O-Cloth has been squeezed hard by competition, and it is still waiting for its dynamic pricing strategy to pay off.

The above examples demonstrate that pricing strategies are complex and that no single strategy suits a firm at all times. There is no guarantee that pricing strategies that work successfully today will continue to do so in the future. Many traditionally successful exporters have recently experienced sales downturns in their foreign markets. One can only speculate on whether a change of pricing strategies could have prevented these downturns. Also, it is not known to what extent other factors (poor market intelligence, weak distribution networks, no product modifications when they were needed, slow delivery, or poor image) were responsible.

The uncertainties of international business make it difficult for executives to select the pricing strategy that is best for their firm. As a result, most firms use the rigid cost-plus strategy until external pressures force them to reconsider. This strategy makes managers feel secure, and it is frequently used when a firm enters the export market. As competition and other external variables grow more intense, however, the firm typically makes exceptions to its pricing policy, moving from rigid to flexible cost-plus pricing. Few firms have attempted to price their export products according to the dynamic conditions of the marketplace. For these firms, the dynamic incremental strategy is usually required, and prices may change frequently in response to competition, the prevailing exchange rate, and other variables.

Most exporting firms appear to establish their pricing policies reactively, changing only when external pressures force the issue. In working this way, however, these firms lose valuable sales and market share during the transition period. Although this strategy may be defensible, three types of lags may result in irreversible damage. The recognition lag is the amount of time between an actual change in the environment and a company's recognition of that change. Reaction lag is the amount of time between the company's recognition of the problem and its decision to react to it. Finally, effectiveness lag is the amount of time needed to implement the decision.

One might conclude that if executives were proactive in their pricing strategy, they might avoid many of the headaches associated with exporting. But how can executives be sure which pricing policy is best for their firms? Considering all the variables that affect price, it is reasonable to assume that different pricing policies should exist for different markets. Furthermore, considering the volatility of foreign markets, one would suspect that these policies should be continuously reviewed and updated. It is not surprising, then, that most executives resort to setting their pricing policies reactively.

A Decision Framework for Export Pricing

Most companies lack a systematic procedure for setting and revising export prices. The absence of a formal decision-making procedure that incorporates and weighs relevant variables has led to the development of the framework described here. It is not intended to replace management judgment, since the business executive is usually in the best position to assess the suitability of various strategies and policies, but simply to provide a systematic framework for arriving at export pricing decisions.

Figure 3 illustrates the steps involved in a formal export price determination process. A brief description of each step is presented below.

FIGURE 3   Decision Process For Export Price Determination

Verify export market potential

Estimate target price range: floor, ceiling, and expected prices

Determine company sales potential at given prices

Analyze import, distribution and transaction barriers

Examine corporate goals and preference for pricing strategy

Select suitable pricing strategy:
  1. Rigid cost-plus
  2. Flexible cost-plus
  3. Dynamic incremental

Check consistency with current price setting

Implementation: Select tactics, distributor prices, and end user prices

Monitor export market performance and make adjustments as necessary

Verification of Market Potential The first step in the analysis gives firm information on the market potential in specific countries. The company can identify market potential for its products by using both formal and informal sources. Formal sources include market-research firms, the U.S. Department of Commerce, banks, and other agencies that provide information on foreign countries. Informal sources include trade shows, local distributors, international trade journals, and business contacts.[15] During this process, those countries that do not demonstrate adequate market potential are dropped from the list of possible markets.

Estimating Target Price Range Once it is determined that a market has sufficient potential, the firm observes the price ranges of substitute or competitive

---

[15] S. Tamer Cavusgil, "Guidelines for Export Market Research," *Business Horizons*, November-December 1985, pp. 27–33.

products in the local market to find its target price range. This consists of three prices:

◆ The floor price, that price at which the firm breaks even;
◆ The ceiling price, the highest price the market is likely to bear for the product; and
◆ The expected price, the price at which the firm would most likely be competitive.

Estimating Sales Potential Assuming that a high enough level of sales potential exists to warrant market entry, management then identifies the size and concentration of customer segments, projected consumption patterns, competitive pressures, and the expectations of local distributors and agents. The landed cost and the cost of local distribution are estimated. The potential sales volume is assessed for each of the three price levels, taking into account the price elasticity of demand.

Analyze Special Import, Distribution, or Transaction Barriers If adequate sales potential exists, management then assesses any special import barriers not accounted for in its earlier efforts. These barriers include quotas, tariffs and other taxes, anti-dumping, price-maintenance, currency-exchange, and other governmental regulations that affect the cost of doing business in that country. In addition, internal distribution barriers must also be assessed. Lengthy distribution channels, high margins, and inadequate dealer commitment may present difficulties for the exporter. Finally, currency supply, payment terms, and financing availability should be reviewed. Is it customary for prices to be negotiable? Do customers expect certain credit or payment terms? Once again, sales potential, market share, and profitability should be analyzed in light of the above information in order to confirm the desirability of market entry.

Corporate Goals and Preference for Pricing After deciding on a target market, some companies may not wish to consider anything but full-cost pricing (either rigid or flexible cost-plus). If desired margins can be achieved, this pricing policy can be implemented. If, however, the desired margins cannot be achieved, the firm can either abort market entry or resort to some form of marginal costing approach. If the firm's management is willing to consider pricing strategies that focus on market rather than profit objectives, it may continue the analysis with a systematic identification of the optimal pricing strategy.

Systematic Selection of Appropriate Pricing Strategy The company needs to arrive at a strategy choice by systematically considering all relevant variables. Management faces a basic choice between a dynamic incremental pricing strat-

FIGURE 4   Criteria Relevant to the Choice Between Full and
             Marginal Costing

Conditions favoring . . . Marginal costing/ Aggressive pricing	Criteria	Conditions favoring . . . Full costing/ Passive pricing
	(a) Firm-specific criteria	
Low	Extent of product differentiation	High
Committed	Corporate stance toward exporting	Half-hearted
Long term	Management desire for recovering export overhead	Short term
Sufficient	Company financial resources to sustain initial losses	Insufficient
Wide	Domestic gross margins	Narrow
High	Need for long-term capacity utilization	Low
High	Opportunity to benefit from economies of scale	Low
	(b) Situation-specific criteria	
Substantial	Growth potential of export market	Negligible
High	Potential for follow-up sales	Low
Continuous	Nature of export opportunity	One-time
High	End-user price sensitivity	Low
High	Competitive intensity	Low
Likely	Opportunity to drive out competition	Unlikely
Favorable	Terms of sale and financing	Unfavorable
Low	Exchange rate risk	High
Low	Cost of internal distribution, service and promotion	High

egy and a cost-plus pricing strategy (either rigid or flexible). Dynamic incremental pricing implies a marginal costing approach, while cost-plus pricing implies full costing.

Figure 4 identifies 15 criteria that help management make choices between the two pricing strategies. Some criteria are derived from the general environment of the firm, while others are unique to the specific export opportunity being considered. Management may choose to weigh each group, as well as individual criteria, in arriving at a choice. Figure 4 spells out the conditions that call for incremental pricing.

Checking Consistency with Current Pricing If a firm is already in the targeted market, the recommended pricing strategy should be compared to the strategy currently in place. If deviations exist, they should be explained and justified. If they cannot be justified, the firm should seriously consider adopting the recommended pricing strategy in order to achieve marketing goals more effectively. It is also important to check for consistency of export pricing policies across export markets to minimize any conflicts (such as inter-market shipping by competing middlemen).

Implementation The exporter will determine specific prices for distributors and end users, in accordance with the recommended pricing strategy, and decide on specific pricing tactics. A strategy may fail in a specific market if execution is not effective or if reaction to change is slow. For example, distributors may vary their margins as a response to price changes. Similarly, distributors may hold a large inventory of products at the old price, creating a lag before the new pricing policy actually becomes effective.

Monitoring Exchange rates can be one of the more volatile variables in international business, especially in developing countries. These rates should be monitored continuously, and the effect of their changes on pricing policy should be evaluated. Variables such as competition, regulations, and price sensitivity can be monitored periodically. As these variables change, the firm can adjust its pricing strategy appropriately. The proposed decision process, therefore, provides a proactive means of establishing pricing policies.

A major implication of this analysis is that no export pricing strategy will fit all of a company's products and markets. International pricing issues are extremely complex, and pricing decisions are fueled by many variables. It is important that the company establish a systematic and periodic approach in selecting a pricing policy. The approach should account for both internal and external variables affecting the firm's export efforts. This framework for export pricing is one such approach. Executives may wish to modify the model in order to better blend it with their firms' perspectives.

A second implication is that many U.S. firms may be overlooking lucrative foreign markets because of their strict adherence to the full-cost pricing approach. Furthermore, this rigid practice may hinder effective market penetration in existing foreign markets. A complete reassessment of the firm's market-share objectives may be needed. Committed exporters will allocate the resources needed to accomplish this task if it becomes necessary.

Finally, there is no guarantee that those pricing policies that are suitable today will work in the future. Changing business trends, exchange rates, consumer preferences, and competition are only a few of the variables that have caught successful exporters off guard. Therefore, a method for monitoring changes in the pricing policy variables should be established. The most volatile variables, such as exchange rates and competitive transaction prices, should be monitored more frequently. Once again, committed exporters will recognize the need for this and allocate the appropriate resources to establish an adequate monitoring system.

Although no best pricing strategy exists, most American firms have adhered to a full-cost approach, often disregarding conditions that are particular to their targeted foreign market. Many companies have abandoned lucrative foreign markets because of seemingly unattractive potentials. Other firms have relinquished sales and market share to local or more aggressive foreign competitors. The full-cost approach is a major deterrent to improving the exports of American businesses.

The establishment of international pricing policies is a dynamic process. Success with one strategy does not guarantee that the same strategy will continue to work. Many companies react passively when global changes make their traditional pricing policies obsolete. Such companies are usually forced to either abandon the market or adapt their pricing strategy to the new conditions. The lag times associated with recognition, reaction, and effectiveness can cause an irreversible deterioration in a company's sales, profits, and market share in the foreign country.

A proactive stance on establishing pricing strategy can often reduce or eliminate these lags, enhancing the firm's flexibility and responsiveness to changing business conditions. To develop a proactive stance, businesses need to establish systematic methods to monitor and evaluate the variables associated with an international pricing policy. Firms that are committed to international business will quickly recognize this and allocate resources accordingly.

The guidelines and decision process discussed in this article have been derived from the experience of exporting firms. Such an empirically-based approach to developing managerial guidelines is appropriate, given the current dearth of export pricing literature. Insights obtained from the field can rip away the shroud of mystery that surrounds export pricing decisions. At the same time, it should be noted that the managerial guidelines offered here are appropriate for a given set of conditions. The seasoned executive will realize that these recommendations are not substitutes for good business judgment. The proposed strategies may need minor modifications to better reflect a company's perspectives and constraints on international pricing.

CONSTITUENTS OF THE INTERNATIONAL TRANSFER PRICING DECISION

Seung H. Kim ◆ Stephen W. Miller

Introduction

As U.S. multinational firms increase their amount of involvement in sophisticated marketing arrangements such as global subsidiaries, joint ventures, and parent-owned distribution systems, the price they charge to these several types of affiliates becomes a complex question. Intracorporate pricing of this type is generally referred to as international transfer pricing, i.e., the pricing of goods and/or services sold from division to division within the corporation.[1] These prices may be varied to achieve a wide variety of results which will further the overall financial strategy of the firm. Profits may be shifted from a parent to an affiliate, or vice-versa, by creating interdivision costs such as sales commissions, fees for contracted services, salaries, interest, rent, purchase premiums, discounts, and royalties.[2] Even though taxes and foreign exchange controls invariably impose restraints, substantial latitude in such pricing is often possible.

An investigation of the existing literature indicates a scarcity of empirical research regarding the practices of U.S. multinational firms in worldwide international transfer pricing. For instance, The Conference Board study of 1970 attempted to analyze the major factors affecting international transfer pricing decisions by U.S. multinational firms.[3] It singled out income tax liability as the most important variable affecting the pricing decision, but made only cursory reference to developing countries. In 1973, Business International Corporation (B.I.C.) conducted research involving the pricing experiences of scores of U.S. international corporations.[4] Similarly, the B.I.C. study did not specifically investigate international transfer pricing decisions in developing countries. Finally, in 1972, Jeffrey Arpan surveyed a number of multinational firms in six major European countries which had wholly-owned subsidiaries in the United States.[5] Arpan's work, while probably the most extensive research conducted by an academician, still concentrated on transfer pricing influences from an advanced country perspective, and again stipulated income tax liability as one of the most important of these influences.

It is apparent, then, that prior research on worldwide transfer pricing decisions by U.S. multinationals has been restricted to the problems of more

---

[1] Vern Terpstra, *International Marketing*, 2nd edition, Holt, Rinehart and Winston, 1978, p. 496.

[2] Richard D. Robinson, *International Business Management: A Guide to Decision Making*, 2nd edition, Holt, Rinehart and Winston, 1978, p. 498.

[3] *Intercompany Transaction in the Multinational Firm*, The Conference Board, New York, 1970, pp. 1–5.

[4] *Setting Intercorporate Pricing Policies*, Business International Corporation, New York, 1973, pp. 5–9.

[5] Jeffrey S. Arpan, *International Intracorporate Pricing*, Preager Publishers, New York, 1972, pp. 3–15.

advanced nations. Additionally, the variable most often designated as having the greatest influence on international transfer pricing is income tax liability, implying that such pricing is defined by the short-term objectives of the multinational firm. However, as the international business environment has changed substantially since 1973, and since prior studies have not paid particular attention to the financial factors which are characteristic of a developing nation, it may well be that present replication of the aforementioned research would result in different conclusions.

The purpose of the study is to establish a theoretical framework for worldwide transfer pricing with specific reference to developing countries. Such pricing should be a part of the overall long-run financial decision-making policy of U.S. corporations which have invested in developing countries. Decision-making for international transfer pricing cannot be made in isolation; it must be related to the overall rate of return on foreign investment, or reasonable return on sales, in developing countries. Transfer pricing is, in this way, directly related to the long-term objectives of the firm. The major factors which influence this form of pricing are varied and specifically related to the financial and economic factors which are characteristic of developing countries.

Methodology

Survey and interview data were utilized in this study. A total of 342 U.S. parent firms, with at least one subsidiary in two of eight specified developing countries, were enlisted as recipients of a mail-survey questionnaire. This comprised the entire population of such parents as listed in the World Trade Academy Press, Inc., of 1978.[6] The eight countries were Korea, Malaysia, Phillipines, Taiwan, Brazil, Colombia, Mexico, and Peru, all having a significant amount of subsidiary activity inherent in their economic structure.

Each of the firms was asked to indicate the degree of importance they attached to each of nine factors that are potential influences on transfer pricing decisions. A scale of one to four was employed, with one signifying high importance, two being medium, three being low, and four being of no importance. The nine factors were as follows:

1. Income tax liability within the host country.
2. Income tax liability within the domestic United States.
3. Tariffs and/or customs duties within the host country.
4. Exchange controls within the host country.
5. Profit repatriation restrictions within the host country.

---

[6] *U.S. Subsidiaries and Affiliates Abroad,* World Trade Academy Press, New York, 1978, pp. 1–312.

6. Quota restrictions within the domestic United States.

7. Credit status of the U.S. parent firm.

8. Credit status of the foreign subsidiary or affiliate.

9. Joint-venture constraints within the host country.

Fifty-two total responses were received after a second mailing. Of this total, 30 U.S. parent firms responded fully, one firm indicated that the data was not available, two firms stated that they did minimal trade with the developing countries and thus there was little use in answering the questionnaire, four responded that they used "arms length" pricing as required by Section 482 under Revenue Ruling 69–630 of the U.S. Internal Revenue Service, and fifteen declined to participate either because of the time and effort needed to fill out the questionnaire or because of the sensitivity of the issue being examined.

The overall response rate was 15.2 percent. (This does not lessen the importance of the research findings; the literature reports other mail-survey return rates that are as low as 15 percent.[7]) Possibly many of those U.S. parents who did not respond at all to the mailing considered the topic to be so sensitive that they preferred no involvement at all. Thus, it appears that management is not inclined to discuss transfer pricing applications to international business freely even when, as in this case, anonymity was assured to all those who participated.

To complement the mail-survey data, personal interviews were conducted with several partners of five of the "big eight" accounting firms, and the controllers of three major U.S. parent multinationals, located in St. Louis, Missouri. Extended interviews with these individuals provided this study with a further, qualitative judgment on the practices of U.S. parent firms with regard to international transfer pricing to their subsidiaries in developing countries.

Analysis of the Data

The mean ratings for each of the nine variable statements are exhibited in Table 1. The mean ratings for each variable were determined for each of the eight countries and, subsequently, a mean was computed for each of the variable statements over all eight developing countries. These means are listed in rank order in Table 2.

As can be seen from the data, a rank order of the importance of each of the variable statements shows a distinctly different array than had been indicated by past studies. As mentioned earlier, previous studies indicated that

---

[7] Kenneth P. Uhl and Bertrom Schores, *Marketing Research: Information Systems and Decision Making*, John Wiley & Sons, Inc., 1969, p. 149, and Walter B. Wentz, *Marketing Research: Management and Methods*, Harper & Row, 1972, p. 83.

TABLE **1**   Mean Ratings of Variable Statement Importance

	Income Tax Foreign	Income Tax U.S.	Tariffs & Custom Duties	Ex-change Controls	Profit Repatria-tion	Quota Restric-tions	Credit Status U.S.	Credit Status Foreign	Joint Venture
KOREA	3.32	3.47	2.94	2.10	2.10	3.43	3.72	3.88	2.59
MALAYSIA	3.19	3.12	2.75	2.38	2.31	3.43	3.78	3.67	2.62
PHILIPPINES	3.11	3.22	2.72	2.16	2.10	3.36	3.76	3.70	2.53
TAIWAN	3.44	3.31	2.81	2.19	2.12	3.43	3.69	3.87	2.44
BRAZIL	3.17	3.21	2.77	2.26	2.09	3.50	3.73	3.70	2.67
COLOMBIA	3.31	3.25	2.88	2.25	2.25	3.54	3.73	3.93	2.50
MEXICO	3.05	3.25	2.60	2.14	2.05	3.53	3.79	3.75	2.56
PERU	3.29	3.41	2.81	2.28	2.28	3.07	3.75	3.82	2.69
MEAN for Variables	3.23	3.28	2.78	2.23	2.16	3.41	3.74	3.79	2.58

Note: The grading scale is as follows: 1 = High importance; 2 = Medium importance; 3 = Low importance; 4 = No importance.

TABLE **2**   Rank Order Nine Variable Statements

Rank Order	Variable Statement	Mean Rating
1	Profit repatriation restrictions within the host country	2.16
2	Joint-venture constraints within the host country	2.58
3	Joint-venture constraints within the host country	2.58
4	Tariffs and/or customs duties within the host country	2.78
5	Income tax liability within the host country	3.23
6	Income tax liability within the domestic U.S.	3.28
7	Quota restrictions within the domestic U.S.	3.41
8	Credit status of the U.S. parent firm	3.74
9	Credit status of the foreign subsidiary or affiliate.	3.79

income tax liabilities were highly important factors affecting international transfer pricing decision-making.[8] However, Table 2 shows that such liabilities are fifth and sixth in ranking order. A decade ago income tax liability was probably the most significant factor, but in international business today it is only one of several factors multinationals should take into consideration in their pricing decisions. In fact, income taxes are perceived not as long run phenomena but as short run charges against current earnings.[9]

International transfer pricing policies should be compatible with the overall objectives of the corporate financial strategy. If a company transfers price segments to a foreign country affiliate where income tax rates are lower, it should not simply be due to the phenomenon of a lower tax rate but because that policy is consistent with the overall financial objective of the firm. Moreover, if a company desires to leave funds in a foreign country and defer U.S. tax payments, compatibility with the company's overall financial objective, and not the advantage of tax deferrals, should be the primary concern. And there must be, as a corollary to the tax deferral advantage, a shortage of working capital, or some other need for additional funds, in the foreign subsidiary. Therefore, the present value of cash flow benefits from deferring tax payments must be greater than the opportunity cost of not using these funds somewhere else.

According to Section 1.861–8 of the U.S. Treasury Regulations, U.S. firms can delay U.S. tax payments by leaving their earnings in a foreign country where the income tax rate is lower, because under present tax law, foreign earnings of a U.S. firm are taxed only when they are repatriated to the parent company.[10] Thus, U.S. multinational firms have the option of taking advantage of a lower tax rate in a foreign country by deferring U.S. tax payments. But, as was previously indicated, this option should not be the only deciding factor in international transfer pricing decisions. Only if the financial advantage of transferring funds from higher tax rate countries to lower tax rate countries outweighs the overall financial benefits of employing these funds in some other manner, should this option be elected.

As shown in Table 2, profit repatriation restrictions and exchange controls within the foreign subsidiary country received the highest ranking orders in an analysis of the variable statements. This is not surprising when it is seen that the two statements are, in fact, interrelated. Exchange controls imposed by many developing countries are often the means of implementing varied restrictions on profit repatriation by U.S. multinational firms.[11] Furthermore, the high

---

[8] Arpan, *op cit.*, p. 101 and the Conference Board, *op. cit.*, pp. 7–9.

[9] David Granick, "National Differences in the Use of Internal Transfer Prices," *California Management Review*, Summer, 1975, pp. 28–32.

[10] James W. Schenold, "A Tool for Maximizing Foreign Tax Credits," *Review*, Price Waterhouse & Company, New York, Vol. 23, No. 2, 1978, pp. 38–51.

[11] S. H. Kim, "Financial Motives of U.S. Corporate Investment Abroad," *California Management Review*, Summer, 1976, pp. 60–65.

rank orders for these statements coincide with the impressions obtained from personal interviews with company controllers and partners of several of the large accounting firms involved in these pricing practices. This result, then, is a dramatization of the well known fact that developing countries make major use of profit repatriation restrictions and/or exchange controls to prevent outflows of foreign capital. This may, of course, be an attempt to compensate for less sophisticated income tax regulations as compared to those in more developed countries.

The fact that U.S. multinational firms employ transfer pricing to circumvent these restrictions on foreign capital outflow bring up yet another problem. For U.S. tax purposes, Section 482 under Revenue Ruling 69–630 of the U.S. Internal Revenue Service provides that all prices charged by U.S. parents to foreign subsidiaries and/or affiliates must be "arms length," or competitive. At first this competitive pricing objective might seem easy to achieve but the several pricing and cost allocation methods allowed under Section 482 make such an attainment much more difficult in practice.[12] A summary of the allowable pricing methods stipulates that, first, a U.S. firm may charge to its outside customers the comparable uncontrolled price, which is that paid by a buyer and seller who are unrelated. Second, a U.S. firm may charge the resale price if a buyer and seller are related. This is accomplished by working down from the actual resale price charged the end customer and reducing it by the appropriate mark-up for the selling subsidiary. Finally, the third method allows a U.S. firm to charge its foreign subsidiary a price consisting of cost plus the appropriate mark-up. As all three of these methods place a heavy reliance on the availability of comparable data from country to country in order to achieve "arms length" standards, the problem compounds itself.[13] Developing countries, in particular, exhibit vastly diverse business and tax regulations. Such factor differences as product quality, terms of sale, level of the market, and market location lead to variable data. Furthermore, pricing and allocating expenses relating to services and intangibles such as administrative and technical services and varied property rights make comparable data even more of an improbability.[14]

Additional complications arise when the several allowable means of allocating costs under Section 482 are taken into account. First, the U.S. parent may choose the full absorption cost method.[15] Here, the full cost of overhead is spread over both domestic and foreign units. Second, the parent may opt for

---

[12] M. Edgar Barrett, "Case of the Tangled Transfer Price," *Harvard Business Review*, May–June 1977, pp. 22, 78.

[13] Samuel B. Cohn, "Constructive Dividends From Section 482 Allocations," *International Tax Journal*, Summer, 1976, pp. 9–15.

[14] Robert Feinscheiber, "Cost Accounting for Intercompany Services," *International Tax Journal*, December 1976, pp. 186–194.

[15] Business International Corporation, *op. cit.*, p. 20.

only direct costs consisting of raw materials, labor, and direct overhead, with the exclusion of depreciation, insurance, and taxes. Finally, a firm may choose the incremental cost method whereby the cost of producing each extra foreign unit is affixed to that unit, once fixed costs for domestic production runs are covered. Thus, not only will dissimilar data result from firms using different cost methods, but different results may come about when the same cost method is used in two different countries with varying actual costs!

The attainment of justifiable "arms length" prices charged by U.S. parents under this Revenue Ruling is even more perplexing when it is noted that there are allowable exceptions. For example, in order that U.S. exporters may not be placed at a disadvantage in establishing new foreign markets, Section 482 provides that prices may, in fact, vary from a "competitive" level within the guidelines of U.S. tax standards when it can be shown that lower transfer prices are necessary for foreign market penetration or to meet foreign competition.[16] Thus, on the one hand, reason would dictate that a U.S. parent would employ higher transfer prices to circumvent host country restrictions on capital outflow while, on the other, it is apparent that the manner in which this may be accomplished is severely restricted.

While the results of this study confirm that profit repatriation restrictions and exchange controls are a predominant influence on the decision to employ transfer pricing, it is also apparent that compliance with U.S. tax regulations made it difficult to build complex transfer pricing networks among divisions located in several different LDC's. Industry sources also warn that transfer pricing should be employed only when such methods are compatible with a firm's overall financial objective, and not just when there is a need to circumvent short-term restrictions on a flow of funds.

The firms surveyed indicated that the third most important factor affecting the use of transfer pricing was joint-venture constraints within the host country. As a general rule, most developing countries impose a 50 percent limitation on foreign ownership when a joint-venture is undertaken. From the developing country's perspective, this serves to preserve national independence from foreign domination and, specifically, to prevent foreign corporations from totally enveloping domestic markets. Hence, the question becomes, how does the U.S. multinational firm recover its investment and obtain a reasonable rate of return on not only the capital investment but on its often substantial purchase of technological and managerial skills, when restrictions on earnings and the amount of foreign equity are imposed by the host country?

Developing countries, as a rule, have generally been lenient with regard to the transfer of funds through royalty and fee payments for managerial and technical skills. They do not consider such payments for technological services

---

[16] George C. Watt, (et al.), *Accounting for the Multinational Corporation*, Financial Executives Research Council, New York, 1977, pp. 463–464.

and management fees as repatriation of earnings. Normally, these charges are determined by the general economic conditions prevailing in the developing country, and the attitude of the local government toward economic development. Those industries that are classified as highly technological are commonly viewed as contributing to the host country's economic development, and the products produced by these industries are, themselves, considered to yield substantial amounts of foreign exchange. Consequently, these firms will receive favorable treatment when negotiating the terms of appropriate royalty and fee payments. In short, transfer pricing may be employed by charging attractive prices through royalty and fee payments when limitations on foreign ownership may be debilitating.

The determination of how much initial equity a U.S. partner should receive in return for technological know-how is made in a similar manner to that of pricing royalties and fees. Industry interviews indicated that the amount of equity is usually based on the foreign firm's estimated ability to contribute to the profits of the joint-venture over a given period of time. Covering the costs of development and delivery of the technology is considered to be a minimum limit, but under no circumstances will U.S. firms accept less than 10 percent of equity value, since a U.S. corporation must own at least this portion of the foreign entity to obtain U.S. tax credits on foreign taxes paid. Thus, whatever the developing country's regulatory limits on joint-ventures may be, it is apparent that the transfer pricing strategy employed should meet the corporation's overall financial objectives.

Table 2 shows that the fourth most important factor is that of tariffs and or customs duties within the host country. As a general principle, U.S. multinational firms tend to charge high tariff countries as low a price as possible, while conforming with the laws and regulations of host countries as well as the United States. At the same time, these lower prices must be compatible with the firm's overall corporate objectives. Hence, a company wishing to penetrate a new foreign market or expand its share of an already existing market would suppress administration, research, and other overhead expenses in establishing transfer prices. These several objectives, then, would be the optimum in establishing a transfer pricing policy consistent with a firm's overall long-run financial decision-making goal.

The seventh most important factor for the companies responding was quota restrictions within the domestic United States. For example, U.S. trade regulations set import quotas for textiles and footwear from Taiwan and Korea and these goods are, in many cases, produced by joint-ventures between those countries and a U.S. parent firm.

The problem of import quota restrictions must be part of the total package in initial joint-venture negotiations. They should not be dealt with after the fact but in the early stages of such negotiations. Instead of using transfer pricing to circumvent the quota restrictions, an appropriate level of return on the parent investment can be obtained through fair negotiated percentages of ownership, justifiable amounts of dividend payments, and appropriate royalty and fee payments. (It may be that the firms surveyed in this study do view quota restrictions as part of the initial negotiation package and, therefore, part of their overall financial and corporate objective, resulting in a fairly low ranking of the importance of this variable to their present transfer pricing policy.)

The final two factors contributing to the transfer pricing decision are the credit status of the U.S. parent firm and the credit status of the foreign subsidiary or affiliate. As shown in Tables 1 and 2, these were ranked eighth and ninth respectively, the lowest in rank and least important to the decision.

It may be possible to bolster a foreign affiliate's credit status by the judicious use of transfer pricing. In fact, many multinational firms allocate only a fixed sum for investment in a foreign host country. For additional funds, the foreign affiliates, many times, have to go into the prevailing local money markets. Moreover, the initiation of a new venture in a foreign country may result in substantial start-up costs with numerous losses before full capacity can be achieved and complete market potentials realized. Thus, if goods are transferred to a foreign affiliate from the U.S. parent at relatively low prices, beginning losses may be substantially reduced or eliminated. The use of low transfer prices gives the foreign affiliate a seemingly sounder financial standing, making foreign lenders more willing to advance needed capital to the enterprise.[17]

This is how the existing literature, at least, has tried to relate credit issues to transfer pricing. Our present research, however, indicates that corporations attach relatively little importance to credit issues. Though past literature did indicate that transfer pricing could serve to switch funds to a foreign affiliate to bolster its balance sheet, it seems that such conclusions were based on earlier cases of U.S. multinationals, wherein young U.S. firms had limited resources to supply to their foreign operations. It appears from the present data that U.S. multinationals today have sufficient capital to provide to their foreign affiliates in the initial start-up stages, without resorting to the later transfer of funds to maintain the financial stability of the operation.

Finally, there appears to be very little importance attached to the credit status of the U.S. parent firm as a determinant of the transfer pricing policy employed, presumably for the same reasons as outlined above.

Summary and Further Implications

The survey data in this study, coupled with personal interviews with several international business practitioners, indicate that worldwide transfer pricing policy is an important integral part of the overall long run financial decision-making policy of U.S. corporations which have invested in developing countries. While there may be a number of immediate objectives that a multinational firm

---

[17] Barrett, *op. cit.*, pp. 20–21.

would wish to meet by the judicious employment of transfer pricing, the use of a particular pricing policy should always be compatible with the long-term objective of the firm. Transfer pricing decisions by U.S. multinational firms become even more critical to the overall financial decision-making apparatus when it is noted that developing countries often exhibit extremely diverse business and tax environments while, at the same time, the thrust of U.S. tax regulations is to push the firm toward equal and competitive prices for all sales, no matter the circumstances of the buyer. Furthermore, the results of this research have shown that restrictions on outflows of foreign capital from subsidiary countries, and not income tax liabilities, are the major influences underlying the establishment of transfer pricing policies by U.S. multinational firms. The employment of transfer pricing to circumvent such restrictions on capital outflows is, as a matter of course, consistent with long-term corporate planning.

The advantages of transfer pricing are obvious but a major criticism of this strategy exists, and it is one that is less apparent because it is internal in nature. Whenever management tampers with its competitive pricing structure, it adulterates the corporate control system.[18] Thus, if the inputs to the system are impure, so are the resulting outputs. This may create a great deal of difficulty in the evaluation of the effective performance of the unit or division, or the management thereof, which is otherwise the appropriate profit center. Nevertheless, personal interviews with controllers of several large multinational firms indicated that industry, in fact, does have a mechanism to evaluate properly those divisions actively using transfer pricing. It is called a *credit-back* system and through it a company may, for example, change its profit center for the export department to the manufacturing division or corporate headquarters, if appropriate. At the same time a company would use a *memo-credit* system, whereby some form of internal designation of performance regarding the overseas profit of the export department is generated by top management for the proper evaluation of that division. Therefore, even if a particular division using transfer pricing shows a loss, the company, as a whole, may show a large consolidated profit, giving appropriate performance credit to the exporting division through this specialized *credit-back* system.

One topic for further research that suggests itself is the effect of floating exchange rates on transfer pricing practices. Our interviews with industry sources suggest that the year 1973 was more of a threshold than had been thought; since that time worldwide exchange rates have fluctuated to a much greater degree than previously. In fact, the countries most often mentioned as having the greatest fluctuations were Mexico, Brazil, Argentina, and the United States, three of which were involved in this study. U.S. multinational firms have

---

[18] James Shulman, "When the Price is Wrong—By Design," *Columbia Journal of World Business,* May–June 1967, pp. 69–76.

experienced financial and economic losses in their foreign operations as a result of exchange rate depreciations. Moreover, since worldwide inflation has affected developing countries to a greater degree than advanced countries, and since purchasing power parity is a major determinant of prevailing exchange rates, the necessity of price adjustments to counter falling exchange rates has become even more critical for U.S. firms with subsidiaries in developing countries.

Before the U.S. dollar devaluations and depreciations of recent years, the use of transfer pricing by U.S. firms was a fairly simple matter. Firms would simply maximize transfer prices to those countries with weaker currencies. But today the traditional hard currency, the U.S. dollar, has become relatively soft. This is where the confusion sets in. How can a U.S. multinational firm, with downward pressure on its own currency, optimize its overall profits when dealing with a foreign subsidiary? Can they invoice their exports in such strong currencies as the German Deutschemark, the Japanese Yen, and the Swiss Franc? This, of course, is a topic that bears further investigation.

As mentioned earlier, international transfer pricing policies must be compatible with the long-range profitability objectives of the firm and cannot be established or altered in major ways for short-term consideration without risking serious consequences. For instance, taxes and tariffs are paid annually, but profitability objectives are long-term and should be devised years in advance. If, in order to meet immediate objectives, short-sighted pricing policies are established by divisional managers, the "ground rules" of the game would change frequently, resulting in pricing policies possibly at variance with long-term corporate objectives and general chaos to the effective management of the system. Nonetheless, a certain degree of pricing flexibility should be allowed, no matter whether the concern is with varying exchange rates, U.S. tax regulations, or differing market potentials.

USING EXPORT SPECIALISTS TO DEVELOP OVERSEAS SALES

John J. Brasch

Several years ago a midwestern manufacturer of medical equipment decided that exporting offered an opportunity to significantly expand sales. Although small, the company was the dominant supplier of its specialty product to the U.S. nursing home market, and it had prospered from sales to Canada as well. Also encouraging were numerous unsolicited inquiries the company had received from other countries.

But while exporting looked promising, the company knew that success in developing overseas markets would take time. It had had a slow and difficult start in U.S. markets, and there was no reason to expect foreign markets to be any different. Moreover, the company's management, already stretched thin, would probably have difficulty devoting sufficient time and effort to these new markets.

At about the same time, a manufacturer of hand tools was trying to figure out how to increase sales through its exclusive representative in Europe. The representative had visited the company's U.S. plant many times and had developed a warm relationship with company officials. During the prior five years, sales to Europe had been $100,000 or more annually.

Although it appreciated this export business, the manufacturer felt that its European sales should be much higher. As in the case of the medical equipment manufacturer, management had neither the time nor the expertise to try to increase sales on its own.

Both the medical equipment and the hand tool manufacturer have since solved their exporting dilemmas by hiring export management companies (EMCs). Export management companies are manufacturers' representatives that sell in world markets. The 800 or so U.S. EMCs tend to be one-person or small-group organizations. They account for approximately 10 percent of all U.S. export sales of manufacturered goods.

The medical equipment company now has exclusive distributors in most European countries and in some Pacific, Latin American, and Middle Eastern countries as well. Its export operations have been profitable for the past two years, and the growth of its export sales has exceeded 50 percent annually for the past three years.

The hand tool company found an export management company that was capable of managing a distribution system in the entire European hardware industry. The EMC reorganized European distribution sales channels in such a way as to maintain the initial distributor's income as a token of appreciation for his past efforts. The hand tool company nearly immediately increased sales eightfold.

In both cases, the export management companies provided marketing management that the manufacturer had been unable to provide.

It is important to note that, in connecting with an EMC, neither company was admitting to any management deficiency. Each decided to focus its internal efforts on domestic markets and to leave the challenge of obtaining and expanding exports to outsiders.

Filling a Small Business Need

Indeed, small companies seldom have the internal capacity for export marketing management. This capacity requires the work of skilled and experienced export managers who have strings of contacts in various countries. Export managers understand foreign cultures. They are up to date on international politics, logistics, taxation, and legal problems. EMCs help fill this small company management deficiency on a contractual basis.

Many EMCs prefer to operate as contract export departments for the manufacturers they represent. Some even use the letterheads of clients as a way to encourage sales since foreign buyers prefer to deal directly with manufacturers and not with third parties. Other EMCs, wary of legal complications, operate under their names only.

EMCs operate as contract export departments by performing all the functions of such departments—doing research and planning; implementing promotional plans by, for instance, attending trade shows and placing advertising; creating distribution channels, which may include the appointment of foreign agents or dealers; processing orders; and reporting to management. In addition, some EMCs assume financial risk in dealing with foreign buyers by guaranteeing payment to their clients or by taking title to goods and collecting independently from customers.

Most EMCs specialize both by geographic area and by industry. For example, a number of EMCs owned by former Cuban nationals are very active and successful in Latin America. In contrast, few EMCs are active in Communist bloc countries, Canada or the South Pacific. Usually EMCs prefer to represent several businesses within each of their specialty industries, which might include machine tools, medical equipment, or computers.

EMCs get compensation either from commissions or from discounts on goods they buy for resale overseas. These commissions and discounts vary according to the extent of service provided and the difficulty of the marketing task. For simple brokering, commissions may be 10 percent or less; but for developing unique channels of distribution, commissions and discounts may range to 30 percent or even 40 percent on occasion. Some EMCs also require that certain start-up expenses be paid; these expenses can range from $5,000 to as much as $50,000.

Locating an Appropriate EMC

Finding the right EMC is no easy task. Several associations of EMCs publish lists of their members, but these lists include only a small percentage of all EMCs since many good firms refuse to involve themselves in groups of competitors. For a list of EMC associations, see the ruled insert. Such lists provide only scant information for screening EMC candidates.

As a consequence, manufacturers usually choose EMCs on the basis of a brief search and minimal analysis. That is not to say that thorough assessment of EMC candidates is impossible.

Ideally, every small company that wishes to should be able to find an EMC that does the following: specializes in its product type, has in place a well-organized and controlled worldwide distribution system, is well-financed and managed, and is willing and eager to devote significant amounts of managerial effort and money to launching a client's products. Such EMCs really do exist, particularly for heavy export industries such as medical products, telephone products, computers, and hand tools.

Initial Contacts

Finding EMCs that specialize in certain industries is usually not difficult. Friendly coexhibiters at trade shows may have suggestions. Some representatives advertise in trade journals. A company can contact an EMC candidate by letter, asking if the agent believes it has something to offer the company.

Initial replies from EMCs will likely be brief, but an EMC that expresses interest warrants at least a phone call and possibly a visit. If in this process the company finds a good match, things will happen fast. An EMC which sees that the manufacturer's product can be easily and cheaply distributed through EMC channels that already exist will aggressively seek a contract and begin distribution. In this situation, little more may be expected from the manufacturer than a contract and the production and shipping of orders.

Unfortunately, things do not usually proceed so smoothly. More often than not, EMCs must assume risks and invest funds to adequately develop export markets.

For example, a medical equipment product line such as the one mentioned at the beginning of this article requires testing in several countries. There may be problems of conversion to metric measure or to 220 voltage. Since new medical equipment must be thoroughly described and explained to potential buyers, advertising and displaying at foreign exhibitions are usually necessary.

Thus, many good EMCs are likely to be cautious about taking on new clients.

Differences Among EMCs

EMCs vary widely in the services they offer clients. For instance, some will accept all credit and collection risks in export transactions, while others will not pay for goods until they are reimbursed.

EMC associations

National Export Company
Gilbert Weinstein, President
65 Liberty Street
New York, New York 10005
212-766-1343

Export Managers Association of California
Stanley Epstein, President
Executive Offices
10919 Van Owens Street
North Hollywood, California 91605
213-935-3500

Overseas Sales and Marketing
Association of America
Peter Reinhard, President
5715 North Lincoln Avenue
Chicago, Illinois 60659
312-334-1502

Export Management Association
  of the Northwest
A.W. Bildsoe, President
815 Oregon Bank Building
319 Southwest Washington
Portland, Oregon 97204
503-223-1323

Some EMCs are traders and some are marketers. Traders are effective at getting orders quickly. They make deals on the basis of contacts—sometimes family relationships—and they operate best in Third World countries, where much business is done on a very personal basis. EMCs that are professional marketers usually seek to carefully define and implement long-term marketing strategies. Rather than make deals, they try to establish stable channels of distribution. While such marketing efforts take longer than simple trading, manufacturers end up with stable markets.

A manufacturer should thus ask a prospective EMC how it expects to obtain orders. A trader will answer that it "has contacts"; a marketer will discuss a long-term plan for selling the product.

EMCs also vary widely in size. They can be new one-person operations, or they can be very large firms with decades of experience. While large, experienced firms may seem to be better choices, small EMCs can often offer more personalized service than large firms, which must often cope with high employee turnover and large client loads.

Small EMCs seem to have different sorts of problems. Because it is so easy to set up EMCs, many are run by entrepreneurs with questionable qualifications in exporting. And like many new ventures, young EMCs have a high mortality rate.

Indeed, the gestation period for an EMC is much longer than for most service businesses—usually it struggles for at least three years before a regular income flow materializes. Weak firms usually fold within the first year or two.

Before entering into an agreement for export representation with a new EMC, then, a manufacturer should closely question the owners about their revenues and expenses as well as the managers about their personal incomes to determine their ability to weather the early storms. A manufacturer should also check with other clients and banks to determine financial stability.

As noted previously, EMCs tend to specialize in geographic areas and product groupings, though a few large, experienced EMCs offer representation in all parts of the world and in many product lines. Such product specialization is an advantage for manufacturers with traditional products but a problem for makers of products that are not sold through standard channels. Makers of products that do not easily fit into the specialties of EMCs may have to make special financial concessions to gain an EMC's commitment to a new effort.

What to Expect

From the EMC's viewpoint, either of the following situations can mean disaster:

1. Sales fail to materialize even though significant manpower and dollars are invested in market development.
2. Sales levels reach such heights that the client takes over the export function in order to save the commissions.

Given this double risk, a manufacturer should not expect an EMC to undertake a massive marketing development investment. For products that complement an EMC's product line, costly marketing efforts are usually not needed. But for products that demand special attention, manufacturers should frankly discuss the market development needs with a potential EMC. If some front-end investment is required, the small company should consider advancing part or all of the amount because whatever market acceptance is gained becomes the manufacturer's asset.

Small business owners should also seek to obtain a specific market development plan from the agent. Like many small ventures, EMCs try to avoid structured planning. If the prospective client wants to know the plan he or she must ask, perhaps repeatedly.

The plan that is finally acceptable should begin with market targeting. While some EMCs might talk about introducing products worldwide immediately, they are better off choosing specific markets.

Finally, small companies should keep in mind that an EMC is really much like a new regional sales manager. To be effective, the EMC must be trained and then supervised. Management needs to manage this resource as it would any other. Small business owners and their subordinates are thus well advised to travel with EMC representatives on some early trips and perhaps attend one or two trade shows with the representatives during the first months of operation. The EMC representatives can learn much from the manufacturers about promoting and selling products.

In hiring EMCs, small companies must be careful not to have unrealistic expectations. The export development process can be quite costly and difficult. Understanding this process can aid small companies in working with EMCs.

READING 26　PARALLEL IMPORT CHANNELS—OPTIONS FOR PRESERVING TERRITORIAL INTEGRITY

Robert E. Weigand

It is sometimes a Herculean leap from marketing plans to real world operations. Operations can fall short. Consider the following typical parallel import vignettes:

- ◆ A pharmaceutical company shipped some of its American made drugs to its distributor in a Central American country, intending to sell at a substantial discount because the local market could not support American prices. The pharmaceuticals did not stay in the foreign market. They were shipped back to the United States to be sold through drug channels that were not part of the American company's plans. The industry now thinks it can legally stop such unauthorized transactions.

- ◆ Suzanne Simpson, an English tourist taking holiday in Miami, bought a place setting of bone Chinaware made in Britain. She didn't pay Britain's substantial value added tax. Further, the dollar was cheaper that day than it had been just a few weeks before when the manufacturer had set its domestic and foreign prices. British manufacturers know these personal imports affect their domestic channels but have not found a way to stop them.

- ◆ Many clever Europeans know that cars are cheaper in Belgium than in nearby countries, the difference largely due to substantial tax differences. European car dealers have been unable to stop the entry of unauthorized imports that parallel their own authorized transactions. This helps explain why Belgium is a substantial exporter of automobiles—more than 25,000 some years—even though it doesn't produce them.

- ◆ It was once possible to buy a new Mercedes Benz in Europe and save money, bypassing the American dealer. The problem is not as great as it once was because many foreign currencies are more expensive than just a few years ago. But foreign dealers may still sell into the American market either because their cost of goods is lower or they accept a lower gross margin when selling to a geographically remote customer. American automobile manufacturers and retailers now think they have an important new law on their side. It was meant to stop car thieves, but it may also stop gray market imports.

Parallel importation occurs when an authentic branded product comes into the domestic market of a foreign country through marketing channels that rival the product's authorized channel or channels. Parallel importation or parallel marketing channels are often called gray marketing for just this reason, and are closely related to the practice of reimportation. This matter was addressed in the *Columbia Journal of World Business* shortly after a significant Supreme Court case in 1988 gave a victory to unauthorized importers.[1] Since that article was published, trademark owners have acquired new tools and strategies—the focus of this article—to combat the practice of parallel markets.

Re-imports are first cousins to parallel imports. They occur when branded products are exported but are returned to the home market, competing with merchandise that moves through the manufacturer's authorized channels. Some reimports are commercially motivated, meaning that astute traders purchase the merchandise overseas because the price is right and it is available, returning it to its country of origin. Other re-imports are personal; business travellers and vacationers bring home branded merchandise because it is cheaper in Hong Kong or an airport shop in Amsterdam than in Boston or Indianapolis. More recently, the process is reversed. The cheaper shops are in the United States; the goods are made in Japan, Korea, or Germany; and the buyers are foreigners who sometimes take the goods back to where they started. Re-imports create many of the very same problems for business strategists as parallel imports.

The legal events that lead to the dilemma, how the problem arises in the international arena, and what those who are responsible for global business strategy can and are doing to protect their channel assets are all worth focusing on especially.

The K Mart Legacy—Limiting the Options

The gray market problem reached a high point in May, 1988, when the U.S. Supreme Court handed parallel importers, such as K Mart Corporation, a nearly complete victory. This landmark case decided that American trademark owners such as Cartier Watches, Duracell Batteries, Seiko Watches, and Fugi Film, generally cannot prevent unauthorized importation of products bearing their own marks or names.[2] In legal terms, the owners' rights to control the trademark are exhausted once ownership changes hands, commonly somewhere in Europe, Hong Kong, or some other offshore jurisdiction. The decision was consistent with long-standing Customs Bureau practices.

---

[1] S. Tamer Cavusgil and Ed Sikora, "How Multinationals Can Counter Gray Market Imports," *Columbia Journal of World Business*, (Winter, 1988), 75–85.

[2] K Mart v. Cartier, Inc., (1988) 486 US 176. See also Hugh J. Turner, Jr., "Grey Market Litigation in the United States District Courts," *North Carolina Journal of International Law and Commercial Regulation*, 11 (Spring, 1986), 349–368; Maureen Beyers, "The Greying of American Trademarks," *Fordham Law Review*, 54 (October, 1985), 83–115; W. Weldon Wilson, "Parallel Importation—Legitimate Goods or Trademark Infringement?" *Vanderbilt Journal of Transnational Law*, 18 (Summer, 1985), 543–576.

Three Routes for Gray Market Goods

There is no end to the imaginative ways used to bring parallel imports to market. Yet, three methods represent the bulk of the gray market imports and are the focus of much of the legal attention.

Case 1

First, and most common, are those products made overseas by American firms. The foreign units may be subsidiaries, joint ventures, or some other entity where there is a commonality of interests with the American company. The foreign affiliate of the U.S. firm may sell to nearby authorized distributors, whether in France, Germany, Italy, and so on. Somewhere in the authorized channel, marketing control is lost; the product gets into the unauthorized channel and some of it is exported to the United States where it competes with similar domestically produced products.

The K-Mart vs. Cartier case made it clear that the controversial Section 526 of the Tariff Act of 1930 does not protect the American firm in such situations. The American firm, although it is the authorized trademark owner, cannot cite the Act to stop unauthorized imports of their watches because the two entities are independent of each other. Largely for this reason, parallel importers are delighted with the Supreme Court's decision.

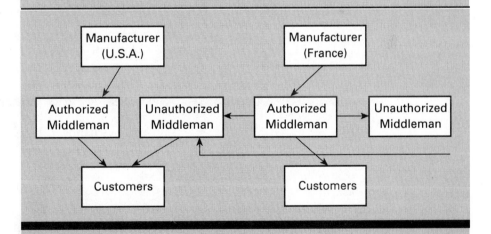

Case 2

Second, a foreign manufacturer may license an American company to be the exclusive importer of a product bearing a foreign name or trademark. The American company registers the foreigner's name, becoming the legal trademark owner in the United States, and agrees to pay royalties. Believing it will be the sole beneficiary of its commercial efforts, the American company develops the market for the product.

Now, suppose that a third party trader purchases an allotment of the product, which was intended for the Spanish market, in Amsterdam. The third party trader then ships the product to Philadelphia to clear customs and to make a profit. However, since 1930, the U.S. Bureau of Customs has interpreted the 1930 Tariff Act so as to prevent goods being brought into the United States by an outside trader.

The Bureau of Customs now prevents these goods from clearing customs unless the American licensee or trademark owner agrees to their importation in writing. This agreement will of course not be given, and thus the importation is stopped. The efforts to create a parallel gray market channel resembling Case 2 have been effectively thwarted. This is good news for American licensees.

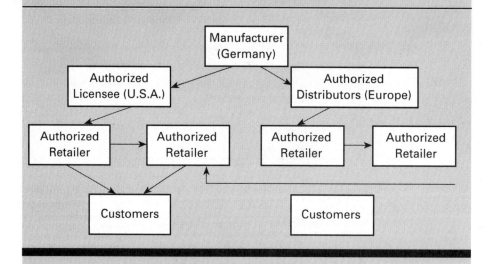

Case 3

A third possibility for a gray market arises when a manufacturer exports from its producing base, only later to have the exports diverted back to the home market. These "re-imports" aren't true parallel imports because there are not authorized imports with which they compete. However they are first cousins to parallel imports because they generate the same sort of concern among the company's authorized middlemen. Re-imports may never pass through any foreign marketing channels, may never even clear customs. They simply sit at an air or sea port for a few days before being loaded onto a return carrier.

This approach is particularly attractive (1) when the manufacturer's strategy is to sell into the foreign market at a substantially lower price than in the home market, due either to the market being poorer or dramatic exchange rate changes, and (2) when the foreign market is geographically close to the home market, thus minimizing the return transport costs.

A current example is occurring in Japan where products are marketed through the country's growing number of discount houses; many of the products are labelled "Made in Japan," but instructions are in Chinese or Korean, suggesting that they were meant for Taiwan, Hong Kong, or Korea.

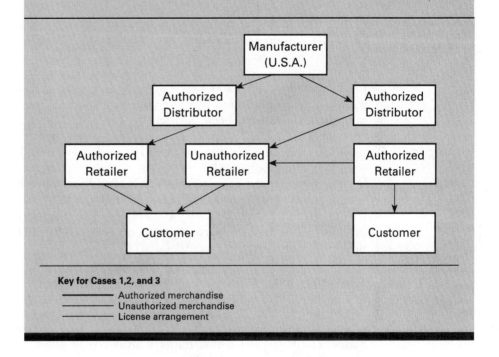

Key for Cases 1,2, and 3

——————— Authorized merchandise
——————— Unauthorized merchandise
——————— License arrangement

Unauthorized marketing channels have a long and tortuous history. In a case now 105 years old, a US District Court largely washed its hands of the parallel importation problem—at least for the time being. A European company granted Appollinaris the exclusive right to import Hunyadi Janos spring water from Hungary. But a clever importer named Scherer learned the water could be bought in Germany, and transported to America; therefore, he could undersell the authorized Hunyadi Janos. Appollinaris sued for protection, arguing that the marketing channels were not the ones intended by either the Hungarian bottler or the American licensee. The New York District Court agreed that Scherer's parallel channel disrupted some well meant plans. But the goods were genuine and thus could not be legally stopped.[3]

---

[3] Appollinaris Co., v. Scherer, (1886) 27 F. 18, SDNY.

In a later case that went to the Supreme Court, an American cosmetics licensee of a French firm was unable to prevent the unauthorized importation of certain cosmetics, even though it believed it was the exclusive importer.[4]

In response to these two cases, particularly the latter, Congress included a paragraph in the Tariff Act of 1922 declaring that imports bearing trademarks owned and registered by a U.S. citizen, corporation, or association cannot be imported unless, "written consent of the owner of such trademark is produced at the time of making entry."[5] The words seem clear enough. Territorialists, led by the Coalition to Preserve the Integrity of American Trademarks, placed much of their faith in this bastardized reconstruction of original Congressional intent. Later, the Supreme Court construed this Section 526 narrowly, deciding that Congress did not mean what it seemed to say. It held in K Mart that Congressional intent was solely to protect American licensees that were marketing products whose trademarks were owned by European and other foreign companies. American licensees have the same rights today. Thus, an American lens manufacturer who has been licensed by, say, Kim's Optics to use the Korean company's intellectual property such as patents or trademarks can prevent Kim's products made in Seoul (or elsewhere) from passing through customs in San Francisco, citing Section 526.

However, parallel importers such as K Mart claim a nearly complete victory because only a small portion of their merchandise falls into the foreign licensor–American licensee category just described. Two categories of gray marketed products are beyond the narrow protection provided by the Court's interpretation of the legislation.

First, the bulk of gray market imports consist of products made by foreign subsidiaries, joint ventures, or otherwise controlled foreign units of American companies or by foreign companies who have no licensee in the United States.

Second, foreign licensees of American companies may produce goods that enter into unauthorized channels, ultimately making their way to the United States. The Court ruled that imports produced by these two classes of units cannot be stopped by the 1922 law.

First Causes

Three factors, sometimes working alone but often in concert, virtually assure that parallel marketing channels will arise unless they can be stopped by trademark owners who seek to protect their authorized channel members. They are (1) exchange rate differences, (2) the power of the discriminating monopolist, and (3) opportunistic behavior by members of administered marketing channels.

Table 1 suggests the ways the three forces just described are different. If the

---

[4] A. Bourjois and Company, Inc., v. Katzel. 692 US (1923), 689.

[5] *Congressional Record—Senate,* (August 19, 1922), 11, 602.

TABLE 1   Topographic Causes and Consequences

Topographic Causes	Flow Direction	Causal Origin	Time Span	Nexus
1. Fluctuating exchange rates	Low valued currency country to high valued	External	Indeterminate	International
2. Discriminating monopolist	Low priced country to high priced country	Manufacturer price policy	Unlimited	International
3. Opportunistic behavior	Random	Distributor perfidy	Unlimited	International or domestic

topographic cause is fluctuating exchange rates, then goods moving into gray market channels can only flow from the low valued currency country to the high valued currency country; the proximate cause is external to the firm; the opportunity will only last until underlying conditions such as the exchange rate or an artificially low purchase price are corrected; and can only occur internationally.

The discriminating monopolist must face the possibility of parallel imports moving from the low priced to the high priced country because of price policies instituted by the manufacturer; the importation will last as long as the policy continues and will take place internationally. (We must ignore here the possibility that the manufacturer may also attempt to price discriminate domestically, as many do.)

And finally, parallel imports that derive from opportunistic channel behavior can occur randomly because distributor opportunism has no particular time limit and can occur either internationally or domestically.

Exchange Rate Differences Like many currencies, the dollar is more or less allowed to find its own value relative to other currencies. The dollar has cheapened relative to the currencies of some of America's most important trading rivals. The global marketer knows that the dollar's deterioration has temporarily lessened the gray market issue in the United States, meaning only that the problem has broken out in other parts of the world. (See *CJWB*, Fall 1989, pp. 18–24.)

Exchange rate fluctuations are more likely to explain gray market transactions if the rate change is swift. If a rate change is protracted it allows the manufacturer to make price adjustments that negate a middleman's potential windfall profits.[6]

---

[6] William Dickey, "Antidumping: Currency Fluctuations As Cause Of Dumping Margins," *International Trade Law Journal*, (Winter, 1981–2), 67.

Exchange rates can be used to explain long term domestic market share won by foreign firms, largely because the cost of acquiring such shares may be purchased when a domestic currency is undervalued. If the domestic currency's value rises, the foreign firm's market share will erode only slowly if at all because the cost of maintaining market share is vastly less than the cost of first earning it.[7] Further, exchange rate changes are not necessarily passed through to middlemen or end users. As domestic currencies gain or lose value vis-a-vis foreign currencies, foreign sellers may elect to reduce or raise price, thus neutralizing the volume effect of currency fluctuations.[8] Although these observations affect international transactions, they do not obviate the need for attention to the issue of parallel imports.

The Discriminating Monopolist Parallel importation can also occur when the strategist tries to price discriminate among markets, charging a lower price in those markets less able to pay and more in high income markets. The concept of price discrimination is nearly faultless, if price strategists can find a way to prevent low priced goods destined for a low income market (or, more accurately, a market composed of buyers who are less willing to pay a higher price) from seeping into the high priced market.[9]

Opportunistic Middlemen Even in the authorized channels where the strategists have carefully selected their distributors, deceitful behavior occurs. An enormous amount of literature suggests disagreement about the nature and use of private property and how opportunism may pay handsomely.[10] Readers must

---

[7] Richard Baldwin, "Hysteresis in Import Prices: The Beachhead Effect," *The American Economic Review*, 79 (September, 1989), 773–785.

[8] Kenneth A. Froot and Paul D. Klemperer, "Exchange Rate Pass-Through When Market Share Matters," 79 *The American Economic Review*, (September, 1989), 637–654.

[9] Joan Robinson, *Economics of Imperfect Competition*. (London: Macmillan and Company, 1934), Chapter 15.

[10] Wroe Alderson, *Marketing Behavior and Executive Action*, (Homewood IL.: Richard D. Irwin, Inc., 1957), 91–97; Kenneth J. Arrow, *The Limits of Organization*, (New York: W. W. Norton and Company, 1974), 23; Robert Axelrod, *The Evolution of Cooperation*, (New York: Basic Books, 1984); R. H. Coase, (1960), "The Problem of Social Costs," *The Journal of Law and Economics*, III (October, 1960), 1–43; Dale F. Duhan and Mary Jane Sheffet, "Gray Markets and the Legal Status of Parallel Importation," *Journal of Marketing*, 52 (July, 1988), 75–83; H. Scott Gordon, "The Economic Theory of a Common Property Resource: The Fishery," *Journal of Political Economy*, 62 (April, 1954), 124–142; Benjamin Klein, Robert G. Crawford, and Armen A. Alchian, "Vertical Integration, Appropriable Rents, and the Competitive Contracting Process," *The Journal of Law and Economics*, 21-2 (1978), 297–326; Frank Knight, *Risk, Uncertainty and Profit*, (New York: Harper and Row, 1965), 254, 260; Gary D. Libecap, "Property Rights in Economic History: Implications for Research," *Explorations in Economic History*, 23, (1986), 227–252; James G. March and Herbert A. Simon, *Organizations*, (New York: John Wiley and Sons, Inc., 1958), 122; Joseph Palamountain, *The Politics of Distribution*, (Cambridge, MA: Harvard University Press, 1955); A. C. Pigou, *The*

look hard to find scholars who argue that preserving channel integrity is rewarding.[11]

Table 2 lays out the calculations an authorized and rational distributor should make in deciding whether to engage in perfidious behavior, meaning making an unauthorized sale to a gray market participant.

Such opportunistic behavior is likely to happen when the middleman's gross margin is disproportionately large relative to the marketing task performed. Further, it is particularly attractive if the transaction occurs outside the distributor's assigned territory. If the sale is geographically remote, the opportunistic distributor may assume that the sale is not made at the expense of the distributor's own full markup sales. Or at least that is the distributor's reasoning until other distributors begin to behave similarly.

How Intellectual Property Owners Can and Do Respond

The K Mart decision was unquestionably a disappointment for those American firms that control their foreign supplier. Even so, there are other options available to those with the stamina and funds to continue the fight. Based on the literature, interviews, and correspondence, the following six methods are commonly used by those who want to protect their intellectual property rights:

Frequent Price Changes Reducing the price differential between the authorized and gray market product is a powerful tool for reducing the attractiveness of the parallel import. The issue quickly becomes a standard exercise in pricing—determining whether the manufacturer takes the brunt of the price reduction or if it is shared with authorized middlemen.

Gray marketers point out—often correctly—that they give the customer just as much as the authorized channel gives. They say that their outlets are clean and convenient, they sell on credit, refund money if not satisfied, provide a store warranty that is as good as the manufacturer's, never sell stale or damaged merchandise, service the product after the sale, and have sales people who know just as much about the product as those in the authorized channel. Most important of all, they do all of the above while undercutting the authorized

Economics of Welfare, (London: Macmillan and Company, 1932), 268, 345; Louis W. Stern and Torger Reve, "Distribution Channels as Political Economies: A Framework for Competitive Analysis," *Journal of Marketing,* 44 (Summer, 1980), 52–64; F. W. Taussig, "Price Maintenance," *American Economic Review,* VI-1, Supplement, (1916), 170–184; R. Eric Reidenback, R. Terence, A. Oliva, "General Living Systems Theory and Marketing," *Journal of Marketing,* 45 (Fall, 1981), 30–37; Oliver Williamson, "Transaction-Cost Economics: The Governance of Contractual Relations," *The Journal of Law and Economics,* 22-2, (1979), 233–261; and ———, *The Economic Institutions of Capitalism,* (New York: The Free Press, 1985).

[11] Robert H. Frank, *Passions Within Reason,* (New York: W. W. Norton and Company, 1988).

TABLE 2   Modelling the Rational Authorized Distributor's Decision

The Problem
The authorized importer in Country X must calculate whether to make a one-time sale of 25,000 units to an unauthorized customer in Country Y.

The Assumptions
Manufacturer is a discriminating monopolist in Country A who charges authorized importers in Countries X and Y 1.0 CUs (currency units) and 1.2 CUs respectively. Authorized importers traditionally have taken a 40% mark-up on delivered price when selling to nearby retailers. Tempted by an opportunity to sell into Y's territory, though no doubt mindful of the prisoner's dilemma (Axelrod), Importer X (perhaps irrationally) decides that the appropriate cost of goods for pricing strategy is 1CU rather than the 1.2CU paid by Y, accompanied by a predatorily low mark-up of 20 percent will assure the sale. The one-time benefit will be 25,000 units sold by X at a .20 mark-up, or 5,000 CUs.

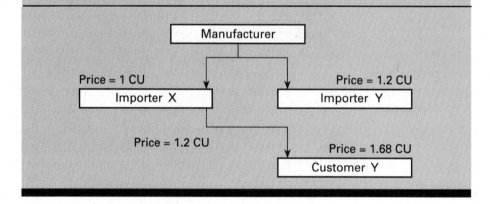

retailers' price. If the customer perceives these arguments to be true, parallel importers are indeed tough rivals.

Reducing retail prices is unpopular among retailers, even though the manufacturer or distributor may also have incurred reduced gross margins. Retailers may understand the gray market issue very well, but believe that something other than reducing their prices should be done.

Even so, it happens. For example, Concord watch dealers were authorized to offer rebates as large as $1,000 to combat unauthorized sales. Advertisements promoting the offer appeared in the country's major newspapers, admitting that exchange rate differences were creating major price differences between America and much of the rest of the world. And in Japan, BMW-Japan reduced its Yen prices so as to discourage customers from making a short trip to a nearby country to purchase an identical car at substantial savings.[12]

---

[12] Robert E. Weigand, "The Gray Market Comes to Japan," *Columbia Journal of World Business* 24 (Fall, 1989), 18–24.

TABLE **2**   (continued)

The Potential Cost

Using probability theory, Importer X believes there are four possible consequences of a clandestine resale. Each has a different cost:

Outcome	Probability	Conditional	Expected
Undiscovered	0.80	0CUs	0CUs
Warning	.05	0	0
Termination	.05	20,000	1,000
Retaliation	.10	15,000	1,500
	1.00		2,500 (EV)

The first two outcomes are costless. The third, termination, incurs the cost of seeking a new supplier and perhaps the loss of future profits discounted to the present value. Assessing the cost of the fourth outcome, retaliation by other authorized importers requires predicting the new, surely lower, gross margin brought by lower margins per unit, whether the lower margins are permanent, and whether the lower margins bring higher unit sales, all discounted to the present value.

Conclusion

The one-time sale should be made.

Dollar Price in Foreign Markets

Second (or third) country currency price quotes are well known to readers of this journal. The most common reason for the practice is to hedge against a currency's deterioration. Global companies sometimes price their merchandise in a foreign currency which they believe is more stable rather than their home country's money. Thus sales contracts may be made in the dollar or Swiss franc, even though the parties are neither American nor Swiss. And global companies do not quote a price to a foreign customer in a declining currency unless the forecasted rate of deterioration is built into the contract.

A second and much less familiar reason for second (or third) country currency price quotes is to reduce opportunistic gray market sales. For example, there was a time when international travellers would purchase only a one-way air ticket from, say, Chicago to Mexico City, paying in dollars. Two weeks later, ready to return home, the traveller would purchase just enough pesos to buy the return ticket, paying for it with more stable American dollars. The traveller had earlier forecasted that the peso would deteriorate in value even during the short visit. Since the airline had not changed its peso price during the two week interval, the traveller pocketed the savings. Today, Mexicana Airlines quotes the price of its international tickets in dollars. Customers can pay in pesos, of course, but the peso quoted in a Mexicana sales office changes every day. Or for another example, Vivitar believes it has discouraged most gray market sales by making sales only in dollars.[13]

Dollar pricing is particularly suited to selling in countries with unstable currencies; presumably customers understand the problem and tolerate it. It is less appropriate in other countries because it means frequent price changes, a practice anathema to modern business.

Work Other Laws, Create New Ones Authorized importers can no longer look to the 1922 legislation for much help. However, the Customs Bureau takes administrative responsibility for reviewing about 400 other pieces of legislation, some of which are quite strict about what can be imported. The task given to attorneys to review pertinent rules is an enormous one, far too great to be explored here. However, some examples show how imaginative business strategists have helped preserve their marketing channels.

The pharmaceutical company that was shipping its product to a Central American country only to learn that it was coming back to the United States, solved the problem rather easily. On products destined for export, it omitted the tiny crimp numbers from the bottom of plastic tubes containing its medicines. The Food and Drug Administration requires such numbers that indicate FDA approval. The company simply told Customs what to look for.

More directly, concern for public health and safety prompted Congress to pass the Prescription Drug Marketing Act to stop what the industry calls "the diversion market," meaning reimports. The new law provides that, ". . . no drug . . . which is manufactured in a State and exported may be imported into the United States unless the drug is imported by the person who manufactured the drug." Thus, pharmaceutical products arriving via unauthorized importers will be seized by the Bureau of Customs.[14]

New York's legislature passed a bill that effectively requires retailers to tell customers whether they are buying an authorized or gray market import.[15] The most common complaints were that the unauthorized products lacked a warranty valid in the United States or the instructions were in a foreign language. In a few instances electrical appliances were wired for direct current homes, not alternating current used by most American homes. California's law allows a retailer to substitute its own express written warranty for the manufacturer's,

---

[13] Vivitar Corporation, Correspondence with Victor Chernick, President, (October 21, 1988), unpaged letter.

[14] Prescription Drug Marketing Act of 1987, Public Law 100–293, (April 22, 1988).

[15] State of New York. General Business Law 218–22.

but only if it provides as much or more protection than that offered by the manufacturer's warranty.[16]

For another example, here at the federal level, the National Highway Traffic Safety Administration has mandated that cars subjected to high theft rates must have identifying numbers indelibly marked on as many as fourteen parts.[17] Thus, if a junkyard has in its inventory a left front fender, decklid, or transmission from a Ford Mustang or Dodge Lancer, the potential customer can know whether the part came from a legitimately junked car or from one that was reported stolen. Every high theft American-made car produced must be marked. But European and Japanese car manufacturers such as Mercedes Benz, BMW, Alfa Romeo, Honda, and Mazda may elect to mark only those units intended for authorized dealers in the United States; all other units will not be marked, a step that would make gray marketing of automobiles far more difficult. The anti-theft legislation is ostensibly designed to reduce car stealing in America, now at a cost of over a billion dollars a year. There is, of course, the added benefit that it could further dry up the gray market.

Household appliances must now be labelled to comply with the Energy Policy and Conservation Act and electronic products are watched for radiation compliance. Proper labels and warnings may be intended to assure public health and safety, but clearly can be used to thwart unauthorized imports.

Channel strategists must be careful. The Norr Pennington doctrine, named after two earlier Supreme Court cases, permits American businesses to work together to encourage legislation, even of the most selfish sort.[18] But it is *not* legal for Americans to engage in sham practices, meaning using legislation for motives other than the purposes for which they are intended.

Finally, America's complex anti-dumping legislation can sometimes be used to prevent parallel imports, particularly if an improper exchange rate is used to calculate a transaction. Gray market importers could handily defend the price of a gray marketed import in comparison with an authorized import if the importer and a collaborating foreign seller were given ample latitude in deciding the date of the transaction and the currency used. However, Customs regulations state that ". . . importers will be expected to act within a reasonable time to take into account price differences resulting from sustained changes in prevailing exchange rates."[19]

---

[16] Ondrea Dae Hidley, "Turning up the Contrast in a Grey Area: California Unleashes the Black Letter Grey Market Goods Act," *Loyola of Los Angeles International and Comparative Law Journal,* 10, (1988), 657–691.

[17] *Federal Register,* Department of Transportation, 51 (March 14, 1986), 8,831–8,840.

[18] Eastern Railway Presidents Conference v. Noerr Motor Freight, (1961) 365 US 127. See also United Mineworkers v. Pennington, (1965) 381 US 657.

[19] *Federal Register,* Department of Commerce, International Trade Administration, II–19, (March 28, 1989), 12,789.

Change the Product Manufacturers often differentiate their products among markets, usually to meet different local tastes, national health or safety rules, packaging requirements, technical standards, income levels, and so on. When the authorized product and the parallel product are dissimilar, it is far more difficult for the customer to compare the two. The persuasive and quite ethical salesperson in an authorized retail outlet can be trained to create doubt in customers' minds by pointing out that the products available in gray market outlets may not be the same quality, as may indeed be the case.

Seiko won a partial victory when it compelled Alexander's to change the wording on its advertisements.[20] Although it could not stop the New York retailer from selling unauthorized imports, it obtained a court order forbidding the retailer from using the expression "list price," thus implying that the watches were identical to the authorized imports. The words "compare with" were acceptable to both sides, acting as a reminder of the advertisement.

Products that are likely gray market candidates sometimes are accompanied by limited warranties that can be used only in the markets for which the product is intended. Warranties may be important to customers where the item is expensive, the manufacturer's reputation for quality is not well known, the retailer is seemingly untrustworthy, and the customer knows there are hidden or complex features of a product that are not readily observable.

Conditional warranties are only guardedly useful. Gray market retailers have fought back by promising their customers that the store will stand behind the merchandise it sells—it will replace or repair faulty merchandise, perhaps refund the purchase price—even if the manufacturer will not. Further, manufacturers are reluctant to exploit the warranty issue because it hints that the customer may confront product failure, even on its authorized imports.

These approaches do not work when the unauthorized retailer has purchased from a domestic supplier who has gained access to goods intended for the American market. Nor do they work when the product differences are inconsequential.

It seems not to have bothered gray market buyers of Swatch watches—intended for the German or French market—on which the days of the week were called Samstag or Dimanche. Nor did it stop Cabbage Patch dolls with German names and adoption papers. Indeed, one gray market retailer may have turned the language difference into an advantage, advertising, "Weine Zeit für Tränen," (No need for tears).[21]

Customers sometimes buy Japanese cameras without warranties, apparently believing that the implicit insurance accompanying the higher priced author-

---

[20] Seiko Time Corporation v. US, et al., (1982) 85–6282. See also "Seiko Wins Order To Get Alexander's To Change Its Ads," *The New York Times*, (August 6, 1982), 31.

[21] "Weine Zeit Fur Tränen," *The New York Times*, Advertisement from Rowe-Manse Emporium, (December 21, 1984), 9.

ized cameras is not worth the premium. Today, 47th Street Photo, a huge New York retailer and avid practitioner of parallel importing, scrupulously states in its advertisements which of its cameras are accompanied by a valid US warranty. It is responding to New York law.

Dealer Termination Perhaps the most powerful reactive strategy available to the manufacturer is to terminate the opportunistic middleman. This is a particularly difficult area because courts have been far less sympathetic to manufacturers who attempt to exercise price controls in the channel than to those who limit their control to non-price matters. However, the Supreme Court recently has affirmed the validity of the Colgate doctrine[22] which permits a seller to announce sales conditions in advance and to terminate dealers who do not abide by those conditions.[23] In another recent case, Sharp Electronic's decision to terminate a price-cutting retailer was upheld; although price maintenance was an issue at stake, Sharp had not attempted to fix a particular price level.[24] Apple Computer's policy statement is short but quite clear about transshippers: "Any Apple dealer or VAR (value added retailer) found to be in violation of the mail-order or transshipping prohibitions will be stripped of its authorized status."[25]

Applying a termination clause toward foreign distributors may be either easier or far more difficult than termination in the United States. Manufacturers must exercise far more caution in some countries than others in selecting distributors and policing their sales; terminating a perfidious middleman can be so costly that it is nearly a useless strategy. Puerto Rico's legislation is so notoriously protective of local dealers that many manufacturers prefer to sell directly into the Commonwealth; on the other hand, termination in many Asian countries is rather simple.

Product Buy-Backs A few manufacturers have gone into the field to buy back the gray market items. Under certain circumstances this may be an effective strategy. The two most important rules are: (1) Establish a channel monitoring system that provides information about how the goods move between producer and retailer. The cost of full problem definition can be large because few miscreant channel members will collaborate in the search effort; and (2) Be assured that the source of the problem has been identified and is moving toward resolution before the repurchasing begins.

---

[22] US v. Colgate (1919), 250 US 300.

[23] Monsanto Company v. Spray-Rite Service Corporation (1984), 465 US 752.

[24] Business Electronics Corporation v. Sharp Electronics Corporation (1988), 486 US 1005, Certiorari denied.

[25] Apple Computer, Inc., *Transshipping and Mail-Order Policy Statement*, (January, 1988), unpaged company document.

Few steps will impress a manufacturer's authorized distributors and retailers quite as much as a buy-back, a declaration that the brand owner is committed to protecting its intellectual property. The cost of the buy-back is a way of purchasing good will in the channel. But there is potentially a darker side: the buy-back cannot easily be proclaimed to the channel while kept secret from the general public.

An End Note

Few commercial events in recent years have generated as much controversy as parallel importation. It confronts a variety of pragmatic issues concerning financial, legal, and marketing matters. But it also involves more ethereal philosophical and ethical questions such as property rights and the right to a free ride on assets owned by others. The genesis of the problem in the United States has shifted; the origin was once due to the low cost American dollar. The problem now more commonly derives from sellers whose strategy includes acting as discriminating monopolists and from opportunistic middlemen who break their allegiance to the channel family.

The issue goes beyond simply whether products will move through controlled or uncontrolled marketing channels. Rather, the struggle confronts two questions: First, whether channel control will increasingly rest with powerful retailers who earn the allegiance of customers, thus dictating the terms under which merchandise is presented to consumer markets. Second, whether manufacturers who now have substantial power in the marketing channel can find the financial, legal, and marketing power to persuade institutional middlemen to remain part of a loyal team. Capitulation is tempting because some of the country's largest retailers have little loyalty to any one manufacturer. Not surprisingly some manufacturers have decided it is easier to join than to fight.

READING 27 **DISTRIBUTION IN JAPAN: PROBLEMS AND CHANGES**

Michael R. Czinkota

ABSTRACT. The Japanese distribution system is frequently characterized as the major non-tariff barrier to imports. This article provides an overview of the existing distribution system in Japan and analyzes its effect on imports. Subsequently, the changes taking place in the system are highlighted and suggestions are made how importers can take advantage of these changes in order to successfully penetrate the Japanese market.

The large and growing Japanese trade surplus with the United States (as well as with most of the other industrialized nations of the world) has led many business, government, and academic leaders, both in the United States and abroad, to accuse Japan of maintaining barriers to the entry of foreign goods. Many of these accusations focus on the Japanese distribution system, which is perceived by a number of analysts to be Japan's primary non-tariff barrier to trade.[1] Studies of the Japanese market that deal with the importation of products refer extensively to the country's complex and highly unique distribution system. The multilayered channel structure, the fact that wholesalers ("tonya") keep on selling to each other, and the atomistic competition among retailers are frequently mentioned. As one report by the Office of the US Trade Representative noted, Japan has a vast distribution network "with more wholesalers and retailers per capita than any of the advanced industrial nations."[2] Western observers often refer to Japan's traditional distribution system as "mysterious, complex, archaic, old fashioned, stubborn, inefficient and anachronistic."[3] As a result, it is frequently believed that "the manner in which the Japanese channels of distribution are structured and managed presents one of the major reasons for the apparent failure of foreign firms to establish major market participation in Japan."[4]

Often, however, the Japanese distribution system continues to be perceived today as it was twenty years ago. Only infrequently are changes and the current dynamism of the system taken into account and reported. It is the purpose of this article to review the major facets of the Japanese distribution system, and

---

[1] Ahern, Raymond J., "Market Access in Japan: the US Experience," *Congressional Research Service,* Report #85–37E, February 14, 1985.

[2] "Japanese Barriers to US Trade and Recent Japanese Government Trade Initiatives," *Office of the US Trade Representative,* Washington, DC, November, 1982, p. 71.

[3] Shimaguchi, Mitsuaki, and Lazer, William, "Japanese Distribution Channels: Invisible Barriers to Market Entry," *MSU Business Topics,* Winter 1979, Vol. 27, No. 1, p. 51.

[4] Ross, Randolph E., "Understanding the Japanese Distribution System: an Explanatory Framework," *European Journal of Marketing,* Vol. 17, No. 1, 1983, p. 12.

to highlight the changes taking place. By better understanding shifts in the wholesaling as well as the retailing sector, firms can better prepare for successful market entry into Japan. Policy-makers, in turn, are provided with information about changes already taking place and future changes needed and worth negotiating for.

This article represents the findings of a small scale exploratory study. Apart from the customary literature review, the results are based on facts and opinions gathered during a series of in-depth interviews in Japan and the United States with 97 individuals from 51 public and private sector institutions. The individuals interviewed included corporate executives, government officials from a variety of bureaus and departments, consultants, academics, and journalists.

Major Features of the Japanese Distribution System

This section will highlight major unique features of the Japanese distribution system. It will briefly trace the underlying reasons for their development, then comment on their effects on the importation of products.

Number of Actors One major feature of the Japanese distribution system is the overwhelming number of companies that participate in it. For example, in spite of its much smaller geographic expansion and population, Japan has about the same number of wholesalers as the United States. Most of these firms have nine employees or less.[5] Only 5.6 percent of Japanese wholesalers have 30 or more employees.[6]

The ratio of wholesale to retail sales in Japan is more than double that in the United States, which indicates the more frequent interaction between wholesalers in Japan than between wholesalers in the United States.[7] Japanese wholesalers sell their goods twice as frequently to other wholesalers as do their counterparts in the United States. Such frequent interaction will, of course, drive up the price of products due to the necessity of every intermediary adding some mark-up.

Japan has also only 10 percent fewer retailers than does the United States. Firms are small (having an average of only 3.6 employees), and their sales are less than half that in the United States.[8] As a result, many of these firms possess a small capital base which permits for only limited flexibility in terms of inventory size and expansion.

Due to this vast number of participants in the distributive process, it is very

---

[5] Tsurumi, Yoshi, "Managing Consumer and Industrial Systems in Japan," *Sloan Management Review,* Fall, 1982, p. 42.

[6] *Commercial Census,* Ministry of International Trade and Industry, 1979.

[7] *Statistics of Commerce,* Ministry of International Trade and Industry, 1981, and *Statistical Abstracts of the United States,* 1984, US Dept. of Commerce, Washington, DC, 1984.

[8] *Statistics of Commerce,* Ministry of International Trade and Industry, 1981.

difficult to find avenues which reach them all. Also, direct distribution to them is often prohibitively expensive. This is particularly true if market penetration is sought outside the urban centers.

Purpose of the Distribution System In the United States, the primary function of intermediaries is seen as improving the efficiency of the distribution system. As the principle of channel geometry has demonstrated, intermediaries are useful economically only if the services and functions they provide are cheaper than the cost of direct distribution. This underlying axiom does not hold true for Japan. Social aims which go beyond pure economics contribute to the continued existence and expansion of smaller channel members. Japanese society has come to accept a degree of tolerated inefficiency within its distribution system to maintain employment and income flows. According to a study by Arthur D. Little, Inc., retailing has come to serve to some extent as a "form of social welfare system".[9] Since Japanese employees are paid a lump sum at retirement rather than an ongoing pension, this payment is often seen by the recipient as an opportunity to set up one's own shop in order to be independent and to derive a steady income. In addition, the Japanese distribution system is used to "absorbing labor during economic downturns in lieu of a more extensive unemployment insurance system."[10]

Both of these factors contribute to the development of small retailers with a small capital base and limited managerial talent. However, given these social aims of the distribution system, the argument of economics alone is often insufficient to effect a restructuring on the macro as well as the micro level. Foreign firms entering the Japanese market must therefore accept the existence of some of this inefficiency in spite of the theoretical possibility of substantial streamlining of the distribution process.

Physical Constraints of Channel Members Geographic constraints have made space a very valuable commodity in Japan. Due to their low level of capitalization, most channel members suffer from substantial lack of storage space. As a result, only small quantities are purchased, and very liberal return privileges exist within the system's channels, extending not only to damaged merchandise but also to merchandise that does not sell easily. While the handling of these returns can be costly, it does permit channel members to carry out a push policy without encountering channel resistance.

The small order size has led to a requirement for frequent replenishments.

---

[9] Arthur D. Little, Inc., "Strategies for Alleviating Recurring Bilateral Trade Problems Between Japan and the United States," in *The Japanese Non-Tariff Trade Barriers Issue: American Views and Implications for Japan-US Relations,* Report to the Japanese National Institute for Research Advancement, May, 1979, p. iv, 249.

[10] Johnson, Chalmers, "The Internationalization of the Japanese Economy," *California Management Review,* No. 25, (Spring, 1983), p. 19.

Even in instances when sophisticated sales forecasting systems are used, immediate channel response to short-term orders is expected.

As a result, factors such as short lead time and secure supplies can often outweigh price competitiveness. Suppliers, particularly those from abroad, are frequently chosen on the basis of order responsiveness. In certain product categories, this responsiveness simply cannot be provided competitively from abroad. For example, many retailers expect delivery time for out of stock products to be less than six hours. In order to provide such short lead times, suppliers need to be located in close vicinity to their customers, a strategy which is very difficult to incorporate into an export philosophy by a foreign firm.

Interaction Among Channel Members One major characteristic of this interaction are the close organizational ties between channel members. The distribution system is often marked by the "keiretsu" relationship, in which producers, distributors, and retailers are all financially linked with each other, either directly or through a banker or trading company. Even management linkage is sometimes possible.[11] As a result, members of the family tend to prefer sourcing from each other to sourcing from the outside. Not only does this phenomenon make it difficult to break into the system, it also continues to haunt the successful firm. For example, while the possibility of selling a unique product is quite high, it must be kept in mind that, once a member of the keiretsu begins producing a similar product, other keiretsu firms may shift their orders to the new producer, leaving the innovator out in the cold. Since the lagtime between innovation and imitation is shrinking continuously, this problem increases in significance for innovators.

This familial sourcing relationship is also marked by close financial ties. Due to the small capital base of many channel members, the role of promissory notes is quite large. Trade credit is liberally extended and delayed payments are readily accepted. In addition, an elaborate system of rebates to channel members is in place. Rebates are provided for channel cooperation, market expansion, and channel innovation.[12] Since small retailers in particular are often highly dependent on financing and rebates, any new firm planning to work with them needs to make provisions to accommodate these needs.

Close ties among channel members, however, do not necessarily have to result from business interdependence and financial dependence alone. The Japanese distribution system also relies heavily upon personal relationships which are built through frequent visits and elaborate courtesies. The maintenance of these relationships is often far more important than the sales level of a certain product or short-term profitability, and includes the occasional provision of money to "send the son to school," frequent exchanges of gifts, friendly discussions, and very little direct pressure to sell. Time is of course the key to

---

[11] *Office of the US Trade Representative,* op. cit., p. 72.

[12] Shimaguchi and Lazer, op. cit., pp. 57–58.

building such relationships, and precisely the one variable which foreign firms in particular cannot benefit from in their initial market penetration efforts. Only a continuous market presence combined with great cultural sensitivity will enable them to start building such relationships.

Active involvement in product and business development is also a major feature of the distribution system. Manufacturers, wholesalers, and retailers interact quite closely and frequently in regard to new product development and product introduction. Successful product introduction needs to be followed up continuously through further product improvements so that channel members see the commitment of the product manufacturers to the product line. Lack of innovation is often seen as a lack of commitment which translates into weak relationships. While local presence is ideal for an importer to obtain input from the channel members, close interaction can also be fostered through frequent visits by both sides. However, regardless of the number of visits, innovation and continuous product refinement is a must in order to demonstrate commitment to the other channel members and to maintain their continued cooperation.

Sales support is another major characteristic of the interaction among channel members. Apart from traditional dealer aids, wholesalers, for example, are expected to supply a substantial number of personnel to retailers to support their product sales. Such support staff often work in the retail store (wearing store uniforms) but are paid for by the wholesaler. The rationale behind this practice is the belief that it is in the interest of the wholesaler and manufacturer to have their own employees selling their products since they are better able to explain the products to the customers than retailer employed personnel. Also expected are thorough product specific sales training and extensive after sale service. Since these dimensions comprise one of the main competitive fields among channel members, foreign suppliers need to ensure that such service and training backup is provided with the product in order to maintain channel goodwill.

Interaction with Consumers

Japanese channel members also work very closely with consumers. One major facet of this interaction is the strong emphasis on quality, form, and presentation. Most channel members insist on carrying only highest quality products and do not tolerate even slight defects and deviations. Much attention is also paid to packaging and wrapping. Sometimes, the cost of packaging may even exceed the value of the product sold.

Retailers also take pride in offering integrated selling systems. For example, product classes are grouped together in similar areas and are enriched by usage demonstrations and supplemental information.

Japanese retailers take on a major counseling role towards their customers, sometimes even going as far as organizing their customers into purchasing clubs. There, retailers register consumers as members of the club and record their purchases. This mechanism permits the retailers to keep sales records and to provide customers with incentives to buy by rewarding them with a bonus once given purchase quantities are reached during the year.

For the foreign firm, this close interaction with consumers again requires proper preparation of the channel members for its products. It also necessitates planning for a "proper fit" of one's products within the palate of a channel member's product offering. Without proper research and closeness to the market, however, this is difficult to achieve.

Changes in the Japanese Distribution System

Over the past decades, the economy of Japan has made significant strides toward a quantitative maturation. Translating this development into a better quality of life has—to some extent—been made the onus of the distribution system. Perhaps this mission is formulated most clearly by the director of the Industrial Policy Bureau of the Ministry of International Trade and Industry (MITI) who stated, "as consumer needs diversify with an emphasis on quality rather than on quantity, it becomes increasingly important for the distribution system to meet these needs."[13]

It is the purpose of this section to explore how responsive the distribution system has been to the changes in the Japanese economy, and what the shifts in the distribution strategies and the emergence of new participants in the distributive process mean to foreign firms. Even though it has been argued "that little distributive change has occurred (in Japan) and that improvement in this sector will take a great deal of time," such changes do occur.[14] In a typical Japanese fashion, they are not coming about with fanfare, but are taking place rather subtly. Nevertheless, they have profound long-term implications for both the Japanese firm as well as the importer.

Increased Distribution Integration The past decade has seen an increase in vertical integration efforts by channel members. Many wholesalers are joining forces or are becoming integrated with manufacturers and other wholesalers.[15] One emerging trend is the formation of manufacturer-wholesalers who produce some merchandise but subcontract out the major part of their production. In addition to manufacturers absorbing wholesalers, wholesalers have also integrated smaller manufacturers into their operations and begun integration into the retail sector. Furthermore, large wholesalers have begun to consolidate their activities with those of their secondary or tertiary partners in order to retain their market positions.

This integration can pose both problems and opportunities for foreign firms. One major problem is the fact that integrated wholesalers and manufac-

---

[13] Konaga, Keiichi, "Future of Japan's Distribution Industry," *Dentsu Japan Marketing/Advertising*, Spring, 1984, p. 1.

[14] Ross, op. cit., p. 12.

[15] Lazer, William, Musata, Shoji, and Kosaka, Hiroshi, "Japanese Marketing: Towards a Better Understanding," *Journal of Marketing*, Spring 1985, Vol. 49, No. 2, p. 79.

turers are more likely to buy from each other than from foreign firms, therefore making penetration more difficult. By the same token, however, wholesalers who grow stronger and larger through integration are able to establish more international linkages, import more, and conduct more direct activities than smaller wholesalers.

The Evolution of Chain Stores The formation of chain stores has become increasingly common in Japan, particularly in the convenience store sector. Since 1977, chain stores have experienced an average annual growth rate of 32 percent. Total sales of the 33 leading chain stores amounted to $3.4 billion in 1982.[16] Seven-Eleven, the largest convenience store chain in Japan, had 2,000 stores by the end of February, 1984, with 350–400 more outlets expected to open every year. These stores are typically located in residential areas, carry only goods needed daily, and are open long hours. In most instances, the stores are owned by an individual on a franchise or volunteer membership basis. The chain management provides owners with training in stocking and management techniques. As a result, 1,800 out of 3,000 stock-keeping units have been replaced by different merchandise in a six month time span in response to consumer needs.[17]

MITI's Industrial Policy Bureau sees the future for smaller retailers mainly in the organization of small stores into voluntary and franchised chains. MITI is apparently willing to lend its support to such developments, since one of its officials stated that "the organization of small retailers is . . . important as they represent the greater part of the Japanese retail industry."[18]

These emerging chain stores can become valuable allies to importers; based on past practices, their willingness to change the composition of merchandise is quite high. In addition, a centralized purchasing function can provide for large-sized orders which would be otherwise difficult to obtain. Finally, centralized distribution can provide many service functions which would be difficult for a foreign supplier to deliver.

The Emergence of Self-Service Stores Even though most traditional Japanese stores have suffered a constant decline in their market share in the past decade, self-service stores have enjoyed rapid real growth. In 1979, self-service stores had a national market share of about 15 percent, compared to just over 5 percent in 1966.[19] This rapid growth indicates the increased acceptance of

---

[16] ———, "In the Convenience Store Sector, Strategic Management is a Must," *Japan Times,* December, 1983.

[17] Sekikawa, Hitomi, "Seven-Eleven Japan Develops About 2,000 Stores," *Distribution Code Center,* (The Distribution Systems Research Institute, Mimeo), February, 1984, p. 1.

[18] Konaga, op. cit., p. 3.

[19] Dodwell Marketing Consultants, *The Structure of the Japanese Retail Distribution Industry 1981/1982,* (Tokyo: 1981), p. 17.

the self-service concept among consumers. The implications of this change are that goods marketed through self-service outlets need to be self-explanatory in nature and familiar to the buyer. Therefore, for new products, firms wishing to use these self-service outlets need to exert a pull strategy, in addition to the traditional Japanese requirements of a push strategy, in order to work with the channel members.

Cash and Carry Wholesaling One newly emerging type of channel member which operates very much contrary to the established notions of the Japanese distribution system is the cash and carry wholesaler. These firms, whose primary competitive tool is price, aim at those channel members who do not need financing, delivery, or service. Frequently their main customers are the very small retailers who come every day to purchase products in small quantities. Cash and carry wholesalers refuse to accept returns from retailers and instead suggest that slow selling merchandise be discounted. They do not develop personal relationships and grant no rebates, bonuses, or special payments.

These cash and carry wholesalers are similarly unconventional in their dealings with manufacturers. Again, no personal relationships are developed. These firms deal with many small manufacturers and select suppliers purely on the basis of product and price competitiveness. Although this method of doing business results in low prices to the end purchaser, such wholesalers often cannot sell national brand merchandise, since many large and well-known manufacturers are unwilling to sell to them for fear of disturbing their well-established channel relations. However, in spite of this handicap, these firms do quite well, based mainly on their high annual inventory turnover, which is often a multiple of that of traditional wholesalers.

Due to their lack of allegiance to any specific manufacturer and their primary focus on price and product, these cash and carry wholesalers have the potential to become good partners of foreign manufacturers.

Increase of Non-Store Retailing Two major types of non-store retailing activities on the increase are mail-order retailing and new retail experimentation. While mail-order retailing has existed in Japan for some time, its international expansion is a novelty. For example, Matsuzakaya, a Nagoya department store, has had a mail-order relationship with a German mail-order firm, Quelle, for years. Customers of Matsuzakaya were able to select Quelle products from a catalogue in Japan. Matsuzakaya then checked the availability of such a selection via air mail. Once availability was confirmed, the customer paid and the merchandise was shipped from Germany. To cut down on the lag-time between merchandise selection and receipt, Matsuzakaya is currently in the process of establishing a direct satellite link with Quelle. Customer catalogue selections will now be transmitted directly to Quelle via computer terminals located in the store in Japan. Merchandise can then be shipped immediately after a check for availability via the on-line system. Thus, the total order lag-time is reduced to two weeks, a facet which makes the mail-order process much more desirable for Japanese customers.[20]

For importers willing to participate in the cost of such on-line ordering systems, new opportunities can be opened up in the mail-order sector. These opportunities are to be found both with current Japanese mail-order firms and firms which can be attracted to the mail-order concept, as well as with the Japanese consumer.

In the area of retail innovation, one particular project should be briefly mentioned. With the support of the Ministry of International Trade and Industry, a two-way interactive cable television system is being developed. This project, which was initiated in 1976, permits the two-way transmission of both voice and picture and allows individuals to request the showing of specific video tapes on their television sets. The program currently experiments with providing retail functions. Large companies are given time slots to explain products and to interact with viewers. A teleshopping program is also offered in which viewers can examine merchandise and obtain price information. While this live program is enjoyed by the viewers, it has not been very enthusiastically received by retailers and has not yet fully resolved the settlement problem as to how customers pay for their orders.

Although the program is operative, it faces big future challenges in the areas of initial investment cost, consumer resistance to costly system purchases, and transmission technology constraints. At the same time, given sufficient acceptance and developmental progress, this avenue of retailing directly to the consumers could provide major opportunities for foreign firms, particularly since this direct distribution would make companies independent from established channel structures.

Restrictions in Department Store Growth While so far the changes enumerated have all presented new opportunities for foreign firms, one major negative trend is also visible. Currently, most imported consumer products in Japan are sold through department stores. This fact is the result of the greater financial capabilities of such stores, their broader international orientation and the composition of their clientele. However, the growth of these stores has been radically curtailed. In the past decade, the so called "large store law" has increasingly restricted the development of larger sized stores. The Ministry of International Trade and Industry and local councils (which need to agree to the opening of new department stores) have imposed many unreasonable restraints and burdens on corporations planning to open such stores. The rationale behind this restriction is the desire to aid small and medium sized stores which run the danger of being run out of business by an increase in department stores.

---

[20] *Kyodo News Release*, (Tokyo), March, 1984.

For the foreign firm attempting to sell consumer products to Japan, this restriction on department store growth presents a major danger because it reduces the growth in the availability of potential major outlets. However, it must be stated that these restrictive measures are being implemented mainly for domestic Japanese policy reasons rather than for purposes of restricting the importation of products.

Major shifts are also occurring in the performance of the physical distribution function in Japan. These are taking place in the area of transportation, warehousing, and information processing.

Changes in the Transportation Function

Changes in the Transportation Function Due to increased urban congestion, channel members are faced with a growing inability to provide competitive delivery service. More and more transportation companies are being formed exclusively for order consolidation purposes. Alone or in cooperation with channel members, such transportation firms can achieve major transport economies; transportation cost savings average about 30 percent and are sometimes as high as 60 percent. The use of consolidation is growing rapidly among channel members because non-users are suffering severely from the competitive advantage of the low transportation cost of users. Turning over the delivery function to outside companies changes the activities of many channel members substantially. Instead of focusing mainly on delivery services, they are now increasingly concentrating on the providing of financing, breakbulk, and assortment services.

For the foreign firm, this trend toward order consolidation offers the opportunity of cooperation with the newly emerging transportation companies. Many of them are not tied to any specific channel members and can provide an important complementary ingredient for competitive distribution in Japan.

The Emergence of Distribution Centers

The Emergence of Distribution Centers Recognizing the increasing problems of congestion, in the late 1960s the Japanese government began to legislate distribution improvements. These legislative efforts resulted in government sponsored joint ventures between small firms, large warehouse companies, and terminals that were designed to create more modern storage and warehouse facilities. In the meantime, manufacturers themselves have begun to join forces to form distribution centers. These newly formed centers contain distribution warehouses, display space, office buildings, and much valued parking space. These warehouse buildings offer efficient space utilization, direct truck access, and fully climatized and largely automated warehousing space. The administration of these centers provides maintenance, security, and common facilities. As a result, tenants need to worry only about their own business.

Although participation in these newly created distribution centers is quite expensive, they can offer new opportunities to foreign firms. Rather than having to rent a multiplicity of depots in each city, one centralized location can now be sufficient. Warehousing also becomes easier due to the distribution center's administrative support, and inventories can be kept more efficiently. Due to the high inventory requirements in Japan, savings in this sector can have a major impact on a corporation's profits.

Improvements in Distribution Information Major emphasis is placed by the distribution channel members and by the Japanese government on improvements in the area of information processing within the distribution system. As a MITI representative noted, "The distribution system is increasingly being required to meet consumer needs more effectively in a maturing industrial society. It must serve not only as a pipeline through which goods flow from producers to consumers, but also as a relay point allowing the information to flow between the two. The information function of the distribution system is expected to increase as the advanced information society develops. In other words, the importance of the distribution system as a relay point for the flow of producer-consumer information will increase as the Japanese economy matures and handles more information."[21]

This increased emphasis on information is apparent when one notes that the distribution system accounts for 43 percent of all computers used in all industries in the country.[22]

One application of this information emphasis is the increased installation of Point of Sale (POS) systems by retailers. This computerized cash register system collects information on all items sold in the store and is used for research, merchandising, and planning. By encouraging consumers to use store credit cards, which are encoded with socio-economic customer data, the POS system can identify consumer segments that purchase certain products, preferred size of product package, and the time of day the products are purchased. Unlike in the United States, Japanese privacy laws do not restrict such information flows. The system is used also for shopping basket analysis, customer traffic analysis and merchandise layout experimentation. Furthermore, it permits more precise demand forecasting, better inventory planning, reduced cash register error, and better personnel utilization.

The use of the POS system reduces the need for employees. However, rather than resulting in layoffs, the freed up employees are used to foster more direct contact with customers, providing them with more information and services. As a consequence, new product introduction is eased, product differentiation is enhanced, and a shift in product mix towards products with high explanatory needs is made possible.

For foreign firms, this information revolution presents numerous opportunities. First of all, market research can be more easily conducted and results more quickly obtained. Secondly, improved information flow can reduce the

---

[21] Konaga, op. cit., p. 1.

[22] Ibid., p. 2.

need for flexible inventory size. Thirdly, countering the trend towards self-explanatory merchandise which occurs through the increased acceptance of the self-service concept, more complicated products can be introduced due to the greater availability of sales personnel.

Conclusions and Perspectives

The Japanese distribution system is undergoing change as a reflection of the shifts occurring in the Japanese economic environment. Facing substantial changes in demand and an increasing unwillingness to pay high prices, channel members have to adjust to remain in business. The current Japanese distribution system serves its market and in most instances serves it well. In cases in which the system is inefficient, changes are coming about. If these changes appear to be slow, it must be kept in mind that change by consensus is always likely to be gradual. However, such changes may sometimes result in distribution configurations in which the process has outpaced the structure, but such situations reflect only a delay in the inevitable.

The thrust for change needs to continue, both on the side of Japan as well as on the part of firms planning to enter the Japanese market. Japanese policy makers need to continue and strengthen their market-opening efforts and carefully weigh the effects of domestic policies on the importation of foreign products. Encouragement should be provided to the development of new distribution channels, the emergence of new channel members, and the use of new distribution processes. The current large store legislation should be seriously reconsidered due to its substantial negative impact on foreign consumer product importation. Finally, some attention should be paid to consumption patterns within the Japanese society, and demand stimulation with concurrent plans for price reductions should be seriously considered.

In turn, prospective importers to Japan should keep in mind the existing Japanese distribution system, with all its constraints. If they wish to work within the system, they must adapt their business practices to it. However, foreign firms should not remain stuck in the perception of Japanese distribution channels formed twenty years ago; rather, they should take advantage of the system's recognized changes. The current saturation of the Japanese home with physical products and the increased desire for innovation and services present unique opportunities. Foreign firms need to work with newly emerging intermediaries and cooperate with the innovators in the distribution process. Armed with the knowledge about changes and opportunities, they need to make a renewed effort to enter the large and potentially very profitable Japanese market.

READING 28   INTERNATIONAL CHANNELS OF DISTRIBUTION AND THE ROLE OF COMPARATIVE MARKETING ANALYSIS

Bert Rosenbloom ◆ Trina L. Larsen

ABSTRACT. To enter international markets successfully, firms need to secure adequate distribution channels for their products in the targeted markets. But gaining access to, as well as developing and maintaining marketing channels in foreign markets requires substantial knowledge of the distribution structures and patterns in those markets. This follows because the so-called standardized (globalized) approach to international marketing strategy does not apply to distribution strategy in foreign markets. Comparative marketing analysis can provide international marketers with the means for obtaining the knowledge needed by providing (1) a substantial literature on distribution in different countries, (2) a variety of methodologies that can provide insights into foreign distribution structures, and (3) by sensitizing international marketers to changing patterns of distribution around the world.

As the 1990s unfold, such terms as *global marketplace, global arena,* and *global competition* are not just some new international business jargon, but realistic descriptions of the international competitive environment as it exists today in an increasing number of industries (Moran 1990). Thus, more and more firms from almost any country around the world will have to sell their products in international markets rather than only domestic ones whether they want to or not (Tung 1990, Keegan 1989, Cateora 1990). In short, international marketing has become a fact of life for growth and even survival in the 1990s and beyond.

Given this increasingly unavoidable need to venture into foreign markets, firms are faced with a host of international marketing strategy questions. Some of the most basic of these are: Do products need to be adapted to the particular foreign markets being targeted or can a global or uniform approach be used (Buzzell 1968, Keegan 1970, Levitt 1983)? How might pricing strategies need to be changed to conform with possible differences in customer demand patterns and elasticities as well as to reflect exchange rate differences (Kressler 1971, Rao 1984, Cavusgil 1988)? Does promotion, especially advertising need to be changed significantly or simply fine-tuned to communicate effectively with different foreign customer segments, or can a more standardized or global approach be used (Peebles, Ryans and Vernon 1978)?

But even if these basic strategy questions and many other related ones are resolved successfully, firms seeking to enter foreign markets must still deal with what is perhaps the most difficult strategic marketing question of all—*how can the firm obtain aggressive and reliable distribution for its products in the foreign markets chosen*? For clearly, without strong distribution channels that can make products conveniently available to final customers, even quality products, competitively

Source: *Journal of Global Marketing*, Vol. 4(4) 1991, pp. 39–54. © 1991 by The Haworth Press, Inc. Reprinted with permission.

priced, and heavily advertised, stand little chance of gaining a foothold in foreign markets, let alone a substantial and sustainable market share.

So, establishing and maintaining international channels of distribution is a crucial, and in many cases the overriding challenge faced by firms seeking to enter foreign markets (Keegan 1989).

The purpose of this article is to show why a knowledge of foreign distribution channels via comparative marketing analysis can be valuable to firms attempting to establish and maintain international distribution channels.

Comparative Marketing and Foreign Distribution Channel Structures

Boddewyn (1981) defines comparative marketing as:

> the systematic detection, identification, classification, measurement, and interpretation of similarities and differences among entire national (marketing) systems or parts thereof.

While comparative marketing analysis as defined above focuses on the macro marketing systems of countries, it can nevertheless be very useful from a micro perspective as well. This is especially the case for the distribution channel "part thereof" of various national marketing systems because it is through comparative marketing analysis that the firm can obtain knowledge and insights about structures and patterns of distribution in foreign countries. In this context then, comparative marketing analysis can become a practical managerial tool—in effect a special type of marketing research capable of providing management with knowledge of "mysterious" foreign distribution channel structures.

Adaptation Versus Standardization of Distribution Channel Strategy

Even if one accepts the argument that comparative marketing analysis can provide a powerful tool for understanding foreign distribution channels, those in the global standardization school of thought would argue that such knowledge is unnecessary. Because marketing strategy can be standardized for countries all over the world, what need is there to learn about the distribution patterns and structures of particular foreign markets?

This question raises yet again the rather old debate about whether international marketing strategies should be standardized (globalized) regardless of differences in the foreign countries in question, or customized (adapted) to meet differences across national environments. Although even a quarter century ago many scholars recognized the benefits of standardization (chiefly economies of scale and a consistent marketing image across nations), the main focus remained on identifying environmental differences that were seen as barriers to standardization (Buzzell 1968, Fayerweather 1969, Keegan 1970). Thus, how firms must adapt their marketing strategies in foreign markets dominated international marketing management thought. But in the early 1980s, the standardization vs. adaptation debate was revived, with renewed vigor. Levitt, in a seminal article (1983) argued that the marketplace was by now truly global, and that firms must standardize their marketing strategies in order to be competitive. According to Levitt, in today's global marketplace, the external pressures for the adaptation of marketing strategies are far outweighed by the benefits resulting from the standardization of marketing strategies. So, according to the globalization school, all the basic strategic components of the marketing mix: product, price, promotion, and distribution should be standardized into one uniform "package" to be offered to any country around the world.

This argument spawned a number of rebuttals which averred that an across the board call for standardization is too simplistic because it makes no allowances for particular types of products or markets (Douglas and Wind 1987, Huszagh, Fox and Day 1985, Hill and Still 1983, Ohmae 1985). Further, some scholars (Douglas and Wind 1987) argued that standardization of marketing strategies is more relevant for some elements of the marketing mix than for others (product and promotion rather than price and distribution). Indeed, limits on the applicability of globalization to distribution strategy was even recognized by Levitt himself because he did *not* advocate the systematic disregard of local or national differences in the formulation of *distribution strategy*. But it is Buzzell (1968) who pointed to the most explicit list of barriers to using a standardized approach to international distribution channel strategy. The most important of these are differences in government restrictions, marketing infrastructure, the character of markets, and industry conditions.

Government Restrictions While it is obviously not possible to list all of the government restrictions which are barriers to the standardization of a firm's distribution strategy, several examples will make the point. Consider the case of Bahrain, where all imports must be channeled through a Bahrain agent; foreigners are not allowed to own trading or marketing agencies (*Bahrain* 1983). In Japan, automobile companies sell cars door-to-door, yet this strategy is not open to them in France, where door-to-door selling is prohibited (Onkvisit and Shaw 1989). Mass-merchandisers of consumer goods in Japan face an obstacle to distribution in the form of the "large-store law," a regulation protecting the position of small shopkeepers in the Japanese economy. To open a store larger than 5,382 square feet, a new retailer must get the permission of the community's retailers, and the law is administered in such a way that it often takes eight to ten years for approval to be granted (Darlin 1988). This affects not only the entry of the new retailer, but the type of products available for purchase, since the small mom-and-pop stores are not likely to stock the large array of goods (including many foreign goods) that the larger retailer would.

There are also many government regulations restricting the types of products that may be sold through particular types of outlets, and when they may be sold. For instance, in Italy municipalities may regulate the product lines which may be handled by retail outlets. In Milan, for instance, a dairy store may sell boiled eggs or boiled rice with oil but may not sell boiled eggs with butter or boiled rice with tomato sauce (Cateora 1990 p. 580). Also in Italy, stores must obtain a license for each type of product they sell, thus limiting the variety of products carried in any one outlet (i.e., some stores may carry soap, but not detergent). In England and Wales there are a number of restrictions on the types of products that may or may not be sold on Sundays. Whiskey and gin may be sold, but dried milk in cans may not; fresh vegetables may be sold, but canned ones may not; and aspirin may be sold, while cough medicine may not. Further, pornographic books may be sold, but Bibles may not (Mosely 1985)!

Finally, many countries (especially civil law countries) have enacted legislation that restricts a firm's ability to terminate or fail to renew channel members. The laws may make it very difficult to terminate a channel member without incurring substantial expense (Giberga 1988). For instance, in Austria, if an agent is terminated without what the law considers just cause, compensation payments to the channel member may range from between one and fifteen years' average commissions (Giberga 1981).

Market Infrastructure One of the most fundamental differences in distribution channel structures across various nations is the number and the variety of outlets available. Channels may not exist for many types of products, or distribution outlets may not be available, especially in outlying rural areas. For instance, in the Philippines, Procter & Gamble, the consummate mass-marketer, sells products door-to-door (Cateora 1990). In other cases, some channels may be dominated by a few giant firms that control access to the market. In Finland, for example, four wholesale-distributor chains carry 92 percent of all non-durable consumer goods in that country. Thus their support is mandatory for significant market penetration (Cateora 1990). In contrast, Japan, a nation with only about 4 percent of the land area and less than half the population of the United States, has about the same number of wholesale-distributors as does the United States, and only 10 percent less retailers (Czinkota 1985).

Another major difference in market infrastructure across nations is the wide variation in the functions and roles of channel members which may differ greatly across nations. One cannot simply assume that a retailer is a retailer is a retailer, and that a wholesaler is a wholesaler is a wholesaler. Consider the case of Japan, where wholesalers play a much greater financial role than do U.S. wholesalers, and as a result gain a great deal of control over the channel (Boddewyn 1981). In some nations, a wholesaler's function may be primarily to break bulk, whereas in other nations, a wholesaler may play a much greater service and promotional role. In Hong Kong it is common for trading companies to handle a tremendous array of products, to the point that they may not realistically have the time to adequately handle any additional products. Also, Hong Kong agents may take on new products without the intention of devoting time and resources to their effective distribution; the purpose of carrying the product may be simply to deny it to the competition (Onkvisit and Shaw 1989).

Character of Markets Socio-cultural differences that affect consumers' shopping patterns are still very much in evidence across national boundaries. For instance, in the United States, a significant portion of the consumption of beverages such as beer takes place in the home, so marketers emphasize retail outlets such as grocery stores, and convenience stores for distribution. In many other countries, however, public areas are the primary place for the consumption of such a product, and the primary outlets are taverns, street vendors, and the like (Cundiff and Hilger 1984).

Another example of the effect of customer characteristics on distribution structure can be seen in MacDonald's first entry in the Netherlands. Lacking knowledge of consumer markets in that country, MacDonald's followed its traditional practice of locating its outlets in the suburbs of Amsterdam, targeting the suburban, car-driving commuter. But, the suburbs are not as popular in the Netherlands. Most people live in the city, and many do not own cars. Additionally, shopping malls are not as prevalent. So MacDonald's had to change its distribution structure by locating its outlets within the city. Kentucky Fried Chicken faced a similar problem in Japan. While people do commute to Tokyo from the suburbs, most do so by train, so many suburban outlets were relatively inaccessible. The firm now concentrates on either inner city locations or near train stations (Onkvisit and Shaw 1989).

Different types of customers may also require alternative channel structures. For instance, for most sales of its tractors and earth moving equipment, Caterpillar uses a network of independent dealers. But when it makes sales to governments such as the United States and the U.S.S.R. a direct channel is used (Czinkota and Ronkainen 1990).

Industry Conditions Competitive structures differ across nations, and in many cases competitors may have control of most available outlets for distribution. Consider the problem Nike faced distributing its products in Europe. The prominent retailers already carried competing brands, such as Puma and Adidas, and were fearful of losing the distribution of these established products if they carried Nike. Thus, Nike had far more trouble securing distributors than it had anticipated (Onkvisit and Shaw 1989).

Cartels or monopolies which control channels can also be a serious obstacle. For instance, in Sweden, all alcoholic beverages must be sold through state-owned and operated outlets. Other examples are a chocolate cartel in Switzerland and the Japan Tobacco and Salt Public Corporation, a state monopoly which controls tobacco imports and charges a fee for distribution.

Levitt (1983) called for innovative solutions, but changing existing distribution systems can be costly and difficult. For instance, in the United States,

Porsche tried to change its distribution from dealers to agents, but following an uproar was forced to abandon the plan (Tinnin 1984).

Increased Understanding of Foreign Channels Through Comparative Marketing Analysis

Although the debate between the global standardization and adaptation approaches still continues, in many areas of international marketing strategy, it does not really apply to the distribution component of international marketing strategy. As discussed above, adaptation of distribution strategy to meet the particular sets of circumstances in foreign environments is likely to be necessary in virtually all cases. Thus, firms seeking to gain distribution for their products in foreign markets have little choice. They must gain knowledge and insight into the distribution structures and patterns in the targeted foreign markets.

Comparative marketing analysis can provide the means for doing so in three ways. First, comparative marketing provides a rich body of literature on distribution structures and patterns in many foreign countries. Second, the methodologies used in comparative marketing can help guide the design and execution of individualized distribution research studies undertaken by firms. Third, exposure to comparative marketing analysis can help increase the decision maker's sensitivity to change as it unfolds in an international context. Each of these benefits is discussed more fully below.

Comparative Marketing Literature As noted above, a rich body of literature on distribution systems exists in comparative marketing, and the publications address a variety of topics of concern to international marketers seeking distribution in foreign markets. One well-developed area of research concerns country- or region-specific analyses of distribution systems. In particular there is a great deal of information regarding distribution structures and patterns in Japan, which is useful because the complex Japanese distribution system is often cited as one of the primary barriers to successful marketing in that nation (Alden 1987, Berney 1986, Czinkota 1985, Luke 1979, Roxx 1983, Rosenberg 1979, Tsurumi 1982).

Another region which has garnered substantial interest in comparative distribution systems is the European Community, an area in which many marketers from all over the world are involved, and in which a great deal of change is expected due to the 1992 economic integration process (Beyma 1989, Kacker 1988, Kelly 1987, Rossant, Galuszka, and Reed 1989).

While not a specific country or region, there are also a number of analyses of distribution systems in developing nations (Chong, 1973; Izraeli, Izraeli, and Meissner, 1976; Goldman, 1974; Wadinambiaratchi, 1965). Distribution systems and consumer shopping patterns in developing nations are typically very different from those in industrialized nations, and companies considering entry into these types of markets would be well advised to consult the literature.

Another critical international distribution issue involves the relationship between manufacturers and channel members. A growing body of literature exists on such issues as how to find, select, motivate, control, and terminate middlemen ("Basic . . ." 1987, "Finding . . ." 1985, Giberga 1986, Masterson 1988, Rosenbloom 1990, Rosson 1984, Sprada 1987). Such information sources in the comparative marketing literature can provide international marketers with the kind of information needed to help overcome distribution system barriers to entry.

Comparative Marketing Methodologies and Distribution Research As discussed earlier, comparative marketing research focuses on the systematic detection, identification, classification, and interpretation of marketing phenomena in different national environments. Several approaches or methodologies have been used in comparative marketing research to achieve these results. The most important of these are institutional comparison, consumer behavior, and statistical analyses.

Institutional Comparison Studies of marketing institutions in various national settings is one of the most common types of comparative marketing research (Boddewyn 1981). Some of this research has been criticized for its superficiality in examining and comparing institutions in different countries. For example, a wholesaler in Japan might be compared with a wholesaler in the United States with little attention paid to the substantive differences between them. Thus,the findings may be misleading at best or completely erroneous at worst. Nevertheless, the fact that some uneven or even poor institutional research has been done does not vitiate the institutional approach. If done diligently, with careful attention given to the definition and description of marketing institutions and structures in various national settings, the institutional comparison methodology can be of great value to the firm seeking to learn more about the marketing institutions in the countries it targets for distribution of its products.

Consumer Behavior Consumer behavior studies undertaken in the context of comparative marketing analysis focus heavily on cross-cultural comparisons of consumer attitudes and behaviors as they relate to the purchase of particular products, responses to advertisements, or to patterns of shopping behavior. Thus, a consumer group in Country X is compared with a consumer group in Country Y, in terms of the different cultural dimensions associated with each group. Differences in these patterns of consumer behavior are then explained in terms of the variation in the cultures of the two groups.

This type of research has also been criticized by comparative marketing scholars because it tends to become confounded by other noncultural variables. For example, Boddewyn (1981) cites an example of hand-to-mouth buying by consumers. Is such behavior accounted for by a stage of economic development variables (such as lack of refrigeration) or a cultural variable (such as a desire for more personal contact with merchants)? Separating these factors is very difficult.

But here again, the fact that the consumer behavior methodology of comparative marketing analysis can be complicated, and even confusing does *not* negate its usefulness as a research tool for the firm seeking to learn more about patterns of consumer shopping behavior in different countries that ultimately determine how products should be distributed in those countries. Indeed, insights about cultural differences can be invaluable for planning distribution channels. Computerland, for example, found that British consumers expect more information and "handholding" in the purchase of expensive technical products, such as personal computers, than Americans. Thus, the use of retail stores to sell personal computers which has worked so successfully for Computerland in the United States, would not work nearly so well in England.

Statistical Analyses The statistical approach to comparative marketing analysis relies on samples drawn from different cultures from which statistical measures are computed and then compared to determine whether statistically significant differences can be found.

Such comparative marketing studies have been severely criticized for their tendency to use very small, non-random samples from which broad generalizations are made (Boddewyn 1981). So, for instance, 50 housewives in France may be compared with 75 from the United States on some small aspect of consumer behavior such as the sources of information used before purchasing a particular product. From this very small convenience sample on a very narrow topic, the researcher might then go on to generalize about "what makes French and U.S. housewives" different (Boddewyn 1981).

Needless to say, such overgeneralizations based on small nonprobability samples can be highly misleading. Yet, is it really more misleading than no information at all? Indeed, much marketing research conducted by firms in their domestic environments is based on small non-random samples. Does this mean then, that such research should not be undertaken or that no domestic marketing research should be done unless large random samples are used? Clearly, this is not the case. The purpose of marketing research, whether conducted in a national or international setting, is to provide additional information which hopefully will reduce the risk associated with making marketing decisions. Hence, to the degree that statistical comparative marketing studies— even those using small nonprobability samples—contribute to that end, they are worthwhile and certainly better than nothing. So, while large random samples in statistical comparative marketing studies would indeed be desirable, the more limited but feasible type of research should not be dismissed.

Sensitivity to Change As noted above, the comparative marketing literature may provide a marketer with information regarding the similarities, and perhaps more notably, the differences that he or she faces when distributing products in foreign markets. But one could argue that situations change, and that some specific information may be outdated. In fact, information regarding nations' legal regulations may become outdated within six months. But this does not negate the relevance of comparative marketing to international marketers. The process of comparative marketing can broaden the outlook of marketers, helping them become aware of differences in the international environment, and making them more sensitive to the changes that are occurring in that environment.

Channel arrangements in other nations may provide marketers with potential strategies in foreign environments as well as in the domestic environment. By studying other distribution structures, a marketer may broaden his outlook to include previously nonexistent alternatives, or do what he is currently doing more efficiently. For instance, European and Asian retailers studied the U.S. process of self-service discount pricing, then introduced the concept in their own countries, and many governments and business executives have studied the Japanese trading companies in order to try to learn from their success (Keegan 1989).

Additionally, there is a great deal of change currently taking place in international distribution patterns, and a marketer should be attuned to these changes and their impact for successful continuation in a market. While change may present international marketers with a threat if they do not adapt to it when necessary, it may also present them with opportunities if they are aware, and ready to take advantage of them. For instance, European retailing, merchandising, and distribution in general, are changing in response to the 1992 economic integration process, and in Eastern Europe marketing infrastructure and patterns are developing from the ground up. A knowledge of how distribution patterns and structures develop, and a more general sense and appreciation for alternative ways of doing things, can give the international marketer an advantage in a period of rapid change which presents a myriad of opportunities as well as threats.

Summary and Conclusion

In order to gain access to international markets, firms need to secure strong distribution channels for their products in foreign markets. But entering, establishing, and maintaining marketing channels in foreign markets requires substantial knowledge of the distribution structures and patterns in those markets because the standardized (globalized) approach to international marketing strategy does not apply to distribution strategy.

Comparative marketing analysis can provide international marketers with the means for obtaining the knowledge needed about foreign distribution structures in three ways: First, the substantial literature on distribution in many countries around the world provides a wealth of valuable information. Second, several methodologies used in comparative marketing analysis such as institutional comparisons, consumer behavior studies in different cultures, and comparative statistical analyses can provide insights into foreign distribution structures and patterns. Finally, the underlying theme and focus of comparative marketing can help to sensitize marketing management to the substantial changes occurring in global patterns of distribution.

REFERENCES

Alden, Vernon R. (1987). Who Says You Can't Crack Japanese Markets? *Harvard Business Review,* (January-February), 52–56.

Basic Question: To Export Yourself or to Hire Someone to Do it For You? (1987, April 27) *Business America,* pp. 14–17.

Berney, Karen. (1986). Competing in Japan, *Nation's Business,* (October), p. 29.

Beyma, Ron. (1989). U. S., European Retailers are Becoming More Transnational, *Europe,* (January-February), p. 20.

Boddewyn, Jean J., (1981). Comparative Marketing: The First Twenty-five Years, *Journal of International Business Studies,* (Spring/Summer), 61–79.

Buzzell, Robert D. (1968). Can You Standardize Multinational Marketing? *Harvard Business Review,* (November/December), 102–113.

Cateora, Philip R. (1990) *International Marketing,* seventh edition, Homewood, IL: Irwin.

Cavusgil, Tamer S. (1988). Unraveling the Mystique of Export Pricing, *Business Horizons,* (May-June), 54–63.

Chong, S. J. (1973). Comparative Marketing Practices of Foreign and Domestic Firms in Developing Countries: A Case Study of Malaysia, *Management International Review,* 6, 91–98.

Cundiff, Edward W., and Hilger, Marye Tharp. (1984). *Marketing in the International Environment,* Englewood Cliffs, NJ: Prentice-Hall, Inc.

Czinkota, Michael R. (1985). Distribution of Consumer Products in Japan, *International Marketing Review,* (Autumn), 39–51.

Czinkota, Michael R., and Ronkainen, Ilkka A. (1990). *International Marketing,* second edition, Chicago, IL: The Dryden Press.

Darlin, D., (1988, November 28). Shelf Control—'Papa-Mama' Stores in Japan Wield Power to Hold Back Imports, *Wall Street Journal,* p.A1.

Douglas, Susan and Wind, Yoram. (1987). The Myth of Globalization, *Columbia Journal of World Business,* (Winter), 19–29.

Fayerweather, John. (1969). *International Business Management: A Conceptual Framework,* New York, NY: McGraw Hill.

Finding a Distributor Takes Planning and Skill: A BI Checklist, (1985, March 8), *Business International,* p. 74.

Giberga, Ovido M. (1981). Laws Restrain Agency Agreement Termination, *Foreign Business Practices,* Washington, DC: Department of Commerce, 86–95.

Giberga, Ovido M. (1986, July 21). The Legal Pitfalls of Negotiating with Foreign Agents, *Business America,* 2–5.

Goldman, Arieh. (1974). Outreach of Consumers and the Modernization of Urban Food Retailing in Developing Countries, *Journal of Marketing,* 8–16.

Hill, J. S., and Still, R. R. (1984). Adapting Products to LDC Tastes, *Harvard Business Review,* (March/April), 92–101.

Huszagh, Sandra, Fox, Richard J., and Day, Ellen. (1985). Global Marketing: An Empirical Investigation, *Columbia Journal of World Business,* (Twentieth Anniversary Issue), 31–43.

Izraeli, Dov, Izraeli, D. N., and Meissner, Frank. (eds.) (1989). *Marketing Systems for Developing Countries,* New York: Wiley.

Kacker, Madhav P. (1988). The Metamorphosis of European Retailing, *European Journal of Marketing,* (no. 8), 15–22.

Keegan, Warren J. (1989). *Global Marketing Management,* fourth edition, Englewood Cliffs, NJ: Prentice Hall.

Keegan, Warren J. (1970). Five Strategies for Multinational Marketing, *European Business,* (January), 35–40.

Kelly, Bill. (1987). The New Wave From Europe, *Sales and Marketing Management,* (November), 45–50.

Kressler, Peter R. (1971). Is Uniform Pricing Desirable in Multinational Markets? *Akron Business and Economic Review,* (Winter).

Luke, Robert H. (1979). Successful Marketing in Japan: Guidelines and Recommendations. In Harold W. Berkman and Ivan R. Vernon (Eds.) *Contemporary Perspectives in International Business,* (pp. 307–315) Chicago: Rand McNally.

Masterson, John T. Jr. (1988, November 21). Drafting International Distributorship and Sales Representative Agreements, *Business America,* pp. 8–9.

Moran, Robert T. (managing editor) (1990). *Global Business Management in the 1990s,* Washington, DC: Beacham Publishing, Inc., pp. ix–xi.

Mosely, Ray. (1985, December 4). Oh, Blimey! Shopping on Sunday, *Chicago Tribune.*

Ohmae, Kenichi. (1985). Becoming a Triad Power: The New Global Corporation, *The McKinsey Quarterly,* (Spring), 2–25.

Ohmae, Kenichi. (1985). *Triad Power,* New York, NY: The Free Press.

Onkvisit, Sak, and Shaw, John J. (1989). *International Marketing: Analysis and Strategy,* Columbus, OH: Mirrill Publishing Co.

Peebles, Dean M., Ryans, John K., and Vernon, Ivan R. (1978). Coordinating International Advertising, *Journal of Marketing,* (Winter), 27–35.

Rao, Vithala R. (1984). Pricing Research in Marketing: The State of the Art, *Journal of Business,* (January), 539–59.

Rosenbloom, Bert. (1990). Motivating Your International Channel Partners, *Business Horizons,* (March-April).

Ross, Randolf. (1983). "Understanding the Japanese Distribution System: An Explanatory Framework," *European Journal of Marketing,* (Winter), 5–15.

Rossant, John, Galuszka, Peter, and Reed, Stanley. (1989, June 26). The Race to Stock Europe's Common Supermarket, *International Business,* pp. 80–82.

Rosson, Philip J. (1984). Success Factors in Manufacturer-Overseas Distributor Relationships in International Marketing. In Erdener Kaynak (Ed.) *International Marketing Management,* (pp. 91–107) New York: Praeger Publishing.

Shimaguchi, Mitsuaki, and Rosenberg, Larry. (1979). Demystifying Japanese Distribution, *Columbia Journal of World Business,* (Spring).

Sprada, Evelyn A. (1987). Distributors: Key to Sales Success, *Export Today,* (Winter-Spring), 33–36.

Tinnin, David B. (1984, April 16). "Porsche's Civil War with Its Dealers," *Fortune,* pp. 63–68.

Tsurumi, Yoshi. (1982). Managing Consumer and Industrial Systems in Japan, *Sloan Management Review,* (Fall), 36–45.

Tung, Rosalie. (1990). Global Orientation in the 21st Century. In Robert T. Moran (Managing Ed.) *Global Business Management in the 1990s,* (pp. 37–44) Washington, D.C.: Beacham Publishing, Inc.

Wadinambiaratchi, George. (1965). Channels of Distribution in Developing Economies, *Business Quarterly,* (Winter), 74–82.

COMPARATIVE EVALUATION OF INTERNATIONAL VERSUS NATIONAL ADVERTISING STRATEGIES

Jacob Hornik

No matter how hard man tries it is impossible for him to divest himself of his own culture, for it has penetrated to the roots of his nervous system and determines how he perceives the world. . . . People cannot act or interact at all in any meaningful way except through the medium of culture.
—*Edward T. Hall,* The Hidden Dimension, p. 188.

Though it is widely accepted that cross-cultural differences in perception exist, there is little empirical evidence actually documenting such differences or suggesting the particular form or pattern they take.

The process of multinational marketing development is associated with substantial growth in international marketing communications (Keegan, 1974). Yet a wide range of considerations, not necessarily relevant for domestic marketing, become highly relevant variables in international marketing decisions. Perhaps this distinction is best seen in the range and nature of alternative advertising strategies and tactics. Notably, the "standardization dilemma" in international advertising: "Does a given concept mean to the people in the other culture what it means to people in the culture in which it was originally developed?", "Should we individualize messages in every country, or standardize messages across countries?" With the exception of Dunn's work (1966, 1967, 1976), international advertising comparisons are almost nonexistent.

The purpose of this paper is to investigate further the "standardization dilemma." First, a multidisciplinary theoretical discussion will add some insight on the controversy. Second, a pilot study will be cited, where comparison has been made between American made ads and Israeli made ads for the same American products promoted in Israel. Third, an attempt will be made to detect some differences in strategy and creativity approaches, and to understand some of the forces that might create disparity.

The overall objective of the research is to develop an understanding of international advertising principles to provide perspective for American advertisers in future business endeavors. It should bring them to grips with the cultural consumer milieu and the attitude and perception of foreign consumers to international advertising messages.

International Marketing Communication

When advertisers convey anything across culture boundaries there may be a great difference between what was intended and what was received. The saying "on the rocks" means one thing in the United States and can hardly be translated to Hebrew. Much of the difficulty in intercultural communication is not just a matter of understanding such sayings, but of understanding nonverbal signals that are generally coded so automatically within a single culture that we are quite unconscious of them (Cole and Bruner, 1971; Harott, 1970).

The international advertiser must constantly be on the alert to cultural variations. Advertising planning, research, segmentation, media selection, creative considerations, and campaign strategies all become more complex when the additional variables of international operations are introduced. Domestic success is no guarantee of predictable success in a different country. Many successful American advertising campaigns failed overseas, because of the failure to understand fully the foreign culture and its social norms (Ricks, Arpan, and Fu, 1974).

The "Standardization Dilemma" The "standardized versus localized" debate in international advertising continues without reaching a consensus. It seems that the lack of agreement is mostly due to the lack of empirical data. Most international advertising studies to date have been descriptive and general, rather than analytical and specific.

There are two schools of thought on approaching the dilemma. The one contends that the differences between countries are of degree, not of direction. Basic human needs are similar everywhere. Therefore, the same products can be sold with similar promotional appeals (Fatt, 1967; Ryans and Donnelly, 1969).

For the other group different cultures usually create different needs, although some basic needs may prevail across cultures. Therefore, people may not be satisfied with similar products and communication appeals (Buzzel, 1968; Harvey and Kerin, 1974).

In some ways, everyone in the world is the same, but at the same time, no two persons in the world are the same. Thus each of us is a cultural communicator and a cultural perceptor. In some cases global marketing communication appears successful. But the limited cases of American Express, Hertz, and Schweppes, who employ the same appeal internationally, all have one thing in common; they are directed toward a rather narrow and somewhat upperclass market in all areas (Pollard, 1976).

The problem with many recent studies in international advertising is that they equate derived product need with perceived message appeal. Certain needs may be the same across cultures because they are to some extent inherent within our biological system (Dichter, 1962). But attitudes and perceptions differ because they are more influenced by culture (Coles and Branner, 1971), tradition (Bond, Nakazato, and Shiraishi, 1975), political systems (Porter, 1972), life style (Linton and Broadbent, 1974), economic system (Kaplan, 1972), and media system (Farace, 1966). Knowledge and identification of culturally related differences in attitude and perception, we contend, are of critical concern for advertising research.

A Theoretical Overview We have examined a variety of text and trade books, conference papers, research studies, and annotated bibliographies in an attempt to discern some general propositions on which the present international advertising concepts appear to be grounded. Based on these, it may be concluded that there are six major propositions which underlie current thinking on the issue, and that each of them is deserving of scrutiny and more empirical evidence.

1. Advertising standardization is not a simplistic concept and should be considered in terms of degree of uniformity rather than in absolute terms (Peebles, Rayons, and Vernon, 1978).

2. Cross-cultural advertising is a distinct and unique form of marketing communication which requires special labeling, attention, instruction and methodology (Printer's Ink, 1966). It calls for added skills—the ability to organize and develop international advertising programs plus the ability to adjust to foreign market conditions influenced by different and varying conditions (Candee, 1963).

3. A fundamental bias in cross-cultural research arises from "ethnocentrism"—from the blindness to the unique and different characteristics of another culture (Van Raaij, 1978). This brought up the "emic-etic issue" in international research (Davidson, 1977; Jones, 1976). Emic is culturally specific research in which an attempt is made to obtain the best possible description of a phenomenon occurring in a particular culture, utilizing concepts employed only in that culture. Etic is the culturally universal approach of studying a phenomenon by utilizing universal concepts. Such concepts are often approximations of emic concepts. Being universal they are suitable for comparative work.

4. Cultural differences between advertisers and consumers might function as boundaries or barriers which must be overcome if understanding and satisfaction are to be achieved (Cole and Bruner, 1971). Since the ad creator (usually advertising agency) is a member of a specific culture, it is assumed that his ads convey messages indicative of particular dispositions that his culture has toward general world themes. This may be especially true when the creator is instructed by the marketing company to prepare an ad conveying a particular message, for the marketer must be sensitive to both the reactions of his countrymen and the reactions of foreigners who may be exposed to the same ad. Thus, ads may be contrasted both within and across countries to determine whether the same interpretations are being made of these ads by members of the respective countries.

5. Learning about a cultural pattern is an important means of reducing uncertainty about the behavior of customers of that culture (Dichter, 1962). Cross-cultural diversities exist. These diversities are the result of

differences in the situation, which consists of cultural values, goals and norms (Munson and McIntyre, 1979; Osgood, 1967; Triandis, 1971), and other forces that may affect the reception and acceptance of messages.

6. Culture is primarily a phenomenon of region or nationality; national identity predicts culture (Brislin, 1973). But parallels between nation and culture should be carefully examined. It is possible to find much greater viability in a "horizontal" analysis based on common occupation, socioeconomic class, or ethnicity (independent of citizenship) which will account for differences in perception (Dunn, 1976). These endorse the logic of market segmentation abroad as well as at home.

The corollary is that communication and culture are so closely bound together that virtually all human communication is culturally linked. When we are engaged in international marketing communication, that communication which takes place as a deliberate form of cross-national advertising, the sender's cultural background affects message form, whereas the receivers' cultural background determines message perception.

Most of the earlier research in cross-cultural perception was carried out to test the "nature-nurture hypotheses" (Segall, 1966). This often involves studies of geometric illusion susceptibility testing the "carpentered world hypotheses" (Jahoda, 1970). More recently, however, the research emphasis has moved from these, to studies of cultural differences in pictorial representation, e.g., the studies of Kaplan (1972), and Deregowski (1972). Lonner and Cvetkovich (1972), for example, were concerned with a study of responses to political cartoons and humor appearing in newspapers around the world. The objective of their study was to determine whether or not differences in perceptions, if they exist, are related to countries of origin of the cartoons. They stated that the "message" of the cartoon, in terms of what the cartoonist is attempting to communicate, might be viewed as one way to assess cultural thematics and cross-cultural communication. Scales were developed to measure reactions to cartoons from different countries and publications.

The issues brought up so far are conceptual in nature, methodological and pragmatic in implication. At this stage of growth and development of the study of cross-cultural promotion, research focus is primarily upon forming the appropriate questions in a fashion reflective of the complexity of the phenomenon under investigation. International marketing communication, therefore, should incorporate a multidisciplinary approach utilizing concepts from management (Ajiteruke and Boddewyn, 1970); communication (Becker, 1969); psychology (Walker, 1971); sociology (Elder, 1976); etc. The current study is an attempt to compare American advertising campaigns versus locally tailored ads for the same American products. Because of some methodological constraints, such as the relatively small sample of ads and respondents, this study should be considered as an illustrative case rather than as a comprehensive treatment to the following hypothesis:

Hypothesis There are no differences in attitudes and perceptions, as measured by the semantic differential, among groups receiving the same product advertisements presented in the form of 1) International American Ads (AmA), 2) Israeli designed ads (IsA), and 3) Neutral, nonidentified ads (NaA).

Method

The study described here is a pilot project in the evaluation of American ads of well-known American products distributed in Israel. Some ads transferred the U.S. approach almost intact (American illustration and translated copy). Other ads were prepared by a local agency in Israel for the same American product. All ads appeared in national Israeli magazines and received in a Starch-type test at least a 15% "Read-most" score.

Analytical Procedure An appropriate way to describe the analysis is by means of a flow chart.

Subjects consisted of a random subsample of 184 housewives taken from 1,800 Home Testing Institute panel members. They were divided at random into

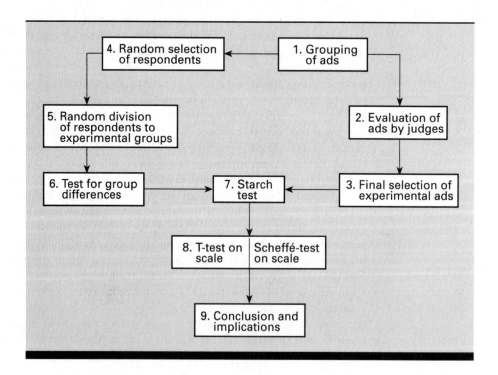

three groups. A t-test was used to determine group differences. There were no significant differences between groups:

t = 1.14, df = 59

t = 0.66, df = 62

t = 1.43, df = 57

t = 2.00 was needed at the .05 level

Hundreds of ads appear each week in Israeli periodicals, and many of these are from international sources promoting other nations' products.

When differences in attitudes and perception are considered, a myriad rival hypotheses which could account for the observed differences must be excluded. Unless these additional factors which could cause the observed differences are controlled, it is not possible to make a valid statement about differences in perception.

An attempt was made to select ads that differ only in one independent variable—cultural attributes (country of origin). Therefore, ad selection was done very carefully in three stages: In the first stage 31 triplicate ads were selected from local magazines. These ads represented AmA for American products marketed in Israel; IsA for the same American products; and NaA for the same products. At the second phase eight local advertising practitioners (three advertising managers, three account executives, and two agency presidents) were consulted. These expert "judges" evaluated the appropriateness of the ads for the intended experiment. The use of expert judges in cross-national research has been strongly recommended as a technique which helps provide for content validity (Straus, 1969). The judges expressed their view as to which triplicate ads maintain the following requirements: (1) Which American-made and Israeli-made ads have strong respective cultural themes, (2) which triplicate ads have the same advertising approach (differing only on cultural theme), (3) which triplicates appeared in the same magazine within a close time span (not exceeding one month), (4) all triplicate ads are about the same size and are either all four color (4/c) ads or all 2/c ads.

In phase three the final selection of ads was done on the basis of ads that fulfill the basic requirements as judged by the practitioners in phase 2. This resulted in six triplicate ads with the same advertising approach to the same product within each triplicate and different approaches and products among triplicates. The ads used in the experiment are described (see List of Advertisements on pages R364–R365).

Two instruments were used

1. First, each single ad was given a Starch method test in order to check respondents' prior exposure and measure recall-recognition. In addi-

TABLE **1**   Experimental Design

Group Advertisements	A	B	C
AmA–Helena Rubinstein	N = 61		
IsA–Helena Rubinstein		N = 64	
NaA–Helena Rubinstein			N = 59
AmA–Fabergé			N = 59
IsA–Fabergé	N = 61		
NaA–Fabergé		N = 64	
AmA–Westinghouse			N = 59
IsA–Westinghouse		N = 64	
NaA–Westinghouse	N = 61		
AmA–Coca-Cola	N = 61		
IsA–Coca-Cola			N =59
NaA–Coca-Cola		N = 64	
AmA–Levis		N = 64	
IsA–Levis	N = 61		
NaA–Levis			N = 59
AmA–IBM		N = 64	
IsA–IBM			N = 59
NaA–IBM	N = 61		

tion, this test assisted in analyzing specific ad features (headline, illustration, copy, etc.)

2. Subjects were presented with three classes of ads. The experimental design is summarized in Table 1.

Immediately after reception of the ads all groups were asked to complete a 9-point semantic differential scale (Dickson and Albaum, 1977; Osgood, 1974) containing three sets of bipolar adjectives and phrases representing their evaluation of ads.

Not understandable	1:2:3:4:5:6:7:8:9:	Understandable
Unappealing		Appealing
Not interesting		Interesting

Table 2 presents the group means for the three evaluative statements. In addition, each respondent was asked to express her view on one open-ended

TABLE 2   Group Scale Values

Group	N	Means	S.D.	95% Confidence Intervals
1. Group A	61	12.2623	3.9871	11.2617 to 13.2629
2. Group B	64	12.9688	3.2610	12.1699 to 13.7677
3. Group C	59	11.8983	4.0073	10.8758 to 12.9208

question (Brislin, Lonner and Thorndike, 1973). This served as a basis to interpret possible variations.

Subjects were instructed not to "figure out the right answer," but to put down their impression on each tested ad. Instruction stated that the purpose of the test is "to find out how you feel about the presented advertisements." Also, the instructions included an example.

It should be stressed that no cross-cultural attempts to develop rating scales for ads have been made. However, the research of Miller and Bacon (1971) was somewhat relevant to our procedure. Their study was concerned with the perception of visual humor. They used a single 7-point humor scale (funny-unfunny) and three 7-point scales which were designed to measure cultural acceptability of the humorous stimulus (a mockery of the famous Playboy Playmate-of-the-Month). This study is theoretically based on the general conceptualization of Miller and Bacon (1971) on visual perception; on Lonner and Cvetkovich's (1972) cross-cultural thematic evaluations; and Davidson's (1977) stand on the "emi-etic issue." He advocates the use of etic concepts and emic measurement procedures in international research.

Results

Starch Analysis The Starch message approach employs the recognition test (Kleppner, 1979). With the ads presented, the respondent tells to what extent she had seen and read each ad prior to the interview. Table 3 summarizes the Starch scores.

ANOVA A one-way analysis of variance was employed on the three semantic differential scales. The results (Table 4) show significant differences between ads at the .01 level.

Scheffé Comparison Scheffé comparisons between each of the three treatment groups produced the following F ratios (Table 5). These tests show that the different ads have different effects on the readers.

TABLE 3   Starch Scores (in percent)

Type of Ad	"Noted" Reader	"Associated" Reader	"Read Most" Reader
A. Helena Rubinstein:			
AmA	57	24	17
IsA	66	41	31
NaA	53	20	15
B. Fabergé:			
AmA	93	76	55
IsA	78	60	38
NaA	59	37	22
C. Westinghouse:			
AmA	53	31	18
IsA	64	37	24
NaA	41	26	15
D. Coca-Cola:			
AmA	64	49	33
IsA	77	58	50
NaA	89	65	61
E. Levis:			
AmA	49	28	20
IsA	62	47	33
NaA	57	31	21
F. IBM:			
AmA	59	44	21
IsA	67	51	29
NaA	51	28	15

Discussion

An attempt was made in this experiment to manipulate stimuli in order to examine the differences in response to culturally-bound ads.

The results of the one-way analysis of variance indicate a rejection of the null hypothesis. The Scheffé comparison indicated that the following ads were significantly different from the others in terms of attitude—more preferred advertisements: IsA-Helena Rubinstein; AmA-Fabergé; IsA-Westinghouse; NaA (American)–Coca-Cola; and the IsA-IBM. In the Levis campaign the Scheffé comparison results couldn't indicate the most preferred ad, though in the Starch test the IsA-Levis received the highest "Read Most" score of 33 percent. It should be noted that in all other cases, the Starch recognition test and the

TABLE 4   One-Way Analysis of Variance for Groups

Source of Variation	Variation: Sum of Square	d.f.	Variance Estimate	Computed F
A. Helena Rubinstein:				
Between	167.0	2	83.50	5.97*
Within	2534.29	181	14.00	
Total	2701.29	183		
B. Fabergé:				
Between	134.95	2	67.48	4.78*
Within	2555.13	181	14.12	
Total	2690.08	183		
C. Westinghouse:				
Between	206.63	2	103.31	13.85*
Within	1350.59	181	7.46	
Total	1557.22	183		
D. Coca-Cola:				
Between	135.17	2	67.59	5.96*
Within	2051.60	181	11.33	
Total	2186.77	183		
E. Levis:				
Between	87.89	2	43.95	4.66*
Within	1706.83	181	9.43	
Total	1794.72	183		
F. IBM:				
Between	164.91	2	82.45	5.94*
Within	2513.30	181	13.89	
Total	2678.21	183		

* $p < .01$, needed $F_{2/181} = 4.61$

attitude-preference test showed quite similar results. In addition, there were no significant differences between the pairs of the other ads as maintained by the Scheffé comparison.

As stated before, this study is exploratory in nature, since the employed sample and advertising campaign make it impossible to generalize the specific findings across all advertising approaches and across other cultures.

Results indicate that there are differences between the ads. Findings suggest the localization of advertising themes in most cases investigated here and perhaps in general. But when the advertising strategy itself is geared towards

TABLE 5   Scheffé Group Comparison in the One-Way Analysis of Variance

Source of Variation	Computed F1/181	Needed F1/150	Probability
A. Helena Rubinstein			
Groups 1 and 2	6.07	3.91	<.05
Groups 1 and 3	2.35		N.S.
Groups 2 and 3	4.17		<.05
B. Fabergé			
Groups 1 and 2	9.23	6.81	<.01
Groups 1 and 3	3.96	3.91	<.05
Groups 2 and 3	1.10		N.S.
C. Westinghouse			
Groups 1 and 2	6.92	6.81	<.01
Groups 1 and 3	2.03		N.S.
Groups 2 and 3	4.16	3.91	<.05
D. Coca-Cola			
Groups 1 and 2	3.94	3.91	<.05
Groups 1 and 3	1.92		N.S.
Groups 2 and 3	7.16	6.81	<.01
E. Levis			
Groups 1 and 2	3.99	3.91	<.05
Groups 1 and 3	6.15		<.05
Groups 2 and 3	4.06		<.05
F. IBM			
Groups 1 and 2	4.24	3.91	<.05
Groups 1 and 3	1.27		N.S.
Groups 2 and 3	6.18		<.05

international appeal (Fabergé—international celebrity), to achieve world-wide corporate image and/or the appeal itself has a common international connotation (Coca-Cola—appetizing appeal), standardization might be employed.

American models are frequently used in international advertising to give sophisticated, cosmopolitan flavor to certain products such as cosmetics and watches. Various social science studies have emphasized the power and importance of physically attractive models in human communication (Backer and Churchill, 1977). From the analysis of the Starch scores and the open-ended questions it seems that it was easier for the Israeli women audiences to identify with the Israeli character in the ad than the more sophisticated culturally different pose of the American model in the American ad. Subjects made statements like "she (the American model) looks different . . ."; "The girls overseas have a different skin . . .", etc. Women, it has been observed, are especially susceptible to the personality lure, especially if the personality is associated with the world of entertainment. Results here indicated the superiority of the American celebrity ad over the Israeli celebrity. The big-name international star for an international product was used to full advantage in the Margaux Hemingway ad. The advertiser established her as a well-known international star and a beautiful, likable character. Her presence seemed to be relevant to the "internationalized" product. Original artwork is ideal for projecting a certain mood, for emphasizing a particular feature (especially in fashion). But, it might be inappropriate in international advertising where unfamiliar symbols and moods might be rejected or misunderstood. In the Levis campaign, it seems that the reader couldn't identify with the fanciful American characters.

In a recent report Dentsu Inc, the famous Japanese advertising agency, showed that Japanese consumers respond best to American ads that emphasize the product's practical advantages (Dentsu, 1978). In the same report they demonstrate differences in advertising approaches between Japan and the United States which are culturally rooted, although there is a considerable influence of the American advertising system on Japan.

Israeli advertising is also patterned very much on the American advertising approach and system. While each country has a somewhat unique marketing structure, advertising techniques have much in common, even in such culturally diverse countries as the United States and Israel. However, the effects of communication between the United States and Israel are filtered through some contrasting cultural norms. For example, it would not be recommended to introduce a Santa Claus in an Israeli ad for American toys. The Israelis do not share other nations' delight in symmetry, or America's passion for completeness. They are more at ease with impression, hints, suggestions. As a consequence, they are skilled at "filling in" the meaning of an illustration or a line of ad copy (Hornik, 1979).

Summary

There are significant differences in the way ads are perceived. The task of mapping out these differences in various cultures is only beginning. While concepts like product attributes are probably universal, and while the product function is probably similar across nations, the exact form of attributes perception in each society might differ considerably. With the existing differences in perceptions, a communicator may be completely bilingual in discussing the ordinary matters of consumption motives yet wholly unreliable in discussing perceptual matters unless he is quite familiar with the attitudes and perceptions of both cultures.

Product (need) universality cannot imply global message appeal. Israeli women certainly share with their American counterparts the passion for beauty.

List of Advertisements Used in the Experiment

Trade	Advertiser	Product/Brand	Origin	Ad Description		
				Illustration	Brief Copy (Translated from Hebrew)	Overall Approach
Cosmetics	Helena Rubinstein	Skin Life Cleanser	American	Beautiful female model—American type	Skin Life by H.R. the Science of Beauty	Power of attractive model
Same	Same	Same	Israel	Beautiful female model—Israeli type	Same	Same
Same	Same	Same	Unidentified (Israel)	Beautiful female model	Same	Same
Cosmetics	Fabergé	Fragrances	American	Celebrity Margaux Hemingway—dominant model	The fabulous Margaux Hemingway introduces the fabulous fragrances from the Home of Fabergé	Celebrity
Same	Same	Same	Israel	Celebrity Rina Mur, 1976 Israel and International beauty queen—dominant model	Rina Mur is proud to announce she enjoys using the fragrance from the Home of Fabergé	Same
Same	Same	Same	Unidentified (Israel)	Beautiful female posing by a line of fragrances	Love means to give, and if you give Fabergé, you give love and happiness	Testimonial
Home appliances	Westinghouse	Refrigerators	American	Close-up on open refrigerator	Economical and saving features of product (shelf space, etc.)	Dramatization of economical details
Same	Same	Same	Israel	Product within a very high-class expensive kitchen	The high quality product from America, the most technologically advanced country in the world.	Snob appeal

Same	Same	Same	Unidentified (Israel)	Close-up on refrigerator	Technical details and color availability	Dramatization of technical details
Soft drinks	Coca-Cola	Coke	American	Product within American scenery (snow)	Coca-Cola-snow-cold	Symbolism—cold
Same	Same	Same	Israel	Product within Israeli famous scenery	The taste of . . .	General—taste
Same	Same	Same	Unidentified (American)	Full Close-up on bottle—refreshing look	Coke for better times	Brand identification
Fashion	Levis	Jeans	American	Cartoon and American symbols (flag, Statue of Liberty)	. . . Get into those Levis cords	Gimmick
Same	Same	Same	Israel	A group of youngsters and Israeli symbols	Levis the true jeans	General
Same	Same	Same	Unidentified (American)	Pair of jeans slacks	The birth of the blue	General
Office equipment	IBM	Typewriter	American	Close-up on machine	The most advanced typewriter for the modern office	General
Same	Same	Same	Israel	Same	The advanced typewriter with bi-language system—Hebrew and other languages	Direct benefit
Same	Same	Same	Unidentified (Israel)	Same	The typewriter by the international giant	General

Both might manifest the same need for cosmetics (i.e. preservation of beauty), but this certainly does not mean that an Israeli woman perceives the American cosmetic ad the same way it is perceived by the American. Therefore, understanding consumer wants, needs, motives and behavior, is a necessary but not a sufficient condition to the development of an effective promotional program.

Cultures vary along many dimensions (Osgood et al, 1975). To bring about any meaningful commercial communication among varying cultures, it is necessary to identify the various dimensions involved and the location of various cultures on each of these dimensions. International marketing communication is possible only to the extent that there are some common dimensions involved, albeit with varying locations. There might be room to translate basic appeals, not necessarily the literal. There are certain appeals that are universal (appetizing appeals). The problem is that it is difficult to identify them. The creative efforts have to be adopted to the cultural and marketing characteristics of each foreign market, preferably on the basis of field research and experiments conducted in the target market. In cases where general themes are found to be universal, standardization might be employed. Otherwise, culture-specific communication messages might have to be constructed.

The operations of multinational firms have been constantly expanding and increasing in complexity. However, research and analysis, instead of leading the way, have not even kept pace. It is apparent that further research is needed to determine more precisely the relative effects of different international advertising tactics. Although the study is limited in its empirical generalizations, results and especially the multidisciplinary theoretical discussion should increase some basic understanding of forces involved in international advertising effectiveness. The results presented here have to be tested in different international marketing communication settings (different products, countries and different advertising approaches). Only by combining "phenomenally identical" and "conceptually equivalent" indicators can reliable and valid comparison be made (Green and White, 1976; Straus, 1969).

In future studies many of the points raised might be used as research hypotheses. The ultimate goal of such research would be the generation of models with the power to predict process and outcome where cultural variability is found.

REFERENCES

Advertising in Japan, Dentsu Inc., Aug. 1978.

Ajiferuke, B. and Boddewyn, J., "Culture and other explanatory variables in comparative management studies," *Academy of Management Journal,* Vol. 13, 1970, pp. 153–165.

Backer, M.J. and Churchill, G.A., "The impact of physically attractive models on advertising evaluations," *Journal of Marketing Research,* Nov. 1977, pp. 538–555.

Becker, S.L., "Directions for intercultural communication research," *Central States Speech Journal,* Vol. 20, Spring, 1969.

Bond, M., Makazato, H., and Shiraishi, D., "Universality and distinctiveness in dimensions of Japanese person perception," *Journal of Cross-Cultural Psychology,* Vol. 6, 1975, pp. 346–357.

Brislin, R., Lonner, W., and Thorndike, R., *Cross Cultural Research Methods,* New York, Wiley, 1973.

Britt, S.H., "Standardizing marketing for the international market," *Columbia Journal of World Business,* Winter, 1974, pp. 39–45.

Buzzel, R.D., "Can you standardize international marketing?" *Harvard Business Review,* Nov-Dec., 1968, pp. 102–113.

Candee, E.J., "International corporate advertising," *Public Relations Journal,* Vol. 19, Oct., 1963, pp. 35–36.

Cole, M. and Bruner, J.S., "Cultural differences and inferences about psychological processes," *American Psychologist,* Vol. 26, 1971, p. 876.

Davidson, A.R., "The etic-emic dilemma: Can methodology provide a solution in the absence of theory?" In Y.H. Poortinga (ed.), *Basic Problems in Cross-Cultural Psychology,* Amsterdam: Swets and Zeitlinger, 1977, pp. 49–59.

Deregowski, J.B., "Pictorial perception and culture," *Scientific American,* 1972, pp. 82–88.

Dichter, E., "The world consumer," *Harvard Business Review,* July, 1962, pp. 113–121.

Dickson, J. and Albaum, G., "A method of developing tailormade semantic differentials for specific marketing content areas," *Journal of Marketing Research,* Feb., 1977, pp. 87–91.

Donnelly, J.H., "Attitudes toward culture and approach to international advertising," *Journal of Marketing,* July, 1970, pp. 60–63.

Dunn, W.S., "The case study approach in cross-cultural research," *Journal of Marketing Research,* Feb., 1966, pp. 26–31.

Dunn, W.S., "Four measures of cross-cultural advertising effectiveness," *Journal of Advertising Research,* Vol. 7, Dec., 1967, pp. 10–13.

Dunn, W.S., "Effect of national identity on multi-national promotional strategy in Europe," *Journal of Marketing,* Oct., 1976, pp. 50–57.

Elder, J.W., "Comparative cross-national methodology," *Annual Review of Sociology,* Vol. 2, 1976, pp. 209–231.

Farace, R.V., "A study of mass communication and national development," *Journalism Quarterly,* Vol. 43, Summer, 1966, pp. 305–313.

Fatt, A.C., "The danger of 'local' international advertising," *Journal of Marketing,* Jan., 1967, pp. 60–65.

Green, R.T., Cunningham, W.H., and Cunningham, I.C.M., "The effectiveness of standardized global advertising," *Journal of Advertising,* 1975, Vol. 4(3), pp. 25–28.

Green, R.T., and White, P.D., "Methodological considerations in cross-national consumer research." *Journal of International Business Studies,* Vol. 7, Fall, 1976, pp. 81–87.

Harott, H., "International communication studies: a critique," in J.W. Markham (ed.), *International Communication as a Field of Study,* Iowa City: University of Iowa Publications, 1970.

Harvey, M. and Kerin, R.A., "Standardization . . . localization: A proposed alternative methodology for the development of multinational promotional campaigns," presented before the American Academy of Advertising, The University of Rhode Island, April, 1974.

Hornik, Jacob, "An empirical investigation of cross-cultural advertising campaigns," in Peter Leeflang and Berend Wierenga (eds.), *8th Annual Meeting of the European Academy for Advanced Research in Marketing,* Groningen, Holland, April, 1979, pp. G48–G68.

"International advertising on the move," *Printer's Ink,* May 13, 1966.

Jahoda, G. and Stacey, B. "Susceptibility to geometric illusions according to culture and professional training," *Perception and Psychophysics,* Vol. 7, 1970, pp. 179–189.

Jones, S., "Integrating emic and etic approaches in the study of intercultural communication," Paper presented at the annual meeting of the International Communication Association. Portland, Oregon, April, 1976.

Kaplan, R., "The dimensions of the visual environment: methodological considerations," in W.J. Mitchell (ed.), *Environment Design: Research and Practice,* Proceedings of the Environmental Design Research Association Conference, Los Angeles, 1972.

Keegan, W.J., *Multinational Marketing Management.* Englewood Cliffs, N.J., Prentice-Hall, Inc., 1979.

Kleppner, O., *Advertising Procedure,* (7th ed.), Englewood Cliffs, N.J., Prentice-Hall, Inc., 1979.

Linton, A. and Broudbent, S., "International life-style comparisons: An aid to marketers," *Advertising Quarterly,* Vol. 44, 1979, pp. 15–18.

Lonner, W.J. and Cvetkovich, G.T., "Scaling responses to political cartoons and cartoon humor," in J.M. Dawson and W.J. Lonner (eds.), *Cross-Cultural Psychology,* Hong Kong University Press, 1972, pp. 214–229.

Miller, C.R. and Bacon, P., "Open- and closed-mindedness and recognition of visual humour," *Journal of Communication,* Vol. 21, 1971, pp. 150–159.

Miracle, G. E., "International advertising principles and strategies," *MSU Business Topics,* Autumn, 1968.

Munson, J.M. and McIntyre, S.H., "Developing practical procedures for the measurement of personal values in cross-cultural marketing," *Journal of Marketing Research,* Vol. 16(1), Feb., 1979, pp. 48–52.

Osgood, C., "On the strategy of cross-cultural research into subjective culture," *Social Science Information,* Vol. 6, 1967, pp. 1–37.

Osgood, C.E., May, W.H., and Miron, M.S., *Cross-Culture Universals of Affective Meaning.* Urbana, Ill.: University of Illinois Press, 1975.

Peebles, D.M., Ryans, J.K., and Vernon, E.R., "Coordinating international advertising," *Journal of Marketing*, Vol. 42(1), January, 1978, pp. 28–34.

Pollard, B., "International advertising: Practical considerations," in H.D. Fischer and J.C. Merill (eds.), *International and Intercultural Communication*, N.Y.: Hastings House, 1976, pp. 286–296.

Porter, R.E., "An overview of intercultural communication," in L.A. Samovar and R.E. Porter (eds.), *Intercultural Communication: A Reader.* Belmont, California: Wadsworth, 1972.

Ricks, D.A., Arpan, J.S., and Fu, M.Y., "Pitfalls in advertising overseas," *Journal of Advertising Research*, Dec. 1974, pp. 47–51.

Ryans, J.K., "Is it too soon to put a tiger in your tank?" *Columbia Journal of World Business*, Vol. 4, 1969, pp. 69–75.

Ryans, J.K., and Donnelly, J.H., "Standardized global advertising, a call as yet unanswered," *Journal of Marketing*, April, 1969, p. 57.

Segall, M., Campbell, D., and Herskovitz, M., *The Influence of Culture on Visual Perception*. New York: Bobbs-Merrill, 1966.

Sheffé, H. *The Analysis of Variance*. New York: John Wiley and Sons, 1959.

Straus, M.A., "Phenomenal identity and conceptual equivalence of measurement in cross-national comparative research," *Journal of Marriage and the Family*, Vol. 31, May, 1969, pp. 233–241.

Sorenson, R.Z., and Weichmann, N.E., "How multinationals view marketing standardization," *Harvard Business Review*, May–June 1975, pp. 38–45.

Triandis, H., Malpass, R., and Davidson, A., "Cross-cultural psychology," *Biennial Review of Anthropology*, Palo Alto, California: Annual Reviews, Inc., 1971.

Van Raaij, W.F., "Cross-cultural research methodology as a case of contrast validity," in H.K. Hunt, *Advances in Consumer Research*, Vol. 5, 1978, pp. 693–701.

Walker, C., Torrance, E., and Walker, T., "A cross-cultural study of the perception of situational causality," *Journal of Cross-Cultural Psychology*, Vol. 2, 1971, pp. 401–404.

READING 30 PITFALLS IN ADVERTISING OVERSEAS

David A. Ricks ◆ Jeffrey S. Arpan ◆ Marilyn Y. Fu

International trade and investment operations are fraught with risk and uncertainty. In fact, the problems encountered by managers of foreign operations are often more difficult than those encountered in domestic operations, and in many instances they have threatened the very survival of the firm.

Many managers fail to realize this, and investors frequently underestimate the difficulties associated with overseas operations. Domestic success is no guarantee of predictable performance in a different environment. Many successful domestic firms have made plans for foreign investments that have missed their mark so widely that these companies have been unable to take advantage of opportunities in even the most promising markets.

When actual results differ widely from planned results, it is often difficult to judge whether the cause was an initial conceptualization error or one of failing to adapt adequately to the environment. Whatever the timing of the decision, however, the basic root of the troublesome uncertainty is most likely the presence of an additional culture in the decision making framework. Different customs, attitudes, and needs render many of a firm's normal procedures inapplicable or untransferable. Awareness of and sensitivity to these often subtle cultural differences may be the major determinant in the success of an international business venture.

Research in this area can identify critical factors in the environment which have caused problems for outsiders in the past so that others can avoid making similar mistakes. This particular research reports investigations and analyses of actual blunders made by executives in advertising and other aspects of international business. All blunders are publicly documented as having been made by real companies in real countries. Taken as a group, they offer some important lessons for international business in the future.

Essentially, a blunder was judged to have occurred if the problem was foreseeable, but a solution was either poorly prepared or entirely overlooked and a significant negative result occurred. Thus, the incorrect translation of an ad into embarrassing wording which would cause adverse reaction would qualify as a blunder, but it would not if the ad had poked fun at a public figure who died shortly after the ad's release. The question of foreseeability is admittedly a crucial one. Every attempt was made to include only examples where the negative result could have been avoided with reasonable foresight and effort.

Findings

Advertising blunders are the most varied and colorful. From the seemingly minute errors of a faulty word in advertising copy, to major problems arising

---

Source: *Journal of Advertising Research,* December 1974, pp. 47–51. Reprinted with permission.

from failing to conduct a thorough market study before committing hundreds of thousands of dollars to a multinational promotional campaign, these blunders have been extremely damaging to the erring firm. Although the circumstances surrounding each situation differ, the core of the problems are primarily due to these few factors: a tremendous optimism about a particular product or product line, vast confidence in business know-how and past success formulas, and failure to fully understand and appreciate the foreign environment.

To illustrate, some advertising blunders are presented which, although somewhat humorous, were often critically injurious to the firms involved.

General Motors made an embarrassing mistake when, in Flemish, "Body by Fisher" translated as "Corpse by Fisher" (Mazze, 1964). In a similar case, Schweppes Tonic Water was rapidly dehydrated to "Schweppes Tonica" in Italy, where "il water" is the idiomatic expression for a bathroom. An American airline operating in Brazil proudly advertised plush "rendezvous lounges" on its jets, only belatedly discovering that "rendezvous" in Portuguese meant a room hired for love-making. Pepsi's familiar ad, "Come Alive with Pepsi" had problems in Germany because the translation of "come alive" meant "come alive out of the grave." Obviously, the ad had to be reworded (*Ad Age*, 1966).

Colgate-Palmolive made an expensive mistake when it introduced its Cue toothpaste in French-speaking countries. Colgate maintained its trademark without knowing that "Cue" was a pornographic work in French (Martyn, 1964).

Faulty laundry soap advertising can clean out sales, as one company discovered in French-speaking Quebec. The firm had come up with numerous new point-of-sale material describing the fantastic cleansing powers of its detergent, boasting that it was particularly suited for the really dirty parts of the wash— "les partes de sale." Sales rapidly declined and the firm later found out to its chagrin that the phrase was comparable to the American idiom "private parts" (Winick, 1961).

Linguistic anomalies are but one class of blunders in advertising. One of Unilever's highly popular detergents was sold under the trademark Radion in Germany, but the product in nearby Austria sold under a different brand name. Although Germany and Austria are independent and distinct in national characteristics, their physical closeness and language similarity permit the use of communications media—such as magazines, television, and radio—common to both nations' audiences. In particular, German media hold a substantial geographical spread in Austria, and the great majority of Austrian housewives are exposed to German advertising in magazines and on television. However, the Austrian exposure to Radion proved a waste since boxes of Radion could not be found on the shelves of Austrian retailers—and its Austrian counterpart could not be immediately recognized by the consumers (Elindor, 1965).

Lack of Cultural Awareness

Although the preceding examples are actual cases of management errors in advertising, they are not the most typical. In fact, most international advertising blunders occur because of a failure to fully understand the foreign culture and its social norms. This can take many forms, ranging from blatant rejection of existing customs and tastes to innocent insensitivity to the environment. One well-intended company, for example, brought upon itself the indignation of foreign participants of its promotional campaign when it elected to use for favors simulated old coins with "$1 billion" engraved on them (*Business Abroad,* 1966). The participants resented the omnipresence of the dollar sign. Germans preferred to see DM, the French the franc, etc. What began as an innocent but well-intended promotional gadget became interpreted as a reflection of the pompous U.S. superiority and all but nullified the efficacy of the promotional campaign.

Advertisements that somehow fail to reflect the local lifestyle often wind up as wasted effort. When General Mills made its attempt to capture the English market, its breakfast cereal package showed a freckled, red-haired, crew-cut grinning kid saying, "See kids, it's great!"—a promotional package that could not be more typically American (McCreary, 1964). General Mills failed to recognize that the British family is not as child-centered as the United States; the stereotype U.S. boy and near banal expression had no appeal to the more formal and aristocratic ideal of the child upheld by the English. As a result, the cereal package repelled the British housewife and wound up untouched on retail shelves.

Similarly, a certain American manufacturer of beauty products decided to court French consumers by using some of the lustrous and arresting advertisements that so successfully captured the American audience (Lenormand, 1964). Unfortunately the advertising missed its audience. The French women did not identify themselves with the exceptionally attractive models because the advertising had been too exaggerated and lacked sufficient realism to elicit the audience's self-identification with the models. The beauty products did not cause Paris to rave and rant, and French women did not choose them.

Another cosmetics firm tried unsuccessfully to woo the Japanese with a lipstick ad campaign that had quite an appeal in Italy (*Business Abroad,* 1967). The ad featured a statue of Nero coming to life with a freakish grin as he saw a girl wearing their particular brand of lipstick. The advertisement struck no accord with the Japanese consumers. Nero was alien to them, the grin was grotesque, and the ad simply had no trace of those characteristics that appealed to the Japanese women. Sham Law, president of the New York consulting firm S. Lall and Associates, had this comment: "The success of an ad in Japan depends largely on the use of a proper appeal. The hard sell is considered extremely impolite. Japanese consumers respond best to ads that emphasize the product's practical advantages."

Warner Lambert's Listerine has also had its share of advertising problems (Diamond, 1969). In Thailand, Warner Lambert filmed commercials about Listerine fashioned after the well-known U.S. TV commercials showing a boy and girl, overtly fond of each other, one advising the other to use Listerine for curing bad breath. Sales remained minimal and company executives were puzzled by the turn of events. Finally, Charlie Tse, Warner Lambert's Southeast Asia area manager noted the catch: such public portrayal of boy-girl relationships was objectionable to the Thai people. The Thai commercial was carefully and quickly adjusted—this time to show two girls discussing Listerine. The ad caught on and increased sales confirmed the effectiveness of the modifications.

Admen have encountered other unusual situations unique to Thailand. A well-known marketer of eye glasses initiated a campaign to promote its spectacles (Carson, 1967). To attract attention, ads and billboards showing cute pictures of animals wearing eye glasses were used. Despite the apparent charm of the portrayals, sales failed to materialize. The marketer only belatedly discovered that Thais regarded animals as a lower level of creation and were unattracted to advertising using animal themes. Similarly, the widely acclaimed Exxon ad, "Put a tiger in your tank," failed to elicit favorable reaction in Thailand (Miracle, 1968). Tigers were simply not symbols of power and strength there.

Additional examples further illustrate the need for careful examination and analysis of marketing labels and advertisements before using them in foreign markets.

A prominent international manufacturer of water recreation products was perplexed when its Malaysian distributors requested that they stop shipment of its products (Carson, 1967). It turned out that in this area where a large number of the people are illiterate, color and shapes served as an important communication medium for the illiterate. Green, to these people, was the symbol of the jungle with its dangers and diseases. Unfortunately for the manufacturer, its international emblem, prominently displayed on its products, was green and people shied away from products stamped with such a fearful omen.

Pepsodent's promise of white teeth was especially inappropriate in many regions of Southeast Asia where betel-nut chewing was an elite habit and black teeth a symbol of prestige (Martyn, 1964). The "wonder where the yellow went" slogan didn't help out either.

As another example of what can be done incorrectly in advertisements, consider the following advertisement which had prominently appeared in magazines and newsmedia of Quebec, Canada (Winick, 1961). A woman, comfortably dressed in shorts, could be seen playing golf with her husband. The caption boldly indicated that the housewife could carefreely enjoy a day on the golf course and still quickly prepare a delicious evening meal for the family by serving the advertised canned fish. Literally everything turned out wrong in this ad. Anthropologists strongly recommended changes because every element shown represented a violation of some aspect of French-Canadian life: Wives were not likely to be golfing with their husbands; women seen in shorts, especially on a high-class golf course, were socially unacceptable, and to top it all, French-Canadians simply did not serve that particular kind of fish as the main course for the evening meal!

It's possible to export what's a good thing in one country to a totally different environment and wind up with no gain. In the following case, the mistake was one of overdoing a good thing in a different situation.

Dow Breweries introduced a new beer, Kebec, in 1963. To highlight the French-Canadian national overtones for the beer, an advertising campaign was especially planned for such emphasis. But in its broad and liberal use of French-Canadian symbols, certain nationalistic emblems were inappropriately included. Loud protests from the public denouncing the company's "profane" use of "sacred" symbols forced Dow to withdraw the campaign within 15 days. The error was unintentional, yet the drastic consumer reaction proved very dear to Dow (Elkin, 1969).

BiNoca similarly offended the Indian public with a seemingly innocuous ad (*The New York Times*, 1967). The ad, placed in certain leading local newspapers, showed an attractive though apparently nude young woman lavishly dousing herself with BiNoca's talcum powder. The following caption was placed on the layout, casually covering strategic portions of her body: "Don't go wild—just enough is all you need of BiNoca talc." The public, accustomed to conservative traditional standards of morality, found the ad indecent, publicly distasteful, and offensive.

Implications

The importance of having an adequate "cultural sensitivity" on the part of decision-makers involved in international operations is well borne out by the findings of this study. Unicultural managements making all the decisions regarding advertising in different cultures seems a high risk strategy. Multi-cultural participation in the planning, decision making, execution, and evaluation stages of an advertising program appears to be a better procedure. Effective use of local foreign nationals would have prevented many, if not all, of the blunders reported in this study—especially those done because the advertisement was translated too literally.

Those knowledgeable in the field of international advertising have advised that the need is to translate basic appeals, not necessarily the literal. No matter how different people are in different countries, one fact remains: there are certain basic appeals that are common to all people, although they may not always be expressed in the same words. The key is to identify and respect the differences in point of view and sensitivities to nuances. Basic appeals can be successfully employed everywhere.

REFERENCES

Advertising Age, May 9, 1966, p. 75.

Business Abroad, When Marketing Abroad: Remove Your Star Spangled Glasses, May 2, 1966, p. 14.

Business Abroad, How to Get Madison Avenue "Sell" into Japanese Ad Campaign, October 30, 1967, pp. 26–29.

Carson, David. *International Marketing: A Comparative Approach*. New York: John Wiley & Sons, 1967.

Carson, Margaret, Admen in Thailand, Singapore Find Unusual Problems, Novel Solutions. *Advertising Age,* November 27, 1967, pp. 3 ff.

Diamond, R.S. Managers Away From Home. *Fortune,* August 15, 1969, pp. 56 ff.

Elindor, Erik. How International Can European Advertising Be? *Journal of Marketing,* April 1965, p. 7.

Elkin, Frederick. Advertising Themes and Quiet Revolutions: Dilemmas in French Canada. *American Journal of Sociology,* July 1969.

League, Frederick A. Why Companies Fail Abroad. *Columbia Journal of World Business,* July-August 1968, p. 55.

Lenormand, J.M. Is Europe Ripe for Integration of Advertising? *International Advertising,* March 1964, p. 14.

Martyn, Howe. *International Business, Principles and Problems.* New York: Collier-Macmillan, 1964.

Mazze, Edward M. How to Push a Body Abroad Without Making It a Corpse. *Business Abroad,* August 10, 1964, p. 15.

McCreary, Edward A. *The Americanization of Europe.* New York: Doubleday & Co., 1964.

Miracle, Gordon E. International Advertising Principles and Strategies. *MSU Business Topics,* Vol. 16, Fall 1968, p. 29.

The New York Times, "Nude in Talc Ad Offends in India," April 29, 1967, pp. 36 ff.

Pryor, Millard H. Planning in a World-Wide Business. *Harvard Business Review,* January-February 1965, p. 130.

Skinner, Wickham. Management of International Production. *Harvard Business Review,* September-October 1964.

Winick, Charles. Anthropology's Contributions to Marketing. *Journal of Marketing,* July 1961, p. 53.

STANDARDIZED INTERNATIONAL ADVERTISING: A REVIEW AND CRITICAL EVALUATION OF THE THEORETICAL AND EMPIRICAL EVIDENCE

Sak Onkvisit ◆ John J. Shaw

ABSTRACT. Standardized international advertising is a highly controversial practice which has attracted a great deal of attention over the last two decades. This paper provides a comprehensive review of related theoretical and research issues. The evaluation includes the examination of empirical evidence based on management and consumer responses. The validity of the three schools of thought (i.e., standardization, localization, and compromise) is critically examined. Finally, the paper proposes a schematic framework which offers a pragmatic solution to the marketing question of whether and when standardization should be employed.

Standardized international advertising, the practice of advertising the same product in the same way in all markets of the world, has generated an ongoing controversy for more than two decades. Yet the interest in this controversial practice continues to be as great as ever. Some recent events underscoring the importance of this issue include: (1) reports of the practice appearing in such influential publications as *Business Week, Fortune,* and *Harvard Business Review;* (2) the attempt of large advertising agencies to use the issue to attract new international clients; (3) nearly 200 educators attending a special session dealing with the subject at the 1985 American Marketing Association conference; and (4) an ongoing debate among some of the most prominent marketing scholars.

Advertising standardization is not just another theoretical concept in search of practical application. It is a significant problem which warrants attention and evaluation. The concept includes far-reaching implications because of its effect on business firms, international trade, advertising agencies, governments, consumers and marketing education.

In the case of business firms, for example, multinational corporations continue to debate the wisdom of the strategy. While such soft-drink giants as Coca-Cola and PepsiCo seem to embrace varying degrees of advertising standardization, other multinationals, such as Nestlé and Volvo, often take the opposite approach. If standardized international advertising is a valid concept, international business managers should strongly consider implementation of this concept and its accompanying benefits, which include decision simplification, ease in execution, cost reductions, operational efficiency, uniform worldwide image, and consistency in customer servicing.

In the broader context of international trade, there is a question of whether standardized advertising, while providing better economies of scale through

---

reduced advertising costs, is an effective means of promoting product sales overseas. Is there the likelihood that the practice will take partial blame for damaging a country's trade performance instead of improving it? This question may be of special interest to the United States, particularly in view of its recent trade problems.

Governments, notably those within less developed countries, can further complicate the acceptance of standardized advertising. Governments often penalize international brands which command strong brand loyalty because they are viewed as a force that reduces the development of domestically branded products which may be physically and functionally equal to the imported brand. As a result, international brands are often taxed more heavily or banned outright. It is possible that standardized advertising may be viewed in the same way as international brands and that the same fate may await standardized advertising. Furthermore, governments may also view standardization as another form of unfair competition because multinational firms can gain cost advantages with standardized campaigns. Local companies, on the other hand, are unable to spread their advertising production costs over other countries and are thus at a distinct disadvantage.

One issue raised in a *Fortune* article is the effect of a standardized campaign on the competition among advertising agencies.[1] Some large agencies have implied that standardized international advertising is a desirable necessity and that only those with international networks can execute the technique successfully. If this claim is true and standardized advertising becomes widespread, it may be the beginning of the end for smaller advertising agencies with no affiliated overseas offices.

Consumer perception and reaction should also be taken into account. If the premise of standardization in advertising is false, its application in the marketplace will work to the disadvantage of the sponsoring firm by reducing sales and profits. From the consumer's viewpoint, the indiscriminate use of standardized advertising can result in misinterpreting the intended message. As a result, one of the important functions of advertising in facilitating the consumers' search process can be seriously impaired. Moreover, there is a possibility that consumers may even resent multi-national corporations' attempts to homogenize their differing tastes and cultures.

From a theoretical standpoint, the validation of the standardization concept could have broader implications which may necessitate a re-examination of the general marketing process. The basis for the need to re-examine the marketing process involves the fact that advertising standardization implicitly assumes consumer homogeneity while the concept of market segmentation, in contrast, assumes consumer heterogeneity. There appears to be a need for examining

---

[1] Fisher, Anne B. (1984), "The Ad Biz Gloms onto 'Global,'" *Fortune*, November 12, 77–78, 80.

the validity and applicability of each strategy in order to try to resolve this apparent contradiction.

The purpose of this paper is: (1) to provide a comprehensive review of the standardized advertising approach in terms of varying perspectives and empirical evidence; (2) to examine the validity of the three schools of thought related to the standardization process; (3) to reconcile the conceptual differences between the notions of advertising standardization and market segmentation; and (4) to utilize a schematic framework in order to provide a pragmatic solution to the marketing question of whether and when standardization should be employed.

Background: A Controversy

The controversy over the standardization of global advertising centers around the appropriateness of variation (or lack of it) within advertising content from country to country. First discussed in 1961 by Elinder,[2] the technique has generated a heated and lively debate among advocates on both sides and has been both praised and condemned. As a result, three schools of thought regarding advertising standardization can be identified: (1) standardization, (2) individualization, and (3) compromise.

Sometimes called the "universal," "internationalized," "common," or "uniform" approach, the standardization school of thought challenges the traditional belief in the heterogeneity of the market and the importance of the localized approach. According to Elinder, "to begin marketing with a local appeal which changes from country to country is about as sensible as stopping a factory's machinery producing a product and setting up production in a number of small national factories—these producing their own national products in short series after their own recipe."[3]

The standardization school of thought assumes that because of better and faster communication there is a convergence of art, literature, media availability, tastes, thoughts, religious beliefs, culture, living conditions, language, and, consequently, advertising. This view holds that even when people are different their basic physiological and psychological needs are assumed to remain the same. Therefore, because of these underlying assumptions, success in advertising depends on motivation patterns rather than geography. This belief is held by Elinder, Roostal, Fatt Strouse, Bronfman, and Levitt, among others. Their typical comments and reactions are echoed by the statements below.

---

[2] Elinder, Erik (1961), "International Advertisers Must Devise Universal Ads, Dump Separate National Ones, Swedish Adman Avers," *Advertising Age*, November 27, 91.

[3] Ibid.

A powerful force drives the world toward a converging commonality, and that force is technology.[4]

Language differences are lightweight—mere feathers, not whole goose.[5]

There is a gradual development of the World Customer who breaks all boundaries . . . Human desires are pretty much alike.[6] Advanced developed nations share "common tastes even where they do not share a common culture." Products "have to appeal to a variety of people in a large number of countries and are designed to meet the highest denominator of these tastes.[7]

The opposite view of standardization strategy is an approach known as "non-standardization," "individualization," "specificity," "localization," or "customization." According to this very traditional school of thought, advertisers must make particular note of the differences among countries. Advertisers must consider barriers such as culture, taste, media availability and other economic considerations. Given these conditions, it becomes necessary to develop specific advertising programs to achieve impact in local markets. This belief is held by such experts as Nielsen, Leighton, Lenormand, Reed, Lipson and Lamont, and McCarthy and Perreault. Their sentiments are reflected by selected statements below.

Lumping foreign nations together under the common and vague headings of 'foreigner'—or, at the other extreme, assuming that they are just like US customers—almost guarantees failure.[8]

A perfect common denominator is essential for standardization, and this denominator has not been found yet.[9]

It is true that all people are motivated by the same basic instincts, sense, affections, passions and aspirations, but the different manner of expressing these

[4] Levitt, Theodore (1983), "The Globalization of Markets," *Harvard Business Review*, 61 (May–June), 92–102.

[5] Elinder, op. cit.

[6] Dichter, Ernest (1962), "The World Customer," *Harvard Business Review*, 40 (July–August), 113–22.

[7] O'Connor, James (1974), "International Advertising," *Journal of Advertising*, 3 (Spring), 9–14.

[8] McCarthy, E. Jerome and William D. Perreault, Jr. (1984), *Basic Marketing*, 8th ed., Homewood, Illinois: Richard D. Irwin.

[9] Lenormand, J. M. (1964), "Is Europe Ripe for the Integration of Advertising?" *The International Advertiser*, 5 (March), 14.

motivations and aspirations can wreck marketing plans and advertising campaigns, as can customs and many other differences.[10]

Because of a tendency for polarization between these two viewpoints, the middle-of-the-road school of thought becomes a desirable voice of moderation. While recognizing local differences and cautioning against a wholesale or automatic use of standardization, the compromise view holds that some degree of advertising uniformity is possible and even desirable. The researchers with this moderate view include Dunn, Ryans, Miracle and Albaum, Keegan, and Peebles, Ryans, and Vernon.

Adhering to the view of this last school of thought, it becomes possible for U.S. marketing techniques to be appropriate under some, but not all, conditions. In general, their appropriateness is a function of product characteristics, consumer characteristics, and environmental variables. Table 1 lists the relevant factors identified by those who hold the moderate view on standardized advertising as being appropriate for use in the international marketplace. These variables are supposed to determine if and when international advertising can be standardized as well as the extent of standardization to be employed.

Some Contemporary Perspectives

Since 1961 the standardization controversy has surfaced once every decade. In the 1980s it was Levitt's turn to inflame the issue. Blaming unnecessary localization on "archaic protectionism" and "medieval accommodation," Levitt unequivocally stated that "a successful global marketing strategy consists of having a common brand name, packaging and communications."[11]

Levitt's article was quite successful in provoking responses. Before long, several well-known scholars offered their own contrasting views. Sheth attempted to clarify the issue by pointing out that emerging "global competition" may have been mistaken for "global markets" which are "more apparent than real."[12] To resolve the issue, Sheth proposed a framework for global markets based on "market needs" and "market resources." Global markets exist and universal marketing is applicable only when both market needs and resources across countries are similar. Otherwise, some kind of segmentation is necessary.

Kotler also has a framework of his own. According to Kotler, the international decision process involves three possible decisions. If a particular product

---

[10] Reed, Virgil D. (1967), "The International Consumer," in *Managerial Marketing*, 3d ed., Eugene J. Kelly and William Lazer, eds., Homewood, Illinois: Richard D. Irwin, 586–600.

[11] Levitt, op. cit.

[12] Sheth, Jagdish (1986), "Global Markets or Global Competition," *Journal of Consumer Marketing*, 3 (Spring), 9–11.

TABLE 1   Factors Affecting the Extent of Standardization

Britt (1974):	Consumption (income group, motive purchase, dictate brand, physical expectations, purchase rate, retail outlet, time in purchase, purpose, amount and usage rate, preparation, with other products) Psychosocial (psychological, social, and economic factors, advertising disadvantages, symbolic content, psychic cost, cosmopolitan, brand name, packaging, pricing, brand loyalty, past advertising strategy, media) Culture (society restrictions, stigma, tradition)
Buzzell (1968):	Market characteristics (physical environment, stage of economic and industrial development, cultural) Industry conditions (product life cycle stages, competition) Marketing institutions (distribution system, advertising media and agencies) Legal restrictions
Cateora (1983):	"The question of standardization or modification depends more on motivational patterns than geography."
Colvin, Heeler, and Thorpe 1980):	Similar purchase motivations permit the strategy of "pattern" standardization of advertising
Dunn (1976):	Thirty-one environmental variables (rate of economic growth, per capita income and distribution of income, average household size, literacy level, education level, vocational training, social class structure, attitudes toward authority, attitudes toward the U.S., degree of nationalism, attitudes toward achievement and work, attitudes toward risk taking, attitudes toward wealth and monetary gain, similarity of ethical and moral standards to U.S., availability of time on commercial broadcast media, availability of satisfactory outdoor media, independence of media from government control, political organization and stability, import/export rate of country, legal restraints on advertising, availability of prototype campaigns, relative importance of visual versus verbal in ad message, experience and competence of personnel in foreign subsidiary and distributor, experience and competence of personnel in foreign agency or branch of U.S. agency, eating patterns and customs, importance of self-service retailing, import duties and quotas, development and acceptance of international trademark, applicability of products' theme or slogan, adequate coverage of market by broadcast media, availability of satisfactory print media)
Kahler (1983):	"Standardization is dependent on a similarity of the motivations for purchase and a similarity of use conditions. For culture-free products such as industrial goods and some consumer durables, the purchase motivations are similar enough to permit high degrees of standardization. Culture-bound products, in contrast, require adaptation."
Keegan (1969):	The choice is a function of (1) the product itself defined in terms of the function or need it serves, (2) the market in terms of the conditions under which the product is used, including the preferences of potential customers and the ability to buy the product in question, and (3) the adaptation costs.

TABLE **1**   (continued)

Keegan (1984):	"For industrial advertising, the possibilities of extension and scale economies in advertising are much greater than in consumer products. Industrial products are bought and used in the same way and for the same reasons in every country." For consumer products, "if the market is global, appeals can be standardized and extended."
Miracle (1968):	The appropriateness of uniform advertising should be determined by (1) type of product, (2) homogeneity or heterogeneity of markets, (3) characteristic and availability of media, (4) types of advertising agency service available in each market segment, (5) government restrictions on the nature of advertising, (6) government tariffs on art work or printed matter, (7) trade codes, ethical practices, and industry agreements, and (8) corporate organization.
Peebles, Ryans, and Vernon (1978):	Six-step program: marketing and advertising strategy and objectives, individual market input, testing, campaign review, budget approval, and implementation
Ryans (1969):	Consumers should be categorized according to their potential receptivity to the standardized technique in order to isolate those who might be responsive from those who might be offended. There are three broad categories: international sophisticate, semi-sophisticate, and provincial.
Terpstra (1983):	Two kinds of relevant variables: production side and market side (consumption system, buying motives, language)

has no international market, this product can be designed for the U.S. market only. If an international market exists and if one product for the world can succeed, universal marketing can then become applicable. But if the one-product-for-all strategy is unlikely to be effective, national/regional adaptations should be planned in advance.[13]

Somewhat more sympathetic and supportive to his Harvard colleague is Porter. Although agreeing with Levitt's assertion that globalization is on the rise, Porter believes that it is necessary to "coordinate" dispersed marketing activities and that international marketing strategy must be part of an international firm's overall worldwide strategy. Consequently, "a change in the direction of more homogenization of needs internationally" does not mean that international marketing should be standardized.[14]

According to Wind, there are many marketing activities to perform, and

---

[13] Kotler, Philip (1986), "Global Standardization—Courting Danger," *Journal of Consumer Marketing*, 3 (Spring), 13–15.

[14] Porter, Michael E. (1986), "The Strategic Role of International Marketing," *Journal of Consumer Marketing*, 3 (Spring), 17–21.

standardization of *all* such activities is only one out of hundreds of strategy combinations. Also for standardized advertising to become an appropriate strategy, the following conditions must hold: (1) homogenization of the world's wants; (2) buyers' willingness to sacrifice preferred product features in favor of lower price and higher quality; (3) economies of scale; (4) preference of a number of global market segments for a uniform physical product and brand image; (5) absence of external constraints; (6) absence of internal constraints; and (7) presence of positive synergy from multi-country operations. Since it is difficult to satisfy all seven conditions, a company should "think globally, act locally."[15]

Other recent works which discuss the standardization issue include Friedmann, Walters, Boddewyn, Soehl, and Picard, and Onkvisit and Shaw. Friedmann feels that the debate can be simplified by considering "the psychological meaning that consumers derive from and ascribe onto products." The relevance of this approach is due to the assumption that "psychological meaning is culturally bound and, therefore, representative of the most relevant variable (i.e., culture) influencing such strategic choices."[16]

Boddewyn, Soehl, and Picard do not believe that Levitt's arguments are grounded in fact. Using the findings of three related studies of the evolution of U.S. companies' marketing activities in the European Community, they admitted that product standardization has increased and that "the standardization of international marketing practices is relatively high and growing in some cases." However, "the standardizations of product, brand, and advertising do not necessarily move apace," and "advertising is more resistant to uniformization than are the other two."[17]

Walters' literature review has led him to conclude that the applicability of standardization is very situation-specific and that, for advertising, "significant uniformity is not common at the level of detailed creative output." Furthermore, "policies of 'total uniformity' . . . are relatively rare."[18] This conclusion is consistent with the observation made earlier by Onkvisit and Shaw who have pointed out that there are conceptual, empirical, and strategic problems associated with standardized advertising. "For standardization in its present form to achieve sweeping influence on a global basis, that will only happen . . . when nations are willing to give up their sovereignty"—an extremely remote likeli-

---

[15] Wind, Yoram (1986), "The Myth of Globalization," *Journal of Consumer Marketing*, 3 (Spring), 23–26.

[16] Friedmann, Roberto (1986), "Psychological Meaning of Products: A Simplification of the Standardization vs. Adaptation Debate," *Columbia Journal of World Business*, 21 (Summer), 97–104.

[17] Boddewyn, J. J., Robin Soehl, and Jacques Picard (1986), "Standardization in International Marketing: Is Ted Levitt In Fact Right?" *Business Horizons* 29 (November/December), 69–75.

[18] Walters, Peter G. P. (1986), "International Marketing Policy: A Discussion of the Standardization Construct and Its Relevance for Corporate Policy," *Journal of International Business Strategies*, 17 (Summer), 55–69.

hood. Therefore, to be preoccupied with standardization is to unduly focus on style over substance.[19]

Although Levitt uses the term "globalization," it is actually just another term for "standardization" which was widely criticized two decades earlier. As such, Levitt's arguments are not exactly new but simply are rephrased as a new presentation of an old idea. Levitt implies that it is myopic not to standardize, a viewpoint not necessarily shared by his contemporary counterparts. Is it possible that Levitt himself may have advocated a new form of marketing myopia? To answer this question, an examination of empirical evidence is necessary.

Empirical Evidence: Fact versus Fiction

The proponents of each school of thought tend to offer opposing viewpoints which are both supported and refuted by real-life examples. In general, their arguments have been based on individual impressions which are subjective and highly judgmental. Consumers could be better served if they were better understood through the scientific collection of empirical data.

Do multinational corporations (MNCs) transfer their advertising campaigns to other countries? As shown in Table 2, the evidence appears to be mixed. According to a Sorenson and Wiechmann study which was based on the responses provided by 27 MNCs, there is a high degree of standardization, with an index of the standardization for promotion decisions among European subsidiaries ranging from 43 percent for media allocation, 56 percent for sales promotion, 62 percent for creative expression, and 71 percent for basic advertising message.[20]

The results of the Sorenson and Wiechmann study, however, should be reviewed with some reservation. First, it concerned only European and U.S. markets, and this geographic limitation may make the results irrelevant for countries with different economic, cultural, and political systems. Second, the methodology allowed advertisement adaptation to be considered as standardization. Third, the responses were influenced by executives' views of these markets as being similar. But as revealed by one study, executives' perceptions could be far from accurate. "Western Europe was never quite as standardized as many home-office executives thought. Some marketing executives do not really know what is and is not being transferred across boundaries."[21]

The economic and cultural environment, as expected, plays a significant

---

[19] Onkvisit, Sak and John J. Shaw (1985), "A View of Marketing and Advertising Practices in Asia and Its Meaning for Marketing Managers," *Journal of Consumer Marketing*, 2 (Spring), 5–17.

[20] Sorenson, Ralph Z. and Ulrich E. Wiechmann (1975), "How Multinationals View Standardization," *Harvard Business Review*, 53 (May–June), 38, ff.

[21] Dunn, S. Watson (1976). "Effect of National Identity of Multinational Promotional Strategy in Europe," *Journal of Marketing*, 40 (October), 50–57.

TABLE 2   Management Responses

Author	Sources of Data	Media Used	Products or Stimuli	Measurement Instrument	Statistical Analysis	Results
Dunn (1966)	Research, marketing, and advertising executives from 30 firms	N/A	Cosmetics, food, drug, beverages, automotive, etc.	Interview/ case studies	Simple tabulation	Marketing executives are pragmatic Ad transfer decisions are based on market, cultural, and media factors.
Donnelly (1970)	121 international advertising managers of leading US manufacturers	N/A	Consumer nondurable goods	Mailed questionnaire, 10-point forced choice bi-directional scale	Percentage and 2-tail t-test	Attitudes toward cultural differences affect advertising practices
Sorenson and Wiechmann (1975)	About 100 executives of 27 multinational firms of consumer packaged goods	N/A	Soft drink, food, soap-detergent-toiletries, and cosmetics	7-point scale	Percentage, paired-comparison	There is a high propensity to standardize advertising practices in spite of differences among countries
Dunn (1976)	71 executives from 35 leading firms	N/A	194 variables for formulating ad strategy	1–7 scale for variable rating	Unknown	Decision-making executives use environmental factors to determine promotional transfer (31 environmental variables)
	76 marketing executives of 30 U.S. and European multinational firms	N/A	—	Focused interview	Unknown	There is an increase in nationalism, and advertising modification is needed
Kaynak and Mitchell (1981)	Starch, Inra and Hooper 1979 World Advertising Expenditures	Print and broadcast	N/A		Percentage	Canadian, British, and Turkish communication practices are different

role in affecting communication practices. According to one cross-national comparison involving Canadian, Turkish, and British techniques, the strategies chosen were influenced by the stage of economic development and other environmental variables such as media expenditures and importance of self-service retailing.[22] In Turkey, the most important modes of communication were word-of-mouth, personal selling, newspaper and radio with very little emphasis on technical information as a basis for persuasion. In contrast, the more developed countries relied more on print and television as well as more written and technical arguments as a persuasive technique. This finding seems to bear out the results reported by Dunn who found that decision-making executives considered certain environmental factors when deciding on their advertising transfer strategy. The Dunn study also showed a resurgence of national identity emerging in western Europe which was accompanied by a decline in the advertising transfer of multinational campaigns.[23]

There is evidence that the attitudes held by international advertising managers of leading U.S. consumer nondurable goods manufacturing firms can influence their international advertising approach. [Those managers who felt that cultural differences were more likely to use decentralized planning and employ local advertising agencies.] In contrast, those from centralized operations tended to agree more with the applicability of standardized advertising.[24]

There is a question of whether these managers' assumptions mentioned above about foreign markets are justified. Managers' perspectives tend to be self-serving and source-oriented (i.e., preoccupied with the message sender's or advertiser's need) rather than receiver-oriented (consumer-oriented). Given this view, it is not sufficient to know what the managers' decisions and assumptions are about various markets. The issue of advertising standardization cannot really be adequately resolved without consumers' input.

Are consumers essentially homogeneous as assumed by the standardized approach? Since it is the main argument used by those who advocate standardization, the validity of the assumption is necessary. Earlier attempts to answer the question relied more on information which was strictly observational and which emphasized colorful idiosyncrasies. While the number of studies in this area is small, the studies are sufficient to shed some light on the issue.

As shown in Table 3, one group of studies concentrates on consumer characteristics and other relevant information without directly measuring how consumers may react to standardized advertisements. For example, one study was interested in innovator characteristics along several dimensions relating to

---

[22] Kaynak, Erdener and Lionel A. Mitchell (1981), "Analysis of Marketing Strategies Used in Diverse Cultures," *Journal of Advertising Research* 21 (June), 25–32.

[23] Dunn, op. cit.

[24] Donnelly, John H., Jr. (1970), "Attitudes toward Culture and Approach to International Advertising," *Journal of Marketing*, 34 (July), 60–68.

TABLE 3   Consumer Characteristics and Indirect Responses

Author	Sources of Data	Media Used	Products or Stimuli	Measurement Instrument	Statistical Analysis	Results
Green and Langeard (1975)	193 randomly selected Texas women and a stratified sampling of 226 French women	N/A	Grocery products and retail services	Mailed and self-administered questionnaires	X^2, percentage, and F test	There are differences in behavior and characteristics between U.S. and French innovators
Green, Cunningham, and Cunningham (1975)	Parallel samples of 95 U.S., 64 French, 49 Indian, and 95 Brazilian college students	N/A	Soft drink and toothpaste	5-point scale translated questionnaires	F test, Scheffé test, X^2	There are disparities in attribute importance structures
Anderson and Engledow (1977)	National systematic random samples of U.S. and German product-testing magazine subscribers	N/A	Major durable goods	5-point scale	Coefficients of congruence and 2-level factor analysis	Information seekers of the 2 countries are similar but far from identical in attitudes and behavior with regard to purchase process and market environment
Boote (1983)	500 randomly sampled women each from United Kingdom, West Germany, and France	N/A	N/A	5-point 29 value scales	Pairwise t-test and Q factor analysis	There are significant differences of values across and within countries

consumption behavior.[25] A comparison of French and American innovators revealed varying demographic characteristics and media habits for both tangible products and services. Another study contrasted information seekers (subscribers to product testing magazines) in the United States and Germany. While there were similarities in attitude and behavior pattern, "the groups are far from

---

[25] Green, Robert T. and Eric Langeard (1975), "A Cross-National Comparison of Consumer Habits and Innovator Characteristics," *Journal of Marketing*, 39 (July), 34–41.

identical and the nature of differences is more apparent from an overall view than from studying individual variables or factors."[26]

For a product to be successfully marketed, its meaningful attributes must be advertised. For advertising standardization to be applicable, such attributes should be equally meaningful to consumers from various countries. However, this kind of attribute uniformity seems to be lacking among consumers in various countries. For example, a study showed that, when college students from the United States, France, India, and Brazil viewed two common consumer products, they used different evaluative criteria by emphasizing different product attributes which were important to them.[27] Evidently, a standardized advertisement employing the same attributes internationally would not have been effective.

One recent study attempted to investigate consumer homogeneity/heterogeneity by using a 29-item value scale to measure psychographic traits in consumers located in Germany, the United Kingdom, and France.[28] The researcher felt that similarities within subgroups of these countries were significant enough to support the use of standardized advertising. For example, he concluded that the fourth British subgroup was "qualitatively similar to the German's second segment." Actually, out of the 14 value statements attributed to this British subgroup, only four of these were also contained in the second German subgroup, with six statements belonging to the first German subgroup and the other four statements not being included in either German subgroup. It thus appears questionable as to the worth of looking for similarities among consumers in such a highly subjective fashion.

A look at Boote's data reveals a totally different picture. First, consumers of the three countries ranked the 29 value statements very differently. Second, the mean ratings of these scales concerning their importance also differed significantly from group to group, as confirmed by the results of T-tests. Third, factor analysis was successful in grouping subjects of similar values, resulting in at least two segments of different lifestyles for each country. Finally, factor analysis also revealed that the number of significant segments varied from country to country. Since the value structure varied across these countries as well as within each country, the evidence, when analyzed carefully, was overwhelmingly against Boote's conclusion and the universal approach of advertising.[29]

The second group of consumer studies (see Table 4) contested the stand-

---

[26] Anderson, Ronald and Jack Engledow (1977), "A Factor Analytic Comparison of U.S. and German Information Seekers," *Journal of Consumer Research,* 3 (March), 185–96.

[27] Green, Robert T., William H. Cunningham, and Isabella C. M. Cunningham (1975), "The Effectiveness of Standardized Global Advertising," *Journal of Advertising,* 4 (Summer), 25–30.

[28] Boote, Alfred S. (1983), "Psychographic Segmentation in Europe," *Journal of Advertising Research,* 22 (December/January), 19–25.

[29] Shaw, John J. and Sak Onkvisit (1983), "Letters to the Editor," *Journal of Advertising Research,* 23 (December), 60–61.

TABLE 4   Consumer Responses To Advertisements

Author	Sources of Data	Media Used	Products or Stimuli	Measurement Instrument	Statistical Analysis	Results
Lorimor and Dunn (1967)	Middle- and upper-class people—200 each from Paris and Cairo	Magazine portfolio-test	Soft drink, cigarette, soap, men's toiletries, and washer	7-step semantic differential in French and Arabic	Factor analysis and correlation	Translated ads are almost as successful as those localized ones
Schleifer and Dunn (1968)	152 marketing and communications students	Magazine	Soft drink, toiletries, cigarette, and wristwatch	Questionnaire	4-way fixed model ANOVA	Ad is more effective when it is associated with a favorable national reference group
Caffyn and Rogers (1970)	1,200 British adults, 100 for each commercial	TV commercials	Soft drink, car, cereal, deodorant, insurance, and analgesic	Check test of 15 words describing commercials	ANOVA	British audiences perceive distinct differences between British and U.S. commercials; U.S. ads are entertaining but less persuasive
Hornik (1980)	184 Israeli housewives randomly divided into 3 groups	Print	Helena Rubinstein, Coke, Levis, Fabergé, IBM, and Westinghouse	9-point semantic differential Starch method test	1-way ANOVA	American, Israeli, and neutral ads are perceived differently
Colvin, Heeler, and Thorpe (1980)	Stratified samples of German, British, and French car buyers—200–300 from each country	N/A	Car photo	Rating of 27 automobile attributes and purchase interest	Conjoint analysis	There is support for the applicability of pattern advertising for common elements while allowing extensive modification for local conditions
Onkvisit and Shaw (1983)	American and foreign students	Print	Wristwatch and soap	Likert scale	Discriminant analysis	The same ads are viewed differently by each group

ardization issue more directly by measuring how groups of consumers responded to a wide range of advertisements—some standardized and some localized. Schleifer and Dunn used four magazine advertisements of everyday consumer products by specifically preparing them in American and Egyptian versions to investigate how attitudes toward a given country might affect the potential persuasiveness of the advertising message. The implication offered by this study was that the national identity of a model and/or product could influence advertising receptivity and that American-related advertisements could be used *if* foreign consumers had favorable attitudes toward the United States.[30]

Caffyn and Rogers asserted how British audiences reacted to different creative approaches for the same or similar products by using six U.S. and six British commercials. While the study did not prove the superiority of either national approach, it did show that British audiences viewed the two groups of commercials differently. "Despite a common language, the social, cultural and marketing differences between the two countries are so great that a commercial which is successful in one country is unlikely to be very successful in the other."[31]

Instead of showing different advertisements to one consumer group as was the case in the Caffyn and Rogers study, another study used the same advertisements with groups of subjects from different countries. American subjects' responses to two advertisements were compared with those of foreign respondents. With these responses as the discriminating variables, discriminant analysis revealed that group differences existed and that the connotative responses to such advertisements varied from group to group. The results indicated that the understanding and interpretation of the advertisements were far from uniform among the respondent groups.[32]

A lack of perceptual homogeneity was also illustrated in a 1980 study by Hornik. In this study, three different versions (international American, Israeli-designed, and neutral or non-identified advertisements) were prepared for well-known American products and were shown to three groups of housewives in Israel—one group for each advertisement version. The one-way ANOVA results indicated differences in attitudes and perceptions among groups receiving the same product advertisements, thus providing endorsement for localized advertisements in general. As explained by Hornik, "product (need) universality cannot imply global message appeal. Israeli women certainly share with their American counterparts the passion for beauty . . . but this certainly does not

---

[30] Schleifer, Stephen and S. Watson Dunn (1968). "Relative Effectiveness of Advertisements of Foreign and Domestic Origin," *Journal of Marketing Research,* 5 (August), 296–98.

[31] Caffyn, John and Nigel Rogers (1970). "British Reactions to TV Commercials," *Journal of Advertising Research,* 10 (June), 21–27.

[32] Onkvisit and Shaw (1983a), "Identifying Marketing Attributes Necessary for Standardized International Advertising," *Mid-Atlantic Journal of Business,* 22 (Winter), 43–57.

mean that an Israeli woman perceives the American cosmetic ad the same way it is perceived by the American." But there is some hope for standardization "in cases where general themes are found to be universal."[33]

One study investigated the applicability of the so-called "pattern standardization." This approach, a cross between standardization and localization, is a strategy which "is designed from the outset to be susceptible to extensive modification to suit local conditions, while maintaining sufficient common elements to minimize the drain on resources and management time." Based on the Ford study in Europe of perceptions of consumers with an intention to buy cars, the results indicated that some single-theme and dual-theme strategies could be employed across certain countries and that some modification was necessary in other instances. Therefore, this advertising system allows "cross-country differences in product perceptions and product attribute preferences."[34]

The empirical studies mentioned and discussed above provide some insights into the practice and desirability of advertising standardization. A summary of findings can be found in Tables 2–4. These studies reveal that the practice, while appearing to be rather widespread, is usually tempered by environmental factors and the extent of market homogeneity. How these variables are perceived by management has a great deal of impact on the implementation of the standardization strategy. However, the evidence points in the direction of a lack of market commonness. In virtually all cases, consumer similarities, if any, are usually overshadowed by market variations and consumer differences which exist within as well as across countries. The findings also indicate that demographic, psychographic, and behavioral differences are quite prevalent.

More empirical evidence is needed to resolve the standardization-localization controversy. Toward this end, additional studies should be conducted with consumers from countries having varying degrees of economic development. Other samples with varying demographics such as age, income, education, and occupation should also be studied since these variables may set the upper limit of the applicability of standardization.

One area within the research that needs clarification is the definition of standardization itself. Strictly speaking, a standardized advertisement is an advertisement which is used internationally with virtually no change in its theme, copy, or illustration, except for translation when needed. More recently, a new view of standardization claims that, as long as the same theme is maintained, an advertisement is still considered standardized even though there is a change in its copy or illustration (e.g., a foreign model is used in an overseas version). This new and broadened definition has clouded the issue because an advertise-

---

[33] Hornik, Jacob (1980), "Comparative Evaluation of International vs. National Advertising Strategies," *Columbia Journal of World Business,* 15 (Spring), 36–46.

[34] Colvin, Michael, Roger Heeler, and Jim Thorpe (1980), "Developing International Advertising Strategy," *Journal of Marketing,* 44 (Fall), 73–79.

ment which used to be viewed as a non-standardized one may now become a standardized advertisement instead.

A more precise definition of standardized advertising, conceptually and operationally, would go a long way toward solving the confusion created by contradictory claims. Is an advertisement standardized *only* when strict translation is involved? Is an advertisement also standardized when the same advertising appeal is retained while employing foreign models (actors)? Is it still standardization when there are minor modifications in the main theme? At what point will an advertisement cease to be a standardized advertisement? These questions suggest that standardization is a matter of degree rather than an all-or-nothing phenomenon, and a scientific investigation should not proceed without an explicit and sound definition of standardization.

Critical Discussion

For an international advertising manager, there are two major issues which affect his decision with regard to standardization: the feasibility of the approach and the desirability of its implementation. Both of these considerations are prerequisites for standardization. A problem can arise where the market may find that the standardization plan is feasible but should not be implemented. On the other hand, this plan may be desirable but not potentially feasible.

The feasibility issue deals with the question of whether there are environmental restrictions or difficulties which may preclude the use of a standardized campaign. The opponents of standardization usually cite three standard problems: local regulations, media and agency availability, and literacy (for print advertisement). The advocates of standardization, in contrast, either discredit the importance of these obstacles or do not believe that such barriers still exist. But as appropriately pointed out by the middle-of-the-road school of thought, the degree of feasibility varies from country to country, creating difficulties in some countries but not in others. Furthermore, the environment may change, and the changes may permit more or less opportunity for standardization in the future. Therefore, this criterion does not generally support the views of either one of the extreme schools of thought but rather is situationally dependent.

A more meaningful question is whether advertising standardization, even if it is feasible, should be used or not. The desirability of use is concerned with reaching consumers effectively and profitably, and the degree of use desirability is likely to vary by product, firm, and country.

Three major criteria determine the degree of use desirability. The first criterion involves the amount of cost savings. Two types of advertising costs should be distinguished: media costs and production costs. Generally speaking, costs for media space and time, when compared to advertising production costs, are relatively much higher. Nevertheless, production costs can be substantial, especially in the field of direct marketing. As noted by Buzzell, the production of films, artwork, and other advertising materials for many companies can cost millions of dollars every year.[35] When costs of creative works (especially for separate campaigns for different countries) are considered as well, the overall production cost can escalate even more. It is this production cost with which standardized advertising is most concerned.

For some firms the saving in advertising production cost may be insignificant, rendering the whole issue moot (if other advantages such as decision simplification and operational ease are not taken into account). For Coca-Cola and PepsiCo, the cost reduction is substantial and is thus desirable. PepsiCo's saving alone from not producing separate films for various markets is about $10 million annually. The overall saving is actually much higher when indirect costs are considered. Such indirect costs include the speed of implementing a campaign, less elaborate staffing of overseas marketing personnel, and the amount of time which management can divert to other marketing activities. Interestingly, this cost criterion, being situationally dependent, generally supports neither the advocates nor the opponents of the universal approach of advertising.

The second criterion of use desirability is communication effectiveness, and it is useful to evaluate advertising standardization on the basis of well-accepted and proven communication principles. The purpose of advertising is to communicate and to persuade, and it is the receiver, not the sender, who is the most important link in the communication process. Since the receiver's particular response is desired, the receiver is the only justification for the source to exist and for communication to occur. It has thus been accepted that an advertiser must "start where the audience is." Without an orientation toward the receiver, breakdowns in communication can happen easily and quickly.

The standardized approach is based on management's view of the existence of a world consisting of homogeneous consumers. This technique is implicitly preoccupied with cost reduction, efficiency, and simplification—factors which are important to managers but not of utmost importance for communication effectiveness or consumer needs. Not surprisingly, standardization tends to increase the likelihood of communication breakdown because an advertiser may fail to encode his message properly and the receiver may be unable to decode the signal. The communication failure may take one of the following forms. First, the standardized message, when irrelevant, will not gain attention and will be ignored. Second, even if not ignored, the message may still not be understood. Lastly, even if understood, the message may not be meaningful or potent enough to influence receivers to take the intended action. Therefore, due to a violation of the principles of effective communication, standardized communication *in its absolute form* is likely to be ineffective.

The final criterion of desirability is consumer homogeneity which, as men-

---

[35] Buzzell, Robert D. (1968), "Can You Standardize Multinational Marketing?" *Harvard Business Review*, 46 (November–December), 102–13.

tioned earlier, is a major assumption of the "standardized school." For the purpose of analysis, consumer homogeneity is classified in two basic ways—national boundary and consumer characteristics. Based on the national boundary, homogeneity can be categorized as vertical (i.e., homogeneous within the same country) or horizontal (i.e., homogeneous across countries). Thus, two countries, while not being vertically homogeneous within their borders, can still be horizontally homogeneous when a particular segment of one country is similar to an equivalent segment of another country.

When consumer characteristics are used as a classification basis, consumer homogeneity may be in the form of demographics on the one hand or in the category of attitudinal responses on another. Attitudinal homogeneity includes such responses as perception, affect, intention, and other forms of behavior such as purchase. It is possible that two consumer groups may differ demographically and yet be alike as far as the attitudinal state is concerned.

If consumers are indeed homogeneous, all other criteria become irrelevant, and the issue of standardization cannot be questioned. But if consumers are not homogeneous as assumed, a standardized advertisement is unlikely to be effective because it may offend consumers in some markets or because it simply fails to appeal adequately to other prospective buyers. Consequently, the adoption of standardization may not improve profit due to a greater proportion of sales decline in relation to any cost saving. If this is the case, standardization should not be used regardless of how feasible it appears to be.

It is virtually impossible to prove the superiority or inferiority of advertising standardization. There are examples of effective standardized advertisements as well as some ineffective ones. Likewise, localized advertisements can be either superior or inferior, depending on the basis of comparison. As a result, there is no valid basis for a direct comparison of the two approaches, and the focus must be on the merits of the homogeneity assumption as a prerequisite for standardization. The results of the literature review mentioned earlier are, surprisingly, in accord in the sense that there is no theoretical nor empirical evidence to support this view. Based on the studies concerning the various dimensions of homogeneity such as demographics, media habits, perceptual similarity and lifestyles, among others, the differences among people from different countries continue to remain as great as ever. Therefore it can be reasonably expected that a standardized advertisement will probably not elicit the same kind of purchase response overseas as it would in the domestic market.

It is not the contention of this paper that all forms of standardization should be excluded from overseas markets nor that it is always desirable to pursue localization. The difference between standardization and localization is in degree rather than in kind. The difference between them should be viewed as occurring along a continuum on a bipolar scale. With a movement toward the "standardized" pole, there is an increase in homogeneity which is accompanied by more opportunity for standardization. As a beginning point for analysis, the United States could be used as the point where "standardization" occurs at this end of the continuum. Perhaps, western Europe, not being too different from the United States, could occupy a spot nearby on the scale, somewhat farther from the "standardized" pole. At the other extreme of the continuum are continents such as Asia and Africa which would be placed much farther out on the scale, away from the "standardized" pole but much closer to the "localized" end, indicating a greater degree of diversity.

One problem faced by marketing managers would be to locate the point along the scale where a particular target market should be positioned based on its similarity to the U.S. market. At some future time, it would be of benefit to marketing scholars if an index could be constructed to incorporate the homogeneity/heterogeneity factors related to a specific country. The purpose for this homogeneity/heterogeneity index would be to then determine the country's position on the scale. Once the location is decided, the extent of standardization versus localization could be determined accordingly.

Advertising Standardization Versus Market Segmentation

It is consumer homogeneity/heterogeneity which provides the major distinction between advertising standardization and market segmentation. For standardization to be achieved, consumer homogeneity is a necessary condition. But market segmentation (as well as the marketing discipline in itself) is based on the heterogeneity assumption. One of the major reasons cited for market segmentation involves a marketing effort concerned with satisfying selected consumer segments differently but more precisely. If consumers are indeed mostly homogeneous, as some marketers may suggest, there would be no need for market segmentation. Due to the bipolar nature of these two points of view, the two marketing strategies have little in common, and it would be inappropriate to advocate using these essentially incompatible concepts together.

One need only examine the U.S. market to see how the domestic market can be segmented along many different variables. For example, the necessity and effectiveness of having specific advertisements aimed at the black segment has been well documented by studies such as Barban and Cundiff.[36] The fact that Coke, McDonald's, Kentucky Fried Chicken, and many others would go through the expense and difficulty of designing advertisements directed at blacks, women, Hispanics, teenagers, etc., makes it clear that economic gains must be derived from devising unique advertising campaigns for different segments. Given the great degree of population diversity, the United States is hardly a melting pot.

It should be noted that market segmentation and advertising standardization, although mutually exclusive, have a common ground in the sense that

---

[36] Barban, Arnold M. and Edward W. Cundiff (1964), "Negro and White Response to Advertising Stimuli," *Journal of Marketing Research*, 1 (November), 53–56.

neither strategy is appropriate at all times. Practically speaking, both frequently occupy a gray area which requires managerial judgment. The suitability of each technique under particular circumstances must be carefully evaluated.

A Framework for Decision Making

The issue underlying the standardization controversy is an artificial one since *perfect* standardization is, in all likelihood, impossible to attain. The real issue then becomes one not of whether standardized advertising should be used but rather *to what extent* it should be used and *under what conditions*. The answer lies in a suitable resolution of the conflict between standardization and segmentation. While standardization contradicts the logic of market segmentation, it is rather ironic that standardization has to be "rescued" by segmentation because it determines when standardization can become potentially applicable on a limited basis. In essence, the appropriateness of standardization is a function of the applicability of market segmentation.

Market segmentation helps in resolving the debate over the use of standardized advertising among academicians and practitioners by providing a practical framework for decision making (see Figure 1). If a market is not segmented, a universal advertisement is appropriate for the total market. However, if that same market is divided into several segments, each segment then requires its own custom-made marketing mix. Under what conditions should the market be segmented? This depends on the five criteria of identification, accessibility, differential response, segment size and cost/profit. Market segmentation is thus applicable and will render standardization useless when (1) the marketer can *identify* his customers' *unique* characteristics; (2) such customers are *accessible* through some *selective* advertising media with minimum waste in promotion; (3) their *responses* to a unique marketing mix will be *favorably different* from those of other segments; (4) the group *size* is *large* enough to justify the special attention being given it; and (5) incremental cost as a result of the segmentation is less than incremental profit. From an advertising perspective, all of the above segmentation criteria must be met in order to rule out the use of advertising standardization. Otherwise, the "one-ad-fits-all" strategy can be used for the total market.

The criteria mentioned above appear to relate well to the factors which have been identified in Figure 1 as being able to affect the extent of advertising standardization. The *identification* criterion is primarily concerned with demographic homogeneity within as well as across countries. *Selectivity*, the second criterion, addresses the issue of media waste and availability. The next criterion, *response*, once again concerns consumer homogeneity, except that, unlike the demographic dimension, the focus is now on attitudinal homogeneity instead. *Size* is the practical criterion which determines the significance of a particular market segment. Finally, the *cost/profit* criterion addresses management's pri-

FIGURE **1**   A Decision-Making Framework For Advertising Standardization

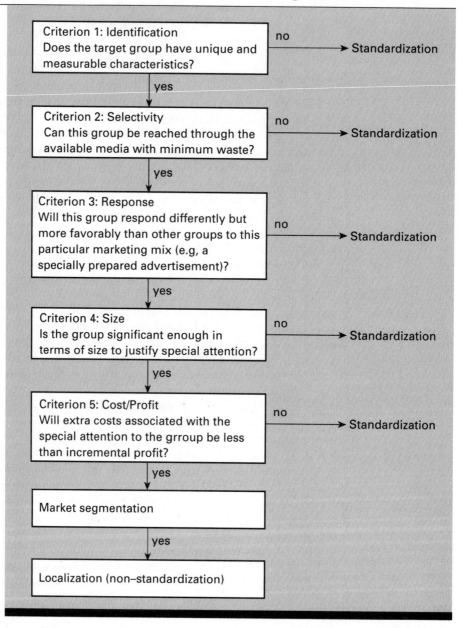

mary concern with the bottom line by considering the extent of cost savings in relation to the amount of incremental profit.

Japanese firms appear to follow the above segmentation/standardization criteria closely. They always design advertisements exclusively for the U.S. market because of its unique characteristics and response, media availability, market size, and great profit potential. In contrast, the Japanese promote in other Asian markets with their own Japanese-designed advertisements perhaps because other Asian markets are similar or because those markets are not economically significant enough to justify non-standardized advertising.

Managerial Implications

For any market and promotional campaign the goals of the campaign (e.g., awareness building, education of product benefits, or sales increase) must be clearly stated. Explicit goals are needed to judge the degree of success or failure of the campaign regardless of whether the campaign is a standardized one or not. An opportunity for standardization may be presented because advertising campaigns for separate markets can have the same goals even though not operating at the same point in time due to being at varying stages of product life cycle in such countries. On the other side of the issue, the same means may not lead to the same goal, and varying tactics may have to be adopted.

As demonstrated by the difficulties experienced in the UK by Philip Morris' Marlboro, Unilever's Lifebuoy, and L'Oreal, the practical aspect of standardized advertising is often overstated, and so is its benefit.[37] Coke and Pepsi are usually cited as examples of successful standardization even though their standard themes (e.g., "It's the Real Thing" and "The Pepsi Generation") are not always easily translated or understood overseas. Also, since Coke and Pepsi standardized advertisements have not been tested against non-standardized versions, there is no evidence showing that a customized advertisement could not have been more effective and increased sales. For some, a question exists as to whether the alleged success of these products is due to standardization or whether it might be camouflaged by the sheer volume of advertising expenditure for these brands. It is interesting to note that PepsiCo, an advocate of standardization, has to use a different brand name for its Mountain Dew lemon-lime drink abroad. Coca-Cola, likewise, found it necessary to alter Sprite's product formulation for it to match the preferences of the Japanese market more closely. As a matter of fact, the cola beverage, often perceived as a universal product, is thought to taste like medicine in some parts of the world. Apparently, a product can be largely universal in many places, but its complete universality may still be an elusive quality.

Marketers should understand that the encouragement of standardization is

---

[37] Fisher, op. cit.

nothing more than a means to an end where appropriate. It should not be considered an end in itself. It serves no useful purpose to strive for world-wide uniformity and conformity if consumers seek diversity and individuality. To be preoccupied with standardization is to overlook the main purpose of advertising, and a realization that this is happening should alert marketers to examine the relevance of their advertising messages. The best advertisements (in terms of appeal and cost) generally maximize profits and should be used regardless of whether they are standardized or customized. For maximum effect, each advertisement should be pre-tested in an international context to determine its impact in terms of attention-getting, comprehension, and persuasion. Marketers should not forget that advertising is supposed to inform and persuade customers effectively. Since market heterogeneity seems to be the rule rather than the exception, there is a high likelihood that a standardized advertisement could disappoint both management and foreign consumers by being unable to perform this function properly.

One cause of the U.S. trade deficit problem is the ethnocentricism of U.S. firms' international marketing policy. The insistence on advertising standardization is a symbol of this viewpoint. Those who insist that American advertisements are effective everywhere should be willing to accept foreign advertisements and values as being just as suitable for the U.S. market—a very unlikely occurrence.

The above discussion should not be interpreted as an endorsement for a polycentric attitude which requires custom-made campaigns for each individual market. Localization, practiced for its own sake, is not necessarily desirable either. A better solution is to take a geocentric or world orientation. Unfortunately, geocentricity is often confused by many with standardization. Standardization is basically a U.S. campaign designed for the U.S. market, but exported to other markets regardless of market considerations. Just because British Airways' TV commercial (which is a takeoff on the "Close Encounters of the Third Kind" movie) was shown in 52 countries, the number of countries where the commercial is shown does not necessarily make the commercial global. A "pretender" is a standardized advertisement disguised as a global one. Geocentricity and standardization are neither synonymous nor compatible.

A geocentric campaign requires the advertisement to be designed for the worldwide audience from the outset to appeal to a shared inter-country denominator while allowing for some modification to suit each market. This approach combines the advantages of standardization (i.e., cost reduction) and individualization (i.e., local relevance and effective appeal).

As a final point, management should distinguish between *standardized programs* and *process*. The process through which marketing programs are developed can be standardized. Notwithstanding, the standardized process does not have to result in standardized marketing programs for overseas markets. Therefore, attention should be devoted to the development of an analytical framework to systematically analyze cross-national market conditions which moderate the appeal of standardization.

Conclusion

Surprisingly, an issue of this magnitude has remained unresolved for a quarter of a century. Management must realize that its primary responsibility is to maximize profits and that cost reduction through standardization is only a secondary objective. Standardization can be achieved at the expense of profit maximization.

"Striking consumer similarities," more often than not, are just an illusion. Although people may share a few common values, such shared coincidences cannot nullify their differences. It is naive to say that people are all alike because, by being human, they have a common, universal denominator. People are human, but human beings are also different with regard to age, sex, culture, nationality, and personality, factors which require the development of different ways to satisfy such characteristic values.

Standardized advertising, in a proper perspective, is prescriptive or normative because it explains how things should be regardless of whether they are a reflection of reality. But until the world is ready to adopt a single language, a single currency, and a single political ideology, it is premature to accept the standardized approach and its sweeping generalization. On a more limited but not necessarily worldwide basis, this technique may be appropriate due to a limited degree of homogeneity which exists in many cultures. The key to the application of standardization is to determine when and where a limited measure of homogeneity exists for some level of standardized advertising. Without the much needed refinements, global standardization is nothing more than a quixotic effort in search of an "impossible dream."

READING 32   CAN SALES PROMOTION GO GLOBAL?

Kamran Kashani ◆ John A. Quelch

Sales promotion in multinational companies has traditionally been a local affair. Subsidiary managers, primarily brand managers, have enjoyed great latitude in the formulation and implementation of promotional programs close to their markets. Although global marketing is influencing traditional decision making in areas such as product line, branding, pricing, and advertising, it has had little influence on sales promotion. But for some companies that may be about to change.

Nestlé's experiences with *laissez-faire* in sales promotion are typical of the problems faced by many multinationals. In the early 1980s, management delegated to the local organizations many decisions that had traditionally been made or strongly influenced by the headquarters. Of all marketing decisions, only branding and packaging were kept at the center. The rest, including consumer and trade promotions, became the domain of the company's country operations around the world.

Although decentralization has helped enhance Nestlé's performance internationally, it has been less than satisfactory in sales promotion. The problem has to do with two developments over time: a worldwide shift in emphasis and budget allocation in favor of sales promotion and away from media advertising, and increasing reliance on price promotion to boost short-term local sales results, particularly in countries with a powerful trade and/or limited electronic media advertising. The outcome: reduced brand profitability, contradictory brand communication, and a serious potential for dilution of brand franchises with consumers.

Today Nestlé is trying to put some central direction back into its worldwide communication practices, including sales promotion. Management is painfully aware of the damage "brand management by calculators" and "commodity promotion" can do to its international brands and their long-term profitability. *Laissez-faire* in sales promotion is no longer considered a virtue at Nestlé.

For some global brands, the importance of promotion in the marketing mix varies dramatically from one country to another. Table 1 illustrates the divergent marketing strategies applied to one consumer packaged goods brand in five countries during 1987.

In this article we will explore the forces challenging the traditional thinking about sales promotion among MNCs. We will examine those factors that make standardization of promotional activities a difficult and risky undertaking. To help clarify the respective roles of headquarters and country management, we will propose a framework for analysis that takes into account a brand's geographic scope and communication objectives on the one hand, and the differ-

TABLE **1**

	U.S.	Japan	U.K.	Canada	Mexico
Total advertising and promotion as a percent of sales	27	33	26	27	1
Advertising percentage	12	39	42	19	68
Consumer promotion %	26	25	25	15	11
Trade promotion %	62	36	33	66	22

ent elements of sales promotion decision making on the other. Finally, we will make recommendations for strengthening management policy toward sales promotion.

Promotion: A Headquarters Concern

Nestlé's uneasiness over the impact of local action on its international brands is just one reason why sales promotions are increasingly becoming a headquarters concern for MNCs. There are additional reasons as well:

Cost. The cost of sales promotion has risen worldwide. For many packaged consumer goods companies, combined consumer and trade promotion expenditures have passed advertising to become the largest single-cost item besides production costs. With increased expenditures has come heightened central management interest in exerting control on how the funds are spent and in improving their productivity.

Complexity. The variety of sales promotions and the frequency with which they are offered have increased over time. Many multinationals have come to realize that their local organizations are not all equipped to deal with this increased complexity in program design, execution, and follow-up.

Global Branding. The visible trend toward establishing uniform brand personalities internationally implies some degree of consistency in brand communication, including sales promotion. Global marketers are aware that a measure of central monitoring is essential for achieving worldwide brand harmony. At the same time, these companies are also realizing that with central coordination, successful local innovations in promotion do not have to stay local. Through their timely transfer to other markets, their success can be reproduced several times around the world.

Transnational Trade. The long-term trend toward retail concentration in certain parts of the world is taking on a new dimension as specialty retailers, mass merchandisers, and buying cooperatives are becoming increasingly transnational in scope. In Europe in particular, nine of the ten largest retailers already have investments in stores outside their home countries. This trend is likely to accelerate when the remaining trade barriers among the 12-member EC are dismantled in 1992. As transnational retailers push for central buying, they will also seek coordinated multinational marketing programs from their vendors. As a consequence, sales promotion, especially trade promotion, will have to become more multinational in tone and coverage.

Promotion: A Local Activity

Although the above factors are working to make sales promotion of increasing concern to headquarters, it still remains primarily a local activity. After all, sales promotion is about motivating *local* consumers and members of the trade to act—to try the product, repurchase it, buy more, switch brands, and so forth. But there are important differences among countries—which country managers eager to retain their decision-making autonomy will quickly point out—that make certain promotion incentives more or less effective.

Economic Development The limited purchasing power in developing countries, often combined with low levels of literacy, poses special problems for marketers. Although theoretically a company has a wide choice of promotional tools, in practice the choice of effective tools is somewhat limited. An international marketer of packaged food products operating in the Philippines must refrain from using high-value, on-pack premiums in consumer promotions; otherwise the final price would be beyond the reach of most consumers. A recent study of the promotional practices of MNCs in developing countries reports that free samples and demonstrations are by far the most widely used consumer promotion tools. On the other hand, the research shows that coupons, wide-spread in developed countries, are rarely used.

Market Maturity National markets frequently differ in their maturity as reflected in overall growth rates and competitive structure. A product might be new to some countries and enjoy few direct competitors, while in others the product might be part of a well-developed, mature, and highly competitive market. Using the same promotional program in these different markets would be inappropriate. Although tools to promote consumer trial (sampling, full-value couponing, and cross promotion with established products and brands) might be appropriate for countries in the early phase, more emphasis on other promotional vehicles (trade allowances and consumer promotions designed to reinforce consumer loyalty) might be more effective in the more mature markets. At any rate, the sales promotion mix should closely reflect local market maturity—including competitive dynamics, which often differ from country to country.

Perceptions Consumer and trade perceptions of promotional incentives are frequently culturally inspired and can vary dramatically from market to market. Coupons, for example, are not widely used in Japan. Since they first appeared in only 1976, the Japanese consumer is still too embarrassed to be seen at a checkout redeeming them. Likewise, in Japan, Lego's "Bunny Set" promotion— the block toys plus a discounted premium offer, a storage case in the shape of a bunny—failed to impress its intended target of mothers, even though the same concept had proven extremely successful in the United States. A post-promotion survey highlighted the reason: unlike their American counterparts, who thought the offering was a great bargain, the Japanese considered the on-pack bunny as superfluous. They objected to the notion of "being forced to waste money on unwanted products." The lesson for international sales promoters: check local perceptions toward particular types of promotion before transferring promotional ideas internationally.

Regulations Laws pertaining to sales-promotion activities differ widely across countries. They govern both the types of promotion that are permissible and the manner in which they are presented. To illustrate, the fair-trade regulations in Japan limit the value of premiums to a maximum of 10 percent of retail price, and no more than 100 yen (about 80 cents). In Malaysia, contests are allowed, but they must involve games of skill and not chance. In Germany, only full-value coupons may be used in consumer promotions. A guide to local legal restrictions on promotions around the world has recently been completed by Boddewyn and Leardi. There are no plans for country-specific regulations on sales promotions and direct-mail practices to be harmonized within the European Community in the run-up to 1992. Currently, only free samples, in-store demos, and reusable packages are permitted in all 12 EC countries.

Trade Structure Local trade structures influence sales promotions. In highly concentrated retailing systems such as in Northern Europe, there is greater pressure on local brand managers from the few powerful trade buyers to emphasize price-oriented trade deals and in-store consumer promotions. The pressure is less acute in Southern Europe, where trade remains fragmented. Promotion offers that the big chains of Northern Europe may dismiss as commonplace could be very appealing in the less promotion-intensive environment of Southern Europe. Indeed, they could be excessively attractive, to the point of damaging a brand's quality image. Also, store facilities differ from country to country. In highly fragmented retailing structures such as Japan's, small store size precludes the use of some promotional tools that occupy store space (in-store sampling, gift-with-purchase offers) or slow down checkout traffic (coupons).

Special Situations There are still other country-specific situations that require decision making close to the local markets. Situations such as state-controlled retailing in Eastern Europe and hyperinflation in Brazil are unique enough to demand the customization of any international promotion scheme. Few trade deals or consumer promotions are offered by companies selling in Eastern Europe; such offers can be a source of embarrassment because they imply to state procurement agents that the marketer's list prices are excessive. However, merchandising assistance in the form of store fixtures, point-of-sale aids, and sales training programs is welcomed. Similarly, Brazil's inflationary environment places constraints on the use of promotional tools:

- With 18 percent inflation per month, there are no temporary price reductions to the trade as are common in North America and Western Europe. Producers give trade incentives by delaying price increases and extending payment terms.
- In Brazil's high-inflation economy, consumer promotions that offer an immediate rather than a delayed value work best. Product samples distributed in stores and in schools (for students to take home to their parents) are much more widely used than cash rebates and coupons. Self-liquidating premiums are preferable to cash rebates because the premium retains its value, though postal delays and theft mean that this type of promotion is still in limited use.
- Widespread coupon use awaits broader consumer understanding of how to redeem coupons, training of store clerks in how to process them, and the development of a coupon redemption infrastructure. In- and on-pack offers are restricted by the prevalence of package tampering in self-service stores.

Drawing the Line

The preceding analysis should have made one point clear. There are still good reasons for leaving sales promotion primarily in the hands of local management. The issue, therefore, is not whether to do away with local autonomy altogether, but how to help improve local practices. In other words, the aim of any attempt at changing the respective roles of headquarters and subsidiary managers should be to upgrade the performance of local promotions—in their overall impact, productivity, and, where appropriate, contribution to international brand franchise building.

To draw the line for the role of headquarters in local sales promotion, one needs to distinguish among local, regional, and global brands. Most MNCs have a mix of brands with different "geographical equities" at different stages of globalization. Each category has its own requirements for central coordination and puts varying demands on local initiatives:

◆ At one extreme are the local brands that do not need international coordination. One example is Nestlé's "Exella" coffee in Japan that, despite its single-country distribution, is the company's largest selling brand of coffee worldwide. "Exella" is considered a Japanese brand and all aspects of the marketing program are managed locally.

◆ At the other extreme are the global brands such as Swatch, Benetton, and Coca-Cola, which have widespread international presence, a high degree of uniformity in brand communications worldwide, and substantial headquarters direction of marketing.

◆ Between local and global brands are regional brands, such as Polaroid's "Image System," which is the company's European brand for its cameras and accessories introduced elsewhere under the "Spectra System" brand. As with many other regional brands aiming for a degree of international harmony, "Image System" is managed by the European headquarters on a pan-European basis.

We believe the role of the center vis-à-vis local management in sales promotion decisions should closely reflect a brand's geographical equity and communication objectives. Broadly speaking, the center's influence should be at its minimum for local brands and at its maximum for global brands. The reverse should be true for the level of subsidiary influence. To be more precise, Figure 1 proposes a framework for defining the source, level, and nature of influence on promotional decisions, using the three brand categories as the starting point. The three possible scenarios of influence and roles shown in the figure are described below.

Global Brands Here the HQ's influence is at its greatest, particularly on new brands conceived and launched as global in scope. The center is assigned the primary task of defining an overall promotional strategy to guide the day-to-day activities of local management. By strategy we mean the guiding principles that reinforce the global brand's international communication objectives, including its positioning. A promotional strategy statement may include guidelines on the relative emphasis on sales promotion versus media advertising in the overall communication budget, the relative weight of consumer and trade promotions, and the appropriate role of price deals versus value-added offers in the promotion mix. Through such guidelines the global product manager aims to protect the integrity of the brand across national markets and convey a consistent

FIGURE 1   Influence and Roles in International Sales Promotion

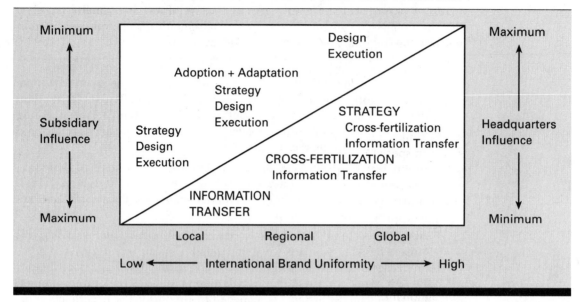

message to consumers and the trade over time. By necessity, these principles have to be broad enough to be implemented in diverse local markets.

In addition to promotional strategy formulation, headquarters is responsible for two other tasks: encouraging cross-fertilization of ideas and practices among the local companies, and facilitating information transfer. A discussion of these other functions is deferred to later sections under regional and local brands.

Whereas the center decides the appropriate promotional strategy for global brands, its implementation is best left to local management. As shown in Figure 1, local management tasks are of two kinds: promotional program design and execution. By design we mean all those decisions that translate the global guidelines into the specific features of each promotion. These features include:

Objective: Is the promotion designed to increase consumer trial or repeat purchase, or obtain store distribution, expanded shelf space, or special displays?

Promotion type: Should sampling, couponing, price packs, rebates, premiums, sweepstakes, or some combination be used?

Product scope: Which products or pack sizes in the brand line should be promoted?

Timing: When should the promotion be run and for how long?

Terms: What, if anything, should the consumer or trade have to do to qualify for the promotion offer?

Program execution involves all other decisions on support activities and logistics necessary for the launch and fulfillment of a promotional offer. This includes the planning of sales force presentations to the trade, working with the manufacturing group or outside suppliers on the production of the promotion offers and associated point-of-purchase support materials, and arranging follow-up evaluation of the promotion's effectiveness.

For global brands, program design and execution are assigned to local management because that is where the local market knowledge—so critical to the campaign's success—typically lies. The center's broad international perspective is simply no substitute for local management's experience and insight. However, special international "events," such as Reebok's recent cosponsorship with Amnesty International of the Human Rights Now! concerts in 14 countries, are an exception to this rule. These promotional events are by necessity conceived and developed at headquarters. Though center driven, international promotion/public relations events often provide an umbrella for complementary individual country promotions directed at the trade, salespeople, and consumers.

Regional Brands When a regional brand strategy calls for the same degree of international uniformity as implied in the case of global brands, then the same rules would apply—headquarters (frequently regional HQ) would contribute the promotional strategy, while the campaign design and execution would be carried out by individual country managements. But the needs of regional brands are not always the same as those of truly global brands. Often the regional management's objectives for a common brand identity are more modest. They tend to focus not so much on standardization as on minimizing contradictory brand communication, avoiding promotional initiatives that upset other local activities across the border, and transferring effective campaign designs to other countries in the region.

When such brand harmonization, rather than standardization, is the overall objective, the center's optimum role in sales promotion can best be defined as cross-fertilization. This function is more than just information transfer, which is also a task assigned to the center, but certainly less than international strategy formulation. The job demands persuasive skills to bring otherwise divergent local practices into harmony.

As shown in Figure 1, the country-level roles for regional brands are defined as adoption and adaptation. They imply a strong local voice in what is adopted from the region and how they are adapted to local conditions. In other words, local management remains fully responsible for a brand's promotional strategy, campaign design, and execution—within the regional policy guidelines, of course.

Local Brands With local brands the degree of local influence on promotional decisions is at its maximum, the need for central coordination is nonexistent, and all decisions on promotional strategy, program design, and execution are local affairs. But this country-level process can still benefit from the broader "collective wisdom" of the international organization. Such would be the case, for example, if local management had knowledge of the practices of sister companies and competitors in similar product categories elsewhere in the world. This information could prove especially valuable in promotion-intensive markets where innovation in program design and execution is an important means of competitive brand differentiation.

The center's task for local brands is information transfer. This is less than cross-fertilization, since it lacks the latter's objective of achieving a degree of international harmonization among country practices. The purpose of information transfer is solely to serve the local managers in their constant search for high-impact sales promotions. The final decisions on what and how to borrow from the outside remain with local management.

Implications for Management Policy

As sales promotion costs rise internationally, their complexity grows over time, and brands and distribution channels take on a global scope, it is natural for top management to question the wisdom of local autonomy in promotional decisions and review ways of achieving greater productivity by exerting more control. However, marketing managers in the operating units may resent headquarters' interference, especially in the larger country organizations with strong traditions of local autonomy and good earnings records. Having recently wrestled with headquarters over global advertising campaigns and worldwide agencies, and having built up their sales promotion budgets at the expense of advertising partly as a result, many will be sensitive to any efforts to erode their control over sales promotion decisions.

We recommend that MNC headquarters first establish agreement on the strategic role and both the actual and intended geographical equity of each brand in its worldwide portfolio. Some brands will be designated local, some regional, and some global. The degree of headquarters involvement in promotion decision making will vary accordingly. Most country managers will be willing to accept some reduction in promotion decision-making authority over regional and global brands because they will still have local brands in their portfolios over which they have complete marketing control. In addition, at least half the promotion budget for the most global of brands is still likely to be devoted to strictly local promotions, as suggested in Figure 2.

Second, we recommend the appointment of an international sales promotion coordinator with recognized expertise in the promotion field, strong persuasion skills, and line marketing experience in one or more operating units. Lego, the Danish global marketer of educational toys, has had a central sales

FIGURE 2   Expected Allocation of Promotion Expenditures According to a
Brand's Geographical Equity

		Sales Promotion Expenditure Mix		
		Local	Regional	Global
Brand Type	Local	100%		
	Regional	75%	25%	
	Global	50%	25%	25%

promotion unit for five years. The international sales promotion coordinator's role would be to:

◆ Promote the transfer of successful promotion ideas among brands and operating units through word-of-mouth, marketing newsletters, and periodic meetings where operating managers from different countries can exchange success stories.

◆ Propose and solicit ideas for regional or global blockbuster or special event sales promotions on appropriate brands, organize regional or global promotion task forces to design and implement them, and persuade the operating units to participate with headquarters in funding these efforts.

◆ Encourage developing countries to use innovative sales promotion techniques as a source of competitive differentiation versus local producers.

◆ Transfer ideas on how to limit trade promotion expenditures from countries where the trade is highly concentrated to those where the trade's power is increasing but not yet dominant.

◆ Develop and present training programs on sales promotion planning, design, and evaluation that will inculcate common standards and procedures among the operating units.

◆ Advise the operating units on solutions to specific promotion problems—without, however, encouraging an excessive dependency on headquarters that could lead to finger pointing if a promotion fails to meet objectives.

◆ Gather performance data on promotions run by all brands in all countries plus data on consumer and trade promotion expenditures and promotion-to-sales and advertising-to-promotion ratios.

◆ Develop standard systems for measuring the effectiveness and efficiency of promotions that country managements can implement—and that can also furnish the data headquarters needs for worldwide promotion evaluation.

◆ Coordinate relations with the company's sales promotion agencies worldwide. The emergence of international sales promotion networks such as KLP suggests that companies may in the future be able to consolidate their worldwide sales promotion expenditures with fewer agencies, as has occurred with advertising.

◆ Oversee on a dotted-line basis the performance of sales promotion staff specialists in the operating units, and provide input to their performance evaluations.

The international sales promotion coordinator's biggest challenges involve regional and global rather than local brands. Once the desired level of uniformity in brand communication across country organizations is determined, the coordinator must use his or her persuasive skills to reduce divergent subsidiary promotion practices that stand in the way of achieving this objective. This is not an easy task; the coordinator must walk a tightrope between traditional subsidiary autonomy on the one hand and the felt need for some degree of harmony in local practices on the other. The coordinator's approach should not be to substitute for local initiatives, but rather to support them through setting broad communications objectives for the brands and laying out useful guidelines for promotional practices that reinforce those objectives. Equally important is consistency over time in the internal communication from headquarters to the operating units. Nothing discredits a global strategy more than sudden shifts in direction. Consistency in internal communication will help achieve the consistency in each brand's external marketing communications, which is the principal motivation for considering a more global approach to sales promotion in the first place.

REFERENCES

Jean J. Boddewyn and Monica Leardi, "Sales Promotions: Practice, Regulation and Self-Regulation Around the World," *International Journal of Advertising*, forth-coming.

John Farrell, "Taking Europe in Your Stride," *Marketing*, November 3, 1988, pp. 45–47.

John S. Hill and Unal O. Boya, "Consumer Goods Promotion in Developing Countries," *International Journal of Advertising*, No. 6, 1987, pp. 249–264.

Laurie Peterson, "Global Promotion," *Promote*, July 4, 1988, p. 6.

READING 33   **GLOBAL OR STATELESS CORPORATIONS ARE NATIONAL FIRMS WITH INTERNATIONAL OPERATIONS**

Yao-Su Hu

The debate on American competitiveness in the world economy has recently been thrown into some disarray. Robert Reich asserts in his essay "Who Is Us?" that in a "borderless" world characterized by "stateless" corporations, it makes no sense to talk of American competitiveness in terms of American-owned corporations, but rather that American competitiveness should be defined in terms of the skills and experience of the American work force.[1] And as Kenichi Ohmae states: "It does not matter who builds the factory or who owns the office building or whose money lies behind the shopping mall or whose equity makes the local operation possible. What matters is that the global corporations . . . act as responsible corporate citizens."[2]

Since these aggressive assertions hinge on the concept of the "global" (or "stateless") corporation, the term deserves careful scrutiny. It has been preceded in the last 30 years by a string of synonyms such as: international, inter-territorial, multinational, transnational, and worldwide. The concept has evolved to the point where it connotes something that has gone beyond nations and has left them behind. Before this, economists talked of "direct foreign investment," which implied the existence of a home nation and "host" (i.e., foreign) countries. In 1960, David I. Lilienthal, who had achieved prominence as Director of the Tennessee Valley Authority and then as Director of the Atomic Energy Commission, launched the expression "multinational corporation."[3] Since then, exaggerated claims have been made about the nature of this newly discovered species and about the inevitable demise of the nation-state. MIT economics professor Charles Kindleberger wrote in 1969: "The international corporation has no country to which it owes more loyalty than any other, nor any country where it feels completely at home . . . The nation-state is just about through as an economic unit . . . The world is too small. It is too easy to get about."[4] What differs between the 1960s and the 1990s is the context of the assertions: in the 1960s, it was the Europeans who worried about U.S. multinationals; now it is the Americans who worry about Japanese and European multinationals.

Source: Copyright 1992 *California Management Review* (Winter). Reprinted with permission.

[1] R. Reich, "Who Is Us?," *Harvard Business Review* (January/February 1990).

[2] K. Ohmae, *The Borderless World* (London: Collins, 1990), p. 194.

[3] Parentage of the term was first pointed out by P. Baran and P. Sweezy, *Monopoly Capital* (London: Penguin, 1966), p. 192. It was confirmed by D. Fieldhouse, "The Multinational: A Critique of a Concept," in A. Teichova et al., *The Multinational Enterprise in Historical Perspective* (Cambridge: Cambridge University Press, 1986).

[4] C.P. Kindleberger, *American Business Abroad* (New Haven, CT: Yale University Press, 1969), lecture 6.

This article addresses some difficult and fundamental questions.[5] What is the nature of the "global," "transnational," or "multinational" corporation? Is it "national" (albeit with foreign or international operations) or is it "stateless" or "global" (by which it is meant that the company has really transcended nations in the sense that it is indifferent as between different countries and has no home nation)? What are the strategic, overall implications for the firm's competitive position in the world economy? And finally, what are the analytical, conceptual implications—i.e., what difference does it make to the way in which we think about the issues, to public debate, and to the research agenda?

Nationality Versus Stateless Globalism in the MNC

The argument that MNCs have become stateless entities stems from the observation that their business operations cross national borders. General Motors makes the Pontiac LeMans in Korea to sell in the United States, Honda makes cars in Ohio that it exports to Japan, and Boeing makes sections of its planes in China, Italy, and Canada for assembly in Seattle.[6] However, this argument is questionable on two counts. First, stateless operations do not necessarily mean stateless corporations; in addition to the geographical spread of the group's operations, there are other criteria that need to be considered before one can consider the group to be stateless—criteria such as the ownership, control, top management, and legal nationality of the group and its components. Second, it does not necessarily follow from the fact that operations cross national boundaries that the nations are of equal importance to the group or that there is no geographical center of gravity.

Some schools of thought label a firm as a "global" or "transnational" corporation simply because it adopts a "global" or "transnational" strategy. Earlier, it was the adoption of a global habit of mind that distinguished the "geocentric" company from the "ethnicentric" and the "polycentric" firm.[7] Apart from the fact that a global strategy has meant different things to different writers, the problem is that a strategy or a habit of mind cannot be quantified. Nor can it be measured unambiguously through its results, for the actual outcome depends not only on the strategy but also on the interplay of internal and external forces.

---

[5] The question of the nationality of the MNC was first raised by Stephen Hymer in his doctoral thesis, published posthumously. See S. Hymer, *The International Operations of National Firms* (Cambridge, MA: MIT Press, 1976). See also U.S. Hu, *The Impact of U.S. Investment in Europe: A Case Study of the Automotive and Computer Industries* (New York, NY: Praeger, 1973), pp. 252–267.

[6] R. Reich, *The Work of Nations* (New York, NY: Knopf, 1991).

[7] Howard Perlmutter, "The Tortuous Evolution of the Multinational Corporation," *Columbia Journal of World Business* (January/February 1969).

Geographical Spread and Scope For a company to be stateless in the sense of being indifferent between nations, a necessary condition is that its operations should be evenly distributed among these nations. This raises the question of what indicators should be used to measure the firm's operations. It seems clear that the distribution of sales or turnover cannot by itself be a satisfactory indicator—for example, a company may be deriving 80 percent of its total sales from foreign countries through exporting, without any foreign manufacturing, yet it would remain clearly anchored in its home nation. The distribution of profits is even more problematic, as this not only depends on the distribution of sales, but is further affected by inter-country transfer pricing.

The geographical distribution of value-added (or net output—i.e., the value of output minus the value of purchased inputs) would be an ideal indicator, but I have not come across a single multinational whose published accounts provide enough data for this to be computed. We therefore have to fall back on the distribution of a firm's assets (total or fixed assets) and of its number of employees as approximate indicators. Table 1 illustrates this for a few of the best-known U.S. multinationals. Many of the German and Japanese multinationals also have less than 50 percent of their operations abroad. On the other hand, many of the British MNCs and MNCs from the smaller European nations such as Switzerland have more than 50 percent of their operations located abroad; this is because of historical reasons or because of economic necessity (i.e., the need to reap economies of scale and scope). At the extreme is Switzerland's Nestlé, which has 95 percent of its assets and 96.5 percent of its employees located outside the home nation.

In cases where less than half of a group's operations are abroad, the home

TABLE 1   The International Scope of Some Multinationals

Company	Percent of total assets outside home country	Percent of total no. of employees outside home country
IBM (1989)	46	44
General Motors (1989)	24	31
Du Pont (1989)	35	24
General Electric (1989)	9	17
Sample Nonbank U.S. MNCs (1988)	22	26

Sources. Computed from company annual reports; U.S. Department of Commerce, Survey of Current Business, June 1990.

country operations are of overwhelming importance to the MNC. Such a firm cannot escape the influence of the home nation's environment. If it is based in a stagnant, declining, or otherwise unfavorable nation, it will be at a disadvantage in relation to competitors based in more dynamic nations. For example, imagine the case of two electronics companies, one American and one Japanese, both of which have 60 percent of their total operations in the home nation. If the Japanese electronics industry grows at 10 percent a year compared to 5 percent a year for the U.S. industry, and if each firm maintains its share of its national industry, the Japanese firm will have a higher overall rate of growth than the U.S. firm if the overseas operations of both grow at the same rate. If the overseas operations grow at 10 percent per annum, the Japanese firm will grow at 10 percent overall, the U.S. company at 7 percent. If the U.S. firm wants to match the Japanese rate of growth, it has to achieve a higher rate of growth of its overseas operations than the Japanese firm achieves on its overseas operations; thus if the Japanese firm's overseas operations grow at 10 percent, the U.S. firm's foreign operations have to grow at 17.5 percent if it is to attain the same overall rate of growth (10 percent). This is a tall order, especially if the U.S. firm has to defend its home market against Japanese competition at the same time. This dependence of the corporation's fortunes on the home nation, depending on the relative weight of home operations, results from the fact that the operations of the global enterprise have a center of gravity or home nation.

What if the group's foreign operations exceed 50 percent of the total? It may be thought that this would put foreign operations on the same footing as domestic operations in the eyes of the headquarters. However, although overseas operations exceed 50 percent in aggregate, this 50 percent is divided between a number of foreign (host) nations. Thus, any individual host nation is likely to account for a much smaller percentage of the corporate total than the home nation. This is illustrated in Table 2.

ICIs case is typical of most MNCs in the world, regardless of their national origins: the home nation is more important, in sheer quantitative terms, to the group than any single foreign country. Furthermore, since governments, civic and business associations, labor unions, and pressure groups are organized and act most effectively within the limits of the nation, the global firm is more susceptible to pressure, persuasion, or requests for cooperation coming from the home nation than from any other country. To put it simply, the home government has within its jurisdiction a much bigger chunk of the group's assets than any individual foreign government. Given that the MNC is a political as well as an economic phenomenon, this differential susceptibility and receptivity is of great importance to the nations concerned. It often is not true, as Kindleberger stated, that the MNC has no country to which it owes more loyalty than any other: self-interest dictates otherwise. It should be noted that the issue here concerns the MNC's differential susceptibility; the fact that the home government may choose not to exert pressure is another matter.

TABLE **2**   International Spread of Imperial Chemical Industries, 1989

	Percent of total net operating assets	Percent of total no. of employees
Overseas operations	62.6	59.1
UK (home base)	37.4	40.9
Continental Europe	15.4	12.5
The Americas	27.5	25.3
Asia Pacific	15.8	12.5
Other countries	3.9	8.9

Source: Company annual report

There are two exceptions to this rule. First, there are companies from small nations, companies like Nestlé, for which a single foreign country (e.g., Germany) may represent a higher percentage of total operations than the home nation. Second, there are "binational" companies which have two home nations or centers of gravity: Shell and Unilever are both based in the UK and the Netherlands, and Asea Brown Boveri is based in Sweden and Switzerland. These two exceptions represent, in this day and age, the most advanced form of internationalization of the corporate entity.

Ownership and Control A global enterprise is normally made up of a parent company, located in the home nation, and a number of subsidiaries in host nations. A subsidiary is like any local company in that it is a legally incorporated entity and has its own legal identity; its distinctive characteristic is that it is owned and/or controlled by another corporation. A subsidiary can be wholly or partly owned by the parent company. Nowadays, partly owned subsidiaries usually involve joint ventures with another parent company or situations in which host-country laws require the presence of local shareholders. There seems to have been a tendency on the part of many MNCs to eliminate shareholdings by the public in their overseas subsidiaries, holdings which owed their existence to historical legacy. In 1959, IBM bought out the 38 percent minority holdings in its UK subsidiary and in 1961 Ford bought out the 46 percent minority shareholdings in Ford England.[8]

---

[8] Y.S. Hu, op. cit., p. 256. The reasons for this preference for 100% ownership are also explained, see pp. 257–259.

At the level of the parent company, ownership and control remain national rather than multinational. Although foreigners may own shares in the publicly quoted parent company, in most cases the majority of the shares are held by individuals and legal entities from the home nation.[9] Control naturally follows, so that both top management and governance rest in national hands. Thus, in terms of ownership and control, there is no doubt that a company like Siemens is German, a company like IBM is American, or a company like Toyota is Japanese. In the case of Nestlé (which has less than 5 percent of its total assets and employees in Switzerland), it is noteworthy that Swiss law allows Swiss companies to exclude foreigners from holding registered shares (which alone carry voting rights) and that Nestlé limits non-Swiss voting rights to 3 percent of the total.[10] In this respect, even a firm such as Nestlé is firmly national rather than transnational or stateless.

The furthest extent to which a group's ownership and control have been internationalized is the case of the "binational" companies, in which the group has two parent companies. The Royal Dutch/Shell Group is 40 percent owned by the Shell Transport and Trading Company PLC (UK) and 60 percent owned by the Royal Dutch Petroleum Company (Netherlands); the two parent companies are owned mainly in their respective home nations. Similarly, the Unilever Group has two parents, Unilever N.V. and Unilever PLC, and Asea Brown Boveri is owned, in equal parts, by ASEA AB (Sweden) and BBC Brown Boveri Ltd (Switzerland).

The multinationalization of shareholdings in the parent companies of global enterprise groups cannot be ruled out for the future. However, many nations will continue in the tradition of viewing the enterprise as much as a community as a commodity.[11] In this tradition, ownership of important chunks of a nation's wealth-producing capacity is seldom left to the vagaries of the market. If foreign shareholdings in a parent company begin to exceed 50 percent, it is often a sign that the firm is losing its status of parent company and becoming the subsidiary of a foreign corporation.

Whatever the ownership and control of the parent company, at the level of the subsidiaries the relationship is crystal clear. Control and ownership rest firmly with the parent. GM controls and owns 100 percent of Opel (Germany), Vauxhall (UK), and all its home and overseas subsidiaries. Ford controls and owns 100 percent of all its overseas subsidiaries except Ford Canada, in which the Canadian government has a minority shareholding. All IBM foreign subsidiaries are wholly owned and controlled by IBM World Trade Corporation in New York, which is wholly owned and controlled by IBM Corporation (also headquartered in New York). European and Japanese multinationals have, by and large,

---

[9] *Business Week* "The Stateless Corporation," May 14, 1990, p. 57.

[10] I. Walter and R. Smith, *Investment Banking in Europe* (Oxford: Blackwell, 1989), pp. 77–79.

[11] See Michel Albert, *Capitalisme Contre Capitalisme* (Paris: Seuil, 1991).

been adopting the same pattern, except where the host government mandates a local partner and/or local shareholdings.

Why do ownership and control matter? Ownership has several important implications. First, the subsidiary's profits accrue to the parent, an entity located in another nation. These profits represent a continuing foreign liability for the host country, and these liabilities increase over time through the reinvestment of earnings. When the profits are remitted to the parent as dividends, usually year after year, the outflow is a subtraction from the host nation's GNP and a debit item in its balance of payments. In relation to the initial investment (part of which may have been financed locally through local borrowing), these profits may be substantial. In the famous case of General Motors–Holden Ltd., the Australian wholly owned subsidiary of General Motors, it was found that the 1953–54 profits after taxes amounted to 560 percent of the original dollar investment and that the dividend declared to the parent, at 46 percent of profits, represented about 8 percent of the dollar export receipts in the Australian balance of payments for 1954–55.[12] While this outflow does not constitute a complete picture of the balance of payments effects of foreign investment for the host nation,[13] it is noteworthy that such outflows are a distinctive feature of MNC subsidiaries: locally owned companies do not accrue profits for a foreign parent.

Second, the fact that a multinational group is owned in a home nation means that the company is normally committed to pay dividends in the currency of the home nation and usually presents its consolidated accounts in that currency. This means that it has a home currency. Assets and cash flows labelled in other currencies carry a risk premium compared to those labelled in the home currency.[14] This may affect the firm's behavior. Everything else being equal, the MNC will prefer to keep its liquid assets in its home currency, and will also prefer to locate new facilities in its home nation.

Third, host nation citizens and institutions, should they wish to, cannot participate directly in the ownership of the local subsidiaries of MNCs based elsewhere, since the shares of the subsidiaries will be entirely in the hands of their parents and will not be traded. This deprives host nation interests and the host government of the possibility of exercising an influence, through local shareholders, on the local subsidiaries of the MNCs. Host nation people can buy shares in the parent company, but they are unlikely to have much voice at that level.

---

[12] E. Penrose, "Foreign Investment and the Growth of the Firm," *Economic Journal* (June 1956).

[13] The balance of payments effects should include the effects on exports, imports, royalties, license fees, etc. as well as the outflow of dividends, and the effects should in theory be assessed against what would otherwise have happened.

[14] Items denominated in foreign currencies incur translation, transaction, and economic exposures to exchange movements. Items denominated in the home currency only incur economic exposure.

The implications of control are no less important. First, although a subsidiary will have, like any local company, a board of directors, the members of the board are selected by, or with the active involvement of, the parent company. The subsidiary's board may contain some of the host nation's most prominent citizens, but their role can only be minor, given that the company is owned and controlled elsewhere. Often the parent company does not expect the local boards to take initiatives, and in many cases half of the board is composed of people from the parent company.

Second, like any local company, a subsidiary will have a CEO and senior executives, but they will have been selected and appointed by the parent company. Where the CEO is not an expatriate from the parent company, he or she will often be a local who has won the confidence of the parent company by, for example, having worked at the headquarters. Often, alongside local managers, expatriates will be holding important positions and, with direct lines of communication to the headquarters, will be making or overseeing important decisions.

Third, even where a subsidiary has been assigned a "global mandate" (i.e., responsibility for a business segment or product line not just in the host nation but throughout the world), certain powers are reserved by the parent and often include: authority to commit capital expenditure above certain limits; borrowing or raising of money; senior appointments; and major new commercial developments.[15]

Fourth, where there are regional headquarters to coordinate and oversee the national subsidiaries in the region, these tend to be headed by home country nationals from the parent company.

Fifth, non-expatriate managers and employees at a subsidiary may have a feeling of second-class citizenship. If a high proportion of a nation's economy is controlled outside, and if this includes strategic or key sectors (i.e., sectors which are quantitatively important, which affect many other sectors or which are key to the future because of high income elasticity of demand, rapid technological progress, and fast growth in labor productivity),[16] it becomes questionable to what extent the nation can really maintain its integrity, coherence, and political independence. Finally, if one accepts that a nation's most important resource is its human resources and that "the power to create wealth, for an enterprise, is the power of decision,"[17] it follows that a nation cannot develop its potential to the fullest if there are not enough nationally based enterprises in which its citizens can exercise the power to make final and integrated decisions.

Global companies are far from being international, multinational, or transnational when it comes to the locus of their ownership and control. If they are

---

[15] See ICI's Annual Report for 1989.

[16] OECD, *The Industrial Policy of Japan* (Paris: OECD, 1972), p. 15.

[17] J.J. Servan-Schreiber, *Le Défi Americain* (Paris: Denoël, 1967), Chapter 4.

viewed by host nations as foreign entities rather than as manifestations of a new world order that transcends national divisions, it is not without justification. It is perhaps for this reason that global enterprises stress "good citizenship" in host nations. However, good citizenship seldom goes so far as the home base giving up any of its control or ownership.

The People A corporation is not only its assets and operations, but also its people. For a global enterprise to have "no country to which it owes more loyalty than any other," its management and workforce must be multinational. What is the reality?

Except for companies such as Nestlé and Shell, the majority of the total number of employees in the corporation is employed in the group's home nation and are home nation citizens. When it comes to positions in senior management or on the parent company's board of directors, the percentage of foreigners (non-home-nation citizens) is not only significantly lower than the percentage of foreigners in the total number of employees, it is minuscule. GM and Ford do not have foreigners on their boards. IBM has only two foreign nationals (one Swiss and one German) sitting on its main board. Only two non-Americans have made it to the top of IBM's managerial hierarchy and they have become famous because of that.

Due to the close geographical proximity of European nations, the EEC's integration, and the fact that educated people in Europe speak a number of languages, European-based global companies tend to be more internationalized in their senior posts. German companies, which have a dual board structure, often have one Swiss and one Dutch national as members of their supervisory boards. Nestlé has an all-Swiss board but a number of non-Swiss senior managers. ICI has one German, one Japanese, and two American (non-executive) directors, and claims that 40 percent of the top 170 executives are not British. Even so, this still means that ICI's home nation (the UK), with 40 percent of the total number of employees, fills 60 percent of the top posts.

The national character of top management is even more pronounced in Japanese companies. Sony is the only major Japanese manufacturer with foreigners on the main board. Local managers in Japanese subsidiaries have a much more "subsidiary" role than those in other MNCs. In Japanese subsidiaries in the United States, the CEO is often Japanese, the American managers hit the promotion ceiling quite soon and are excluded from the inner councils, and the senior American managers rarely call the shots and are frequently relegated to playing a high-profile public-relations role.[18] There is nothing surprising in all this, since he who pays the piper calls the tune. The global enterprises of today are usually national or binational at best, especially at the senior management level. The few foreigners admitted to the parent board or top posts are

---

[18] *Business Week*, December 17, 1990. pp. 50–52.

admitted precisely because of their compatibility with the national style and character so that their presence should have little disruptive impact on the national character of the firm.

Legal Nationality and Taxation In legal terminology, there is no such thing as a multinational or global company. At present, there is no international law under which a transnational or supranational company can be formed and have legal existence in several nation-states. Even the European Community, arguably the most integrated group of nations in the world, has so far, after many years of discussion, failed to agree on the legal basis for a European company. Companies can only be formed under national law, and they acquire the nationality, citizenship, or domicile of the country under whose law they are incorporated. The parent company has the nationality of the home nation, the subsidiaries of the respective host nations in which they were created. Each is subject to a different national law, which determines the legal limitations on its behavior. Thus legal nationality affects corporate behavior, since what is legal in one nation may be illegal in another (e.g., a company's buy-back of its own shares or the creation of "floating charges" on its assets as collateral for borrowing); and what is mandated in one nation (e.g., codetermination in German law) may not be required in another.

The separate legal personality of the parent and its subsidiaries means that the parent is not automatically held liable for its subsidiary's liabilities. The concept of limited liability applies to any shareholder, whether that refers to a private individual or a parent corporation. This means that the global enterprise is able to hide behind the legal principles of separate legal personality and limited liability to avoid taking responsibility for the actions of a subsidiary that it owns and controls. In a limited number of cases (such as the Bhopal disaster), the courts have been able to "lift the veil" and to hold the parent or the group responsible. In general, however, this is exceptional and the law on corporate groups is not well-developed.[19]

Under international law, legal nationality is a necessary condition for obtaining the diplomatic protection of the State concerned; however, it may not be a sufficient condition.[20] In order to rule out tax havens and flags of convenience, international law seems to require, in addition to legal nationality (which is simply a matter of place of incorporation), a real and effective link between the corporation and the State. Evidence of such a link can be constituted by control or ownership.

---

[19] See P. Blumberg. "The American Law of Corporate Group," and D. Muchlinski, "Group Liability and the Multinational Enterprise," papers presented at the University of Warwick Workshop on Corporate Control and Accountability, June 30–July 2, 1991.

[20] See Barcelona Traction, Light and Power Co. Ltd. (Belgium v. Spain), International Court of Justice 1970, and Nottebohm (Liechtenstein v. Guatemala), ICJ 1953 (111) and ICJ 1955 (93).

The case of MNCs raises an interesting question for which there is no clear legal answer. If, for example, IBM Germany needed diplomatic protection in Eastern Europe, to whom should IBM turn to for such protection: the U.S. Government or the German Government? Much would depend on the circumstances. The company would probably prefer protection by the more powerful nation's government. MNCs from small nations may prefer U.S. diplomatic protection if they have significant operations in the United States. It is significant that in the case of exports of automobiles from Japanese "transplants" in the United States to the EEC, the Japanese have apparently left the matter of their diplomatic representation in the EEC to the U.S. Government.

Another interesting question arises in cases where a company changes its legal nationality for tax or political reasons (usually by creating, in a country with a favorable tax and/or political regime, a holding company which then owns the former parent company and/or its subsidiaries—as was the case with the "moves" by Tetra Pak to Switzerland, by Jardine Matheson to Bermuda, and by the Hong Kong Bank to Britain). To which government will it turn for diplomatic protection in case of need? The government of the country where its holding company is now incorporated (and where its head office may, but need not, be located) or the government of the former country where the bulk of its assets, operations, and people are still located? In the case of the moves from Hong Kong to Britain or Bermuda, the problem is masked by the fact that the sovereign power remains the same (Hong Kong and Bermuda being British colonies). Tetra Pak, cited by Ohmae as an example of the freedom to move, is a company which achieved fiscal emigration from Sweden to Switzerland. It is now facing a very large fine (US$85 million) by the EEC Commission for anti-competitive behavior.[21] Will it get diplomatic protection from the Swedish or from the Swiss government, or neither?

The extra-territorial application of U.S. laws in the territorial jurisdiction of other sovereign nations results partly from the problems surrounding the definition of corporate nationality. For the purposes of certain laws, the United States has adopted the position that the law should apply to all U.S. nationals, and U.S. nationals have been defined to include not only U.S. corporations but also their subsidiaries abroad. This has led to conflicts with nations which define corporate nationality in terms of the place of incorporation. Where a clear conflict of laws can be demonstrated, the host nation has been able to intervene and to prevail by invoking the principle of territoriality. It should be noted, however, that, in the absence of such conflict of laws, there is little that the host nation can do about the fact that instructions and decisions flow one way in any hierarchical system.

Taxation is a key interface between the State and the business corporation. From the point of view of a nation's tax authorities, there are key differences

---

[21] *International Herald Tribune,* July 23, 1991 and July 25, 1991.

between a home-based company with foreign operations and a company which is a subsidiary of a foreign parent corporation. In nations that adopt the worldwide principle of taxation (the United States, Britain, and most OECD countries), the home government can de jure tax the home-based MNC on its worldwide earnings by virtue of the fact that the subsidiaries' earnings accrue to the parent. Tax deferral (whereby foreign subsidiaries' earnings are not taxed until remitted to the parent as dividends) and foreign tax credits (whereby tax paid abroad can be credited against home country tax liabilities) are concessions with regard to the principle of worldwide taxation. With regard to a foreign-based MNC, the tax authorities can, as a rule, only tax the locally generated earnings of the local subsidiary, since the parent and sister companies are not owned by the local company and hence their earnings do not belong to it. De facto, there are also important differences. The home government has access to the consolidated accounts of the home-based MNC, can require additional data through the head office, and can tax the group accordingly. With the local subsidiary of a foreign-based MNC, the problem of determining what the local earnings are is clouded by the problem of inter-country transfer pricing[22] and various charges (royalties, license fees, etc.) payable to the parent and sister companies. Consolidated accounts are of little help since there is no right to tax the worldwide earnings of the group, and access to the head office is more distant. With a home-based group, transfer pricing may alter the inter-country allocation of declared profits, but as long as there is no leakage out of the system, it does not alter the group's total profits and hence its potential tax liability to the home government.

In sum, with home-based MNCs, not only is the tax potential higher, the scope for tax avoidance or evasion is smaller. It is important to note that most advanced nations have tax rules or Treasury regulations designed to prevent fiscal emigration, the transfer of assets to foreign entities, and other moves where gaining a tax advantage is the main objective, with unauthorized moves resulting in severe tax liabilities on hidden reserves or deemed gains and/or criminal penalties.

Although the global firm is exposed to many jurisdictions, it usually has a home government and a home tax authority. It therefore has a legal and a fiscal nationality that matters to it more than others.

The International Competitive Advantage of the Firm

Consider the German chemical industry, the Swiss pharmaceutical industry, and the Japanese computer industry, which are world-class leaders in their fields. Assume that the American chemical industry, or pharmaceutical industry, or

---

[22] *Newsweek,* "How Multinational Firms Use Transfer Pricing to Evade At Least $20 Billion in U.S. Taxes," April 15, 1991.

computer industry is in danger of losing its international competitive advantage because the environment in the home nation has become unfavorable. Couldn't a U.S.–based company, by establishing a local presence in Germany, Japan, or Switzerland, tap into the foreign nation's competitive advantage and so offset its own, home-based disadvantage? The problem lies in the relativity of competitive advantage. Although tapping into German, Japanese, or Swiss innovations, ideas, skills, aptitudes, attitudes, dynamism, or other sources of advantage would probably add to the U.S.–based firm's advantage, it is likely that the German, Japanese, or Swiss companies would benefit even more from these sources of advantage. They are, after all, operating in their own environment and system. They have been there for a long time and are expected to remain there for a long time. The companies are staffed, managed, and owned by citizens who are members of the same national community. Their self-respect, as well as the esteem in which they hold each other, is intimately connected with this membership, and loyalty to the nation is a paramount commitment of all citizens.[23] Social memory, as a system for ensuring serial equity among groups by remembering who made sacrifices in the past,[24] works only if there is long-term (if not permanent) membership and involvement; it works better if there is a multiplicity of ties and networks. Social memory functions in a nation but not between nations. Foreigners and foreign entities may never gain full acceptance into a national community and its social memory—or even if they do, it requires a very long time. Moreover, top people like to deal with top people, and the local head of a foreign-based group may be perceived as a subordinate who has to report elsewhere. Thus, irrespective of whether explicit "discrimination" exists or not, it is unlikely that a U.S.–based firm can, even with a local presence, plug into a foreign nation's sources of advantage as effectively as competitors who are based, owned, controlled, and managed locally. Furthermore, competitive advantages that can be derived from locating in third countries (e.g., low cost locations) are equally available to the German, Japanese, or Swiss companies; they cannot, therefore, represent a source of *differential* advantage for American firms. Thus: *The primary source of a company's international competitive advantage lies in its home nation; foreign sources of advantage can supplement national sources but cannot be sufficient as a substitute.*

The possibility of joint ventures or strategic alliances with world-class competitors does not alter the thrust of this argument. To get a possible partner

---

[23] H. Morgenthau, *Politics Among Nations* (New York, NY: Knopf, 1978), p. 494.

[24] W. Ouchi, *The M-Form Society* (New York, NY: Avon, 1986), various chapters. A social memory consists of a network of civic, business, and government associations/institutions that not only can remember who has been cooperative and who has been selfish, but also has the ability to reward and punish when the time comes. A social memory is what was called a sense of community, a sense of responsibility, a sense of civic-mindedness. Serial equity is equity which is achieved over a long period of time, so that a group that is disadvantaged today knows that its sacrifices will not be forgotten.

interested in cooperating with one, one must have something to offer, i.e., one must possess a competitive advantage. In industries characterized by rapid technological progress, the nature of this advantage will be intimately linked to continuous innovation, improvement, and investment, and hence it is likely that competitive advantage will be generated in the home nation. In sectors with slow technological developments, competitive assets such as distribution networks or market shares erode less quickly with time; and hence they may be more independent of the current status of the firm's home base. Thus: *In industries with rapid technological progress, strategic alliances are no substitute for creating and sustaining competitive advantage at home.*

What about companies like Nestlé which has 95 percent of its total operations located outside the home nation or Philips with an estimated 85 percent of assets abroad? These companies may be owned, controlled, and managed from the home nation, but surely the home base, with such a small weight in total operations, is not central to the maintenance of competitive advantage? The competitive advantage of Nestlé may be based partly on its national qualities, real or perceived: Swiss quality, Swiss standards, Swiss thoroughness or meticulousness, Swiss management, and the reputation of all things Swiss in the eyes of foreigners. If so, severing the links with the home nation and with Swiss people and attitudes would severely disadvantage the company. The impact of the home nation's reputation is likely to be more pronounced in some service industries than in manufacturing industries. In buying services, which are "experience" goods rather than "inspection" goods, reputation can be of decisive importance, and reputation is often national. In banking, moreover, the home nation's performance affects its banks' ability to raise funds in international markets and the price they have to pay. Thus: *The reputation and qualities of the home nation may be an important source of advantage for a firm operating internationally, in spite of the fact that the home nation may account for only a small percentage of worldwide assets and operations.*

It is noteworthy that almost all of the so-called MNCs (for which such data is available) do the bulk of their R&D in the home nation. For example, a 1983 survey of 23 German MNCs showed that 83 percent of their R&D personnel was concentrated in the home nation (which accounted for only 65 percent of total employment). [25] Du Pont has 90 percent of its R&D personnel in the United States in 1989 (compared with 65 percent of its total assets and 76 percent of its total employment).[26] The same tendency appears to be more pronounced in small country "multinationals": for Philips, 40 percent of R&D is said to be concentrated in the home nation, which accounts for only 15 percent of total assets. Another way of saying this is that, within the MNC, the

---

[25] M. Wortmann, "Multinationals and the Internationalization of R&D: New Developments in German Companies," *Research Policy* (April 1990).

[26] Annual report.

R&D intensity is higher for the parent company at home than for overseas subsidiaries. Thus, for the sample of German MNCs mentioned above, R&D intensity (in terms of manpower) was 9.6 percent in Germany compared to 3.6 percent abroad. This is nothing new. The nation where the bulk of a company's R&D takes place indicates where the strategic core of its innovative effort lies. Innovation requires integrated and strategic decision making. In innovative activities, the home nation is the locomotive, assuming a leading role out of proportion to its weight in total operations. Thus: *The home nation is the center of a firm's innovative efforts, and it is where strategic and integrated decisions are made.*

Consider the case of "multinationals" who suffer from an unfavorable home environment but who have "strong" overseas operations established at a time when the home nation was more dominant and dynamic. Couldn't the group maintain its overall strength by relying on its overseas strength to compensate for its domestic weakness? The problem again lies in the relativity of competitive advantage. The overseas subsidiaries in Germany or Japan may indeed be strong in relation to the parent company, but this does not mean that they are necessarily strong in comparison with their local (German or Japanese) competitors. What happens then? A senior executive of the Japanese subsidiary of a foreign chemicals company commented: "Twenty years ago I spent every night at the best restaurants in Tokyo, being entertained by the chief executives of major Japanese companies, who wanted to gain access to our technology through joint ventures or licensing. . . . Today. . .no one asks me out to dinner anymore."[27] It becomes only a matter of time before profits and market shares tumble.

It is possible that, at some point in time, an overseas subsidiary may show a better profitability than the parent company. This may be the result of the home and host nations being in different phases of the business cycle. It may be due to the fact that the subsidiary is the global home base for a segment or product line that is going through good times. More commonly, however, it may simply be the consequence of the particular foreign market being more protected than the home market; for example, in the 1980s, the European automotive markets were more protected against Japanese competition than was the U.S. market. Whatever the case, this differential profitability is likely to be a temporary phenomenon and will not contribute to the competitive advantage of the parent or the subsidiary unless the profits are reinvested in continuous improvement and innovation.

Another problem is that when the parent company is under siege, it will milk or sell its overseas subsidiaries to save itself. Faced with falls in earnings in the short term, the likelihood of hostile raids, criticism by shareholders, and a generally short-term mentality, U.S. companies have been selling their stakes in Japan.[28] For example, faced with the need to reduce borrowing and with a

---

[27] *The McKinsey Quarterly* (Winter 1990), p. 24.

[28] *Business Week,* March 12, 1990, pp. 20–21.

quarterly loss, Avon Products sold its Japanese subsidiary for $408 million in February 1990. In 1991, Chrysler sold half of its stake in Mitsubishi Motors for $592 million to smooth over a third-quarter plunge in profits. Honeywell sold half of its stake in Yamatake-Honeywell for $407 million in 1989. And in Britain, the engineering group Davy Corp., faced a half-year loss and a collapse in its share price, sold its German subsidiary, the jewel in the crown, Zimmer AG, to the Metallgesellschaft group for DM 228 million in cash, in February 1991.[29] Thus: *Lack of international competitiveness at home is unlikely to be compensated by overseas operations, but may result in the harvesting of the latter.*

Finally, what about the possibility of shifting the home base to take advantage of a more favorable environment? If a company has 60 percent or more of its assets, operations, and people in one country, it is hard to see how it could transfer the 60 percent wholesale to another country. Shifting the home base is not the same thing as shifting a *divisional* headquarters or changing the registered office (i.e., the legal address) of the holding company for political or tax reasons. What can be located abroad is the home base for a particular segment, business, or product line, especially when it is new to the company and/or the group's involvement results from the acquisition of an existing company abroad, which then becomes the home base for that business. Despite its global mandate, however, the subsidiary would still have to report to a parent company. Moreover, the shifting of the registered office for tax avoidance purposes is severely controlled. As for *corporate* headquarters, it is simply not effective to have it far removed from the nation where most of the operations are located. Thus: *The company as a whole cannot easily move its home base; it needs its home nation and has a strong interest in contributing to make it a dynamic and competitive base.*

Implications and Conclusions

Well-known companies such as IBM, General Motors, Sony, Honda, Matsushita, Philips, Unilever, Nestlé, Thomson, Hyundai, Daewoo, Tatung, and so on have been variously called by many names—the international, multinational, transnational, global, or stateless corporation. Are these companies national or are they what these adjectives suggest, something that transcends and is separate from nations? To answer this question, the following criteria should be applied:

◆ In which nation or nations is the bulk of the corporation's assets and people located?

---

[29] *International Herald Tribune*, February 7, 1991 and February 8, 1991.

◆ By whom are the local subsidiaries owned and controlled, and in which nation is the parent company owned and controlled?

◆ What is the nationality of the senior positions (executive and board posts) at the parent company, and what is the nationality of the most important decision makers at the subsidiaries in host nations?

◆ What is the legal nationality of the parent company? To whom would the group as a whole turn for diplomatic protection and political support in case of need?

◆ Which is the nation where tax authorities can, if they choose to do so, tax the group on its worldwide earnings rather than merely its local earnings?

The relevance and significance of corporate nationality are revealed as one goes over the questions. These criteria usually produce an unambiguous answer: that it is a national corporation with international operations (i.e., foreign subsidiaries).

There are two exceptions to this answer. First, there are, as noted earlier, the binational companies which are owned, controlled, and staffed in two home nations, and whose assets have two centers of gravity. Secondly, there are the firms from small nations, for whom the home nation accounts for a small percentage of total assets and operations; however, companies such as Nestlé, Philips, and Ericsson satisfy all the other criteria for being Swiss, Dutch, or Swedish, and it is noteworthy that the Swiss, Dutch, or Swedes have no doubt in their minds as to the national character of these enterprises.

Thus, apart from the binational companies, there are no multinational, transnational, or global enterprises, only national firms with international operations.

Who Is Us? If we think in terms of MNCs, TNCs, or global firms, the power of associations and connotations will draw our attention towards the imagery of a single world economy, in which Reich's question "Who is us?" becomes irrelevant. In this borderless world, the behavior of the global corporation is said to be driven solely by pure economic rationality on a global scale. If a nation loses out in, say, the global firm's location of new investment, the possibility of bias or discrimination is *ex hypothesi* ruled out, because of this assumption of "rationality." If, on the other hand, we recognize these firms to be national firms with international operations, we will ask whether they are American, Japanese, German, Swiss, Dutch, British, or what? If corporations are no longer transnational or global, then depending on who we are, they are either national or foreign.

What about foreign companies that undertake manufacturing, even R&D and design, in the United States and that provide employment to American workers and managers? Reich implies that these firms may be more American than American corporations that have international operations.[30] To address his question "who is us?" we can apply the criterion of corporate nationality and compare Toyota, Nissan, and Honda (which have production facilities in the United States) with Ford and GM (which have extensive international operations).

◆ *Center of Gravity*—In 1989, GM had 76 percent of its assets and 69 percent of its employees in the United States. Ford and GM produce 55 to 65 percent (in units) of their worldwide output of cars in the United States. For Honda, arguably the most internationalized of all Japanese automotive manufacturers, the United States represented only 22 percent of total manufacturing workers worldwide as of March 1991 (63 percent of total assets and total employees being concentrated at home). Honda, Nissan, and Toyota produce 70 percent to 90 percent (in units) of their total output at home. Thus, the United States matters much more to U.S. firms than to their foreign rivals; the destiny of U.S. companies is more tied to that of the United States, and they are likely to be particularly receptive to demands and pressures from the United States.

◆ *Ownership and Control*—Honda US, Toyota US, and Nissan US are owned and controlled by their parent companies in Japan, which themselves are owned and controlled in Japan. The subsidiaries' profits accrue to the parents. The home currency is the Yen. The U.S. subsidiaries are not listed on U.S. stock exchanges and so cannot be owned directly by Americans. The important decisions are made by the Japanese. GM and Ford are majority owned by U.S. citizens and institutions, and are controlled from the United States by Americans. Their worldwide profits accrue to the United States. The home currency is the dollar.

◆ *People*—There are no non-Japanese on the parent company boards of Honda, Toyota, and Nissan or in their top management positions. The U.S. workers and managers of these companies are a minority compared to their counterparts in Japan. with Ford and GM, top management and the parent board are American, and the U.S. workforce is the majority.

◆ *Legal Nationality*—Toyota US is a U.S. corporation because it is incorporated in the United States, but the parent company is Japanese. In the event of a conflict of interest, Toyota may ask the Japanese government or the Japanese lobby to intervene in the United States. Ford or GM could never call on a foreign government to intercede with the U.S. government.

◆ *Tax Domicile*—Ford and GM pay U.S. taxes on a worldwide basis; Honda,

---

[30] Reich (1990), op. cit.

Toyota, and Nissan pay U.S. taxes on a local basis, i.e., on the basis of the income in the United States.

Thus, because of the special nature of the links between the corporation and its home nation and because of the citizenship of the majority of its owners, managers, and workers, a "national" company with international operations is "one of us." It is entitled to support from its home nation, if only because it usually pays more tax to the home government than to any other government.

Corporate Nationality and National Competitiveness Companies tend to concentrate their mainstream innovative efforts and strategic decision making in the home nation. This means that the most important and the most skill-intensive jobs will be located in the home nation, and that exports will be generated on the back of innovation. This process enhances the nation's standard of living.

Foreign companies may make the United States their home base for a particular business segment or product line, but their home nation remains their home base for the corporate group as a whole. Foreign companies may indeed provide jobs and carry out R&D, engineering, or design in the United States but it would be interesting to compare the R&D intensity of foreign-owned subsidiaries in the United States with that of their parents and that of U.S. corporations. It is also noteworthy that, even with such a localized manufacturer as Honda in the United States, recent federal and private studies show that the "domestic content" or local valued-added of its cars is not as high as had hitherto been thought.[31]

Implications for Theory, Research, and Pedagogy If, as I have argued, the multinational corporation does not exist, how would this affect the theory of the multinational corporation? The existence of the theory could be preserved by arguing that the expression "MNC" is to be understood as merely a shorthand for national or binational firms with international operations. If so, uniformity will be replaced by diversity. The search for a universal theory will no longer be possible, once the umbrella term has been discarded. Instead, we will recognize that there are differences and similarities in the international operations of firms from different home nations, with regard to:

◆ Why do they go abroad? What are the differences and similarities in the motives for going abroad, and in the transferable competitive advantage that makes it possible to go abroad successfully?

◆ How do they operate abroad? Do firms from different nations show

---

[31] *Business Week*, "Honda, Is It an American Car?" November 18, 1991.

different patterns as between exporting, producing abroad, licensing, joint venture, subcontracting, and so on?

◆ Where do they go? Do firms from different nations have different geographical preferences?

Similarly, the search for universal, uniform recipes on how to manage the transnational or global enterprise would give way to a more complex and variegated view. Not only do parent companies from different home bases display different practices and values, but, within the same corporate group, there may be differences between the parent and each of its overseas subsidiaries, depending on the strength of local institutions, practices, and values.[32] And these differences may continue to exist as long as nations continue to be the focus of people's sense of belonging and identification as well as a major component of their personal identities. This view of the nation as "community" (but as national community, endowed with the attributes of independence, continuance for the future, and sovereignty) to which people belong (and to which their forefathers belonged and their descendants will belong) may help to explain why the removal of barriers need not undermine the vitality of nations. This is confirmed by the experience of history, which shows that the world was more borderless in the period 1870–1913 than it is today, in the sense that the barriers to trade, capital movements, and migration were lower then.[33] Yet nations, and the frenzied nationalism that led to war, had not withered away.

Although this article has focussed on the concept of nationality, to recognize the existence of nations is not the same thing as to advocate nationalism. Nor is the sense of belonging to a national community incompatible with membership of both sub-national communities and of the world community. To quote the founding father of the national school of political economy: "As the individual chiefly obtains by means of the nation and in the nation mental culture, power of production, security, and prosperity, so is the civilization of the human race only conceivable and possible by means of the civilization and development of the individual nations."[34]

---

[32] The transfer of management practices between national systems is discussed by Richard Whitley, *Societies, Firms and Markets in East Asia* (forthcoming), Chapter 8.

[33] *The Economist,* "The State of the Nation-State," December 22, 1990.

[34] Friedrich List, *The National System of Political Economy* (originally published in 1841), Chapter 15.

READING 34   JOINT VENTURES IN THE FACE OF GLOBAL COMPETITION

Benjamin Gomes-Casseres

ABSTRACT. This article presents a framework that helps managers decide when to use a joint venture to do business abroad. It recommends a joint venture when a firm needs to expand its capabilities to compete successfully, but not when it will merely exploit an existing advantage. A joint venture is also not recommended when there are potential conflicts of interest between the partners. If a firm prefers whole ownership but host government policies restrict foreign ownership, some multinational corporations prefer not to invest, but managers can often bargain for exceptions to restrictive policies. A firm is usually in a strong bargaining position if it brings advanced technology or is willing to make major investments. Governments tend to have the upper hand if they control access to an attractive domestic market.

American firms seem to have discovered a new strategy for competing abroad: joint ventures. Until a decade ago, many U.S. multinational companies (MNCs) shunned joint ventures, arguing that shared ownership led to loss of control and profits. As one General Motors executive put it, "If it was worth doing, it was worth getting all the benefits." In search of ways to bolster their global competitive advantages, these same firms are now finding new merits in joint ventures. (Let us define a joint venture as any affiliate of an MNC where the equity is partly owned by another firm, usually one from the host country. This definition excludes non-equity cooperative ventures, such as licensing.)

General Motors is a case in point. Until the early 1970s, it owned 100 percent of the equity in each of its subsidiaries abroad. By 1975, six of GM's forty foreign subsidiaries were owned jointly with another firm, usually one from the host country. Since then, twelve out of twenty of GM's new foreign subsidiaries have been joint ventures! In the United States itself, the company launched its joint venture with Toyota in 1983, a cornerstone of its strategy to expand its small-car offerings. GM's joint ventures in Korea (with Daewoo) and Japan (with Isuzu and Suzuki) are also important elements in this strategy.

General Motors is not alone in its new-found love for joint ventures. Evidence from industries as diverse as cosmetics and computers suggests that, after insisting on whole ownership abroad in the 1960s, U.S. multinationals began to use joint ventures more extensively in the early 1970s.[1] This trend

---

[1] In 1969, 31 percent of the new foreign manufacturing ventures of large U.S. multinationals were jointly owned with local partners, compared with 41 percent six years later. See B. Gomes-Casseres, "Joint Venture Cycles: The Evolution of Ownership Strategies of U.S. MNEs, 1945–1975" in *Cooperative Strategies in International Business,* eds. F. J. Contractor and P. Lorange (Lexington, MA: Lexington Books, 1988).

seems to have accelerated in the early 1980s, to the point where one prominent international consultant claimed that "no company can stay competitive in the world today singlehandedly."[2] Among the U.S. firms forming major joint ventures abroad are Honeywell (with France's Bull and Japan's NEC), AT&T (with Italy's Olivetti and Holland's Philips), and Whirlpool (also with Philips). In addition, scores of firms have recently entered the Chinese or South Korean markets with joint ventures: these include Johnson & Johnson, Gillette, Heinz, Procter & Gamble, Corning Glass, W.R. Grace, Xerox, General Electric, Rohm & Haas, McCormick, and Allied-Signal.

Business leaders and researchers cite five main reasons for the rising popularity of joint ventures. First, the governments of many countries with attractive domestic markets—including China and South Korea—try to restrict foreign ownership. Second, many U.S. firms have found that host country partners could help them enter new markets quickly by providing management expertise and local connections.[3] Such help is particularly important because of the intensifying competition from European and Japanese carmakers, which is a third reason for U.S. firms' increasing use of joint ventures. These competitors are often willing to settle for joint ventures in host countries where U.S. firms have insisted on whole ownership.[4] Fourth, foreign firms, especially from Europe and Japan, have become more attractive joint venture partners for U.S. multinational corporations as their technological capabilities and market presence have grown. Finally, in many industries global scale is becoming a distinct advantage in R&D and production, leading all but the largest firms to consider joint ventures as a way to achieve such scale and share risks.[5]

Joint Versus Whole Ownership

This evidence suggests that joint ventures can be more useful in global competition than managers of U.S. multinational corporations thought just a decade ago. But does this mean that the old reasoning was wrong? By no means. Joint ventures still entail huge costs when used at the wrong time. The loss of control is real, as are the risks of creating new competitors, damaging the firm's reputation, and eroding its technological edge.

As a result of such costs, joint ventures are often unstable. GM and its South

---

[2] Kenichi Ohmae quoted in "Are Foreign Partners Good for U.S. Companies?" *Business Week,* 28 May 1984.

[3] Extensive anecdotal evidence on the role of joint ventures in providing local connections in China and Japan can be found in S. Goldenberg, *Hands across the Ocean* (Boston: Harvard Business School Press, 1988).

[4] Evidence for the automobile, automotive parts, food, computer, and pharmaceutical industries is in L.G. Franko, "New Forms of Investment in Developing Countries by U.S. Companies: A Five Industry Comparison," *Columbia Journal of World Business,* Summer 1987, pp. 39–56.

[5] See T. Hout et al., "How Global Companies Win Out," *Harvard Business Review,* September–October 1982, pp. 98–108.

Korean partner Daewoo are blaming each other for the disappointing exports from their formerly promising joint venture. Disagreements between AT&T and its computer partner Olivetti have also made the pages of the business press. And a highly profitable joint venture between the chemical firms Hercules and Montedison was quietly dissolved when the latter bought the former's shares. These are not isolated cases. Empirical studies suggest that anywhere between one-third and two-thirds of joint ventures eventually break up.[6]

But why do so many firms enter into joint ventures that eventually cost them headaches and money? There are two explanations for instability in any joint venture. First, the partners simply made a mistake: they formed a joint venture when it may not have been the best thing to do, or they joined up with the wrong partner. Second, their initial decision was right, but conditions changed so that the joint venture was no longer useful.[7] In both cases, the joint venture form itself is not to blame. It is more likely that the process for deciding when to use joint or whole ownership was inadequate.

There is a time and a place for joint ventures in a firm's global strategy. Recognizing that time and place allows a firm's managers to avoid partnerships that end in costly divorces. It also allows them to evaluate from time to time, before serious disagreements arise, whether their joint ventures are still useful. This article presents a framework to help managers decide when a joint venture is appropriate, and when it is not.

Host Government Restrictions But even when an MNC prefers to own all the equity in a subsidiary, it may not be able to do so. Governments of countries such as India, Mexico, China, and even France try to encourage joint ventures with local firms in a variety of ways. In China, for example, major sectors are reserved for local firms or joint ventures. The French government might use subtler ways to favor local firms and joint ventures, such as national standards and preferential procurement.

Does this mean that the MNC's choice between joint and whole ownership is irrelevant in these cases? No. All governments with restrictive ownership policies have, at one time or another, made exceptions for firms insisting on

---

[6] In one McKinsey and Coopers & Lybrand study, 70 percent of the joint ventures broke up. See "Corporate Odd Couples," *Business Week,* 21 July 1986, pp. 100–105.

In L.G. Franko's pioneering work on the topic, one third of the joint ventures were eventually dissolved. See his *Joint Venture Survival in Multinational Corporations* (New York: Praeger, 1971).

[7] Two articles in the Summer 1987 *Columbia Journal of World Business* present unconventional views on joint venture instability. My own "Joint Venture Instability: Is It a Problem?" analyzes the two types of explanations noted in the text. It also suggests that joint ventures can often be transitional forms that are expected to give way to whole ownership after they achieve their purpose. If so, joint venture instability is a sign of success, not failure.

Roehl and Truitt argue that partner disagreements are not only inevitable, they are also useful. See T.W. Roehl and J.F. Truitt, "Stormy, Open Marriages Are Better: Evidence from U.S., Japanese, and French Cooperative Ventures in Commercial Aircraft," *Columbia Journal of World Business,* Summer 1987.

whole ownership. IBM, for instance, recently negotiated a wholly owned subsidiary in Mexico. Foreign investors in India, too, have found creative ways to respond to the government's demands; sometimes they retained management control of critical activities, while at other times they gained exceptions to the demand for shared equity.[8] In their efforts to attract foreign investors, the governments of South Korea, Venezuela, and even China are also softening their ownership restrictions.

Firms preferring whole ownership in such restrictive countries might thus be able to bargain for an exception. But not every MNC has the bargaining chips necessary to pull this off. My framework also helps managers identify the strengths and weaknesses of their firms in such negotiations.

Evidence from a variety of sources supports the guidelines presented below. I used statistical data collected at Harvard in the 1970s to identify when and why U.S. multinational corporations chose to use joint ventures in the past, and when they did not (see the Appendix).[9] The results of this analysis are consistent with studies based on recent, but more limited, data from researchers at Wharton.[10] I also interviewed more than forty international executives from five major global companies to understand the dilemmas they faced. I learned that many factors influenced the ownership decision, but that only the few discussed here were critical.

Deciding When to Use a Joint Venture

Assuming that managers are free to choose the ownership structure for a foreign venture, the decision should depend on their strategies for managing the firm's capabilities and geographic scope. The role of the venture in these strategies influences the *costs and benefits of joint as compared with whole ownership*.[11]

---

[8] See D. J. Encarnation and S. Vachani, "Foreign Ownership: When Hosts Change the Rules," *Harvard Business Review,* September–October 1985, pp. 152–160.

[9] The data was collected by the Harvard Multinational Enterprise Project, as described in J. P. Curhan et al., *Tracing the Multinationals: A Sourcebook on U.S.–based Enterprises* (Cambridge, MA: Ballinger, 1977).

[10] See S. J. Kobrin, "Trends in Ownership of U.S. Manufacturing Subsidiaries in Developing Countries: An Interindustry Analysis" in Contractor and Lorange (1988).

[11] For recent theoretical perspectives on the costs and benefits of joint ventures, see my "Ownership Structures of Foreign Subsidiaries: Theory and Evidence," *Journal of Economic Behavior and Organizations,* in press;

E. Anderson and H. Gatignon, "Modes of Foreign Entry: A Transaction Cost Analysis and Propositions," *Journal of International Business Studies,* Fall 1986, pp. 1–26; and

J. Hennart, "A Transaction Cost Theory of Equity Joint Ventures," *Strategic Management Journal,* July–August 1988, pp. 36–74.

Pioneering work on this topic appears in J. M. Stopford and L. T. Wells, Jr., *Managing the Multinational Enterprise: Organization of the Firm and Ownership of the Subsidiaries* (New York: Basic Books, 1972).

Expanding or Exploiting Capabilities Whether a joint venture is appropriate depends on the capabilities and goals of the firm. In the GM-Toyota joint venture, each partner contributed in an area in which the other was weak. GM brought its U.S. distribution network to the deal, and Toyota brought its small-car designs and efficient manufacturing methods. Outside the U.S. market, too, GM's need for a low-cost manufacturing base for small cars led to its joint venture with Daewoo in Korea. This venture was to sell 200,000 compact cars in the United States through GM's Pontiac Division. For Daewoo, it was a way to compete against Hyundai in the U.S. market.

The joint venture between AT&T and Olivetti, too, was motivated by complementary capabilities of the two firms. AT&T had little experience doing business abroad, and wanted to sell its minicomputers in Europe. Olivetti, on the other hand, was relatively strong in Europe, but wanted to sell its personal computers in the United States. A similar combination of goals and capabilities brought together Honeywell, Bull, and NEC. The three companies had long-standing supply and licensing relationships, but decided in 1987 to integrate their computer operations further through a freestanding, jointly owned venture. NEC was to supply technology for high-end computers; Honeywell offered an extensive distribution network and customer base in the United States; and Bull was strong in midsize computers and in the French market.

Some Risks of Joint Ventures. These strategies contrast strikingly with those of other firms I studied. Managers from both Gillette and Johnson & Johnson insist that joint ventures are anything but ideal, at least in their core businesses. Gillette's technological edge in making razor blades makes it unnecessary for them to cooperate with other firms. Furthermore, such cooperation might risk sacrificing the high quality standards for which Gillette blades are known worldwide. Gillette headquarters staff make sure subsidiaries maintain these standards by monitoring their raw material supplies, furnishing process equipment, and regularly spot checking final products. Joint venture partners would have little to add to this process and might dilute the control exercised from headquarters.

A commitment to quality and central control is also what drives Johnson & Johnson to shun joint ventures. J&J's business depends greatly on intangible assets such as trademarks, patents, and reputation. Sharing control of such assets with another firm might risk eroding these competitive advantages. For example, a local partner might cut corners to sell in markets where quality was not valued highly, and so hurt J&J's reputation in other areas. Royalty agreements could provide some protection in these areas, reported one executive, but 100 percent ownership provides the best assurance. This is another case where the MNC has little to gain, and much to lose, from a joint venture.

Even J&J, however, uses joint ventures in some situations. It entered the Japanese pharmaceuticals market with a joint venture, partly because of the presence of strong local competitors who had more experience in pharmaceuticals than did J&J. The company also turned to a joint venture to enter the French consumer products market, after failing with a wholly owned venture. French companies had well-established reputations and distribution networks in this market; J&J found that the only effective way to compete with them was to join them.

Ownership Tradeoffs: Capability. These cases suggest that *a joint venture is more appropriate when the firm seeks to expand its capability into new fields, and less appropriate when it aims to exploit an existing competitive advantage.* In GM's joint ventures in Japan and Korea, AT&T's in European computers, and J&J's in French consumer products, a joint venture was used to expand the firm's capabilities through cooperation with a partner that had the needed know-how and market position. On the other hand, in their core businesses Gillette and J&J (and GM in the 1960s) merely exploited the competitive advantages that they already had. Usually a partnership was unnecessary—and in fact it could dilute the firm's advantages.

The competitive advantages of multinational corporations are typically based on their organizational know-how and skills, or on intangible assets such as patents, trademarks, and reputation. By their very nature, such advantages cannot be readily bought from outsiders, as is the case, for example, with machinery, labor, or raw materials.[12] But MNCs can acquire such advantages through a joint venture with another firm, which typically involves some transfer of personnel, provision of training and advice, and cooperative marketing and research. Joint ventures are thus more than just convenient financial vehicles for geographical expansion—indeed, they may be costly mistakes where that is their only rationale. Rather, successful joint ventures are arrangements to acquire capabilities and assets that cannot be purchased through arm's-length transactions.

The examples cited above also illustrate the importance of choosing the right joint venture partner. In each case, the U.S. firm chose a partner that could complement its capabilities—one that was strong in precisely those areas in which the U.S. firm was weak. In this sense, the first criterion for choosing a partner is that the firms be different. The potential for joint gains is greater the more *dissimilar* the partners. But it is also important that their goals be compatible, as discussed in the next section.

My statistical analyses supported these conclusions. I found that U.S. MNCs were less likely to form joint ventures in their core business than in fields in which they had less experience. Similarly, those with extensive experience abroad were less likely to form joint ventures than others, and all seemed to prefer whole ownership in countries with which they were relatively familiar.

---

[12] See D. J. Teece, "The Multinational Enterprise: Market Failure and Market Power Considerations," *Sloan Management Review,* Spring 1981, pp. 3–17.

Firms in businesses that depended on intangible assets such as proprietary technical know-how and product image were particularly unlikely to form joint ventures, as these advantages could be eroded by a misbehaving partner. The case data suggests, however, that local firms can sometimes add to an MNC's local market image when they have established brands and distribution networks.

And even in industries where proprietary technical know-how was important, those firms that needed to *acquire* technology to compete effectively often used joint ventures to do so. Thus high-technology firms exhibited two extreme behaviors: either they were dead set against joint ventures or else they found these arrangements critical to success. Until recently IBM took the former position; firms like Honeywell and AT&T now argue the latter. Which side of the debate these high-technology firms are on depends, once again, on whether they are exploiting or expanding their technological capabilities.

Global or Local Scope   The cases discussed above begin to illustrate another factor important to the choice of ownership structure. In insisting on wholly owned subsidiaries, both Johnson & Johnson and Gillette were concerned with the effect of the joint venture on their *global strategies*. Both maintained global quality standards that upheld their image and reputation worldwide. The risk of a joint venture stemmed from the fact that the partner, often a local firm, was concerned only with *local strategies,* where lower standards might suffice.

This is one specific illustration—probably the most important one—of the old adage that partners in a joint venture need to have compatible goals. That is a second criterion in selecting a partner. In contrast with the condition about complementary capabilities, here the greater the *similarity* between the partners, the lower the likelihood of conflicts. Of course, the geographic scopes of no two firms are alike, especially not those of multinational corporations and local partners. But the goals that each has for the joint venture should be alike, which can often be the case for MNCs following multidomestic, rather than global, strategies.[13]

Ownership Tradeoffs: Scope.   The potential for conflict between an MNC's global strategy and a host country partner's more localized concerns appears in many forms. Firms pursuing a global strategy often incur costs in one location to benefit their operations elsewhere.[14] Local profits in such cases are secondary to global profits. But a local partner would, of course, be concerned only with

---

[13] The distinction between global and multidomestic strategies rests on whether the MNC integrates its worldwide operations or pursues separate strategies in each host country. See Hout et al. (1982).

[14] See G. Hamel and C.K. Prahalad, "Do You Really Have a Global Strategy?" *Harvard Business Review,* July–August 1985, pp. 139–148.

local profitability, and so would try to block policies that represented net costs to the joint venture but net benefits to the MNC. This suggests that *joint ownership with a local firm may not be appropriate for ventures that are to be integrated into the MNC's global strategy.*

IBM followed this rule religiously in the 1960s and 1970s. Originally, IBM had managed its six plants in Europe independently of each other, as each served a local market. In the early 1960s the firm decided to merge them and manage them as parts of an integrated regional system. Products and components were traded among the plants, and all followed similar marketing and product strategies. Since then, explained former CEO Jacques Maisonrouge, "The control issue [has become] critical, because optimization of the whole system was not equal to optimization of the subparts."[15] Partly because joint venture partners would be interested only in optimization of the "subpart" in which they had a share, IBM has traditionally insisted on whole ownership.

The recent disagreements between General Motors and its South Korean partner also point to a conflict of interest based on differences in geographic scope. The joint venture's sales in the United States were running 33 percent below target in mid-1988, and Daewoo lost $40 million on the deal in the first half of that year alone. Daewoo and Korean auto analysts blamed GM for failing to promote the car in the United States and for not placing a high priority on it. On the fact of it, GM would seem to have stronger incentives for promoting car sales from its wholly owned divisions than from the joint venture. Similarly, Daewoo wants to expand in its local market, but GM is cold to the idea. As a result, Daewoo has been forced to turn to Japanese suppliers for technology to make a new inexpensive "people's car," a pet project of the president of Korea.[16]

Global Strategies and Expanding Capabilities. The relationship between the U.S. firm Hercules and Montedison, Italy's chemicals giant, illustrates both aspects of the joint venture decision: management of capabilities and of geographic scope. In 1982, Montedison launched a strategy to "internationalize" the company by using joint ventures. According to one of the company's top planners, joint ventures would be used "where Montedison had good technology and decent business positions, and where it needed to grow, but couldn't do so alone." Two such fields were polypropylene plastics and pharmaceuticals.

Montedison developed a new polypropylene process that slashed electricity costs by 30 percent and steam use by 90 percent. The process also used a lower-grade raw material than other technologies then on the market, and the finished product had a number of advantages. But Montedison's global market position in polypropylene was weak. It held about 17 percent of European capacity, but had failed to enter the U.S. market with a wholly owned subsidiary

---

[15] Talk at Harvard Business School, 17 April 1985.

[16] See "Is the GM-Daewoo Deal Running on Empty?" *Business Week,* 12 September 1988, p. 55.

some years earlier. The costs of learning to operate in an unfamiliar environment and building market share from scratch proved too high for Montedison.

Hercules was the dominant polypropylene producer in the United States. It also had the largest market share worldwide, just slightly ahead of Shell. In addition, Hercules was strong in areas where Montedison was weak: product applications and marketing. On the other hand, Hercules was weak in process technology, having traditionally depended on licenses from Montedison.

This combination was ideal for a joint venture. Montedison could expand its capabilities in downstream activities and in the U.S. market, while Hercules could do the same in upstream activities. Himont, a new fifty-fifty joint venture between the companies, thus became the world market leader when both parents transferred their polypropylene businesses to it in 1983. Montedison's new technology was installed in all Himont plants, and the joint venture adopted Hercules's successful marketing strategies. In this case, Montedison's global strategy did not seem to conflict with the goals of Hercules, because the latter, too, operated on a global scale.

But such conflicts did appear in another joint venture between these two companies. Before launching Himont, Montedison and Hercules each owned 50 percent of Adria Labs, a pharmaceutical company in the United States that sold a highly successful anticancer drug. To Montedison, Adria was primarily a sales arm of its pharmaceutical division, which developed and produced the drug. But Hercules wanted Adria to be the core of a new, self-sufficient company capable of manufacturing its own products. The costs of such an effort seemed to conflict with Montedison's plans to integrate Adria into its global strategy, which called for introducing to the U.S. market a number of new drugs developed in Italy. As in the case of IBM's regional integration in Europe, control of this venture seemed critical to Montedison. So, at the same time that Hercules and Montedison formed Himont, they also shifted majority ownership of Adria Labs to Montedison.

My statistical analysis yielded additional evidence of the link between global strategies and ownership. It suggested that vertical integration between a joint venture and its partners could affect the likelihood of conflicts between them. Subsidiaries that sold a substantial share of their output to the MNC or to other subsidiaries in the MNC's system were less likely than others to have joint ownership. Such sales might be part of a global strategy in which each subsidiary produces what it is best at. The transfer prices used in these transactions are likely to be a perennial source of conflict with local joint venture partners. The MNC will want prices that maximize its global profits, which implies shifting profits to wholly owned subsidiaries. The local partner will, of course, want just the opposite.

The effect of vertical integration inside the host country was different. When an MNC's venture depended on raw material inputs from local suppliers, particularly when there were few suppliers, it was likely to have joint ownership. In such situations, MNCs apparently find it advantageous to give the supplier a stake in the venture to assure a constant supply. Transfer prices for the inputs might be a problem here too, but the local supplier has an even greater incentive to insist on high transfer prices if it does not own a share of the venture.

Negotiating with Host Governments

If, based on the analysis above, MNC managers decide that a joint venture is the best structure for a foreign subsidiary, then the host government is likely to agree. Almost without exception, host government policies have aimed to encourage, not discourage, joint ventures. So it is the multinational corporation preferring *whole* ownership that may have to negotiate with restrictive host country governments.[17]

In such ownership negotiations, MNC managers make tradeoffs among a number of issues, including ownership. An analysis as described above should precede these negotiations, because it suggests why the firm needs whole ownership and how important this is. For example, if control really is "critical," as IBM claimed, then the point should probably not be conceded in negotiations. But if the firm only mildly prefers whole ownership, it may well decide to trade this issue off against others.

The ability of the host government to make the MNC change its position on ownership depends on what it can offer the firm in return. The same is true for the firm's ability to gain an exception to the government's rules. This ability of one party to get its way reflects its *bargaining power* in negotiations. Case and statistical studies suggest that the bargaining power of firms and host governments vary according to the circumstances of the investment.[18]

MNC Strength: Contributions to Country Goals

IBM's ownership negotiations with India in 1978 and with Mexico in 1985 suggest when MNCs can expect to "win" at the bargaining table. The governments of both countries had rules restricting foreign ownership of manufacturing subsidiaries. In the first case, the government enforced this rule strictly, and IBM ended up divesting from India rather than ceding 60 percent of its existing operations to local investors.

---

[17] Of course, in many countries there are other terms to negotiate with host country governments, such as capacity licenses, foreign exchange allocations, tax rates, and so on. This discussion focuses on negotiations about ownership structures.

[18] Theoretical discussions and empirical evidence on the role of bargaining power in ownership negotiations are in my "MNC Ownership Preferences and Host Government Restrictions: An Integrated Approach" (Boston: Harvard Business School, working paper, 1988);

N. Fagre and L.T. Wells, Jr., "Bargaining Power of Multinationals and Host Governments," *Journal of International Business Studies,* Fall 1982, pp. 9–23; and

S. J. Kobrin, "Testing the Bargaining Power Hypothesis in the Manufacturing Sector in Developing Countries," *International Organization* 41 (1987): 609–638.

In the second case, IBM gained a rare exception to the Mexican rules, and set up a wholly owned venture to manufacture personal computers. What made the difference?

One difference between the two cases was that Mexico in 1985 was more desperate for foreign investment than India was in 1978. India was pursuing a fairly successful strategy of self-sufficiency and nonalignment that led it to want local control of an indigenous computer industry. Foreign investment was valued only because it brought in skills that contributed to this goal. Clearly, IBM could supply these skills, but so could a number of second-tier U.S. and European companies that were willing to share ownership with Indian firms.[19] IBM, for its part, felt that yielding to India's demand for a joint venture would set precedents that it could not afford, given its previously untarnished record of complete ownership worldwide.

The situation in Mexico was different. The country had just endured its second foreign exchange crisis in a decade and was well on its way to a third. This situation led the Mexican government to soften its restrictions on foreign investment, much as other developing countries had been doing. Mexico, too, wanted computer technology, but in addition it wanted foreign investors for the capital they would bring in, the exports they could generate, and the confidence they might instill in the country's recovery.

IBM's promise to transfer technology to Mexican firms and export a major part of the output from its Mexican operations proved to be just the sweetener the government needed to approve the wholly foreign-owned investment. During the negotiations, IBM agreed to triple its planned investment to $90 million, export 90 percent of the output, and help the Mexicans set up, run, and fund a semiconductor development center. IBM also agreed to a number of provisions that favored local producers: it promised to buy inputs from local suppliers, develop a local dealer network, and sell its final output in the domestic market at prices that were 15 percent above international levels. (This last provision implicitly protected higher-cost domestic producers.)

The key bargaining chips that IBM wielded in this negotiation were its *technology* and *degree of commitment to the host market*. In high-technology fields with high barriers to entry, producers from developing countries usually cannot break into world markets without the help of a global firm. And many governments, following Japan's example, are promoting precisely these types of industries. The ownership regulations in a number of countries explicitly make exceptions to projects in high-technology sectors. But even when such exceptions are not mandated by law, MNCs contributing to the host government's goals are in a strong bargaining position in ownership negotiations.

MNCs making major commitments to restrictive host countries are also

---

[19] See J.M. Grieco, "Between Dependence and Autonomy: India's Experience with the International Computer Industry," *International Organization* 36 (Summer 1982): 609–632.

more likely than others to gain an exception to the ownership rules. My statistical studies suggested that the bargaining power of the MNCs increased with the size of their investment. Aside from the inflow of capital, host country governments also seem to value the substantial managerial skills and domestic linkages that accompany major projects. These factors seem to have been important in the case of IBM in Mexico.

Government Strength: Attractive Markets Historically, the host governments that have had most success enforcing ownership restrictions were those with *attractive domestic markets*. Numerous U.S. firms were forced to form joint ventures in Japan in the 1960s and 1970s, or to license their technologies, because that was the only way to get access to the booming Japanese market. Today, China is using its large and rapidly growing market to gain concessions from MNCs. Until April of 1986, the Chinese government refused to approve wholly foreign-owned ventures; since then W.R. Grace and others have set up such facilities. But the Chinese have continued to encourage joint ventures through a variety of incentives, and foreign firms are often more than willing to comply. Gillette, for example, did not hesitate to set up a joint venture in China, even though it insisted on whole ownership elsewhere. Johnson & Johnson has already formed two joint ventures there; it owns 50 percent of one venture making pharmaceuticals and tampons, and 60 percent of one making Band-Aid bandages.

India, Mexico, and Brazil also have used the attraction of their domestic markets to force MNCs to form joint ventures with local firms. One reason IBM went out of its way to reach an agreement with Mexico was to gain access to the Mexican market and use it as a base to develop a Latin American business. Smaller countries imposing ownership restrictions, such as those in the Andean Common Market, have had much less success. In these instances, foreign investors sometimes preferred to stay away altogether rather than give in to the government's demands.

Alternative Strategies for Firms. Even when the country offers an attractive market, however, managers may feel that the risks of joint ownership in some ventures are too high. What are they to do? First, they should consider whether the venture could be modified to reduce these risks. Maybe the subsidiary could be set up to sell exclusively in the domestic market, rather than in world markets, thus reducing the need for control that stems from following a global strategy. Gillette and Johnson & Johnson seem to have done that in China. Where this is not possible, the solution may well be to decline to invest altogether. My statistical analysis indeed showed that ventures in restrictive countries tended to be less tightly integrated than others into the MNC's networks.

A second option for firms that are forced to concede on the ownership issue is to seek concessions on aspects of control that are less publicly visible.

Sometimes restrictive governments hold their ground on the ownership issue, but allow MNCs to have management control of the operations. Gillette, for example, owns only 49 percent of a ballpoint pen business in Mexico, but controls general administration, manufacturing, finance, and product quality through a management contract. General Motors' managers, too, have found that host country governments are usually more willing to make concessions on management control issues than on the basic demand for some local participation.

The Future of Joint Ventures

Partly for reasons cited above, more and more MNCs have been forming joint ventures abroad in recent years. Are we thus seeing the passing of the traditional form of investing abroad, the wholly owned subsidiary? The answer to this question affects the way global firms will be managed in the 1990s. It depends on trends in the factors that determine the costs and benefits of joint ventures.

The current popularity of joint ventures is not unique. Between 1955 and 1961, the share of joint ventures in the new investment of large American MNCs went from 28 percent to 55 percent. But just as rapidly that share fell to 31 percent in 1969.[20] The 1970s saw another increase in the use of joint ventures abroad, to a new level that seems to have been sustained into the 1980s.

The reasons behind the ebb and flow of joint ventures in the past seem to lie in the changing global strategies of the multinational corporations. The 1950s are sometimes referred to now as a "flag-planting" period; U.S. firms rushed abroad to establish footholds in many countries at the same time. Forming joint ventures with local firms was an ideal way to enter new markets quickly. But the trend in the 1960s was toward consolidation and integration of the firms' global networks, as suggested by the IBM Europe example cited above. Conflicts with joint venture partners, who had purely local concerns, became more common in this period. The U.S. firms thus shunned joint ventures in this period, and even bought out many of the partners who had been useful earlier. This patten may well repeat itself in the future.

Joint Ventures and Globalization   One trend sometimes credited with the popularity of joint ventures in the 1980s is the widening of the competitive arena from national to global markets. Marketers call this the "globalization" of markets; industry analysts point to the increasing need to pursue worldwide economies of scale and scope; and trade statistics reflect the rising competition from a myriad of foreign sources. These trends are probably affecting all industries, even though some, such as telecommunications, are changing more dramatically than others.

---

[20] For a detailed analysis of historical trends in joint venture formation, see my "Joint Venture Cycles" in Contractor and Lorange (1988).

Globalization forces led Montedison to launch the polypropylene joint venture with Hercules. Montedison was traditionally an Italian producer, with minor operations in other European countries. But in the early 1980s all the major chemical firms elsewhere became global competitors. Firms like Hoechst, BASF, ICI, and Dow not only exported from their home bases, but also manufactured abroad, raised capital on international markets, and formed supply and other relationships with each other. These companies used their strengths in one country to help them compete in others, and they drew on technological and managerial resources from several countries.

Montedison's joint venture with Hercules was an effort to move in one leap into the league of global chemical producers. As such, it illustrates how *globalization encourages joint ventures when it drives firms to expand their capabilities and access to markets.* Similarly, firms might form joint ventures to do R&D in industries where costs could not be recouped in national markets alone, such as in telecommunications. Or they might join forces to draw on scientific resources in various countries, as is happening in biotechnology.

But there is another side to the globalization of industries. Firms with operations in various countries often find it profitable to manage these in an integrated way, using one plant to supply the other, or following common marketing and manufacturing strategies. Globalization here implies greater central control of worldwide operations; joint ventures are more of a hindrance than a help in this process. Thus, *globalization discourages joint ventures when it drives firms to integrate their worldwide operations.* Given this tendency, it is not surprising that, once Himont established its position as a leader in global polypropylene production. Montedison bought out Hercules's share.

Opposing forces are thus likely to drive the choice of ownership structure for foreign subsidiaries in global industries. The tension between the need to expand globally and the need to control the network is likely to be felt in industry after industry. International managers will thus continue to struggle with this dilemma in the future. That prospect is clearly better than simply following the current joint venture fad, or blindly pursuing the old preference for whole ownership.

A Final Checklist

A substantial body of evidence now exists to guide managers struggling with this dilemma. The framework I have presented suggests that six questions are critical. For every proposed business investment abroad, managers should ask these questions.

What ownership structure do we prefer, if we are free to choose? In answering this question managers should consider the next two questions. Even when there are restrictions on foreign ownership, it is important to start with this question, because it prepares the firm for negotiations.

Can we exploit an existing competitive advantage, or will we need to expand our capabilities to compete successfully? The stronger the latter possibility, the more attractive a joint venture will be. Of course, a firm may have an advantage in one area, such as technology, but still need to expand its capabilities in another, such as marketing. A joint venture partner should then be chosen to complement the firm's existing capabilities.

Will we be following a globally integrated strategy? If so, a joint venture with a local partner can lead to costly conflicts of interest. The key is to make sure that the partners agree on the level—global or local—at which profits are to be maximized. Potential problems may arise when the MNC supplies or buys from the joint venture, when quality standards exceed requirements of the local market, and when exports from the venture compete with those of the MNC's other subsidiaries.

If the host government restricts foreign ownership, do we have the bargaining power to win an exception? Answering this depends on answering the next question. If the firm's bargaining power is limited, it should consider modifying its strategy for the new business so that whole ownership is no longer critical. It is often possible to learn to live with a forced joint venture by limiting the scope of the venture and negotiating management contracts.

What will we contribute to the country's goals, and how much will we depend on the host government? The key here is whether the firm's contributions to the country are valued highly by the government. Firms bringing advanced technology and willing to make major investments are generally in a strong bargaining position. Conversely, the host government's bargaining position will be stronger the more attractive the domestic market is to the MNC.

Will answers to these questions change with industry evolution? The firm's ownership strategies are likely to vary over time, just as they vary across industries and countries. Thus, each proposal should be evaluated on its own merits. Moreover, a decision made today may need to be revised later. Managers sensitive to the global evolution of their businesses will be able to avoid unnecessary surprises and costs in joint ventures.

Appendix

The framework presented in this article is based partly on extensive statistical analysis of data from almost 200 large American MNCs collected in the 1970s by Harvard's Multinational Enterprise Project. This database is still the most detailed and comprehensive one available on the activities of U.S. MNCs abroad. The sample used here contained information on ownership structure and other characteristics of 1,877 subsidiaries in a broad cross section of countries and industries. I added country variables from the World Bank and industry variables from the Profit Impact of Marketing Strategies (PIMS) database to the Harvard data. I then used binomial regression methods to develop and test a model describing the conditions under which the MNCs chose joint or whole ownership for the subsidiaries in existence in 1975. I tested the applicability of this cross-sectional model over time with earlier data from the same database. Finally, the results of this analysis were complemented with case data on five large MNCs gathered through field interviews in 1985. The statistical results were consistent with these cases, as well as with statistical data collected by other researchers in the 1980s. Further details on the statistical results are in my "Ownership Structures of Foreign Subsidiaries: Theory and Evidence," forthcoming, and "MNC Ownership Preferences and Host Government Restrictions: An Integrated Approach" (1988).

COMPETITION FOR COMPETENCE AND INTERPARTNER LEARNING WITHIN INTERNATIONAL STRATEGIC ALLIANCES

Gary Hamel

ABSTRACT. Global competition highlights asymmetries in the skill endowments of firms. Collaboration may provide an opportunity for one partner to internalize the skills of the other, and thus improve its position both within and without the alliance. Detailed analysis of nine international alliances yielded a fine-grained understanding of the determinants of inter-partner learning. The study suggests that not all partners are equally adept at learning; that asymmetries in learning alter the relative bargaining power of partners; that stability and longevity may be inappropriate metrics of partnership success; that partners may have competitive, as well as collaborative aims, vis-à-vis each other; and that process may be more important than structure in determining learning outcomes.

The Research Question

A skills-based view of the firm It is possible to conceive of a firm as a portfolio of core competencies on one hand, and encompassing disciplines on the other, rather than as a portfolio of product-market entities (Prahalad and Hamel, 1990). As technology bundles, core competencies make a critical contribution to the unique functionality of a range of end-products. An example is Honda's expertise in powertrains, which is applied to products as diverse as automobiles, motorcycles, generators, and lawn mowers. Encompassing disciplines include total quality control, just-in-time manufacturing systems, value engineering, flexible manufacturing systems, accelerated product development, and total customer service. Such disciplines allow a product to be delivered to customers at the best possible price/performance trade-off. Core competencies and value-creating disciplines are precisely the kinds of firm-specific skills for which there are only imperfect external markets, and hence form the raison d'etre for the multinational enterprise (Buckley and Casson, 1985; Caves, 1971; Teece, 1981).

Conceiving of the firm as a portfolio of core competencies and disciplines suggests that inter-firm competition, as opposed to inter-product competition, is essentially concerned with the acquisition of skills. In this view global competitiveness is largely a function of the firm's pace, efficiency, and extent of knowledge accumulation. The traditional 'competitive strategy' paradigm (e.g., Porter, 1980), with its focus on product-market positioning, focuses on only the last few hundred yards of what may be a skill-building marathon. The notion of competitive advantage (Porter, 1985) which provides the means for computing product-based advantages at a given point in time (in terms of cost and differentiation), provides little insight into the process of knowledge acquisition and skill building.

Core competencies and value-creating disciplines are not distributed equally among firms. Expansion-minded competitors, exploiting such firm-specific advantages, bring the skill deficiencies of incumbents into stark relief. The present study was unconcerned with why such discrepancies in skill endowments exist, but was very concerned with the role international strategic alliances might play in effecting a partial redistribution of skills among partners. While 'globalization' has been widely credited for provoking a shift to collaborative strategies (Ghemawat, Porter and Rawlinson, 1986; Hergert and Morris, 1988; Ohmae, 1989; Perlmutter and Heenan, 1986), the ways in which strategic alliances either enhance or diminish the skills which underlie global competitiveness have been only partially specified. *The goal of the present research was to understand the extent to which and means through which the collaborative process might lead to a reapportionment of skills between the partners.*

While skills discrepancies have been recognized as a motivator for international collaboration (Contractor and Lorange, 1988; Root, 1988), the crucial distinction between acquiring such skills in the sense of gaining *access* to them—by taking out a license, utilizing a subassembly supplied by a partner, or relying on a partner's employees for some critical operation—and actually *internalizing* a partner's skills has seldom been clearly drawn. This distinction is crucial. As long as a partner's skills are embodied only in the specific outputs of the venture, they have no value outside the narrow terms of the agreement. Once internalized, however, they can be applied to new geographic markets, new products, and new businesses. For the partners, an alliance may be not only a means for trading access to each other's skills—what might be termed *quasi-internalization*, but also a mechanism for actually acquiring a partner's skills—*de facto internalization.*

A conception of strategic alliances as opportunities for *de facto* internalization was suggested during a major research project on 'competition for competence' in which the author participated (Prahalad and Hamel, 1990). In that study managers often voiced a concern that, when collaborating with a potential competitor, failure to 'out-learn' one's partner could render a firm first dependent and then redundant within the partnership, and competitively vulnerable outside it. The two premises from which this concern issued seemed to be that (1) few alliances were perfectly and perpetually collusive, and (2) the fact that a firm chose to collaborate with a present or potential competitor could not be taken as evidence that that firm no longer harbored a competitive intent vis-à-vis its partner. Indeed, when it came to the competitive consequences of inter-partner learning, the attitudes of some managers in the initial study had shifted from naiveté to paranoia within a few short years. This seemed to be particularly true for managers in alliances with Japanese partners. What was lacking was any systematic investigation of the determinants of inter-partner learning.

Methodology

Thus the research objective was theory development rather than theory extension. The parameters which controlled the choice of research design were: (1) a belief that existing theoretical perspectives illuminated only a small part of the collaborative phenomenon; (2) a desire to identify the determinants of a certain class of collaborative outcomes, i.e., inter-partner learning; and (3) the consequent need for observation that was administratively fine-grained, multi-level and longitudinal. These considerations made inevitable the choice of a research design based on the principles of grounded theory development (Glaser and Strauss, 1967; Mintzberg, 1978; Pettigrew, 1979; Seyle, 1964). Because patterns of causality are extremely complex in most real-world administrative systems, traditional deductive-analytic methodologies force the researcher to declutter the phenomenon by: (1) substituting crude proxies for difficult-to-measure determinants or outcomes; (2) assuming away some of the multidimensionality in causal relationships; and/or (3) narrowing the scope of research. In doing so, much of the potential value of the research is lost. The problem is not that the resulting theories are under-tested (i.e., they fail a test of rigor), but that they are under-developed (i.e., they are so partial in coverage that they illuminate only a fragment of the path between choice, action, and outcome). For the purposes of this study a decision was made not to prematurely prune the collaborative problem into a shape that would fit within the constraints of a deductive methodology.

Grounded theory development proceeded in two stages. In the first stage the goal was to illuminate the basic dimensions of a theory of inter-partner learning. To this end an attempt was made to maximize underlying differences among cases in order to discover those concepts or theoretical categories that were most universal (where the data across cases were most similar), and those that were entirely idiosyncratic (where the data across cases were most divergent). Interviews were initially conducted with 74 individuals across 11 companies concerning nine international alliances. The number of individuals interviewed within each company ranged from three to 11, with six the average. Interviews were typically two hours in length, though a few consumed an entire day. Given concerns over confidentiality on the part of participating firms, several of the participating firms requested anonymity. The 11 firms in the study ranged in size from under $500 million in sales to more than $50 billion. Four of the companies were domiciled in the United States, four within the European Community, and three in Japan. Each firm derived at least 30 percent of its revenue from outside its domestic market. Industries covered included aerospace, chemicals, semiconductors, pharmaceuticals, computers, automobiles, and consumer electronics. In every company managers with responsibility for strategic alliances from both divisional and business unit levels were interviewed. Approximately 40 percent of the interviews were with functional supervisors or first-line employees who worked regularly across the collaborative membrane. Seven of the participating firms had a partner within the sample of 11 firms; in this way both 'sides' of three on-going partnerships were observed. Thus inter-case diversity was achieved along the dimensions of partner nationality and industry affiliation, and agreement type (equity-based joint ventures versus long-term co-marketing, design, and supply relationships).

The anxiety over asymmetric learning expressed by managers in the earlier study was confirmed in the first stage interviewing process. Concerns were of three broad types: (1) concern over the *intent* of partners (collaborative versus competitive, internalization of partner skills versus mere access); (2) concern over the 'openness' of the firm to its partner—what came to be termed *transparency;* and (3) concern over the firm's ability to actually absorb skills from its partner, i.e. *receptivity.* As the core categories that came to constitute the formal internalization model, *intent, receptivity,* and *transparency* were identified as prospective determinants of inter-partner learning. Also emerging from the first round of interviewing was a proposed linkage between learning and inter-partner bargaining power, and, consequently a notion of collaboration as a 'race to learn.'

Having illuminated an overarching formal model, the second stage of research aimed at understanding in detail the processes and mechanisms through which intent, receptivity, and transparency impacted on learning outcomes. This was accomplished through a second round of case-based research, termed 'theoretic sampling' (Glaser and Strauss, 1967: 45–77), because the choice of which cases to compare is directed by the emerging theory. By selecting cases where the researcher hoped to find both maximum and minimum variance along the dimensions of the core model, it was possible to amplify the core model. A further criterion to be satisfied was the need to gain even deeper, more extensive access to the individuals involved in the process of collaborative exchange than had been achieved in first stage interviewing, and to ensure that access was gained to both sides of the collaborative membrane. This was deemed necessary if the researcher was to have any hope of measuring, however crudely, the migration of skills between partners, the criticality of those skills (and hence the extent to which they should be valued and protected or sought by each partner), and ultimately, the competitive consequences of those skill transfers.

These requirements were met in the following ways. Two partnerships, involving five firms (one partnership was triadic), were selected for intensive study. Inter-case differences were minimized to the extent that both partnerships comprised a European firm (or firms) on one side, and a Japanese firm on the other. Thus it was possible to compare the behavior of the European firms, one with another, and the behavior of the Japanese partners, one with another. Both alliances were more than five years old at the time the study commenced, both had received substantial media attention, and were regarded as two of the most important and 'successful' Euro-Japanese alliances. Both partnerships were set within the electronics industry.

At the same time there were potentially significant differences between the cases: one centered around professional products with a 3–5-year life cycle, and the other around a consumer product with a 6–12-month life cycle. One of the European partners had a clear corporate strategy for core competence building, the others did not. The locus of activity for one partnership was based in Europe, the other in Japan. One partnership involved regular and intensive collaboration across the membrane, the other periodic inter-working. One partnership was a joint equity venture, the other a mixture of long- and short-term development and supply contracts. And of course there was the opportunity to compare the behavior of partners based in very different national contexts. The first stage interview process, as well as much of the anecdotal evidence (e.g., *Business Week,* 1989), suggested this difference in national origin might be crucial to learning outcomes.

Each of the five partners agreed to provide access to facilities as well as to key managers and operating employees. Each of the partners also agreed to submit to a minimum of 40 hours of interviewing. While single, week-long research visits were made to the Japanese partners, repeated research visits, extending over two years, were made to the European partners. Interviewing continued until saturation of core categories—intent, transparency, and receptivity—was achieved, i.e., new properties of the categories were no longer emerging. Relying on archival data, as well as interviews with industry analysts, two detailed industry briefing notes were prepared. The detailed research reports which summarize the output of the second stage interviewing are contained in Hamel (1990).

Findings

The six major propositions which grew out of the data are summarized in Table 1. They will be discussed in turn, and the evidence which produced them briefly summarized.

Competitive collaboration Though not always readily admitting it, several partners clearly regarded their alliances as transitional devices where the primary objective was the internalization of partner skills. As one Japanese manager put it:

> We've learned a lot from [our partner]. The [foreign] environment was very far from us—we didn't understand it well. We learned that [our partner] was very good at developing. Our engineers have learned much from the relationship.

A European manager stated that:

> [Our partner] was passionately hungry to find out the requirements of the users in the markets they wanted to serve. We were priming the market for them.

TABLE **1**   A theory of inter-partner learning: Core propositions

1. *Competitive collaboration*

   (a) Some partners may regard internalization of scarce skills as a primary benefit of international collaboration.

   (b) Where learning is the goal, the termination of an agreement cannot be seen as failure, nor can its longevity and stability be seen as evidence of success.

   (c) Asymmetries in learning within the alliance may result in a shift in relative competitive position and advantage between the partners outside the alliance. Thus some partners may regard each other as competitors as well as collaborators.

2. *Learning and bargaining power*

   (a) Asymmetries in learning change relative bargaining power within the alliance: successful learning may make the original bargain obsolete and may, *in extremis,* lead to a pattern of unilateral, rather than bilateral, dependence.

   (b) The legal and governance structure may exert only a minor influence over the pattern of inter-partner learning and bargaining power.

   (c) A partner that understands the link between inter-partner learning, bargaining power, and competitiveness will tend to view the alliance as a race to learn.

3. *Intent as a determinant of learning*

   (a) The objectives of alliance partners, with respect to inter-partner learning and competence acquisition, may be usefully characterized as internalization, resource concentration, or substitution.

   (b) An internalization intent will be strongest in firms which conceive of competitiveness as competence-based, rather than as product-based, and which seek to close skill gaps rather than to compensate for skills failure.

   (c) A substitution intent pre-ordains asymmetric learning; for systematic learning to take place, operators must possess an internalization intent.

4. *Transparency as a determinant of learning*

   (a) Asymmetry in transparency pre-ordains asymmetric learning: some firms and some skills may be inherently more transparent than others.

   (b) Transparency can be influenced through the design of organizational interfaces, the structure of joint tasks, and the 'protectiveness' of individuals.

5. *Receptivity as a determinant of learning*

   (a) Asymmetry in receptivity pre-ordains asymmetric learning: some firms may be inherently more receptive than others.

   (b) Receptivity is a function of the skills and absorptiveness of receptors, of exposure position, and of parallelism in facilities.

6. *The determinants of sustainable learning*

   Whether learning becomes self-sustaining— that is, whether the firm eventually becomes able, without further inputs from its partner, to improve its skills at the same rate as its partner—will depend on the depth of learning that has taken place, whether the firm possesses the scale and volume to allow, in future, amortization of the investment needed to break free of dependence on the partner, and whether the firm possesses the disciplines of continuous improvement.

A manager in a Japanese firm that had to contend with a persistently inquisitive European partner believed that:

> The only motivation for [our European partner] is to get mass manufacturing technology. They see [the alliance] as a short circuit. As soon as they have this they'll lose interest.

This manager believed that the partner would see eventual termination of the agreement as evidence of successful learning, rather than of a failed collaborative venture.

While no manager in the study claimed a desire to 'deskill' partners, there were several cases in which managers believed this had been the outcome of the collaborative process. In these cases the competitive implications of unanticipated (and typically unsanctioned) skill transfers were clearly understood, albeit retrospectively. The president of the Asia-Pacific division of an American industrial products company was in no doubt that his firm's Japanese partner had emerged from their 20-year alliance as a significant competitor:

> We established them in their core business. They learned the business from us, mastered our process technology, enjoyed terrific margins at home, where we did not compete in parallel, and today challenge us outside of Japan.

The divisional vice-president of a Western computer company had a similar interpretation of his firm's trans-Pacific alliance:

> A year and a half into the deal I understood what it was all about. Before that I was as naive as the next guy. It took me that long to see that [our partner] was preparing a platform to come into all our markets.

Yet another manager felt a partner had crossed the line distinguishing collaboration from competition:

> If they were really our partners, they wouldn't try to suck us dry of technology ideas they can use in their own products. Whatever they learn from us, they'll use against us worldwide.

Recognizing the potential danger of turning collaborators into competitors, a senior executive in a Japanese firm hoped his firm's European partners would be 'strong—but not too strong.'

The proposition that partners possessing parallel internalization and international expansion goals would find their relationships more contentious than partners with asymmetric intents arose, in part, from observing the markedly different relationships that existed between three partners in a triadic alliance. The British firm in the alliance, possessing neither an internalization intent nor global expansion goals, enjoyed a placid relationship with its Japanese partner. However, the French and Japanese firms in the alliance, each possessed of ambitious learning and expansion goals, were often at loggerheads. A technical manager in the Japanese firm remarked that:

> The English were easier to work with than the French. The English were gentlemen, but the French were [not]. We could reach decisions very quickly with the English, but the French wanted to debate and debate and debate.

This seemed to be a reaction to the difficulty of bargaining with a partner who possessed equally ambitious learning goals.

In general, whenever two partners sought to extract value in the same form from their partnership—whether in the form of inter-partner learning benefits or short-term economic benefits, managers were likely to find themselves frequently engaged in contentious discussions over value-sharing. The relationships where managers were least likely to be troubled by recurring arguments over value appropriation were those where one partner was pursuing, unequivocably, a learning intent and the other a short-term earnings maximization intent. In such relationships—there were three—one partner was becoming progressively more dependent on the other. That the British firm mentioned above ultimately withdrew from the business on which the alliance was based suggested a fundamental proposition: just as contentiousness does not, by itself, indicate collaborative failure (some managers recognized they had to accept a certain amount of contentiousness as the price for protecting their core skills and gaining access to their partner's), an abundance of harmony and good will does not mean both partners are benefiting equally in terms of enhanced competitiveness. Collaborative success could not be measured in terms of a 'happiness index.'

Learning and bargaining power The link between learning and bargaining power emerged clearly in several cases, one of which is briefly summarized here. A European firm in the study had entered a sourcing agreement with a Japanese partner in the mid-1970s, and later, partly through the use of political pressure, had succeeded in enticing the Japanese partner into a European-based manufacturing joint venture to produce a sophisticated electronics product that had, heretofore, been sourced by the European firm from Japan. At the time the joint venture was entered, the European firm established a corporate-wide goal to gain an independent, 'worldclass,' capability to develop and manufacture the particular product. This was seen as part of a broader corporate-wide effort to master mass manufacturing skills that were viewed as crucial to the firm's participation in a host of electronics businesses. Over the next seven years, the European firm worked assiduously to internalize the skills of its Japanese partner. By the late 1980s the firm had progressed through six of the seven 'steps' it had identified on the road from dependence to independence—where the journey began with a capability for assembling partner-supplied sub-assemblies using partner-specified equipment and process controls, and ended with a capability for simultaneous advance of both product design and manufacturing disciplines (i.e., design for manufacturability, component miniaturization, materials science, etc.), independent of further partner technical assistance.

In interviews with both the European firm and its Japanese partner, it became clear that the bargaining power of the Continental firm had grown as its learning had progressed. For the European firm, each stage of learning, when complete, became the gateway to the next stage of internalization. Successful learning at each stage effectively obsolesced the existing 'bargain,' and constituted a de facto query to the Japanese partner: '*Now* what are you going to do for us?' As the firm moved nearer and nearer its goal of independence, it successively raised the 'price' for its continued participation in the alliance. The Japanese partner also learned through the alliance. Managers credited the venture with giving them insight into unique customer needs and the standards-setting environment in Europe. However, the Japanese firm could not easily obsolesce the initial bargain; this due not to any learning deficiency on its part, but to the difficulty of unwinding a politically visible relationship.

The notion of collaboration as a race to learn emerged directly from the interview data. As one Western manager put it:

> If they [our partner] learn what we know before we learn what they know, we become redundant. We've got to try to learn faster than they do.

Several Western firms in the study seemed to have discovered that where bargaining power could not be maintained by winning the race to learn, it might be maintained through other means. In a narrow sense managers saw collaboration as a race to learn, but in a broader sense they saw it as a race to remain 'attractive' to their partners. A European manager stated:

> You must continually add to the portfolio of things that make you desirable to your partner. Many of the things that [our partner] needed us for in the early days, it doesn't need now. It needed to establish a base of equipment in Europe and we have done this for them. You must ensure that you always have something to offer your partner—some reason for them to continue to need you.

Managers in a Japanese firm whose European partner had shown a high propensity to learn, believed that ultimate control came from being ahead in the race to create next-generation competencies. Leadership here brought partial control over standards, the benefits of controlling the evolution of technology, and the product price and performance advantages of being first down the experience curve. One senior manager put it succinctly:

> Friendship is friendship, but competition is competition. Competition is about the future and that is R&D.

Here was a suggestion that partners in competitive alliances may sometimes be more likely to view collaboration as a race to get to the future first, rather than a truly cooperative effort to invent the future together. Again, this provided evidence of a subtle blending of competitive and collaborative goals.

The greater the experience of interviewees in administering or working within collaborative arrangements, the more likely were they to discount the extent to which the formal agreement actually determined patterns of learning, control, and dependence within their partnerships. The formal agreement was seen as essentially static, and the race for capability acquisition and control essentially dynamic. As the interviewing progressed it became possible to array the factors which interviewees typically associated with power and control. Power came first from the relative pace at which each partner was building new capabilities internally, then from an ability to out-learn one's partner, then from the relative contribution of 'irreplaceable' inputs by each partner to the venture, then from relative share of value-added, then from the operating structure (which partner's employees held key functional posts), then from the governance structure (which partner was best represented on the board and key executive committees), and finally from the legal structure (share of ownership and legally specified terms for the division of equity and profits). On this basis it was possible, for several of the alliances, to construct a crude 'relative power metric.' For the triadic partnership mentioned above (British, French, and Japanese), relative power was apportioned as per Table 2.

While the legal and managerial power of the British partner was at least equal to that of its counterparts, it failed almost totally to exploit other potential sources of power and control. The British firm's failure to keep pace with its partners in learning and competence-building made its acquisition by one of its partners, or some other ambitious firm, almost inevitable. By way of contrast, the French firm, with no advantage in terms of ownership or executive authority, was able to substantially increase its control of the relationship through a rapid pace of learning. The French firm had substantially increased its R&D budget, hoping eventually to counterbalance its Japanese partner's faster pace of new product development and competence-building. Although the French firm's equity stake remained at 33 percent through most of the 1980s, it continued to enhance its bargaining power by internalizing the skills of its Japanese partner and gaining an ever-increasing share of value-added. From the very different experiences of the British and French firms in this alliance came the proposition that power vested in a particular firm through the formal agreement will almost certainly erode if its partners are more adept at internalization or quicker to build valuable new competencies.

The perspectives on bargaining power and learning which emerged from the case analysis also gave rise to propositions regarding the longevity of

TABLE 2   Relative power of partners in a triadic alliance[1] (ranked by perceived importance as determinants of bargaining power)

	British	French	Japanese
1. Relative pace of competence building[2]		+++	+++++
2. Relative success at inter-partner learning		++++	++
3. Relative criticality of inputs[3]		++	+++
4. Relative share of value-added[4]	+	++	++++
5. 'Possession' of key operating jobs[5]	++	++	+
6. Representation on governing bodies[6]	++	+	+
7. Legal share of ownership[7]	+	+	+

[1] The number of plus signs indicates the relative power within the joint venture that each partner gained from each factor.

[2] Managers in the Japanese partner believed their firm was innovating more rapidly than its European partners in the areas of miniaturization, production engineering, and advanced technologies.

[3] For most of the venture's early history product designs, process equipment, and high-precision components were supplied exclusively by the Japanese partner.

[4] By 1985 European content was approximately 50 percent. The French partner supplied a greater share of the European content than the British partner.

[5] The Managing Directors of the two European plants were Europeans. At each plant a Japanese employee held the Deputy Managing Director's post.

[6] Each partner was responsible for appointing two representatives to the Supervisory Board and one representative to the Management Board. The agreement stipulated that a European was to be President of the Supervisory Board. An executive seconded from the British partner occupied this position.

[7] Each of the three partners held 33.33 percent of the joint venture's equity.

rivalrous alliances. In general, it appeared that competitively oriented partners would continue to collaborate together so long as they were: (1) equally capable of inter-partner learning or independent skills development, and/or (2) both substantially smaller, and mutually vulnerable, to industry leaders.

Three broad determinants of learning outcomes emerged during the study and constitute the core of the internalization model. *Intent* refers to a firm's initial propensity to view collaboration as an opportunity to learn; *transparency* to the 'knowability' or openness of each partner, and thus the potential for learning; and *receptivity* to a partner's capacity for learning, or 'absorptiveness.' While there was much a firm could do to implant a learning intent, limit its own transparency, and enhance its receptivity, there seemed to be some inherent determinants of inter-partner learning, more or less exogenous to the partnership itself, that either predisposed a firm to positive learning outcomes, or rendered it unlikely to successfully exploit opportunities to learn. These are outlined in Table 3, and will be discussed below, along with more 'active' determinants or learning outcomes.

Intent as a determinant of learning The only collaborative intent that was consistent across all firms in the study was *investment avoidance*. In some cases this seemed to be a partner's sole objective. Five of the seven Western firms in the study that had alliances with Japanese partners, had not possessed an internalization intent at the time they entered their Asian alliances. Possessing what came to be called a *substitution* intent, these firms seemed satisfied—at least in the beginning—to substitute their partner's competitiveness in a particular skill area for their own lack of competitiveness. Insofar as it could be ascertained, the Japanese counterparts in these alliances seemed to possess explicit learning intents—with one possible exception. This apparent asymmetry in collaborative goals between Western and Japanese partners is deemed significant because in no case did systematic learning take place in the absence of a clearly communicated internalization intent.

In cases where one partner had systematically learned from the other, great efforts had been made to embed a learning intent within operating-level employees. One project manager recalled that at the outset of the alliance his divisional vice president had brought together all those with organization-spanning roles and told them:

> I wish we didn't need this partnership. I wish we knew how to do what our partner knows how to do. But I will be more disappointed if, in three years, we have not learned to do what our partner knows how to do.

In one firm where learning did not take place, the blame was put on a failure to clearly communicate learning objectives to those with inter-organizational roles:

> Our engineers were just as good as [our partner's]. In fact, their's were narrower technically, but they had a much better understanding of what the company was trying to accomplish. They knew they were there to learn; our people didn't.

A manager in a company with a record of successful learning from partners described what had been done to embed a learning intent:

> We wanted to make learning an automatic discipline. We asked the staff every day, 'What did you learn from [our partner] today?' Learning was carefully monitored and recorded.

While several Western firms had adopted defensive learning intents, as they came to understand the internalization goals of their Japanese partners, none

TABLE 3   Inherent determinants of inter-partner learning:
A comparison of prototypes

	Factors associated with positive learning outcomes	Factors associated with negative learning outcomes
Strength of internalization intent		
1. Competitive posture vis-à-vis partner	Co-option now, confrontation later	Collaboration instead of competition
2. Relative resource position versus corporate ambitions	Scarcity	Abundance
3. Perceived pay-off—capacity to exploit skills in multiple businesses	High; alliance entered to build corporate-wide core competencies	Low; alliance entered to 'fix' problems in a single business
4. Perspective on power	Balance of power begets instability	Balance of power begets stability
Transparency (organizational)		
5. Social context	Language and customs constitute a barrier	Language and customs not a barrier
6. Attitude towards outsiders	The clan as an ideal: exclusivity	The 'melting pot' as ideal: inclusivity
Transparency (skills)		
7. Extent to which skills are context-dependent	Skills comprise tacit knowledge embedded within social systems	Skills comprise explicit knowledge held by a few 'experts'
8. Relative pace of skills enhancement	Fast	Slow
Preconditions for receptivity		
9. Sense of confidence	Neither under-confidence nor over-confidence in its own capabilities	Either under-confidence or over-confidence in its own capabilities
10. Need to first unlearn	As a newcomer, little that must be forgotten before learning can begin	As a laggard, much that must be unlearned before new skills drive out old
11. Size of skills gap with industry leaders	Small	Substantial
12. Institutional versus individual learning	Capacity for 'summing up' and transferring individual learning	Fragmentation (vertical and horizontal) frustrates learning

of these firms could demonstrate that systematic learning had taken place. That the alliance could be a laboratory for learning seemed to be a difficult message to convey, once the alliance had become widely viewed as simply an alternative to internal efforts, as one manager commented:

> When the deal was put together some of us were skeptical, but we were told this was the wave of the future and we'd have to learn to rely on [our partner]. So we relied on them; boy, did we rely on them. Now we're hearing [from senior management] that we shouldn't rely on them *too* much; we have to keep some kind of 'shadow' capability internally. Well, I think we've gotten this message a bit late. Letting [our partner] do the tough stuff has become second nature to us.

To summarize the argument thus far, learning took place by design rather than by default, and skill substitution or surrender by default in the absence of design. In situations where there was a marked asymmetry in intent, the migration of skills between partners could not be accurately characterized as merely 'leakage' (Harrigan, 1986). The competitive consequences of skills transfers, as well as the actual migration of skills, was often unintended, unanticipated, and unwanted by at least one of the partners. This seems to be the fate that befell Varian Associates, a U.S. producer of advanced electronics including semiconductors. Reflecting on its joint venture with NEC, one of Varian's senior executives concluded that 'all NEC had wanted to do was to suck out Varian's technology, not sell Varian's equipment' (Goldenberg, 1988: 85).

What factors might account for observed differences in intent? Whether or not a firm possessed an explicit internalization intent seemed to be a product of: (1) whether it viewed collaboration as a more or less permanent alternative to competition or as a temporary vehicle for improving its competitiveness vis-à-vis its partner; (2) its relative resource position vis-à-vis its partner and other industry participants; (3) its calculation of the pay-off to learning; and (4) its preference for balanced vs. asymmetric dependence within the alliance. Taking these proposed determinants in turn, it was mentioned earlier that several partners had developed defensive internalization intents upon discovering the learning goals of their partners. The majority of Western firms in the study appeared to have initially projected their own substitution intents onto their partners. These firms tended to describe the logic of their collaborative ventures in terms of 'role specialization,' 'complementarity,' 'centers of excellence,' and so on. Such descriptors evinced a view of collaboration as a stable division of roles based on the unique skill endowments of each partner, rather than as a potentially low-cost route to replicating partner skills and erasing initial dependencies.

With one exception, those Western partners that had lacked an initial internalization intent had all been substantially larger than their Japanese partners at the time their alliances were formed. The assumption seemed to be that relative size was a good proxy for relative skill levels. A U.S. manager summarized the attitude that had prevailed a decade earlier when the firm entered its first major Japanese alliance: 'We invented the industry. What could we possibly learn from an up-start in Japan?' An executive in their Japanese partner reflected on difference in the two partners' attitudes toward learning:

> When we saw [our larger Western partner] doing something better, we always wanted to know why. But when they come to look at what we are doing, they say, 'Oh, you can do that because you are Japanese,' or they find some other reason. They make an explanation so they don't have to understand [what we are doing differently].

An abundance of resources, and a legacy of industry leadership, whether real or perceived, made it difficult for a firm to admit to itself that it had something to learn from a smaller partner.

The intent to learn also appeared to be a function of the firm's calculation about the pay-off to learning. In those firms where the internalization intent was strongest and most deeply felt, the skills to be acquired from the partner were seen as critical to the growth of the entire company, and not just the competitiveness of a single product or business. This was in contrast to firms where competitiveness was defined solely in end-product terms, and where top management had no explicit plans for building corporate-wide skills. Here alliances were viewed as short cuts to a more competitive product line (by relying on a partner for critical components or perhaps entire products), rather than as short cuts to the internalization of skills that could be applied across a range of businesses. Without clear corporate goals for competence building, and a deep appreciation for the critical contribution of core competence leadership to long-term competitiveness, individual businesses appeared unlikely to devote resources to the task of learning.

The perceived pay-off to learning was also influenced, in some cases, by a partner's calculation of the cost of continued dependence. Managers in the study identified a range of potential costs that could be associated with dependency in a core skill area: an inability to thwart a partner intent on entering the firm's prime markets: or the obverse—being constrained from entering an emerging market, or having one's entry slowed by a powerful partner; the risk of being 'stranded' by a collaborator who pre-emptively ended the relationship; or being disadvantaged when the financial terms of the agreement are re-negotiated. Japanese partners, in particular, seemed to view strategic alliances as second-best options. A group of managers interviewed in one firm expressed an opinion, quite vehemently, that their company would never accept a situation in which it was, over the long term, dependent on a Western partner for an important aspect of its product-based competitiveness—this despite the fact that several of that firm's foreign partners were in just such a dependency position. Not surprisingly, this firm possessed a strong internalization intent.

There may be a reason why Japanese firms, in particular, seemed adverse to the very notion of symmetrical dependency between partners. Nakane (1970) has shown that social organization in Japan is based on the notion of dependence. The parent-child analogy is applied to the government and its public, employers and employees, managers and subordinates, and large firms and their suppliers. In this view a 'balance of power' brings indeterminateness and instability to a relationship, while a clearly disproportionate allocation of power, that is, dependence, brings cohesion and consistency. The preference of Japanese managers for unequivocable decision-making power in foreign subsidiaries and joint ventures has been well documented (Ballon, 1979; Ouchi and Johnson, 1974). Indeed, when asked to consider a hypothetical American-Japanese joint venture located in the United States, Japanese managers felt that future trust would be highest if Japanese, rather than American, managers occupied the most powerful positions, and if Japanese managers, rather than Americans, had responsibility for initiating key decision processes such as capital budgeting (Sullivan and Peterson, 1982).

It seems unlikely that many Japanese managers would disagree with Harrigan's (1986: 148) assertion that:

> Managers can be as crafty as they please in writing clauses to protect their firm's technology rights, but the joint venture's success depends on trust.

But when Japanese managers list 'trust' as one of the most important conditions for a successful joint venture (Block and Matsumoto, 1972), they may be speaking not of the trust that comes from what Buckley and Casson (1988) term 'mutual forbearance,' but from unequivocal dependence. If knowledge is power, and power the father of dependence, one can expect Japanese firms to strive to learn from their partners.

Transparency as a determinant of learning Whereas intent established the desire to learn, transparency determined the potential for learning. Some partners were, for a variety of reasons, more transparent—more open and accessible—than others. Of course, every partner intended to share some skills with its opposite number. Even in firms with an inherently 'protective' stance vis-à-vis their partner, some degree of openness was accepted as the price for enticing the partner into the relationship and successfully executing joint tasks. Yet many managers drew a distinction between what might be termed 'transparency by design,' and 'transparency by default.' The concerns managers expressed were over unintended and unanticipated transfers.

Such concerns arose in cases where managers believed their partner's learning had gone for beyond what was deemed essential for the successful performance of joint tasks, to encompass what was necessary to internalize skills. A partner's learning could be both more intensive than foreseen in the formal agreement, and more extensive. The greatest sense of 'unfairness,' and the greatest sense of failure in managing transparency, was observed in those firms where a partner's learning had extended to skill areas that were not explicitly part of the formal agreement. This often seemed to be the cases in OEM sourcing arrangement where an up-stream partner had used the alliance to gain insights into customer needs and market structure. A European-based manager described the process thus:

> Anytime we demanded unique features for the European market [in a product sourced from Japan, our Japanese partner] wanted a complete justification for each item. They wanted to understand why we wanted certain product features, competitors' product information, customer perceptions, all the market-based things. You can get fifteen years of accumulated wisdom across the table in two hours.

Broadly, there appeared to be at least five inherent, *ex ante* determinants of transparency: (1) the penetrability of the social context which surrounded the partner; (2) attitudes towards outsiders, i.e. clannishness; (3) the extent to which the partner's distinctive skills were encodable and discrete; and (4) the partner's relative pace of skill-building.

While this exploratory study cannot provide an answer to the question, 'Are Japanese partners inherently less transparent than their Western counterparts?' what can be said is that nearly all the Western partners in the study believed this to be the case. The study suggested that there were indeed systematic, though not irreversible, asymmetries in transparency between Western and Japanese partners. Typical was the comment of one Western manager:

> Despite the fact that we were [in Japan] for training, I always felt we were revealing more information about us than [our Japanese partners] were about themselves.

Interestingly, no Japanese manager expressed an opinion that Western partners might be inherently less transparent than Japanese partners. Peterson and Schwind (1977) found similar evidence of asymmetry in transparency between Japanese and Western alliance partners. In their study of international joint ventures located in Japan, 'communication' was the problem mentioned most often by both expatriate and Japanese managers. However, for expatriate managers 'difficulty in receiving exact information and data' from their Japanese partners ranked a close second, mentioned by 87 percent of U.S. expatriate respondents. The next most noted problems, 'reluctance to report failures,' and 'no open discussion of problems,' further reflect the frustration these managers felt in extracting information from their Japanese partners. However, no Japanese manager mentioned access to information as a major annoyance in dealing with Western partners.

It seems plausible to propose that this asymmetry in perceptions of relative opaqueness rests at least in part on the extent to which a firm's knowledge base is context-bound (Terpstra and David, 1985). Contextuality refers to the 'embeddedness' of information in social systems. In general, knowledge in Oriental cultures is more contextual than information in Occidental cultures (Benedict, 1946). Form and content, ritual and substance cannot easily be disentangled. Context-dependent knowledge (for example, principles of industrial relations in Japan) is inherently less transparent than context-free knowledge (e.g., the principles of the transistor).

Japanese employees working within Western partners seemed to more easily gain acceptance by peers, and more quickly become insiders, than was the case in reverse. For example, a divisional vice president managing a joint European-Japanese design effort within Europe remarked that:

> We were conscious of [our partner's employees] on-site and did try to keep information exchange on a need-to-know basis. However, after a while, they ceased to be different. We played badminton together, we went to the same parties and restaurants. They became close friends.

While several Western managers, with employees working in Japanese-based alliances, expressed concerns over the fact that their staff might 'go native,' no Japanese manager expressed such a concern in the reverse case. Several managers, both Western and Japanese, expressed the opinion that the 'openness' of Western cultural and organizational contexts facilitated the assimilation of partner employees, while the sense of 'clan' possessed by Japanese staff made them sensitive to the risk of revealing competitively useful information to a partner. The same European manager who commented on the easy social integration of Japanese team members also recalled that:

> Once the contract was signed, [the Japanese partner] had a view of what we needed to know to complete the project. They were totally open in this regard, but totally closed on all other issues. They had well-defined limits in terms of what they would tell us. The junior guys would tell us nothing unless a senior person was there.

The point here is not that Japanese organizations are clannish. That point has been made before (Ouchi, 1980). Instead, it is that where clannishness is high, opportunities for access will be limited, and transparency low. As a member of a clan, an employee involved in a partnership can be expected to retain a sense of identity with, and loyalty to, the parent. When conflicts arise which reflect an incongruity between parent and partner goals, a clan member will search for solutions consistent with the parent's goals.

An asymmetry in language skills often exacerbated inherent constraints on transparency such as clannishness and complexity. That operating employees in Western firms almost universally lacked Japanese language skills and cultural experience in Japan served to limit the transparency of their Asian hosts. One engineer from a European company recalled his frustration in working with a partner in Japan:

> Whenever I made a presentation [to our partner] I was one person against ten to twelve. They'd put me in front of a flip chart, then stop me while they went into a conversation in Japanese for ten minutes. If I asked them a question they would break into Japanese to first decide what I wanted to know, and then would discuss options in terms of what they might tell me, and finally would come back with an answer.

Not only did it appear that some organizations were more penetrable than others, it appeared that some types of knowledge were inherently more deeply buried in the social context of the firm than others. Explicit knowledge was more encodable than tacit knowledge—it could be transferred in engineering drawings, extracted from patent filings, etc., and discrete knowledge was more easily extracted from a partner than systemic knowledge. In general, it appeared that specific technologies (e.g., a microprocessor chip design), were more transparent than deep-seated competencies (e.g., value-engineering skills), and that market intelligence flowed more easily than knowledge of leading edge manufacturing know-how. Thus an asymmetry in the nature of the skills contributed by each partner to the venture could, *ceteris paribus*, preordain asymmetric learning. In partnerships where one firm brought product designs and market experience to the table, and other (typically Japanese) manufacturing competence, the partner contributing production skills seemed to benefit from an inherently lower level of transparency. For while it did not appear that a firm could transfer product designs to its partner without revealing, perhaps inadvertently, a great deal of implicit market information, it was possible for the producing partner to ship back finished products without revealing much of what comprised its manufacturing competence.

The pace of a firm's innovation also seemed to determine its transparency to its partner. In some cases one partner's speed of innovation out-ran the other's pace of absorption. One fast-moving partner believed it could afford to be very open in terms of access, and yet remain essentially opaque, given its rapid pace of product development. Managers in this Japanese firm believed that their rate of new product introduction was between four and five times faster than that of their partner. Despite their partner's avowed learning intent, managers in this firm felt relatively unconcerned:

> We are very convinced that our R&D speed is faster than [our partner's]. This is our ultimate protection [against partner encroachment].

The researcher was reminded of the old adage about the difficulty of drinking from a fire hose.

Partners employed a wide variety of active measures to limit transparency.

In one firm, all partner requests for information and access were processed through a small 'collaboration department.' Staff from this department attended virtually all meetings between managers and staff of the two partners. In this way they were able to control the 'aperture' through which the partner gained access to people and facilities. Out of this case grew the notion of a 'gatekeeping' role: one or more individuals charged with monitoring knowledge flows across the collaborative membrane.

Another determinant of relative transparency position appeared to be the number of people from each partner seconded to the other, or, more generally, the extent to which the nature of joint tasks required regular and intensive intermingling of staff from the two partners. At one extreme was the task of jointly designing a car, where the need to mate together powertrain, body, and suspension required intensive cross-membrane interaction, and made both partners highly transparent to each other. At the other extreme was the much simpler task of specifying single 'plug-in' components to be supplied by a partner.

Firms in the study also sought to limit their transparency to ambitious partners by restricting the collaborative agreement to a narrow range of products or markets. One manager argued that:

> If you source the *entire* product in, there is a lot greater transfer of design skills—your partner gets to see everything. What you should do is design components, source from multiple places, and then do integration and manufacturing yourself.

Another firm saw site selection and control as key issues in limiting transparency:

> It helps to have a joint company in a third location: this helps to protect you. You don't let your partner do joint work on your site. And if you have a third site you can decide what you put in and what you don't.

Given the fact that the process of collaborative exchange took place not at senior management levels, but at operating levels, the management of transparency depended, ultimately, on the ability and willingness of operators to sometimes say 'no' to a partner's requests for information or access. The extent to which operating employees had an explicit sense of the need to protect information from bleeding through to a partner varied widely across the sample firms. One project manager was surprised by how close-mouthed his partner's engineers were:

> Everyone I met within [our partner] seemed to operate with well-defined limits on what they would tell us. Their engineers were very guarded with technical details.

Sometimes I had to appeal to higher level managers to get information critical to the project's success.

In one firm senior managers explicitly recognized the tensions that could arise when operating employees were asked to work in a collegial way to make the alliance a success, and at the same time had a responsibility for limiting the partner's access to core skills. One way out of this dilemma was to give operators the right to escalate partner requests for information.

It appeared that firms which could rely on passive or 'natural' barriers to transparency had an inherent advantage over partners that could not. This was not only because natural barriers to transparency seemed to be the most difficult to overcome, but also because active measures were sometimes regarded by partners as provocative. When U.S. firms have relied on contractual clauses and other active means to limit transparency, they have often been accused of acting in bad faith, or undermining trust (Ballon, 1979). To the extent that passive barriers can substitute for active measures, a partner may be able to claim for itself the high ground of trust and openness, and yet still benefit from almost unassailable barriers to partner encroachment.

Receptivity as a determinant of learning If intent establishes the desire to learn, and transparency the opportunity, receptivity determines the capacity to learn. Just as there were active and passive determinants of transparency, so there were of receptivity. In several cases, when questioned as to why they had apparently learned more than their Western partners, Japanese managers answered, in essence, 'We had the attitude of students, and our Western partners the attitude of teachers.' Ballon would no doubt accept such a generalization:

> When looking at the West from outside the Western Hemisphere, one attitude stands out. It is just how anxious Americans and Europeans are to *teach* the rest of the world (1979: 27).

Humility may be the first prerequisite for learning. However, the distinction between teachers and students rested on more than just cultural stereotypes.

Generating an enthusiasm for learning, that is, an attitude of receptivity, among operating employees seemed to depend largely on whether the firm entered the alliance as a *late-comer*, or as a *laggard;* i.e. whether the alliance was seen by the majority of employees as a proactive choice to support ambitious growth goals (the perspective of late-comers), or as an easy 'way out' of a deteriorating competitive situation (the perspective of laggards). Where a firm had become a laggard, and had come to think of itself as such, middle-level managers and operators appeared more likely to adopt an acquiescent attitude towards dependency and learning opportunities. While they sometimes saw learning as a laudable goal, they possessed little enthusiasm for the task. Perhaps not surprisingly, in firms that had struggled to maintain their competitiveness in a particular product/market, and had failed, alliances tended to be seen by operating-level employees as confirmation of their failure, and not as a means to rebuild skills. A sense of resignation was not conducive to receptivity.

The stigma of failure did not attach itself to firms using alliances to build skills in new areas, i.e., closing skills 'gaps' as opposed to compensating for a skills failure. The European partner mentioned earlier could not have claimed to possess world-class manufacturer skills at the time it entered its alliance with a Japanese partner. Yet it had succeeded, through its own efforts, in dramatically improving the productivity of its color television manufacturing in the five years preceding the joint venture, and had come close to Japanese productivity levels. It had also doubled its share of the European color television market in the decade preceding the alliance. Thus it was not difficult for employees to regard the partnership as a multiplier, rather than as a substitute, for internal efforts.

Organization learning theory suggests that laggards may confront two cruel paradoxes. First, learning often cannot begin until unlearning has taken place (Burgleman, 1983b; Hedberg, 1981; Nystrom and Starbuck, 1984). This is particularly true where the behaviors that contributed to past success have been deeply etched in the organization's consciousness. The problem of unlearning is not only a cognitive problem—altering perceptual maps—but a problem of driving out old behavior with new behavior. The link between changed cognition and changed behavior is probably more direct in individuals (Postman and Underwood, 1973; Watzlawick, Weakland and Fisch, 1974) than it is in large multinational companies (Prahalad and Doz, 1987). Current patterns of behavior in large organizations are typically 'hard-wired' in structure, in information systems, incentive schemes, hiring and promotion practices, and so on (Argyris and Schon, 1978). The implication here is that unlearning will be a significant hurdle for a laggard attempting to compensate for past skill failure. For a late-comer using an alliance to build skills in a new area, unlearning is not a prerequisite. Receptivity will not be impaired by employees clinging to past practices.

Second, while a reduction in organizational slack typically precipitates the search for new knowledge (Cyert and March, 1963), the complete absence of slack just as surely frustrates learning (Burgelman, 1983a). Some slack is necessary if the organization is to search for new approaches, experiment with new methods, and embed new capabilities. Learning is a luxury which can be afforded by those with some minimum complement of time and resources. A small crisis abets learning, a big crisis limits learning. Of course it has been argued that collaboration may be a timely and low-cost mechanism for acquiring new skills. But even here, as learning progresses from knowledge-gathering to capability-building, investment needs escalate. A firm may understand how its partner achieves a certain level of performance, but not have the resources needed to embed that understanding through staff development and investment in new facilities. Again, the results of the study support the contention that learning is most likely to occur in the middle ground between abundance and arrogance on one side, and deprivation and resignation on the other.

To these two paradoxes may be added a third: the greater the need to learn, i.e., the farther one partner is behind its counterpart, the higher the barriers to receptivity. Simply put, to replicate the skills of a partner, a firm must be able to identify, if not retrace, the intermediate learning 'steps' between its present competence level and that of its partner. After visiting the most advanced manufacturing facility of a Japanese partner, a manager in one Western firm remarked:

> It's no good for us to simply observe where they are today, what we have to find out is how they got from where we are to where they are. We need to experiment and learn with intermediate technologies before duplicating what they've done.

If the skills gap between partners is too great, learning becomes almost impossible.

The notion of receptivity was seen to apply to the corporate body, as well as to individual receptors. Individual learning became collective learning when (1) there existed a mechanism for 'summing up' individual learning, i.e., first recording and then integrating the fragmentary knowledge gained by individuals, and (2) learning was transferred across unit boundaries to all those who could benefit in some way from what had been learned. It was evident in the study that firms with a history of cross-functional teamwork and inter-business coordination were more likely to turn personal learning into corporate learning than were firms where the emphasis was on 'individual contributors' and 'independent business units.' A senior manager in a Japanese partner commented on the internal relationships that had aided its learning, and hindered, it believed, its partner's learning:

> Within [my firm] there is a great deal of mutual responsibility. Responsibility is a very grey area in Japan; many people are involved. There is much more overlap in responsibility than in [our Western partner] where information seems to be compartmentalized. [Our partner] thought we asked too many questions, but in [my company] information is shared with many people even if they are not directly involved. Engineers in [one department] want to know what is happening in design [in another department] even if that is not related to their direct responsibilities.

On the other side of the relationship a Western manager offered a similar perspective:

> [In joint meetings, staff] groups [from our Japanese partner] would almost always be multi-disciplinary, even for technical discussions. [They] clearly wanted to understand the implications of our technology. You had the feeling that most of the [their] people who were sitting in the [joint] meetings were there only to learn. We would have never taken anyone into such a meeting without a direct interest in what was being discussed.

In terms of active determinants, receptivity depended upon, above all else, the diligence with which those with greatest access to the partner approached the task of learning. One firm in particular appeared to conceive of inter-partner learning as a rigorous discipline. This firm's success in internalizing partner skills suggests that such a conception may be a prerequisite for systematic learning. A senior executive in the company described its 'inch-by-inch' efforts to learn from its partner:

> You need to be incredibly patient, but eventually you would get what you wanted. In the event of the slightest breakdown, you had to ask [our partner], 'What now?' We acquired the know-how very slowly in this way, by finding out all the little mistakes [we were making], by repeatedly asking questions, and by forcing them, little by little, to yield technical information.

In this case receptivity seemed to thrive as long as top management continued to express an active interest in what was being learned. Top management's commitment to learning was exhibited first through a clear intent to establish a world-class consumer electronics manufacturing competence, secondly through the hiring of a wholly new executive group, and thirdly through a constant stream of investment to build up a physical plant as closely parallel to that of the partner as possible. Given initial estimates that it would take between three and five years for the firm to 'catch up' with its Japanese partner, top management believed its unwavering enthusiasm for, and attention to, the partnership was critical to a positive learning outcome. Internalizing new skills via an alliance would seem to require a reasonably long attention span on the part of top management.

The personal skills of receptors also influenced receptivity. The European partner referred to above had assembled a collaborative team with the necessary skills to observe, interpret, apply, and improve upon partner skills. One member of the team came from the watch-making industry, and others from successful precision-engineering firms. The average age of team members was estimated to be 35 years. The relatively young age of the team, and the fact that few were tainted with the burden of past failure, reduced the need for 'unlearning.' The team also benefited from a liberal training budget. For this company it was not enough to embed, through goal setting and daily reinforcement, a learning discipline, receptors had to be competent to receive. This meant that their skills had to parallel, as closely as possible, those from whom they were learning.

Determinants of sustainable learning Whether a skills gap closed through inter-partner learning later re-opened seemed to depend on several factors, all of which can be summarized under the general heading of a *capacity for self-sustaining learning*. The critical point here is that intercepting a partner's skills at a point in time appeared to be a lesser challenge than matching a partner's underlying rate of improvement over time. To break free of dependence a firm had, first, to match its pace of absorption to its partner's pace of innovation, and then to equal or better its partner's capability for autonomously and continuously improving those skills. NEC, when it formed its alliance with Honeywell in the early 1960s, was much smaller than its partner. Nonetheless, NEC ultimately reversed its initial dependency. Those few firms in the study that were committed to turning the tables of dependency appeared to agree that matching a partner's pace of autonomous improvement depended on: (1) capturing know-why as well as know-what from their partners, (2) mastering the disciplines of continuous improvement, and (3) achieving global scale.

Two firms in the study recognized that, as long as they operated at regional scale, they could not fully apply the lessons learned from partners operating at global scale. Both firms made large international acquisitions with the express goal of amortizing investment in world-scale facilities that paralleled those of their partners. Both firms found that as their learning agendas shifted from technology to competence, from discrete skills to systematic skills, and from know-how to know-why, their pace of learning had slowed. It was clear to both partners that building a foundation for autonomous improvement demanded insight into the underlying dynamic which drove their partner's pace of innovation. Again, this was a substantial challenge, particularly for Western firms, as at least some of the impetus behind the innovative pace of their Japanese counterparts appeared to be culturally idiosyncratic (Baba, 1989; Imai, 1986; Itami, 1987).

Discussion

Though this research grew out of an interest in skills-based competition (Nelson and Winter, 1982; Dierickx and Cool, 1989; Quinn, Doorley and Paquette, 1990; Prahalad and Hamel, 1990; Barney, 1990; Teece, Pisano and Shuen, 1990), it is also important to set it within the context of existing research on the management of strategic alliances. The way in which the present study both complements and challenges prior research on collaboration is now discussed.

Collaboration as a transitional stage Joint ventures and other non-market inter-firm agreements have typically been pictured as an intermediate level of integration between arm's-length contracts in open markets and full ownership (Nielsen, 1988; Thorelli, 1986). But where the goal of the alliance is skills acquisition, an alliance may be seen, by one or both partners, not as an optimal compromise between market and hierarchy, to use Williamson's (1975) nomenclature, but as a half-way house on the road from market to hierarchy. In this sense the alliance is viewed not as an alternative to market-based transactions or full ownership, but as an alternative to other modes of skill acquisition. These might include acquiring the partner, licensing from the partner, or developing the needed skills through internal efforts. There are several reasons collaboration may in some cases be the preferred mode of skills acquisition.

For some skills, what Itami (1987) terms 'invisible assets,' the cost of internal development may be almost infinite. Complex skills, based on tacit knowledge, and arising out of a unique cultural context may be acquirable only by up-close observation and emulation of 'best in class.' Alliances may offer advantages of timeliness as well as efficiency. Where global competitors are rapidly building new sources of competitive advantage, as well as enhancing existing skills, a go-it-alone strategy could confine a firm to permanent also-ran status. Alliances may be seen as a way of short-circuiting the process of skills acquisition and thus avoiding the opportunity cost of being a perpetual follower. Motorola's reliance on Toshiba for re-entry to the DRAM semiconductor business seems to reflect such a concern. Internalization via collaboration may be more attractive than acquiring a firm in total. In buying a company the acquirer must pay for nondistinctive assets, and is confronted with a substantially larger organizational integration problem.

Capturing value versus creating value There are two basic processes in any alliance: *value creation* and *value appropriation*. The extent of value creation depends first on whether the market and competitive logic of the venture is sound, and then on the efficacy with which the two partners combine their complementary skills and resources; that is, how well they perform joint tasks. Each partner then appropriates value in the form of monetary or other benefits. In general, researchers have given more attention to the process of value creation than the process of value appropriation. The primary concern of both the transactions cost (Hennart, 1988) and strategic position (e.g., Harrigan, 1985) perspectives is the creation of joint value. Transactional efficiency gained through quasi-internalization is one form of value creation; improvement in competitive position is another. Both perspectives provide insights into why firms collaborate; neither captures the dynamics which determine collaborative outcomes, and the individual monetary and long-term competitive gains taken by each partner. Making a collaborative agreement 'work' has generally been seen as creating the preconditions for value creation (Doz, 1988; Killing, 1982, 1983). There is much advice on how to be a 'good' partner (Goldenberg, 1988; Perlmutter and Heenan, 1986)—firms are typically urged to build 'trust' (Harrigan, 1986; Peterson and Shimada, 1978)—but little advice on how to reap the benefits of being a good partner.

There appear to be two mechanisms for extracting value from an alliance: bargaining over the stream of economic benefits that issues directly from the successful execution of joint tasks, and internalizing the skills of partners. These 'value pools' may be conceptually distinct, but they were shown to be related in an important way. Bargaining power at any point in time within an alliance is, *ceteris paribus,* a function of who needs whom the most. This, in turn, is a function of the perceived strategic importance of the alliance to each partner and the attractiveness to each partner of alternatives to collaboration. Depending on its bargaining power a partner will gain a greater or lesser share of the fruits of joint effort. An important issue then is what factors prompt changes in bargaining power. Some factors will be exogenous to the partnership. A change in strategic priorities may suddenly make a partnership much more or much less vital for one of the partners (Franko, 1971). Likewise, a shift in the market or competitive environment could devalue the contribution of one partner and revalue the contribution of the other. Rapid change in technology might produce a similar effect (Harrigan, 1985). However, there is one determinant of relative bargaining power that is very much within the firm's control: its capacity to learn.

While Westney (1988) and Kogut (1988) recognize that learning may be an explicit goal in an alliance, they do not specify the critical linkages between learning, dependency, and bargaining power. Conversely, while Pfeffer and Nowak (1976) and Blois (1980) correctly view alliances as mechanisms for managing interorganizational dependence, they do not take a dynamic view of interdependence, and hence miss the linkage between learning and changes in relative dependency. If bargaining power is a function of relative dependence it should be possible to lessen dependency and improve bargaining power by out-learning one's partner. Most bargains obsolesce with time (Kobrin, 1986); by actively working to internalize a partner's skills it should be possible to accelerate the rate at which the bargain obsolesces. This seems to have been the motivation for Boeing's Japanese partners in recent years (Moxon, 1988). It was clearly the motivation of two of the Japanese partners in the study.

The process of collaborative exchange Researchers have tended to look at venture and task structure when attempting to account for partnership performance. An equally useful perspective might be that of a *collaborative membrane*, through which flow skills and capabilities between the partners. The extent to which the membrane is permeable, and in which direction(s) it is permeable determines relative learning. Though researchers and practitioners often seem to be preoccupied with issues of structure—legal, governance, and task (Harrigan, 1988; Killing, 1983; Schillaci, 1987; Tybejee, 1988) the study suggests that these may be only partial determinants of permeability. Conceiving of an alliance as a membrane suggests that access to people, facilities, documents, and other forms of knowledge is traded between partners in an on-going process of *collaborative exchange*. As operating employees interact day-by-day, and continually process partner requests for access, a series of *micro-bargains* are reached on the basis of considerations of operational effectiveness, fairness, and bargaining power. Though these bargains may be more implicit than explicit, out-learning a partner means 'winning' a series of *micro-bargains*. The simple hypothesis is that the terms of trade in any particular micro-bargain may be only partially determined by the terms of trade which prevailed at the time the macro-bargain was struck by corporate officers. A firm may be in a weak bargaining position at the macro level, as NEC undoubtedly was when it entered its alliance with Honeywell in the computer business in the early 1960s, but may be able to strike a series of advantageous micro-bargains if, at the operational level, it uniquely possesses the capacity to learn. Restating the bargaining power argument ad-

TABLE 4   Distinctive attributes of a theory of competitive collaboration

	Traditional perspective	Alternative perspective
Collaborative logic	Quasi-internalization	De-facto internalization
Unit of analysis	Joint outcomes	Individual outcomes
Underlying process	Value creation	Value appropriation
Success determinants	Form and structure (macro-bargain)	Collaborative exchange (micro-bargains)
Success metrics	Satisfaction and longevity	Bargaining power and competitiveness

vanced earlier, the cumulative impact of micro-bargains will, to a large extent, determine in whose favor future macro-bargains are resolved.

Success metrics Where internalization is the goal, the longevity and 'stability' of partnerships may not be useful proxies for collaborative success. Nevertheless, they have often been used as such (Beamish, 1984; Franko, 1971; Gomes-Casseres, 1987; Killing, 1983; Reynolds, 1979). A long-lived alliance may evince the failure of one or both partners to learn. It was interesting to note in the study that, despite collaborative agreements in Japan with Japanese firms spanning several decades, several Western partners were still unable to 'go it alone' in the Japanese market. By way of contrast, there were few cases in which Japanese firms had remained dependent on Western partners for continued access to Western markets (though in one case the Japanese partner ultimately acquired its European partner). Likewise, an absence of contention in the relationship is not, by itself, an adequate success metric. A firm with no ambition beyond investment avoidance and substitution of its partner's competitiveness for its own lack of competitiveness may be perfectly content not to learn from its partner. But where a failure to learn is likely to ultimately undermine the competitiveness and independence of the firm, such contentedness should not be taken as a sign of collaborative success. The theoretical perspective on collaboration developed in this paper is summarized in Table 4.

Acknowledgement

The author would like to thank the Gatsby Charitable Foundation for funding the research on which this article is based. In addition, thanks are due the two referees for their constructive suggestions.

REFERENCES

Argyris, C. and D. A. Schon. *Organizational Learning,* Addison-Wesley, Reading, MA, 1978.

Baba, Y. 'The dynamics of continuous innovation in scale-intensive industries,' *Strategic Management Journal,* **10,** 1989, pp. 89–100.

Ballon, R. J. 'A lesson from Japan: Contract, control, and authority,' *Journal of Contemporary Business,* **8**(2), 1979, pp. 27–35.

Barney, J. B. 'Firm resources and sustained competitive advantage.' Unpublished manuscript, Department of Management, Texas A&M University, 1990.

Beamish, P. W. 'Joint venture performance in developing countries.' Unpublished doctoral dissertation, University of Western Ontario, 1984.

Benedict, R. *The Chrysanthemum and the Sword,* reprint (1974), New American Library, New York, 1946.

Block, A. and H. Matsumoto. 'Joint venturing in Japan.' *Conference Board Record,* April 1972, pp. 32–36.

Blois, K. J. 'Quasi-integration as a mechanism for controlling external dependencies,' *Management Decision,* **18**(1), 1980, pp. 55–63.

Buckley, P. J. and M. Casson. *Economic Theory of the Multinational Enterprise: Selected Papers,* Macmillan, London, 1985.

Buckley, P. J. and M. Casson. 'A theory of cooperation in international business.' In F. J. Contractor and P. Lorange (eds). *Cooperative Strategies in International Business,* D.C. Heath, Lexington, MA, 1988, pp. 31–53.

Burgelman, R. A. 'A model of the interaction of strategic behavior, corporate context and the concept of strategy,' *Academy of Management Review,* **8**(1), 1983a, pp. 61–70.

Burgelman, R. A. 'A process model of internal corporate venturing in the diversified major firm,' *Administrative Science Quarterly,* **28**(2), 1983b, pp. 223–244.

Business Week. 'When U.S. joint ventures with Japan go sour,' 24 July 1989, pp. 14–16.

Caves, R. E. 'International corporations: The industrial economics of foreign investment, *Economica,* February 1971, pp. 1–27.

Contractor, F. J. and P. Lorange. 'Why should firms cooperate: The strategy and economic basis for cooperative ventures.' In F. J. Contractor and P. Lorange (eds), *Cooperative Strategies in International Business,* D.C. Heath, Lexington, MA, 1988, pp. 3–28.

Cyert, R. M. and J. G. March. *A Behavioral Theory of the Firm.* Prentice-Hall, Englewood Cliffs, NJ, 1963.

Dierickx, I. and K. Cool. 'Asset stock accumulation and sustainability of competitive advantage,' *Management Science,* December 1989, pp. 1504–1514.

Doz, Y. 'Technology partnerships between larger and smaller firms: Some critical issues.' In F. J. Contractor and P. Lorange (eds), *Cooperative Strategies in International*

Business, D.C. Heath, Lexington, MA, 1988, pp. 317–328.

Franko, L. G. *Joint Venture Survival in Multinational Corporations,* Praeger, New York, 1971.

Ghemawat, P., M. E. Porter and R. A. Rawlinson. 'Patterns of international coalition activity.' In M. E. Porter (ed.), *Competition in Global Industries,* Harvard University Press, Boston, MA, 1986, pp. 345–365.

Glaser, B. G. and A. L. Strauss. *The Discovery of Grounded Theory: Strategies for Qualitative Research.* Aldine, New York, 1967.

Goldenberg, S. *International Joint Ventures in Action: How to Establish, Manage and Profit from International Strategic Alliances,* Hutchinson Business Books, London, 1988.

Gomes-Casseres, B. 'Joint venture instability: Is it a problem,' *Columbia Journal of World Business,* Summer 1987, pp. 97–102.

Hamel, G. 'Competitive collaboration: Learning, power and dependence in international strategic alliances.' Unpublished doctoral dissertation, Graduate School of Business Administration, University of Michigan, 1990.

Harrigan, K. R. *Strategies for Joint Ventures.* Lexington Books, Lexington, MA, 1985.

Harrigan, K. R. *Managing for Joint Venture Success.* Lexington Books, Lexington, MA, 1986.

Harrigan, K. R. 'Joint ventures and competitive strategy,' *Strategic Management Journal,* **9.** 1988. pp. 141–158.

Hedberg, B. L. T. 'How organizations learn and unlearn.' In P. C. Nystrom and W. H. Starbuck (eds). *Handbook of Organizational Design,* Oxford University Press, London, 1981.

Hergert, M. and D. Morris. 'Trends in international collaborative agreements,' In F. J. Contractor and P. Lorange (eds). *Cooperative Strategies in International Business,* D.C. Heath, Lexington, MA, 1988, pp. 99–109.

Hennart, J. 'A transaction cost theory of equity joint ventures,' *Strategic Management Journal,* July–August, **9,** 1988, pp. 36–74.

Imai, M. *Kaizen: The Key to Japan's Competitive Success,* Random House, New York, 1986.

Itami, H. with T. W. Roehl. *Mobilizing Invisible Assets.* Harvard University Press, Cambridge, MA, 1987.

Killing, J. P. 'How to make a global joint venture work,' *Harvard Business Review,* May–June 1982, pp. 120–127.

Killing, J. P. *Strategies for Joint Venture Success.* Praeger, New York, 1983.

Kobrin, S. J. 'Testing the bargaining hypothesis in the manufacturing sector in developing countries,' Unpublished manuscript, 1986.

Kogut, B. 'Joint ventures: Theoretical and empirical perspectives,' *Strategic Management Journal,* **9**(4), 1988, pp. 319–322.

Mintzberg, H. 'Patterns in strategy formulation,' *Management Science,* **24**(9), 1978, pp. 934–948.

Moxon, R. W., T. W. Roehl and J. F. Truitt. 'International cooperative ventures in the commercial aircraft industry: Gains, sure, but what's my share.' In F. J. Contractor and P. Lorange (eds), *Cooperative Strategies in International Business,* D.C. Heath, Lexington, MA, 1988, pp. 255–278.

Nakane, C. *Japanese Society.* University of California Press, Berkeley, CA, 1970.

Nelson, R. R. and S. G. Winter. *An Evolutionary Theory of Economic Change,* Belknap Press, Cambridge, MA, 1982.

Nielsen, R. P. 'Cooperative strategy,' *Strategic Management Journal,* **9**, 1988, pp. 475–492.

Nystrom, P. C. and W. H. Starbuck.; 'To avoid organizational crises, unlearn,' *Organizational Dynamics,* **12**(4), 1984, pp. 53–65.

Ohmae, K. 'The global logic of strategic alliances,' *Harvard Business Review,* March–April 1989, pp. 143–155.

Ouchi, W. G. 'Markets, bureaucracies, and clans,' *Administrative Science Quarterly,* **25**, 1980, pp. 129–141.

Ouchi, W. G. and R. T. Johnson. 'Made in America (under Japanese management),' *Harvard Business Review,* September–October 1974, pp. 61–69.

Perlmutter, H. V. and D. H. Heenan. 'Cooperate to compete globally,' *Harvard Business Review,* March–April 1986, pp. 136–152.

Peterson, R. B. and H. F. Schwind. 'A comparative study of personnel problems in international companies and joint ventures in Japan,' *Journal of International Business Studies,* **8**(1), 1977, pp. 45–55.

Peterson, R. B. and J. Y. Shimada. 'Sources of management problems in Japanese-American joint ventures,' *Academy of Management Review,* **3**, 1978, pp. 796–804.

Pettigrew, A. M. 'On studying organizational cultures,' *Administrative Science Quarterly,* **24**(4), 1979, pp. 570–581.

Pfeffer, J. and P. Nowak. 'Joint ventures and inter-organizational interdependence,' *Administrative Science Quarterly,* **21**, 1976, pp. 398–418.

Porter, M. E. *Competitive Strategy: Techniques for Analyzing Industries and Competitors,* Free Press, New York, 1980.

Porter, M. E. *Competitive Advantage,* Free Press, New York, 1985.

Postman, L. and B. J. Underwood. 'Critical issues in interference theory,' *Memory and Cognition,* **1**, 1973, pp. 19–40.

Prahalad, C. K. and Y. Doz. *Multinational Mission,* Free Press, New York, 1987.

Prahalad, C. K. and G. Hamel. 'The core competence and the corporation,' *Harvard Business Review,* May–June 1990, pp. 71–91.

Quinn, J. B., T. L. Doorley and P. C. Paquette. 'Building leadership in high technology industries: Focus technology strategies on services innovation.' Unpublished paper presented at the Second International Conference on Managing the High Technology Firm, University of Colorado, Boulder, CO, 10 January 1990.

Reynolds, J. I. *Indian-America Joint Ventures: Business Policy Relationships.* University Press of America, Washington, DC, 1979.

Reich, R. B. and E. D. Mankin. 'Joint ventures with Japan give away our future,' *Harvard Business Review,* March–April 1986, pp. 78–86.

Root, F. R. 'Some taxonomies of cooperative arrangements.' In F. J. Contractor and P. Lorange (eds), *Cooperative Strategies in International Business,* D.C. Heath, Lexington, MA, 1988, pp. 69–80.

Schillaci, C. E. 'Designing successful joint ventures,' *Journal of Business Strategy,* **8**(2), 1987, pp. 59–63.

Seyle, H. *From Dream to Discovery: On Being a Scientist,* McGraw-Hill, New York, 1964.

Sullivan, J. and R. B. Peterson. 'Factors associated with trust in Japanese-American joint ventures,' *Management International Review,* **22**(2), 1982, pp. 30–40.

Teece, D. J. 'The multinational enterprise: Market failure and market power considerations,' *Sloan Management Review,* **22**(3), 1981, pp. 3–17.

Teece, D. J., G. P. Pisano and A. Shuen. 'Firm capabilities, resources, and the concept of strategy,' CCC Working Paper No. 90-8, Center for Research in Management, University of California at Berkeley, 1990.

Terpstra, V. and K. David. *The Cultural Environment of International Business.* South-Western, Cincinnati, OH, 1985.

Thorelli, H. B. 'Networks: Between markets and hierarchies,' *Strategic Management Journal,* **7**, 1986, pp. 37–51.

Tybejee, T. T. 'Japan's joint ventures in the United States.' In F. J. Contractor and P. Lorange (eds), *Cooperative Strategies in International Business,* D.C. Heath, Lexington, MA, 1988, pp. 457–472.

Watzlawick, P., J. H. Weakland and R. Fisch. *Change.* Norton, New York, 1974.

Westney, D. E. 'Domestic and foreign learning curves in managing international cooperative strategies.' In F. J. Contractor and P. Lorange (eds), *Cooperative Strategies in International Business,* D.C. Heath, Lexington, MA, 1988, pp. 339–346.

Williamson, O. E. *Markets and Hierarchies: An Analysis and Antitrust Implications.* Free Press, New York, 1975.

COUNTERTRADE: A POWERFUL GLOBAL COMPETITIVE STRATEGY FOR U.S. INTERNATIONAL TRADERS

Pavlos Michaels

Introduction

In recent years, there has been a proliferation of requirements for countertrade (barter) in international trade (Verzariu, 1984). This has resulted from the increasing number of developing countries that endorse or encourage such arrangements.

Furthermore, increases in countertrade transactions result from other compensatory impositions requiring reciprocal asset transfers, which in many cases may involve demands for domestic content and coproduction in the importing country. These latter arrangements are increasingly being required for civil contracts in government agency procurements (Verzariu, 1984).

A major reason for the tremendous increase in countertrade is that today the international financial community is in an extremely vulnerable position. Specifically, the inability of Third World Countries to pay off their outstanding debt is challenging the stability of the system (Kirpalani, 1985). In reality, many LDC's do not have the foreign currency reserves to purchase fundamental industrial imports and, thus, find countertrade a viable mechanism for obtaining imports without increasing their debt.

On the other hand, exporters are forced to participate in these countertrade transactions if they wish to increase or, in certain cases, maintain a viable export market. It has become increasingly important for multinational and international banks to understand the intricacies involved in countertrade as its use in international business transactions widens.

Since world trade is a major economic issue of the 1980s, the United States will need to increase the volume of its exports to continue its economic growth. Such an increase is necessary not only as an attempt to reduce the trade deficit, but also in response to present global economic conditions. These conditions will force the United States to participate in an increasingly greater number of countertrade transactions.

This paper, based on an extensive review of the literature on countertrade, attempts to address some of the major issues involved in countertrade within the framework of the contemporary international business environment. Its narrow focus is to investigate and determine the potential for U.S. firms to use countertrade to increase their competitiveness.

Source: Reprinted by permission, *SAM Advanced Management Journal*, Summer 1989, Society for Advancement of Management, Vinton, VA 24179.

Literature Review

Nature of Countertrade Each countertrade transaction is unique, but most transactions share a set of common but not standard characteristics. Basically, there are five major forms of countertrade: (1) barter, (2) parallel barter or counterpurchases, (3) compensation deals or "payback," (4) switch trading or "clearings," and (5) buy-back arrangements (Cateora, 1987, p. 504). One should recognize that these five broad categories are by no means mutually exclusive. Combinations of the traditional with the innovative are being introduced all of the time. For definitions, explanations, and mechanisms of countertrade transactions, the reader is advised to consult any international marketing books which deal with the topic of countertrade, such as Cateora (1987), Cundiff and Hilger (1988), Kirpalani (1985), and other specialized books on countertrade, such as Verzariu (1984).

International Trade and Countertrade Trends Countertrade transactions are definitely increasing (Cateora, 1987; Kirpalani, 1985; Cundiff & Hilger, 1988). Some estimates rank countertrade as high as one third (or 33 percent) of all international transactions (Cooper, 1984; Kirpalani, 1985). Cundiff and Hilger (1988) estimate its magnitude at 30 percent, while the International Trade Administration of the U.S. Department of Commerce estimates 5 percent to 20 percent (Verzariu, 1984). The majority of the conservative estimates, however, are closer to 20 percent (Cateora, 1988).

Regardless, it is evident that a significant amount of all international trade today involves some form of countertrade transaction—a trend expected to increase substantially in the near future. Much of the increase will be from trading with Third World countries (*Business International*, 1985, pp. 353–354). Currently, an estimated 50 percent or more of all international trade with Communist-bloc countries involves countertrade (Walsh, 1985).

The U.S. Government Position on Countertrade The U.S. government is becoming much more attentive to the potential impact of countertrade on the U.S. economy. The Reagan Administration, although it did not take a formal position, did not support countertrade in theory, which it viewed as a violation of the principle of free trade.

> [According to Verzariu (1984),] A long-standing objective of U.S. trade and monetary policy during the post–World War II years has been the development of an open, nondiscriminatory, and multilateral trading system which avoids restrictive trade practices. The U.S. Government policy on countertrade is consistent with its general policy to oppose all interferences with market forces by governments, whether they are mandated countertrade arrangements or other restraints on trade. Free and fair trade based on mutually acceptable trading relations is essential for a strong U.S. economy and continued growth in U.S. exports.

. . . The U.S. Government strongly opposes government-mandated countertrade because such practices are enforced for other-than-economic objectives, resulting in governmental interferences with international market forces. Governmental intrusions in the international marketplaces generally lead to distorted world trade and production patterns and place competitive American exporters at a disadvantage. (p. vi)

The United States, like most other developed nations, hesitates to take a position on countertrade for two reasons: (1) lack of knowledge on the subject, and (2) lack of available data on the economic impact of such transactions. Presently, U.S. trade officials have no measure to determine the amount of U.S. imports that result from countertrade transactions. However, according to an International Trade Commission report, U.S. exports exceed imports received through countertrade during any given period. This is true because the value of goods exported by American companies usually exceeds that of the goods that make up the countertrade obligation (United States International Trade Commission, 1985).

The government is also concerned with the growth in tax evasion, bribery, dumping, and unfair competition as a result of increased countertrade activities. However, the deterioration of the multilateral trade system and the growth of bilateral agreements remains the primary concern to government officials (Verzariu, 1984).

The U.S. government does not seem to know how to react to this archaic yet modern tool of international trade known as countertrade. The government does not promote countertrade but does not actively intervene in private sector involvement in countertrade and, ironically, participates in such activity itself (Verzariu, 1984).

The Commerce Department has established services for U.S. companies involved in countertrade by providing advice on negotiating tactics, market information, and by selling countertraded goods in the United States. The government is even more directly involved in countertrade transactions known as "industrial offsets."

Furthermore, the U.S. Department of Defense arranges cooperative policies encouraging defense industry co-assembly and co-production with other NATO-country defense firms. The U.S. government also engages in barter in the export of surplus agricultural goods. It is apparent from these statements that the U.S. Government needs to research extensively the effects of countertrade, domestically and globally, and develop and implement policy actions that reflect its position. With the continued growth in countertrade, time seems to create a fluctuating, passive yet negative attitude towards countertrade; instead, solid decisions need to be made.

Position of U.S. Business American firms have been more reluctant to participate in countertrading than many of their foreign competitors (Gundiff and

Hilger, 1988). They seem to be unwilling to adjust to different conditions and, in this case, to deviate from customary cash sales. In contrast, Western European and Japanese firms have the longest history of countertrade because of their trading experience with Eastern Europe. U.S. firms have been slow to accept the concept and practice countertrade, preferring to lose a sale rather than become involved in unfamiliar situations and transactions. In fact, a survey by Martin and Ricks (1985) of several hundred U.S. firms involved in international trade indicated that a majority would refuse a countertrade offer.

This attitude seems to stem from inexperience with countertrade and, as a respondent candidly replied to the Martin and Ricks (1985) survey, "We don't need the hassle. We have enough business without it." The truth of the matter is, however, that regardless of prevailing U.S. attitudes, demands for countertrade will increase, and many firms will find they have little or no choice but to submit to hassles or problems of countertrade (Martin and Ricks, 1985).

While a good number of U.S. firms avoid barter or countertrade arrangements in general, others are profitably involved. One excellent example is Pepsi-Cola, which has a barter arrangement with Russia.

From the American free enterprise perspective, the Government's position is correct in theory. But what happens when one faces the realities of the international market? At this point, the international market is of more concern than the U.S. market alone. American firms do not favor countertrading, yet this method of transaction may offer them the only access to markets with soft currencies or to state trading markets (Cundiff and Hilger, 1988; and Kirpalani, 1985).

Does Countertrade Have Any Virtues?

Welt (1985) says, "Countertrade? Better than No Trade." He goes on to explain by giving five reasons why purchasers impose countertrade obligations. The reasons are the following: (1) to preserve hard currency, (2) to improve balance of trade, (3) to gain access to new markets, (4) to upgrade manufacturing capabilities, and (5) to maintain prices of export goods.

From the exporter's perspective, the literature shows that four major reasons motivate an exporter to participate in a countertrade agreement: (1) To take advantage of sales opportunities. More and more developing countries and centrally planned economies are demanding obligatory countertrade arrangements as the only acceptable form of international trade; (2) For Western firms participating in countertrade offers the potential of establishing a long-term source of supply, particularly for firms engaged in "buy-back" agreements; (3) To gain prominence in new markets. Countertrade lends itself to trading during recessionary periods; (4) To lower tax and tariff obligations. This can be done if both parties involved understate the value of the transaction.

Does Countertrade Have Any Drawbacks?

To do justice to the topic, we examine the matter both from the macro- and the microeconomic perspective. Let us begin with the macroeconomic perspective. From the macroeconomic perspective, there are several drawbacks, according to opponents of countertrade. The first and most frequently cited criticism is that it undermines the principles of both GATT and IMF, which are to promote open, multilateral trade among member nations. Although it is argued that bilateral agreements using countertrade better serve the needs of individual countries, critics counter by saying that countertrade is a disguised form of protectionism and an underlying force in the potential breakdown in the multilateral system.

Another negative aspect of countertrade is its complexity and risk. The countertrade transaction generally involves two contracts which must cover a range of factors: price, quantity, quality, and delivery of two separate transactions across national boundaries. Implementing the contracts is a separate but equally difficult task. The risks associated with the political, legal, economic, and cultural environment in the importing country add to the overall complexity and time commitment involved in drafting and implementing the contracts.

The increased cost of countertrade is a major consideration for firms engaging in it. The use of middlemen is standard procedure; coupled with the volume of paperwork and the bureaucratic red tape involved in such a trade agreement, the use of middlemen increases the cost of the deal between 20 percent and 40 percent.

A primary concern from the government's perspective is that countertrade encourages uncompetitive trade practices. This also indicates the need for a well-defined policy that specifically addresses such issues. The distortion of the true values of the deal increases the potential for tax evasion. Transfer pricing and the evasion of income taxes is another issue that is a concern to those trying to regulate countertrade activity. Countertrade deals can also be used to disguise illegitimate bribes. U.S. exporters may make improper payments to foreign officials to avoid the Foreign Corrupt Practices Act of 1977.

It is apparent that countertrade presents some very real threats to such institutions as GATT and the IMF. Although countertrade may only be a short-term solution to many of the persistent problems in the global economy, it seems to be working fairly well.

From the microeconomic perspective, there are a number of disadvantages offered in the literature. First, the crucial problem confronting a seller in countertrade negotiations is determining the value and potential demand of the goods offered for exchange (Cateora, 1987). This is complicated further when there is inadequate time to conduct a market analysis.

A second drawback is the risk involved. The western exporters' concerns range from political stability in individual export markets to unexpected shifts in official regulatory policies in the importer's country which may affect the exporter's trade arrangements or his investments.

Finally, another drawback of countertrade is the need for a special type of preparation—entirely different from other preparations American firms undertake as they engage in trade using money as the medium of exchange.

U.S. Economic Trends and Hopes

In recent years, the big question "Can America Compete?" has been raised continuously (*Business Week,* April 20, 1987), but no acceptable or satisfactory final answer has been given. The U.S. economy has been sluggish for years, despite fiscal and monetary stimuli (*Business Week,* April 20, 1987). Now, faced with the urgent need to reduce its budget and trade deficits, America may well see its enviable standard of living decline (*Business Week,* April 20, 1987).

Looking at the U.S. economic outlook and comparing it to that of other countries, it is easy to accept Senator Lloyd Bentsen's statement that, "We are in the competitive fight of our lives" (*American Excellence in a World Economy.* 1987). Furthermore, Americans may aspire to accommodate former President Ronald Reagan's dream in regard to "the new challenge to America":

> "Yes, in the year 2000, we want America to be number one—and climbing for the stars . . . (The) . . . quest for excellence . . . is a great national understanding that will challenge all Americans to be all they can be, to work together to seek new opportunities, to be the very best in a strong and growing international economy— an international economy that gives us both the challenge of competition and, as it grows and we grow with it, the promise of a century of prosperity ahead." (*American Excellence in a World Economy,* 1987, p. 1).

In brief, discussion about U.S. competitiveness should focus on three analytical categories:

> *Productivity* as a function of how well-off we are relative to other countries in the world; *spending patterns* as they are reflected in our trade deficits; and *trade performance* as it bears directly on the competition between U.S. industry and the industries of other trading nations (*Excellence in a World Economy,* 1987, p. 5).

Countertrade as a Global Competitive Marketing Strategy

America cannot continue ignoring the changing international economic realities. The United States should not retreat into isolation by erecting trade barriers, capital controls, or restrictions on foreign trade and investment. Rather, the United States must fight for market access, fair treatment, and an open free world economy. Efforts to avoid adjustment will damage its citizens' living standards, not protect them (Michaels, 1988). Americans should as always welcome competition and not fight against it. We should remember that competitiveness is a means of raising living standards (*American Excellence in a World Economy,* 1987).

Considering the countertrade and the U.S. economic trends simultaneously, and some of the special conditions within which countertrade takes place, the need for countertrade in a global competitive strategy seems to be absolutely essential. Two questions need to be answered: (1) Why should countertrade be used as a competitive strategy? and (2) How should countertrade be used by U.S. firms to be a successful strategy?

Why Should Countertrade Be Used as a Competitive Strategy? The reviewed literature shows that over 80 countries use or require countertrade exchanges, and also that countertrade has been growing both absolutely and as a portion of international trade. A final but very important factor is that countertrade is part of dynamic environmental changes and global competitive marketing strategies.

For our purpose, strategy is defined as the grand design (masterplan or blueprint) that specifies how to deploy the resources of a firm to achieve its organizational objectives, with emphasis on the long-range perspectives and taking into account the environment and its dynamic changes. Similarly, competitive international marketing strategy is defined as the grand design or masterplan used by a firm to enable it to compete more effectively to strengthen its market position in the international market (Porter, 1980).

In brief, due to the requirements of strategic marketing, the United States must use countertrade as a competitive international marketing and trade strategy. It is imposed by the circumstances of the international and global marketing arena. The option to reject countertrade is not available to the United States unless it wants to be left out of the mainstream international market and suffer the consequences. Let us remember that the United States has been experiencing an era of affluence and rapid growth as a result of being in the mainstream of the industrial revolution and international trade (Kirpalani, 1985; Michaels, 1988).

The international marketing environment (and even more the global one) requires that Americans change, and the faster we embrace the challenge of change, the earlier and greater will be the benefits (*American Excellence in a World Economy,* 1987). The acceptance of countertrade as a competitive international marketing strategy is concluded to be both imposed by the circumstances and absolutely imperative for U.S. firms, based on the reviewed literature.

How Should U.S. Firms Use Countertrade as a Global Strategy?
Companies need to make a series of strategic decisions pertaining to their international and global marketing operations. For example, they need first to decide on whether to become an international company. Second, an international firm must decide on its geographic concentration for business—i.e.,

whether its business or operations should locate in developing or industrialized countries. Third, a firm must choose the particular countries to be entered. Fourth, a decision has to be made on the strategy to use to penetrate each country or market selected. Fifth, a firm has to decide which marketing mix to offer in its international operations in general, and in each selected country target market in particular.

Jeannet and Hennessey (1988, p. 240) offer a conceptual model on international strategies, which may serve our purposes very well in this case. The remainder of this section ties into the Jeannet and Hennessey model.

A deliberate global expansion policy is pursued by firms which are motivated by profit potential through market expansion (Jeannet and Hennessey, 1988). For U.S. firms in particular, market extension should also be used as a defensive strategy to maintain sales, volume, and profits due to the deep penetration of their domestic market by strong foreign competitors.

Growth rates vary significantly among countries. In low-growth countries, which are also faced with a shortage of foreign exchange, the firm might suffer a competitive disadvantage unless it is willing to accept the required countertrade conditional exchanges. This market reality must be understood, and firms must be prepared to accept developing and less developed countries in their market portfolios.

The country selection decision is one of the components of an international marketing strategy. The country selection may not present a major problem under normal circumstances. But what happens when many countries practice countertrading and the United States needs markets due to, say, trade deficits and loss of both domestic and international market share? The options may be limited, forcing the United States to resort to countertrade, also, since there may not be enough countries operating according to U.S. desires.

After target countries are chosen for market entry, a firm must decide how to enter them. The options range from a very low level of involvement, investment, and commitment (such as various forms of exporting) to more involved and investment-intensive forms of entry (such as company-owned sales subsidiaries or even manufacturing subsidiaries (Kirpalani, 1985). Countertrade may be the only feasible and viable entry strategy in some cases, and should be used.

Marketing-mix programs are significant in a domestic market and likewise in foreign markets. Besides, the United States is only one out of over 160 to 170 countries in the world. Although standardization is favored over adaptation by many for good reasons, we cannot standardize everything to fit the American business system. Therefore, countertrade may have to be used if American firms are sincerely honest in their desire to compete in the international market arena.

To manage the international marketing process, a situation analysis is definitely required. But a situation analysis also shows that countertrade is a fact of international trade, and a strategy which has proven successful in many cases.

Therefore, countertrade can be neither ignored or rejected as a way of managing the international marketing process.

To compete successfully in international marketing, firms need to pay attention to their geographic expansion. A firm decides on extent of internationalization it desires by choosing a position on a continuum ranging from entirely domestic to a global reach where the company devotes its entire marketing strategy to global competition. Of course, each level of internationalization profoundly changes the way a company competes and requires different strategies with respect to marketing programs, planning, organization, and control of the international marketing effort.

Again, countertrade may be a viable (though imposed) competitive strategy in international marketing. Countertrade is the best strategy for expanding into such markets as the Third World, and the Eastern Bloc, where foreign currency shortages and other factors make countertrade necessary (Kirpalani, 1985). In the final analysis, the decision boils down to whether U.S. firms want to take advantage of foreign markets or not.

Product-market strategy is the second key dimension in the strategy of an international company—the first being geographic extension. To what extent should a company become a supplier of a wide range of products aimed at several or many markets? Should a company become the global specialist in a certain area by satisfying one or a small number of target segments and doing this in most major markets around the world? Do U.S. companies have a choice under the prevailing international and national conditions as presented above? Once again, countertrade may be (or rather is) a good option strategy these days.

Summary

Competitive strategies for international marketing represent the focus of this paper as they pertain to countertrade. When firms compete in the international market, their competitive strategies are likely to depend on their resources and their competition (Jeannet & Hennessey, 1988). A company must be able to adapt to any differences in competition on a country-by-country or country-by-group-of-countries basis. This situation makes it necessary for U.S. firms to use countertrade as a competitive international and global marketing strategy.

Firms (U.S. firms, especially) increasingly find that, for competitive reasons, they must operate internationally to survive. During this past decade, a changing international market environment has considerably influenced company choices. As a result, many formerly domestic firms have become multinationals. Subsequently, an increasing number of firms have adopted a global strategy and, in the process, developed a new business philosophy. It is at this juncture that U.S. firms face a challenge: To adopt a new way of thinking and accept countertrade as a viable option in competitive international strategies.

Conclusions

It is apparent from this discussion that the U.S. government needs to study the issue of countertrade and develop a policy including regulatory actions, if necessary, to monitor countertrade actions. The most successful strategy would be to collaborate with other Western nations so that the policy would be universally acceptable and applicable. It is also a practical solution, since most of the major Western industrialized nations (excluding France) have not yet developed a policy. The government should also continue providing assistance to the private firms engaging in countertrade, and perhaps develop these services to include insurance.

In many ways, countertrade is contradictory; for example, it undermines the multilateral trading system. But it is precisely the failures of this system that have given rise to countertrade and its continued growth. Countertrade has both an expansionary as well as contradictory effect on world trade. Countertrade can be used to avoid payment of debts, but can also serve as a force to collect debts. The long-term effects of countertrade remain unknown, but it is time for the U.S. government to abandon its neutral to negative approach, establish consistent policies and recognize that countertrade will continue to grow as a tool in the international trade environment.

Finally, academicians need to study countertrade further to understand its mechanics. Simultaneously, they need to research the attitudes of American traders, as well as the actual and perceived problems encountered. Such an undertaking would provide fruitful assistance to both American international or global marketers and the U.S. Government in developing supportive programs and policies.

REFERENCES

American Excellence in a World Economy: A Report of the Business Roundtable on International Competitiveness (1987). Washington, D.C.: The Business Roundtable on International Competitiveness.

Banks, Gary (1983). "The Economics and Politics of Countertrade," *The World Economy,* (June), 159–182.

Cateora, Phillip R. (1987). *International Marketing* (6th ed.). Homewood, IL: Irwin.

Chase Manhattan Bank N.A. (1986), "Countertrade." Countertrade Unit, May 1986.

Cooper, Richard (1984). "By Bartering, Dealers Avoid Laying Out Cash for Goods," *Merchandising,* April, 93–96.

Cundiff, Edward, and Hilger, Marye Tharp (1988). *Marketing in the International Environment* (2nd ed). Englewood Cliffs, NJ: Prentice Hall.

De Miramon, Jacques (1985), "Countertrade: An Illusory Solution," *OECD Observer,* (May), 24–29.

Fielke, Norman (1983), "Barter in the Space Age," *New England Economic Review,* (November/December), 34–41.

Huh, K. M. (1983), "Countertrade: Trade Without Cash?" *Finance and Development,* (December), 14–16.

Jeannet, Jean-Pierre and Hennessey, Hubert D. (1988). *International Marketing Management.* Boston: Houghton Mifflin Company.

Kirpalani, V. H. (1985). *International Marketing.* New York: Random House.

Lipsey, R. G. and Lancaster, Kelvin (1955), "The General Theory of Second Best," *Review of Economic Studies,* 11–32.

Lochner, Scott J. (1985), "Countertrade and International Barter." *The International Lawyer,* Summer.

Martin, Everett G. and Ricks, Thomas E. (1985), "Countertrading Grows as Cash-Short Nations Seek Marketing Help," *The Wall Street Journal,* March 13, p. 1.

Michaels, Pavlos (1988). "Protectionism and Its Real Meaning for the United States: New Problems, New Approaches." in David L. Moore (Editor) *Marketing: Forward Motion.* Williamsburg, VA: Atlantic Marketing Association Proceedings, pp. 857–867.

Mirus, Rolf and Young, Bernard (1986), "Economic incentives for Countertrade." *Journal of International Business Studies,* (Fall), 27–39.

Pennar, Karen (1987), "Can America Compete?" *Business Week,* April 20, pp. 45–69.

Porter, Michael E. (1980). *Competitive Strategy.* New York: The Free Press.

Smith, W. R., Jr. (1988). "Countertrade: Forms, History and Economic Efficiency," in John H. Summey and Paul J. Hensel (Eds.) *Strategic Issues in a Dynamic Marketing Environment*—Southern Marketing Association 1988 Proceedings. Carbondale, IL: Southern Illinois University at Carbondale.

The Economist (1987), May 9, 61–62.

United States International Trade Commission (1985). *Assessment of the Effects of Barter and Countertrade Transactions on U.S. Industries:* Report on Investigation No. 332–185 Under Section 332 of the Tariff Act of 1930 (USITC Publication 1766). Washington, D.C.: United States International Trade Commission.

Verzariu, Pompiliu (1984). *International Countertrade: A Guide for Managers and Executives.* Washington, D.C.: U.S. Department of Commerce, International Trade Administration.

Walsh, James I. (1985), "Mandated Countertrade: Methods and Issues." *Export Today,* Fall, pp. 57–67.

Welt, Leo G. B., "Trade Without Money: Barter and Countertrade," New York: Law and Business, Inc., 1984.

Welt, Leo G. B., "Countertrade? Better than No Trade," *Export Today,* Spring 1985.

READING 37 **FOUR WINNING STRATEGIES FOR THE INTERNATIONAL CORPORATION**

John Fayerweather

ABSTRACT. The international corporation must look carefully at the global environment and its own capabilities. Only after a thorough assessment of these factors will a company be able to choose from among the four most prevalent global strategies outlined in this article.

IBM and Singer are both dominant global firms in their respective major fields, computers and sewing machines. For both, foreign operations provide about 50 percent of volume. But the international strategies of the two companies are strikingly different. In what ways and why? The analysis which follows digs down to the roots of the explanation, developing the logic of the four basic strategy models prevalent in current global operations.

Fundamentally, strategy formulation for the international corporation (IC) is no different from that for any firm. The basic requirements are a sound assessment of the capabilities of the firm and perceptive determination about how those capabilities may be employed effectively within the operating environment. There are, however, a number of special characteristics of the global context that result in distinctive elements of strategy formulation for the IC.

To lay the groundwork for discussion of strategy models, these distinctive elements must be examined: the more significant of the environmental factors to which the IC must adapt, the particular capabilities of the IC, and the role of control in IC strategy.

Looking at the Environment

The unique and critical environmental features for the IC are largely related to the prominence of nations as the basic institutions of the world economy and polity and the importance of national goals. These appear constantly as reference points to which the strategic capabilities of the IC must be related. Two broad goal sets dominate: economic progress and political control.

Economic Progress The daily preoccupation of nations around the world and their governments is with furtherance of economic progress. An assortment of subgoals are recognized as central for this purpose, each having important relevance to the operations of ICs.

Expansion of industrial facilities is the sine qua non for increased output

Source: Reprinted from *Journal of Business Strategy* (New York: Warren, Gorham & Lamont). © 1981 Research Institute of America, Inc. Used with permission.

of goods and services. It is also the primary m
employment, a pressing need in the LDCs with th
an important consideration even in the develop
payments is a chronic concern in virtually all cc
of foreign exchange is a critical determinant of a
for industrial expansion, materials for industrial output, a
meet consumer desires that cannot be produced internally. To
balance of payments situation, nations constantly seek to cut back on non
tial imports, increase inputs of foreign capital, and expand exports. Finally,
improvement of the technological capabilities of a country is perceived as
essential for industrial growth. Toward that end, a country seeks both technology in itself and the improvement of the technological capabilities of its people.

Political Control Political control is an objective both for its own sake and as
a means for furthering economic progress. All nations today adhere at least to
some degree to the concept that economic progress requires central direction
by the national government. National leaders perceive, therefore, that it is
important to their ends that they have a high degree of control over economic
decision making, including the nature of new investment, the allocation of
funds both internally and in international transactions, and related factors.
More broadly, they recognize that control of national affairs is dependent upon
the power of the nation in international affairs. In an economically interdependent world, each nation's share of the global wealth and its role in global
decision making are dependent upon its power status. Conversely, to the extent
that other nations are stronger, each nation finds that aspects of internal affairs
are heavily influenced by interests of outsiders rather than those of its own
people. Thus, it is of continuing importance to its goal of controlling its own
affairs to strengthen itself in the international arena.

Assessing Capabilities

Within this context, the first step in strategy formulation is for management to
identify the basic strong points of its operations. This process is sound in
general, since the strengths of a company give it a competitive edge and must,
consequently, be the focus of overall emphasis in strategy. The process takes on
a special importance in international operations, however, because the strengths
of a company very often turn out to be the elements that are valued by host
nations. They compose, therefore, a significant part of the bargaining leverage
that the IC can employ at the negotiating table.

Each company, of course, has a unique set of capabilities. However, most of
the areas of strength of ICs fall into a limited number of categories, each with
particular strategy implications. The following outline provides a useful general
scheme for analysis which each firm can adapt for its own needs. Broadly, the

special capabilities of firms in international business are analyzed under two headings, resource strengths and global capabilities.

Resource Strengths The traditional rationale for the wide range of international business transactions has been the flow of resources from countries where they are plentiful or available at low cost to countries offering good demand and satisfactory price. ICs fit into this tradition, their strategies being based to a very large extent on resource capabilities. However, the resources in which their strengths are prominent take quite varied forms and there have been significant shifts in their character in recent years. Thus, the IC management needs to assess carefully both its resource capabilities and the needs for them around the world to lay an adequate base for its strategy. Four general types of resource capability exist: skills, capital, labor, and raw materials.

Technological and Managerial Skills. The prominence of technical and managerial skills among the resource capabilities of international corporations is readily observed. Every IC with some patented products or processes, a good R&D program, and a competent management will mark them down as key components of its resource capabilities. However, the assessment for strategy formulation cannot stop at that broad level. The management must ask a number of more refined questions about its skill capabilities to determine what sort of strategy they lead to.

In considering technical skills, here are some key questions to be answered:

♦ Are the skills quite unique, or do competitors have comparable capabilities? If the former is true, as in a case like IBM, the company works from great strength in its strategy, whereas in the latter case, it is forced to work from a weaker position or to seek other aspects of capabilities as sources of strength.

♦ Is the company constantly developing new technological innovations, or is its technology relatively stable? In the former case, a company may project a strategic position in which foreign countries are continuously seeking its services, while in the latter, host countries may see no value in relations with the firm beyond the minimum necessary to acquire existing technological skills.

♦ How difficult is it to learn and apply the skills? If skills are relatively simple to absorb, the strategy for transmitting them will typically be much less sophisticated than that where the technology is of a complex nature requiring continuing controls, supervision, and other forms of contact between the IC and application situations.

♦ What is the ability of host nation personnel and companies to absorb technology? If the ability is relatively low, the strategy of the IC should be based on a much more fully integrated delivery system than is needed where the host competence is high. The difference here is well illustrated by comparing Japan, which absorbed a tremendous body of IC technology from the United States and other countries largely through licensing and minority joint venture arrangements, with relatively underdeveloped nations in which fully controlled subsidiaries staffed for extended periods by expatriates are required for optimum effectiveness.

The answers to these questions for each corporation are continually changing, with major shifts observable over relatively short periods. Until the early 1960s, U.S. international corporations had a wide technological lead in many product areas. However, the Europeans and now the Japanese have caught up and in some cases surpassed American ICs in technology in a number of fields. Thus, in a large portion of cases, corporations, which may have built their early international strategies on relatively strong technological capability, must readjust to the realities that they are on a par with a number of competitors. Likewise, as the technological competence in many less-developed host nations has risen rapidly, the strategic importance of IC technological capabilities has declined relatively.

Transmission of managerial skills is more complex in general than that of technological skills, but over the long haul it may be equally or more important to the strength of an IC's international strategy. Because they rest heavily on human behavior rather than physical-mechanical processes, managerial skills are much more difficult to transmit and acquire. For this reason, strategy based on their transmission is harder to develop and manage. By the same token, however, its competitive potential and possibilities for long-term strength are considerable, especially in light of the continuing improvement of managerial systems and methods in home countries of ICs. Accepting the general proposition that ICs generally have a transmittable capability in their managerial skills, the manager must again ask more precise questions about the situation of his company.

◆ What managerial skills are appropriate for the level of development of host nations? For example, sophisticated consumer behavior interviewing may work well in Europe but be overcomplicated both for managers and for economic utility in Nigeria.

◆ How do the managerial skills relate to cultural contexts in host nations? Intensive superior-subordinate conferences with target setting and appraisal may, for example, be a useful export for management development in Australia but run counter to cultural patterns in Indonesia.

Capital. The role of capital in the strategies of international corporations has changed substantially over the years. In earlier times, the simple process of transmitting funds from the parent company to establish factories abroad was a major component of international strategies because other sources of funds were relatively limited and establishment of fully owned subsidiaries was the dominant strategy mode. By the mid-1970s, the provision of home country capital had fallen to a much smaller role in IC strategies, both because of the greater availability of other sources in host countries and international capital markets (e.g., Eurodollars) and because of the greater frequency of alternative strategies, such as licensing and joint ventures.

At the same time, other aspects of capital have become more prominent in strategy formulation as the structure of overseas investments of ICs has grown, including overseas production facilities and global marketing systems. The production and full utilization of each form of capital calls for careful attention in strategy formulation.

Since the greater portion of foreign investment has been made in the past decade or so, the majority of foreign production sites and facilities may be presumed to be relatively satisfactory. However, for older factories and increasingly for the current generation, significant questions must be posed in the assessment of resources available to the IC in light of changing conditions both internally and externally. How do the costs of each factory compare with those of competing facilities, particularly in other countries where labor and other costs may be appreciably lower? How suitably are the facilities positioned in relation to changes in market demand?

Global marketing systems, including distribution channels, advertising structure, and brand names, have always been one of the great strengths of international corporations. They have taken on a new significance as a capital resource, however, because of the strong thrust of less-developed countries toward development of markets for export of manufactured goods in the past few years. There are substantial advantages to the LDCs in utilizing these well-established marketing systems as compared with employing alternatives or setting up their own distribution methods.

For the most part, this utilization has taken place internally within the organizations of international corporations, fostered substantially by external incentives. That is, the main pattern of evolution has been for ICs to increasingly utilize plants in Southeast Asia, Mexico, Brazil, and a few other countries as export supply points, fostered by the LDCs' providing export incentives. Assessing how well the IC's international marketing structure is positioned to serve this process can therefore pay off handsomely because expansion of exports ranks as a top priority for most LDCs.

Labor. Because of their parochial viewpoint, many international corporations have experienced labor as a competitive weakness rather than as a resource until quite recently. In the early 1960s in particular, a number of U.S. ICs along with purely domestic corporations suffered severely from the influx of imports from Japan and other low-wage-cost countries. The more competent IC managements now perceive that labor is a resource that they can use to their own advantage just as effectively as their competitors did. In the assessment of this resource, however, questions must be asked to determine how great its value is and in what ways it can be used. Is the value-weight-volume relationship of a product such that it can be shipped substantial distances making effective use of wage-cost differences? Is it feasible to break down production processes so that labor-intensive aspects can be performed in low-wage areas and components shipped for assembly in marketing centers? To what extent in such a system are there problems of training, quality control, and maintenance of continuity in flow of products?

Raw Materials. The typical manufacturing IC does not count among its major resources raw materials in the same sense as a mining or petroleum firm. Nonetheless, many manufacturing ICs have a degree of control over raw materials which is important for their international strategies. For example, chemical and phamaceutical companies produce intermediates (a blend of raw materials and skills) which are essential for end-product producers in many countries. To the extent that this is the case in any particular IC, the resource assessment therefore should include the relative competitive strength that raw material resources provide to the firm.

Global Capabilities

The unique capabilities of the international corporation compared with those of an essentially national corporation lie in its capacity to organize activities on a global basis. Although the transmission of resources may be accomplished by national corporations, only the international corporation is structured to integrate economic activities from a worldwide point of view. The global unification capabilities offer substantial opportunity for competitive advantage. On the other hand, there are strong forces working toward fragmentation of operations, including the economic and cultural differences among countries and the distinctive aspects of the national interests of each which are pressed by their national governments in negotiations with ICs. Thus, the second major aspect of assessment of strategic capabilities lies in examining the relative weights of these influences for unification and fragmentation of operations. The analysis focuses on the area of global capability central to basic strategy, the product delivery system.

The product delivery system incorporates the company's product lines, research and development program, logistic system, and sales promotion efforts. Great economic advantage can theoretically be achieved by a high degree of global unification of all aspects of this system through the economies of scale, avoidance of wasteful duplication of effort, and location of activities in low-cost areas. However, opposing influences, both in the past and currently, impose a substantial amount of fragmentation in the systems of virtually all companies.

Product Lines: Standardization versus Diversity. One key consideration of unification is product line. The capabilities for unification in the other aspects are all dependent to a substantial degree on the extent of standardization of company product lines around the world. Thus, the pressure of the advantages to be gained through unification in the other aspects provides strong pressures for standardization of product lines.

The great majority of companies do stick within broad product categories throughout their worldwide operations except in unusual circumstances; for example, Singer took up life insurance in Brazil to help cover the overhead of its retail stores when imports of sewing machines were cut off in the 1950s. However, within their broad product categories, companies typically have substantial diversity either for historical reasons (acquisitions or decentralized product decision making in earlier periods) or because of current conditions such as variations in local tastes, standards of living, and climate. The incentives to move in the direction of adapting to these variations are considerable since, after all, it is market penetration and market share that are fundamentally the keys to corporate growth. The strategy assessment, therefore, must carefully weigh the potentials in this fragmentation direction against the considerable potential advantages from standardization and unification in other aspects of the product delivery system.

Research and Development: To Centralize or Not? The advantages of a unified approach to worldwide research and development are compelling. Centralization of R&D reduces wasteful duplication of effort, makes communication among technical personnel more efficient, and generally provides better coordination with global sales and production management. By comparison with R&D efforts of essentially national companies, a unified global R&D system permits amortization of R&D costs over a much broader base. Thus, it is competitively feasible for the IC to mount a higher level of R&D effort than competitors operating on a more limited or fragmented basis. The practical impact is such that the great majority of international corporations do virtually all of their research in a limited number of facilities in their home countries with overseas technical work largely confined to development resulting in minor product modifications to fit local tastes, styles, and the like.

This general pattern is highly unsatisfactory to host nations, however. In their quest for both economic progress and political strength, they give a high priority to building up their own technical capability. The typical parent IC research and development organization, while it provides technological benefits to foreign countries, is not perceived as building up their long-term technical capability. What host nations seek is for ICs to establish R&D facilities within their borders to train their people and provide on-the-spot innovative capabilities.

Besides this political pressure, there are additional considerations that favor some distribution of R&D facilities outside of the home nation. In particular, it is a means for effectively using technical personnel of other countries, and of being more responsive to market demands by closer proximity to local sales organizations. In combination, these considerations have led a few companies, particularly the larger ones, to establish some global dispersion of R&D facilities, typically with units in Europe and to a lesser degree in Latin America and Japan. In some cases, the full R&D effort for a particular product line may be allocated to one of the foreign units, thus preserving to a substantial degree the operational benefits of a unified system, simply shifting the geographical site of R&D work.

These varied elements suggest that the prevailing pattern of unified R&D represents the strongest capability of the international corporation but that there is sufficient logic for departure from it in some cases. Thus, each corporation must make a careful assessment of the balance of factors in its own case for this aspect of the product delivery system.

Production Systems: Local or Global in Scope? The potential capabilities from a unified global logistic system are just as promising as those from unified R&D activities. One can conceive a system in which a limited number of factories of optimum economic scale are located in sites with the lowest cost of labor and materials supplying markets all over the world. Unfortunately, this is far from the reality. There are major influences, both internal and external, that militate against unification of logistic systems.

Among the internal factors, product characteristics are often a significant consideration. The volume or weight of products may result in transportation costs that eliminate all or a good portion of the advantages gained through large-scale plants or lower-cost sites. History is another consideration, companies being reluctant to close down established facilities and make new investments, particularly if benefits from logistic efficiency are modest. Finally, proximity of production facilities to markets facilitates coordination of sales and production activities. Thus, gains in marketing effectiveness are observed by many companies to offset the limited benefits that might be provided by greater efficiency in the logistic system.

The external factors for the most part revolve around the nation-oriented drive to maximize local production regardless of global efficiency considerations. In the less-developed countries, governments pressing for industrial development have established barriers to imports (tariffs and quotas), causing ICs to establish factories serving the local national market only, with costs well above those of products made in major factories serving export systems. In the developed countries, the governmental actions are typically less forceful but present nonetheless. They are motivated in part by balance-of-payments difficulties, for which one solution is restricting imports. A second factor of growing strength is the drive of organized labor in each country to hold onto existing production of ICs as well as restricting competitive imports.

As a consequence of these external and internal influences, the extent of global unification of IC logistic systems is confined to a few patterns in which benefits are great enough to outweigh the deterrents or the latter are relatively modest. Quite commonly, production is centralized on a regional basis in which the transportation and marketing communication deterrents are minor and economies of scale are substantial. This approach is particularly common where external factors have deliberately favored it, notably in the European Economic Community and to a lesser but slowly expanding degree in other regional economic groups, like the Latin American Free Trade Area and the Andean Common Market. The second pattern of growing importance is the structure tying facilities in LDCs to markets in developed countries, with emphasis on the effective transmission of labor resources noted earlier.

Gearing Sales Promotion to the Audience. The global unification capabilities of the IC in sales promotion are substantially less both in theory and practice than those in R&D and logistics. There are some efficiencies in use of common marketing methods throughout an IC, including interchange of ideas and experience about similar products among units. Some gains are feasible through centralization of preparation of advertising material. Utilization of media with global or regional distribution requires a centralized approach. However, the benefits achieved in these ways are modest and a large portion of sales promotion efforts are necessarily oriented to the local level. It is essential to their effectiveness that they be finely attuned to differences in consumer attitudes and competitive conditions. So the practical possibilities of unified global approaches are limited. Nonetheless, with variations among industries, they offer sufficient advantage so that they must be included in the strategic assessment process.

The Importance of Control

Control assumes a critical role in strategic planning because of the importance attached to it by both host nations and international corporations. For the former, the decision-making power held by the IC is a serious detraction from the capability of the nation to control its own affairs, the significance of which was stressed above. For the international corporation, on the other hand, control of its foreign operations is of fundamental importance.

The IC has a fiduciary responsibility to its stockholders which requires that it exercise adequate supervision of the performance of corporate assets. Managements commonly perceive this responsibility as calling for the ability to control the main decisions affecting corporate operations. In more concrete terms, key aspects of global operations call for a substantial degree of central control if they are to be effective, including transmission of skills and coordination of global product delivery.

Conflict is the inevitable outcome of these well-founded desires of both the host nations and the ICs for control. To achieve most satisfactory resolution of the conflict requires a full understanding of the objectives being sought through control and the means of achieving them. The ultimate outcome in each situation will be determined in large measure by the power of each party, but substantial accommodation of interests and effective direction of power may be achieved if the perception of the situation is clear on both sides.

The Role of Ownership Of particular importance in this stage of strategy assessment is a full comprehension of the role of ownership, an element in control that is badly misunderstood by many people, both in host nations and international corporations. Ownership is commonly perceived to be the major determinant of control. This perception stems from the obvious fact that the owners have ultimate voting power over major corporate decisions and the choice of key personnel. However, as applied to the ownership by ICs of subsidiaries in foreign countries, there is substantially more to control than that.

In the first place, regardless of the degree of ownership by the parent IC, a wide range of decisions on subsidiary operations is either potentially or actually controlled by host governments, including investments, repatriation of funds, and employment of expatriates. The implication of this fact for the IC is that obtaining ownership control may in fact be substantially less useful than it believes because the actual degree of control obtained is limited. The implication for the host nation is that forcing ICs to give up or share ownership with local nationals may not be as worthwhile or necessary as it perceives because the specific objectives sought may be more effectively obtained through direct controls exerted on the subsidiary decision making.

Just as the host nation may achieve control directly without national ownership participation, so the international corporation may exert substantial control even from a minority position under certain circumstances. The key to this sort of control lies in the possession by the IC of some continuing source of strength that gives it leverage in decision making in relation to local partners. The most common sources of this form of strength are a continuing flow of new technology, superior management competence, and control of export marketing channels that are important to the venture.

A second critical point is that the control effects achieved by sharing ownership with local nationals depend greatly upon the character of the latter. So far as an IC is concerned, an agreeable or silent partner may in many cases make little difference in the outcome of its decision making whereas a difficult partner may complicate control in directions quite apart from any control influences intended by the host government. By the same token, whether or not the host government achieves significant control gains through ownership by its host nationals in the affiliates of ICs depends upon the amenability of the local investors to government influence, which will vary considerably with their politics, personalities, and power.

Economic Effects To further complicate this picture, there are diverse views as to the economic effects of shared ownership. The basic presumption of host nations is that minimizing foreign equity reduces the long-term outflow of income from the country. Whether or not this is a valid assumption depends upon assessment of the continuing value of the capital involved and the profitability of each particular venture. More complex are questions about the structural effect of shared ownership. As a practical matter, ICs with limited resources and the necessity to build the greatest strength for long-term operations generally treat affiliates differently. This treatment depends upon the degree of ownership in respect to what is important to host nations. In particular, they are much less likely to assign research and development functions to operations in which they have lower ownership shares. They are also inclined to give such units a less important role in global logistic systems. It is both more profitable and simpler to handle decision making if those plants used as export sources are fully or at least majority-controlled.

These considerations lead to a wide variety of current viewpoints toward shared ownership. In some countries, there is very strong pressure on international corporations to give up majority ownership of affiliates. The Andean group countries are typical of this end of the spectrum. New investors or those seeking the free trade benefits of the Andean Common Market are expected to divest themselves of majority ownership within ten to fifteen years. At the other end of the spectrum are some countries that place no pressures on companies to give up ownership. Thus, each IC in each country situation must carefully assess how shared ownership would specifically affect its operations as well as determining what the objectives and outlook of the government are to decide what range of flexibility may be found within which it may negotiate for its own interests.

How ICs Respond: Four Strategy Models

The assortment of factors considered in the assessment process will lead to different conclusions for strategy in each company situation. It is impractical, therefore, to set forth detailed strategy recommendations for international corporations in general. However, it is feasible to outline the main dimensions of a few strategy models which are logical outcomes of the assessment process outlined here and which may be observed as common patterns in international business. The key elements of the models are outlined in Table 1 including the corporate capabilities underlying them, the form of economic return anticipated, the requirements for effective operation including critical points subject to negotiation with host governments, and the power available to the IC in the negotiation process.

Dynamic High-Technology Model The dynamic high-technology strategy assumes an IC capability for generating a continuing flow of product and process innovations for which demand exists in foreign countries. The profitability of the strategy rests upon arrangements rewarding the IC for transmitting the skills. The chief alternatives are satisfactory profit margins for exports of com-

TABLE **1**   Strategy Patterns for International Corporations

	IC Capabilities	Economic Return System	Operating Structure Requirements	IC Power Factors
Dynamic high-technology model	Continuing flow of technically significant new products	Steady flow of payments in royalties or from sales margins	Sustained high-quality R&D program. Reasonable control of application of technology abroad	Strong, based on desire of host nations for future technological innovations
Low- or Stable-technology model	Useful technological skill but low sophistication or slow change	Full income realized in a short period	A short-term transmission arrangement: sale or turnkey installation Sufficient control to assure income payment	Relatively weak, dependent on value of technology and competition
Advanced management skill model	High competence in marketing or other management fields	Steady flow of dividends from ongoing operations	Continuing integrated operations in fields with management skill competitively effective	Weak due to low priority for management skills
Unified-logistic labor-transmission model	High value to weight/volume ratio. High labor intensity in production. Strong global marketing system	Regular flow of dividends from either production units or marketing system	Low-cost production sites Strong global marketing organization Standardized products Highly integrated control of operations Full ownership preferred	Strong based on high priority for exports in producing countries. Weak in importing countries

pleted products or components, royalties for the use of technology, and dividends from competitively profitable operation of overseas affiliates.

The most essential requirement for the satisfactory pursuit of this strategy is the maintenance of a strong R&D program that will generate the continuing flow of new technology. The importance of this requirement must be stressed because host nation pressure on ICs to expand R&D within their countries may jeopardize it. The risk for the IC is that distributing R&D among a number of host countries may reduce the efficiency and effectiveness of technological work so that the heart of the strategy is weakened. Thus, concessions to host nation desires in this regard must be given grudgingly and carefully. The chief possibilities are that minor development work may be allocated to foreign affiliates or that large segments of work on a particular product line may be allocated to major R&D facilities in particular countries. If the latter type of concession is made, however, it is essential that full control over the foreign unit be assured, including ownership, because of the possible loss of proprietary rights to products that are essential to the economic base of the strategy.

The second essential requirement is that sufficient income be generated by the operating arrangements so that the global R&D program can be adequately financed. In the current trend of host nation negotiations, particularly in less-developed countries, this requirement is increasingly difficult to achieve. LDCs in the past few years have become much more aggressive in trying to reduce the balance of payments cost of paying for imported technology. Mexico, for example, in 1973 passed a new law calling for review of all technology agreements and is systematically requiring the reduction of royalties in a substantial number of cases.

Some degree of control over foreign affiliates is required in this strategy, but not as much as in some other strategies. A key assumption is that a substantial degree of effective managerial control can be achieved simply through the leverage of the continuing provision of technology. The minimum essential requirement is sufficient control over the application and quality of the technological work of the foreign affiliate so that the economic base of the transmission process is not weakened over the long term. That is, the IC must be able to assure that the technology is used in such a way that satisfactory products are produced. Otherwise, the affiliate will not continue to generate income that will flow back to the IC. This degree of control can be achieved by relatively limited means, such as a quality-control arrangement with an independent licensee if the latter is a competent manufacturing organization. Beyond this minimum essential, the IC stands to gain by achieving greater degrees of control over the foreign affiliate. As a general matter, the effectiveness of the application of its technology will usually be greater if it has full control over the personnel employed in the foreign affiliates and key decisions in the operating processes. Furthermore, the greater the ownership, the more readily and completely the IC may obtain full financial benefits from the technological capabilities.

The strength of the IC in negotiating these points depends essentially upon the quality of its technological capabilities. A company with a significant competitive lead in a field whose technology is considered very important to host nations commands strong power in such a strategy. Leaders in specialized fields, like computers and pharmaceutical products, are typical examples. Companies with somewhat less essential technologies or whose work is closely matched by competitors are in a less-strong position. Firms producing nuclear reactors and various types of industrial machinery provide examples of this sort.

Stable- or Low-Technology Model   The second strategy model assumes the IC has capability in a technological field that has a relatively slow rate of innovation (e.g., steel) or in which the technology is of a rather unsophisticated character (e.g., cement). The economic returns in such circumstances must usually be based on one-shot or quite short-term arrangements unless other factors provide supplementary strength. That is, the IC's strategy calls for a system in which the technology in effect is sold in one immediate transaction or over some given period required to effectively transfer the skills involved. As compared with the first model, there can be no presumption of continuing income over an extended period.

The operating requirements for this strategy call for the same sort of short-term viewpoint. The key requirements are a sufficiently secure financial arrangement to assure adequate return coupled as may be appropriate to sufficient control over operations to support that financial return. The specific form these arrangements may take will vary considerably according to the country circumstances.

The simplest approach is an arrangement in which the technology is sold outright. In some cases, this may merely amount to selling a piece of machinery with an instruction book or perhaps the brief service of an engineer to assist in the installation and start-up process. More complex arrangements grade up to the turnkey contract for large industrial installations in which the IC undertakes full responsibility for construction of a plant and managing it for a period of years until local personnel are competent in its operation.

The other general approach to this strategy is the establishment of licensees, joint ventures, or fully owned subsidiaries with a guarded time horizon perspective. Host country attitudes are generally not favorable to the long-term income costs of arrangements like this based on relatively stable or low-sophistication technology. However, the general foreign investment policies or other conditions at a given moment in a country may permit an international corporation to establish a fully owned operation. In doing so, the IC must realistically recognize that in the future, perhaps not far down the road, adverse host national attitudes may assert themselves. Such has been the case in many situations in less-developed countries, resulting in pressures on ICs with weak technological positions to divest all or part of their ownership and terminate licensing agreements from which continuing benefits were not apparent to the host government officials. Thus, the strategy of a corporation in setting up operations should presume a relatively short-term payout against the risk of termination.

Although the power of the international corporations pursuing this strategy varies with the extent of competition and the degree of sophistication of their technology, the presumptions underlying the strategy assume that they do not have a particularly strong bargaining position.

Advanced Managerial Skill Model The third general strategy pattern is based on one or more areas of management expertise. The notable examples of this sort of strategy are found among international corporations in consumer nondurable fields whose competitive strength is based on advanced marketing skills often combined with related management competence in organization, personnel, budgeting, and finance. The economic returns in this type of strategy call for a continuing operational system that generates a steady flow of business with a high operating margin.

While in theory it might be possible to implement the advanced management strategy through management contracts or minority joint venture arrangements, in practice majority operating control seems to be a key requirement. Since advanced managerial skills incorporate a large degree of behavioral, nonscientific competence, it is extremely difficult to transmit them through anything but a well-integrated organization system. Thus, effective strategies of this sort are typically found in those firms that have a broad network of fully controlled foreign subsidiaries in which management personnel work together over extended periods and acquire a thorough knowledge both of the management skills involved and of how to relate to other people in the organization.

ICs find themselves in a relatively weak position in pursuing this strategy if resistance is encountered in host nations. The resistance is generally greatest among less-developed countries which regard advanced managerial skills in areas like marketing of consumer goods with substantial skepticism. They give a low priority to this sort of skill as compared with technological skills and take a negative view therefore toward earnings involving balance of payments costs to the nation derived from their application. Among more-advanced countries, there is greater acceptance of the value of managerial skills, particularly in the leading countries which have ICs of their own whose earnings are based on competence of this sort. Still, even in these countries, the IC is in a relatively weak bargaining position in the pursuit of this strategy because little national benefit is perceived from the skills involved.

Unified-Logistic Labor-Transmission Model Three elements of corporate capability are essential requirements for the fourth strategy model. First, the product involved must have a high enough ratio of value to weight and volume so that transportation over substantial distances is economically feasible. Second, the production processes must be sufficiently labor-intensive so that economic advantage greater than transportation costs is achieved by locating production in low-wage areas. Third, the IC must have an effective global marketing organization. Electronic products, sewing machines, and, to some extent, automobiles are examples of products that fit these criteria.

The economic return from the logistic strategy comes from achieving a satisfactory profit margin through the combination of the first two factors with a steady flow of business based on the third factor. The system is financially flexible so that the profit may be taken in whatever proportions are appropriate from the production locations or the marketing system.

The implementation of this strategy calls for a well-integrated and efficient global system. Furthermore, the system must have a substantial capacity for flexibility and change over time because elements essential to it are subject to considerable change. Most important are changes in wage costs which can radically alter the basis for the logistic structure. For example, in the early 1960s,

Japan was a sound production site for inclusion in such a strategy, but with the rapid rise of wage levels there, it has become a poor competitive location compared with Southeast Asian countries. A different form of evolution is the transition of Brazil from a highly unstable political and economic status to a strong position in the mid-1970s with a booming economy providing a superior sourcing site for inclusion in a global logistic scheme.

The need for flexibility over time dictates essential elements to be included in the implementation of this strategy. It is important that there be a high degree of standardization of products so that production sites may be used interchangeably as sources for the marketing organization. Since maintenance of low costs is central to the logic of the strategy, continuing effort to improve efficiency of operations is required. Assuming the probability that rises in wage levels in some locations emerge as more favorable sites, the strategy requires a continuing study of production locations and a sound concept as to how production mobility will be accomplished.

The control elements in implementation are also critical. To tie together widely separated production and marketing units, there must be tight internal control. Market forecasts and production plans must be worked out carefully and changes in them transmitted rapidly. Clearly, quality control must be maintained effectively. There must also be thorough coordination within the system as to changes in products and particularly in the evolution of production site mobility.

Given all of these requirements, it appears that a high degree of control by the international corporation is desirable, including full ownership of all units in the system. Without this degree of ownership some questions become very difficult to deal with. In particular, the transfer of sourcing from one production site to another will raise very troublesome questions if there are equity partners in the foreign units. Likewise, the extensive questions of pricing between production and marketing units are much more complicated when ownership partners are involved.

In both of these matters, it may in fact be preferable as an alternative to full ownership to work with no ownership at all, handling the production phase of the strategy through manufacturing contract arrangements with independent national firms. Prices in these circumstances can be bargained over directly and cutbacks in sourcing accomplished within the terms of the contractual arrangements. However, independent manufacturers, particularly in less-developed countries with low-wage costs, which are the natural production sites in this strategy, may be less than fully satisfactory when it comes to reliability in meeting production schedules and quality standards. Thus, the achievement of full ownership control is highly desirable for this strategy though lesser degrees of control are feasible.

The negotiating power available to an IC pursuing this strategy is great in the host countries serving as production sites and weak in those composing only marketing outlets. Among the former, with the desire to expand exports to improve their balance of payments and increase employment, the IC pursuing this strategy is looked on with great favor. In many cases, for example, the 100 percent ownership desired may be obtained on the basis of proposed export volume despite general nationalistic policy opposing foreign control of production facilities. The weakness of the IC in the marketing countries stems, of course, from the opposite psychology. The desire to reduce imports to help the balance of payments is often reinforced strongly by local manufacturers and unions protecting national production units. Where the latter are particularly strong, the IC may find that it cannot achieve entry for foreign production or that the entry is limited by quotas or tariffs. A number of European countries, for example, have been quite resistant to imports from Japan and other Asian countries. However, the IC does have substantial support in the pursuit of this general strategy from the international consensus favoring greater access for exports of less-developed countries into the industrial areas, which has been pressed by UNCTAD and given substantive commitment through the agreements for preferential tariff treatment for imports of manufacturers from LDCs.

Composite Strategies The four strategy models have been set forth separately to facilitate analysis. Some firms can clearly be identified with just one model. However, the strategies of many firms combine the characteristics of two or more. The automobile companies, for example, blend a moderate level of technology and highly competent managerial skills with increasing use of unified-logistic labor-transmission capabilities. In an operating sense, the coexistence of strategies does not appreciably alter the analysis presented here. However, it can make a major difference in relations with host societies.

As we have noted, two of the models embody strength in relations with host nations, namely those based on high-technology transmission or on export logistics, while two carry little power in this respect, those based on weak technology or on advanced management skills. In a combination strategy it may be possible to use the strength of one of the former to offset the weakness of the latter and thus make profitable use of the capabilities it embodies which otherwise might not be effectively employed internationally. IBM's strength in relations with host nations, for example, is strong primarily because of its technological superiority. In fact, however, it is widely recognized that IBM's marketing competence vaulted it to the lead in its field, and it continues today to use that skill as a major basis for its profitability abroad. Singer represents a different combination, its greatest strength lying in the availability of its global marketing system to serve export plants like Brazil and Taiwan utilizing a technology for basic sewing machines little different from that of other leading firms in the field.

READING 38   **HOW TO TAKE YOUR COMPANY TO THE GLOBAL MARKET**

George S. Yip ◆ Pierre M. Loewe ◆ Michael Y. Yoshino

ABSTRACT.   Deciding how to deal with the globalization of markets poses tough issues and choices for managers. There are both external business forces and internal organizational factors to consider. External business forces revolve around the interaction of industry drivers of globalization and the different ways in which a business can be global. Understanding this interaction is key to formulating the right global strategy. Internal organizational factors play a major role in determining how well a company can implement global strategy. This paper provides a systematic approach to developing and implementing a global strategy.

Most managers have to face the increasing globalization of markets and competition. That fact requires each company to decide whether it must become a worldwide competitor to survive.[1]

This is not an easy decision. Take the division of a multibillion-dollar company, a company that's very sophisticated and has been conducting international business for more than fifty years. The division sells a commodity product, for which it is trying to charge 40 percent more in Europe than it does in the United States. The price was roughly the same in the United States and in Europe when the dollar was at its all-time high. The company built a European plant which showed a greater return on investment with that European price. But the dollar has fallen and, if the company drops its European price to remain roughly the same as the U.S. price, the return on the plant becomes negative, and some careers are in serious jeopardy. So it is attempting to maintain a 40 percent European price premium by introducing minor upgrades to the European product.

But its multinational customers will have none of it. They start buying the product in the United States and transshipping it to Europe. When the company tries to prevent them from transshipping, they go to a broker, who does the work for them; they still save money.

The manufacturer doesn't have a choice. It's working in a global market. And it's going to have to come up with a global price. But management is fighting a losing battle because it is unwilling to make the hard strategic and organizational changes necessary to adapt to global market conditions.

European and Japanese corporations also face these kinds of organizational roadblocks. Large European firms, for example, historically have been more multinational than U.S. companies. Their international success is due, in part,

[1] See Theodore Levitt's arguments in "The Globalization of Markets," *Harvard Business Review*, May–June 1983, pp. 92–102. For a counterargument, see Susan P. Douglas and Yoram Wind, "The Myth of Globalization," *Columbia Journal of World Business*, Winter 1987, pp. 19–29.

to decentralized management. The companies simply reproduced their philosophy and culture everywhere, from India to Australia to Canada. They set up mini-headquarters operations in each country and became truly multinational with executives of different nationalities running them.

Now they are having problems running operations on a worldwide basis because these multinational executives are fighting the global imperative. In one European company, for example, the manager running a Latin American division has built an impenetrable wall around himself and his empire. He's done very well, and everyone has allowed him to do as he pleases. But the company's global strategy requires a new way of looking at Latin America. The organization needs to break down his walls of independence. So far, that's proved next to impossible.

Japanese companies face a different set of problems. On the whole, they have followed a basic, undifferentiated marketing strategy: make small Hondas, and sell them throughout the world. Then make better Hondas, ending up with the $30,000 Honda Acura. It's incremental, and it has worked.

Now, however, the Japanese must create various manufacturing centers around the globe and they're facing many difficulties. They have a coordinated marketing strategy and have built up infrastructures to coordinate marketing, which requires one particular set of skills. But now they've begun to establish three or four major manufacturing operations around the world, and they need a different set of skills to integrate these manufacturing operations. In addition, many Japanese companies are trying to add some elements of a multinational strategy back into their global one.

American multinationals have tended to take a different path. The huge domestic market, combined with cultural isolation, has fostered an "us-them" mentality within organizations. This split has made it difficult to fully adapt to the needs of international business. Until recently, overseas posts have been spurned. A marketing manager for new products in a U.S. consumer products company told us that running the sizable United Kingdom business would be a step down for him. As a result of others' similar views, many American firms face two conflicting challenges today. They need to complete their internationalization by increasing their adaptation to local needs, while at the same time they need to make their strategies more global.

But some companies are better off not trying to compete globally because of the difficulties of their internal situation. The CEO of one midwest manufacturer decided that his company had to go global to survive. He gave marching orders. And the organization marched. Unfortunately, they started marching over a global cliff. For example, they set up a small operation in Brazil since they had targeted South America as part of their global strategy. But the executives they appointed to run the operation had never been outside the United States before, and the company started losing money. Company analysis found that going global was just too unnatural to its cultural system and that a viable strategic alternative was to stay in the United States and play a niche strategy.

Most international companies have grappled with the types of problems we have been describing, and have tried to find a solution. This paper provides a framework for thinking through this complex and important issue. In particular the framework addresses the dual challenge of formulating and implementing a global strategy. Readers may find the framework a convenient way to analyze globalization issues.

The Dual Challenge

Managers who want to make their businesses global face two major challenges. First, they need to figure out what a global strategy is. Then, when they know what to do, they have to get their organizations to make it happen.

Different Ways of Being Global

Developing a global strategy is complicated by the fact that there are at least five major dimensions of globalization. These are:

- ◆ Playing big in major markets.
- ◆ Standardizing the core product.
- ◆ Concentrating value-adding activities in a few countries.
- ◆ Adopting a uniform market positioning and marketing mix.
- ◆ Integrating competitive strategy across countries.

Each of these can offer significant benefits:

Playing Big in Major Markets Playing big in major markets—countries that account for a sizable share of worldwide volume or where changes in technology or consumer tastes are most likely to start—brings these benefits:

- ◆ Larger volume over which to amortize development efforts and investments in fixed assets.
- ◆ Ability to manage countries as one portfolio, including being able to exploit differences in position along the product life cycle.
- ◆ Learning from each country.
- ◆ Being at the cutting edge of the product category by participating in the one or two major countries that lead development.

Standardizing the Core Product The local managers of multinational subsidiaries face strong pressures to adapt their offerings to local requirements. This gets the company laudably close to the customer. But the end result can be such great differences among products offered in various countries that the overall business garners few benefits of scale.

The core product can be standardized while customizing more superficial aspects of the offering. McDonald's has done well with this approach—Europeans and Japanese may think they are eating the same hamburgers as Americans, but the ingredients have been adapted for their tastes. A French McDonald's even serves alcohol. But the core formula remains the same.

Concentrating Value-adding Activities in a Few Countries   Instead of repeating every activity in each country, a pure global strategy provides for concentration of activities in just a few countries. For example, fundamental research is conducted in just one country, commercial development in two or three countries, manufacturing in a few countries, and core marketing programs developed at regional centers, while selling and customer service take place in every country in the network. The benefits include gaining economies of scale and leveraging the special skills or strengths of particular countries. For example, the lower wage rates and higher skills in countries such as Malaysia or Hong Kong have encouraged many electronics firms to centralize worldwide assembly operations in these countries.

Adopting a Uniform Market Positioning and Marketing Mix   The more uniform the market positioning and marketing mix, the more the company can save in the cost of developing marketing strategies and programs. As one company told us, "Good ideas are scarce. By taking a uniform approach we can exploit those ideas in the maximum number of countries." Another benefit is internal focus. A company may struggle with numerous brand names and positionings around the world, while its rivals single-mindedly promote just one or two brands. There also are marketing benefits to a common brand name as international travel and cross-border media continue to grow. In consolidating its various names around the world, Exxon rapidly achieved global focus and recognition. Coca-Cola, Levis, and McDonald's are other companies that have successfully used a single-brand strategy. Mercedes, BMW, and Volvo not only use the same brand name throughout the world, but also have consistent images and positionings in different countries.

Integrating Competitive Moves Across Countries   Instead of making competitive decisions in a country without regard to what is happening in other countries, a global competitor can take an integrated approach. Tyrolia, the Austrian ski-binding manufacturer, attacked Salomon's stronghold position in its biggest market, the United States. Rather than fighting Tyrolia only in the United States, Salomon retaliated in the countries where Tyrolia generated a large share of its sales and profits—Germany and Austria. Taking a global perspective, Salomon viewed the whole world—not just one country—as its competitive battleground.

Another benefit of integrating competitive strategy is the ability of a company to cross-subsidize. This involves utilizing cash generated in a profitable,

Example of Global Strategy: Black & Decker

Black & Decker, manufacturer of hand tools, provides an example of a company that is pursuing a global strategy. In the past decade, Black & Decker was threatened by external and internal pressures. Externally, it faced a powerful Japanese competitor, Makita. Makita's strategy to produce and market standardized products worldwide made it a low-cost producer, and enabled it to increase steadily its share in the world market. Internally, international fiefdoms and nationalist chauvinism at Black & Decker had stifled coordination in product development and new product introductions, resulting in lost opportunities.

In response, Black & Decker decisively moved toward globalization. It embarked on a major program to coordinate new product development worldwide to develop core standardized products that can be marketed worldwide with minimal modification. The streamlining in R&D also offers scale economies and less duplication of effort, and new products can be introduced more quickly. It consolidated worldwide advertising by using two principal agencies, gaining a more consistent image worldwide. Black & Decker also strengthened the functional organization by giving functional managers a larger role in coordinating with the country management. Finally, Black & Decker purchased General Electric's small appliance business to achieve world-scale economies in manufacturing, distribution, and marketing.

The globalization strategy initially met with skepticism and resistance from country management due to entrenched factionalism among country managers. The CEO took a visible leadership role and made some management changes to start the company moving toward globalization. Today, in his words, "Globalization is spreading and now has a life of its own."

high-market-share country to invest aggressively in a strategically important but low-market-share country. The purpose is, of course, to optimize results worldwide.

Industry Drivers of Globalization

How can a company decide whether it should globalize a particular business? What sort of global strategy should it pursue? Managers should look first to the business's industry. An industry's potential for globalization is driven by market, economic, environmental, and competitive factors (see Figure 1).[2] Market forces

---

[2] For related frameworks on the role of industry forces in global strategy, see Thomas Hout, Michael E. Porter, and Eileen Rudden, "How Global Companies Win Out," *Harvard Business Review,* September–October 1982, pp. 98–109. Also Porter, "Changing the Patterns of International Competition," *California Management Review,* Winter 1986, pp. 9–40; and Porter, editor, *Competition in Global Industries,* Boston, MA: Harvard Business School Press, 1986. Bruce Kogut takes a somewhat different view in "Designing Global Strategies," *Sloan Management Review,* Summer 1985, pp. 15–28, and Fall 1985, pp. 27–38.

FIGURE **1**   External Drivers of Industry Potential for Globalization

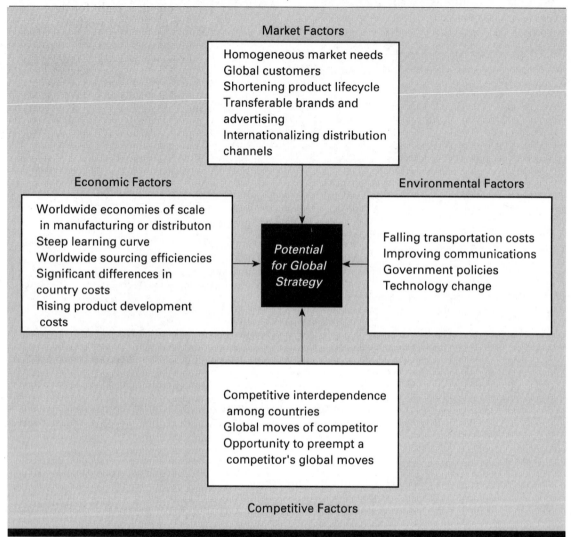

determine the customers' receptivity to a global product; economic factors determine whether pursuing a global strategy can provide a cost advantage; environmental factors show whether the necessary supporting infrastructure is there; and competitive factors provide a spur to action.

The automotive industry provides a good example of all four forces. People in the industry now talk of "world cars." A number of *market factors* are pushing the industry toward globalization, including a mature market, similar demand trends across countries (such as quality/reliability and fuel efficiency), shortening product life cycles (e.g., twelve years for the Renault 5, eight for the Renault 18, and five each for the Renault 11 and Renault 9), and worldwide image-building. Similarly. *economic factors* are pushing the automotive industry toward globalization. For example, economies of scale, particularly on engines and transmissions, are very important, and few country markets provide enough volume to get full benefits of these economies of scale. Similarly, many car manufacturers have now moved to worldwide sourcing. In the *environmental* area, converging regulations (safety, emissions) and rapid technological evolution (new materials, electronics, robotics), all requiring heavy investment in R&D and plant and equipment, also are moving the industry inexorably toward globalization. Finally, *competitive* factors are contributing to globalization. Witness the increasing number of cooperative ventures among manufacturers—Toyota-GM, Toyo Kogyo-Ford, Chrysler-Mitsubishi. These ventures are putting pressure on all automotive manufacturers to go global.

In summary, managers wrestling with globalization issues should first analyze the four sets of industry forces to determine whether they compete in an industry that is global or globalizing. Next they need to assess how global their companies are, and how global their competitors are, along the five dimensions defined previously. This step—which is illustrated in the Appendix—helps define the broad direction of the strategic moves needed to change their company's global competitive posture. A very difficult part remains: assessing whether the organization has the capacity to go global.

Organizational Factors in Globalization

Organizational factors can support or undercut a business's attempt to globalize.[3] Therefore, taking a close look at how the organization will affect the relative difficulty of globalization is essential. Four factors affect the ability of an organization to develop and implement global strategy: organization structure, management processes, people, and culture (see Figure 2).[4] Each of these aspects of organization operates powerfully in different ways. A common mistake, in implementing *any* strategy, is to ignore one or more of them, particularly the less tangible ones such as culture.

---

[3] For a discussion of organizational issues in global strategy, see Christopher A. Bartlett, "MNCs: Get Off the Reorganization Merry-Go-Round," *Harvard Business Review,* March–April 1983, pp. 183–146; Christopher A. Bartlett and Sumantra Goshal, "Tap Your Subsidiaries for Global Reach," *Harvard Business Review,* November–December 1986, pp. 87–94. Also Gary Hamel and C. K. Prahalad, "Do You Really Have a Global Strategy?" *Harvard Business Review,* July–August 1985, pp. 139–148; and C. K. Prahalad and Yves L. Doz, *The Multinational Mission: Balancing Local Demands and Global Vision,* New York: The Free Press, 1987.

[4] For global marketing strategy, see John A. Quelch and Edward J. Hoff, "Customizing Global Marketing," *Harvard Business Review,* May–June 1986, pp. 59–68.

FIGURE **2**   Internal Factors That Facilitate a Global Strategy

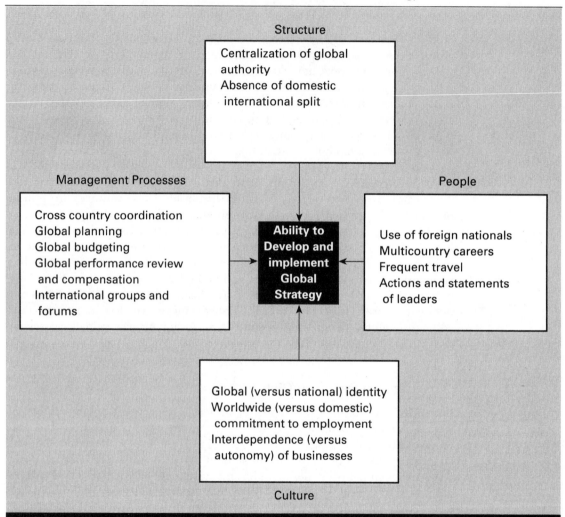

Organization Structure

Centralization of global authority. One of the most effective ways to develop and implement a global strategy is to centralize authority, so all units of the business around the world report to a common sector head. Surprisingly few companies do this. Instead, they are tied for historical reasons to a strong country-based organization where the main line of authority runs by country rather than by business. In a company pursuing a global strategy, the business focus should dominate the country focus. It's difficult, but necessary.

Domestic/international split. A common structural barrier to global strategy is an organizational split between domestic and international divisions. The international division oversees a group of highly autonomous country subsidiaries, each of which manages several distinct businesses. A global strategy for any one of these businesses can then be coordinated only at the CEO level. This split is very common among U.S. firms, partly for historical reasons and partly because of the enormous size of the U.S. market. Ironically, some European multinationals with small domestic markets have separated out not their home market but the U.S. market. As a market they find it difficult to get their U.S. subsidiaries to cooperate in the development and implementation of global strategy. In one European company we know, the heads of worldwide business sectors go hat in hand to New York to solicit support for their worldwide strategies.

Management Processes While organization structure has a very direct effect on management behavior, it is management processes that power the system. The appropriate processes can even substitute to some extent for the appropriate structure.

Cross-country coordination. Providing cross-country coordination is a common way to make up for the lack of a direct reporting structure. Some consumer packaged goods companies are beginning to appoint European brand managers to coordinate strategy across countries.

Global planning. Too often strategic plans are developed separately for each country and are not aggregated globally for each business across all countries.[5] This makes it difficult to understand the business's competitive position worldwide and to develop an integrated strategy against competitors who plan on a global basis.

Global budgeting. Similarly, country budgets need to be consolidated into a global total for each product line to aid the allocation of resources across product lines.[6] Surprisingly few companies do this.

Global performance review and compensation. Rewards, especially bonuses, need to be set in a way that reinforces the company's global objectives. An

---

[5] For a discussion of different types of global strategic planning, see Balaji S. Chakravarthy and Howard V. Perlmutter, "Strategic Planning for a Global Business," *Columbia Journal of World Business,* Summer 1985, pp. 3–10; and David C. Shanks, "Strategic Planning for Global Competition," *Journal of Business Strategy,* Winter 1985, pp. 80–89.

[6] See John J. Dyment's discussion of global budgeting in "Strategies and Management Controls for Global Corporations," *Journal of Business Strategy,* Spring 1987, pp. 20–26.

electronics manufacturer, for example, decided to start penetrating the international market by introducing a new product through its strongest division. The division head's bonus was based on current year's worldwide sales, with no distinction between domestic and international sales. Because increasing his domestic sales was easier—and had a much quicker payoff—than trying to open new international markets, the division head didn't worry much about his international sales. Predictably, the firm's market penetration strategy failed.

International groups and forums. Holding international forums allows exchange of information and building of relationships across countries. This in turn makes it easier for country nationals to gain an understanding of whether the differences they perceive between their home country and others are real or imagined. It also facilitates the development of common products and the coordination of marketing approaches. For example, a French manufacturer of security devices uses councils of country managers, with different countries taking the lead on different products. While this approach is time-consuming, the company has found that this reliance on line managers makes it easier for various countries to accept the input of other countries, and thus for global approaches to be pursued by all.

People Being truly global also involves using people in a different way from that of a multinational firm.

Use foreign nationals. High-potential foreign nationals need to gain experience not only in their home country, but also at headquarters and in other countries. This practice has three benefits: broadening the pool of talent available for executive positions; demonstrating the commitment of top management to internalization; and giving talented individuals an irreplaceable development opportunity. United States companies have been slow to do this, particularly at the most senior ranks.

Promoting foreigners, and using staff from various countries, has often paid of. In the 1970s, an ailing NCR vaulted William S. Anderson, the British head of their Asian business, to the top job. Anderson is widely credited with turning around NCR. A French packaged goods manufacturer undertook seven years ago to move its European staff from country to country. Today, of fifteen staff members working at headquarters, seven are French, three are English, three are German, and two are Italian. The company credits this practice—among others—for its remarkable turnaround.

Require multicountry careers. Making work experience in different countries necessary for progression, rather than a hindrance, is another step that helps a company become truly global. One electronics manufacturer decided to make a major push into Japan, but an executive offered a transfer there was loath to take it. He was unsure a job would remain for him when he came back. As he put it, "The road to the executive suite lies through Chicago, not Osaka."

Travel frequently. Senior managers must spend a large amount of time in foreign countries. The CEO of a large grocery products company we have worked with spends half his time outside the United States—a visible demonstration of the importance and commitment of the company to its international operations.

State global intentions. The senior management of a company that wants to go global needs to constantly restate that intention and to act accordingly. Otherwise, the rank and file won't believe that the globalization strategy is real. One test among many is the prominence given to international operations in formal communications such as the chairman's letter in the annual report and statements to stock analysts.

Culture Culture is the most subtle aspect of organization, but, as shown below, it can play a formidable role in helping or hindering a global strategy.

Global (versus national) identity. Does the company have a strong national identity? This can hinder the willingness and ability to design global products and programs. It can also create a "them and us" split among employees. One firm was making a strong global push, and yet many of its corporate executives wore national flag pins! European companies are generally well in advance of both American and Japanese firms in adopting a global identity.

Worldwide (versus domestic) commitment to employment. Many American companies view their domestic employees as more important than their overseas employees and are much more committed to preserving domestic employment than to developing employment regardless of location. This often leads them to decide to keep expensive manufacturing operations in the United States, rather than relocate them to lower-cost countries. This puts them at a competitive cost disadvantage and threatens their overall competitive position.

Interdependence (versus autonomy) of business. A high level of autonomy for local business can also be a barrier to globalization.

In sum, the four internal factors of organization structure, management processes, people, and culture play a key role in a company's move toward globalization.

For example, a company with a strong structural split between domestic and international activities, management processes that are country—rather than business—driven, people who work primarily in their home countries, and a parochial culture is likely to have difficulty implementing integrated competitive strategies. If the analysis of external drivers has shown that such strategies are necessary for market, competitive, environmental, or economic reasons, top management needs to either adapt the internal environment to the strategic moves the company needs to make—or decide that the profound organizational changes needed are too risky. In the latter case, the company should avoid globalization and compete based on its existing organizational strengths.

Conclusion

There are many ways to pursue a global strategy. Industry forces play a major role in determining whether going global makes sense. An analysis of a company's competitive position against the five dimensions of globalization—major market participation, product standardization, activity specialization, uniform market positioning, and integrated competitive strategy—helps define the appropriate approach for a globalization strategy. Finally, and very importantly, the ability of the organization to implement the different elements of global strategy needs to be considered.

Matching the external and internal imperatives is critical. For example, we have worked with a company whose culture included the following characteristics:

- ◆ A high degree of responsiveness to customers' requests for product tailoring.
- ◆ A strong emphasis on letting every business and every country be highly autonomous.
- ◆ A desire for 100 percent control over foreign operations.
- ◆ A commitment to preserving domestic employment.

The difficulty the company found in pursuing a globalization strategy is illustrated in the strategy/culture fit matrix in Figure 3. The matrix helped management articulate the pros and cons of the three major options they could pursue: a pure global strategy with an organizational revolution; a series of incremental changes in both strategy and organization, leading to a mixed strategy of globalization/national responsiveness; and an explicit rejection of globalization, accompanied with a conscious decision to build on the company's existing organizational and cultural characteristics to develop a pure national responsiveness strategy. This enabled them to make fundamental and realistic choices rather than assuming the unavoidable dominance of strategy over organization and of globalization over national responsiveness.

Competing globally is tough. It requires a clear vision of the firm as a global competitor, a long-term time horizon, a concerted effort to match strategy and organization changes, a cosmopolitan view and a substantial commitment from the top. But the result can be the opportunity to gain significant competitive

FIGURE 3   Identification of High-Risk Areas in Implementing a Global Strategy

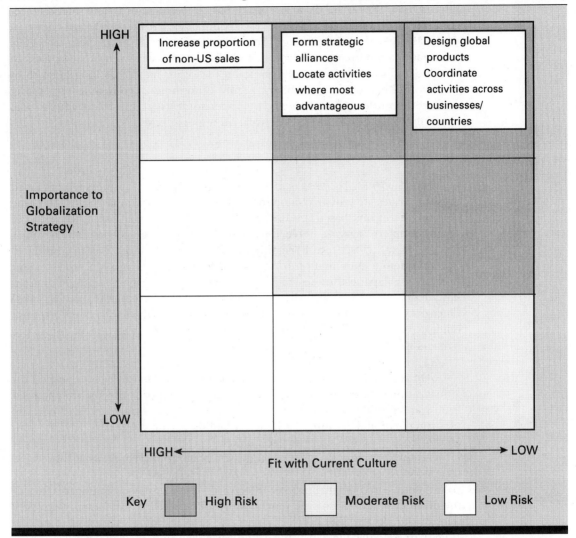

advantage through cost, focus, and concentration, and improved response to customers' needs and preferences.

Appendix

To illustrate use of the global strategy framework, or global strategy audit, we summarize here the experiences of two companies, both of them multibillion-dollar multinationals. One company, disguised as "TransElectronics," is a U.S.-

based concern operating in many aspects of electronics. The other company, disguised as "Persona," is a European-based manufacturer and marketer of consumer packaged goods. The two companies provide different views of the challenge of global strategy. TransElectronics is still developing as a fully multinational company and faces the challenge of accelerating that process to become a global competitor. Persona, on the other hand, has long been thoroughly multinational, with many highly autonomous companies operating around the world. Its challenge is to temper some aspects of that multinational autonomy to compete more effectively on a global basis.

TransElectronics

Step 1—Identify business unit. All six TransElectronics business sectors faced pressing issues of global competition. The Communications Sector had one division, Electron, based in the United States, that sold what we will call "transcramblers" against fierce European and Japanese competition. A major market, Japan, closed until recently to foreign competition, was beginning to open through a combination of TransElectronics' efforts and U.S. government pressure on Japanese trade barriers. So developing a global strategy for transcramblers was a high priority for TransElectronics. A complication was that Electron was not a stand-alone business unit—other units had related responsibilities. As we will describe, this split of responsibilities was one of the major barriers to Electron's implementation of a global strategy.

Step 2—Evaluate industry potential for globalization. Market factors pushed for globalization: there were few differences among countries in what they wanted from transcramblers. On the other hand, few global customers existed because of strong national boundaries between public sector customers (PTTs), who accounted for a large share of the market.

Economic factors strongly pushed for globalization. There were substantial scale economies and learning effects, sourcing efficiencies could be gained by consolidating manufacturing, and Electron's labor costs—a significant part of the product's total cost—were much lower in Puerto Rico and Taiwan than they were in the United States.

Environmental factors also pushed for globalization. The privatization of some national PTTs was opening up previously closed markets, and products were becoming more standardized in Europe around a common format. An offsetting factor was local content requirements in many countries.

Competitive forces were also in line. Electron's major competitors (European and Japanese) took a global product approach with fewer price levels and minimum product customization. They also had largely centralized their manufacturing activities in just one or two countries each.

In conclusion, strong external forces pushed the transcrambler industry toward globalization. Not only was globalization already high, it was likely to continue increasing.

Step 3—Evaluate current extent of globalization.

Market participation. Electron was quite global in its market participation. Its sales split among countries closely matched that of the industry.

Product standardization. Electron's product line was highly standardized—in fact, more so than its executives realized. They initially thought that their product was not standard across countries because 40 percent of the product cost was in a decoder that was different in each country. But digging deeper, however, they discovered that within the decoder only the software was unique. Furthermore, the software was embodied in purchased parts (masked ROMs). Therefore, there was no difference in the manufacturing process, only in the inventory to be kept. Also, the cost of developing the unique software was amortized over a large sales base. As a result, what initially appeared to be 40 percent nonstandard turned out to be 3 percent nonstandard.

Activity concentration. Electron's R&D and purchasing activities were specialized in the United States, but much of their manufacturing was dispersed across the United States, Puerto Rico, Taiwan, and Europe. Marketing was primarily done in the United States. Selling, distribution, and service were by necessity done locally but were not coordinated across countries. Electron's competitors were all much more centralized and coordinated.

Marketing uniformity. The product positioning of transcramblers was consistent across countries, as was that of Electron's competitors. If anything, TransElectronics' marketing policies were too uniform, given a rigid pricing policy that did not allow Electron to adapt to the wide variations in price across countries. As a result, Electron did not use price as a strategic weapon.

Integration of competitive moves. Electron did not integrate its competitive moves across countries, nor did its competitors.

Step 4—Identify strategic need for change in the extent of globalization. From the previous analyses, Electron concluded that its extent of globalization was significantly lower than the industry potential, and lower than its competitors' globalization. Furthermore, the industry potential for globalization was steadily increasing. It was clear that Electron had a strong need to develop a more global strategy. The next issue was whether Electron would be able to implement such a strategy.

Step 5—Evaluate organizational factors.

Structure. TransElectronics' structure worked in two major ways against a global strategy. First, TransElectronics operated with a strong domestic/international split within each sector. Second, worldwide responsibilities for Electron's business were scattered throughout the organization. The Elec-

The Steps of the Global Strategy Audit

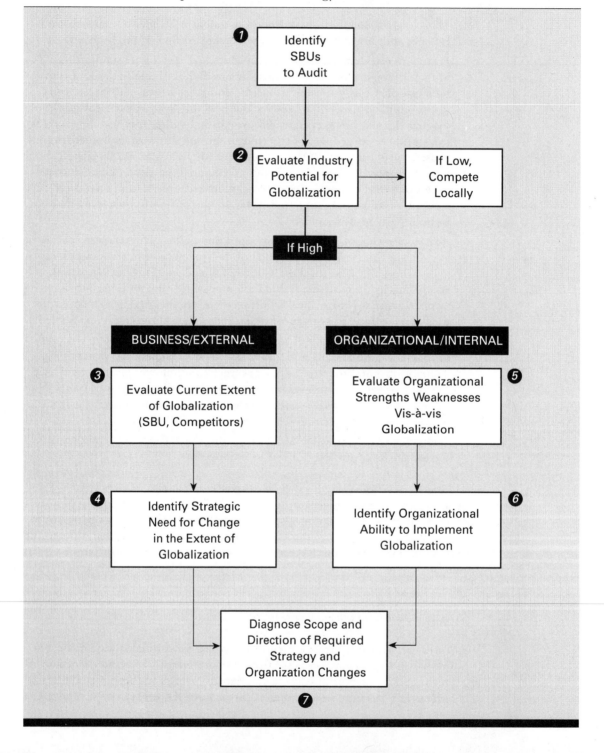

tron division itself had responsibility for some product development, some manufacturing, and some marketing. Other divisions in the United States and overseas shared these responsibilities. Selling was the responsibility of both local non-U.S. countries, and in the United States, of a totally separate distribution group for the entire communications sector. In effect, there was no one manager below the sector head who had global authority over transcramblers.

Management Processes. The budget process worked against a global approach. The Electron division budgeted only a total number for overseas sales, without country targets. The International Group in the Communications Sector set country quotas for the entire sector, without product quotas or product-by-country quotas. The strategic planning process did not help either. The Electron division and the International Group developed separate plans simultaneously. There were no international components in the bonus for domestic managers.

People. TransElectronics' employee practices worked against a global approach. There were few foreign nationals in the United States at either corporate or divisional levels. There were many foreign nationals overseas, but these were mostly in their home countries, and there was little movement between international and domestic jobs. In particular, the U.S. divisions were reluctant to give up people, and overseas assignments were not seen as being part of a desirable career track.

Culture. TransElectronics' corporate culture worked against a global view in both obvious and subtle ways. At the obvious level, TransElectronics was very much an American company with a "them-us" mentality. Indeed, the chairman had made speeches calling for increased trade barriers against Japanese firms. More subtly, TransElectronics had a very strong culture of being responsive to customer requests for product tailoring, born of a heritage of selling exclusively to a very small number of automotive customers. This culture worked strongly against attempts to standardize globally.

Step 6—Identify organizational ability to implement globalization. TransElectronics clearly had a very low organizational ability to develop a global strategy for transcramblers. They had certainly experienced many difficulties in their fitful attempts at doing so.

Step 7—Diagnose scope and direction of required changes. In summary, the most important business changes that Electron had to make were to exploit more opportunities for product standardization and to specialize somewhat more where different activities (particularly manufacturing) were conducted.

More widespread changes were needed in terms of management and organization. While many aspects of these needed to change, the most implementable change was in terms of management process. TransElectronics adopted for the transcrambler business a global strategic planning process and globally based evaluation and compensation. These relatively modest changes would pave the way for future acceptance of the more radical changes needed in organization structure, people, and culture.

Persona

Step 1—Identify business unit. As in the case of Electron, there were difficulties in defining the relevant business unit. Persona had operating companies around the world that sold many kinds of personal-care as well as other household products. The global strategy audit was conducted for one particular product, "hairfloss," that was sold around the world.

Step 2—Evaluate industry potential for globalization. Market factors pushed strongly for globalization: market needs were very much the same around the world within income categories—higher-income countries were earlier users of the new variants and ingredients that were introduced every few years. Brand names and advertising were also widely transferable—some competitors used just one major brand name and essentially the same advertising campaign around the world.

Economic factors were less important, given that product costs were only about 25 percent of total costs, economies of scale were low, and price was not a major basis of competition. Also the low value-to-weight ratio of hairfloss made it uneconomical to ship far. Nonetheless, there was some centralized manufacturing on a multicountry regional basis, e.g., parts of Western Europe, Southeast Asia, and Africa.

Environmental factors did not particularly favor globalization. In Western Europe, however, the increasing importance of multicountry media, particularly satellite television with wide reception, and of the European Economic Community, pushed for regional, if not global, approaches.

Competitive behavior was the major force pushing the industry to globalization. Persona faced three major worldwide competitors, multinationals like itself. Two of these competitors took a much more standardized approach than Persona—they concentrated their resources behind the same one or two brands of hairfloss in each. In contrast, Persona tended to market three or four brands in each country, and these brands were different among major countries. Persona's competitors also were quick to transfer successful innovations from one country to the next, while Persona's brand fragmentation hindered its efforts. This global fragmentation seemed to be a major reason behind Persona's slipping market share and profitability.

Persona concluded that there were strong external forces pushing the hairfloss industry toward globalization—at least to the extent of coordinated regional operations—and this push toward globalization was likely to increase in the future.

Step 3—Evaluate current extent of globalization.

Market participation. Persona participated in markets that accounted for almost 90 percent of worldwide (excluding communist countries) hairfloss volume. The largest competitor, not Persona, participated in almost 100 percent.

Product standardization. Persona's hairfloss product line was quite highly standardized around half a dozen variants. Persona generally marketed a large number of variants in wealthier countries, but the variants were still basically the same across countries.

Activity concentration. Like most consumer packaged goods multinationals, Persona practiced very little specialization by country. Persona fielded a full business operation in most countries.

Marketing uniformity. On this dimension of globalization Persona was severely lacking because of its multiple brands, multiple product positionings, and multiple advertising campaigns.

Integration of competitive moves. Persona did not do much to integrate its competitive moves across countries, although it had begun recently to experiment with such attempts.

Overall, Persona's actual extent of globalization was somewhat lower than that of its competitors.

Step 4—Identify strategic need for change in the extent of globalization. In conclusion, while Persona's worldwide hairfloss strategy was quite global in some respects, the lack of marketing uniformity was the biggest problem. The key variables that Persona could manipulate were brand name and positioning. First, to increase local marketing muscle, Persona needed to reduce the number of brands in each country to two. Second, to achieve the benefits of global market uniformity, they had three broad alternatives:

1. A different brand but common positioning for each product variant in each country.
2. A common regional brand and positioning.
3. A common global brand and positioning.

Because Persona already had strong brand names around the world that it did not want to abandon, and because a common positioning would achieve most of the benefits of uniformity, the company concluded that the second alternative was best. The next issue was whether Persona would be able to implement such a strategy.

Step 5—Evaluate organizational factors.

Structure. Persona's structure made it difficult to develop and implement a global strategy. Persona operated with a strong geographic structure that was overlaid with a worldwide product direction function at corporate. This function, however, had advisory rather than direct authority over the individual country businesses. Furthermore, the direction function did not include the United States.

Management processes. The budget and compensation systems worked against global strategy. These were done on a strictly local basis, although aggregated geographically. But there was no mechanism to encourage local participation in a worldwide effort. A strategic plan was developed globally, but local acceptance was voluntary.

People. On this score, Persona was very capable of implementing a global strategy. Its managers were drawn from all over the world, and transfers both among countries and to and from corporate were common.

Culture. Culture was the biggest barrier. Persona had a very strong culture of giving autonomy to its local managers. Although corporate leaders increasingly wanted to give direct orders on strategy, they were loath to risk the possible loss of local accountability and commitment.

Step 6—Identify organizational ability to implement globalization. Like Trans-Electronics, Persona also had a low organizational capacity for global strategy but for somewhat different reasons.

Step 7—Diagnose scope and direction of required changes. In summary, the most important business changes that Persona had to make in hairfloss were to reduce its number of brands in each country and to develop a common brand by region and common positioning for each major product variant.

Organizationally, changing the structure would create too much disruption. What was needed was a greater willingness by corporate to push countries to adopt a global approach. A first step was a directive that all countries should launch the new "high-gloss" variant within a six-month period. Persona hoped that a successful experience of common action would start moving the culture toward greater acceptance of global strategies.

Further Steps. A global strategy audit provides four concrete outputs:

◆ An assessment of how global the industry is today and is likely to become in the future.

◆ An understanding of how global the firm's approach is today and how it compares to its competitors and to the industry potential for further globalization.

◆ An identification of the organizational factors that will facilitate or hinder a move toward globalization.

◆ A broad action plan, specifying strategic and organizational change priorities.

The audit, in and of itself, does not provide the details of a competitive strategy. If its output has shown that adopting some form of global strategy is indeed desirable, the audit needs to be followed by another effort aimed at developing a detailed global strategy. Among the decisions that will need to be made are the definition of a competitive posture in various countries (i.e., in what part of the world should we compete on our own, and in what part should we form alliances?); the articulation of specific functional strategies (manufacturing, marketing, financial, etc.) and, for each function, of the appropriate balance between global and local approaches (for example, all elements of manufacturing could be global, while some elements of marketing, such as sales promotion, might remain local); and the adoption of organizational mechanisms aimed at reinforcing the strategic objectives sought.

However, the audit provides a relatively simple and quick way to get answers to some of the most complicated questions facing corporate management today. It also greatly facilitates the undertaking of the strategy development phase that follows, because it has identified the major thrusts that are needed. Furthermore, it has the potential for avoiding major errors—such as a move toward globalization when none is warranted. Finally, it sensitizes the organization to the issues and to the commitments needed if it really decides to compete globally.

READING 39 CHANGING PATTERNS OF INTERNATIONAL COMPETITION

Michael E. Porter

When examining the environmental changes facing firms today, it is a rare observer who will conclude that international competition is not high on the list. The growing importance of international competition is well recognized both in the business and academic communities, for reasons that are fairly obvious when one looks at just about any data set that exists on international trade or investment. Figure 1, for example, compares world trade and world GNP. Something interesting started happening around the mid-1950s, when the growth in world trade began to significantly exceed the growth in world GNP. Foreign direct investment by firms in developing countries began to grow rapidly a few years later, about 1963.[1] This period marked the beginning of a fundamental change in the international competitive environment that by now has come to be widely recognized. It is a trend that is causing sleepless nights for many business managers.

There is a substantial literature on international competition, because the subject is far from a new one. A large body of literature has investigated the many implications of the Heckscher-Ohlin model and other models of international trade which are rooted in the principle of comparative advantage.[2] The unit of analysis in this literature is the country. There is also considerable literature on the multinational firm, reflecting the growing importance of the multinational since the turn of the century. In examining the reasons for the multinational, I think it is fair to characterize this literature as resting heavily on the multinational's ability to exploit intangible assets.[3] The work of Hymer and Caves among others has stressed the role of the multinational in transferring know-how and expertise gained in one country market to others at low cost, and thereby offsetting the unavoidable extra costs of doing business in a foreign country. A more recent stream of literature extends this by emphasizing how the multinational firm internalizes transactions to circumvent imperfections in various intermediate markets, most importantly the market for knowledge.

There is also a related literature on the problems of entry into foreign markets and the life cycle of how a firm competes abroad, beginning with export or licensing and ultimately moving to the establishment of foreign subsidiaries.

Source: Copyright 1986 by The Regents of the University of California. Reprinted from the *California Management Review,* Vol. 28, No. 2, Winter 1986. By permission of The Regents.

[1] United Nations Center on Transnational Corporations, *Salient Features and Trends in Foreign Direct Investment* (New York, NY: United Nations, 1984).

[2] For a survey, see R. E. Caves and Ronald W. Jones, *World Trade and Payments,* 4th ed. (Boston, MA: Little, Brown, 1985).

[3] There are many books on the theory and management of the multinational, which are too numerous to cite here. For an excellent survey of the literature, see R. E. Caves, *Multinational Enterprise and Economic Analysis* (Cambridge, England: Cambridge University Press, 1982).

FIGURE **1**   Growth of World Trade

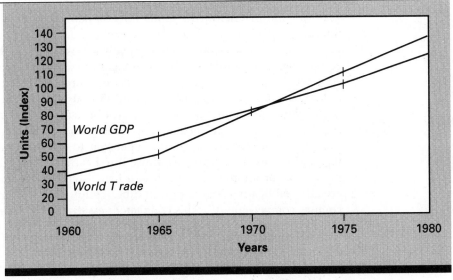

Vernon's product cycle of international trade combines a view of how products mature with the evolution in a firm's international activities to predict the patterns of trade and investment in developed and developing countries.[4] Finally, many of the functional fields in business administration research have their branch of literature about international issues—e.g., international marketing international finance. This literature concentrates, by and large, on the problems of doing business in a foreign country.

As rich as it is, however, I think it is fair to characterize the literature on international competition as being limited when it comes to the choice of a firm's international strategy. Though the literature provides some guidance for considering incremental investment decisions to enter a new country, it provides at best a partial view of how to characterize a firm's overall international strategy and how such strategy should be selected. Put another way, the literature focuses more on the problem of becoming a multinational than on strategies for established multinationals. Although the distinction between domestic firms and multinationals is seminal in a literature focused on the problems of doing business abroad, the fact that a firm is multinational says little if anything about its international strategy except that it operates in several countries.

[4] Raymond Vernon, "International Investment and International Trade in the Product Cycle," *Quarterly Journal of Economics*, Vol. 80 (May 1966):190–207. Vernon himself, among others, has raised questions about how general the product cycle pattern is today.

Broadly stated, my research has been seeking to answer the question: what does international competition mean for competitive strategy? In particular, what are the distinctive questions for competitive strategy that are raised by international as opposed to domestic competition? Many of the strategy issues for a company competing internationally are very much the same as for one competing domestically. A firm must still analyze its industry structure and competitors, understand its buyer and the sources of buyer value, diagnose its relative cost position, and seek to establish a sustainable competitive advantage within some competitive scope, whether it be across-the-board or in an industry segment. These are subjects I have written about extensively.[5] But there are some questions for strategy that are peculiar to international competition, and that add to rather than replace those listed earlier. These questions all revolve, in one way or another, around how a firm's activities in one country affect or are affected by what is going on in other countries—the connectedness among country competition. It is this connectedness that is the focus of this article and of a broader stream of research recently conducted under the auspices of the Harvard Business School.[6]

Patterns of International Competition

The appropriate unit of analysis in setting international strategy is the industry, because the industry is the arena in which competitive advantage is won or lost. The starting point for understanding international competition is the observation that its pattern differs markedly from industry to industry. At one end of the spectrum are industries that I call *multidomestic,* in which competition in each country (or small group of countries) is essentially independent of competition in other countries. A multidomestic industry is one that is present in many countries (e.g., there is a consumer banking industry in Sri Lanka, one in France, and one in the United States), but in which competition occurs on a country-by-country basis. In a multidomestic industry, a multinational firm may enjoy a competitive advantage from the one-time transfer of know-how from its home base to foreign countries. However, the firm modifies and adapts its intangible assets to employ them in each country and the outcome is determined by conditions in each country. The competitive advantages of the firm, then, are largely specific to each country. The international industry becomes a collection of essentially domestic industries—hence the term "multidomestic." Industries where competition has traditionally exhibited this pattern include

---

[5] Michael E. Porter, *Competitive Strategy: Techniques for Analyzing Industries and Competitors* (New York, NY: The Free Press, 1980); Michael E. Porter, "Beyond Comparative Advantage," Working Paper, Harvard Graduate School of Business Administration, August 1985.

[6] For a description of this research, see Michael E. Porter, ed., *Competition in Global Industries* (Boston, MA: Harvard Business School Press, forthcoming).

retailing, consumer packaged goods, distribution, insurance, consumer finance, and caustic chemicals.

At the other end of the spectrum are what I term *global* industries. The term global—like the word "strategy"—has become overused and perhaps under-understood. The definition of a global industry employed here is an industry in which a firm's competitive position in one country is significantly influenced by its position in other countries.[7] Therefore, the international industry is not merely a collection of domestic industries but a series of linked domestic industries in which the rivals compete against each other on a truly worldwide basis. Industries exhibiting the global pattern today include commercial aircraft, TV sets, semiconductors, copiers, automobiles, and watches.

The implications for strategy of the distinction between multidomestic and global industries are quite profound. In a multidomestic industry, a firm can and should manage its international activities like a portfolio. Its subsidiaries or other operations around the world should each control all the important activities necessary to do business in the industry and should enjoy a high degree of autonomy. The firm's strategy in a country should be determined largely by the circumstances in that country; the firm's international strategy is then what I term a *"country-centered strategy."*

In a multidomestic industry, competing internationally is discretionary. A firm can choose to remain domestic or can expand internationally if it has some advantage that allows it to overcome the extra costs of entering and competing in foreign markets. The important competitors in multidomestic industries will either be domestic companies or multinationals with stand-alone operations abroad—this is the situation in each of the multidomestic industries listed earlier. In a multidomestic industry, then, international strategy collapses to a series of domestic strategies. The issues that are uniquely international revolve around how to do business abroad, how to select good countries in which to compete (or assess country risk), and mechanisms to achieve the one-time transfer of know-how. These are questions that are relatively well developed in the literature.

In a global industry, however, managing international activities like a portfolio will undermine the possibility of achieving competitive advantage. In a global industry, a firm must in some way integrate its activities on a worldwide basis to capture the linkages among countries. This will require more than transferring intangible assets among countries, though it will include it. A firm may choose to compete with a country-centered strategy, focusing on specific market segments or countries when it can carve out a niche by responding to whatever local country differences are present. However, it does so at some

---

[7] The distinction between multidomestic and global competition and some of its strategic implications were described in T. Hout, Michael E. Porter, and E. Rudden, "How Global Companies Win Out," *Harvard Business Review* (September/October 1982), pp. 98–108.

considerable risk from competitors with global strategies. All the important competitors in the global industries listed earlier compete worldwide with coordinated strategies.

In international competition, a firm always has to perform some functions in each of the countries in which it competes. Even though a global competitor must view its international activities as an overall system, it has still to maintain some country perspective. It is the balancing of these two perspectives that becomes one of the essential questions in global strategy.[8]

Causes of Globalization

If we accept the distinction between multidomestic and global industries as an important taxonomy of patterns of international competition, a number of crucial questions arise. When does an industry globalize? What exactly do we mean by a global strategy, and is there more than one kind? What determines the type of international strategy to select in a particular industry?

An industry is global if there is some competitive advantage to integrating activities on a worldwide basis. To make this statement operational, however, we must be very precise about what we mean by "activities" and also what we mean by "integrating." To diagnose the sources of competitive advantage in any context, whether it be domestic or international, it is necessary to adopt a disaggregated view of the firm. In my newest book, *Competitive Advantage,* I have developed a framework for doing so, called the value chain.[9] Every firm is a collection of discrete activities performed to do business that occur within the scope of the firm—I call them value activities. The activities performed by a firm include such things as salespeople selling the product, service technicians

---

[8] Howard V. Perlmutter, "The Tortuous Evolution of the Multinational Corporation," *Columbia Journal of World Business* (January/February 1969), pp. 9–18. Perlmutter's concept of ethnocentric, polycentric, and geocentric multinationals takes the *firm* not the industry as the unit of analysis and is decoupled from industry structure. It focuses on management attitudes, the nationality of executives, and other aspects of organization. Perlmutter presents ethnocentric, polycentric, and geocentric as stages of an organization's development as a multinational, with geocentric as the goal. A later paper (Yoram Wind, Susan P. Douglas, and Howard V. Perlmutter, "Guidelines for Developing International Marketing Strategies," *Journal of Marketing*, Vol. 37 (April 1973: 14–23) tempers this conclusion based on the fact that some companies may not have the required sophistication in marketing to attempt a geocentric strategy. Products embedded in the lifestyle or culture of a country are also identified as less susceptible to geocentrism. The Perlmutter et al. view does not link management orientation to industry structure and strategy. International strategy should grow out of the net competitive advantage in a global industry of different types of worldwide coordination. In some industries, a country-centered strategy, roughly analogous to Perlmutter's polycentric idea, may be the best strategy irrespective of company size and international experience. Conversely, a global strategy may be imperative given the competitive advantage that accrues from it. Industry and strategy should define the organization approach, not vice versa.

[9] Michael E. Porter, *Competitive Advantage: Creating and Sustaining Superior Performance* (New York, NY: The Free Press, 1985).

performing repairs, scientists in the laboratory designing process techniques, and accountants keeping the books. Such activities are technologically and in most cases physically distinct. It is only at the level of discrete activities, rather than the firm as a whole, that competitive advantage can be truly understood.

A firm may possess two types of competitive advantage: low relative cost or differentiation—its ability to perform the activities in its value chain either at lower cost or in a unique way relative to its competitors. The ultimate value a firm creates is what buyers are willing to pay for what the firm provides, which includes the physical product as well as any ancillary services or benefits. Profit results if the value created through performing the required activities exceeds the collective cost of performing them. Competitive advantage is a function of either providing comparable buyer value to competitors but performing activities efficiently (low cost), or of performing activities at comparable cost but in unique ways that create greater buyer value than competitors and, hence, command a premium price (differentiation).

The value chain, shown in Figure 2, provides a systematic means of displaying and categorizing activities. The activities performed by a firm in any industry can be grouped into the nine generic categories shown. The labels may differ based on industry convention, but every firm performs these basic categories of activities in some way or another. Within each category of activities, a firm typically performs a number of discrete activities which are particular to the industry and to the firm's strategy. In service, for example, firms typically perform such discrete activities as installation, repair, parts distribution, and upgrading.

FIGURE 2   The Value Chain

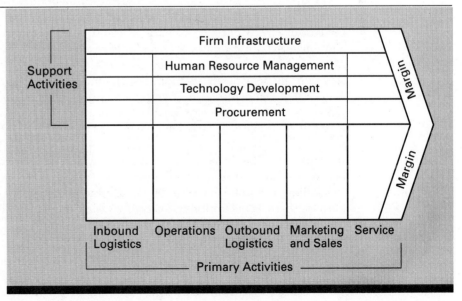

The generic categories of activities can be grouped into two broad types. Along the bottom are what I call *primary* activities, which are those involved in the physical creation of the product or service, its delivery and marketing to the buyer, and its support after sale. Across the top are what I call *support* activities, which provide inputs or infrastructure that allow the primary activities to take place on an ongoing basis.

Procurement is the obtaining of purchased inputs, whether they be raw materials, purchased services, machinery, or so on. Procurement stretches across the entire value chain because it supports every activity—every activity uses purchased inputs of some kind. There are typically many different discrete procurement activities within a firm, often performed by different people. Technology development encompasses the activities involved in designing the product as well as in creating and improving the way the various activities in the value chain are performed. We tend to think of technology in terms of the product or manufacturing process. In fact, every activity a firm performs involves a technology or technologies which may be mundane or sophisticated, and a firm has a stock of know-how about how to perform each activity. Technology development typically involves a variety of different discrete activities, some performed outside the R&D department.

Human resource management is the recruiting, training, and development of personnel. Every activity involves human resources, and thus human resource management activities cut across the entire chain. Finally, firm infrastructure includes activities such as general management, accounting, legal, finance, strategic planning, and all the other activities decoupled from specific primary or support activities but that are essential to enable the entire chain's operation.

Activities in a firm's value chain are not independent, but are connected through what I call linkages. The way one activity is performed frequently affects the cost or effectiveness of other activities. If more is spent on the purchase of a raw material, for example, a firm may lower its cost of fabrication or assembly. There are many linkages that connect activities, not only within the firm but also with the activities of its suppliers, channels, and ultimately its buyers. The firm's value chain resides in a larger stream of activities that I term the value system. Suppliers have value chains that provide the purchased inputs to the firm's chain; channels have value chains through which the firm's product or service passes; buyers have value chains in which the firm's product or service is employed. The connections among activities in this vertical system also become essential to competitive advantage.

A final important building block in value chain theory, necessary for our purposes here, is the notion of *competitive scope*. Competitive scope is the breadth of activities the firm employs together in competing in an industry. There are four basic dimensions of competitive scope:

◆ *Segment* scope, or the range of segments the firm serves (e.g., product varieties, customer types);

- *Industry* scope, or the range of industries the firm competes in with a coordinated strategy;
- *Vertical* scope, or what activities are performed by the firm versus suppliers and channels; and
- *Geographic* scope, or the geographic regions the firm operates in with a coordinated strategy.

Competitive scope is vital to competitive advantage because it shapes the configuration of the value chain, how activities are performed, and whether activities are shared among units. International strategy is an issue of geographic scope, and can be analyzed quite similarly to the question of whether and how a firm should compete locally, regionally, or nationally within a country. In the international context, government tends to have a greater involvement in competition and there are more significant variations among geographic regions in buyer needs, although these differences are matters of degree.

International Configuration and Coordination of Activities A firm that competes internationally must decide how to spread the activities in the value chain among countries. A distinction immediately arises between the activities labeled downstream on Figure 3, and those labeled upstream activities and support activities. The location of downstream activities, those more related to the buyer, is usually tied to where the buyer is located. If a firm is going to sell in Japan, for example, it usually must provide service in Japan and it must have salespeople stationed in Japan. In some industries it is possible to have a single sales force that travels to the buyer's country and back again; some other specific

FIGURE 3   Upstream and Downstream Activities

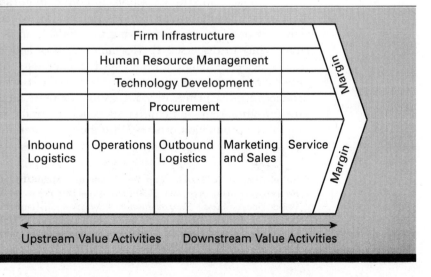

downstream activities such as the production of advertising copy can also sometimes be done centrally. More typically, however, the firm must locate the capability to perform downstream activities in each of the countries in which it operates. Upstream activities and support activities, conversely, can at least conceptually be decoupled from where the buyer is located.

This distinction carries some interesting implications. The first is that downstream activities create competitive advantages that are largely country-specific: a firm's reputation, brand name, and service network in a country grow out of a firm's activities in that country and create entry/mobility barriers largely in that country alone. Competitive advantage in upstream and support activities often grows more out of the entire system of countries in which a firm competes than from its position in any one country, however.

A second implication is that in industries where downstream activities or buyer-tied activities are vital to competitive advantage, there tends to be a more multidomestic pattern of international competition. In industries where upstream and support activities (such as technology development and operations) are crucial to competitive advantage, global competition is more common. In global competition, the location and scale of these potentially footloose activities are optimized from a worldwide perspective.[10]

The distinctive issues in international, as contrasted to domestic, strategy can be summarized in two key dimensions of how a firm competes internationally. The first is what I term the *configuration* of a firm's activities worldwide, or where in the world each activity in the value chain is performed, including in how many places. The second dimension is what I term *coordination*, which refers to how like activities performed in different countries are coordinated with each other. If, for example, there are three plants—one in Germany, one in Japan, and one in the United States—how do the activities in those plants relate to each other?

A firm faces an array of options in both configuration and coordination for each activity. Configuration options range from concentrated (performing an activity in one location and serving the world from it—e.g., one R&D lab, one large plant) to dispersed (performing every activity in each country). In the latter case, each country would have a complete value chain. Coordination options range from none to very high. For example, if a firm produces its product in three plants, it could, at one extreme, allow each plant to operate with full autonomy—e.g., different product standards and features, different steps in the production process, different raw materials, different part numbers.

---

[10] Buzzell (Robert D. Buzzell, "Can You Standardize Multinational Marketing," *Harvard Business Review* [November/December 1980], pp. 102–113); Pryor (Millard H. Pryor, "Planning in a World-Wide Business," *Harvard Business Review*, Vol. 23 [January/February 1965]); and Wind, Douglas, and Perlmutter (op. cit.) point out that national differences are in most cases more critical with respect to marketing than with production and finance. This generalization reflects the fact that marketing activities are often inherently country-based. However. this generalization is not reliable because in many industries, production and other activities are widely dispersed.

FIGURE **4**   Configuration and Coordination Issues by Category of Activity

Value Activity	Configuration Issues	Coordination Issues
Operations	• Location of production facilities for components and end products	• Networking of international plants • Transferring process technology and production know-how among plants
Marketing and Sales	• Product line selection • Country (market) selection	• Commonality of brand name worldwide • Coordination of sales to multinational accounts • Similarity of channels and product positioning worldwide • Coordination of pricing in different countries
Service	• Location of service organization	• Similarity of service standards and procedures worldwide
Technology Development	• Number and location of R&D centers	• Interchange among dispersed R&D centers • Developing products responsive to market needs in many countries • Sequence of product introductions around the world
Procurement	• Location of the purchasing function	• Managing suppliers located in different countries • Transferring market knowledge • Coordinating purchases of common items

At the other extreme, the plants could be tightly coordinated by employing the same information system, the same production process, the same parts, and so forth. Options for coordination in an activity are typically more numerous than the configuration options because there are many possible levels of coordination and many different facets of the way the activity is performed.

Figure 4 lists some of the configuration issues and coordination issues for several important categories of value activities. In technology development, for example, the configuration issue is where R&D is performed: one location? two locations? and in what countries? The coordination issues have to do with such things as the extent of interchange among R&D centers and the location and sequence of product introduction around the world. There are configuration issues and coordination issues for every activity.

Figure 5 is a way of summarizing these basic choices in international strategy on a single diagram, with coordination of activities on the vertical axis and configuration of activities on the horizontal axis. The firm has to make a set of choices for each activity. If a firm employs a very dispersed configuration—placing an entire value chain in every country (or small group of contiguous countries) in which it operates, coordinating little or not at all among them—then the firm is competing with a country-centered strategy. The domestic firm that only operates in one country is the extreme case of a firm with a country-centered strategy. As we move from the lower left-hand corner of the diagram up or to the right, we have strategies that are increasingly global.

Figure 6 illustrates some of the possible variations in international strategy. The purest global strategy is to concentrate as many activities as possible in one country, serve the world from this home base, and tightly coordinate those activities that must inherently be performed near the buyer. This is the pattern adopted by many Japanese firms in the 1960s and 1970s, such as Toyota. However, Figures 5 and 6 make it clear that there is no such thing as one global strategy. There are many different kinds of global strategies, depending on a firm's choices about configuration and coordination throughout the value chain. In copiers, for example, Xerox has until recently concentrated R&D in the United States but dispersed other activities, in some cases using joint-venture partners to perform them. On dispersed activities, however, coordination has been quite high. The Xerox brand, marketing approach, and servicing procedures have been quite standardized worldwide. Canon, on the other hand, has had a much more concentrated configuration of activities and somewhat less coordination of dispersed activities. The vast majority of support activities and manufacturing of copiers have been performed in Japan. Aside from using the Canon brand, however, local marketing subsidiaries have been given quite a bit of latitude in each region of the world.

A global strategy can now be defined more precisely as one in which a firm seeks to gain competitive advantage from its international presence through either concentrating configuration, coordination among dispersed activities, or both. Measuring the presence of a global industry empirically must reflect both dimensions and not just one. Market presence in many countries and some export and import of components and end products are characteristic of most global industries. High levels of foreign investment or the mere presence of multinational firms are not reliable measures, however, because firms may be managing foreign units like a portfolio.

Configuration/Coordination and Competitive Advantage Understanding the competitive advantages of a global strategy and, in turn, the causes of industry globalization requires specifying the conditions in which concentrating activities globally and coordinating dispersed activities leads to either cost advantage or differentiation. In each case, there are structural characteristics of an industry that work for and against globalization.

The factors that favor concentrating an activity in one or a few locations to serve the world are as follows:

- ◆ Economies of scale in the activity.
- ◆ A proprietary learning curve in the activity.
- ◆ Comparative advantage in where the activity is performed.
- ◆ Coordination advantages of co-locating linked activities such as R&D and production.

FIGURE **5**   The Dimensions of International Strategy

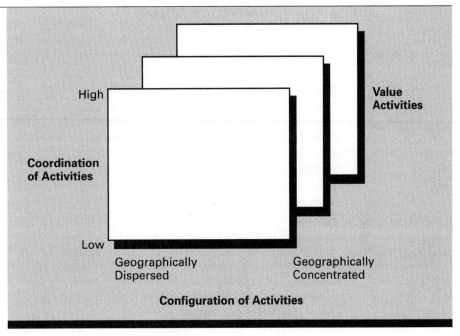

FIGURE **6**   Types of International Strategy

	Geographically Dispersed	Geographically Concentrated
High Coordination of Activities	High Foreign Investment with Extensive Coordination among Subsidiaries	Purest Global Strategy
Low	Country–Centered Strategy by Multinationals with a Number of Domestic Firms Operating in Only One Country	Export–Based Strategy with Decentralized Marketing

Value Activities

The first two factors relate to *how many* sites an activity is performed at, while the last two relate to *where* these sites are. Comparative advantage can apply to any activity, not just production. For example, there may be some locations in the world that are better places than others to do research on medical technology or to perform software development. Government can promote the concentration of activities by providing subsidies or other incentives to use a particular country as an export base, in effect altering comparative advantage— a role many governments are playing today.

There are also structural characteristics that favor dispersion of an activity to many countries, which represent concentration costs. Local product needs may differ, nullifying the advantages of scale or learning from one-site operation of an activity. Locating a range of activities in a country may facilitate marketing in that country by signaling commitment to local buyers and/or providing greater responsiveness. Transport, communication, and storage costs may make it inefficient to concentrate the activity in one location. Government is also frequently a powerful force for dispersing activities. Governments typically want firms to locate the entire value chain in their country, because this creates benefits and spillovers to the country that often go beyond local content. Dispersion is also encouraged by the risks of performing an activity in one place: exchange-rate risks, political risks, and so on. The balance between the advantages of concentrating and dispersing an activity normally differ for each activity (and industry). The best configuration for R&D is different from that for component fabrication, and this is different from that for assembly, installation, advertising, and procurement.[11]

The desirability of coordinating like activities that are dispersed involves a similar balance of structural factors. Coordination potentially allows the sharing of know-how among dispersed activities. If a firm learns how to operate the production process better in Germany, transferring that learning may make the process run better in plants in the United States and Japan. Differing countries, with their inevitably differing conditions, provide a fertile basis for comparison as well as opportunities for arbitraging knowledge, obtained in different places about different aspects of the business. Coordination among dispersed activities also potentially improves the ability to reap economies of scale in activities if subtasks are allocated among locations to allow some specialization—e.g., each R&D center has a different area of focus. While there is a fine line between

---

[11] A number of authors have framed the globalization of industries in terms of the balance between imperatives for global integration and imperatives for national responsiveness, a useful distinction. See, C. K. Prahalad, "The Strategic Process in a Multinational Corporation," unpublished DBA dissertation, Harvard Graduate School of Business Administration, 1975; Yves Doz, "National Policies and Multinational Management," an unpublished DBA dissertation, Harvard Graduate School of Business Administration, 1976; and Christopher A. Bartlett, "Multinational Structural Evolution: The Changing Decision Environment in the International Division," unpublished DBA dissertation, Harvard Graduate School of Business Administration, 1979. I link the distinction here to where and how a firm performs the activities in the value chain internationally.

such forms of coordination and what I have termed configuration, it does illustrate how the way a network of foreign locations is managed can have a great influence on the ability to reap the benefits of any given configuration of activities. Viewed another way, close coordination is frequently a partial offset to dispersing an activity.

Coordination may also allow a firm to respond to shifting comparative advantage, where shifts in exchange rates and factor costs are hard to forecast. Incrementally increasing the production volume at the location currently enjoying favorable exchange rates, for example, can lower overall costs. Coordination can reinforce a firm's brand reputation with buyers (and hence lead to differentiation) through ensuring a consistent image and approach to doing business on a worldwide basis. This is particularly likely if buyers are mobile or information about the industry flows freely around the world. Coordination may also differentiate the firm with multinational buyers if it allows the firm to serve them anywhere and in a consistent way. Coordination (and a global approach to configuration) enhances leverage with local governments if the firm is able to grow or shrink activities in one country at the expense of others. Finally, coordination yields flexibility in responding to competitors, by allowing the firm to differentially respond across countries and to respond in one country to a challenge in another.

Coordination of dispersed activities usually involves costs that differ by form of coordination and industry. Local conditions may vary in ways that may make a common approach across countries suboptimal. If every plant in the world is required to use the same raw material, for example, the firm pays a penalty in countries where the raw material is expensive relative to satisfactory substitutes. Business practices, marketing systems, raw material sources, local infrastructures, and a variety of other factors may differ across countries as well, often in ways that may mitigate the advantages of a common approach or of the sharing of learning. Governments may restrain the flow of information required for coordination or may impose other barriers to it. The transaction costs of coordination, which have recently received increased attention in domestic competition, are vitally important in international strategy.[12] International coordination involves long distances, language problems, and cultural barriers to communication. In some industries, these factors may mean that coordination is not optimal. They also suggest that forms of coordination which involve relatively infrequent decisions will enjoy advantages over forms of coordination involving on-going interchange.

---

[12] See, for example, Oliver Williamson, *Markets and Hierarchies* (New York, NY: The Free Press, 1975). For an international application, see Mark C. Casson, "Transaction Costs and the Theory of the Multinational Enterprise," in Alan Rugman, ed., *New Theories of the Multinational Enterprise* (London: Croom Helm, 1982); David J. Teece, "Transaction Cost Economics and the Multinational Enterprise: An Assessment," *Journal of Economic Behavior and Organization* (forthcoming, 1986).

There are also substantial organizational difficulties involved in achieving cooperation among subsidiaries, which are due to the difficulty in aligning subsidiary managers' interests with those of the firm as a whole. The Germans do not necessarily want to tell the Americans about their latest breakthroughs on the production line because it may make it harder for them to outdo the Americans in the annual comparison of operating efficiency among plants. These vexing organizational problems mean that country subsidiaries often view each other more as competitors than collaborators.[13] As with configuration, a firm must make an activity-by-activity choice about where there is net competitive advantage from coordinating in various ways.

Coordination in some activities may be necessary to reap the advantages of configuration in others. The use of common raw materials in each plant, for example, allows worldwide purchasing. Moreover, tailoring some activities to countries may allow concentration and standardization of other activities. For example, tailored marketing in each country may allow the same product to be positioned differently and hence sold successfully in many countries, unlocking possibilities for reaping economies of scale in production and R&D. Thus coordination and configuration interact.

Configuration/Coordination and the Pattern of International Competition

When benefits of configuring and/or coordinating globally exceed the costs, an industry will globalize in a way that reflects the net benefits by value activity. The activities in which global competitors gain competitive advantage will differ correspondingly. Configuration/coordination determines the ongoing competitive advantages of a global strategy which are additive to competitive advantages a firm derives/possesses from its domestic market positions. An initial transfer of knowledge from the home base to subsidiaries is one, but by no means the most important, advantage of a global competitor.[14]

An industry such as commercial aircraft represents an extreme case of a global industry (in the upper right-hand corner of Figure 4). The three major competitors in this industry—Boeing, McDonnell Douglas, and Airbus—all have

---

[13] The difficulties in coordinating are internationally parallel to those in coordinating across business units competing in different industries with the diversified firm. See Michael E. Porter, *Competitive Advantage: Creating and Sustaining Superior Performance* (New York, NY: The Free Press, 1985), Chapter 11.

[14] Empirical research has found a strong correlation between R&D and advertising intensity and the extent of foreign direct investment (for a survey, see Caves, 1982, op. cit.). Both these factors have a place in our model of the determinants of globalization, but for quite different reasons. R&D intensity suggests scale advantages for the global competitor in developing products or processes that are manufactured abroad either due to low production scale economies or government pressures, or which require investments in service infrastructure. Advertising intensity, however, is much closer to the classic transfer of marketing knowledge to foreign subsidiaries. High advertising industries are also frequently those where local tastes differ and manufacturing scale economies are modest, both reasons to disperse many activities.

global strategies. In activities important to cost and differentiation in the industry, there are compelling net advantages to concentrating most activities and coordinating the dispersed activities extensively.[15] In R&D, there is a large fixed cost of developing an aircraft model ($1 billion or more) which requires worldwide sales to amortize. There are significant economies of scale in production, a steep learning curve in assembly (the learning curve was born out of research in this industry), and apparently significant advantages of locating R&D and production together. Sales of commercial aircraft are infrequent (via a highly skilled sales force), so that even the sales force can be partially concentrated in the home country and travel to buyers.

The costs of a concentrated configuration are relatively low in commercial aircraft. Product needs are homogenous, and there are the low transport costs of delivering the product to the buyer. Finally, worldwide coordination of the one dispersed activity, service, is very important—obviously standardized parts and repair advice have to be available wherever the plane lands.

As in every industry, there are structural features which work against a global strategy in commercial aircraft. These are all related to government, a not atypical circumstance. Government has a particular interest in commercial aircraft because of its large trade potential, the technological sophistication of the industry, its spillover effects to other industries, and its implications for national defense. Government also has an unusual degree of leverage in the industry: in many instances, it is the buyer. Many airlines are government owned, and a government official or appointee is head of the airline.

The competitive advantages of a global strategy are so great that all the successful aircraft producers have sought to achieve and preserve them. In addition, the power of government to intervene has been mitigated by the fact the there are few viable worldwide competitors and that there are the enormous barriers to entry created in part by the advantages of a global strategy. The result has been that firms have sought to assuage government through procurement. Boeing, for example, is very careful about where it buys components. In countries that are large potential customers, Boeing seeks to develop suppliers. This requires a great deal of extra effort by Boeing both to transfer technology and to work with suppliers to assure that they meet its standards. Boeing realizes that this is preferable to compromising the competitive advantage of its strongly integrated worldwide strategy. It is willing to employ one value activity (procurement) where the advantages of concentration are modest to help preserve the benefits of concentration in other activities. Recently, commercial aircraft competitors have entered into joint ventures and other coalition arrangements with foreign suppliers to achieve the same effect, as well as to spread the risk of huge development costs.

---

[15] For an interesting description of the industry, see the paper by Michael Yoshino in Porter, ed., op. cit., (forthcoming).

The extent and location of advantages from a global strategy vary among industries. In some industries, the competitive advantage from a global strategy comes in technology development, although firms gain little advantage in the primary activities so that these are dispersed around the world to minimize concentration costs. In other industries such as cameras or videocassette recorders, a firm cannot succeed without concentrating production to achieve economies of scale, but instead it gives subsidiaries much local autonomy in sales and marketing. In some industries, there is no net advantage to a global strategy and country-centered strategies dominate—the industry is multidomestic.

Segments or stages of an industry frequently vary in their pattern of globalization. In aluminum, the upstream (alumina and ingot) stages of the industry are global businesses. The downstream stage, semifabrication, is a group of multidomestic businesses because product needs vary by country, transport costs are high, and intensive local customer service is required. Scale economies in the value chain are modest. In lubricants, automotive oil tends to be a country-centered business while marine motor oil is a global business. In automotive oil, countries have varying driving standards, weather conditions, and local laws. Production involves blending various kinds of crude oils and additives, and is subject to few economies of scale but high shipping costs. Country-centered competitors such as Castrol and Quaker State are leaders in most countries. In the marine segment, conversely, ships move freely around the world and require the same oil everywhere. Successful competitors are global.

The ultimate leaders in global industries are often first movers—the first firms to perceive the possibilities for a global strategy. Boeing was the first global competitor in aircraft, for example, as was Honda in motorcycles, and Becton Dickinson in disposable syringes. First movers gain scale and learning advantages which are difficult to overcome. First mover effects are particularly important in global industries because of the association between globalization and economies of scale and learning achieved through worldwide configuration/coordination. Global leadership shifts if industry structural change provides opportunities for leapfrogging to new products or new technologies that nullify past leaders' scale and learning—again, the first mover to the new generation/technology often wins.

Global leaders often begin with some advantage at home, whether it be low labor cost or a product or marketing advantage. They use this as a lever to enter foreign markets. Once there, however, the global competitor converts the initial home advantage into competitive advantages that grow out of its overall worldwide system, such as production scale or ability to amortize R&D costs. While the initial advantage may have been hard to sustain, the global strategy creates new advantages which can be much more durable.

International strategy has often been characterized as a choice between worldwide standardization and local tailoring, or as the tension between the economic imperative (large-scale efficient facilities) and the political imperative (local content, local production). It should be clear from the discussion so far that neither characterization captures the richness of a firm's international strategy choices. A firm's choice of international strategy involves a search for competitive advantage from configuration/coordination throughout the value chain. A firm may standardize (concentrate) some activities and tailor (disperse) others. It may also be able to standardize and tailor at the same time through the coordination of dispersed activities, or use local tailoring of some activities (e.g., different product positioning in each country) to allow standardization of others (e.g., production). Similarly, the economic imperative is not always for a global strategy—in some industries a country-centered strategy is the economic imperative. Conversely, the political imperative is to concentrate activities in some industries where governments provide strong export incentives and locational subsidies.

Global Strategy versus Comparative Advantage Given the importance of trade theory to the study of international competition, it is useful to pause and reflect on the relationship to the framework I have presented to the notion of comparative advantage. Is there a difference? The traditional concept of comparative advantage is that factor-cost or factor-quality differences among countries lead to production of products in countries with an advantage which export them elsewhere in the world. Competitive advantage in this view, then, grows out of *where* a firm performs activities. The location of activities is clearly one source of potential advantage in a global firm. The global competitor can locate activities wherever comparative advantage lies, decoupling comparative advantage from its home base or country of ownership.

Indeed, the framework presented here suggests that the comparative advantage story is richer than typically told, because it not only involves production activities (the usual focus of discussions) but also applies to other activities in the value chain such as R&D, processing orders, or designing advertisements. Comparative advantage is specific to the *activity* and not the location of the value chain as a whole.[16] One of the potent advantages of the global firm is that it can spread activities among locations to reflect different preferred locations for different activities, something a domestic or country-centered competitor does not do. Thus components can be made in Taiwan, software written in India, and basic R&D performed in Silicon Valley, for example. This international

---

[16] It has been recognized that comparative advantage in different stages in a vertically integrated industry sector such as aluminum can reside in different countries. Bauxite mining will take place in resource-rich countries, for example, while smelting will take place in countries with low electrical power cost. See R. E. Caves and Ronald W. Jones, op. cit. The argument here extends this thinking *within* the value chain of any stage and suggests that the optimal location for performing individual activities may vary as well.

specialization of activities within the firm is made possible by the growing ability to coordinate and configure globally.

At the same time as our framework suggests a richer view of comparative advantage, however, it also suggests that many forms of competitive advantage for the global competitor derive less from *where* the firm performs activities than from *how* it performs them on a worldwide basis; economies of scale, proprietary learning, and differentiation with multi-national buyers are not tied to countries but to the configuration and coordination of the firm's worldwide system. Traditional sources of comparative advantage can be very elusive and slippery sources of competitive advantage for an international competitor today, because comparative advantage frequently shifts. A country with the lowest labor cost is overtaken within a few years by some other country—facilities located in the first country then face a disadvantage. Moreover, falling direct labor as a percentage of total costs, increasing global markets for raw materials and other inputs, and freer flowing technology have diminished the role of traditional sources of comparative advantage.

My research on a broad cross-section of industries suggests that the achievement of sustainable world market leadership follows a more complex pattern than the exploitation of comparative advantage per se. A competitor often starts with a comparative advantage–related edge that provides the basis for penetrating foreign markets, but this edge is rapidly translated into a broader array of advantages that arise from a global approach to configuration and coordination as described earlier. Japanese firms, for example, have done a masterful job of converting temporary labor-cost advantages into durable systemwide advantages due to scale and proprietary know-how. Ultimately, the systemwide advantages are further reinforced with country-specific advantages such as brand identity as well as distribution channel access. Many Japanese firms were fortunate enough to make their transitions from country-based comparative advantage to global competitive advantage at a time when nobody paid much attention to them and there was a buoyant world economy. European and American competitors were willing to cede market share in "less desirable" segments such as the low end of the producer line, or so they thought. The Japanese translated these beachheads into world leadership by broadening their lines and reaping advantages in scale and proprietary technology. The Koreans and Taiwanese, the latest low labor cost entrants to a number of industries, may have a hard time replicating Japan's success, given slower growth, standardized products, and now alert competitors.

Global Platforms The interaction of the home-country conditions and competitive advantages from a global strategy that transcend the country suggest a more complex role of the country in firm success than implied by the theory of comparative advantage. To understand this more complex role of the country, I define the concept of a *global platform*. A country is a desirable global platform in an industry if it provides an environment yielding firms domiciled in that country an advantage in competing globally in that particular industry.[17] An essential element of this definition is that it hinges on success *outside* the country, and not merely country conditions which allow firms to successfully master domestic competition. In global competition, a country must be viewed as a platform and not as the place where all a firm's activities are performed.

There are two determinants of a good global platform in an industry, which I have explored in more detail elsewhere.[18] The first is comparative advantage, or the factor endowment of the country as a site to perform particular activities in the industry. Today, simple factors such as low-cost unskilled labor and natural resources are increasingly less important to global competition compared to complex factors such as skilled scientific and technical personnel and advanced infrastructure. Direct labor is a minor proportion of cost in many manufactured goods and automation of non-production activities is shrinking it further, while markets for resources are increasingly global, and technology has widened the number of sources of many resources. A country's factor endowment is partly exogenous and partly the result of attention and investment in the country.

The second determinant of the attractiveness of a country as a global platform in an industry are the characteristics of a country's demand. A country's demand conditions include the size and timing of its demand in an industry, factors recognized as important by authors such as Linder and Vernon.[19] They also include the sophistication and power of buyers and channels and the product features and attributes demanded. Local demand conditions provide two potentially powerful sources of competitive advantage to a global competitor based in that country. The first is *first-mover advantages* in perceiving and implementing the appropriate global strategy. Pressing local needs, particularly peculiar ones, lead firms to embark early to solve local problems and gain proprietary know-how. This is then translated into scale and learning advantages as firms move early to compete globally. The other potential benefit of local demand conditions is a baseload of demand for product varieties that will be sought after in international markets. These two roles of the country in the success of a global firm reflect the interaction between conditions of local supply, the composition and timing of country demand, and economies of scale and learning in shaping international success.

---

[17] The firm need not necessarily be owned by investors in the country, but the country is its home base for competing in a particular country.

[18] See Porter, *Competitive Advantage*, op. cit.

[19] See S. Linder, *An Essay on Trade and Transformation* (New York, NY: John Wiley, 1961); Vernon, op. cit., (1966); W. Gruber, D. Mehta, and R. Vernon, "R&D Factor in International Trade and International Investment of United States Industries," *Journal of Political Economics*, 76/1 (1967):20–37.

The two determinants interact in important and sometimes counterintuitive ways. Local demand and needs frequently influence private and social investment in endogenous factors of production. A nation with oceans as borders and dependence on sea trade, for example, is more prone to have universities and scientific centers dedicated to oceanographic education and research. Similarly, factor endowment seems to influence local demand. The per capita consumption of wine is highest in wine-growing regions, for example.

Comparative disadvantage in some factors of production can be an advantage in global competition when combined with pressing local demand. Poor growing conditions have led Israeli farmers to innovate in irrigation and cultivation techniques, for example. The shrinking role in competition of simple factors of production relative to complex factors such as technical personnel seem to be enhancing the frequency and importance of such circumstances. What is important today is unleashing innovation in the proper direction, instead of passive exploitation of static cost advantages in a country which can shift rapidly and be overcome. International success today is a dynamic process resulting from continued development of products and processes. The forces which guide firms to undertake such activity thus become central to international competition.

A good example of the interplay among these factors is the television set industry. In the United States, early demand was in large screen console sets because television sets were initially luxury items kept in the living room. As buyers began to purchase second and third sets, sets became smaller and more portable. They were used increasingly in the bedroom, the kitchen, the car, and elsewhere. As the television set industry matured, table model and portable sets became the universal product variety. Japanese firms, because of the small size of Japanese homes, cut their teeth on small sets. They dedicated most of their R&D to developing small picture tubes and to making sets more compact. In the process of naturally serving the needs of their home market, then, Japanese firms gained early experience and scale in segments of the industry that came to dominate world demand. U.S. firms, conversely, cut their teeth on large-screen console sets with fine furniture cabinets. As the industry matured, the experience base of U.S. firms was in a segment that was small and isolated to a few countries, notably the United States. Japanese firms were able to penetrate world markets in a segment that was both uninteresting to foreign firms and in which they had initial scale, learning, and labor cost advantages. Ultimately the low-cost advantage disappeared as production was automated, but global scale and learning economies took over as the Japanese advanced product and process technology at a rapid pace.

The two broad determinants of a good global platform rest on the interaction between country characteristics and firms' strategies. The literature on comparative advantage, through focusing on country factor endowments, ignoring the demand side, and suppressing the individual firm, is most appropriate in industries where there are few economies of scale, little proprietary technology or technological change, or few possibilities for product differentiation.[20] While these industry characteristics are those of many traditionally traded goods, they describe few of today's important global industries.

The Evolution of International Competition

Having established a framework for understanding the globalization of industries, we are now in a position to view the phenomenon in historical perspective. If one goes back far enough, relatively few industries were global. Around 1880, most industries were local or regional in scope.[21] The reasons are rather self-evident in the context of our framework. There were few economies of scale in production until fuel-powered machines and assembly-line techniques emerged. There were heterogeneous product needs among regions within countries, much less among countries. There were few if any national media—the *Saturday Evening Post* was the first important national magazine in the United States and developed in the teens and twenties. Communicating between regions was difficult before the telegraph and telephone, and transportation was slow until the railroad system became well developed.

These structural conditions created little impetus for the widespread globalization of industry. Those industries that were global reflected classic comparative advantage considerations—goods were simply unavailable in some countries (who then imported them from others) or differences in the availability of land, resources, or skilled labor made some countries desirable suppliers to others. Export of local production was the form of global strategy adapted. There was little role or need for widespread government barriers to international trade during this period, although trade barriers were quite high in some countries for some commodities.

Around the 1880s, however, were the beginnings of what today has blossomed into the globalization of many industries. The first wave of modern global competitors grew up in the late 1800s and early 1900s. Many industries went from local (or regional) to national in scope, and some began globalizing. Firms such as Ford, Singer, Gillette, National Cash Register, Otis, and Western Electric had commanding world market shares by the teens, and operated with integrated worldwide strategies. Early global competitors were principally American and European companies.

Driving this first wave of modern globalization were rising production scale economies due to advancements in technology that outpaced the growth of the world economy. Product needs also became more homogenized in different

---

[20] Where it does recognize scale economies, trade theory views them narrowly as arising from production in one country.

[21] See Alfred Chandler in Porter, ed., op. cit., (forthcoming) for a penetrating history of the origins of the large industrial firm and its expansion abroad, which is consistent with the discussion here.

countries as knowledge and industrialization diffused. Transport improved, first through the railroad and steamships and later in trucking. Communication became easier with the telegraph then the telephone. At the same time, trade barriers were either modest or overwhelmed by the advantages of the new large-scale firms.

The burst of globalization soon slowed, however. Most of the few industries that were global moved increasingly towards a multidomestic pattern—multinationals remained, but between the 1920s and 1950 they often evolved towards federations of autonomous subsidiaries. The principal reason was a strong wave of nationalism and resulting high tariff barriers, partly caused by the world economic crisis and world wars. Another barrier to global strategies, chronicled by Chandler,[22] was a growing web of cartels and other interfirm contractual agreements. These limited the geographic spread of firms.

The early global competitors began rapidly dispersing their value chains. The situation of Ford Motor Company was no exception. While in 1925 Ford had almost no production outside the United States, by World War II its overseas production had risen sharply. Firms that became multinationals during the interwar period tended to adopt country-centered strategies. European multinationals, operating in a setting where there were many sovereign countries within a relatively small geographical area, were quick to establish self-contained and quite autonomous subsidiaries in many countries. A more tolerant regulatory environment also encouraged European firms to form cartels and other cooperative agreements among themselves, which limited their foreign market entry.

Between the 1950s and the late 1970s, however, there was a strong reversal of the interwar trends. As Figure 1 illustrated, there have been very strong underlying forces driving the globalization of industries. The important reasons can be understood using the configuration/coordination dichotomy. The competitive advantage of competing worldwide from concentrated activities rose sharply, while concentration costs fell. There was a renewed rise in scale economies in many activities due to advancing technology. The minimum efficient scale of an auto assembly plant more than tripled between 1960 and 1975, for example, while the average cost of developing a new drug more than quadrupled.[23] The pace of technological change has increased, creating more incentive to amortize R&D costs against worldwide sales.

Product needs have continued to homogenize among countries, as income differences have narrowed, information and communication has flowed more freely around the world, and travel has increased.[24] Growing similarities in

---

[22] Ibid.

[23] For data on auto assembly, see "Note on the World Auto Industry in Transition," Harvard Business School Case Services (#9–382–122).

[24] For a supporting view, see Theodore Levitt, "The Globalization of Markets," *Harvard Business Review* (May/June 1983), pp. 92–102.

business practices and marketing systems (e.g., chain stores) in different countries have also been a facilitating factor in homogenizing needs. Within countries there has been a parallel trend towards greater market segmentation, which some observers see as contradictory to the view that product needs in different countries are becoming similar. However, segments today seem based less on country differences and more on buyer differences that transcend country boundaries, such as demographic, user industry, or income groups. Many firms successfully employ global focus strategies in which they serve a narrow segment of an industry worldwide, as do Daimler-Benz and Rolex.

Another driver of post–World War II globalization has been a sharp reduction in the real costs of transportation. This has occurred through innovations in transportation technology including increasingly large bulk carriers, container ships, and larger, more efficient aircraft. At the same time, government impediments to global configuration/coordination have been falling in the postwar period. Tariff barriers have gone down, international cartels and patent-sharing agreements have disappeared, and regional economic pacts such as the European Community have emerged to facilitate trade and investment, albeit imperfectly.

The ability to coordinate globally has also risen markedly in the postwar period. Perhaps the most striking reason is falling communication costs (in voice and data) and reduced travel time for individuals. The ability to coordinate activities in different countries has also been facilitated by growing similarities among countries in marketing systems, business practices, and infrastructure—country after country has developed supermarkets and mass distributors, television advertising, and so on. Greater international mobility of buyers and information has raised the payout to coordinating how a firm does business around the world. The increasing number of firms who are multinational has created growing possibilities for differentiation by suppliers who are global.

The forces underlying globalization have been self-reinforcing. The globalization of firms' strategies has contributed to the homogenization of buyer needs and business practices. Early global competitors must frequently stimulate the demand for uniform global varieties; for example, as Becton Dickinson did in disposable syringes and Honda did in motorcycles. Similarly, globalization of industries begets globalization of supplier industries—the increasing globalization of automotive component suppliers is a good example. Pioneering global competitors also stimulate the development and growth of international telecommunication infrastructure as well as the creation of global advertising media—e.g., *The Economist* and *The Wall Street Journal*.

Strategic Implications of Globalization

When the pattern of international competition shifts from multidomestic to global, there are many implications for the strategy of international firms. While a full treatment is beyond the scope of this paper, I will sketch some of the implications here.[25]

At the broadest level, globalization casts new light on many issues that have long been of interest to students of international business. In areas such as international finance, marketing, and business-government relations, the emphasis in the literature has been on the unique problems of adapting to local conditions and ways of doing business in a foreign country in a foreign currency. In a global industry, these concerns must be supplemented with an overriding focus on the ways and means of international configuration and coordination. In government relations, for example, the focus must shift from stand-alone negotiations with host countries (appropriate in multidomestic competition) to a recognition that negotiations in one country will both affect other countries and be shaped by possibilities for performing activities in other countries. In finance, measuring the performance of subsidiaries must be modified to reflect the contribution of one subsidiary to another's cost position or differentiation in a global strategy, instead of viewing each subsidiary as a stand-alone unit. In battling with global competitors, it may be appropriate in some countries to accept low profits indefinitely—in multidomestic competition this would be unjustified.[26] In global industries, the overall system matters as much or more than the country.

Of the many other implications of globalization for the firm, there are two of such significance that they deserve some treatment here. The first is the role of *coalitions* in global strategy. *A coalition is a long-term agreement linking firms but falling short of merger.* I use the term coalition to encompass a whole variety of arrangements that include joint ventures, licenses, supply agreements, and many other kinds of interfirm relationships. Such interfirm agreements have been receiving more attention in the academic literature, although each form of agreement has been looked at separately and the focus has been largely domestic.[27] International coalitions, linking firms in the same industry based in different countries, have become an even more important part of international strategy in the past decade.

International coalitions are a way of configuring activities in the value chain on a worldwide basis jointly with a partner. International coalitions are proliferating rapidly and are present in many industries.[28] There is a particularly high incidence in automobiles, aircraft, aircraft engines, robotics, consumer electron-

---

[25] The implications of the shift from multidomestic to global competition were the theme of a series of papers on each functional area of the firm prepared for the Harvard Business School Colloquium on Competition in Global Industries. See Porter, ed., op. cit., (forthcoming).

[26] For a discussion, see Hout, Porter, and Rudden, op. cit. For a recent treatment, see Gary Hamel and C. K. Prahalad, "Do You Really Have a Global Strategy?" *Harvard Business Review* (July/August 1985), pp. 139–148.

[27] David J. Teece, "Firm Boundaries, Technological Innovation, and Strategic Planning," in L. G. Thomas, ed., *Economics of Strategic Planning* (Lexington, MA: Lexington Books, 1985).

[28] For a treatment of coalitions from this perspective, see Porter, Fuller, and Rawlinson, in Porter, ed., op. cit., (forthcoming).

ics, semiconductors, and pharmaceuticals. While international coalitions have long been present, their character has been changing. Historically, a firm from a developed country formed a coalition with a firm in a lesser-developed country to perform marketing activities in that country. Today, we observe more and more coalitions in which two firms from developed countries are teaming up to serve the world, as well as coalitions that extend beyond marketing activities to encompass activities throughout the value chain.[29] Production and R&D coalitions are very common, for example.

Coalitions are a natural consequence of globalization and the need for an integrated worldwide strategy. The same forces that lead to globalization will prompt the formation of coalitions as firms confront the barriers to establishing a global strategy of their own. The difficulties of gaining access to foreign markets and in surmounting scale and learning thresholds in production, technology development, and other activities have led many firms to team up with others. In many industries, coalitions can be a transitional state in the adjustment of firms to globalization, reflecting the need of firms to catch up in technology, cure short-term imbalances between their global production networks and exchange rates, and accelerate the process of foreign market entry. Many coalitions are likely to persist in some form, however.

There are benefits and costs of coalitions as well as difficult implementation problems in making them succeed (which I have discussed elsewhere). How to choose and manage coalitions is among the most interesting questions in international strategy today. When one speaks to managers about coalitions, almost all have tales of disaster which vividly illustrate that coalitions often do not succeed. Also, there is the added burden of coordinating global strategy with a coalition partner because the partner often wants to do things its own way. Yet, in the face of copious corporate experience that coalitions do not work and a growing economics literature on transaction costs and contractual failures, we see a proliferation of coalitions today of the most difficult kind—those between companies in different countries.[30] There is a great need for researching in both the academic community and in the corporate world about coalitions and how to manage them. They are increasingly being forced on firms today by new competitive circumstances.

A second area where globalization carries particular importance is in *organizational structure*. The need to configure and coordinate globally in complex ways creates some obvious organizational challenges.[31] Any organization struc-

---

[29] Hladik's recent study of international joint ventures provides supporting evidence. See K. Hladik, "International Joint Ventures: An Empirical Investigation into the Characteristics of Recent U.S.–Foreign Joint Venture Partnerships," unpublished Doctoral dissertation, Business Economics Program, Harvard University, 1984.

[30] For the seminal work on contractual failures, see Williamson, op. cit.

[31] For a thorough and sophisticated treatment, see Christopher A. Bartlett's paper in Porter, ed., op. cit., (forthcoming).

ture for competing internationally has to balance two dimensions; there has to be a *country* dimension (because some activities are inherently performed in the country) and there has to be a *global* dimension (because the advantages of global configuration/coordination must be achieved). In a global industry, the ultimate authority must represent the global dimension if a global strategy is to prevail. However, within any international firm, once it disperses any activities there are tremendous pressures to disperse more. Moreover, forces are unleashed which lead subsidiaries to seek growing autonomy. Local country managers will have a natural tendency to emphasize how different their country is and the consequent need for local tailoring and control over more activities in the value chain. Country managers will be loath to give up control over activities or how they are performed to outside forces. They will also frequently paint an ominous picture of host government concerns about local content and requirements for local presence. Corporate incentive systems frequently encourage such behavior by linking incentives narrowly to subsidiary results.

In successful global competitors, an environment is created in which the local managers seek to exploit similarities across countries rather than emphasize differences. They view the firm's global presence as an advantage to be tapped for their local gain. Adept global competitors often go to great lengths to devise ways of circumventing or adapting to local differences while preserving the advantages of the similarities. A good example is Canon's personal copier. In Japan, the typical paper size is bigger than American legal size and the standard European size. Canon's personal copier will not handle this size—a Japanese company introduced a product that did not meet its home market needs in the world's largest market for small copiers! Canon gathered its marketing managers from around the world and cataloged market needs in each country. They found that capacity to copy the large Japanese paper was only needed in Japan. In consultation with design and manufacturing engineers, it was determined that building this feature into the personal copier would significantly increase its complexity and cost. The decision was made to omit the feature because the price elasticity of demand for the personal copier was judged to be high. But this was not the end of the deliberations. Canon's management then set out to find a way to make the personal copier saleable in Japan. The answer that emerged was to add another feature to the copier—the ability to copy business cards—which both added little cost and was particularly valuable in Japan. This case illustrates the principle of looking for the similarities in needs among countries and in finding ways of creating similarities, not emphasizing the differences.

Such a change in orientation is something that typically occurs only grudgingly in a multinational company, particularly if it has historically operated in a country-centered mode (as has been the case with early U.S. and European multinationals). Achieving such a reorientation requires first that managers recognize that competitive success demands exploiting the advantages of a global strategy. Regular contact and discussion among subsidiary managers seems to be a prerequisite, as are information systems that allow operations in different countries to be compared.[32] This can be followed by programs for exchanging information and sharing know-how and then by more complex forms of coordination. Ultimateiy, the reconfiguring of activities globally may then be accepted, even though subsidiaries may have to give up control over some activities in the process.

The Future of International Competition

Since the late 1970s, there have been some gradual but significant changes in the pattern of international competition which carry important implications for international strategy. Our framework provides a template with which we can examine these changes and probe their significance [see Figure 7]. The factors shaping the global configuration of activities by firms are developing in ways which contrast with the trends of the previous thirty years. Homogenization of product needs among countries appears to be continuing, though segmentation within countries is as well. As a result, consumer packaged goods are becoming increasingly prone toward globalization, though they have long been characterized by multidomestic competition. There are also signs of globalization in some service industries as the introduction of information technology creates scale economies in support activities and facilitates coordination in primary activities. Global service firms are reaping advantages in hardware and software development as well as procurement.

In many industries, however, limits have been reached in the scale economies that have been driving the concentration of activities. These limits grow out of classic diseconomies of scale that arise in very large facilities, as well as out of new, more flexible technology in manufacturing and other activities that is often not as scale sensitive as previous methods. At the same time, though, flexible manufacturing allows the production of multiple varieties (to serve different countries) in a single plant. This may encourage new movement towards globalization in industries in which product differences among countries have remained significant and have blocked globalization in the past.

There also appear to be some limits to further decline in transport costs, as innovations such as containerization, bulk ships, and larger aircraft have run their course. However, a parallel trend toward smaller, lighter products and components may keep some downward pressure on transport costs. The biggest change in the benefits and costs of concentrated configuration has been the sharp rise in protectionism in recent years and the resulting rise in nontariff

---

[32] For a good discussion of the mechanisms for facilitating international coordination in operations and technology development, see M. T. Flaherty in Porter, ed., op. cit., (forthcoming). Flaherty stresses the importance of information systems and the many dimensions that valuable coordination can take.

FIGURE 7   Future Trends in International Competition

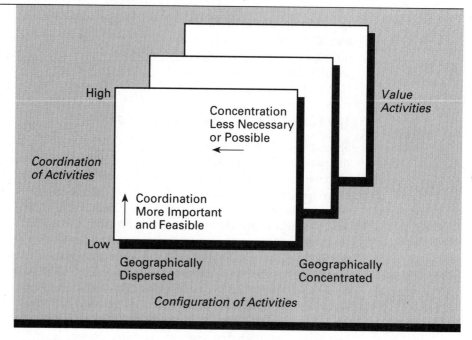

barriers, harkening back to the 1920s. As a group, these factors point to less need and less opportunity for highly concentrated configurations of activities.

When we examine the coordination dimension, the picture looks starkly different. Communication and coordination costs are dropping sharply, driven by breathtaking advances in information systems and telecommunication technology. We have just seen the beginning of developments in this area, which are spreading throughout the value chain.[33] Boeing, for example, is employing computer-aided design technology to jointly design components on-line with foreign suppliers. Engineers in different countries are communicating via computer screens. Marketing systems and business practices continue to homogenize, facilitating the coordination of activities in different countries. The mobility of buyers and information is also growing rapidly, greasing the international spread of brand reputations and enhancing the importance of consistency in the way activities are performed worldwide. Increasing numbers of multinational and global firms are begetting globalization by their suppliers. There is also a sharp rise in the computerization of manufacturing as well as

---

[33] For a discussion, see Michael E. Porter and Victor Millar, "How Information Gives You Competitive Advantage," *Harvard Business Review* (July/August 1985), pp. 149–160.

other activities throughout the value chain, which greatly facilitates coordination among dispersed sites.

The imperative of global strategy is shifting, then, in ways that will require a rebalancing of configuration and coordination. Concentrating activities is less necessary in economic terms, and less possible as governments force more dispersion. At the same time, the ability to coordinate globally throughout the value chain is increasing dramatically through modern technology. The need to coordinate is also rising to offset greater dispersion and to respond to buyer needs.

Thus, today's game of global strategy seems increasingly to be a game of coordination—getting more and more dispersed production facilities, R&D laboratories, and marketing activities to truly work together. Yet, widespread coordination is the exception rather than the rule today in many multinationals, as I have noted. The imperative for coordination raises many questions for organizational structure, and is complicated even more when the firm has built its global system using coalitions with independent firms.

Japan has clearly been the winner in the postwar globalization of competition. Japan's firms not only had an initial labor cost advantage but the orientation and skills to translate this into more durable competitive advantages such as scale and proprietary technology. The Japanese context also offered an excellent platform for globalization in many industries, given postwar environmental and technological trends. With home market conditions favoring compactness, a lead in coping with high energy costs, and a national conviction to raise quality, Japan has proved a fertile incubator of global leaders. Japanese multinationals had the advantage of embarking on international strategies in the 1950s and 1960s when the imperatives for a global approach to strategy were beginning to accelerate, but without the legacy of past international investments and modes of behavior.[34] Japanese firms also had an orientation towards highly concentrated activities that fit the strategic imperative of the time. Most European and American multinationals, conversely, were well established internationally before the war. They had legacies of local subsidiary autonomy that reflected the interwar environment. As Japanese firms spread internationally, they dispersed activities only grudgingly and engaged in extensive global coordination. European and country-centered American companies struggled to rationalize overly dispersed configurations of activities and to boost the level of global coordination among foreign units. They found their decentralized organization structures—so fashionable in the 1960s and 1970s—to be a hindrance to doing so.

As today's international firms contemplate the future, Japanese firms are rapidly dispersing activities, due largely to protectionist pressures but also be-

---

[34] Prewar international sales enjoyed by Japanese firms were handled largely through trading companies. See Chandler, op. cit.

cause of the changing economic factors I have described. They will have to learn the lessons of managing overseas activities that many European and American firms learned long ago. However, Japanese firms enjoy an organizational style that is supportive of coordination and a strong commitment to introducing new technologies such as information systems that facilitate it. European firms must still overcome their country-centered heritage. Many still do not compete with truly global strategies and lack modern technology. Moreover, the large number of coalitions formed by European firms must overcome the barriers to coordination if they are not to prove ultimately limiting. The European advantage may well be in exploiting an acute and well-developed sensitivity to local market conditions as well as a superior ability to work with host governments. By using modern flexible manufacturing technology and computerizing elsewhere in the value chain. European firms may be able to serve global segments and better differentiate products.

Many American firms tend to fall somewhere in between the European and Japanese situations. Their awareness of international competition has risen dramatically in recent years, and efforts at creating global strategies are more widespread. The American challenge is to catch the Japanese in a variety of technologies, as well as to learn how to gain the benefits of coordinating among dispersed units instead of becoming trapped by the myths of decentralization. The changing pattern of international competition is creating an environment in which no competitor can afford to allow country parochialism to impede its ability to turn a worldwide position into a competitive edge.

GLOBAL STRATEGIC PLANNING: A MODEL AND RECENT DEVELOPMENTS

William A. Dymsza

ABSTRACT. This article develops a comprehensive, dynamic model of strategic planning for multinational corporations. The model depicts many aspects in MNC strategic planning systems, while recognizing that many variations exist among companies. Within the context of the model and experience of companies, certain approaches to competitive assessment, focusing on strategic issues, portfolio planning, and threat/opportunity analysis, are emphasized. Finally, the article examines recent ways in which MNCs have been fine-tuning their strategic planning to deal with rapidly changing global environments, to meet new competition, and to achieve profitability and other goals.

Introduction

One of the most important developments in management has been the much greater emphasis that multinational companies have placed on strategic planning as a framework for decision making.

Over the years the process of strategic planning has been refined and fine-tuned by multinational companies to make it more significant in decision making. Confronted with rapid—often discontinuous—changes and with greater uncertainty in their business across the world, managements of multinational companies have developed a more analytical framework for planning as a basis for making decisions. These managements want to anticipate and adapt to future changes and uncertainties rather than be victims of them. They want to employ their corporate resources—management, personnel, technologies, business know-how, funds, and other assets—in a more efficient and productive way to attain their corporate objectives. They want to explore global opportunities for profits and service to their consumers, to reduce threats, uncertainties, and exposure to risk, and to achieve greater competitive efficiency, along with profitability objectives around the world. As a result, multinational companies are making greater use of strategic planning as a key management process.

Unique Aspects of International Strategic Planning: Types of Decisions

Even though many aspects of international strategic planning are similar to those of domestic business planning, some important differences do exist, creating uniqueness and complexity. For example, the types of decisions that strategic planning should help a multinational company to make are as follows: In what region and what countries and when should a company expand its

---

Source: *Journal of International Business Studies*, Fall 1984, pp. 169–183. Reprinted with permission.

international commitments in funds, technology, management, know-how, and personnel? Should it enter a new country? What type of entry should it undertake in countries with opportunities: exporting, licensing, direct investments, management contracts, other arrangements? What are the opportunities/risks in various countries in different modes of entry? In what countries should it expand its existing plants, undertake new investments, make acquisitions? What product adaptations should it make and what new products should it introduce in various countries? To what extent should it change its marketing and product mixes in different countries? What should the company do about exchange risk, political vulnerability, and adverse governmental controls and regulations? Should it disinvest or phase out business in certain countries? Where should it raise funds for its worldwide operations? Should it go into joint ventures with private firms or government enterprises abroad, and under what conditions? What management development programs should it undertake at headquarters and its affiliates abroad?

Differences in International Business Management

The range of choices shown above indicates the complexity of international strategic planning and some of the respects in which the process differs from planning for domestic business. The differences between strategic planning for international business and domestic operations arise from the complexity of undertaking business in foreign countries with different and changing political, regulatory, economic, sociocultural, business, and other environments. Further, risk dimensions in international business vary, often change, and are difficult to ascertain precisely.

Strategic and Operational Planning

Multinational companies engage in 2 basic types of planning: 1) strategic or long-term planning, and 2) operational or tactical planning.[1] Strategic planning, which often involves a time dimension of 3 to 7 years (often 5 years) is the most significant type of planning in establishing the future directions and major courses of action for the multinational corporation. Strategic planning involves formulation of key objectives and goals for the corporation and its global system of enterprises, including the determination of strategies that allocate corporate resources among units in various countries to achieve the established objectives.

---

[1] For more elaborate discussion of international strategic and operational planning, see George A. Steiner and Warren M. Cannon, *Multinational Corporate Planning* (New York: Macmillan Co., 1966), Chapter 1; Derek F. Channon, *Multinational Strategic Planning* (New York: Amacom, 1978); and William A. Dymsza, *Multinational Business Strategy* (New York: McGraw Hill, 1972), Chapters 3, 4.

Operational planning, on the other hand, encompasses highly detailed plans, procedures, and budgets for the company and its international units, usually for a period of one or 2 years. The operational plans serve as a framework for day-to-day decision making and also as a basis for the monitoring and control systems. Some multinational companies may also have very long-range plans of 15 to 20 years (for example, to develop new high-technology products); certain petroleum companies may project supply-demand in oil for 2 decades or longer as part of their planning. But the strategic planning with a time period of 3 to 7 years (often 5 years) and the operational planning (usually for a year) constitute the basic types of business planning that are crucial for management of multinational corporations.

It should be emphasized that strategic planning constitutes a major responsibility of top management at headquarters because nothing less than the future of the multinational corporation is at stake; executives of divisions, regional offices, and national subsidiaries are generally also involved. Under operational planning, on the other hand, not only the top but also the middle layer managers and the functional staff of country affiliates, regional offices, and divisions of the corporation participate in the process. The operational plans of all units should be interrelated with the strategic plans and approved by the top management of the multinational corporation.

Model of Multinational Strategic Planning

Figure 1 shows a model for comprehensive strategic planning for multinational corporations.[2] This model starts with a reevaluation of company philosophy, mission, or definition of business and then moves to a managerial audit of the strengths and weaknesses of all units and the total enterprise, an assessment of competition in national markets, and an evaluation and projection of key political, legal, economic, cultural, regulatory, technological, and business factors in major countries and regions. After an analysis of major opportunities and risks and specification of key strategic issues by major units around the world, the multinational company formulates objectives and global strategies for the corporation, divisions, and national subsidiaries, with contingency plans to deal with changing and unexpected developments, and action programs to achieve implementation of the strategies. On the basis of the strategic plan, the units of the corporation determine the operational plans, including detailed budgets. A control system regularly monitors performance against targets in the tactical plans and budgets. From time to time (for example, annually), the corporation revises and recycles its strategic plan to adapt to changes that have taken place.

---

[2] For other models and discussion, see William H. Davidson, *Global Strategic Management* (New York: John Wiley & Sons, 1982), Chapter 8.

FIGURE 1   Model for Comprehensive Strategic Planning for MNCs

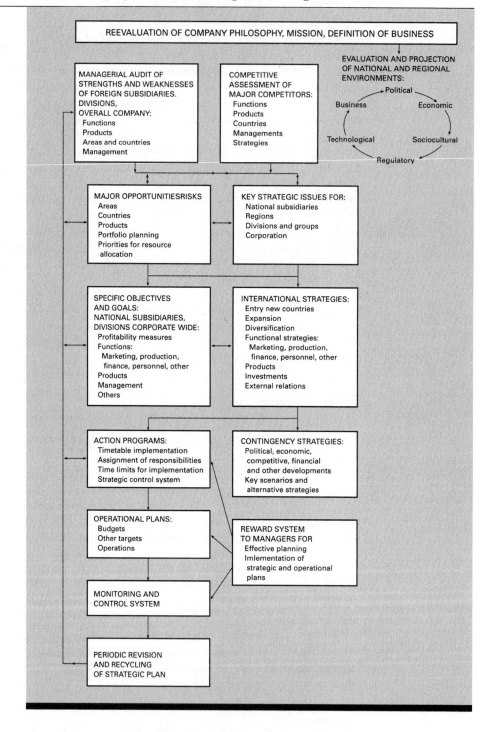

The model presented in Figure 1 brings out the components that comprise a comprehensive system of international strategic planning. This represents one of many possible models. Multinational corporations vary considerably in the scope, format, emphasis, and process of their strategic planning. Some corporations have highly comprehensive systems of strategic planning that vary in major ways from the model; other companies have simpler processes of planning. Yet, this model depicts many aspects that are widely found in strategic planning systems of multinational corporations, and should be considered as a dynamic model in a highly interdependent process. Each phase and all components have many interactions, forward flows, and feedbacks involving much vertical and lateral communication between top management, corporate staff, the planning officers, and international managers.

A major issue in international strategic planning is the extent to which the planning process should be structured in a formal manner. The alternative would be to have a less structured, more flexible strategic planning process. Some companies, such as a major international pharmaceutical company, opt for a less structured process, since the top management believes that such a process provides for more innovative planning with room for more entrepreneurial decision making and initiative. On the other hand, most multinational corporations find that structured strategic planning works more effectively in involving management at all levels, including the staff officers along with the planning officials. A structured planning process can also encourage innovation, creativity, and initiative by key country, regional, division, and corporate levels.

The model for strategic planning is a multidimensional one involving corporate headquarters, groups, divisions, regional offices, and national subsidiaries in a top-down and bottom-up process of planning. In other words, it represents a combination of centralized and decentralized planning in which all units of the enterprise around the world participate. The major responsibility for strategic planning rests with the line managers of all units, with assistance from planning and functional staff officers at all levels. The top management of the multinational corporation, however, has the primary responsibility for determining the overall global directions and objectives and for coordinating the strategies of all units worldwide.

This model provides for major flexibility in the needs of companies for integrated or adaptive planning and some balance between the two.[3] Integrated planning involves global unification of functional, product, or other strategies, and centralization of decisions, particularly in production, finance, R&D, and investments. Adaptive planning comprises differentiation and responsiveness to diversity of country environments. Multinational corporations characterized by

---

[3] See R. F. Vancil and Peter Lorange, "Strategic Planning in Diversified Companies," *Harvard Business Review,* January-February 1975, pp. 81–90.

high technology or rapid technological change, complex sourcing, and high economies of scale often require integrated planning.[4] On the other hand, firms with somewhat limited economies of scale, mature products in the product cycle, and major emphasis on marketing, and those facing diversity in consumer tastes and government regulations need considerable adaptive planning. Most multinational corporations have to achieve some balance between integration and adaptation in their strategic planning and operational decisions.

The strategic planning process and resource allocation based on it can be used as a catalyst to achieve convergence among managers on key decisions and consensus-building among executives whose priorities and perceptions vary widely.[5] It can create pressures for interaction among managers, for convergence of views, and for conflict resolution. A reward system for effective participation in the planning process and for achievements of goals and subgoals fosters such a business climate.

The model also coordinates the international control system with operational and strategic planning of the enterprise and its units around the world. This fosters implementation of strategic and operational plans. Implementation is also fostered by deep involvement of top management in the planning process, dissemination of key aspects of corporate plans, and rewards to managers for effective strategic planning and implementation.

Every aspect of the strategic planning and control process is important in this model; but, because some aspects are well known and because space is limited, the balance of this paper will focus on competitive assessment, strategic issues, portfolio planning, and opportunity/risk analysis, with examples.

Competitive Assessment

The competitive audit assesses actual and potential competition faced by the corporation in countries, regions, and worldwide, particularly in major country markets.[6] The audit involves analysis of industry, technology, product cycle and product development, and of substitute product trends in major markets. The auditing company then identifies major competitors in country markets, their types of operation, their business policies and practices, and their key strengths and weaknesses. The performance of units of the company is compared with that of competitors in matters such as sales growth, share of market, market/expense costs, quality of products, product change and innovation, labor productivity, costs of manufacturing, physical facilities and scale of operations, profit

---

[4] W. H. Davidson, *Global Strategic Management*, p. 317.

[5] See Yves Doz and C. K. Prahalad, "Patterns of Strategic Control within Multinational Corporations," *Journal of International Business Studies*, this issue.

[6] For a more comprehensive discussion, see D. F. Channon, *Multinational Strategic Planning*, pp. 73–76.

margins, various measures of profitability, and competence of management and personnel. The analysis should also deal with companies that are producing and marketing substitute products and with potential competitors in national markets. Figure 2 shows a comprehensive format for assessment of competition in major countries. Figure 3 shows criteria used by a marketing-oriented multinational company in assessing competitive position in key product/country markets.

Some precise quantitative data about major competitors may be difficult to obtain. With a systematic effort, however, much of the information can be estimated or pieced together from annual reports (required in some countries), and from trade journals, company magazines, statistical analyses, and other sources. The country subsidiaries should maintain systematic information about major competitors, updated for strategic planning purposes.

From such quantitative performance comparisons and exercises of qualitative judgments, the corporation should be able to assess strengths and weaknesses of major competitors in various countries and regions. It should also be able to determine competitive advantages that it has over other companies in specific countries; it should lead from these strengths in its strategies. For example, companies that find they have one or more competitive advantages in proprietary product lines, product design, brand names, advertising, distribution, or manufacturing costs in various countries should emphasize these strengths in determining their strategies. Generally, it is more important to lead with competitive strengths than to allocate resources to overcome weaknesses.

Certain multinational companies try to ascertain the key strategies of major competitors in product/country markets in order to respond to them better. For example, from its competitive assessments, a major diversified electronics company ascertains major competitors in many key product/country markets. Using its competitive information, the company simulates strategic plans for its major competitors as if for its own enterprise. These strategic plans formulated for competitors enable the electronics company to establish more realistic strategic plans to deal with existing and emerging competition in specific country/product markets.[7]

Strategic Issues

Some companies require the managers of each country subsidiary, regional office, and division to determine 3 or 4 strategic issues that will have the most significant impact on their business during the planning period. This requires the managements of each unit to analyze profoundly and concentrate on a few

---

[7] Information obtained in personal interview with an official on the Strategic Planning Staff of the electronics company.

FIGURE 2   Major Factors in International Competitive Assessment*

Key Resources	Production	Marketing	Management Processes— Developments
Management • HQ, groups, divisions • National subsidiaries	Physical Capacity • Countries Plants and Equipment • Location	Marketing Mix • Divisions • Regions • Countries	Organization • Centralization • Decentralization • Line and staff
Local Managers • In top, middle positions • National • Subsidiaries	• Size and type • Age • Automation Economies of Scale	Products • Product mix • New product introduction • Adaptation of products • Product differentiation	Information and Control System • Accounting system • Computerized systems
Engineering, technical, administrative skilled manpower in major countries	Productivity Global or Regional Rationalization	Brand Names and Trademarks	Strategic and Operational Planning Management Development • Corporate level • Divisions • National subsidiaries
Technology • Patents in key countries • Production processes • Product know-how • Effectiveness of R&D	Human Resources • Managerial, technical workforce • Labor unions • Turnover	Market Segmentation Customer Service Distribution • Type • Effectiveness	Development of National Managers Personnel and Staffing Practices • Experience • Longevity • Turnover • Replacement
Capital and Financial Resources • Global • Regional • Major countries		Promotion • Expenditures • Type and media • Effectiveness Price • Type	Reward Systems Corporate Value System
Business Know-how		Investment and Expenditures • On various aspects of market development	

* Key factors in the company are evaluated in relation to major competitors.

key issues. The management should be able to determine such strategic issues from a careful study of their business and analysis of trends in the industry, technology, key environmental factors, competition, and emerging opportunities.

Examples of strategic issues are the following: major new competition emerging in some countries; adverse changes in government and increased

FIGURE 3   Criteria for Assessing Competitive Position

Factor	Competitive Position		
	Strong	Moderate	Weak
Market position	#1 or #2	Included in top 6	Not among top 6
Relative market share (percentage)	30 percent or higher	15–30 percent	Less than 15 percent
Relative growth	Exceeds market average growth by 20 percent	±20 percent of market average growth	Lags market average growth rate by 20 percent or more
Relative pricing	High (a leader)	Moderate (a follower)	Low
Cost comparison and productivity per worker	Low cost advantage	About average for industry	High costs
Product quality level	Favorable	Neutral	Unfavorable
Innovation	Market leader—consistently first with new products, new technology, and so on	About even with other competitors	Lags market consistently in new products/services
Marketing strength	Recognized as leader in market	About average for industry	Generally lower than industry
Advertising/promotion activity	High	Moderate	Low
Managerial competence	Favorable	Neutral	Unfavorable
Overall ranking	Strong	Moderate	Weak

political vulnerability; conversely, favorable changes in the regulatory climate in countries with changing governments; requirements for new product innovations and improvements; needed refurbishment of marketing effort, including promotion and distribution; need for development of more competent middle and top local managers in the subsidiary; and emerging increases in raw material costs.

Other strategic issues can emphasize the need to adapt existing products, introduce new products, engage in more effective market segmentation, improve external relations, develop appropriate technology in labor-intensive developing countries, investigate ways to increase labor productivity, improve relations with labor unions, and provide effective incentives for national managers. In the mid-1970s, a major multinational pharmaceutical company shifted to a less structured strategic planning system that emphasized strategic issues at the country, regional, and corporate levels.[8] This led to less structured strategic planning with more management concentration on critical issues affecting the company's future business. The pharmaceutical's operational planning continued to be highly structured and related to its control and monitoring system. Another highly diversified multinational conglomerate, on the other hand, requires its country and product managers to focus on 2 or 3 critical strategic issues in order to establish more realistic goals within the context of the corporation's broad objectives in growth of profits and its style of management—one that fosters confrontation by line and staff managers from headquarters, regions, countries, and products.

Companies that require managers of national subsidiaries, regional officers, and divisions to develop key strategic issues find that such development establishes more focus on their strategic planning on emerging opportunities and threats to business in various areas of the world. The process can also lead to the formulation of more innovative and realistic strategies.

Portfolio Planning and Opportunity/Analysis

From the analysis of key environmental factors in major countries, combined with the managerial and competitive audits and a focus on strategic issues, multinational corporations can generally pinpoint the countries with the most promising opportunities in relation to risk. Many companies have adopted strategic portfolio planning, however, which is a more sophisticated approach to determining priorities for allocation of corporate resources in complex enterprises with a portfolio of businesses.[9] This approach establishes criteria for evaluating, allocating resources to, and planning the future direction of a portfolio of businesses involving a combination of several product lines in a number of countries.

Companies utilizing portfolio planning typically take the following steps:[10]

1. Redefine various businesses as strategic business units (SBUs), often different from the operating units. The SBUs may be defined by product/country market or, occasionally, product/country units.

2. Use a portfolio matrix to determine the attractiveness and competitiveness of SBUs. Common grids are the Boston Consulting Group Mar-

---

[8] Information about the planning of the pharmaceutical and multinational conglomerate was obtained in personal interviews with officers of the companies.

[9] See D. F. Channon, *Multinational Strategic Planning*, Chapter 4.

[10] See Philippe Haspeslagh, "Portfolio Planning: Uses and Limits," *Harvard Business Review*, January-February 1982, pp. 58–73.

ket growth/share matrix, the General Electric industry attractive-ness/business position matrix, and the Shell Directional Policy Mix.

3. On the basis of this framework, assign strategic missions to SBUs and allocate resources to each of them over the planning period.

Based upon his survey of more than 300 of the *Fortune* "1000" companies and his other studies, Haspeslagh shows that portfolio planning is widely used by large enterprises in the United States—many of them multinational.[11] According to him, the real issue is not which portfolio grid to use, but the definition of strategic business units and assignment of strategic missions to them. Decisions on strategic missions require broad analysis of industry/product characteristics, competitive positions, anticipated responses by major competitors, available financial resources, and interactions with other businesses in the portfolio.[12] Managerial judgments, involving the weighing of significant trade-offs, also play an important part in assignment of strategic missions and allocation of resources.

Most U.S. multinational companies that use portfolio planning define their strategic business units by products in the American and foreign markets. The SBUs for planning commonly differ from the organizational operational units. Thus, these companies encounter problems of coordinating management of the SBUs and the operational units of the enterprise in the United States and in foreign countries. Further, multinational companies encounter some difficulties of integrating the country environmental factors and the product dimensions in determining missions of SBUs and allocation of resources to them. As multinational companies gain experience with portfolio planning and integrate it into strategic planning and management, however, they find that it becomes an effective managerial process.

An Example of Portfolio Planning in a Multinational Food Company

Portfolio planning can be illustrated by a brief example of the Boston Consulting Group matrix used since 1977 by a major multinational food company's international operations.[13]

The food corporation defines its strategic business units by product brands in international markets. As shown in the Product Grid in Figure 4, the position of each strategic business unit is evaluated in a 4-box matrix based upon relative market share and market growth. This establishes the business units as: 1) stars

---

[11] Ibid., pp. 61–62.

[12] Ibid., pp. 61–63, 65–66.

[13] This example of portfolio planning by international operations of the multinational food company was provided by the strategic planning officer at a meeting of the American Management Association.

FIGURE **4**   Product/Brand Grid

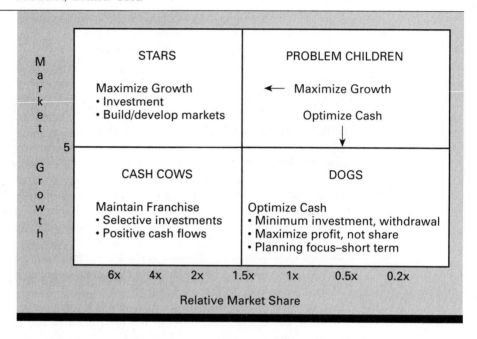

and candidates for investment and building markets; 2) cash cows to maintain the franchise for selective investments and positive cash flows; 3) problem children to watch carefully; and 4) dogs, to optimize cash, minimize investment, maximize profit rather than share of market, and consider for possible divestment. This portfolio planning process provides a role for each product/brand in country markets and results in a means of allocating resources, clarifying priorities, and fostering communications.

The portfolio management of the multinational food company is more sophisticated than may appear on the surface. The company evaluates the performance of SBUs (products/brands in country markets) in the past, present, and future. It engages in forecasting future market growth and market share of SBUs using computerized models, with alternative assumptions. As shown in Figures 5 and 6, the management attempts to ascertain whether the SBUs are going to experience a success sequence—moving from problem children to stars—or a disaster sequence—moving from stars to problem children and dogs. The top international management works with the country and regional managers in the evaluation process that considers the importance of each product/brand, the outlook for innovation, the relationship between various brands, current and future competition, and risk in various country markets in resource allocation. The process requires the management to make

FIGURE **5**   Success Sequence

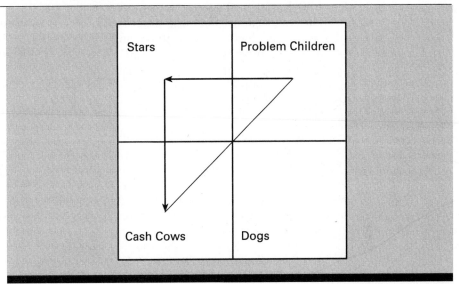

FIGURE **6**   Disaster Sequence

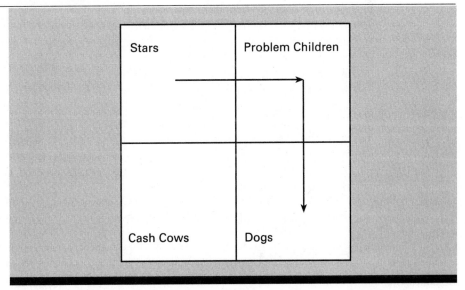

judgments on how the multinational food company plans to manage its portfolio of SBUs, with evaluation of appropriate trade-offs.

The international planning officer of the food company emphasized that support by the chief executive officer and top management is crucial. Portfolio planning has to be integrated with the management process; it has to have a specific time frame for actions and implementation. Functional and educational support are essential, along with patience and flexibility. Further, the top management has to have an effective system of strategic review and control of performance.

Some companies experience difficulties in coordinating portfolio planning for their domestic and overseas units as a result of major differences in country characteristics and variations in risk. Managers can also encounter difficulties in resource allocation to SBUs where facilities and resources are shared among SBUs. Further, portfolio planning may not be suitable for many new international activities or for those that require a period of nurturing before explosive growth takes place.

Example of a Multinational Corporation's Threat and Opportunity Analysis on a Country Basis

A major diversified multinational electronics company initiated a joint international planning project between corporate strategic planning staff and the international division in the late 1970s to propose changes in the strategic planning process for the corporate and strategic business unit, with the objective of developing strategic plans that would be more responsive to fast-changing environmental and competitive forces.[14] The electronics company wanted to ensure a better matching of country opportunities and needs with SBU strengths and needs. A key aspect of this project was a threat and opportunity analysis of major countries, based upon a number of criteria of political, economic, regulatory, and competitive environments. For each country, the project group developed an environmental profile, a profile of company participation, and specific opportunities and threats by product/country markets and type of involvement—along with corporate response options.

For example, in 1977 the project group made quantitative impact estimates of potential losses in sales, based upon identifying major threats on a country-by-country and product-by-product basis for 1982. These estimates reflected the probability of occurrence, considering the significance of projected sales and assuming no effective counter-strategies.

On the other side of the coin, with respect to opportunity analysis, the project group identified opportunities from all sources on a country-by-country

---

[14] This example is based upon a paper given to the author by an official after personal interviews at company headquarters.

and product-by-product basis. It estimated incremental opportunities—the additional sales that the electronics company was expected to attain in 1982 over and above current plans and/or opportunities that had already been identified. The estimates were considered to be rough, as they were restricted to major opportunities and were highly discounted to reflect corporate capabilities. Because incremental opportunities were conducted on a country-by-country basis, the estimates understated regional opportunities that were available through regional coverage and rationalization in certain areas, such as, the EEC. They also did not consider possible incremental opportunities through synergism.

From this study, the project group concluded that the company should plan more effectively for risk containment and opportunity exploitation. This required new emphasis on defensive strategic thrusts because of the changed international outlook. The name of the game in strategic planning was going to involve more international risk management—establishing priorities for investments, potential investment limits by countries, more stringent risk assessment of new ventures, and synergistic contingency planning. Finally, the electronic corporation's top management and staff would have to engage in more corporate-level overviews of the company's current and future involvement in a limited number of key countries and to establish priorities in the strategic planning process.

The project group proposed a new strategic vocabulary, as shown in Figure 7, and a 9-block Incremental Opportunity/Defensive Posture matrix classifying major countries, as shown in Figure 8.

FIGURE 7   Strategic Vocabulary

Defensive Posture	
Risk	**Response**
1. High-risk countries	A defensive posture—to protect
2. Medium-risk countries	A manage risk situation
3. Low-risk countries	A posture to monitor
Opportunity Orientation	
Opportunities	**Classification**
1. High incremental opportunities	A growth country
2. Medium incremental opportunities	An enhance country
3. Low incremental opportunities	A hold country

FIGURE 8   Incremental Opportunity/Defensive Posture Matrix

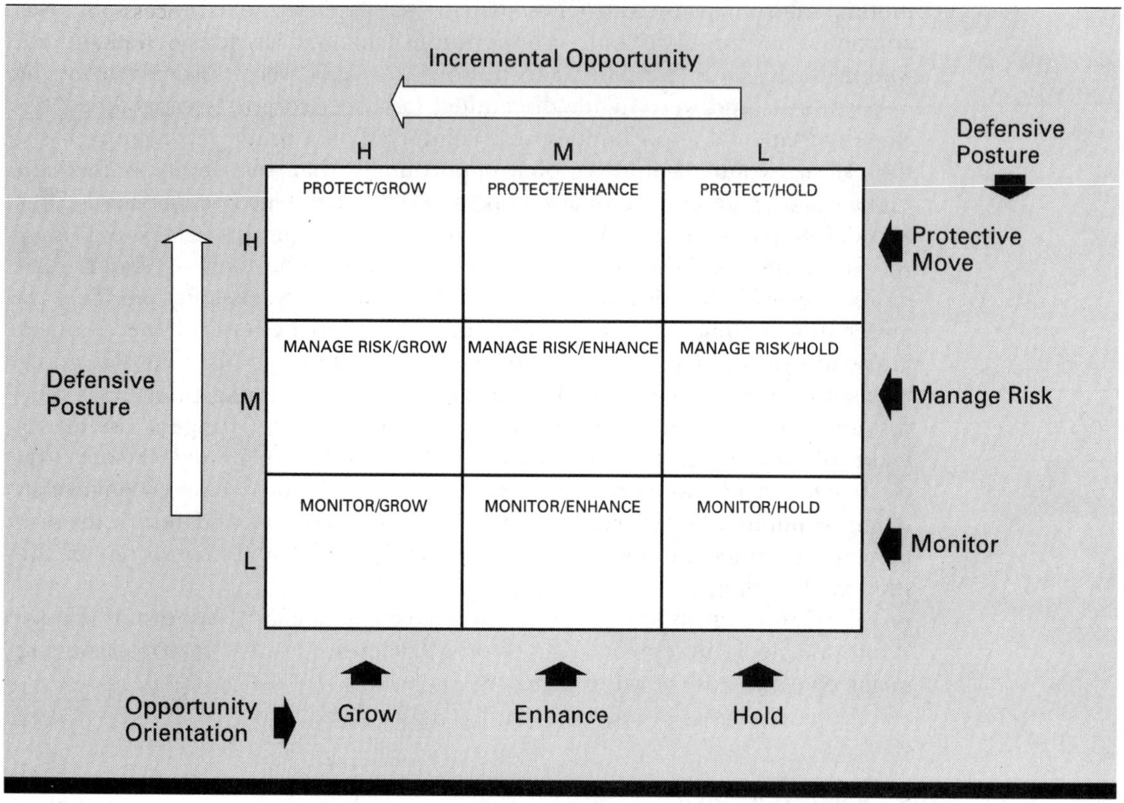

From the 9-box matrix, the major countries were classified according to the new vocabulary that designated priorities.

The protect/grow countries received first priority in planning; the management risk/grow countries and protect/enhance countries were given second priority. One of the conclusions from these priorities was that the multinational electronics corporation needed to bring the total strength of the company to bear on its international business, in a combination of exploiting opportunities and defending its positions. In order to do this, it should establish early positions in high-growth country markets; it should shift resources to nations with the greatest potential, particularly nations with undeveloped human and natural resources. The electronics company's future business in these nations should include not only permanent export participation, but also licensing, low-risk direct investment, and types of joint ventures. Corporate strategic planning would play an important part in this process, in conjunction with the international division, the global product divisions, the strategic business units, and the country managements.

The threat/opportunity analysis added an important dimension to the global strategic planning of the electronics company. This process in itself, however, did not enable the management of the company to foresee and develop strategies to deal with the consequences of certain major political and economic changes that emerged in the late 1970s and the early 1980s—such as, the rise of the radical, Moslem government in Iran, the declining income of the OPEC countries, and rising foreign debt of many developing countries in Latin America and elsewhere; nor did this process correctly ascertain changes in growth patterns in many countries as a result of the severe economic recession in the 1980s.

The electronics company found that it had to improve its forecasting of political, economic, and competitive changes to utilize effectively its threat/opportunity analysis in its strategic planning. Further, it had to engage in more contingency planning, in action programs that assigned specific responsibilities to managers for follow-through and implementation, and in more effective strategic and operational controls.

With rapid and unforeseen changes taking place in many areas, a number of other multinational companies have been utilizing early warning systems—focusing on key indicators—which they relate to contingency plans and action programs. This has enabled some multinationals to adapt more readily to major environmental changes in a timely fashion. Nevertheless, early warning systems do not necessarily alert multinational companies to critical emerging problems in major countries and to environmental changes and discontinuities.

All in all, the threat/opportunity analysis shown above provides a systematic way for the multinational corporation and its international, product and SBU managements to undertake more effective international risk management in the strategic planning process. However, the system requires sophisticated forecasting, comprehensive evaluation of key environmental factors and sound management judgment. It also requires periodic reevaluation, along with comprehensive assessments of future political risk, socio-economic changes, competitive developments, contingency planning, and effective strategic and operational control.

Recent Trends and Concluding Comments

The emphasis of many multinational companies on competitive assessment, strategic issues, portfolio planning, and opportunity risk analysis—as shown in this discussion and examples—fits within the context of the comprehensive model of global strategic planning outlined at the beginning of this paper. This generalized model shows many aspects of global strategic planning that U.S. and European multinationals utilize for their global management, although many variations exist. These companies have been developing strategic planning systems that fit their business requirements, including their country and product involvement, customer orientation, style of management, and corporate culture.

Faced with increased change and uncertainty and a more competitive international environment, multinational companies have been fine-tuning their strategic planning systems. A number of them have been moving into more integrative planning in order to rationalize utilization of resources on a global basis. Another trend has been to develop more formalized strategic planning with line and staff managerial involvement at headquarters, regional, and country levels. These companies have often utilized computerized forecasting models, expanded use of portfolio planning to determine resource allocation to SBUs, engaged in more rigorous assessment of actual and potential competition in country/product markets, developed strategies that emphasize productivity improvement and cost reductions of all units around the world, and planned longer-term investments in modernizing plants, research and development, marketing programs, and management development. Through portfolio planning and hard-headed management, multinational companies have striven to increase their return on investments by concentrating on their profitable and promising product lines and divesting country and product operations that have not been achieving their earnings goals or that do not fit within their long-term company mission or definition of their business. These companies have given more attention to international risk management and exploitation of their unique advantages.

On the other hand, some multinational companies have moved to somewhat less structured and more flexible strategic planning. For example, a major pharmaceutical company and other multinational companies emphasize global strategic issues, innovative planning, and entrepreneurial initiatives. Several multinationals have different time dimensions and formats for business planning by headquarters, divisions, and country affiliates. A major diversified electronics company—long a leader in global management by strategic planning—has shifted away from highly sophisticated, time-consuming models developed by its corporate strategic planning staff. This company, with a new chief executive officer, has substantially reduced its planning staff and has concentrated its strategic planning on key high technology businesses in which the company is a leader, on more down-to-earth portfolio planning to allocate resources in order to obtain rate of return earnings goals, on divestment of business that does not fit the corporate mission, and on development of more entrepreneurship in management. Whether companies have engaged in more or less structured strategic planning, they have required line managers at all levels to assume major responsibility in the process.

With the increased competition from Japanese multinational companies, a major issue is the emphasis of U.S. companies on longer-range strategic management versus bottom-line profitability results from year-to-year operations. Some scholars have maintained that Japanese enterprises have a longer-term managerial perspective, whereas U.S. multinational and other companies, despite strategic plans, place primary emphasis upon the operational plans, budgets, and rate of return results in the short term. Many U.S. managers of country subsidiaries, regional offices, divisions, and other units believe that they will be evaluated primarily by their profitability results annually rather than by their involvement in and implementation of strategic plans. Further, bonuses, incentive programs, and advancement in the corporate hierarchy are often based upon short-term profitability achievements.

Such an orientation, despite major emphasis upon strategic planning by managers at all levels, does not foster longer-term strategic management. Yet, the author's studies show that many top managements of multinational corporations have placed emphasis on longer-term planning of the future directions of their global enterprises and on achieving some balance between longer-term and short-term results. But in some cases, what may be required is more effective strategic controls and positive incentives for effective strategic planning and implementation at the subsidiary, regional, division, and corporate levels in order to emphasize management by strategic planning globally.

This paper has presented a generalized model of global strategic planning and various approaches to competitive assessment, strategic issues, portfolio planning, and opportunity/risk analysis in business planning by multinational companies. Recent trends show that multinational corporations continue to strive to devise strategic and operational planning and control systems that will enable them to manage their international and domestic business more effectively in an era of rapid, sometimes discontinuous, changes.

A COMPARISON OF THE ETHICAL BEHAVIOR OF AMERICAN, FRENCH, AND GERMAN MANAGERS

Helmut Becker ◆ David J. Fritzsche

ABSTRACT. A cross-cultural comparison of the indicated ethical behavior of managers was conducted in order to determine whether behavior varies by ethical setting. Data were collected using a series of vignettes representing the following types of ethical problems: (1) coercion and control, (2) conflict of interest, (3) the physical environment, (4) paternalism, and (5) personal integrity.

In his treatise on law completed in the thirteenth century, Saint Thomas Aquinas stated that "natural law" encompasses the preservation of human life, the promotion of family life, an orderly social life, and the quest for knowledge. According to Velasquez and Rostankowski (1985), the underlying features of natural law are: (1) People of every nationality are bound together by certain fundamental principles of right and wrong, (2) human nature provides the basis of these fundamental principles, and (3) adult natural reasoning abilities provide all adults with an awareness of these fundamental moral principles.

Natural law is considered to transcend national boundaries. It is viewed as taking precedence over those national laws which are thought to be unjust or immoral. This position was taken, for example, by the Allies in their trials of German and Japanese military leaders following World War II (Appleman, 1954). National law does not create morality just as morality does not necessarily find expression in the written law. Thus it is possible for an act to be legal in a particular country and not moral when judged by a higher order of natural law. Alternatively, an act may have a moral basis in natural law, yet be illegal under some national law.

The morality of business decisions may be evaluated using three different ethical theories: utilitarianism, rights, and justice (Beauchamp and Bowie, 1983; Cavanagh, 1984; and Velasquez, 1982). Classical utilitarian philosophy was developed in the writings of the English philosophers Jeremy Bentham (1798) and John Stuart Mill (1861). The German philosopher Immanuel Kant (1797) and the English philosopher John Locke (1690) both developed theories of rights. The theory of justice can be attributed to Aristotle with important recent developments provided by the American philosopher John Rawls (1971). While these theories provide a normative theoretical basis for evaluating business decisions, they are difficult to operationalize for research purposes. Unfortunately they also do not always lead to the same conclusion. In some situations, one theory may lead to a judgement that a decision is moral while another theory may generate an opposite conclusion.

In management literature, values have been dealt with from a number of perspectives. Some writers have focused on the pressures of the business environment and have provided advice for improving the ethical aspects of business behavior (Boling, 1978; Purcell, 1975). Others have discussed the teaching of ethics to present and future managers (Barach and Nicol, 1980; Purcell, 1972). There is a growing body of empirical investigations of ethical beliefs and behavior of managers (Becker and Fritzsche, 1981; Brenner and Molander, 1977; Carroll, 1978; Fritzsche and Becker, 1983, 1984; Krugman and Ferrell, 1981).

The empirical literature on business ethics has been limited to examining the ethics of business managers in one country. In the United States the popular press has allocated a great deal of space to the ethics of American businessmen operating in other countries. Little work has been done comparing the ethical beliefs and behavior of managers across cultures. This is surprising given the attention created by the passage and implementation of the Foreign Corrupt Practices Act. The present study is an attempt to fill this void. It compares the ethical beliefs and behavior of managers across cultural boundaries in order to explore the question: How and to what extent do ethical beliefs and behavior vary by cultural setting?

Study Design

Data were collected via mail surveys of marketing managers in France, Germany, and the United States. The managers sampled in the United States were members of the American Marketing Association. The German respondents were subscribers to *Absatzwirtschaft Zeitschrift für Marketing,* a German marketing journal. The French managers consisted of a sample drawn from individuals listed in *Annuaire des VIP du Marketing.* Samples of French and U.S. respondents were selected using the systematic random sampling process with the starting position obtained from a random number table. The authors were unable to obtain an address list of German marketing managers. However, the above-mentioned German publication did agree to publish the questionnaire in an issue of its journal and to include a request for readers to return the completed questionnaire. A total of 124 usable questionnaires was received from the U.S. sample, 70 were received from the German sample and 72 were received from the French sample. The response rate ranged from 14 percent for the French sample to 21 percent for the U.S. sample.

The questionnaire contained vignettes based on diverse categories of ethical problems managers might face in their day-to-day activities. Some of the problems were selected from issues addressed in two books dealing with business ethics (Barry, 1979; Beauchamp and Bowie, 1979); others were chosen from issues addressed at the Summer Institute on Ethical Issues in the Management of Public and Private Institutions sponsored by the Society for Values in Higher Education (Dill, Donaldson, Goodpaster, and May, 1979). The problem categories consisted of (1) coercion and control, (2) conflict of interest, (3) the physical environment, (4)paternalism, and (5) personal integrity. References to these categories can be found in the ethics literature in writings of authors of many nationalities. Thus, these categories were considered to be universal.

A case of coercion and control exists when a manager feels compelled by an external force to make a specific decision. This may involve the use of threats, extortion, or other sources of power. When a manager has more than one interest which, if mutually pursued, may result in injury to individuals or to the firm, a conflict of interest situation exists (Beauchamp and Bowie, 1979). The physical environment is a special case of conflict of interest where one of the affected parties is the environment. A personal integrity problem exists when a decision raises issues of conscience. Finally, a paternalism problem involves balancing the respect for individual autonomy with the commitment to consumers' welfare.

The five categories of ethical problems were framed into a series of ten vignettes, two for each ethical problem category. Based upon material from the business ethics texts and the Summer Institute on Ethical Issues cited above, each vignette presented a different decision scenario. Respondents were asked to indicate the decision that they would make based upon their personal values as well as the economic and business factors existing in the scenarios. In addition, respondents were asked to indicate the rationale or reason for their specific response.

The ten vignettes were pretested on a group of marketing managers drawn from the local chapter of the American Marketing Association. In addition, the vignettes were critiqued for content validity by a group of individuals working in the field of business ethics. The group consisted of philosophers, business practitioners engaged in corporate social responsibility activities, and business professors. The pretest results and the comments received from the ethics group were used to revise the vignettes. The vignettes were then placed in the questionnaire in random order. After the data were collected from the American sample, the data were evaluated for face validity. The weaker of the two vignettes from each problem category was dropped from the study. The remaining five vignettes, which appeared to possess construct validity, were used to collect data from the French and the German respondents. The authors were able to classify the response to the open-ended questions associated with each vignette by one of the three types of ethical theory discussed above, utilitarian, rights, or justice (Cavanagh and Fritzsche, 1985).

The questionnaire was translated into French and German. The French translation was performed by a professor who teaches French for business at a Midwestern university. The German translation was completed by one of the authors, a native of Germany now teaching business in the United States.

The vignette approach was used because it contains a common background of information for understanding and responding to an ethical problem. Such background would have to be assumed by the respondents if simple questions were utilized. By adding situational detail, vignettes can provide for more standardized stimuli across respondents and improved data quality (Alexander and Becker, 1978).

It should be noted that the responses to the vignettes do not represent actual management behavior. Rather the responses represent behavior that managers indicated they would take when faced with specific ethical dilemmas. The extent to which their indicated behavior differs from what their actual behavior would be is unknown.

Findings

A comparison of the demographics of the three samples resulted in the following observations: Nearly 60 percent of the French and one half of the German respondents classified themselves as upper level management compared to one quarter of the U.S. respondents. Approximately one half of the U.S. sample reported its position as middle management while only a third of the German managers and a fifth of the French managers indicated middle level responsibilities. Of the remainder, 15 percent of the U.S. and 9 percent of the German respondents stated they were junior executives. There were no French junior executives. Somewhat curiously, however, 25 percent of the French respondents indicated that they occupied "other" positions.

The educational level, as measured by degrees and years of education, showed few differences among the three survey countries. Reflecting the popularity of the MBA degree in the United States, 58 percent of the American respondents said they hold masters or equivalent degrees compared with 29 percent of the German and 26 percent of the French managers. However, consistent with national census figures, the German and French samples included a significantly higher proportion of doctorate degree holders, 26 percent and 28 percent respectively compared to only 2 percent for the U.S. respondents. Thus, the total proportion of advanced degree holders was comparable among all three respondent groups. The French sample tended to be somewhat older on the average and the German sample somewhat younger than their U.S. counterparts. A significantly greater proportion of American respondents was female, 19 percent, compared to only 4 percent of the French and 3 percent of the German samples.

The responses to the vignette were recorded on an 11-point scale range from "definitely would not" (equals 0) to "definitely would" (equals 10) perform the act propositioned in each decision scenario. The results are presented by type of ethical problem investigated. French, Germany, and American samples are compared both on the basis of the scale responses and also on the basis of the rationale provided for individual answers. In cases where more than one rationale was provided by a respondent, the first rationale was selected for analysis as it was assumed to be the primary rationale. It should be noted, however, that not all individuals responding to a vignette provided their underlying reasons. The number of respondents from each country providing a rationale for a vignette is noted at the bottom of each table. The calculated percentages are based upon the number of respondents providing a rationale for the vignette decision.

Vignette No. 1—Coercion and Control

> Rollfast Bicycle Company has been barred from entering the market in a large Asian country by collusive efforts of the local bicycle manufacturers. Rollfast could expect to net 5 million dollars per year from sales if it could penetrate the market. Last week a businessman from the country contacted the management of Rollfast and stated that he could smooth the way for the company to sell in his country for a price of $500,000.

If you were responsible, what are the chances that you would pay the price?

The responses were examined with the help of one-way analysis of variance (ANOVA). In addition, the Scheffe a posteriori test was used to analyze differences across response. Given the conservative nature of the Scheffe procedure, a level of significance of $p < .10$ was judged to be appropriate.

The ANOVA procedure revealed a mean difference among the three samples at the $p < .000$ level of significant (see Table 1). As indicated by the Scheffé test, this over-all mean difference resulted from significantly different responses of the U.S. managers and their European counterparts. While French and German managers differed little from each other, the U.S. respondents were significantly less likely than both to pay the bribe as described in Vignette No. 1.

An examination of the rationale provided by the respondents yielded several findings. Forty-seven percent of the American managers said that the action was a bribe, unethical, illegal, or against company policy. This compares to 15 percent for the French and 9 percent for the German managers with similar comments. Thirty-eight percent of the German managers responded that either "competition forces us to take the offer" or "it is simply the price to be paid to do business" in that country; 55 percent of the French managers believed likewise. However, 45 percent of the German managers gave reasons which did not fit into any of the above categories. These responses were scattered across the 11-point scale. It is interesting to note that while only 6 percent of the Germans and 15 percent of the French stated it was an acceptable practice in other countries, 22 percent of the U.S. managers took this position. The U.S. managers were more concerned with the ethical and legal aspects of this vignette while the French and German managers tended to be more concerned with successful business practices.

The greater emphasis by the U.S. managers on the legal aspects of the vignette may be traced to the passage of the Foreign Corrupt Practices Act in 1977 by the United States Congress. Both France and Germany have laws prohibiting bribery or corruption of public officials; and French laws even

TABLE 1   Comparison of French, German, and United States Response to
               Vignette No. 1—Coercion and Control

Source	Degree of Freedom	Sum of Squares	F	Probability
Between Groups	2	312	11.01	.000
Within Groups	259	3670		

	Country	Mean		
	French	6.9^1		
	German	5.8^1		
	United States	4.0		

	Percent of Respondents		
Rationale for Response	French	German	United States[2]
Bribe, unethical	9%	9%	23%
Illegal under Corrupt Business Practices Act	3	0	16
Against company policy	3	0	8
Competition forces us to take offer	0	9	3
An acceptable practice in other countries	15	6	22
Is not unethical, just the price paid to do business	55	29	14
No one is hurt	0	2	4
Other	15	45	9
TOTAL	100%	100%	100%
Number of respondents providing rationale	34	65	107

[1] Mean responses which did not differ significantly from each other per the Scheffé test.
[2] Totals do not add to 100 due to rounding.

extend the prohibition of bribery to employees of private enterprises (The French Penal Code, 1960). But neither country has legislation in place which makes it a crime to bribe or corrupt a public or private official of another country (Goldstein, 1979). However, the German Federal Court of Justice ruled that a contractual arrangement made in a foreign country which resulted from a bribe of a public official must also be rejected in Germany. The rejection was based upon the fact that bribery is illegal within the foreign country as well as within Germany. Furthermore, the court held it to be unethical for a German organization to bribe a foreign government official (Bundesgerichtshof, 1985). Although there is a lack of legislation barring foreign payments, concern appears to be mounting in the court system.

Vignette No. 2—Conflict of Interest

Jack Brown is vice president of marketing for Tangy Spices, a large spice manufacturer. Jack recently joined a business venture with Tangy's director of purchasing to import black pepper from India. Jack's new company is about to sign a five year contract with Tangy to supply their black pepper needs. The contract is set at a price 3 cents per pound above the current market price for comparable black pepper imports.

If you were Brown, what are the chances that you would sign the contract?

As shown in Table 2, there was no significant difference in the mean response of the three groups to the *conflict of interest* vignette. The marketing managers from all three countries were unlikely to sign the contract.

The U.S. managers tended to state that the act would be dishonest or a conflict of interest. The French and German managers were more likely to take the position that one should look out for one's own interest. It should be noted that both the French and German managers gave a much larger proportion of "other" reasons than the U.S. respondents. Most of the French "other" responses indicated that they would *not* sign the contract. The majority of the German "other" responses did likewise. However, nearly a third of the German respondents indicated a high likelihood of signing the contract.

Vignette No. 3—Physical Environment

Master Millers has developed a special milling process which yields a wheat flour which when used for bread provides a lighter, more uniform texture than conventionally milled wheat flour. Unfortunately, the process gives off more dust than the emission control equipment presently installed can handle and still maintain emissions within legal limits. Due to lack of availability, the company is unable to install new emissions control equipment for at least two years; however, if it waited that long to introduce the new process, competitors would very likely beat it to the market.

The general manager wants to use the new process during the third shift which runs from 10 p.m. to 6 a.m. By using the process at that time, the new flour could be introduced and the excess pollution would not be detected due to its release in the dark. By the time demand becomes great enough to utilize a second shift, new emission control equipment should be available.

TABLE **2**   Comparison of French, German, and United States Response to Vignette No. 2—Conflict of Interest

Source	Degree of Freedom	Sum of Squares	F	Probability
Between Groups	2	11	.52	.594
Within Groups	246	2474		

Country	Mean
French	2.4
German	2.7
United States	2.2

Rationale for Response	Percent of Respondents		
	French	German	United States*
Dishonest—stealing from the company	10%	12%	19%
Conflict of interest	23	29	45
Base decision on best price for Tangy	6	2	9
Five-year contract gives Tangy advantage over inflation	0	2	10
Why not? Should look out for own interest	16	10	5
Agreement prohibiting such action signed with the company	0	2	2
Other	45	43	11
TOTAL	100%	100%	100%
Number of respondents providing rationale	31	59	94

* Totals do not add to 100 due to rounding.

If you were responsible, what are the chances you would approve the general manager's request?

Before examining the data pertaining to this vignette, it may be instructive to review the environmental policy of France and Germany. Both France and Germany enacted major environmental legislation in 1974 (Gross and Scott, 1980). The French legislation resulted in Decree number 74–415 of 13 May 1974 (Decree Concerning the Control of Polluting Emissions, 1979). In 1978, the French Council of Ministers approved a bill creating an Air Agency which is responsible for the quality of the atmosphere (Cabinet Approves Legislation, 1979). This agency has the authority to shut down polluting installations when pollution readings reach a prespecified level and to place a permanent limit on pollution emissions in certain areas.

In 1971, the German government proclaimed environmental protection to be an independent public goal (Federal Environmental Agency, 1985). In 1974, the German government passed legislation creating the Federal Emissions Control Law which was claimed to be one of the most restrictive environmental laws in Europe (Ullmann, 1983). That same year the Federal Environmental Agency was established with headquarters in Berlin. Its objectives include conducting studies of environmental impact and to provide scientific assistance and advice to the federal government (Federal Environmental Agency, 1985). The law authorized licensing of establishments which "are particularly liable to cause harmful effects on the environment . . ." (Federal Emission Control Law). Permits are granted and the law is enforced by the Federal states.

Both France and Germany have had environmental legislation in place for some time. However, one must question the effectiveness of environmental policy enforcement. Reports of particle emissions in both France and Germany declining 50 percent over the period 1970 to 1975 (The State of the Environment, 1979) appear to indicate that policy has had a positive effect. There is also evidence that the French environmental policy may have resulted in higher levels of water pollution than the German policy. This may be due to the lower level of environmental consciousness in France (Knoepfel and Weidner, 1983 and French Prefect Agrees, 1980). On the whole, however, the environment appears to be an important public policy issue in both countries.

On the question of environmental pollution in Vignette No. 3, the results from the data analysis seem to reflect national patterns (see Table 3). The ANOVA procedure showed a statistically significant difference among the mean responses of the three groups. While the Scheffé test found no significant difference between the French and German responses, the U.S. responses were statistically different from both the French and Germans. The French and German managers ranged from neutral to slightly in favor of approving production without the benefit of emission controls. The U.S. managers were not likely to approve the request if it meant polluting the environment.

When one looks at the rationale for the responses, one notes a much greater concern for the legal aspects of the action by the U.S. managers, 24 percent compared to 6 percent for both the French and the German managers. The French and German managers are somewhat more likely to reason that the pollution will not hurt the environment. The German managers are also somewhat more likely to state that competition forces them to approve the use of the process. There is a large "other" component for the French and German managers which tends to be scattered across the response scale.

The implementation of environmental policy by the various governments

TABLE **3**   Comparison of French, German, and United States Response to Vignette No. 3—Physical Environment

Source	Degree of Freedom	Sum of Squares	F	Probability
Between Groups	2	293	13.0	.000
Within Groups	261	2947		

	Country	Mean		
	French	5.7[1]		
	German	5.2[1]		
	United States	3.3		

	Percent of Respondents		
Rationale for Response	French	German	United States[2]
It would be illegal	6%	6%	24%
Concern for the environment—life	13	18	16
Risk of getting caught with resulting negative consequences too great	6	6	15
The pollution would not really hurt the environment	31	21	18
Not their fault, equipment would be installed if available	0	0	8
Competitors force one to take these measures	3	11	3
Large potential gain with low risk	16	0	5
Other	25	38	13
TOTAL	100%	100%	100%
Number of respondents providing rationale	68	63	103

[1] Mean responses which did not differ significantly from each other per the Scheffé test.
[2] Totals do not add to 100 due to rounding.

differs between countries. (See, for example, Knoepfel and Weidner for differences between France and Germany). The managers in the current study must have been aware of environmental concerns in their own country. If policy is enforced more or less rigidly in one country compared to another, this may affect the perceived morality of the decisions in the two countries.

Vignette No. 4—Paternalism

Ted Jones, Senior Editor of J & P Publishing Company, has just received a manuscript from one of his most successful authors. It provides the most authoritative account, yet published, of the history of the development of the atomic bomb. However, the final chapter contains a detailed description of how the bomb is made. Jones has tried to convince the author to omit the last chapter stating that such information should not be made readily available to the mass market in paperback form. The author believes the chapter is critical to the success of the book and thus will not agree to its deletion.

If you were Jones, what are the chances that you would publish the book?

The response of the French, German and U.S. managers did not differ significantly for this vignette as shown in Table 4. All three groups were reluctant to publish a book containing instructions on how to build the bomb.

In terms of the rationale for the response, more U.S. managers appeared to believe the publication would be too dangerous to world safety. The perceived danger was aggravated by the feeling of helplessness in confronting international terrorism. Here again, a large number of European responses were classified as "other." These responses tended to cluster at the low end of the scale, indicating a negative response, with some scatter across the scale for all three groups. The opposition to publishing the book was borne out by a wide variety of personal reasons.

Vignette No. 5—Personal Integrity

John Ward is working in product development for an auto parts contractor. Ward's firm received a large contract last summer to manufacture transaxles to be used in a new line of front-wheel-drive cars which a major auto manufacturer plans to introduce in the near future. The contract is very important to Ward's firm which has recently fallen on hard times. Just prior to obtaining the contract, half of the firm's employees, including Ward, had been scheduled for an indefinite layoff.

Final testing of the assemblies ended last Friday and the first shipments are scheduled for three weeks from today. As Ward began examining the test reports, he discovered that the transaxles tended to fail when loaded at more than 20 percent over rated capacity and subjected to strong torsion forces. Such a condition could occur with a heavily loaded car braking hard for a curve down a mountain road. The results would be disastrous. The manufacturer's specifications call for

TABLE 4   Comparison of French, German, and United States Response to Vignette No. 4—Paternalism

Source	Degree of Freedom	Sum of Squares	F	Probability
Between Groups	2	55	2.0	.136
Within Groups	261	3539		

	Country	Mean	
	French	3.8	
	German	2.9	
	United States	2.8	

	Percent of Respondents		
Rationale for Response	French	German	United States*
Too dangerous to world safety	26%	35%	45%
Concerned with legal ramifications	6	0	7
Average person could not build bomb even if given information	9	3	3
Don't see responsibility as being theirs	0	0	7
Those who want this information can get it now from other sources	15	21	23
May create image detrimental for company	3	5	5
Other	38	37	11
TOTAL	100.%	100%	100%
Number of respondents providing rationale	69	63	104

* Totals do not add to 100 due to rounding.

the transaxle to carry 130 percent of its rated capacity without failing. Ward showed the results to his supervisor and the company president who indicated that they were both aware of the report. Given the low likelihood of occurrence and the fact that there was no time to redesign the assembly, they decided to ignore the report. If they did not deliver the assemblies on time, they would lose the contract. John must now decide whether to show the test results to the auto manufacturer.

If you were Ward, what are the chances that you would notify the auto manufacturer?

In this vignette, a response close to 10 indicates that the manager would report the negative test results to the auto manufacturer (i.e., blow the whistle). The results in Table 5 show that respondents from all three countries are likely to "blow the whistle." However, the statistical difference among the respondent groups is significant, as the French and U.S. managers were even more likely to blow the whistle than were the Germans.

When one examines the rationale for the responses, it becomes clear that the U.S. managers, followed by the French managers, appear to be much more concerned about the chances of injury or death to people. The French managers are more likely to believe that the company has a responsibility to the public. Some U.S. managers and a slightly greater percentage of German managers responded that Ward has no additional responsibility after he reported to his superiors. The French and German responses again fell into the "other" category to a greater extent than their U.S. counterparts. These responses were scattered across the 11-point scale for the Germans without any discernable trend. The French were more concentrated in the upper half of the scale reflecting their greater probability of blowing the whistle.

Discussion

Comparing the responses of the French, German, and American managers surveyed in this study, several interesting patterns emerge. Some of these patterns exhibited national-cultural idiosyncrasies; others reflected cross-cultural universals inherent in moral principles suppositioned by natural law. For instance, the problem involving the paternalism issue (Vignette No. 4) was dealt with in a highly cautious, conservative manner by a large majority of respondents. All three national groups tended to reject publication of a recipe book for the construction of an atomic bomb. Although a sizeable proportion of the sample from each country believed the information could be obtained elsewhere, the universal sentiment was to reject the decision alternative, which was perceived as having the potential of inflicting incalculable harm on all mankind.

The same general pattern was observed for the conflict of interest problem (Vignette No. 2). A large majority of respondents said they would refuse to sign a non-competitive contract with a supplier which was in part owned by a company officer. The obvious conflict of interest was perceived rather strongly. Indeed, the sample members took a firmer stand on avoiding this conflict situation than they took on any other vignette. To give in to the pressure on signing the high-priced contract was universally interpreted as a normal weakness which must not be condoned.

TABLE 5   Comparison of French, German, and United States Response to Vignette No. 5—Personal Integrity

Source	Degree of Freedom	Sum of Squares	F	Probability
Between Groups	2	91	3.8	.023
Within Groups	260	3083		

Country	Mean
French	7.8[1]
United States	7.7[1]
German	6.4

Rationale for Response	Percent of Respondents		
	French	German	United States[2]
Chances of causing injury or death too great to remain silent	30%	14%	52%
The company has a responsibility to the public—criminal and dishonest to remain silent	21	11	12
Risk to firm's image, profitability and long run potential too great to remain silent	18	18	13
Risk of injury or death too low to halt sale	3	2	4
Profits are what is important	0	2	0
Ward has no additional responsibility, loyalty will help keep him silent	3	18	11
Other	24	37	8
TOTAL	100%	100%	100%
Number of respondents providing rationale	33	63	113

[1] Mean responses which did not differ significantly from each other per the Scheffé test.
[2] Totals do not add to 100 due to rounding.

In Vignette No. 3 the conflict of interest context was altered. It focused upon the benefit that may accrue to the firm (rather than the individual) at the expense of the physical environment. The French and German managers were more likely to side with their employer and to participate in what they perceived as a relatively minor infraction of environmental law. The American respondents were less likely to approve a production run which would result in illegal air pollution.

When a physical injury to a third party would result directly from the negligence on the part of the respondents' firm, the managers universally tended to side with the injured party (Vignette No. 5). While whistle blowing is not a respected activity in most business circles, many of the respondents said they would put their jobs on the line and "blow the whistle" if it would help to prevent a potentially serious injury to an innocent individual. Among the German respondents the whistle blowing tendency was slightly less pronounced. One might hypothesize that this is so because Germans in general may have a greater tendency to follow the authority of their immediate supervisors. This would be especially the case here, since there is no law backing the whistle blower.

If one accepts the legality of an act as defining the limits of acceptable behavior, it may appear quite easy to explain the greater willingness of the European managers to pay the bribe in the coercion and control case (Vignette No. 1). However, while the French and German managers were more likely to pay the bribe than were their U.S. counterparts, they still showed some reservations which had nothing to do with the law. If the responses had been based purely upon the law, the European mean response would have been expected to be much closer to ten. Nevertheless, one might reach the conclusion that while ethics play a part in management decision making, it is easier to be ethical when the law is behind one's decision.

If one were to generalize, the U.S. managers were noticeably more concerned with ethical and legal questions. Their French and German counterparts appeared to worry more about maintaining a successful business posture. To be sure, there was some overlapping of responses; however, the differences remained.

Some of the response differences may be the result of differing laws and regulations within the countries. Certainly, recent court decisions on company liability would bear this out for some of the responses of U.S. managers. Also, incentives in a culture for specific actions are reflected in business decisions. Consequently, there appear to be differences as well as universals in the ethical behavior of French, German, and U.S. managers.

Of course, the findings of this relatively small study should be corroborated by additional studies focusing in more detail upon the nature of the differences among the groups. A major objective should be to document the ethical behavior of the groups vis-à-vis each other. Business leaders and public policy makers within their respective countries can determine whether the behavior of their managers is acceptable by national as well as international standards. If it is, no change is needed; if it is not, the information provided by such studies may help them channel business behavior in more desirable directions. Better understanding of ethical beliefs and behavior across national-cultural boundaries would appear to be mandated within the multinational context of the business environment.

The above findings have important implications for the management of multinational corporations. If in fact the ethical behavior of managers varies across cultures, management should consider the consequences of ethical incongruence when developing staffing plans for its organization. Placing foreign managers in a culture which is incongruent with their values is likely to lead to strife within the facility as well as possible problems with customers, suppliers, and governmental bodies. It may also result in illegal behavior.

Data from the current study indicate that the ethical dimensions of management behavior across cultures vary with the type of ethical problem faced. There appears to be little difference in conflict of interest settings and little acceptance of such behavior in any of the three countries. Paternalistic activities also do not appear to be cause for concern, at least when they have a potentially large impact on society. However, issues involving coercion and control, the physical environment and personal integrity may be cause for concern.

If one is dealing strictly with the legal aspects, Europeans operating in the United States or U.S. managers operating in Europe must be briefed upon the legal ramifications of foreign payments. One would also hope that good business practices dictate that the ethics of such payments be considered. Reports indicate that European managers would like to see an end to foreign payments (Goldstein, 1979). However, the end does not appear to be in sight (Rubin, 1982).

Differences in environmental regulations should also be included in an orientation program when managers are moving from Europe to the United States or vice versa. As important as the regulations themselves is the manner in which they are implemented. In addition to the legal aspects of the environment, some time should be spent on the ethical aspects of dealing with the environment. Ethical concern for the environment was shown on both sides of the Atlantic.

When dealing with issues of personal integrity, multinational corporations are advised to orient their employees to what personal integrity means within the host country. As suggested above, one could surmise for example, that the difference between the Germans and the French and U.S. managers' response to the personal integrity vignette is more due to the greater respect for authority shown by Germans than it is to real differences in ethical values.

The findings should alert multinational corporations to the fact that more attention must be given to orienting new managers to the differing values in the foreign countries and the policies appropriate for the facilities in those countries. What may be assumed as common knowledge when transferring employees within a country may require special attention when transfers are made across cultures. Special attention should be given to familiarizing new employees from other countries with the code of ethics of the facility, written or unwritten.

REFERENCES

Alexander, Cheryl S. and Becker, Henry Jay. "The Use of Vignettes in Survey Research," *Public Opinion Quarterly,* 1978, 42, 93–104.

Appleman, John. *Military Tribunals and International Crimes.* Indianapolis: Bobbs-Merrill Company, Inc., 1954.

Barach, Jeffery A. and Nicol, Elizabeth A. "Teaching Ethics in Business Schools," *Collegiate News and Views,* 1980, Fall, 5–8.

Barry, V. *Moral Issues in Business.* Belmont, CA: Wadsworth, 1979.

Beauchamp, Thomas L. and Bowie, Norman E. *Ethical Theory and Business.* Englewood Cliffs, NJ: Prentice-Hall, 1979.

Becker, Helmut and Fritzsche, David J. "Moral Unterliegt Pragmatik," *Absatzwirtschaft-Zeitschrift für Marketing,* 1981, 23, 66–80.

Bentham, Jeremy. *An Introduction to the Principles of Morals and Legislation* (1789). New York: Hafner, 1948.

Boling, T. Edwin. "The Management Ethics 'Crisis': An Organizational Perspective," *Academy of Management Review,* 1978, 3, 360–365.

Brenner, Steven N. and Molander, Earl A. "Is the Ethics of Business Changing?" *Harvard Business Review,* 1977, 55, 57–71.

Bundesgerichtshof (German), Urteil vom 14.3 1985—IZR 168/82.

"Cabinet Approves Legislation to Create New Air Agency Coordinating all Programs," *International Environment Report: Current Report,* 1979, 2, 5, 665.

Carroll, A. B. "A Survey of Managerial Ethics: A Post Watergate View," *Business Horizons,* 1975, 18, 75–80.

Cavanagh, Gerald F., S. J. *American Business Values* (2nd ed.). Englewood Cliffs, NJ: Prentice-Hall, Inc., 1984.

Cavanagh, Gerald F., S. J. and Fritzsche, David J. "Using Vignettes in Business Ethics," *Research in Corporate Social Performance and Policy.* (Ed. Preston) Vol. 7. Greenwich, CT: JAI Press Inc., 1985.

"Decree Concerning the Control of Polluting Emissions into the Atmosphere and Certain Uses of Thermal Energy," *International Environment Report: Reference File 2,* 1979, 47.

Dill, D. D., Donaldson, T. J., Goodpaster, K. E., and May, W. W. *Syllabi for the Teaching of Management Ethics.* A publication of the Summer Institute on Ethical Issues in the Management of Public and Private Institutions, 1979, New Haven, CT.

Federal Environmental Agency: A Selection of Recent Publications, Berlin, Germany: Federal Environmental Agency, 1985.

The French Penal Code. Gerhard O. W. Mueller (ed.), South Hackensack, NJ: Fred B. Rothman and Company, 1960.

"French Prefect Agrees to Apply German Standards for Battery Plant, *International Environment Report: Current Report,* 1980, 3. 9, 403–4.

Fritzsche, David J. and Becker, Helmut. "Ethical Behavior of Marketing Managers," *Journal of Business Ethics,* 1983, 2, 291–299.

Fritzsche, David J. and Becker, Helmut. "Linking Management Behavior to Ethical Philosophy—An Empirical Investigation," *Academy of Management Journal,* 1984, 27, 167–175.

Goldstein, E. Ernest. "European Views of United States Anti-Bribery and Anti-Boycott Legislation," *Northwestern Journal of International Law and Business,* 1979, 1, 2, 363–370.

Gross, Andrew C. and Nancy E. Scott. "Comparative Environmental Legislation and Action," *International and Comparative Law Quarterly,* 1980, 29, 650–651.

Kant, Immanuel. *The Metaphysical Elements of Justice* (1797). (tr. J. Ladd) New York: Library of Liberal Arts, 1965.

Knoepfel, Peter and Helmut Weidner. "Implementing Air Quality Control Programs in Europe: Some Results of a Comparative Study," *International Comparisons in Implementing Pollution Laws,* (Paul B. Downing and Kenneth Hanf, eds.) Boston, MA: Kluwer-Nijhoff Publishers, 1983.

Law for the Prevention of Harmful Effects on the Environment Caused by Air Pollution, Noise, Vibration and Similar Phenomena. 15 March 1974 (Bundesgesetzblatt Part. I, pp. 721, 1193), as amended by the Law Amending the Law to Introduce the Penal Code, 15 August 1974 (Bundesgesetzblatt Part I, p. 1942).

Krugman, Dean M. and Ferrell, O. C. "The Organizational Ethics of Advertising: Corporate and Agency Views," *Journal of Advertising,* 1981, 10, 21–30.

Locke, John. *The Second Treatise of Government* (1690). New York: Liberal Arts Press, 1952.

Mill, John Stuart. *Utilitarianism* (1863). Indianapolis, IN: Bobbs-Merrill Company, Inc., 1957.

Purcell, Theodore V. "A Practical Guide to Ethics in Business," *Business and Society Review,* 1975, 43–50.

Purcell, Theodore V. "Do Courses in Business Ethics Pay Off?" *California Management Review,* 1977, 19, 50–58.

Rawls, John. *A Theory of Justice.* Cambridge, MA: Belknap, 1971.

Rubin, Seymour. "International Aspects of the Control of Illicit Payments," *Syracuse Journal of International Law and Commerce,* 1982, 9, 1, 315–323.

"The State of the Environment in OCED Countries: A First Assessment," *OCED Observer,* 1979, 15–25.

Ullman, Ariel A. "The Implementation of Air Pollution Control in German Industry," *International Comparisons in Implementing Pollution Laws,* (Paul B. Downing and Kenneth Hanf, eds.) Boston, MA: Kluwer-Nijhoff Publishers, 1983.

Velasquez, Manuel G., S. J. *Business Ethics.* Englewood Cliffs, NJ: Prentice-Hall, Inc., 1982.

Velasquez, Manuel, S. J. and Rostankowski, Cynthia. *Ethics: Theory and Practice.* Englewood Cliffs, NJ: Prentice-Hall, Inc., 1985.

ETHICS: ARE STANDARDS LOWER OVERSEAS?

Andrew W. Singer

When American business people venture abroad, a common view is that they're wandering into an ethical no-man's-land, where each encounter holds forth a fresh demand for a "gratuity," or baksheesh.

William C. Norris, who founded and for many years headed Control Data Corporation, says, "No question about it. We were constantly in the position of saying how much we were willing to pay" to have a routine service performed overseas. Norris recalls frequently facing situations such as: "The computer is on the dock, it's raining, and you have to pay $100 to get it picked up. . . ."

In South America, firms often face a "closed bidding system" when dealing with that region's large, nationalized companies, says John Swanson, a senior consultant of communications and business conduct at Dow Corning Corporation. He says that his company has been locked out of the South American market at times because it refused to pay the bribes necessary to get that business.

In Japan, bids for government construction jobs are routinely rigged, according to one former U.S. Government official who asked to remain anonymous—a result of Japanese firms purchasing "influence" from politicians.

Donald E. Petersen, former chairman and chief executive officer of the Ford Motor Company, cites ethical challenges in much of the developing world. "Give me a military dictator with absolute power, and it doesn't matter if he's South American or African or Asian—you've got problems."

Is the United States More Ethical?

Is this common perception borne out by reality? Are business standards overseas in fact lower than those at home? In 1987, Touche Ross, the accounting firm (now Deloitte & Touche), surveyed a range of U.S. business executives, members of Congress, and business school deans. Asked to rank the top five countries in terms of ethical standards, respondents placed the United States first, followed by the United Kingdom, Canada, Switzerland, and West Germany.

Some differences were found among respondent groups. Business school deans, for instance, put Japan at the top of their list—while business executives did not rank Japan among their top five at all.

When asked about the survey, William Morris says, "I agree with the second group. Control Data tried unsuccessfully for 15 years to get into the Japanese market. They kept us out with laws and subterfuges until they could catch up [to the U.S. computer industry]. Then they opened up to U.S. firms. I think that is very unethical."

Source: Reprinted by permission by the Conference Board from Across The Board, September 1991, pp. 31–34.

Referring to the *keiretsu*, the famed Japanese business groups, Norris says, "In our country, we call that collusion."

Many U.S. executives agree that from a business ethics standpoint, the Japanese are a special case. Take gift giving. "It is an important part of how they conduct themselves," says Donald Petersen. Often, there is little thought given to the idea: "Give me the business and I'll give you a gift."

When dealing with the Japanese, Petersen found that it was futile to try to convince them of the superiority of the American approach to business, in which, for instance, the receipt of gifts of any value in the course of a business transaction is frowned upon as a potential conflict of interest. His solution when dealing with the Japanese was simply to present the policy of accepting no gifts of any value as an American idiosyncrasy.

Bruce Smart, former U.S. Undersecretary of Commerce for International Trade, says that the Japanese are very consistent in sticking to their standards. However, those standards—which accept practices such as companies buying influence from politicians—may sometimes be looked at askance by U.S. eyes. Still, if by business ethics one means consistency with standards, "then the Japanese are probably very ethical," says Smart. Probably fewer Japanese executives cheat on their business expense sheets than Americans, Smart opines.

Underdeveloped Nations: "You'll be Tested Constantly"

In general, U.S. executives see only minor differences in business ethics as practiced in the United States, Canada, and Northern Europe. But most agree that there are some departures in the practice of business ethics when it comes to Southern Europe—Italy and Spain, for instance—and a tremendous difference in the underdeveloped nations.

"Based on my 40 years at Ford, there were no more difficult problems with ethical standards in Europe than here," says Petersen. But among the underdeveloped nations—particularly those countries with autocratic governments in which power is absolute and concentrated—it is often ordinary practice to hold out a hand for a bribe, or to take a company official for a slow walk through customs, until he gets the message that a "grease" payment is required.

Petersen maintains that a company can adhere to high standards—prohibiting bribery or even grease payments—and still function. "It's difficult. You'll be tested constantly, and at times you'll think you've lost business. But if you have a service that they want, they'll come around."

A "Holier-Than-Thou" Attitude

Not all agree that the United States is justified in taking such a superior position. "We have a tendency to take a 'holier-than-thou' attitude," says John A. Seeger, management professor at Bentley College in Waltham, Massachusetts. He maintains that U.S. standards are artificial and naïve rather than too high.

"We are often prepared to pay bribes because we hear that's expected—but that's because we hear from people who want bribes," says Seeger, explaining that managers don't often speak with the people who don't pay or receive bribes. "We expect to be held up, and so we get held up. It is the classic self-fulfilling prophecy."

When discussing overseas ethical standards, there is a danger of stereotyping people. Seeger, in fact, recently wrote a prize-winning management case based on a real incident in which the owner of a Persian Gulf company, Sameer Mustafa, an Arab, refused to bribe the engineer in charge of a Gulf construction project—and suffered economically as a result. Not *only* Americans have an abhorrence of bribery, Seeger suggests.

Kent Druyvesteyn, staff vice president of ethics at General Dynamics Corporation, agrees that we should put away ideas of American superiority when discussing ethics. Too often, says Druyvesteyn, ethical discussions take the form of: "We really do things well here. But when we go abroad, they do things so badly."

William S. Lipsman, associate general counsel of the Sara Lee Corporation, recently returned from a two-year assignment in the Netherlands. He says that he found litigation ethics standards in Europe to be higher than those in the United States. Business there is conducted on a more personal basis, Lipsman explains. "The concept that you, as a business leader, would sue another business without first sitting down at a meeting, face-to-face, is unheard of."

Bruce Smart doesn't even place the United States in the top echelon when it comes to national business standards. The Canadians, British, Australians, and perhaps even the Germans rate higher, in his view. His thinking: A kind of noblesse oblige still exists among the business classes in those countries. Conversely, in the United States, where there is a less entrenched business group, the prevailing attitude is that you make it whatever way you can. This attitude reached its apotheosis in the 1980s with the insider trading scandals on Wall Street, which Smart describes as "the biggest ethical blot on U.S. business" in recent memory.

Whether U.S. standards are in fact higher than those abroad is likely to remain a moot point. But in one respect the United States stands alone: It is the only nation that has sought to legislate moral business conduct overseas.

Can We Legislate Morality?

Passed in the late '70s in the wake of Watergate and the overseas bribery scandals, the Foreign Corrupt Practices Act (FCPA) made it a felony for U.S. companies to obtain business by paying off foreign government officials. From its inception, the FCPA has been controversial. "Managers in other countries often chuckle at the United States hoping to export its morality in the form of the Foreign Corrupt Practices Act," says Gene Laczniak, management professor at Marquette University in Milwaukee.

"It's anachronistic in today's world," says William Norris, the former Control

The Murky Land of the FCPA

The Foreign Corrupt Practices Act (FCPA) became law in 1977 in the wake of foreign bribery scandals involving U.S. companies that shook the governments of Belgium, the Netherlands, Honduras, Italy, and Japan. One of the most notorious incidents involved an estimated $25 million in concealed payments made overseas by Lockheed Corporation in connection with sales of its Tristar L-1011 aircraft in Japan. This culminated in the resignation and subsequent criminal conviction of Japanese Prime Minister Kankuie Tanaka.

The FCPA, which makes it a crime for a U.S. corporation to bribe officials of foreign governments to obtain or increase business, is controversial, in part, because it seeks to forge a distinction between "bribes" (which it deems illegal) and "gratuities" (which the FCPA permits). The difference is murky, according to the FCPA's critics.

"The law marked the difference between gratuities paid to low-level officials and payments made to authorities," writes Duane Windsor in his book, *The Foreign Corrupt Practices Act: Anatomy of a Statute.* "In many countries a payment to a customs official is a matter of course and a matter of economic necessity. A customs official may backlog an order or hinder a shipment by elaborately checking each imported item. The detrimental effect to the shipment is obvious. In response, lawmakers sought to delineate gratuities and bribes very clearly. But in reality the definition of gratuities was so vague that some people felt it had a chilling effect [on business]"–A.W.S.

Data chief. "It's like the antitrust laws in many ways. The world has passed it by." (The antitrust laws, enacted at the turn of the century, originally embodied a strong ethical element: The Government didn't want the nation's enormous "trusts" to run roughshod over the "little guy." That worked fine as long as the U.S. economy was an isolated system, say critics. But now antitrust laws may be inhibiting large U.S. firms from competing in the international arena.) In any case, says Norris, most U.S. companies don't want to become involved in activities such as bribing foreign officials.

R. John Cooper, executive vice president and general counsel of Young & Rubicam Inc., the New York–based advertising agency, makes a similar argument. The FCPA was enacted at a time when the competitive position of U.S. companies in the world was stronger—or at least perceived to be stronger—than it is today, Cooper points out. In 1970, the United States was the source of 60 percent of the world's direct foreign investment. By 1984, according to the United Nations, that figure had dropped to 12 percent. Japanese, European, and East Asian firms have picked up much of the slack, launching economic forays even into America's own backyard.

The United States risks becoming economically hamstrung by statutes such as the Foreign Corrupt Practices Act, suggests Cooper. "We have to reexamine some of these high-toned notions."

In the late 1980s, Young & Rubicam and three of its executives were indicted on a conspiracy charge under the FCPA. The Government asserted that the company had "reason to know" that one of its Jamaican agents was paying off that country's Minister of Tourism to obtain advertising business. In order to avoid a lengthy trial, the company paid a $500,000 penalty, says Cooper.

One outcome of that experience is that Young & Rubicam now has a policy that forbids even facilitating payments. Facilitating (or grease) payments are considerations to secure some ordinary service in a country, such as getting a ship unloaded in a harbor, or having a telephone installed. These are permitted under the FCPA.

Shouldering an Ethical Burden

According to Cooper, Young & Rubicam's recent experience "puts us in a position in which we're very reluctant to engage in a very common practice in some foreign countries: hiring people with relationships, who have the ability to generate business from official sources." The company can't go near such people, Cooper says. With increasingly heated international competition, the act is out of date, he says. It puts too much of a burden on U.S. corporations to know everything about their foreign agents—a burden not shouldered by foreign competitors.

The FCPA might have been an "overreaction" on the part of Congress to events such as Watergate and the overseas bribery scandals, suggests John Swanson of Dow Corning (see sidebar on page R597), "We're competing out there with strong and vibrant economies—Japan, the Common Market. We're a player but not a dominant player. We can't have this legislation that is clearly not understood [but which] has such an effect on the viability of trade."

The FCPA brings back bitter memories for William Norris. Some years ago, Control Data Corporation was prosecuted by the U.S. Government under the Foreign Corrupt Practices Act for making payments in Iran.

"I never felt we did anything wrong," says Norris, explaining that the company was conforming to the laws of Iran. (In 1978, Control Data Corporation pleaded guilty to three criminal charges that it made improper payments to unnamed foreign officials. It was fined $1,381,000 by the U.S. Customs Service.) Looking back on his long tenure as Control Data's chief executive, Norris says that settling—and not fighting—that case was one of the few things that he ever regretted.

But the FCPA also has its defenders. "It's a tough trade-off," admits Marquette's Laczniak, but the bottom line is that the "U.S. public doesn't want its companies to secure business by paying huge sums of money to foreign officials." The FCPA, in other words, is really just a reflection of the prevailing values of American society.

"I have sort of a hard time arguing that it should be repealed," says Bruce Smart. Bribing foreign officials tends "to run counter to the idea of democratic representative government. If we countenance bribery, we make it more difficult for those people to find a better way to do business."

As for the idea that U.S. standards have to be adjusted to reflect the new economic realities: "That's an ancient argument, morally," says General Dynamic's Druyvesteyn. "It's one that goes back to Deuteronomy, in the Bible. 'Sure, things are rough. We've had a drought, and the sheep aren't fat. We may have to add a little to the weight.'"

The Slippery Slope of Grease Payments

What about facilitating, or grease, payments, which are permitted under the FCPA as long as they are documented? Such payments are the norm for doing business in some parts of the world. Indeed, government employees are often intentionally underpaid in the expectation that they will receive such gratuities.

The issue of facilitating payments is addressed in Dow Corning's ethics code. "The company felt in the early 1980s that if it didn't put it in the code, it would be like the ostrich with its head in the ground," explains John Swanson. Because grease payments are going on in many parts of the world, they should be recognized.

If the company sends a person to Mexico, and his household possessions are locked up on the dock, and he can't get them delivered to his house without a facilitating payment, then Dow Corning will pay it, says Swanson. "We don't like it. But to get that person to work a few weeks early, we will do it."

What did William Norris do when a big computer was stuck on the dock for want of a $100 payment? "I told them to pay the $100." To fail to make the grease payment in that instance would be "carrying it too far," says Norris. In many other cases, though, Control Data refused to yield to such extortion, and the company lost sales as a result.

"It depends upon what amount of money is involved," says Gene Laczniak. "If you are paying small amounts of money to individuals just to do their jobs [and that is part of the country's culture], then that is just the cost of doing business in that part of the world. But if the money is paid to sway people to make decisions that they would not otherwise make, then that is subverting the nature of the free market system," says Laczniak. "I don't think anyone wants the system to work that way."

Joanne Ciulla, a professor at the University of Pennsylvania's Wharton School, acknowledges that facilitating payments can be somewhat problematic. In many developing countries, bureaucracies are hopelessly inefficient, she says. One is, in effect, paying for an efficient service within an inefficient system.

This presents some moral problems. If everyone uncomplainingly pays facilitating payments, a government has no incentive to be efficient. On the other hand, there is not a whole lot one company can do to change the system. Ciulla is reluctant to recommend that companies "fight windmills" by banning such payments in toto. What companies can do, she suggests, is put pressure on governments to clean up their act. Airing such concerns might have an impact in the long run.

The argument that U.S. global standards are too high, however, is "totally absurd," in Ciulla's view. People sometimes overlook the deleterious effects that bribery has on developing countries, where the widespread practice impedes the development of a free market, she says. "How do you develop if you can't open a fruit stand without paying a bribe?"

She notes that even where bribery and corruption is widely practiced, it's not condoned—at least officially. Even in the Dominican Republic—considered by many to be one of the most corrupt places on earth—no one says bribery is okay, Ciulla points out. No one bribes publicly, it's done privately.

Barbara Burns, a public relations consultant and a member of the board of directors of the International Public Relations Association, says that in some South American countries, notably Brazil, it is not unusual for public relations professionals to pay to have favorable stories for corporate clients placed in publications, often by remunerating a journalist. "But everyone knows which publications these are—so placement is not so valuable to the client," says Burns. "And if you start paying off, it undermines your credibility, and finally your business." She adds that there are also many high-quality publications in Brazil that can't be "bought."

From a company's point of view, the practice of giving grease payments can be economically hazardous—apart from possible legal sanctions. "It's very hard to figure out the expenses. How do you anticipate costs?" asks Ciulla. Governments change, and a "contact" may fall from favor. How much additional extortion might one face down the road?

Integrity Has Its Rewards

Adhering to higher standards doesn't have to have negative economic consequences, suggests Dow Corning's Swanson. Some years ago, Dow Corning surveyed its top customers. These customers found the company wanting in certain areas, namely response time and certain quality issues. On the positive side, the customers said: "We know you're a company of integrity, and that you stand behind your products, people, and service." Because of the company's integrity, says Swanson, "they gave us a three-year period of grace to improve our response times and quality. Otherwise, they might have taken their business to a foreign competitor."

U.S. standards are too high, then? "I don't carry that feeling with me," says Donald Petersen. "In general, I wouldn't want to see us say it's okay to reduce our standards to those of others."

And while William Norris is opposed to legislation like the FCPA—which was badly drawn and arbitrarily enforced, in his view—he doesn't recommend that U.S. companies compromise their high standards when operating abroad, either. "I don't think it's necessary to reassess those standards," says Norris. "It's better to lose a deal now and then than to lower standards, which will demoralize the workforce." In the long run, he sees high ethical standards simply as part of a quality management approach toward business.

FOSTERING ETHICAL MARKETING DECISIONS*

Gene R. Laczniak ◆ Patrick E. Murphy

ABSTRACT. This article begins by examining several potentially unethical recent marketing practices. Since most marketing managers face ethical dilemmas during their careers, it is essential to study the moral consequences of these decisions. A typology of ways that managers might confront ethical issues is proposed. The significant organizational, personal, and societal costs emanating from unethical behavior are also discussed. Both relatively simple frameworks and more comprehensive models for evaluating ethical decisions in marketing are summarized. Finally, the fact that organizational commitment to fostering ethical marketing decisions can be accomplished by top management leadership, codes of ethics, ethics seminars/programs, and ethical audits is examined.

Most marketing decisions have ethical ramifications whether business executives realize it or not. When the actions taken are "proper," the ethical dimensions go unnoticed and attention centers upon the economic efficiencies and managerial astuteness of the decisions. But such is not always the case. When a marketing decision is ethically troublesome, its highly visible outcomes can be a public embarassment or sometimes worse. Consider the following examples which are drawn from recent newspaper reports:

1. Between 1982 and 1986, Norelco knowingly sold a water purification system whose filtration mechanisms were contaminated with methylene chloride—a probable carcinogen. Basically, Norelco's so-called *Clean Water Machine* contained a carbonated filtration system which was sealed with a methylene-chloride-based glue which then seeped into the water. Norelco engineers were quickly aware of the problem but the judgement of the company was that the risk to individual consumers was slight because the leakage was likely minimal. At least, this was Norelco's public posture after questions about the product began to emerge. One wonders whether the company hoped to continue sales while they redesigned the filter, thereby eliminating the negative publicity stemming from the public disclosure of this (ironically) toxic clean water machine.[1]

2. Because of the glut of new products and limited amounts of shelf space, large supermarket chains are demanding upfront payments called "slotting fees" in order to stock new products. Supermarket

---

Source: Reprinted by permission of *Journal of Business Ethics* 10: 259–271, 1991.

* This article is based on material in *The Higher Road: A Path to Ethical Marketing Decisions*, Allyn & Bacon, 1992.

[1] 'Norelco Sold Water Purifier That It Knew Could Be Hazardous': 1988, *Milwaukee Journal*, (October 9), p. 13A.

chains justify this practice primarily because they have very narrow profit margins and because unsuccessful new products are costly to remove from the shelves. Some firms claim that *such practices discriminate* against small manufacturers who are without the ability to pay the large amounts that are demanded. For example, Safeway asked $25,000 from a small Montana specialty foods producer to have its pizzas placed in freezer cases in its California stores. Other manufacturers complain of the practice because many of the slotting fees are privately negotiated and as they are often made in cash, they become especially subject to abuse.[2]

3. Because tobacco manufacturers have been heavily criticized in the United States and other developed countries about safety of cigarette smoking, they have looked to the third world as the major source of their growth. Developing countries now consume about one-third of the $200 billion worth of cigarettes sold in the world. Moreover, many of these developing countries have been targeted as the major sources of tobacco promotion in the immediate future. Often, tobacco companies develop relationships in conjunction with the local government which collects a substantial proportion of the product price in the form of sales taxes. To make matters worse, several tobacco companies admit that many of the brands sold to developing countries contain more tar and nicotine than in cigarette brands sold in developed countries.[3]

4. Manufacturers sometimes "dump" products which are declared unsafe for one reason or another in their initially targeted market and move those products to other areas of the world. In these latter countries regulators have not made the "unsafe" designation or existing regulations haven't caught up to safety standards applicable in the original market. One of the most blatant recent cases of abuse had to do with the output of some Bavarian dairies which had been ordered to destroy their product. The milk was radioactively contaminated by the Chernobyl nuclear disaster because the German cows had grazed on contaminated grass. In any event, two train loads of milk were intercepted as they were about to be shipped to Egypt.[4]

---

[2] Gibson, R.: 1988, 'Space War: Supermarkets Demand Food Firms' Payments Just to Get on the Shelf,' *Wall Street Journal* (November 1), Sec. A, p. 1.

[3] Mulson, S.: 1985, 'Smoking Section: Cigarette Companies Develop Third World as a Growth Market,' *Wall Street Journal* (July 5), p. 1.

[4] Tagliabue, J.: 1987, 'Keeping Tainted Foods Off Third World Shelves,' *New York Times* (February 2), p. B2.

5. Travel agents have been increasingly accused of not keeping the best interest of their clients in mind. In some cases, they have attempted to capture for their own accounts frequent flyer points which have not been credited to existing customer files. In other cases, the travel agents participated in sweepstakes sponsored by airline or rental car companies. These sweepstakes allow for an improved chance of "winning the game" based on the amount of business directed toward a particular airline or rental car company. The net result is that without the customers knowing it, clients might be steered into higher cost travel options as this is in the best interest of the travel agent.[5]

6. As Americans became increasingly health conscious, advertising stressed the health and nutritionally related benefits of various food products. This has led to numerous cases of misleading or exaggerated claims. For example, ads running in several women's magazines are urging women to drink more milk in order to prevent osteoporosis (the development of brittle bones that can fracture easily). What the ads do *not* say is that many dairy products (e.g., whole milk) are high in fat content and can contribute to high cholesterol levels and as a result, heart disease. Similarly, many cereal manufacturers have now promoted the supposed health benefits of consuming "all bran" cereals. One recent headline for a two page ad about Kellogg's cereals screamed, "Grab a weapon in the war against cancer."[6] This occurred because of the statistical linkage of certain bran and fibrous material consumption to low rates of intestinal cancer. Yet, what the advertising omits is the fact that there is great debate in the medical community about what the proper level of fiber consumption should be and the fact than an over consumption of fiber—a mistake uninformed consumers might make—can lead to a neglect in the diet of other sources and nutrition valuable for needed vitamins and minerals.[7]

The examples could continue. The items cited above are meant to be illustrative of the point that there are various areas of marketing—including product management, international issues, retailing, advertising, distribution, and pricing—that can raise ethical questions about appropriate marketing practice. The recent spate of business ethics scandals including the Wall Street insider trading scams, the price gouging by numerous defense contractors and the check

---

[5] Rose, L.: 1988, 'Travel Agents' Games Raise Ethics Issues,' *Wall Street Journal* (November 23), p. B1.

[6] 'The Food/Health Supplement,:' 1989, *New York Times Magazine* (April 16), Part 2.

[7] Morris, B.: 1985, 'Rise in Health Claims in Food Ads Can Help and Mislead Shoppers,' *Wall Street Journal* (April 2), p. 33.

overdraft scheme by the former E. F. Hutton brokerage firm has only heightened the skepticism of the American public to business practices.

How Does the Public Feel About Business?

Analysts who track the public pulse seem to have established a perception of business and marketing which is less than flattering. Consider the following statistics which seem to show that Americans generally distrust business and business people.[8]

◆ A *Business Week/Harris poll* indicated that white collar crime is thought to be very common (49 percent) or somewhat common (41 percent) and that 46 percent (most in any category) believe that the ethical standards of business executives are only fair.

◆ A 1987 *U.S. News and World Report* survey reports that the majority of the American public believes that most business people regularly participate in ethical transgressions such as taking home office supplies, padding expense accounts, and using small amounts of organizational funds for personal purposes.

◆ A 1987 *Time* study suggests that 76 percent of the American public saw a lack of business ethics in business managers as contributing to the decline of U.S. moral standards.

◆ A 1988 *Touche Ross* survey of the business community reported that the general feeling (even among business people) is that the problems concerning business ethics which have been portrayed in the media have not been overblown or exaggerated.

From a marketing standpoint, it is even more distressing to realize that among various categories of business professionals those holding marketing positions are viewed to be among the *least* ethical. For example, in a 1983 Gallup study judging the ethicalness of various occupations, the categories salespeople and advertising practitioners were ranked at the bottom of the honesty and ethical standards scale.[9] This disturbing public opinion probably developed because of the unethical practices of a minority. Yet, because of data like these all marketers are too often construed as hawkers, pitchmen, con-artists, and cheats. This festers a cancer which gnaws on the integrity of marketing practitioners everywhere.

---

[8] Reported in Robin, D. P., and R. E. Reidenbach: 1989, *Business Ethics: Where Profits Meet Value Systems* (Prentice-Hall, Englewood Cliffs, N.J.), p. 4.

[9] Gallup Poll (1983), 'Honesty and Ethical Standards,' Report No. 214 (July).

Does the Typical Marketing Manager Face Ethical Problems?

Over the years, some marketing managers have argued that they are relatively exempt from ethical dilemmas or that such moral pressures do not generally affect them. In reality, most studies confirm that between 65 and 75 percent of all managers do indeed face an ethical dilemma at some point in their career. An ethical dilemma is defined for our purposes as confronting a decision that involves the trade-off between lowering one's personal values in exchange for increased organizational or personal profits. Thus based upon the reports of practicing managers, it appears that most marketing executives are *not* free from dealing with ethical concerns. If anything, the percentages referenced above underestimate the number of marketers who face ethical dilemmas because some may not recognize one when it confronts them. Judging from the questions being raised about the propriety of marketing practices on all its fronts, the proposition that many marketing decisions have significant moral consequences seems a truism.

Can Emphasizing Ethics Make a Difference?

The point has sometimes been made that preaching ethics in an organization does not have an effect upon the behavior of managers. This view was captured in the old adage which states "scruples, either you got 'em or you ain't." For years, the Harvard Business School and other colleges of business did not bother to teach business ethics on the supposition that efforts along these lines would most likely prove fruitless. Underlying this approach is a stream of research that indicates moral development occurs at a rather early age and by the time an individual enters a business organization, his/her moral sensibilities are rather established and somewhat immutable.[10] There is evidence that this viewpoint is probably in error, as various organizational case studies have consistently shown that the ethical gyroscopes of managers can be spun about by organizational actions and economic pressures.[11]

One way to establish how ethical concern might be of value to an organization is to visualize the archetypal ways in which managers might confront an ethical issue.[12]

First, you have the *crook*. This kind of individual looks at a particular

---

[10] Kohlberg, L.: 1969, 'Stage and Sequence: The Cognitive Developmental Approach to Socialization,' in D. A. Gaslin (ed.), *Handbook of Socializations Theory and Research* (hereafter cited as Kohlberg, Stage and Sequence), pp. 347–480 (Rand McNally: Chicago).

[11] Brenner, S. and E. Molander: 1977, 'Is The Ethics of Business Changing?', *Harvard Business Review* (January/February), pp. 52–71.

[12] Adapted from Martin, T. R.: 1986, 'Ethics in Marketing: Problems and Prospects,' *Marketing Ethics: Guidelines for Managers*, Laczniak and E. Murphy (eds.) (D. C. Heath and Company: Lexington, MA). pp. 3–5.

marketing situation, realizes that it has negative ethical consequences, *knows* that taking the action would be morally wrong but consistently goes ahead and takes that action—presumably for personal reward and the (short-term) economic gain of the organization. Such unethical, and often criminal activity, exists in a minority of the population including marketing executives. Most companies will attempt to purge such individuals from the organization when their pattern of action becomes evident. Others, however, may tolerate such behavior if the actions lead to economic rewards for the organization. In any event, concern for ethical issues by the organization will probably not influence the behavior of this type of individual.

A second kind of manager might be called the *good samaritan*. This manager looks at a decision with potential ethical consequences and, based upon some method of moral reasoning and personal principles, generally arrives at what is arguably an ethical and just resolution of the decision. Like the crook, such highly principled good samaritans, who almost always recognize the ethical consequences of their actions and then can reason to appropriate conclusions without respect to the organization, are relatively rare.

The third type of manager might be called the *seeker*. This manager genuinely wants to do the right thing but does not always have the appropriate information or awareness. Seekers may be required to make decisions having ethical consequences but they may not recognize an ethical choice. This type of manager can clearly benefit from ethical education as well as a greater degree of stated ethical concern by the organization. Such managers need to be made aware of the potential ethical consequences of marketing decisions as well as the trade-offs that exist among the alternative actions that are available when making a decision with substantial ethical consequences. We suspect the number of managers falling into the "seeker" category is fairly substantial and especially describes those younger or less experienced marketers.

The fourth type of manager—the *rationalizer*—presents the most difficult situation. The rationalizer recognizes that certain decisions have ethical consequences, but they generally will find a way to justify the most economically expedient solution whether it is ethical or not. That is, they have the ability to recognize that there are moral consequences to particular decisions, but in their mind they can find a reason why in their situation the normal moral cautions do not apply. Obviously, this sort of manager can benefit from heightened ethical concern in the organization. This is particularly true when that concern takes a form which teaches a method of moral reasoning that can be applied to marketing decisions or compels them to act ethically because they fear organizational sanctions.

The upshot of this discussion is that at the extremes, efforts to stimulate ethical concern by organizations will not change managerial behavior. Certain managers (i.e., crooks) will be predisposed to act unethically and others (i.e., good samaritans) will try to do the right thing regardless of the organizational posture. However, in the middle ranges, where one suspects we find most managers, there would appear to be a sufficiently large number either looking for moral guidance (i.e., seekers) or not having the necessary background or fortitude (i.e., the rationalizers) to reason through morally difficult problems. For organizations concerned with improving their ethical climate, the ability to influence seeker- and rationalizer-type managers becomes a valuable strategic window of opportunity. Those managers who do not regularly recognize the ethical implications of their decision are in need of having their ethical sensitivities raised by ethics education. Those who recognize the situation with moral consequences but cannot properly deal with them are in need of education in the realm of ethical reasoning. It may be that via ethics seminars or even some customized "paper and pencil" tests, organizations can learn what percentage of their managers most likely fall into each category. Then, ethics codes, programs, or education can be tailored to fit the ethical needs of the companies' executives.

Why Should Marketing Organizations Attempt to Foster Ethical Behavior?

Besides the obvious answer that being ethical is simply the proper thing to do—a point which will be developed later—marketers should be ethical because not to be so will likely generate significant personal, organizational and societal costs.[13] Consider first the personal costs. If an action is illegal as well as unethical (as many such actions are), the manager who makes the questionable ethical decision can be held personally liable. The case of the Foreign Corrupt Practices Act of 1977 (which applies to U.S. based organizations) that prohibits the bribery of foreign officials to obtain overseas contracts illustrates this point.[14] For each violation—that is, the payment of a bribe—the organization is subject to a one million dollar fine. More significant, however, the manager responsible for this payment is subject to a $10,000 fine per violation and a maximum of five years in prison. Relatedly, the courts are increasingly disposed to incarcerate executives shown to be responsible for violations of the law which endanger consumers.[15] For instance, a manager who premeditatedly decides to market an unsafe product (the managers responsible for the earlier mentioned Norelco decision come to mind) are subject to criminal and personal liability. Criminal liability, of course, is the harshest of penalties but there are other negative outcomes. Organizations which take their ethical reputation seriously will not

---

[13] Based upon Laczniak, G. R. and P. E. Murphy: 1986, 'Incorporating Marketing Ethics Into The Organization,' *Marketing Ethics: Guidelines for Managers* (D.C. Heath and Company, Lexington, MA), pp. 98–100 (hereafter cited as Laczniak and Murphy, *Marketing Ethics*).

[14] Kaikati, G. and W. A. Label: 1980, 'Americal Bribery Legislation: An Obstacle to International Marketing,' *Journal of Marketing* (Fall), pp. 38–43.

[15] Laczniak and Murphy, *Marketing Ethics*.

hesitate to terminate employees who violate ethical and professional norms. This is an obvious gesture which communicates an organization's seriousness of purpose concerning the maintenance of an ethical culture. Needless to say, such terminations will affect the future career prospects of these individuals, not to mention the personal embarassment that goes along with being fired.

There are also substantial *organizational costs* resulting from unethical behavior when ethical transgressions by a company become publicized. Typically, these take the form of reduced sales and a loss of goodwill. A classic case is the experience of the Nestlé Company with their marketing of infant formula in Third World countries.[16] In that particular situation, Nestlé attempted to aggressively market infant formula, as a substitute for mothers' breast milk, in less developed countries. Nestlé seemed to pay little attention to the fact that the proper use of infant formula requires sanitary conditions and a fairly high literacy rate on the part of mothers. Because these conditions were not present, infants incurred a substantially higher rate of malnutrition than if they had been fed mothers' milk. As these circumstances became known, the result was a public relations nightmare as well as a balance sheet catastrophe for Nestlé. The derogatory publicity along with a substantial loss of sales was due to various boycotts of Nestlé products worldwide.

A similar case involves the Beech Nut Company which continued to sell a cheap, chemical based substitute juice as a real apple juice for babies, primarily to maintain its cash flow.[17] The company denied any wrongdoing even after the evidence had plainly been generated which would find the company guilty of hundreds of counts of premeditated product fraud. In this situation, the reputation of Beech Nut—a company marketing to children and one dependent upon fostering an image of safety and care—has probably become irreconcilably besmirched because of the actions of a few unscrupulous managers.

Finally, there are enormous *societal costs* which are generated by the unethical behavior of organizations. First, a consumer, who is tricked into buying a product that he/she does not need or who ends up paying substantially more for a product or service than is justified, incurs a surplus economic cost as well as some resentment toward the marketing system. Some groups such as the poor, the old, the handicapped, the mentally feeble, children, and recent immigrants are particularly vulnerable to unethical selling practices. Besides the economic or physical pain suffered by victims of unethical marketing practice, there is a general damage to the credibility of the existing economic system which requires a high level of trust to operate smoothly. Whether one believes in a free market economy or a planned economy, most business analysts agree that it is the economically efficient firm with the superior product that should

---

[16] Sethi, S. P. and J. E. Post: 1979, 'The Marketing of Infant Formula in Less Developed Countries,' *California Management Review*, Vol. XXI, No. 4, pp. 35–48.

[17] Trauk, J.: 1988, 'Into The Mouths of Babes,' *New York Times Magazine* (July 24) p. 17.

be rewarded, rather than the dishonest firm which gains a perceived advantage via misrepresentation. Yet, when a competitive situation exists wherein an unethical marketing practice generates a short-term benefit for less efficient firms, the advantages of the supposedly efficient marketplace are shortcircuited and shift toward the unethical firm. Needless to say, if questionable marketing practices happen to a greater extent, further erosion of confidence by the American public in the marketing system occurs.

Frameworks for Ethical Decision Making

What standards do marketers use in order to grapple with questions that may have ethical implications? Historically, most marketers and business executives have gravitated toward a utilitarian method of problem solving. Applied to an ethical situation in a marketing context, the reasoning employed by many managers would take the form of a cost/benefit analysis. Businesspeople, because of their training, are naturally prone to talk about concepts such as "maximizing profitability" and "concern for the bottom line." Profitability essentially translates into the excess of revenue over cost. It does not require a great stretch of the marketing manager's imagination to apply a similar sort of thinking to an ethical context. Thus, managers often operate with a rule that essentially says, "make decisions such that the benefits to the firm exceed the costs incurred by the firm to the greatest extent possible." Depending upon how a manager defines "benefits" and "costs" one might arrive at different conclusions. If the emphasis is upon economic criteria (such as short-term profits) it is easy to see how a fair amount of the ethical analysis conducted by business executives gives great weight to economic outcomes which evaluate how various options would benefit stockholders in the near term.

Thus looking at situations from their potential influence upon short-run profitability, one can see how an organization rationalizes taking a product (for example, a toy dart gun) which has been declared unsafe in one market and attempts to sell it in another market where the regulation might not apply. The rationale: the organization does not have to write-off the inventory—a major cost. The inherent danger of the product might be arguable. Who is to say definitely that a plastic, rubber tipped dart gun is any more or less dangerous than a baseball? The sale of the product is perfectly legal, thereby protecting a revenue stream. In short, economic considerations often prevail over other possible perspectives like whether "toy guns" are a proper plaything or whether a firm should tolerate any product that has a likelihood of severely injuring a child.

This is not to say that there are no other shorthand decision rules besides utilitarian cost/benefit analysis which are used by business people. Other expeditious frameworks for ethical decision making have been articulated as useful. The extent to which these thumbnail frameworks have been utilized by marketers in particular situations has not been systematically studied. Some of the maxims which might aid a marketer facing an ethical dilemma are the following:[18]

> *The Golden Rule*—act in a way that you would expect others to act toward you.
>
> *The Professional Ethic*—take only actions which would be viewed as proper by an objective panel of your professional colleagues.
>
> *Kant's Categorical Imperative*—act in a way such that the action taken under the circumstances could be a universal law of behavior for everyone facing those same circumstances.
>
> *The TV Test*—a manager should always ask, would I feel comfortable explaining this action on TV to the general public?

Some thumbnail rules are difficult to apply in specific situations. At times, the application of one more rule of thumb to the same situation seems to suggest an entirely different solution. For example, if every sales rep pads his/her expense account by 15 percent because customary gratuities (i.e., tips) are not technically reimbursable, the *professional ethic* might dictate the practice is OK despite its variance from the letter of company policy. In contrast, the *categorical imperative* might be interpreted as suggesting that as a "universal rule" padding an expense account is not acceptable.

Still, such maxims can have considerable value. One wonders whether the product manager who permitted the Norelco Clean Air Machine to continue to be sold—knowing that methylene chloride might be leaking into the carbon filtration system—could possibly feel comfortable explaining those actions to the general public on TV. Similarly, the professional ethic can be extremely useful for those sub-specialties in business that have a code of professional conduct which covers certain re-occurring situations. For example, various groups of professional marketing researchers have developed detailed codes of ethics which cover commonly encountered situations by their peer group. Included, for instance, in many marketing research codes of ethics would be dictums that stipulate that respondent confidentiality should be protected when it is promised, that data which does not confirm the hypothesized findings of the researcher is not suppressed, that the limitations of various statistical methods are identified in the research report, and so forth.

Whatever frameworks are used, the consensus regarding what constitutes proper ethical behavior in a decision making situation tends to diminish as the level of analysis proceeds from the abstract to the specific. Put another way, it is easy to get a group of managers to agree *in general* that a practice is improper;

---

[18] Laczniak, G. R.: 1983, 'Business Ethics: A Manager's Primer,' *Business* (January–March), pp. 23–29 (hereafter cited as Laczniak, *Business*).

however, casting that practice in a very specific set of circumstances usually reduces consensus. For example, most managers would agree with the proposition that "business has the obligation to provide consumers with facts relevant to the informed purchase of a product or a service." However, let us test this proposition in a specific situation.

> Suppose we have a manufacturer of cleaning concentrate whose directions call for mixing one part of the concentrate with four parts of water; suppose further that this cleaning concentrate has been sold in this manner for 25 years. Now, assume that an issue of *Consumer Reports* indicates that the product will clean just as effectively if mixed with one part concentrate to eight parts water. Thus, consumers need only use one half as much concentrate. Does the company have an ethical responsibility to inform customers of this fact?

Again, most managers *agree* that business has the obligation to provide consumers with facts relevant to an informed purchase. But does such an informed purchase include full disclosure of this *new information,* especially if further product testing in different situations would produce different results?

Because of the difficulty of applying such general principles to specific case situations, a number of researchers have begun to investigate what factors account for the particular decisions of managers in an ethical context. In an effort to aid their investigations, some of these researchers have begun to formulate *models* which stipulate the factors which come into play as a marketing manager arrives at an "ethical" decision.

Models of Marketing Ethics

The Moral Development Model This approach draws partly upon the analysis of educational psychologist Lawrence Kohlberg, who studied the moral development of adolescents.[19] Basically, Kohlberg postulated that over time individuals develop moral systems which are increasingly complex although there was no guarantee that any particular individual moves beyond the initial and most fundamental stage of moral development. Essentially, Kohlberg saw three broad levels of cognitive moral development. These were:

◆ *The preconventional stage* where abiding concern of the individual would be resolving moral situations with the individual's own immediate interests and consequences firmly in mind. An individual at the preconventional level would give strong weight to the external rewards and punishments which would be most likely to affect them. Normally, this

---

[19] Kohlberg, Stage and Sequence.

stage includes a strong emphasis upon literal obedience to rules and authority.

◆ *The conventional stage.* Individuals at the conventional stage have progressed to a level where their ethical decision making mode takes into consideration the expectations of some significant referent group and larger society. What constitutes moral propriety has to do with a concern for others, however, still motivated most directly by organizational rules. Such rules are tempered by keeping loyalties and doing one's duty to society.

◆ *The principled level.* This is the highest stage of moral development. Individuals who reach this level solve their ethical problems in a manner that goes beyond the norms and laws that are overtly applicable to a situation. Proper conduct certainly includes upholding the basic rights, values, and legal contracts of the society, but beyond that such individuals seem to subscribe to universal ethical principles which they believe that all members of society should follow in similar situations.

What the Moral Development model implies is that the ethical sophistication of managers can increase over time. The major difference among the various stages of moral development according to this approach is that as the manager moves to a higher level of moral development the individual is able to take more factors into consideration, especially factors which go beyond personal self interest. Two major implications of the Moral Development model are that (a) some managers will be less sophisticated than others in terms of the considerations they bring to bear to a decision with potentially moral consequences. At the most basic level, some managers will operate almost totally from the standpoint of egoistic self interest. And (b), perhaps there are interventions that organizations can bring to bear which will compel managers to higher levels of moral development—assuming this is a goal which is seen as in the interest of the organization.

The Contingency Model Another model has been developed by Ferrell and Gresham.[20] In addition to the usual individual factors that might influence an ethical decision, their approach suggests two major intervening issues that will determine whether a manager acts ethically or not. There are: the *opportunity* to engage in potentially unethical action and the *relative influence* (positive or negative) *of reference groups,* especially peers and top management. With regard to the role of these reference groups, the model stipulates that when contact with peers is great, peers will have a greater degree of influence upon ethi-

---

[20] Ferrell, O. C., and L. Gresham: 1985, 'A Contingency Framework For Understanding Ethical Decision Making in Marketing,' *Journal of Marketing* (Summer), pp. 87–96.

cal/unethical behavior. Conversely, when the interaction with top management is substantial, the attitudes communicated by top management will have a strong formulative role in shaping the behavior of subordinate managers concerning ethical decisions. For example, sales reps often operate in a fairly autonomous fashion in the field with limited contact with management. In such cases, the attitudes of peers regarding ethical issues would likely be more influential than the opinions of management.

With respect to the *opportunity* to engage in unethical behavior, it is not surprising that the model postulates that the greater the opportunity to engage in such behavior the more likely an individual will do so—all other things equal. The proclivity to favor an unethical option is tempered of course by the rewards and punishments which are operating in a particular manager's environment. That is to say, unethical behavior is discouraged by codes of ethics which prohibit certain activities. Similarly, when punishments are enacted for violation of certain professional conduct, unethical behavior is less likely to occur. In the absence of such sanctions, the probability of a manager acting unethically increases.

The contribution of the Contingency Model is that it shows individual values are not the sole arbiter of ethical behavior; peer and supervisor influence is also extremely important. With respect to the role of top management, there is an old organizational adage which suggests that the business enterprise is but a lengthened shadow of the person at the top. In all probability, the posture of top management may be the single most important factor determining ethical behavior in an organization.[21] Similarly, the notion of opportunity to act unethically simply underscores the common sense notion that options which are not available will not generally be taken.

The Reasoned Action Model Other approaches to the study of ethics have taken the "rational man" approach.[22] The basic idea is that a typical individual will approach an ethical problem from a rather calculating perspective. First, the person must perceive that a situation has ethical dimensions. At this point, several evaluations take place. One involves a judgement concerning the inherent rightness or wrongness of the ethical question [at issue]. Either basic or sophisticated principles are used to arrive at this judgement. A second step involves a determination of what the perceived consequences of acting ethically or unethically are. The probability that each of those consequences will occur are then subjectively calculated taking into consideration the importance of each outcome. The ultimate ethical judgement arrived at by the manager is the result of judgement concerning the norms of behavior (i.e., the evaluation

---

[21] Baumhart, R. C.: 1961, 'How Ethical Are Businesses?,' *Harvard Business Review* (July–August), p. 6.

[22] Hunt, S. D., and S. Vitell: 1986, 'A General Theory of Marketing Ethics,' *Journal of Macromarketing* (Spring), pp. 5–16.

regarding the rightness or wrongness of the action) in conjunction with the evaluation of the net gain from each outcome adjusted for the probability of its happening. What all this means is that managers will systematically weigh the possible options and outcomes in light of their individual value system. One of the essential problems of the approach is that it never clearly specifies whether the evaluations are made from the standpoint of the person, the manager as representing the organization or the manager taking into account the various stakeholders (i.e., consumers, employees, etc.) of the firm.

Although this model may seem complicated upon first exposure, it is not terribly complex. Brought down to its essentials, it implies the following:

1. If managers perceive a situation which requires an action which may have ethical consequences, they will attempt to elaborate the alternative outcomes of the options available to them.

2. In coming to a decision as to which option to choose, managers will weigh factors including the inherent rightness or wrongness of the act itself, the probability that acting in a particular way will lead to certain payoffs, and the values of those payoffs.

3. All of this will lead to formation of an ethical judgment which will culminate in the *intention* to take a particular action. Whether the action is actually taken or not can still be mitigated by various situational factors such as the likelihood of getting caught.

Again, the value of models like those described is that they elaborate important issues which bear upon ethical decision making. Whether these factors deal with the moral development of the individual manager, the influence of top management or peer groups, the opportunity to engage in particular actions, or the value of various outcomes to the manager, they are all organizational aspects which can be adjusted to possibly improve the firm's ethical posture. Perhaps the greatest shortcoming of such models is that they are basically descriptive. While they elaborate factors that come into play when managers might take an action with moral consequences, such approaches generally avoid making any moral judgments about the propriety of various actions.

The organization which is interested in *improving* rather than simply understanding the ethical decisions which take place in marketing, needs (a) an organizationally mandated sequence of ethical reasoning that a manager can utilize, and (b) organizational commitment by top management to an ethical culture. Each of these topics is treated briefly below.

A Sequence of Questions to Improve Ethical Reasoning

One approach to more normatively deal with ethical issues is to require managers to proceed through a sequence of questions which essentially test whether the action that they contemplate is ethical or has possible ethical consequences. A battery of such questions might include the following:[23]

> *Question 1:* Does the contemplated action violate law?
>
> *Question 2:* Is the contemplated action contrary to widely accepted moral obligations? (Such moral obligations might include *duties of fidelity* such as the responsibility to remain faithful to contracts, to keep promises, and to tell the truth; *duties of gratitude* which basically means that special obligations exist between relatives, friends, partners, cohorts, and employees; *duties of justice* which basically have to do with obligations to distribute rewards based upon merit; *duties of nonmaleficence* which consists of duties not to harm others; *duties of beneficence* which rest upon the notion that actions should be taken which improve the situation of others—if this can be readily accomplished.)[24]
>
> *Question 3:* Does the proposed action violate any other special obligations which stem from the type of marketing organization at focus? (For example, the special duty of pharmaceutical firms to provide safe products, the special obligation of toy manufacturers to care for the safety of children, the inherent duty of alcohol manufacturers to promote responsible drinking.)
>
> *Question 4:* Is the *intent* of the contemplated action harmful?
>
> *Question 5:* Are there any major damages to people or organizations that are likely to result from the contemplated action?
>
> *Question 6:* Is there a satisfactory alternative action which produces equal or greater benefits to the parties affected than the proposed action?
>
> *Question 7:* Does the contemplated action infringe upon the inalienable rights of the consumer (such as the right to information, the right to be heard, the right to choice, and the right to redress)?
>
> *Question 8:* Does the proposed action leave another person or group less well off? Is this person or group already a member of a relatively underprivileged class?

The questions outlined need not be pursued in any lockstep fashion. If none of the questions uncover any potential conflicts, clearly the action being contemplated is quite likely to be ethical. However, if the sequence of queries does produce a possible "conflict," this does not necessarily mean that the action being proposed is unethical per se. There may be unusual intervening factors

---

[23] Adapted from Laczniak, G. R.: 1983, 'Frameworks For Analyzing Marketing Ethics,' *Journal of Macromarketing* (Spring), pp. 7–18.

[24] Ross, W. D.: 1930, *The Right and The Good* (Clarendon Press, Oxford).

which would still allow the action to ethically go forward. For example, suppose it is determined that the contemplated action is a violation of the law. Perhaps the law is unjust and thus, there could be a moral obligation for an organization to transgress the law. Similarly, suppose there is an alternative action which could be taken which would produce equal or greater good for a larger number of individuals. However, the implementation of this alternative would bankrupt the existing organization. In such a situation, the taking of the alternative action (rather than the contemplated action) is very likely not required.

Organizational Commitment to an Ethical Culture

The sequence of questions discussed can enhance the moral reasoning ability of managers. However, the organization can take other steps which attempt to shape the *behavior* of managers by virtue of the organizational environment in which they operate. Several possible steps are addressed here. These actions can influence the organizational culture in the long term.[25]

Top Management Leadership A primary factor in setting a firm's ethical tone is the posture and seriousness of purpose communicated by top managers toward this issue. Most studies of business and marketing ethics make this quite clear.[26] As Deal and Kennedy point out in their book, *Corporate Cultures,* managers give extraordinary attention to those matters stressed in the corporate value system. These values are personified more often than not by the top executive in the organization.[27]

It is commonly accepted that companies are over-managed and under-led. Leadership is important in all aspects of the firm, but it is critical in the ethics area. Examination of CEOs' characteristics typically list integrity as an indispensible ingredient. For instance, James Burke, former CEO of Johnson & Johnson, directed managers to evaluate the company's successful corporate credo. These efforts are credited as being responsible for the swift product recall and sensitive reaction to the infamous Tylenol poisonings. Another illustration of leadership and integrity is Lee Iacocca's stance regarding Chrysler's past practice of disconnecting odometers of cars while driven by company executives. Iacocca admitted the firm had made a mistake in judgment and promised that the practice would never happen again.[28]

---

[25] Partially adapted from: Laczniak and Murphy, *Marketing Ethics,* pp. 100–104.

[26] Laczniak, *Business.*

[27] Terrence E. Deal and Allen A. Kennedy (1982), *Corporate Culture: The Risks and Rituals of Corporate Life* (Addison-Wesley Publishing Co., Inc., Reading MA).

[28] Patrick E. Murphy, 'Implementing Business Ethics,' *Journal of Business Ethics,* December 1988, pp. 907–915.

Codes of Ethics These statements are ideally the articulation of corporate values in a moral context. One recent report indicated that 75–80 percent of all major corporations have established codes of ethics.[29] Such codes can help vitalize the organization, but some are simply "public relations boilerplate" or "motherhood and apple pie" statements. In fact, one study indicated that most existing codes are primarily legalistic in orientation.[30]

Although a few firms, such as the aforementioned example of Johnson & Johnson, have a short and general corporate credo, most companies delineate their ethical stance in a formal and longer code of ethics. These codes commonly address issues like conflict of interest, treatment of competitors, the right to privacy, gift giving, and political contributions. Despite their limitations, a recent survey stated that codes are perceived to be *the* most effective way to encourage ethical corporate behavior.[31]

We propose that for codes to have the maximal impact, they should be:

Publicized and Communicated to the Organization. New employees are usually asked to read and sign off on the code during their orientation. However, the code is quickly forgotten if it is never mentioned again. Firms should regularly communicate with marketing personnel about the code and publicize it in departmental memos and meetings. Some firms, including Michigan National Bank, require that employees read and affirm their commitment to the code on an annual basis.

Specific To avoid vagueness, the code should offer specific guidance to sales and marketing executives. Words that have vague meanings should be avoided. In the gift giving and receiving area, words like nominal, token, or modest should not be used. Some firms do follow this type of policy. For example, Waste Management tells employees that gifts should not exceed $100 in aggregate annual value and Donnelly Mirrors' code states "If you can't eat it, drink it, or use it up in one day, don't give it or anything else of greater value."

Pertinent. In our examination of codes of ethics, we are continually struck by how similar they are. More thought needs to be given on placing pertinent information in the code. The point is that each organization has certain areas that are particularly likely to encounter ethical abuse, and these concerns are

---

[29] W. Mathews (1987), 'Codes of Ethics: Organizational Behavior and Misbehavior,' in Fredrick (ed.) *Research in Corporate Social Performance and Policy* (JAI Press, Inc., Greenwich, CT), pp. 107–130.

[30] Donald P. Robin et al., 'A Different Look at Codes of Ethics,' *Business Horizons,* January–February 1989, pp. 66–73.

[31] Touche Ross, *Ethics in American Business* (Touche Ross & Co., New York) January 1988.

ones on which the code should focus. For instance, toy companies must make special provisions for protecting the safety of children. Mail order firms should address the question of their return policy and how they handle merchandise damaged in shipping. Companies that spend millions of dollars on promotion and advertising need to detail their advertising philosophy as well as what program vehicles or media they will or will not use.

Enforced. To gain the respect of managers and their subordinates, the code of marketing conduct must be enforced. Sanctions should be specified and punishments meted out. What the particular sanctions for a given violation would entail depends on the violation. For example, padding an expense account for the first time may result in a salesperson losing his or her commission for a period of time, while a manager who induces employees to use bait-and-switch tactics might be dismissed. Specifically, Baxter's (formerly Baxter-Travenol) code states that violators will be terminated.

Revised To remain current, codes should be revised periodically. They need to be living documents to reflect changing worldwide conditions, community standards, and evolving organizational policies. For example, Caterpillar instituted its code in 1974 and revised it in 1977 and 1982. Johnson & Johnson's credo came into being in 1945 and was modified slightly in 1979 as a result of the credo challenge meetings.

Ethics Seminars/Programs A number of organizations choose to hold periodic seminars for marketing managers that deal with the question of ethics. Each manager might be required to attend one seminar every several years. The purpose of such educational modules is not so much to provide exact answers to particular questions as to sensitize managers to potential ethical problems that fall within the domain of their responsibilities. The programs or seminars may take the form of helping managers develop their capability to morally reason or involve the discussion of hypothetical case situations which treat circumstances that could conceivably arise.

There are several avenues that firms can travel in developing these ethics seminars or programs. One option is a modest effort such as having a speaker or panel at a dealer meeting or corporate conference. For instance, a recent market research conference sponsored by Drakett Company (a Bristol Myers subsidiary) included such an ethics module where several ethically-charged cases were discussed. A second possibility is longer "in-house" conferences or off-site meetings on the subject. Polaroid held a series of ethics conferences several years ago. Probably the most extensive ethics seminar is conducted by Chemical Bank. Their "Decision Making and Corporate Values" program is a two-day, off-site, seminar aimed at the VP level. Discussion centers around ethics cases, such as credit approval, branch closings, foreign loans, and insider trading—all developed from interviews with Chemical personnel.[32]

A third type of program was undertaken a couple years ago at McDonnell Douglas. The firm distributed three ethics books to all employees of the company. The revised code and other material followed the previously mentioned points for a well-constructed code. The company also instituted a company-wide ethics training program for both white and blue collar employees.[33] Even though McDonnell Douglas undertook this extensive ethics program, some of its marketing executives were implicated in a subsequent defense contractor scandal. Thus, there are no guarantees that ethics programs or seminars will institutionalize ethics within all parts of the firm.

Ethical Audits Increasingly, firms are finding that unless they monitor their ethical performance, it will be taken for granted. As a result, some companies have developed systematic procedures which allow the organization to determine whether its employees are taking the commitment to ethical and social responsibility seriously. This process can involve the utilization of an outside consultant or perhaps a special ethics committee of the board of directors empowered to periodically evaluate operations against a prescribed set of standards.

Perhaps the company with the longest and most complete ethical audit program is Dow Corning, based in Midland, Michigan. The firm started using face-to-face audits at its plants over a decade ago and holds about twenty of these meetings annually. The number of participants in these four to six hour meetings range from five to forty. The auditors meet with the manager-in-charge the evening before so as to ascertain the most pressing issues. Actual questions often come from a relevant section in the corporate code and are adjusted to the audit location. Sample questions are: Do any of our employees have ownership or financial interest in any of our distributorships? Have our sales representatives been able to undertake business conduct discussions with distributors in a way that actually strengthens our ties with them? A Business Conduct Committee oversees the audits and then prepares a report for the Board. The manager who heads this effort says there are no shortcuts to implementing this program because it requires much time and extensive interaction with the people involved.[34]

---

[32] Patrick E. Murphy, 'Creating Ethical Corporate Structures,' *Sloan Management Review,* Winter 1989, pp. 81–86.

[33] Murphy, *Journal of Business Ethics.*

[34] Murphy, *Sloan Management Review.*

Conclusion

To return to an earlier point, some managers when given the opportunity to act unethically, especially when that action will lead to *personal gain,* will choose to be unethical. All marketing managers will not behave like saints any more than one could expect perfect behavior from all doctors, lawyers, or college professors. Nevertheless, for the organization that takes its ethical duties seriously, the provision of mechanisms to help managers better morally reason through ethical problems and the establishment of a corporate culture which will help direct managerial actions toward beneficial ends goes far in the establishment of an ethically enlightened marketing organization.

A TRAVELER'S GUIDE TO GIFTS AND BRIBES

Jeffrey A. Fadiman

"What do I say if he asks for a bribe?" I asked myself while enduring the all-night flight to Asia. Uncertain, I shared my concern with the man sitting beside me, a CEO en route to Singapore. Intrigued, he passed it on to his partners next to him. No one seemed sure.

Among American executives doing business overseas, this uncertainty is widespread. Consider, for example, each of the following situations:

♦ You are invited to the home of your foreign colleague. You learn he lives in a palatial villa. What gift might both please your host and ease business relations? What if he considers it to be a bribe? What if he *expects* it to be a bribe? Why do you feel uneasy?

♦ Your company's product lies on the dock of a foreign port. To avoid spoilage, you must swiftly transport it inland. What "gift," if any, would both please authorities and facilitate your business? What if they ask for "gifts" of $50? $50,000? $500,000? When does a gift become a bribe? When do you stop feeling comfortable?

♦ Negotiations are complete. The agreement is signed. One week later, a minister asks your company for $1 million—"for a hospital"—simultaneously suggesting that "other valuable considerations" might come your way as the result of future favors on both sides. What response, if any, would please him, satisfy you, and help execute the signed agreement?

♦ You have been asked to testify before the Securities and Exchange Commission regarding alleged violations of the Foreign Corrupt Practices Act. How would you explain the way you handled the examples above? Would your explanations both satisfy those in authority and ensure the continued overseas operation of your company?

Much of the discomfort Americans feel when faced with problems of this nature is due to U.S. law. Since 1977, congressional passage of the Foreign Corrupt Practices Act has transformed hypothetical problems into practical dilemmas and has created considerable anxiety among Americans who deal with foreign governments and companies. The problem is particularly difficult for those conducting business in the developing nations, where the rules that govern payoffs may differ sharply from our own. In such instances, U.S. executives may face not only legal but also ethical and cultural dilemmas: How do

Source: Reprinted by permission of *Harvard Business Review.* "A Traveler's Guide to Gifts and Bribes," by Jeffrey A. Fadiman, July-August 1986. Copyright © 1986 by the President and Fellows of Harvard College; all rights reserved.

businesspeople comply with customs that conflict with both their sense of ethics and this nation's law?

One way to approach the problem is to devise appropriate corporate responses to payoff requests. The suggestions that follow apply to those developing Asian, African, and Middle Eastern nations, still in transition toward industrial societies, that have retained aspects of their communal traditions. These approaches do not assume that those who adhere to these ideals exist in selfless bliss, requesting private payments only for communal ends, with little thought of self-enrichment. Nor do these suggestions apply to situations of overt extortion, where U.S. companies are forced to provide funds. Instead they explore a middle way in which non-Western colleagues may have several motives when requesting a payoff, thereby providing U.S. managers with several options.

Decisions and Dilemmas

My own first experience with Third World bribery may illustrate the inner conflict Americans can feel when asked to break the rules. It occurred in East Africa and began with this request: "Oh, and Bwana, I would like 1,000 shillings as Zawadi, my gift. And, as we are now friends, for Chai, my tea, an eight-band radio, to bring to my home when you visit."

Both *Chai* and *Zawadi* can be Swahili terms for "bribe." He delivered these requests in respectful tones. They came almost as an afterthought, at the conclusion of negotiations in which we had settled the details of a projected business venture. I had looked forward to buying my counterpart a final drink to complete the deal symbolically in the American fashion. Instead, after we had settled every contractual aspect, he expected money.

The amount he suggested, although insignificant by modern standards, seemed large at the time. Nonetheless, it was the radio that got to me. Somehow it added insult to injury. Outwardly, I kept smiling. Inside, my stomach boiled. My own world view equates bribery with sin. I expect monetary issues to be settled before contracts are signed. Instead, although the negotiations were complete, he expected me to pay out once more. Once? How often? Where would it stop? My reaction took only moments to formulate. "I'm American," I declared. "I don't pay bribes." Then I walked away. That walk was not the longest in my life. It was, however, one of the least commercially productive.

As it turned out, I had misunderstood him—in more ways than one. By misinterpreting both his language and his culture, I lost an opportunity for a business deal and a personal relationship that would have paid enormous dividends without violating either the law or my own sense of ethics.

Go back through the episode—but view it this time with an East African perspective. First, my colleague's language should have given me an important clue as to how he saw our transaction. Although his limited command of English caused him to frame his request as a command—a phrasing I instinctively found offensive—his tone was courteous. Moreover, if I had listened more carefully, I would have noted that he had addressed me as a superior: he used the honorific *Bwana*, meaning "sir," rather than *Rafiki* (or friend), used between equals. From his perspective, the language was appropriate; it reflected the differences in our personal wealth and in the power of the institutions we each represented.

Having assigned me the role of the superior figure in the economic transaction, he then suggested how I should use my position in accord with his culture's traditions—logically assuming that I would benefit by his prompting. In this case, he suggested that money and a radio would be appropriate gifts. What he did not tell me was that his culture's traditions required him to use the money to provide a feast—in my honor—to which he would invite everyone in his social and commercial circle whom he felt I should meet. The radio would simply create a festive atmosphere at the party. This was to mark the beginning of an ongoing relationship with reciprocal benefits.

He told me none of this. Since I was willing to do business in local fashion, I was supposed to know. In fact, I had not merely been invited to a dwelling but through a gateway into the maze of gifts and formal visiting that linked him to his kin. He hoped that I would respond in local fashion. Instead, I responded according to my cultural norms and walked out both on the chance to do business and on the opportunity to make friends.

The Legal Side Perhaps from a strictly legal perspective my American reaction was warranted. In the late 1970s, as part of the national reaction to Watergate, the SEC sued several large U.S. companies for alleged instances of bribery overseas. One company reportedly authorized $59 million in contributions to political parties in Italy, including the Communist party. A second allegedly paid $4 million to a political party in South Korea. A third reportedly provided $450,000 in "gifts" to Saudi generals. A fourth may have diverted $377,000 to fly planeloads of voters to the Cook Islands to rig elections there.

The sheer size of the payments and the ways they had been used staggered the public. A U.S. senate committee reported "corrupt" foreign payments involving hundreds of millions of dollars by more than 400 U.S. corporations, including 117 of the *Fortune* "500." The SEC described the problem as a national crisis.

In response, Congress passed the Foreign Corrupt Practices Act in 1977. The law prohibits U.S. corporations from providing or even offering payments to foreign political parties, candidates, or officials with discretionary authority under circumstances that might induce recipients to misuse their positions to assist the company to obtain, maintain, or retain business.

The FCPA does not forbid payments to lesser figures, however. On the contrary, it explicitly allows facilitating payments ("grease") to persuade foreign officials to perform their normal duties, at both the clerical and ministerial levels. The law establishes no monetary guidelines but requires companies to keep reasonably detailed records that accurately and fairly reflect the transactions.

The act also prohibits indirect forms of payment. Companies cannot make payments of this nature while "knowing or having reason to know" that any portion of the funds will be transferred to a forbidden recipient to be used for corrupt purposes as previously defined. Corporations face fines of up to $1 million. Individuals can be fined $10,000—which the corporation is forbidden to indemnify—and sentenced to a maximum of five years in prison. In short, private payments by Americans abroad can mean violation of U.S. law, a consideration that deeply influences U.S. corporate thinking.

The Ethical Side For most U.S. executives, however, the problem goes beyond the law. Most Americans share an aversion to payoffs. In parts of Asia, Africa, and the Middle East, however, certain types of bribery form an accepted element of their commercial traditions. Of course, nepotism, shakedown, and similar practices do occur in U.S. business; these practices, however, are both forbidden by law and universally disapproved.

Americans abroad reflect these sentiments. Most see themselves as personally honest and professionally ethical. More important, they see themselves as preferring to conduct business according to the law, both American and foreign. They also know that virtually all foreign governments—including those notorious for corruption—have rigorously enforced statutes against most forms of private payoff. In general, there is popular support for these anticorruption measures. In Malaysia, bribery is publicly frowned on and punishable by long imprisonment. In the Soviet Union, Soviet officials who solicit bribes can be executed.

Reflecting this awareness, most U.S. businesspeople prefer to play by local rules, competing in the open market according to the quality, price, and services provided by their product. Few, if any, want to make illegal payments of any kind to anybody. Most prefer to obey both local laws and their own ethical convictions while remaining able to do business.

The Cultural Side Yet, as my African experience suggests, indigenous traditions often override the law. In some developing nations, payoffs have become a norm. The problem is compounded when local payoff practices are rooted in a "communal heritage," ideals inherited from a preindustrial past where a community leader's wealth—however acquired—was shared throughout the community. Those who hoarded were scorned as antisocial. Those who shared won status and authority. Contact with Western commerce has blurred the ideal, but even the most individualistic businesspeople remember their communal obligations.

Contemporary business practices in those regions often reflect these earlier ideals. Certain forms of private payoff have endured for centuries. The Nigerian practice of *dash* (private payments for private services), for example, goes back to fifteenth century contacts with the Portuguese, in which Africans solicited "gifts" (trade goods) in exchange for labor. Such solicitation can pose a cultural dilemma to Americans who may be unfamiliar with the communal nuances of non-Western commercial conduct. To cope, they may denigrate these traditions, perceiving colleagues who solicit payments as unethical and their culture as corrupt.

Or they may respond to communal business methods by ignoring them, choosing instead to deal with foreign counterparts purely in Western fashion. This approach will usually work—up to a point. Non-Western businesspeople who deal with U.S. executives, for example, are often graduates of Western universities. Their language skills, commercial training, and professional demeanor, so similar to ours, make it comfortable to conduct business. But when these same colleagues shift to non-Western behavior, discussing gifts or bribes, Americans are often shocked.

Obviously, such reactions ignore the fact that foreign businesspeople have more than one cultural dimension. Managers from developing countries may hold conflicting values: one instilled by exposure to the West, the other imposed by local tradition. Non-Western businesspeople may see no conflict in negotiating contracts along Western lines, then reverting to indigenous traditions when discussing private payments. For Americans, however, this transition may be hard to make.

My experience suggests that most non-Westerners are neither excessively corrupt nor completely communal. Rather, they are simultaneously drawn to both indigenous and Western ideals. Many have internalized the Western norms of personal enrichment along with those of modern commerce, while simultaneously adhering to indigenous traditions by fulfilling communal obligations. Requests for payoffs may spring from both these ideals. Corporate responses must therefore be designed to satisfy them both.

Background for Payoffs

Throughout non-Western cultures, three traditions form the background for discussing payoffs: the inner circle, future favors, and the gift exchange. Though centuries old, each has evolved into a modern business concept. Americans who work in the Third World need to learn about them so they can work within them.

The Inner Circle Most individuals in developing nations classify others into some form of "ins" and "outs." Members of more communal societies, influenced by the need to strive for group prosperity, divide humanity into those with whom they have relationships and those with whom they have none. Many Africans, for instance, view people as either "brothers" or "strangers." Relationships with brothers may be real—kin, however distant—or fictional, extending to comrades or "mates." Comrades, however, may both speak and act like kin, address one another as family, and assume obligations of protection and assistance that Americans reserve for nuclear families.

Together, kin and comrades form an inner circle, a fictional "family," devoted to mutual protection and prosperity. Like the "old boy networks" that operate in the United States, no single rule defines membership in the inner circle. East Africans may include "age mates," individuals of similar age; West Africans, "homeboys," all men of similar region; Chinese, members of a dialect group; Indians, members of a caste. In most instances, the "ins" include extended families and their friends.

Beyond this magic circle live the "outs": strangers, aliens, individuals with no relationship to those within. Communal societies in Southern Africa, for example, describe these people in all their millions as "predators," implying savage creatures with whom the "ins" lack any common ground. The motives of outsiders inspire fear, not because there is danger but simply because they are unknown. Although conditioned to display courtesy, insiders prefer to restrict both social and commercial dealings to those with whom they have dependable relationships. The ancient principle can still be found in modern commerce; non-Western businesspeople often prefer to restrict commercial relationships to those they know and trust.

Not every U.S. manager is aware of this division. Those who investigate often assume that their nationality, ethnic background, and alien culture automatically classify them as "outs." Non-Western colleagues, however, may regard specific Westerners as useful contacts, particularly if they seem willing to do business in local fashion. They may, therefore, consider bringing certain individuals into their inner circles in such a manner as to benefit both sides.

Overseas executives, if asked to work within such circles, should find their business prospects much enhanced. These understandings often lead to implicit quid pro quos. For example, one side might agree to hire workers from only one clan; in return the other side would guarantee devoted labor. As social and commercial trust grows, the Westerners may be regarded less and less as aliens or predators and more and more as comrades or kin. Obviously, this is a desirable transition, and executives assigned to work within this type of culture may wish to consider whether these inner circles exist and if so, whether working within them will enhance business prospects.

The Future Favor A second non-Western concept that relates to payoffs is a system of future favors. Relationships within the inner circles of non-Western nations function through such favors. In Japan, the corresponding system is known as "inner duty" or *giri*. On Mt. Kenya, it is "inner relationship," *uthoni*. Filipinos describe it as "inner debt," *utani na loob*. All systems of this type assume that any individual under obligation to another has entered a relationship in which the first favor must be repaid in the future, when convenient to all sides.

Neither side defines the manner of repayment. Rather, both understand that some form of gift or service will repay the earlier debt with interest. This repayment places the originator under obligation. The process then begins again, creating a lifelong cycle. The relationship that springs from meeting lifelong obligations builds the trust that forms a basis for conducting business.

My own introduction to the future favors system may illustrate the process. While conducting business on Mt. Kenya in the 1970s, I visited a notable local dignitary. On completing our agenda, he stopped my rush to leave by presenting me a live and angry hen. Surprised, I stammered shaky "thank-yous," then walked down the mountain with my kicking, struggling bird. Having discharged my obligation—at least in Western terms—by thanking him, I cooked the hen, completed my business, eventually left Kenya, and forgot the incident.

Years later, I returned on different business. It was a revelation. People up and down the mountain called out to one another that I had come back to "return the dignitary's hen." To them, the relationship that had sprung up between us had remained unchanged throughout the years. Having received a favor, I had now come back to renew the relationship by returning it.

I had, of course, no such intention. Having forgotten the hen incident, I was also unaware of its importance to others. Embarrassed, I slipped into a market and bought a larger hen, then climbed to his homestead to present it. Again I erred, deciding to apologize in Western fashion for delaying my return. "How can a hen be late?" he replied. "Due to the bird, we have *uthoni* [obligations, thus a relationship]. That is what sweetens life. What else was the hen for but to bring you here again?"

These sentiments can also operate within non-Western commercial circles, where business favors can replace hens, but *uthoni* are what sweetens corporate life. Western interest lies in doing business; non-Western, in forming bonds so that business can begin. Westerners seek to discharge obligations; non-Westerners, to create them. Our focus is on producing short-term profit; theirs, on generating future favors. The success of an overseas venture may depend on an executive's awareness of these differences.

The Gift Exchange One final non-Western concept that can relate to payoffs is a continuous exchange of gifts. In some developing nations, gifts form the catalysts that trigger future favors. U.S. executives often wish to present gifts appropriate to cultures where they are assigned, to the point where at least one corporation has commissioned a special study of the subject. They may be less aware, however, of the long-range implications of gift giving within these cultures. Two of these may be particularly relevant to CEOs concerned with payoffs.

In many non-Western commercial circles, the tradition of gift giving has evolved into a modern business tool intended to create obligation as well as affection. Recipients may be gratified by what they receive, but they also incur an obligation that they must some day repay. Gift giving in these cultures may therefore operate in two dimensions: one meant to provide short-term pleasure; the other, long-range bonds.

This strategy is common in Moslem areas of Africa and Asia. Within these cultures, I have watched export merchants change Western clientele from browsers to buyers by inviting them to tea. Seated, the customers sip at leisure, while merchandise is brought before them piece by piece. The seller thus achieves three goals. His clients have been honored, immobilized, and placed under obligation.

In consequence, the customers often feel the need to repay in kind. Lacking suitable material gifts, they frequently respond as the merchant intends: with decisions to buy—not because they need the merchandise but to return the seller's gift of hospitality. The buyers, considering their obligation discharged, leave the premises believing relations have ended. The sellers, however, hope they have just begun. Their intent is to create relationships that will cause clients to return. A second visit would mean presentation of another gift, perhaps of greater value. That, in turn, might mean a second purchase, leading to further visits, continued gifts, and a gradual deepening of personal and commercial relations intended to enrich both sides.

The point of the process, obviously, is not the exchanges themselves but the relationships they engender. The gifts are simply catalysts. Under ideal circumstances the process should be unending, with visits, gifts, gestures, and services flowing back and forth among participants throughout their lives. The universally understood purpose is to create reciprocal good feelings and commercial prosperity among all concerned.

Gift giving has also evolved as a commercial "signal." In America, gifts exchanged by business colleagues may signal gratitude, camaraderie, or perhaps the discharge of minor obligations. Among non-Westerners, gifts may signal the desire to begin both social and commercial relationships with members of an inner circle. That signal may also apply to gifts exchanged with Westerners. If frequently repeated, such exchanges may be signals of intent. For Americans, the signal may suggest a willingness to work within a circle of local business colleagues, to assume appropriate obligations, and to conduct business in local ways. For non-Western colleagues, gifts may imply a wish to invite selected individuals into their commercial interactions.

Approaches to Payoffs

While U.S. corporations may benefit from adapting to local business concepts, many indigenous business traditions, especially in developing regions, are alien to the American experience and therefore difficult to implement by U.S. field personnel—as every executive who has tried to sit cross-legged for several hours with Third World counterparts will attest.

Conversely, many non-Western administrators are particularly well informed about U.S. business practices, thus permitting U.S. field representatives to function on familiar ground. Nonetheless, those willing to adapt indigenous commercial concepts to U.S. corporate needs may find that their companies can benefit in several ways. Through working with a circle of non-Western business colleagues, and participating fully in the traditional exchange of gifts and favors, U.S. executives may find that their companies increase the chance of preferential treatment; use local methods and local contacts to gain market share; develop trust to reinforce contractual obligations; and minimize current risk, while maximizing future opportunities by developing local expertise.

Corporations that adapt to local business concepts may also develop methods to cope with local forms of payoff. Current approaches vary from culture to culture, yet patterns do appear. Three frequently recur in dealings between Americans and non-Westerners: gifts, bribes, and other considerations.

Gifts: The Direct Request This form of payoff may occur when key foreign businesspeople approach their U.S. colleagues to solicit "gifts." Solicitations of this type have no place in U.S. business circles where they could be construed as exploitation. Obviously, the same may hold true overseas, particularly in areas where shakedown, bribery, and extortion may be prevalent. There is, however, an alternative to consider. To non-Western colleagues, such requests may simply be a normal business strategy, designed to build long-term relationships.

To U.S. businesspeople, every venture is based on the bottom line. To non-Western colleagues, a venture is based on the human relationships that form around it. Yet, when dealing with us they often grow uncertain as to how to form these relationships. How can social ties be created with Americans who speak only of business, even when at leisure? How can traditions of gift giving be initiated with people unaware of the traditions? Without the exchange of gifts, how can obligations be created? Without obligations, how can there be trust?

Faced with such questions, non-Western business colleagues may understandably decide to initiate gift-giving relationships on their own. If powerful, prominent, or wealthy, they may simply begin by taking on the role of giver. If less powerful or affluent, some may begin by suggesting they become recipients. There need be no dishonor in such action, since petitioners know they will repay with future favors whatever inner debt they incur.

The hosts may also realize that, as strangers, Americans may be unaware of local forms of gift giving as well as their relationship to business norms. Or they may be cognizant of such relationships but may have no idea of how to enter into them. In such instances, simple courtesy may cause the hosts to indicate—perhaps obliquely—how proper entry into the local system should be made. Such was the unfortunate case with my East African colleague's request for the eight-band radio.

Cultural barriers can be difficult to cross. Most Americans give generously, but rarely on request. When solicited, we feel exploited. Solicitations may seem more relevant, however, if examined from the perspective of the non-Western peoples with whom we are concerned.

Often, in societies marked by enormous gaps between the rich and the poor, acts of generosity display high status. To withhold gifts is to deny the affluence one has achieved. Non-Western counterparts often use lavish hospitality both to reflect and to display their wealth and status within local society. When Americans within these regions both represent great wealth through association with their corporations and seek high status as a tool to conduct business, it may prove more profitable for the corporation to give than to receive.

In short, when asked for "gifts" by foreign personnel, managers may consider two options. The first option is to regard each query as extortion and every petitioner as a potential thief. The second is to consider the request within its local context. In nations where gifts generate a sense of obligation, it may prove best to give them, thereby creating inner debts among key foreign colleagues in the belief that they will repay them over time. If such requests indeed reflect a local way of doing business, they may be gateways into the workings of its commercial world. One U.S. option, therefore, is to consider the effect of providing "gifts"—even on direct request—in terms of the relationships required to implement the corporation's long-range plans.

Bribes: The Indirect Request A second approach to payoffs, recurrent in non-Western business circles, is the indirect request. Most Third World people prefer the carrot to the stick. To avoid unpleasant confrontation, they designate third parties to suggest that "gifts" of specified amounts be made to those in local power circles. In explanation they cite the probability of future favors in return. No line exists, of course, dividing gifts from bribes. It seems that direct solicitation involves smaller amounts, while larger ones require go-betweens. On occasion, however, the sums requested can be staggering: in 1976, for example, U.S. executives in Qatar were asked for a $1.5 million "gift" for that nation's minister of oil.

U.S. responses to such queries must preserve both corporate funds and executive relationships with those in power. While smaller gifts may signal a desire to work with the local business circles, a company that supplies larger sums could violate both local antipayoff statutes and the FCPA. Conversely, outright rejection of such requests may cause both the go-betweens and those they represent to lose prestige and thus possibly prompt retaliation.

In such instances, the FCPA may actually provide beleaguered corporate executives with a highly convenient excuse. Since direct compliance with requests for private funds exposes every U.S. company to threats of negative publicity, blackmail, legal action, financial loss, and damage to corporate image, it may prove easy for Americans to say no—while at the same time offering nonmonetary benefits to satisfy both sides.

U.S. competitors may, in fact, be in a better situation than those companies from Europe and Japan that play by different rules. Since the principle of payoffs is either accepted or encouraged by many of their governments, the companies must find it difficult to refuse payment of whatever sums are asked.

Nor should the "right to bribe" be automatically considered an advantage. Ignoring every other factor, this argument assumes contracts are awarded solely on the basis of the largest private payoff. At the most obvious level, it ignores the possibility that products also compete on the basis of quality, price, promotion, and service—factors often crucial to American success abroad. U.S. field representatives are often first to recognize that payoffs may be only one of many factors in awarding contracts. In analyzing U.S. competition in the Middle East, for instance, one executive of an American aircraft company noted: "The French have savoir faire in giving bribes discreetly and well, but they're still not . . . backing up their sales with technical expertise." The overseas executive should consider to what degree the right to bribe may be offset by turning the attention of the payoff seekers to other valuable considerations.

Other Considerations: The Suggested Service A third approach, often used by members of a non-Western elite, is to request that U.S. companies contribute cash to public service projects, often administered by the petitioners themselves. Most proposals of this type require money. Yet if American executives focus too sharply on the financial aspects, they may neglect the chance to work other nonmonetary considerations into their response. In many developing nations, nonmonetary considerations may weigh heavily on foreign colleagues.

Many elite non-Westerners, for example, are intensely nationalistic. They love their country keenly, deplore its relative poverty, and yearn to help it rise. They may, therefore, phrase their requests for payoffs in terms of a suggested service to the nation. In Kenya, for example, ministerial requests to U.S. companies during the 1970s suggested a contribution toward the construction of a hospital. In Indonesia, in the mid-1970s, a top executive of Pertamina, that nation's government-sponsored oil company, requested contributions to an Indonesian restaurant in New York City as a service to the homeland. In his solicitation letter, the executive wrote that the restaurant was in fact intended to "enhance the Indonesian image in the U.S.A., . . . promote tourism, . . . and attract the interest of the U.S. businessmen to investments in Indonesia."

Westerners may regard such claims with cynicism. Non-Westerners may not. They recognize that, even if the notables involved become wealthy, some portion of the wealth, which only they can attract from abroad, will still be shared by other members of their homeland.

That belief is worth consideration, for many elite non-Westerners share a second concern: the desire to meet communal obligations by sharing wealth with members of their inner circle. Modern business leaders in communal cultures rarely simply hoard their wealth. To do so would invite social condemnation. Rather, they provide gifts, funds, and favors to those in their communal settings, receiving deference, authority, and prestige in return.

This does not mean that funds transferred by Western corporations to a single foreign colleague will be parceled out among a circle of cronies. Rather, money passes through one pair of hands over time, flowing slowly in the form of gifts and favors to friends and kin. The funds may even flow beyond this inner circle to their children, most often to ensure their continued education. Such generosity, of course, places both adult recipients and children under a long-term obligation, thereby providing donors both with current status and with assurance of obtaining future favors.

In short, non-Western colleagues who seek payoffs may have concerns beyond their personal enrichment. If motivated by both national and communal idealism, they may feel that these requests are not only for themselves but also a means to aid much larger groups and ultimately their nation.

A Donation Strategy

Requests for payoffs give executives little choice. Rejection generates resentment, while agreement may lead to prosecution. Perhaps appeals to both communal and national idealism can open up a third alternative. Consider, for example, the possibility of deflecting such requests by transforming private payoffs into public services. One approach would be to respond to requests for private payment with well-publicized, carefully tailored "donations"—an approach that offers both idealistic and practical appeal.

This type of donation could take several forms. The most obvious, a monetary contribution, could be roughly identical to the amount requested in private funds. Donating it publicly, however, would pay off important foreign colleagues in nonmonetary ways.

At the national level, for instance, the most appropriate and satisfying corporate response to ministerial requests for "contributions" toward the construction of a hospital, such as occurred in Kenya, might be actually to provide one, down to the final door and stethoscope, while simultaneously insisting that monetary payments of any kind are proscribed by U.S. law.

The same principle can apply at local levels. Top executives of smaller companies, faced with requests for funds by influential foreign counterparts, might respond by donating to medical, educational, or agricultural projects at the provincial, district, or even village level, focusing consistently on the geographic areas from which those associates come. The donation strategy can even operate at interpersonal levels. How, for example, would my African colleague have reacted had I responded to his request by offering to "donate" whatever would be needed for a special feast—including a radio?

U.S. executives could also weave "other considerations" into the donation, encouraging foreign colleagues to continue business interaction. Many U.S. companies now simply donate funds. Those in Bali, Indonesia, contribute large sums to local temples. Those in Senegal donate to irrigation projects. Companies in South Africa support 150 Bantu schools for black Africans.

Yet donations alone seem insufficient. To serve as an alternative to payoffs, the concept should have practical appeal. Consider, for example, the story of a Western company in Zaire. During the 1970s, Zaire's economy decayed so badly that even ranking civil servants went unpaid. As a result, key Zairian district officials approached officers of the Western company, requesting private funds for future favors. Instead, the company responded with expressions of deference and "donations" of surplus supplies, including goods that could be sold on the black market. The resulting cash flow enabled the officials to continue in their posts. This in turn allowed them to render reciprocal services, both to their district and to the company. By tailoring their contribution to local conditions, the company avoided draining its funds, while providing benefits to both sides.

There are many ways to tailor donations. At the most obvious level, funds can support social projects in the home areas of important local colleagues. Funds or even whole facilities can be given in their names. Production centers can be staffed by members of their ethnic group. Educational, medical, and other social services can be made available to key segments of a target population based on the advice of influential foreign counterparts. Given the opportunity, many non-Westerners would direct the contributions toward members of their inner circles profiting from local forms of recognition and prestige. These practices, often used in one form or another in the United States, can provide non-Western counterparts with local recognition and authority and supply a legal, ethical, and culturally acceptable alternative to a payoff.

Donating Services United States companies may also deflect payoff proposals by donating services, gratifying important foreign colleagues in non-monetary fashion, and thus facilitating the flow of future business. In 1983, for example, a British military unit, part of the Royal Electrical and Mechanical Engineers, planned an African overland vehicle expedition across the Sahara to Tanzania. On arrival, they were "expected" to make a sizable cash donation to that nation to be used in support of its wildlife.

Usually this meant meeting a minister, handing over a check, and taking a picture of the transfer. Instead, the British assembled thousands of dollars worth of tools and vehicle parts, all needed in Tanzanian wildlife areas for trucks on antipoaching patrols. Tanzania's weakened economy no longer permitted the import of enough good tools or parts, which left the wildlife authorities with few working vehicles. As a result, wild-game management had nearly halted. By transporting the vital parts across half of Africa, then working alongside local mechanics until every vehicle was on the road, the British reaped far more goodwill than private payments or even cash donations would have gained. More important, they paved the way for future transactions by providing services meant to benefit both sides.

Donating Jobs A third alternative to private payoffs may be to donate jobs, particularly on projects meant to build goodwill among a host nation's elite. In the 1970s, for example, Coca-Cola was the object of a Middle Eastern boycott by members of the Arab League. Conceivably, Coca-Cola could have sought to win favor with important individuals through gifts or bribes. Instead, the company hired hundreds of Egyptians to plant thousands of acres of orange trees. Eventually the company carpeted a considerable stretch of desert and thereby created both employment and goodwill.

More recently, Mexico refused to let IBM become the first wholly owned foreign company to make personal computers within its borders. Like Coca-Cola in Egypt, IBM employed a strategy of national development: it offered a revised proposal, creating both direct and indirect employment for Mexican nationals, in numbers high enough to satisfy that nation's elite. Such projects do more than generate goodwill. Those able to involve key foreign colleagues in ways that lend prestige on local terms may find they serve as viable alternatives to bribery.

Good Ethics, Good Business

Three strategies do not exhaust the list. U.S. executives in foreign countries should be able to devise their own variants based on local conditions. Each approach should further social progress while offering local status instead of U.S. funds. Americans may find their non-Western colleagues more inclined to do business with corporations that lend prestige than with those whose representatives evade, refuse, or simply walk away. It should not harm a company to gain a reputation for providing social services instead of bribes. A corporation that relies too much on payoffs will be no more respected within non-Western business circles than developing nations that rely too much on payoffs are now respected in U.S. business circles.

Similarly, since the legal dilemma would be resolved, home offices might respond more favorably to overseas requests for funds. Whereas funding for private payments remains illegal, proposals to "donate" the same amounts toward host-nation development could be perceived as public relations and cause-related marketing. Home offices should not fear legal action. While the FCPA prohibits payments to foreign political parties, candidates, or officials with discretionary authority, nowhere does it prohibit the use of funds to aid developing societies, and it requires only that companies keep detailed records that accurately and fairly reflect the transactions.

Businesspeople can also resolve the ethical dilemma. Turning private payoffs into public services should meet both U.S. and corporate moral standards. While one measure of corporate responsibility is to generate the highest possible returns for investors, this can usually be best achieved within a climate of goodwill. In contemporary Third World cultures, this climate can more often be created by public services than by private payoffs. To sell cola, Coke did not bribe ministers, it planted trees. Certainly, host governments will look most favorably on companies that seek to serve as well as to profit, especially through "gifts" that show concern for local ways.

Finally, the cultural dilemmas can also be resolved. Non-Western business practices may be difficult to comprehend, especially when they involve violations of U.S. legal, commercial, or social norms. Nonetheless, U.S. business options are limited only by our business attitudes. If these can be expanded through selective research into those local concepts that relate to payoffs, responses may emerge to satisfy both congressional and indigenous demands. What may initially appear as begging, bribery, or blackmail may be revealed as local tradition, cross-cultural courtesy, or attempts to make friends. More important, when examined from a non-American perspective, mention of "gifts," "bribes," and "other valuable considerations" may signal a wish to do business.

NAME INDEX

SUBJECT **INDEX**